T5-CVP-218

BILINGUALISM *and* BILINGUAL EDUCATION

BILINGUALISM
and
BILINGUAL EDUCATION
A COMPARATIVE STUDY

E. Glyn Lewis

Foreword by Bernard Spolsky

UNIVERSITY OF NEW MEXICO PRESS

Albuquerque

Library of Congress Cataloging in Publication Data

Lewis, E Glyn.
    Bilingualism and bilingual education.

    Bibliography: p.
    Includes index.
    1. Bilingualism. 2. Education, Bilingual.
I. Title.
P115.L4   404'.2   79-55982
ISBN 0-8263-0532-6

Manufactured in the United States of America.
Library of Congress Catalog Card Number 79-55982.
International Standard Book Number 0-8263-0532-6.
First Edition.
Copublished in Great Britain by Pergamon Press, Ltd., Oxford.

Cyflwynedig i Lois a Nesta

Contents

TABLES

FIGURES

Acknowledgments

The greater part of this study was written between 1975 and 1977. Some of the material was gathered earlier while I was co-director of the Languages Research Project at the University College of Wales at Swansea on behalf of the Schools Council and while I conducted research for the International Educational Assessment's comparative study of the "Teaching of English as Foreign Language in Ten Countries." I am grateful for the financial support of these two organizations which enabled me to conduct enquiries that were offshoots of the main projects. Earlier the Ministry of Education for England and Wales provided assistance that enabled me to spend some time on various occasions in the Soviet Union studying the teaching of languages, and especially the problems associated with bilingualism in education. The study could not have been completed, and the American aspects hardly glanced at, but for generous financial support by the Ford Foundation. To Mr. Mel Fox and Miss Marjorie Martus who facilitated the grant that I received for research and study I am especially indebted.

A large portion of my research in the United States was done while at the University of New Mexico at Albuquerque. The administrators of the University were very helpful in granting me research facilities, and I am particularly grateful to Dr. Bernard Spolsky, Dean of the Graduate School, who forestalled every difficulty. The Seminars that he arranged enabled me to profit from the experience of many faculty members and graduate students with long experience and deep scholarship in this field. It would be impossible to name all the members who contributed to my edification, but Dr. Vera John-Steiner, who together with her husband, Stan Steiner, were most hospitable at their Santa Fe home, may be taken as representative. Dr. Ellen Spolsky will never know how much her kindness and hospitality meant to me during my several short visits to Albuquerque as well as during my semester at the University there.

Without the cooperation of teachers, graduate students, and others in the United States, and elementary and secondary school pupils and their parents in Wales who participated in the attitudes survey, a central part of the research would have failed. I am also greatly indebted to those people in New Mexico, Texas, Dade County, Miami (Florida), and New York who completed the questionnaires. To Professor Theodore Andersson of Austin, Texas, and Mr. Armando Cotayo of Hunter College, New York, who helped in obtaining satisfactory samples of teachers, I am particularly indebted.

Professor Andersson has always been a source of information and inspiration, as has Professor Joshua Fishman as well. The latter, though he must be absolved from the shortcomings of the study, bears a responsibility for its appearance in view of the inspiration of his own studies and his encouragement over many years. Dr. Sarita Schotta, of the Bilingual Education Section of the National Institute of Education, Washington, D.C., was always ready to let me have relevant information concerning national developments, as was Dr. Frederick Shaw of the New York City Department of Education in a more limited field. Dr. Tom Hopkins of the Bureau of Indian Affairs Research Center at Albuquerque has been extremely helpful in connection with the study of bilingual education in Indian communities and in identifying sources of information and supplying materials.

I am indebted to the University of New Mexico Press for undertaking, at an early stage of its development, the publication of the volume; to its former director, Mr. Hugh Treadwell, for discussing it with me; and especially to Dr. David Holtby, who edited a difficult text with care and contributed not a little to making its transatlantic crossing less difficult than it might have been.

My main debt is to my wife, Valmai, who has provided the most helpful environment possible for the completion of this work.

E. Glyn Lewis
Porthcawl, Mid-Glamorgan

Foreword

The choice of language education policy is among the most critical and complex issues facing modern societies. In the world as a whole, it is the exception rather than the rule that a child comes to school already speaking the language, dialect, or variety that society and school consider to be ideal. Schools either teach in or teach the standard dialect of the standard language. For various reasons, this is seldom the variety spoken at home by most people. This sets up a language barrier between home and school, and leads to a conflict in values that is painful and difficult to resolve.

For most of the world, the standard language of the school, usually a world language, has come to represent the modern technological culture with which it is associated: a culture involved with large cities and complex states, with mass media and high energy consumption, with individual citizens submerged in complex impersonal organizations. The standard language is part of this modern world that has grown up over the last four hundred years or so, sharing a place in it with television and computers, automobiles and apartment buildings. It has a great number of attractive features: it clearly represents a high culture, with great possibilities for individual development (witness the changing role of women in modern societies), improved standard of living and health, and new and existing art forms. But in recent years we have started to realize that modernism is flawed, perhaps even fatally, as we see how technological developments have threatened to destroy our environment and how mass societies threaten the existence of the individual. One response to this challenge has been a return to traditionalism, for many people associated with ethnic identity and languages. Some go as far as to argue for separatism: only by returning to old ways and living in small separate communities do they believe we can regain identity. It is fine to maintain traditional values, but hard to do this if it means giving up the desirable features of modern life. It's good to be a traditional Navajo, but hard to have to carry water three miles every day to one's home. It is good to live in a village, but difficult to do this at the cost of availability of good medical care. Traditional social values are fine, but not when they lead to the social stagnation that characterizes many traditional groups, where every man's place is clearly marked from birth, and every woman's place is clear, and several notches below.

Language policies match these choices, because it is the standard world language that gives access to the benefits of modernism, and it is the local language that provides contact with ethnic and local traditions. Two antithetical approaches are offered to the challenge. The first is to modernize, to assimilate even at the cost of losing ethnic and linguistic identity. This is the essence of what is usually called transitional bilingual education, programs where children who come to school speaking a local language are expected to switch at some stage (including in some extreme cases at the schoolroom door) to another. The competing approach is to maintain separateness, as completely as possible, at whatever cost. This is one rationale behind proposals for bilingual maintenance programs, with their hope of maintaining traditional values, language, and society intact. It requires either the forced isolation suffered for so long by linguistic minorities in the United States or the self-chosen separatism of religious groups like the Amish or the Chassidim for such an approach to succeed, but there are many who favor it.

There are those who argue that there is a third possibility, a possible synthesis between these tensions, a resolution that takes the best features of both modernism and traditionalism. "Bilingual education", writes E. Glyn Lewis in his pioneering study of its history, "is only partly, and to my way of thinking only secondarily, concerned with simple maintenance and conservation. If it is to be worth anything, it needs to make certain that out of the discrete cultural elements a new unity is born" (Lewis, in Cooper and Spolsky, 1977a: 30).

Of all scholars in the field of bilingual education, it has been Lewis who has led the way in recognizing not just the universality of bilingual education but the universal significance of the basic issues it is concerned with. His contributions to the field have been enormous. His study of bilingualism and bilingual education in the ancient world and of developments through the middle ages provided a time depth so often lacking in social sciences. His detailed analyses of bilingualism and bilingual education in Wales and in the Soviet Union provided not just a model for description, but identified many of the theoretical bases for understanding the field. His latest contribution, first set out in a number of papers but now brought to maturity in the present volume, has been to make clear the value of international comparative studies.

Perhaps more than any other scholar, Lewis has helped American educators to realize the international dimensions of the field, which made particularly appropriate his collaboration with James Alatis in organizing the 1978 Georgetown Roundtable with that title. In his closing remarks at that conference, Lewis added a new note, when he argued convincingly that a theory of pedagogy is essentially not so much scientific as it is moral: it is neither predictive nor normative, but provides scope for the making of value judgments and the application of moral criteria. He concludes with a recognition that the choices are ultimately contradictory and irreconcilable:

> Where we are faced with the choice between equally sacred claims and values, what, as teachers and citizens, can we do? Tension does not entail conflict unless we will it so. We accept tension and so promote pluralism. The latter is not only governed by a number of principles but it also engenders at least one principle which, while valuable in itself, ensures that tension and the intrinsic conflict of values is creative rather than destructive. This principle is tolerance . . . (Lewis, in Alatis, 1978: 680)

This present volume will be another major contribution to the field, for it combines careful observation of bilingual education in three major parts of the world—the Soviet Union, the Celtic countries of Western Europe, and the United States—with a pioneering attempt to outline a theory of bilingualism and bilingual education. Lewis has had long acquaintance with the problems of Celtic speakers in Western Europe, both as an inspector of schools and a professor in Wales; his studies of bilingualism and bilingual education in the Soviet Union have become classic; and his opportunities over recent years to observe bilingual education in the United States have left many of us waiting to learn his impressions and judgments. Using these three cases, and comparing and contrasting them, Lewis is able to explore the nature of social and individual bilingualism, its consequences, and the various policy choices made to deal with real and perceived problems. By studying the various rationales and justifications proposed for various kinds of programs, he analyzes the basic tensions that underlie language education policy in these three parts of the world, and so is able to look at the basic issue of the continuing tension between modernism and tradition. This book, appearing fifty years after the 1928 Luxembourg International Conference, will, I believe, come to serve as a mark of the maturity of the study of bilingualism and bilingual education.

Bernard Spolsky
University of New Mexico
Albuquerque, New Mexico

Part One

Theoretical Framework

One

Types of Bilingual Communities and Other Variables

INTRODUCTION

It has been claimed that "a comparative study is essentially an attempt so far as possible to replace the names of systems (countries) by the names of concepts or 'variables'" (Noah, 114). The comparative study of bilingual education both within and between national systems, according to that definition, is an attempt to replace the labels attached to types of programs by the names of the variables. Depending upon the prevailing or historical circumstances, different constellations of these variables result in different programs. The interaction of the various characteristics of each system of bilingual education creates unique patterns, and our interest is the investigation of how various systems derive from different combinations of identical elements. Concentrating on a particular school, a particular school system, or on any one specific national system of bilingual education may enable us to examine in depth a limited area, but only comparison enables us to recognize what meaning attaches to what we discover. The identification of these variables is undertaken in this chapter along with an analysis of the most fundamental of these factors, namely types of bilingual community—the social and linguistic environment in which any bilingual program is set.

SOURCES OF HETEROGENEITY AND
THEIR VARIABLE IMPACT

Inherent in our study is a consideration of aspects of heterogeneity, whether it be of linguistically distinct clans, tribes, nationalities, nations, or states. There would be no need to provide a bilingual education if there were not already some degree of heterogeneity or, alternatively, if it were not the intention to promote it. The most immediate aspect of heterogeneity that a bilingual education seeks to accommodate or to promote is linguistic, but it would be naive to conceive of linguistic diversity independently of other forms of heterogeneity.

Linguistic diversity of groups in a society is associated with at least eight other aspects of heterogeneity (Linz and Miguel). First, ethnic groups in a country may differ in levels of economic development, as with Yakuts and Russians, or in the United States with immigrants and Anglos, or even with different minorities among themselves. Second, they may differ in social structure, as do Tatars and Russians or Daghestanis and Georgians in the Soviet Union, or Amerindians and Anglos in the United States. Third, the availability of education and the quality of what is available may differ from one ethnic group to another: for instance, the differences between Russian and non-Russian medium schools in any part of the Soviet Union, or the education of Amerindians, Mexican-Americans or Puerto Ricans on the one hand and Anglos on the other in the United States.

Cultural practices and traditions of a group (which may not always be identified with language affiliation) are a fourth aspect of heterogeneity and vary greatly. There are, for example, differences between the cultures of native-speaking Russians and those members of non-Russian speaking groups who have adopted Russian as their native tongue but retained their traditional cultures. Fifth, religious differences may distinguish linguistic groups as they do in the case of Jews, Christians, and Muslims in the Soviet Union or in the case of Muslims, Jews, a variety of Christian denominations, and other religions in the United States. The degree of the groups' political participation is a sixth facet of diversity, and it may differ as is the case with the Puerto Ricans compared with Anglos in the United States, or the Jews compared with any other ethnic group in the Soviet Union. Apart from participation, the political traditions of the groups in contact may differ as do the English and the Afrikaans, or the Bantu and either of the two white races in the Republic of South Africa. Seventh, there are differences in values, norms, and basic personality traits, like those which distinguish Mexican-Americans on the one hand and Anglos on the other. Finally, there exist variations in patterns and traditions of family life, including the differences between groups in the patrilinear or matrilinear lines of authority (a relevant consideration in the maintenance of language in mixed marriage), or nucleated as opposed to extended family patterns, affecting the influence of the older generations on language maintenance. All these sources of heterogeneity which may be present in different combinations are usually associated in varying degrees with linguistic differences.

The education of a bilingual child occurs amidst some if not all these aspects of heterogeneity. Educators must take account of as many as possible of these linguistically associated variables because in a bilingual program we do not set out merely to teach two languages but rather to educate a person who possesses or needs to possess two languages. Chomsky (1976) has suggested that a reaction to any feature of the environment— for example, to different languages in the case of the bilingual child—is most likely to be "structure dependent." This implies that the significance of bilingualism is determined by its relation to the total structure of political, economic, and religious institutions. Elements of such institutional structures may be associated with differences in language, and because of that they constitute groups of variables that have to be included in the design of any research or evaluation of bilingual education.

Furthermore, the nature of a bilingual program relates directly to its position in the *partial* structural complexes which together constitute the total social structure. One such partial structure is the mainstream system of education, which refers to one the majority are exposed to. In a heterogeneous society, this is usually monolingual, and for that reason (having no special linguistic features) it may be referred to as unmarked—especially the procedures which determine entry to and retention within it.

With one or two notable exceptions, research on bilingual education has ignored the embedment of bilingualism within the complex of other forms of heterogeneity. For this reason, most reports on bilingualism have tended to be restricted and uninteresting.

DIFFUSION VARIABLES

While within-country differences, whether of class or ethnic affiliations, may have been declining in most modernized societies, it has been suggested that "at least between 1900 and 1960 inter-country differences have been increasing" (Deutsch, 1966:7). This is because while differences themselves decline, the awareness of differences may intensify. In fact this is the usual process. As the minority is compressed it becomes more volatile. Deutsch's conclusion supports the argument that investigators must begin understanding these differences by developing cross-national studies, but the value of such research is often questioned because cross-national influences seemingly are not strong. In fact, though, contacts are extensive because diffusion variables are present in such factors as increased communication. Thus, the provision of bilingual education in one country may be affected by the existence of such programs in other contiguous or distant countries. For example, the movement toward an autonomous system of education in Quebec will probably have a powerful effect on attitudes toward bilingual education in the United States (New York *Times*, 3 January 1977). In Britain, education of immigrants has been shaped by advances in the United States with TESOL (Teaching English to Speakers of Other Languages) programs as well as based on the historical provision of bilingual education for the Welsh-speaking minority.

SETTINGS

A second type of variable in heterogeneity is "settings," and it refers to the differences in the immediate context of the provision of bilingual education in different countries or for different ethnic groups within a single country. The typology of settings may consist of historical, external, institutional, behavioral, or community-type variables.

Historical Settings

An examination of the historical setting is important for understanding ethnic groups in a country. For instance, in the United States ethnic groups belong to several historical types: they are either indigenous or immigrant. The indigenous are either autochthonous or incorporated. To the indigenous group belongs the Amerindian populations, while the incorporated include the Hispanics who already inhabited the areas that were taken over or conquered. The immigrants either have historical and linguistic ties with some group already settled in the country, for instance the Puerto Ricans and Cubans with the Hispanics; or they are "free floating" immigrant groups like the Europeans, Asians and Middle Easterners, historically and linguistically unconnected with the indigenous; or they are involuntary immigrants like the blacks. Their history both within the United States and prior to their settlement in the country powerfully influences the chances of national acceptability of any kind of bilingual education among succeeding generations. There is, for instance, an acknowledged difference between the attitudes of the Spanish-speaking and Italian immigrant groups in the United States. Based on discussions with Hispanics and Italians, especially in New York City, it appears that Spanish-speaking groups seek the establishment of a system that is outside the mainstream, while the Italian immigrants prefer to seek modifications and concessions within the dominant system.

The same importance of setting is found in considering the background of Soviet, Belgian, British, or South African bilingualism. In the Soviet Union, bilingual education continues to be influenced—if not determined—

by the perpetuation of colonialism; consequently, the provision of such an education is regarded as belonging almost exclusively to the realm of politics and governed by political exigencies. In Britain, bilingual programs are influenced by different political-historical considerations, namely the gradual decolonization of the Celtic minorities. In either case, the historical antecedents must be studied before the provision of bilingual education can be understood or improved. This theme is developed in another of my research studies (Lewis, E. G., 1978e).

Institutional Settings

Institutional variables are central to a comparative study of bilingual education. Heterogeneous societies, however complex or simple they may be, tend to institutionalize the practice of linguistically differentiated communication. They prescribe rules of communication and codes that apportion languages to different areas of social life—like religion, or politics and administration, or education. Communication in all these areas is regulated by networks of explicit rules and conventions that determine the specific roles of the various languages. Increasingly, anthropologists are helping to describe such rule systems; and increasingly, too, psychologists are interested in discovering how such rule systems, or institutionalized behaviors, are internalized by individuals—especially by different ethnic groups. Such developments account for the growing interest in the study of the "ethnography of speaking" and the analysis of the institutionalized constraints on communication by minority groups (Philips, 1970).

Concerning the education of bilingual children, institutional variables affect the characteristics of particular ethnic groups and the relationship between educational provision for minorities (not simply ethnic minorities) and the system of mainstream education. For instance, it is important to take into account the degree of centralization characteristic of the mainstream system and how that responds to the needs of minority groups, who often live in certain limited areas and who want to design and control programs that best suit their needs and their expressed wishes. Similarly, bilingual education cannot be studied satisfactorily unless we take into account the relation of other types of minority education, for instance the education of handicapped children or religious minorities, to the mainstream system and the provision for linguistic minorities.

It is interesting to compare political institutions in different countries to determine their receptivity to bilingual programs. Although the relatively open and liberal system of the United States, especially where differentiated general education is concerned, would seem to favor bilingual provision for minorities more so than is the case in the closed, authoritarian system of the Soviet Union, this is not so. Ethnic groups in the USSR have a greater range of options than have ethnic groups in the United States, and theoretically these options are more widely diffused through the USSR. The fact that there are considerable and sometimes insurmountable difficulties in the way of individuals or groups seeking to take up the options is irrelevant to the principle. Minorities in the United States, unlike those of the Soviet Union, have for the most part few *group* rights. Apart from the Amerindians and Mexican Americans, American minorities lack distinctive tribal or national territories on which they might base any such rights. The contrary is the case in the Soviet Union where specific constitutional and territorial bases for bilingual education exist.

To take another example, bilingual education became possible in Britain when the educational system in Wales became institutionally autonomous, though not independent of that of England. Subsequently, the bilingual program has matured in step with the growth of institutional autonomy. The relation between autonomy and bilingualism is also seen in Switzerland. Institutional autonomy there is great, and because of that the linguistic arrangement of the Confederation works well. The difficulties of providing a satisfactory bilingual education in Switzerland occurs only where the linguistic differences are not institutionalized satisfactorily, as is the case of minorities within a canton. For example, the Jura French-speaking population are unable to obtain satisfaction for their linguistic-educational claims from the official German Canton authorities.

Structure dependence, a function of the interaction of institutional variables, changes from ethnic group to ethnic group and from country to country. Thus, the provision of bilingual education is integral to the mainstream system in Wales, the Soviet Union, and Belgium; however, it is usually peripheral to the mainstream in the United States. Sometimes, though, in America it is independent of or parallel to the mainstream, and this is the most characteristic provision for the Amerindian groups, especially those on reservations.

We cannot study a system of bilingual education unless we have an understanding of the mainstream system as well as of the structural relationships of the two systems—bilingual and mainstream. Institutional variables are the key to these relationships because they reflect the attitudes and policies prevailing. Institutions are agencies for crystallizing or consolidating individual attitudes. It is by means of institutions that attitudes acquire and are able to exert the political influence necessary to bring about modifications in the present system. Therefore, institutions are likely to be the key to the understanding of the relations between different levels or categories of education. Consequently, we may have two subsets of variables—those that characterize the provision for bilingual children and those that characterize the mainstream system. Moreover, a study of the subset of variables must focus on cross-national or cross-systemic relationships and variations in the provision of education for different ethnic groups, as well as on the effects on minority education of different degrees of reluctance or willingness on the part of mainstream systems to offer bilingual education. Without being committed to establishing a system of bilingual education, some nations at a particular point in their development (and usually for the sake of expediency) are prepared to adopt rudimentary forms of bilingual education. This was the case in Wales up to 1871.

To compare Soviet with Canadian, British, or American education, for instance, we need first to analyze how the treatment of other minorities in those countries compares with the educational provision for the linguistic minority and then to assess how differences in the treatment of *different* linguistic groups are correlated with the mainstream educational system. In the Soviet Union, for example, this would mean comparing the provision for bilinguals with the provision for handicapped children; additionally, it would require comparing the provision for Kazakh bilingual education to the provision for Georgian bilinguals and the relationship in each of those two cases to the mainstream, Russian-medium instruction. In the United States, it would involve comparing attitudes about language provision for different types of immigrant groups—for instance long standing European immigrants compared with more recent European or Asian groups, the Hispanics and Amerindian groups, as well as relating such differentiated provision (if the provision is in fact differentiated) to the mainstream system in particular localities. Such relationships between the two subsets of variables might be considered in terms of discrete stage analysis or of process analysis, where *changes* in the one structure—mainstream—are related to changes in the other—bilingual systems. Furthermore, the sources of change in economic, political, demographic, and other institutions would need to be analyzed according to their possible relationship to changes in the provision of types of education, especially bilingual education.

In making comparisons involving cross-national differences within and between mainstream and bilingual education programs, at least two kinds of institutional variables need to be taken into account. The first concerns the methods of selecting and retaining students—the age of initial selection, the criteria for selection, and the existence of built-in mechanisms to correct errors or aberrations in selection. Furthermore, differences in the total length of the process of formal education, differences in the total weekly exposure to formal education, and differences in the phasing of formal education (as between pre-school, elementary, secondary and post-secondary) are all aspects of the institutionalization of bilingual education and mainstream system. In the Soviet Union, significant differences exist between mainstream and bilingual systems of student education, and somewhat similar differences are found between mainstream and bilingual teacher education programs (Lewis, E. G., 1972).

The second kind of institutional variable concerns the relationship between the educational system and "status rigidity;" that is, the degree to which and the manner in which high and low status groups are associated with either bilingual or mainstream education. The type of education involved varies according to the ascribed status of the groups. High status may favor the advantaged in the case of mainstream education while negative status may determine selection of bilingual programs. The latter appears to be the case in the United States where often by law bilingual education is tied to low income status. So far as concerns European/Bantu bilingualism in South Africa, low status is attached to European/Bantu bilingualism; but so far as English/Afrikaans bilingual education is concerned, status is irrelevant. Status is relevant in the Soviet Union in the sense that the Russians, who tend to be the most prestigious group, do not favor bilingual education for themselves. In British schools, status rigidity influences the manner in which certain ethnic groups are selected, and the degree to which they are retained in certain educational programs. Status is not correlated with the education of bilinguals in Wales; but so far as immigrant bilinguals are concerned, their selection for and retention in the system of education is adversely affected by their low status.

Status rigidity and selection-retention variables may be associated also with the status or condition of marginality, a key concept in the analysis of bilingual communities. It should, therefore, enter into the set of institutional variables, or alternatively be included in community type variables. While "marginality" is an important general concept, its incidence as well as its effect on individuals may vary with the operation of such institutional variables as we have mentioned. A so-called marginal person may be conditioned from birth by his existence on the borders of two languages and cultures, and the educational and other institutions to which he is exposed may reinforce his marginal status. Irrespective of the length of his contact or the type of education he experiences, he may share his marginality with large numbers of his primary group and because of their numbers and the length of their marginal existence they create their own institutions. Such forces exert their influence at any or at all stages of the development of individuals—early childhood, adolescence, or adulthood.

A person involved in institutionalized marginality may not experience the major frustrations about social expectations that afflict those marginals who do not belong to groups where marginality is institutionalized. The individual who shares with a large number of others the condition of marginality belongs to a settled community developing its own institutions, but those who lack such a linguistic or cultural solidarity are not equally protected against pressures from the dominant cultures. Regardless of whether marginality is institutionalized or not, it is an important factor in understanding the acceptability of bilingual education to such groups and the formation of their attitudes toward it.

Behavioral Settings

We are concerned in this study with systems of education rather than with the behavior of students, teachers, or parents. In our use, therefore, behavioral variables reflect the way in which systems behave. One aspect of this behavior in a mainstream system is how it satisfies the aspirations of a minority. The system may be able to manipulate demands for bilingualism because of its success in promoting social mobility for minorities. The way in which the mainstream system behaves in this respect has a marked, possibly a determining influence, on attitudes about the need for or the type of bilingual education when it is provided.

For instance, during the last century the success of the mainstream system of education in Britain—especially as it promoted the upward mobility of Welsh and Scots—tended to legitimize it or at least to mute the criticisms of the delay in advancing bilingual education until the last half of the century. This is also true of new immigrants to Canada. In the Soviet Union at the present time, the overwhelming stress placed on Russian-medium schools at the expense of national-language medium schools is justified by the close meshing of the mainstream educational provision to the promotion of the social mobility of the minorities. The pressure for vernacular (and in consequence bilingual) education in most African countries did not become apparent until a significant proportion of the native populations had succeeded in advancing themselves economically and socially. The same is true for most minorities in the United States where the main stimulus for bilingual education is economic and social advancement.

The demand for bilingual education among some members of a minority group and its rejection by others in the same group, or the demand for it by some ethnic groups and not by others, cannot be understood unless the behavior of the mainstream, unmarked system of education is analyzed to determine its variable economic impact on different ethnic groups and on different elements within the same group. Such an analysis necessitates the identification of the forces that shape the mainstream system and the attitudes of minorities toward it.

The variables involved in the analysis of the mainstream system, as we conceive it, have to do with its comprehensiveness: how far it embraces all social strata and particularly what we may refer to as "ethnic strata." Many of the social and political tensions that are associated with the demand for bilingual education have their origin in and derive their significance initially from differences in the economic development of minorities compared with the dominant group. Other differences, like those of language and ethnicity assume importance because of their association with economic and political subordination. This argument does not invalidate the proposition that at a certain point in economic development, when the standard of life enjoyed by minorities has improved perceptibly and they have developed their own elites, language and ethnicity "take off" irrespective of economic considerations as independently powerful factors in promoting bilingual education.

All systems of education in heterogeneous societies—whether education is class stratified and monolingually oriented, or in broad terms classless and linguistically heterogeneous, or class stratified and linguistically heterogeneous—have to do with the distribution of power in society. To a very considerable extent this is at the root of whatever demand there may be for bilingual education or the reluctance to provide it, whether in the United States, Canada, Britain, Belgium, or the Soviet Union. The distribution and the maintenance of power depend on how society defines the valued populations—the types of people whom it regards most highly. In Britain before the development of bilingual education, the valued population did not represent all groups equally: the peripheral Celtic stratum was subordinated. This has changed step-by-step with the provision of more widely embracing bilingual education, so that now it is not uncommon for the traditional ethnic minorities to be overrepresented in the professions as well as in politics and administration. The Soviet Union, though less successfully, has sought to use the mainstream system of education to mobilize all ethnic minorities as participants in the total society. This is not the case in other heterogeneous societies like those of Southern Africa.

We come back, therefore, to the consideration set out earlier, namely that before we can understand the demand for a bilingual education we need to know the extent to which the varied expectancies—political, economic, cultural—of the minorities are being already met without recourse to bilingual education. This kind of understanding requires more than statistical accounts such as the relative sizes of various minority representations in the professions.

An analysis of the guidelines adopted to secure a just equilibrium between groups—whether those guidelines are based on aristocratic, paternalistic, meritocratic, or egalitarian philosophies—must be based on an understanding of the salient differences within the general attitudes to life of individuals and groups. For instance, the Welsh demand for bilingual education was motivated not only by economic aspirations but also by an egalitarian and meritocratic philosophy of education that contrasted with the paternalistic and aristocratic philosophy guiding the unmarked, mainstream system of education in Britain. In the Soviet Union, it is not only the fact of their economically more advanced status that causes the Baltic countries, for example, to press for vernacular (and therefore bilingual education) as opposed to Russian-medium schooling, but it also stems from their prior involvement with the egalitarian systems of education in the democratic countries to the north and west of them. Only a comparative study will reveal whether causal relations exist between the demand for bilingual education (emphasizing the vernacular) and levels of economic advance and types of educational philosophy adhered to. In the United States, the history of the earlier immigrants was that economic advance dampens the ardor for bilingual education, and the spirit of egalitarianism has resulted in a reluctance to emphasize ethnicity, or ethnic group claims as distinct from the rights of individuals.

External Settings

These have to do with a country's relationships with other states, far and near. Such relationships help to create the ambience for educational initiatives at home. For instance, Soviet attitudes to the "nationalities problem" (to which bilingual education is subordinate) has tended to vary with changes in foreign policy or with the threat and resolution of external conflict. Bilingual education, in terms of relatively liberal attitudes to vernacular education, has been favored when Soviet officials wanted to separate and isolate nationalities within the USSR from nations, such as Iran, possessing the same or closely related languages. The Soviet Union realized that by favoring the vernacular within the USSR they were ensuring a linguistic and cultural divergence from the foreign variant. Bilingual education also advanced during the peaceful period under Kruschev as a part of his policy of accommodating nationalities after a considerable decline during the War of Liberation led by Stalin. Prior to that war and now again under Brezhnev, vernacular education received little encouragement and receives hardly more support under Brezhnev; the emphasis, instead, is on the consolidation of Soviet as opposed to nationality rights. In the United States, attitudes to some enemy aliens like Germans and Japanese during two major foreign wars, or a concern for ethnic groups who are thought to be oppressed by unsympathetic regimes, like the Cubans or political refugees from Europe and elsewhere, has tended to affect the provision of bilingual education not only for those specific groups, but generally as well.

Community-Type Settings

The final type of setting is that which characterizes the type of bilingual community for which bilingual education is thought desirable. Some of these community-type variables are physical, some historical, some are demographic, and others are political or cultural. Hitherto, our consideration of the provision of bilingual education as well as our conceptualization of it has been restricted largely because we have failed to take account of community differences, a failure deriving from a lack of even a rudimentary typology of such communities. What is attempted here is merely an adumbration of such a typology, and much more work will have to be done to ensure an adequate analysis of community types.

GEOGRAPHICALLY ISOLATED COMMUNITIES

We distinguish first between communities that are relatively stable and those that are mobile, and bilingualism has been characteristic of both communities. Sometimes such stable groups are very large and not isolated. The different language groups constituting the Swiss Confederation (German, French, Italian, and Romansch) include in each case some geographically isolated areas as well as some dense urban populations. Furthermore, each of the four language groups is and has been relatively stable for many decades. The German-speaking population is over three million, and during the last century and a quarter its relative size has not changed by more than 3.5 percent. The French-speaking population accounts for over a million, and their relative strength has changed by less than 2.3 percent. In the case of the Italians, the figures are 200,000 and 3.4 percent; for the Romansch, the data are 42,000 and 0.1 percent (Mayer, 1956: 478). Stability of language affiliation may therefore characterize very large and to some extent densely urban communities.

Such stable communities, however, tend to be both small in relation to the total population of the country as well as isolated. They are usually members of geographically distinct and relatively closed linguistic groups, consisting of peasant communities tied to the land and possessing only rudimentary systems of communication. It is for these reasons that many of them have been able to preserve their native language though surrounded by superior numbers associated with more prestigious cultures. In some instances an isolated area may continue for centuries to maintain long historical traditions of complex patterns of bilingualism. For instance, Quechua is one of the principal languages of the Andean highlands of South America, and regardless of their different cultural backgrounds virtually all inhabitants of large areas of the *sierra* from Ecuador to northern Argentina are Quechua speakers. There is an isolated region in southern Peru and northern Bolivia where Aymara is the native language. Many of the speakers of both languages are bilingual in Spanish. In spite of the pressure of Spanish, which has been considerable for centuries, isolation has helped to maintain the local languages against powerful odds.

Another instance is provided by the North Caucasus of the Soviet Union. The area is inhabited by some fifty different nationalities speaking their own languages or distinct dialects. Such linguistic diversity necessitated the use of a lingua franca for wider communication, while at the same time bilingualism characterized groups contiguous to one another and in frequent contact. Russian was little known before 1917, the local Azeri language acting as a lingua franca. In Daghestan, according to the 1886 census, the number speaking Russian was about 0.1 percent and the degree of bilingualism arising from the contact of local languages was higher than that involving the use of the powerful Russian language. Their isolation guaranteed an ability to maintain their languages against the pressure of powerful neighbors. Also representative of Soviet communities isolated by their habitat are the Peoples of the North, relatively stable linguistically—according to the 1970 census—though with high levels of local bilingualism as distinct from bilingualism involving Russian: Even 17.6 percent; Nanai 9.4 percent; Udegei 10.1 percent; Nganasans 15.7 percent; Yukagirs 32.8 percent.

Isolation is a considerable factor in the history of Welsh language maintenance. In 1891, the thirteen counties that constituted the principality until the redefining of boundaries in 1974, belonged to one of three categories. First were those with very high Welsh language maintenance— 90 percent and over. These areas are in the far west highland areas. The counties where language maintenance was very low are on the English border, along the rivers running into England and on the low-lying seaboard, north and south. The intermediate category contained highly industrialized areas, and for that reason they had acquired communication systems that broke down their isolation. All the high-level maintenance counties have behaved identically linguistically during the last hundred years. Although the level of Welsh has declined in the whole of Wales about 50 percent, in the isolated counties it has been 20 percent. Similarly, the maintenance of the Irish language is a function of isolation. The Irish Gaeltacht, the stronghold of the national language, is in the far west of the country. In the most isolated area of Galway, 43 percent were monolingual Irish in 1961, 52.2 percent were bilingual, and only 4.7 percent had no competence in Irish. The Scots Gaelic-speaking area likewise is extremely isolated—restricted almost entirely to the Northern Highland counties and the Islands. The Gaelic-speaking zone can be divided into these three categories: the Mainland counties of Sutherland and Perth together with parts of Argyll, Inverness, Ross and Cromarty; the Inner Hebrides; and the Outer Hebrides. The first, the least remote of the isolated north, are by now almost completely anglicized. Of the Inner Hebrides, none of the inshore islands now has a majority of Gaelic speakers, while the third category—the Outer Hebrides—though gradually losing out to the English language still represents the Gaelic stronghold (See Chapter 3).

In Finland, Norway, and Sweden, the Lapps in their isolation are comparable to the Soviet Peoples of the North. It is true that in all three cases contact with the majority language is exerting pressure on the local language, but "communication between the two groups occurs without the loss of homogeneity" (Guggenheim and Hoem, 1967: 24). In the case of the Norwegian Lapps, the young children have little or no knowledge of the majority language, and in Kautokeino the primary school is organized to provide for the two groups separately (ibid.: 25).

ENCLAVES

The communities to which we have referred, though isolated, are not confined to a restricted or limited area but are diffused over wide stretches of country. Some communities, however, although they may be comparatively large are not only isolated but enclosed. Their enclosure may be due to any one, or more, of several factors. Some such communities are the vestigial remnants of much larger linguistic groups that have been in decline over centuries and exist now as core settlements. For instance in the USSR, Yagnobi has survived because of the gradual movement of its speakers from their relatively low lying home into the mountains where they are concentrated and isolated from other Pamiri dialects. Speakers of Uygur form small concentrations in the Fergana Valley where they are surrounded by Uzbeks as well as by the dominant Tadzhiks and Kirghiz. Vogul is spoken by enclavic groups in the Urals east of Perm, and Ostiak is encountered still farther east towards Tobolsk. There are small concentrations of speakers of Turkish in the Crimea, remnants of those introduced into that area by the Ottoman Turks. Among the most interesting cases for bilingual education at present, though hardly numerically significant as groups, are enclaves of Albanians, Croats, and Greeks still maintaining their native languages in the Italian Mezzogiorno after many centuries. In the absence of official statistics, it is estimated that between 10,000 and 15,000 speakers of Greek dialects are concentrated on the Salentina Peninsula and east of Reggio, the last remains of a population of Byzantine origin who invaded Italy between the sixth and tenth centuries. In the Molise province in Italy, there were in 1954 about 4,000 Croat speakers, a very small proportion of those who settled there in the fifteenth and sixteenth centuries in order to escape the Turkish invasions of Croatia. The population of Albanian origin is estimated at over a quarter of a million, about a third of whom maintain their native tongue. Over thirty villages constituting Albanian enclaves exist in Calabria. The Italian Ministry of Education, up until 1965 at least, promoted courses for teachers of Albanian bilingual children (London *Times*, 7 July 1965).

In eastern Switzerland, and in the eastern Alps generally, a number of Romance dialects are still spoken. Engadin is recognized as an official language for the area, though those who speak the language are bilingual in German or Italian. Rumanian dialects are spoken in various enclavic communities of herdsmen in the Balkans, and these people are also bilingual, being able to speak Serbian, or Bulgarian, or Greek according to the country in which the enclave exists. A much larger enclave results from the presence of the indigenous Finnish-speaking population in the northernmost Arctic region of Sweden known as Norrbotten. Though the figure has declined since 1930 when the last official census of Finnish speakers in Sweden was taken an estimated 20,000 speakers of Finnish inhabit the Norrbotten enclave. Slightly larger enclaves are found in many other areas of the world. In India, the Khasi of Assam, the Burushaski in Gilfit, and language groups of the Tibeto-Burmese Himalayas are a few examples (Emmeneau, 1956: 5). Enclaves in some African territories represent fairly large groups of recently arrived immigrants, as in Uganda where "they remain relatively isolated from the villages in which they settle" (Doob, 1961: 19). Enclaves of ethnic and linguistic minorities are the bridgeheads sometimes of more extensive colonization, as in the case of colonists in North America.

The enclaves we have described are quite small compared with the total population in which they are embedded demographically and geographically, but there are several instances of large, national enclaves. The Sorbs or Wends of Lusatia (Lausitz) in Eastern Germany are such a case. Though they have now declined to under 100,000, at the end of the nineteenth century they numbered well over 166,000. They are the survivors of the Slavonic tribes who once occupied most of the territory between the rivers Elbe and Oder. Linguistically, they are of West Slavonic origin, speaking one of the eleven Slavonic languages in Europe. A similar enclave is constituted by the Fries in North Friesland (Netherlands). The Dutch language has usurped Fries in West Friesland, and the German language has largely obliterated the Fries enclave in East Friesland. In the more isolated North Friesland, however, the language is still spoken and taught in elementary schools among a population of over 10,000, over 70 percent of whom speak the language.

Farther south, in Spain, France, and Italy, large linguistic enclaves exist as well, and in some instances such enclaves straddle national or state boundaries. For instance, Languedoc is the area more appropriately known as Occitanie where Provençal or *langue d'oc*, is spoken. The region accounts for nearly a third of the area of metropolitan France and is inhabited by a quarter of the French population. Of these, about ten million have some knowledge of the language. The Italian region of Piedmont includes ten valleys linked linguistically to Provençal. It would be difficult to regard as an enclave such a vast area with so many millions speaking the language were it not for the fact that state policy in France and Italy isolates the language politically, culturally, and socially. In such a case, the attitude of the state transforms a national language into an enclavic one. The same is true of the Basque situated on both sides of the western Pyrenees. Four-fifths of the area in which Basque is spoken lies in Spain. Of the total population of the southern Basque region, in 1970 an estimated two million spoke the language. The total population of the northern Basque country is approximately 200,000 (1970), and it is estimated that nearly a half of this total have some knowledge of the language, though very few of them are less than fifty years old. As in the case of Provençal, the attitude of the Spanish and French state has made a linguistic and political enclave of a strong national language. This is the situation of Catalan also, except that it exists in several enclaves in nonmetropolitan Spanish territories as well as in Spain itself. The main body of speakers of Catalan live on Spain's eastern coast between Alicante and the Pyrenees, but they are also found on the Balearic Islands of Majorca and Minorca, Ibiza, and Fomentera, as well as in the area of Alghero in Sardinia. About six million live in the Catalan-speaking areas, and of this total five million speak the language. There are about 260,000 Catalans on the French side of the Pyrenees around Perpignan. It is also spoken in the Republic of Andorra and used there for official purposes. Though Breton does not have speakers outside France, its situation is very much the same as that of Basque, Catalan, and Provencal: it is a national language that has been forced into an enclavic status because of illiberal language policies.

A more tolerant, accommodating attitude toward language is evident when we consider the linguistic situation in Yugoslavia. Of the total population in the census of 1972, eight million were listed as Serbs (39 percent), four million were listed as Croats (22 percent), 1.6 million as Slovenes (8.2 percent), nearly 1.2 million as Macedonians (6 percent) and 500,000 as Montenegrins (2.5 percent). In each of these cases, there is national recognition of the language, though in several cases the number of speakers is less than those of national enclaves in other countries we have referred to. In addition, nonindigenous minorities like Albanians, Hungarians, Slovaks, Rumanians, Czechs, and Italians—all of whom tend to be confined to their own restricted locales—have considerable linguistic autonomy. In the case of Yugoslavia, therefore, we have languages which, were they spoken by similar or approximately the same numbers in France or Spain, would have to be regarded as enclavic, but are here fully national.

So far we have referred to communities whose languages are now almost vestigial and have become enclavic because of their limited numbers and their subordination to the language or languages surrounding them. In other cases, the enclavic languages remain large and in some instances they are increasing in size but are isolated and enclaves because the state policy restricts their currency and denies their national status. There is still a third type of enclave, in which a part of the area where a national language is spoken is transferred by treaty to another state where it becomes a linguistic minority. Examples are the Germans of North Schleswig who were transferred to Denmark, and the Danes of South Schleswig who were transferred to Germany. The Alsatians on the borders of France and Germany are another example. At present, Alsace is within the jurisdiction of France, although all but approximately 1.7 percent of its one and a half million residents speak dialects of German. The Germans of the Eastern Cantons of Belgium are another example of an artificial enclave created by treaty. In the Walloon province of Liège live an enclavic community of over 62,000 whose native language is German. The South Tyrol became part of the Italian state after 1919 when the area was transferred from the former Austrian state, Bolzano, to give the area its Italian name, has a population of over 400,000 of which 26,000 are German-speaking. In the same area is another enclave, the Ladin speaking population of over 15,000. The Slovenian enclave in Trieste has had an even more eventful history of shifting allegiance and yet maintains its linguistic integrity.

So far as the United States is concerned, isolated communities and enclaves of the kinds to which we have referred affect the Native American population and some of the Spanish-speaking populations, but not immigrants. The enclaves of Native Americans (where they are not to be included in the category of segregated groups) are vestiges of communities that have inhabited the area for many centuries but whose numbers have now declined catastrophically. One instance are the Oneidas of Wisconsin; there are very few who are monolingual in Oneida, and those few are at an advanced age. Many of them know both Oneida and English equally well, and the remainder know Oneida to some extent, some better than English. They constitute an enclave gradually being claimed by the surrounding dominant English-speaking environment (Swadesh, 1948).

Only infrequently are enclaves of immigrants in the United States found because of purely geographic isolation. Thus, for example, the proportion of the total United States population concentrated inside Standard Metropolitan Statistical Areas (SMSA's) is much lower than the proportion of those of foreign or mixed parentage, or of the foreign born. Within the SMSA's, the percent of the total population living in the rural areas is proportionately higher than the first or second generation immigrants. The proportion of the total population living outside SMSA's and in the rural parts of non-SMSA's is much higher than the proportion of first and second generation immigrants. Immigrants are not attracted to most areas where they may be isolated (Table 1.1).

On the other hand, although about 95 percent of first and second generation immigrants live inside SMSA's or in urban districts outside such areas, at least half of the Indians of the United States still live on reservations. Many Indians commute to nearby industrial centers, but the relative isolation of the reservation promotes the maintenance of their native languages. The isolation of Eskimo settlements also ensures that the English language, when it is acquired, has to compete with the use of

TABLE 1.1 Urban/Rural Proportions of Total and Immigrant Populations in the United States and the NE

Type of Population	Total	Inside SMSA					Outside SMSA			
		Total	Central Cities	Other Urban	Rural Non-Farm	Rural Farm	Total	Urban	Rural Non-Farm	Rural Farm
United States										
Total	100	63.3	32.5	23.1	6.5	0.9	37.0	14.3	16.1	6.6
Foreign or Mixed Parents	100	77.2	40.8	30.6	5.1	0.7	22.8	10.7	8.4	3.6
Foreign Born	100	83.8	52.2	27.0	4.0	0.6	16.2	8.3	6.2	1.7
North East										
Total	100	79.0	38.8	31.9	7.8	0.7	20.9	9.6	9.9	1.4
Foreign or Mixed Parents	100	84.7	43.7	35.0	5.6	0.3	15.3	8.7	5.9	0.7
Foreign Born	100	87.9	55.8	27.8	3.9	0.3	12.3	7.0	4.5	0.7

Source: *U.S. Census of Population, 1960* (Quoted Taeuber, 1971: p. 121).

the native language. The children of Nicolai, an extremely isolated native community, all speak the Upper Kustokwi language. The same is true of the Upper Tanana language in Titlin and Northway. Such examples could be multiplied (Kari and Spolsky, 1973: 14). Further consideration is given later in this study to the rurality of the indigenous Americans and the Spanish Americans. At this point, it is sufficient to emphasize that the types of isolated linguistic communities we have identified elsewhere in the world exist in the United States also, and that every statistically measurable socio-economic, demographic, and derivatively linguistic characteristic reflects significant differences between the isolated rural and the concentrated urban native populations. Age and sex differences, the rate of intermarriage, and the size and structure of the families all substantiate the association between isolation and the maintenance of the native language together with English in the United States (Office of Special Concerns, Vol. III: 17).

"BOUNDED" COMMUNITIES

At this point, the distinction should be made between communities isolated because of physical or geographical conditions or because of the language policy of the state and those that are closed because of their traditional social structure and way of life. The latter may, of course, be isolated physically but their "closedness" is not exclusively a function of isolation: their stability and "boundedness" is an inherent characteristic of the group. This is observed in the case of the Pueblos, who live in small, settled farming villages and have done so for over 1,500 years. Because of their "bounded" nature, language becomes a symbol of solidarity. Difference in language or dialect can be used as a symbol of solidarity only if there is a clear and conscious awareness of the boundary between "us" and "them" (Mather, 1973: 43).

This is also found with the Daghestanis of the North Caucasus. Their boundedness is reflected in the fact that though a high level of local bilingualism exists, the level of native language maintenance is also exceptionally high. For instance, the Tsakhars are 43.5 percent bilingual, but they also have 96.5 percent native-language maintenance. Apart from the Nogai, the native-language maintenance is not below 93 percent, and it is worth noting that in their case the level of bilingualism is also low at 1.1 percent. Northern Soviet nationalities retained well into the twentieth century their traditional closed social structures: the majority of them did not develop beyond the limits of early, even primitive, bounded communal systems. They existed as communities of separate clans and tribes. Before the acceleration of immigration, the elaboration of a Russian oriented system of education, and the introduction of better communications, these ethnic groups had high levels of native language maintenance—in 1926, for instance, Udegei had 85 percent, Saami 85 percent, and

Nivkh 97 percent. Once their boundedness is relaxed, their language affiliation is threatened; consequently, in 1970 the three nationalities referred to had levels of language maintenance of 55.1 percent, 56.2 percent and 49.5 percent respectively.

The characteristic of boundedness becomes more apparent when we consider Native American tribes other than Pueblo, types "who formed no permanent communities and no bounded speech community. The largest permanent social unit was the family, larger groupings being temporary and ephemeral" (Miller, 1975: 5). These were bands who tended to move freely; their place of residence was dictated by the availability of crops and animals. There was a great deal of resettling by groups and individuals but not by larger entities (Sherzer, 1973: 783). This involved some shifting from group to group, principally in the form of intermarriage. The history and the traditions of such open groups have created attitudes that have a powerful bearing on their contemporary way of life; particularly affected are their attitude to the native tongue, which does not play the same part in consolidating ethnic identity as it does in the stable and bounded communities. Bilingualism and shift of language dominance, involving tribal languages as well as between tribal languages and English, are more easily facilitated in the more mobile bands.

But, however produced, relative boundedness of a community does not preclude complex linguistic relationships. For example, in the Creek Confederacy, although "Muskogee or Creek were numerically and politically the dominant languages, there were also minority groups speaking other languages, so that. . .the linguistic situation within the Confederacy was one of great complexity" (Haas, M. R., 1945: 69). A bounded, stable way of life has not entailed remaining in ignorance of other Pueblo language: Hano-Hopi bilingualism and Spanish, English, and Pueblo bilingualism attest to complex language contacts. But the Pueblos are highly conscious of their linguistic identity and careful not to undermine the significance their language has for the maintenance of their way of life (Dozier, 1970). Consequently, the impact of the colonial languages on such Pueblo languages as Tewa, Taos, and Keresan is slight. Speakers of those languages have adapted to the Spanish and English civilizations not by borrowing but rather by coining new words and extending the meaning of words already in the basic stock. However, some Pueblo groups have been more culturally affected than others by outside influences, and today they are less bounded than they were. This is the case of Isleta Pueblo (Leap, W. L., 1973).

LOCAL OR PERIPHERAL BILINGUALISM

Most of the nationalities we have referred to, whether isolated, enclavic, or bounded tend to be rural, peasant communities: in fact, the dominant view of anthropologists, particularly in America, is that the peasantry is the typical closed, bounded community. Many of them appear to be bounded as much by their historical traditions and by particular aspects of their cultures, especially religion, as by their evident geographical and social isolation. Because their closedness is partly a function of their isolation, and because they have long histories of occupying their isolated territories, their bilingualism is the result of contact with comparable neighboring communities rather than of contact with either dominant and embracing groups or with a widely diffused language. It is local or peripheral bilingualism, characteristic of the linguistic borderlands. This, as we have pointed out, is the case in the North Caucasus, in the Soviet North, and in the Fergana Valley. The last named has been farmed for thousands of years and is one of the most densely populated agricultural areas in the world. It is divided among Kirghiz, Uzbeks, and Tadzhiks, and its high mountainous defiles have isolated pockets and indentations of those major linguistic groups as well as other minorities like the Uygurs. Bilingualism is characteristic of these groups, but it is principally the result of local, peripheral contacts rather than of the spread of any one major language, and certainly not the consequence of Russian penetration. For instance, as determined from census figures (Lewis, E. G., 1972), the enclaved Uygurs are well above the average for local and peripheral bilingualism (9.3 percent) and well below the average in respect of knowledge of Russian as an auxiliary language. Additionally, their level of native language maintenance is high—88.5 percent.

There are numerous examples of such local or peripheral bilingualism in the United States, including the Shoshoni and North Paiute living near each other in Utah and Wyoming (Miller, W., 1972). There Shoshoni and North Paiute bilingualism exists in conjunction with English, just as in the case of the Uygur with local bilingualism in the Fergana Valley being concurrent with Russian. Again in the United States, along the border between Washo and North Paiute, local bilingualism resulted in such a mixture of the two languages that some tribesmen were regarded as "half Paiute" (Downs, 1973). In other instances, such bilingualism has helped to produce American pidgins like the Chinook jargon of the Pacific Northwest (Bright, 1973: 717). Reference has already been made to local bilingualism within the Creek Confederacy, as well as between Hanos and Hopi, and in the Isleta Pueblo.

Local, peripheral bilingualism involving two minority languages is far more prevalent in the Soviet Union than it is in the United States partly because of the greater diffusion of English over Russian as a lingua franca. Inter-minority bilingualism, like local dialects, tends to be eliminated by the diffusion of a dominant language. Another reason peripheral bilingualism is common in the USSR is that differences in kinds of contact are more numerous there than in North America. Ethnic and linguistic groups have been brought within the Soviet Union by changes in international boundaries, but Russian is not the only language to which incorporated groups are oriented. Such incorporated "aliens" include Poles, 12.7 percent of whom within the Soviet Union are bilingual in a language other than Russian. Rumanians also have high levels of local bilingualism—16.3 percent within the Ukraine. Greeks in the Donetsk Oblast as well as in western and southern Georgia have 14.5 percent bilingualism involving local languages. Hungarians in the Transcarpathian Oblast have 9.8 percent bilingualism involving Hungarian and Ukrainian. Thirty-six percent of the Kurds are bilingual in Armenian, Georgian, or Kirghiz.

A second type of contact is produced by historical, long-standing enclaves in which a language has evolved through contact with languages spoken mainly outside a country. This is the case of the Gagauz of Moldavia, who in addition to their own language, have a command of Moldavian. Many also know the neighboring Bulgarian language. Their Gagauz language reflects earlier contacts with Greek and Turkish (Baskakov, 1973). In the United States, such contacts are paralleled mainly by historical local contacts between indigenous Amerindians, Eskimo and Aleuts, or Mexican-Americans.

SEGREGATED

Ethnic-linguistic groups may be isolated or constitute themselves as enclaves in urban as well as in rural and remote areas. Such segregated communities may occupy barrios or ghettos within a city. The pejorative connotations of those two places suggest the segregated occupants are usually repressed minorities. Like the rural isolated groups, they tend to be closed and relatively stable linguistic areas, especially in the United States because they are continuously reinforced from outside. These areas are well defined urban closed communities, often the product of generations of involuntary and voluntary social, psychological, and linguistic introversion. Additionally, their linguistic segregation may be reinforced by other group characteristics such as color, race, religion, or nationality: in Britain for example, Chinese, Cypriots, Indians, and Pakistanis occupy identifiable areas of London, Birmingham, and other large metropolitan complexes. In the United States, Mexican-Americans tend to congregate in distinctly Spanish neighborhoods, brought about sometimes when the traditional Mexican plaza, the center of community life, was by-passed by the new railway, as in Albuquerque, New Mexico. The Puerto Ricans of New York City and other American metropolises are another instance (Fishman, 1971a), as are the Cubans in Miami, Florida.

In whatever manner such segregated areas come to be created, they are urban enclaves and bounded communities. They help to create attitudes to language similar to those of the rural bounded communities—it perpetuates their distinctive ethnic background, and its use is a means of maintaining group solidarity. In 1974, nearly all the Spanish-speaking children of Dade County (Miami, Florida) were concentrated in three contiguous school districts, constituting an urban enclave. The levels of language maintenance in the total area reflected the varying degrees of residential concentration. In the three most densely concentrated Spanish-speaking areas, an average of 40 percent of the students were heavily Spanish-dominant requiring special instruction in English. Only 11 percent of the students in the less concentrated areas were dominant in Spanish and required special English instruction (Dade County, 1975). In the Soviet Union, apart from the position of the Jews, the tendency towards segregation is closely related to industrialization, urbanization, and immigration. Moreover, linguistic-ethnic segregation does exist in the USSR, and it has the same consequences for language maintenance as elsewhere. Such segregation affects the locally dominant group as much, if not more than the immigrants who, in any Soviet urban setting, tend to be diffused and diversified.

The local ethnic group is homogenous, and because of the extremely rapid development of large towns they may become minorities in their traditional place of residence, as is the case of the Spanish in Albuquerque. This is equally true of Tashkent where, of the total population of 1,385,000 in 1970, only 37 percent were Uzbeks; nearly 40 percent were Russians, the remainder being Tatars, Jews, Ukrainians, and twenty smaller minorities. Of the Uzbek, 78 percent lived in the "old" traditional district, so that approximately 400,000 (less than a third of the total population of the city) lived in a separate, segregated area. The remainder of the total population occupied the "new town." The degree of the "boundedness" of the old town native community is reflected by the far lower ratio of intermarriages, the higher level of native language maintenance, and the lower level of Russian usage than in the "new" town.

MOBILITY OF POPULATIONS

Introduction

Different types of community—physically isolated, enclavic, bounded, or segregated—are just one set of variables in bilingualism. Another variable is mobility—movement both within and across linguistic, ethnic, and national boundaries. Such mobility has taken several forms; yet few studies have been made of the differential effects of those several types of movement on language maintenance. This paucity of research may be due partly to the lack of interest in historical aspects of the sociology of language as compared with studies of current sociolinguistic complexes. Where so many different kinds of linguistic minorities are involved, as in the United States and the Soviet Union, it is important to consider those aspects of their historical development that condition their current behaviors. A second reason for the neglect of migration studies as they relate to language may be a common belief that migration is a pathological rather than a normal process: "the dominance of functionalist and integrationist influences in the interpretation of social change have resulted in the migrant being defined as a deviant person, a 'marginal man'" (Jackson, J. A., 1969: 3). A third reason is a failure to conceptualize the issues, to advance a general theory embracing as many forms as possible of social and linguistic change engendered by migration. This failure to conceptualize is tied very closely to the fact that although "the social sciences have long recognized the importance of migration as a factor in social change. . .there have not yet been any systematic attempts to develop an anthropological analysis of migration" (Kasdan, 1970:1). Such an anthropological analysis inevitably embraces considerations of language.

As an aspect of social and linguistic anthropology, however, the study of kinds of population movement and their differential effect on language has to be undertaken within a wider context. Migration is a demographic problem: it influences sizes of populations; it is an economic problem because a shift in density of population is often due to imbalances in standards of living; it takes in considerations of social-psychology since issues of motivation and attitudes are involved; it is also a sociological problem because migration may influence social structures and cultural systems (Jansen, 60; see also Volkov, 19). Historical factors are involved in the differential growth rates found in the United States, Canada (Quebec especially), and the USSR; historical factors also help to maintain some languages, like French in Quebec, against the pressure of other languages. The Soviet demographer S.I. Bruk (1971) attributes primary responsibility for such variations to differences in traditional social backgrounds and traditional attitudes. Population movement represents "an alloy of several elements—social, psychological, ideological and rational" (Tatevosayan, 112). It is significant that in none of the studies referred to is education or language included as a major aspect of the influence of migration.

Among the aspects of population movement which are intimately involved in considerations of language contact are the functions that mobility fulfills: Zavatskaya, (1963) identifies three. First, an accelerating function, exemplified in Wales and the Soviet Union, where in both cases movement of populations increased the speed at which ethnic and linguistic contact had been proceeding for centuries. The second function is to redistribute populations, and one of the major differences between the Soviet Union and the United States is that while this redistributive function predominates over all others in the USSR, in the United States it is the "receptive" or accumulative function which is most characteristic. The final function is selective—differences in the age and sex compositions of migrant groups are important for language and characterize all the countries we are concerned with.

Another aspect of the wider context of the study of migration and its effects on language is the motivation of mobility. Usually migration has been regarded as exemplifying the results of the "push" of unfavorable economic conditions at home and the "pull" of more favorable circumstances elsewhere. In the U.S., this was the view of A. L. Haddon (1912) and Numelin (1937); Duncan (1959: 90) saw "migration as the main mechanism of adjustment to the redistribution of economic opportunity caused by national resource development and technological change which impinge unequally on industries and areas." Students of the Soviet Union tend toward the same conclusion. Parming (1972: 64) in his analysis of changes in Estonia between 1935 and 1970 offers three explanations. "First, we suspect that a majority of the immigrants during 1944–49 arrived involuntarily. It is difficult to understand why up to 180,000 people wished to migrate from other sections of the USSR to Estonia. Second, the most powerful explanation for the period since the mid 1950s is that Estonia has a 'pull factor', possessing the Soviet Union's highest standard of living and the most Western Culture. And thirdly, Estonia has no local labour resources." The immigration of agricultural workers from the West of England to help supply the industrial labor force of South Wales at the end of the nineteenth century was similarly motivated by the push of a depressed agricultural industry in South West England and the pull of a labour deficit in the industrial areas of Wales (Lewis, E. G., 1978b).

However, migration with the processes of demographic assimilation which may result from it is not a simple phenomenon nor is linguistic assimilation inherent to either of them: if it occurs, it is a product of the kinds of aspirations and motivations that stimulated movement. Hence, the results of inter-state or international migration may differ from local, rural to urban, within-rural, or within-urban area migration. The linguistic consequences of internal movements of native peoples (for example Amerindians, Spanish) may differ from those of the international migration. In theory, language and ethnic cultures are distinguishable from purely demographic transitions, but in fact all are aspects of historical evolutions and of transformations of ethnic heritages. Thus, while economic motivations may be sufficient explanations of some migrations they cannot account entirely for the early settlement of the English in the U.S., nor of Dutch, German, Swedish, Norwegian, and French attempts at colonizing and later immigration. Economic security was only one goal early American settlers sought—personal, group, civic, and religious freedom counted for as much or more with many of them. Other recurring motivations are the instinctive disposition to seek new lands, the satisfaction of a psychological urge to overcome danger, the inclination to rob, the attractiveness of conflict, and the pressure of mightier neighbors or inter-tribal struggles. The behavior of migrants toward their native languages and toward the languages of their new homes is influenced by the attitudes which impelled them to migrate in the first place.

Furthermore, the migrant does not simply react to his new surroundings—geographical, cultural, or linguistic. A large number possess a "cognitive model. . .as to the nature and goals of migration" (Philpott, 1970: 74). These goals affect their perception of the areas they leave and shape attitudes about their new social environment. "The composite memory of things past is a significant variable in any analysis of immigrant experience, yet it has often been ignored or given scant significance" (Jackson, J. A., 2). For instance, the immigrant may continue to express a lively and practical concern for the politics of his homeland. This is undoubtedly the case of the Cubans. Lebanese migrants to the United States have been known to have had a similar active interest in their native conflicts (Sweet, 1978: 180). The same is true of the Jews who may relate as instinctively to Israel or to the Soviet Union (whether they originate from that country or not) as they do to the United States. Whatever their commitments to their areas of origin (and they are far from being exclusively political or even broadly social), there is no doubt that concentrations of immigrants in the United States—Asians in California, Italians in New York, Puerto Ricans in New Jersey and Palestinians and Lebanese in Detroit—constitute networks of relationships with the homeland. They assist families and friends to migrate and settle in specific localities, thus reinforcing the original culture and language in strategic 'closed' communities.

While it is theoretically possible to establish a continuum on the basis of migrant motivation and ideology—ranging from those at one extreme whose total commitment and orientation are toward the new country or areas of settlement to those at the other extreme who are equally committed to their former homes—in practice the migrants reach a compromise. One aspect of this is the establishment of a network of social controls that to a greater or lesser extent help to maintain a degree of conformity to the social and cultural norms of the sender country or area and its language appropriate in the new setting. Such networks are reflected in the increasing number of Puerto Rican Studies programs in schools and colleges which, whether they are meant specifically to do so or not, serve to revitalize and maintain identity and solidarity among the minority. In addition, institutions such as the Taller Boricua Museo del Barrio and Taller Loiza, in New York and New Jersey to say nothing of Aspira and its activities, help to nourish the relationship of a Puerto Rican to the homeland as well as to provide appropriate centers around which the network of Puerto Rican interests and associations can be knit. Nowadays language, even more than religion, is fundamental to the functioning of such networks, and the degree to which the language is maintained depends upon the motivation of the immigrants who are catered for: whether they are voluntary or involuntary migrants: whether the impulse to their migration was favorable or hostile; whether the prospect of return is left open or not; and whether, if voluntary, the goals of migration were idealistic and utopian (the creation of a new world) or the immediate satisfaction of material needs.

Such considerations affect most linguistically heterogeneous countries although the degree of their importance in those countries varies. But there are some considerations that help us to differentiate fundamentally between some countries. For instance, it is customary to refer to Russian mobility as being almost exclusively territorial (or limited to movement on land) and that of Britain as only partly territorial (affecting the Celts) but oceanic in respect of emigration to America and other countries and in respect of immigration at present from former colonies. This will be elaborated when we consider international migration specifically. There are other considerations of a political nature with considerable relevance to the study of the linguistic aspects of mobility. The Soviet Union is a confederation of territorially and linguistically distinct nations and nationalities while the United States is not. In the Soviet Union, international migration is synonymous with internal mobility. In the United States and Britain, internal migration does not involve international migration. Furthermore, in the Soviet Union we have (ethnically and linguistically at least) a closed society of linguistic groups—migration results only in their distribution, whether within or across the frontiers of Soviet nationalities. The United States, Canada, and Britain are open societies—the nature of the frontier in each case is such as to ensure that to a large degree mobility is synonymous with receptivity of new groups. We may or may not prefer the advantages of the closed to those of the demographically open society, but we cannot ignore the differences or the implication of those differences for language.

Such differences focus on the relative importance of different kinds of frontiers, of which we can distinguish those which are to all intents and purposes objective, from subjective frontiers. The former frontiers include those created or sanctioned by history—politically and therefore in most areas ethnically determined, or frontiers that are physically objective, created by seas, rivers, and mountains. Other frontiers are social and psychological, imposed or acquiesced in for ideological or emotional reasons. Language differences in the USSR tend to be related to objective boundaries, save in the case of the Jews. Languages are identified with territories and these territories have geographically or historically determined objective frontiers. They belong to the category of 'European frontiers'. This is also the case in Britain in terms of the Celts, but not where new minorities are involved for whom linguistic frontiers ignore territorial boundaries and are more often than not coincidental with social-psychological or attitudinal divisions. This tends to be the case in the United States also except for the Southwest and even there strictly speaking only in respect of the Amerindian population. In Canada, the provincial status of the French-speaking population approximates to the status of territorial-defined nationalities in the USSR.

Differences between objective and subjective frontiers are associated with ease or difficulty of linguistic group mobility. In the United States, linguistic frontiers tend to be impermanent and shifting, corresponding little to administrative boundaries. In the USSR they are permanent, determinate, and coincide with national boundaries. Whatever linguistic groups occupy a city like Chicago—successive layers of Germans, Italians, Czechs, Poles, Slovaks, Lithuanians from Europe, and then Puerto Ricans—cleavages along lines of educational achievement, occupation, and economic status have transcended and cut across older associations by ethnicity and national origin. Such is not the case in the Soviet Union where language differences in large cities are maintained while social, cultural, educational, and economic differences tend to be eroded. In Britain, especially so far as concerns newly arrived minorities, but to some extent also in the case of Welsh and other Celtic speakers, the situation is akin to that of the United States and Canada; social divisions and frontiers transcend linguistic differences or linguistic lines of demarcation.

Type of Movement

In studying the factors which affect bilingualism, the first requirement is to identify, distinguish, and define the various types of movement. Gonzalez (1967) classifies 'labor migrations' (which is our main concern) according to whether they are seasonal, temporary nonseasonal, recurrent, continuous, or permanent removal. This is a satisfactory classification for general purposes, but the one proposed for this study is better suited to the considerations of the relation of population movement to language contact and consequent bilingualism. Therefore, first within-national mobility in its several forms is to be considered followed by a consideration of forms of international migration. Because some countries, like the Soviet Union, are federations of nations and for that reason migration may be simultaneously intra-and international, the distinction is not categorical.

NOMADISM AND SEASONAL MIGRATION

The most primitive form of migration is 'nomadism', which frequently is misconceived as unplanned or irregular wandering; however, its most salient characteristic is cyclical movement of groups within a limited geographical compass. Soviet Nomads, such as Kazakhs and Tatars of the Steppe, followed regular patterns from a winter camp through a spring route to a summer pasture and so back over an autumn passage to the winter camp again. In the United States, the Apache were also a nomadic group. "They were without systems of agriculture or permanent habitation but lived in temporary symbiotic relations with the Pueblos" (Dozier, 1970: 3). Although in a limited fashion it still persists among some small Indian and Eskimo groups, nomadism is no longer a significant form of movement in North America.

Nomadic peoples still remain in the Soviet Union and until fairly recently were an important aspect of life in Central Asia and the Far North. The Kazakhs have represented the nomads of the Steppes as distinct from the sedentary Turkic tribes—Uzbeks, Karakalpaks, and Iranian Tadzhiks. The Kazakhs were divided into several "hordes" with hardly any fixed or really regular locations. The Turkmen, on the other hand, tended to establish firm locations, and each of the several tribes centered on an oasis. Their locations contributed toward creating 'bounded communities', conscious of separate identities, dialect, and language differences, which was not the case to the same extent with the Kazakhs. Nomadism resulted in avoidance of the pressures exerted by the presence of any one major language, like Russian, and it has also been a powerful force, as was the case with Semitic languages in the Middle East, in promoting the diffusion of a tribal language among those with whom they came into contact (Whatmough, 21). A variant of nomadism is seafaring, and it has been responsible for the diffusion of Austro-nesian languages and in creating (after periods of low level bilingualism) such 'mixed languages' as Russenorsk, spoken by Russian merchants and the Norwegian fishermen of the Arctic—a lingua franca with selective elements of Russian and Norwegian grammar. This was a case of spurious bilingualism because each group spoke the same jargon but believed it spoke the other's language. (Sommerfelt, 33). The nomads of the Soviet Far North represent a type of movement that, while it prevailed as their characteristic mode of life, facilitated the maintenance of their language against the pressure of Russian. Many of them are reindeer herders and still remain nomads, visiting settlements only at long intervals. Their grasp of Russian is relatively low. Only 29 percent of the Yukagirs and 32.5 percent of the Itelmen, for instance, claim to have learned some Russian. In fact the level of competence of that proportion is low: children of these nomads, when they are placed in boarding schools, need to have intensive preliminary instruction in "zero grades" before being allowed into the regular classes. The Lapps of Norway are a similar case and are now recognized as belonging to one of three groups according to their levels of acculturation and linguistic assimilation. The three groups are Nomadic Lapps, Rural Lapps living in permanent settlements, and Village Lapps who belong to relatively densely populated centers. The life of the Nomadic Lapp is based on the migratory pattern of the reindeer they herd. In the spring and autumn of each year, they move to the coast, to the mountains, and then back again. All able boys above a certain age—and frequently whole families—are involved. The education of the children recognizes the differences between the three groups, each of whom attends at different times of the year and follows a differently organized curriculum. While the Village Lapps are proficient in Norwegian and attend the same classes as the Norwegians, the Nomadic Lapps are linguistically dominant in Lapp and able to use only a very few words of Norwegian. The Rural Lapps are linguistically less assimilated than the Village Lapps. Although they attend the same school as the nomads, they do so at different levels and contact between them is limited (Guggenheim and Hoem, 1967).

SEASONAL MIGRATION

Seasonal migration differs from nomadism. It usually is the movement of only a very few members of a total group, who tend to be motivated by individual, sometimes idiosyncratic goals rather than by group traditions. Because it involves a small number, such seasonal migrations have been thought to lack much significance for language change and bilingualism. But the study of the influence of small numbers of Welsh cattle drovers in the seventeenth and eighteenth-century as a source for infusing English into the Welsh language suggests that even a few whose seasonal migrations were regular may have had a considerable influence. (Collyer, 1976). Whether we are concerned with seasonal migration or with nomadism, the effects of such types of migration on language contact cannot be ignored and should be contrasted with the influence of settled communities. In the United States, Voegelin refers to this in considering the languages of the Great Basin: "The vagueness or indeterminateness in establishing language barriers in the Great Basin may be accounted for in part by seasonal migrations and, more generally, a fondness for moving about in 'wider areas' whether economically motivated or to relieve the isolation of living (otherwise) in contact with none other than members of a few families. . .One suspects less vagueness in determining where the language barriers lie in Pueblo societies." (Voegelin, 1973: 1107).

Nomadism and seasonal migration are both temporary in their demographic incidence; the regularity of nomadism and the frequency of individual seasonal migration, though, make it certain that the effect of contact is permanent. This is exemplified in the case of the Aldan district of the Yukut ASSR (USSR), which is a typical mining district in the Far North. Because of the effect of migration, less than 30 percent of the population is indigenous and only 78 percent of them claim the local language as their mother tongue. The immigrant population has always been temporary or transient. Before the arrival of Russian gold prospectors, the native population numbered 2,000 in 1897. By 1970, the population had increased to 61,000—only 33 percent of whom were indigenous. The number of migrants has far exceeded the present size of the population: between 1950 and 1959 over 100,000 arrived and as many left. The population has three layers: the native Aldans, who constitute a permanent core equal to a third of the population; migrants, most of them Russians who remain for three to eight years with their families, constituting 40 percent of the inhabitants. They are not there long enough to be assimilated and are a stubborn Russian enclave, drawing Aldans to them. Third, seasonal migrants remaining for short periods and reinforcing continuously the Russian second layer (Khodachek, 1973).

Temporary and seasonal migration frequently reinforces the influence of more permanent immigrants and so effectively intensifies the threat to a local language. Additionally, it facilitates changes in the areas from which the temporary workers migrate. The effect seasonal workers have on language maintenance will be discussed later in terms of agricultural, Welsh-speaking workers moving in and out of new industrial centers in South Wales during the first phase of industrial development. Unlike the case of the Aldans, the language of the receiving area was reinforced because the temporary workers were themselves Welsh. It was the Welsh area from which the Welsh-speaking migrants departed that experienced the eroding influence of migration. They might stabilize the proportion of Welsh to English in the industrial areas, but their regularly repeated cycles of migration and return changed the situation of the Welsh language in their original homes.

COMMUTING

Commuting is a variant of nomadism and seasonal migration. The cycle of migration is more rapid—daily or weekly rather than seasonal. Partly because of its frequency and regularity as well as because the commuter tends to be involved with large numbers of speakers of other languages in urban areas, commuting has had and is having significant influences on language maintenance and in promoting bilingualism. The commuter becomes a culture broker, an intermediary between groups usually at different levels of socio-cultural development. Tabouret-Keller points to situations of the linguistic hinterland of Toulouse where 30 percent of the population are industrial workers, 40 percent of them commuting daily into the city. Consequently the number of those who speak the *langue d'oc* or Provençal national language has declined as the number of commuters increased. Where commuting is less convenient and the working population remains on the land—as is the case in another village—the language is maintained (Tabouret-Keller, 1972:365–72). Robert Cooper's studies of the interaction of different linguistic groups in Ethiopian market places point to the same results on the languages of the *market migrants*

(Cooper, 1969). The commuting practices of American Indians on the reservations usually involve not only adults who travel to work but also children who travel to school. The effects of such commuting is all the greater because it involves not only differences between languages—for example, Navajo and English—but the very basis of the language's survival, the way of life of the tribe. The effect of commuting must be considered in its relationship to the individual commuter as well as to the community to which he belongs. Studies of language contact generally focus on the groups in contact, but the Indians are a case where the contact is primarily established by individuals acting outside the group but affecting it nevertheless.

MIGRATION

Voluntary

A more significant population movement is permanent migration—a moving away of a *collectivity* from one location to another. This movement of a collectivity does not necessarily involve the permanent departure of the whole tribe or nation from its original home, but rather the diffusion of large segments over new territories where they come into contact with several different language and ethnic groups. This was the case of the Celts who spread from their original home in southern Germany and part of Bohemia into almost the whole of Central Europe, including Czechoslovakia. Later they penetrated east towards Thrace, south into transalpine Italy, the whole of Gaul and most of Spain, before moving farther west to the British Isles. As a result, they created important bilingual communities that are represented in the languages still spoken in France and Britain. A less familiar example of the movement of a collectivity is that of the Yakut nation now inhabiting Northern Siberia. Their folklore and the lexical content of their language shows that they lived in Southern Siberia and knew about tigers and leopards but not about polar foxes or ptarmigans. Their terminology relating to material culture has traces of deep involvement with far distant more advanced countries in the East—central Asia, Iran, and China. Thirty-three percent of the Yakut lexicon is Mongol. They moved northward along the River Lena and entered on a new stage of their history. With their higher culture they were able to push out the indigenous tribes they came into contact with or, more importantly, subjected them to their culture and to the use of the Yakut language. Moving thousands of miles to their present home in the north, they helped to create new cultures and new languages— for example Okladnikov—arising out of their contacts. These are not isolated instances: the linguistic history of Europe and Asia has been determined by such large movements of peoples and by the kind of mixed language communities thus created.

At present, such movements in the USSR may follow one of three courses: they may be restricted within the boundaries of an ethnic group; or they may proceed across such boundaries without, however, crossing national or administrative frontiers; or they may involve moving into a different national republic. We shall have occasion later to refer to permanent migration across ethnic as well as across Soviet national or republic boundaries. For the moment, it is necessary to emphasize that while such migrations are crucial to the promotion of bilingualism in the Soviet Union, at present the main type of population movement has been local and the main source of urban growth has been the surrounding linguistically homogenous rural population. Two-thirds of new urban populations come from such rural areas (Perevedentsev, 1970: 34).

The movement of ethnic groups within the United States—for instance speakers of Spanish within and from the Southwest—is well known, and the general trends may be seen by considering two examples of Indian migration. The first concerns a large group of Sahaptian who migrated into the State of Washington, some of them crossing the Cascade Mountains where they intermarried with the incumbent Salishan tribes. Boas noted that in consequence "the present dialects of this region are practically identical with the neighboring Salishan dialects" (Boas, 1940: 220). The second instance concerns the Creek Indians who, before their forcible removal in the nineteenth century to what is now Oklahoma, migrated to Alabama voluntarily (albeit under pressure from colonial invaders). The Creek language, like some of the minority languages with which they came into contact, is a Muskogean language. Other non-Muskogean languages like Shawnee helped to create a complex pattern of bilingualism in which Creek was the salient feature. Most speakers of the minority languages shifted to Creek, though some adopted other minority languages in preference (Swanton, 1952: 12–31, 215).

However, not all such migrations in the United States involved relocating the rural, indigenous Amerindian or Spanish populations. Interstate movements have been a continuing characteristic, and such movements of both native and foreign born intensifies the influx that international immigration represents.

In fact, for more than a century the ratio of stable to migrant population in the United States has not changed significantly (Columns D and E in Table 1.2), nor has the proportion of the population who have migrated across state boundaries changed. While there was an early reduction at the turn of the first half of the last century, the tendency is for inter-state migration to accelerate slightly each decade (Column C). Until 1930, the foreign born maintained a fairly high rate of interstate migration which has since declined quite considerably (Column B). This is largely due to the native component (which includes all third generation immigrants, many of whom still maintain a non-English language) increasing in the most heavily populated areas that were once heavily weighted with foreign born populations.

TABLE 1.2. Proportion of Total U.S. Population Each Decade
According to Migrant Status, 1850–1960

A	B	C	D	E
		Born in		
Date of	Foreign	Another		
Census	Born	State	Migrant	Non-migrant
1850	11.2	21.3	32.5	67.3
1860	15.0	21.0	36.0	63.8
1870	14.4	19.9	34.3	65.7
1880	13.3	19.1	32.4	67.6
1890	14.8	17.7	32.5	66.9
1900	13.6	17.8	31.4	68.3
1910	14.7	18.4	33.1	66.5
1920	13.2	19.2	32.4	67.2
1930	11.6	26.7	32.3	67.3
1940	8.8	20.4	39.2	60.3
1950	6.9	23.5	30.4	68.4
1960	5.4	24.8	30.2	66.6

Source: Extracted from several tables in U.S. Bureau of the Census, *Historical Statistics of the United States*, 1960.

Such high ratios of migrant to stable population, and the relatively high ratios of foreign born migrants in the total migrant ratio over such a long period, makes for considerable ethnic and linguistic convergence and is contrary to the experience of the Soviet Union until very recently. Another feature of migration making for such convergence is second stage (or urban to suburban) migration of either the foreign born or their children born in the United States. Such a movement also implies the abandonment of relatively closed urban communities, where the ethnic language is heavily reinforced, for more open or at least more dispersed suburban locations where that reinforcement is less evident.

Involuntary Migration

Deportation, evacuation, forcible resettlement, and slavery are all forms of involuntary migration, and their impact on language has been recorded often enough. In each case communities, sometimes whole nations, may be involved; in others, only individuals are affected. Even when communities or whole ethnic groups are involved, they may be resettled as groups or dispersed in very small numbers. The nature of the language contact and the bilingualism that ensues depends on the size and cohesiveness of the group relative to the area of settlement and the status of the cultures associated with the languages. As we shall see, this is particularly important in considering the linguistic destiny of African immigrants shipped as slaves to the United States. Some of the first American settlers were refugees; and though the cause of expulsion or the pressure which people are unable to withstand have changed from time to time, such involuntary movements still account for an important element of international migration into the United States. (See Chapter 4.) It has recently affected the Jews, Czechs, Ukrainians, Hungarians, Cubans, and many others. However, those who are expelled or feel unable to remain at home usually look forward to a time when they may return. More so than most immigrants, they have a reason to cling to their native language however much they acquire English as well. Unlike the enslaved migrants, they also usually have the advantage of being able to choose their location on arrival. They are generally drawn to communities consisting of the nationality they represent.

The part played by slaves in the historical progress of bilingualism, while it should not be overestimated, cannot be ignored. In some areas their numbers were very large: in Xenophon's time, the slaves in Lauricum outnumbered the total population of some of the smaller Greek city-states (Finley, 1959: 153). Philip of Macedon colonized Thrace with Greek and Macedonian slaves—the large settlements bearing such titles as "the city of slaves" or "the city of adulterers" (Jones, A. H. M., 1956: 4). Such colonies tended to be linguistically and ethnically heterogeneous: the Greek slave trade extended to Italy, Illyria, Armenia, Arabia, Palestine, Egypt, and even Ethiopia, though the principal sources were Asia Minor and Syria, and lower Danube, and the Black Sea Coast. Romans added Ligurians, Sardinians, Spaniards, Gauls, and Germans. Augustan wars in Spain, Germany, the Alpine areas, and Illyricum and Panonia put large numbers of slaves on the market (ibid). In this mix, the Celtic element was probably larger than has been credited. It did not cease with the decline of Rome. Genoa had close links with the east through slavery. There were slaves in every Italian town—the ports and the interior, and they were a socio-linguistic fact affecting the lives of all classes, not only a few noblemen or patricians.

Intermarriage of slaves facilitated a complete blending of races. They were easily assimilated after a time but not before periods of bilingualism. The slave "was a product of Graeco-Roman civilization, an example of Rome's strange power of absorbing and assimilating aliens" (Gordon, M. L., 1924: 110). Their influence varied according to their occupations. The proportion in domestic service must have been considerable at all times: they were employed in secretarial and managerial posts as bank managers, and as interpreters, tutors, and teachers (ibid. 185). Their impact on bilingual education was significant (Lewis, E. G., 1976).

Africans migrated involuntarily to North America to be used as chattel slaves on plantations and small farms, in mines and forests, and small towns and cities. The Afro-American element of the population of the United States is large and influential. As a dynamic minority developing its own ideology that reflects its own culture nurtured in Afro-American bounded communities, it has had a great influence on the thinking of linguistic minorities without itself, I believe, being a *linguistic* minority and so capable of posing a strictly *bilingual* as distinct from a minority problem. But their exclusion from the category of linguistic minorities is due not to the "difficulty posed by forced migration to the preservation of any or all cultural and social continuities" (Mintz, 1961 and 1970). Forced migration of cohesive Indian bands and tribes did not prevent them from maintaining their languages. Nor has the forcible removal of some Soviet nationalities killed off their languages (Lewis, E. G., 1972). Likewise, the enslavement of Greeks in Rome produced a rich bilingual society (Lewis, E. G., 1976).

The particular circumstances of African slavery in North and South America did make it virtually impossible for their languages to be maintained. The slaves were members of diverse ethnic and linguistic groups. Although it may not be the case that the slaves were deliberately heterogenized in order to reduce their resistance, the fact is that the working gangs of slaves were invariably ethnically and linguistically composite. Over the centuries, to preserve their dignity and self-identity they had to create a new culture, based largely on their memory of the old ways. Their culture was alien in a way that the cultures of European, and later, Asian immigrants were not. To a considerable extent, the European cultures are simply variants of a Western culture of which the United States is part. By the time Asian immigrants made their contribution, a great deal was known about their cultures because of commercial contacts with the West. One should not ignore, though, the "antiyellow" racism of the late nineteenth century in places like Seattle and San Francisco. The African slaves were isolated linguistically and, more important, culturally. They were unable to justify the retention of their language. In conditions of linguistic heterogeneity, cultural isolation, and economic and physical subordination to a dominant homogeneous race, they had to acquire the English language. Although radical dialectal modifications occurred, English was the language of communication within and between groups. Outside the United States, the African immigrants in contact with colonial languages have created new dialects. This also happened in the United States with Gullah in South Carolina being the best example.

Afro-American self-consciousness and solidarity, as it came to be expressed in the 1960s, supplied a large part of the inspiration of the interest in bilingual education as a minority phenomenon. Though Blacks are conscious of their own dialects of English, they do not qualify or need to participate in bilingual programs as distinct from programs for the education of minorities, ethnic studies, and bicultural programs that take account of special dialects. The evidence is that they do not wish to develop bilingualism.

Other forms of involuntary migration have characterized the United

States, the Soviet Union, and Europe in general and have had a significance for language maintenance and bilingualism. Much of the migration
of Indians was involuntary. Often the tribes were forced to move by
adverse climatic conditions, as did the Hopi at the end of the eighteenth
century. They migrated and were given succor by the Havasupai, and
their friendly relationship endured throughout the nineteenth century.
English became their lingua franca. The Zuñi also sheltered the Hopi,
and bilinguals were encouraged to act as intermediaries and interpreters.
The history of the Mohawk is interesting because, though they lived
peaceably among the Dutch and English colonists in the Mohawk River
Valley of New York State, they and most of the Iroquois chose the "wrong"
side in the Civil War and were forced to migrate northwards toward
Ontario and Montreal (Chafe, 1973: 1171). The Choctaw Indians of the
Mississippi are the descendants of the Choctaws who remained after the
compulsory removal of the great majority in the early nineteenth century.
The Western Shoshoni were removed to the reservation of Owyhee in
northern Nevada and approximately 500 of them remain there. All these
were group migrations so that large and cohesive communities existed in
contact with new languages.

The story of the Navajo "long walk" is part of the historical memory of
that nation. Corralled by Kit Carson in 1864, 8,000 Navajos were forcibly
moved 300 miles from northeast Arizona to New Mexico. Such forced
migrations had occurred earlier with other Indians, for when Texas came
into the Union in 1845 an agreement with the United States provided for
removal of its Indians to Indian Territory. Such removals reflected the
operation of a three-phase policy that has had ambiguous consequences
for Indian languages—the three aspects being concentration, reservation,
and allotment. The tribes were usually removed in large numbers and
remained cohesive groups in the areas in which they settled, and as a
consequence they were able and indeed obliged to maintain their language as the only means of within-group communication. The reservation
became an insular experience where contact with other groups was limited, and whatever bilingualism there was did not endanger the native
language. The present strength of the Navajo language is due largely to
the concentration and reservation aspects of Indian policy. This was not
the case of the Huron who, although they survived defeat at the hands of
the Iroquois, were scattered in all directions and in very small groups.
Consequently, they were unable to maintain their own language as they
came into contact with numerous groups speaking different languages
(Chafe, 1973: 1170). Forcible removal by colonizing English was prac-
ticed by other colonizers too: it happened after the French-Indian Wars of
1763.

Involuntary transfer of numerous people has occurred in Europe as
well: Bulgarians from Rumania, Greece, Yugoslovia, and Turkey; Greeks

from Bulgaria and Turkey; as well as Turks from Greece after the Balkan Wars in the early part of this century. All these created linguistic minorities in the host country. During the period 1923–39, new linguistic minorities were created in Europe by racial, political, and religious persecution. Two hundred thousand persons were forced to leave Italy, some moving into neighboring countries where they still form linguistic enclaves and some going to the United States. About 450,000 fled from Germany to other Western European countries, America, and Palestine. Also affected by the expulsion of linguistic minorities after the First World War were Hungarians from Rumania and Yugoslavia, Serbs from Hungary, Poles from Siberia, France, and Germany, and Germans from territories they lost after defeat. These transfers helped to remove rather than to create minorities, but they also introduced bilinguals into fairly homogeneous areas in their resumed homelands. The 400,000 Armenians forced by the Turks to flee to the USSR helped to create bilingual communities of Armenians in Georgia as well as other areas of the Soviet Union outside Armenia.

Involuntary group migration in the form of group deportation (as distinct from slavery to which further reference is made in Chapter 2) has characterized periods of Tsarist and Soviet history also. The Tsar issued a decree in 1854 to deport Muslims inland from the Crimea, and the example was not disregarded by the Soviet regime. The Russian revolution of 1917 and the Civil War of 1917–23 forced over 1.5 million speakers of Russian, Ukrainian, Georgian, and Armenian to flee the country and set up homes, usually in group settlements in Central and Western European countries as well as Asia, North America, and other parts of the world. These involuntary migrants created bilingual communities in the host countries. Simultaneously Turks, Greeks, and Armenians fled from their traditional homes in southern Russia and returned mainly to Turkey and Greece. In such cases, linguistic minorities within Russia were removed or diminished. Religious persecution in the USSR resulted in the involuntary migration of about 10,000 Mennonites to Canada thus creating a typical enclave bilingual community in that country.

The process of expulsion was resumed later. In 1941 the Germans of the Volga were removed, some one million of them to Altayskiy Krai, Novosibirskaya, and Omskaya Oblasts (Roof, 1961: 2). Between 1942–44, 134,000 Kalmyks, 75,000 Karachai, 500,000 Chechens and Ingushi, as well as over 40,000 Balkars were deported into linguistically and ethnically alien areas. For example, Chechens and Ingushi were sent beyond Frunze and into the Petropavlovsk regions where they were forced into cultural and linguistic contact with the indigenous peoples. The Chechens were deprived of any support for their own language and culture (*Sovetskiy Kirgiz*, 1956). One of the most harshly treated groups were the Estonians, whose high level of education and culture made deportation into backward areas particularly onerous. For instance in late 1944, 30,000 Estonians were sent into labor service elsewhere in the USSR, and additional deportations were carried out in 1945. In 1949, another and one of the largest mobilizations of forced labor occurred; by early 1950, 129,000 Estonians had been deported. In addition, many had fled into Germany on two occasions and into Sweden and Finland. The reserve of native speakers of Estonian was depleted, and the impact of the Russian-speaking immigrants was greatly intensified (Parming, 55–56, 61). Furthermore, the nature of the language contact forced upon the Estonians affected their attitude to Russian and to bilingualism. On both matters, Estonian attitudes are less favorable than those of other Baltic countries, especially in Latvia (Kholmogorov).

In addition to such punitive forced migration, the evacuation of large proportions of ethnic communities occurred in Russia during the Second World War. It has been estimated that the total evacuation in the eighteen months from the middle of 1941 to the end of 1942 was close to 20 million. It involved the settling of large numbers of Slavic-speaking peoples among minorities within the Russian Republic, in the Urals and Western Siberia, and in parts of Central Asia and Kazachstan. The evacuation was temporary, but many years after the war 15 percent of the original evacuees remained in their settlement areas (Pokshishevskiy, 1969c).

Part Two

Case Studies

Two

The Soviet Union:

Colonization and Immigration

INTRODUCTION: THREE CASE STUDIES

Part Two of this book is on the historical development and the current extent of multilingualism in the Soviet Union, the Celtic countries, and the United States. The variables that may be said to have operated in producing such multilingual countries can be divided into two categories— on the one hand primary variables that have to do with the causes of direct contact between different groups, including geographical conditions and military and political developments; on the other, secondary variables that have to do with the nature of the contact that has been established. An example of the latter is the attitudes of the population toward language in contact, including religious, commercial, and educational considerations, as well as such demographic factors as the size of the language groups and the age and sex distribution of such populations. Both primary and secondary variables are subsumed within an overarching category of historical development. The geography of contiguous countries or ethnic groups, and especially their spatial distribution, assumes importance mainly from the manner in which they are exploited either to safeguard the isolation of the relevant groups or to create new or better means of communication between them. The military, economic, and political variables are aspects of the history of the group. At any point in time, then, the linguistic heterogeneity of a particular country, however produced, can be understood only if its historical development is studied. The early history of language contact in the lands around or near the Mediterranean, important though it is for its own sake, is even more important in illuminating the origins and later development of the widespread diffusion of Celtic languages and their contact with most European languages, the influence of Greek on Byzantine cultures in contact with Slav populations, which later helped to produce the Russian Empire, and the gradual evolution of separate languages like Spanish and French from the merging of the languages that constituted the pattern of multilingualism in the respective countries. The colonizing of the Americas, in turn, is part of the history of language spread in Europe and should "ideally be approached as an outward expansion of European populations" (Taeuber, 1971).

In the following three chapters, I center the study on the working of two or three of the more fundamental primary variables, particularly colonization and immigration, introducing the secondary variables as they become relevant in each of the three cases. A fuller treatment of these secondary variables, especially ideological, attitudinal, pedagogical, and legal, I have reserved for the third part of this study. Of the primary variables, geography is fundamental but it is not a dynamic phenomenon—one cannot significantly change the natural boundaries between peoples so that if geography alone decided the nature of language contact it would remain peripheral rather than widespread. On the other hand, colonization and migration are eminently dynamic forces and produce changes in the nature of contacts between peoples. Consequently, while the geographical variable is implicit in the working of all the other variables (because it helps to decide the limitations of communication networks), it is the study of colonization and migration that contributes most to our understanding of the growth of multilingual societies.

The present linguistic and ethnic composition of the populations of the Soviet Union, the Celtic countries, and the United States is the product of the conquest of some territories, the more or less pacific acquisition of others, as well as colonization and massive migration, all acting on primordial native groups and interacting with each other. Two types of colonization have produced language contact: the first is the traditional European process associated with the conquest of stable nations and nationalities. This has been exemplified from the twelfth to the fourteenth century and beyond by the Germanic colonization of eastern European lands, mainly east of the Elbe River. That colonization was facilitated by political and social arrangements as well as by force. German law was imposed on existing Slav towns as well as new settlements. The important point is that "the colonization took place within an already established Slav people who had a more or less compact organization and who resisted the new-comers and when necessary shut them out" (Braudel, 62), as the Caucasus peoples did the Russians. The successive wars for European domination have conformed to the same pattern and have involved the redefinition of linguistic frontiers rather than the populating of new and comparatively empty lands.

The story of the colonizing of the Russian empire belongs to this European tradition. It is true that the Russian occupation of Siberia involved moving against small numbers of very primitive peoples in a vast and comparatively empty space. But the Russian Empire had already been founded by following a different process. In the sixteenth century peasant colonization of nationalities such as the Nogais, Tatars, and other established nations occurred on the Volga, Don, and Dniester. In the nineteenth century the incorporation of the Caucasus and Turkestan brought the Russians face to face with equally, if not in fact more advanced, Islamic civilizations. Unlike the colonizers of North America, the Russians (with the exception of Siberia) did not possess a *tabula rasa* on which to engrave their record of colonization.

Similarly, the colonization of the Celtic-speaking periphery of Britain—Wales, Scotland, and Ireland, as well as Brittany, the Celtic area of France—belongs firmly within the European tradition. The Celtic areas were not empty spaces; they had established social systems and were civilized nations speaking languages with which were associated literatures richer in some respects than those of their conquerors. The fate of the Scots, Irish, and Welsh bears a resemblance to what was to happen to the Ukrainians, Georgians, Armenians, and others in the Soviet Union, and to the Slavs beyond the Elbe. This is very different from the colonization of North America. It cannot be denied that the European nations who followed the Spanish and Portuguese to that continent had to contend not only with the primitive Amerindian tribes but with their powerful European precursors just as the English had to contend with the French. But that contention was very largely for the possession of unoccupied or almost unoccupied territories. The Amerindian tribes, like those of Siberia (from whom some of the Amerindian peoples had descended), were small and scattered. With the exception of the Pueblos, they were largely nomadic. The same processes were exemplified in Brazil where the indigenous Indians slipped away when the Portuguese appeared. The newcomers dispersed over more or less empty land, so that in less than a century, like the Spanish in the North, the Portuguese had overrun—though not occupied—a very large portion of territory that was to become Brazil. The real problem was not the old population (they were either annihilated or had vanished), but the creation of a new nation in empty space.

In the New World a different type of colonizing process occurred. Many different peoples were attracted from many parts of the world. An intensive process of ethnic and linguistic convergence resulted, and the colonial movement is centripetal. In Europe the process has been one of divergence: the colonial process is centrifugal. The English diffused to assimilate the peripheral Celtic lands to the north and west of Britain as well as North America. The Russians, from the Muscovite home, have spread to the European West and sought out the diverse Asian nations of the South and East. Differences in the nature of population movement have produced differences in attitudes to language. The United States, in spite of its English language dominance, has been a nation of *induced* diversity. Diversity was an inescapable consequence, whatever attempts were made to ignore it. The American problem has always been to ensure unity without entirely obliterating diversity; on the other hand, Russia and now the Soviet Union, like the English in Britain, set out to *acquire* diversity. Russia was always able to enforce unity, by the military strength of the Mongol hordes, then by the Tsars, by the cult of the Orthodox Church, and now by the promotion of a single party and a uniform ideology. The English, too, enforced unity by military strength and the state religion. From the point of view of England and Russia, the problem has been to accommodate the inescapable diversity of the colonized nations within a uniform political system, without sustaining that diversity. While the United States admitted diversity, the Soviet Union and England have sought it. The different processes of colonization have resulted in different emphases on aspects of the intractible problem of the relation of linguistic unity and diversity.

Another important point of difference is that the national minorities in the Soviet Union have very strong territorial bases for their languages— they are in fact conquered people who have been drawn into an empire but not removed from their ancestral homes. In the United States, with the exception of the Spanish-speaking population and the Native Americans, there are no territorial bases for the minority languages, although if history had treated the German colonials differently there might have been.

While it is proper and necessary to distinguish between the Old and New World types of colonization, it would be imprudent to disregard at least two features that are common to both, or at least establish a continuity between them. The diffusion of the dominant language in both cases has depended on the prior completion of a long period of national mobilization and consolidation. Several smaller linguistic groups within the small state of early Russia had to be forged into a single nation before the state could begin its imperial progress. Similarly, before the North American continent could experience the presence of a multiplicity of new peoples, the pioneering colonial nations had to forge their own domestic unity. Before Spain could begin to expand in the New World, Catalans, Castilians, Valencians, Andalusians, and Aragonese had to be united as one state under a single king. In Britain, the English tribes had to be unified and then the Celts—Welsh, Irish, and Scots—had to be assimilated to safeguard that unity and provide a springboard for expansion. One of the reasons Spain preceded Britain in colonizing North America was its earlier completion of the phase of national unification. The same process of consolidation operated in Russia. They were a prelude to the imperial expansion that took them to Alaska, to which we shall refer in detail later.

There is no mistaking the continuity of the process of expansion within the colonizing countries and progress to and within the areas they colonized. This fact has been emphasized by other writers who had been concerned mainly with British expansion. Rowse (1957) writes of "the continuity of expansion within these islands and that across the oceans especially the phase of it which is crucial for modern history, namely that across the Atlantic to the peopling of North America." The same is true of the Soviet Union in respect of its lands. Some historians, like Henri Pirenne, argued in several works that earlier attempts to colonize failed because the Americas did not supply a need: America (when the Vikings discovered it) was lost as soon as it was gained because Europe did not yet need it. But another reason may be that Europe was not yet ready to take advantage of the New World. That readiness involved a sufficiently powerful and unified state to support and to provide the base for the enterprise. So far as the Soviet Union is concerned, the readiness to take advantage of new opportunities was based on the gradual concentration of power within the small Muscovite state, and the process of colonization has fed on the success of repeated adventures. For the United States, the unification of both Spain and the British Isles was a powerful force for the successful imperial ventures across the Atlantic. Furthermore, the British who participated in the actual process of American colonization in the early stages were those who had been involved also in the colonization of the Celtic periphery of the English Kingdom—Gilbert, Raleigh, and Grenville from Celtic Cornwall; Lloyds, Morgans, Vaughans, and Trevors from Wales.

Thus a consideration of the colonization of the lands immediately adjacent to the early Muscovite state is vital to the study of the development of linguistic heterogeneity in the Soviet Union, just as a consideration of the colonization of the Celtic fringe is relevant to the study of the same phenomenon in the United States. Much of the data drawn upon for these case studies is from census returns, and a consideration of the parameters of that source is offered in Appendix One.

COLONIZATION AND IMMIGRATION IN THE SOVIET UNION

Russian Colonization

The processes of consolidation operated in Russia and were a prelude to the imperial expansion that took it on to Alaska. Slav consolidation of their place on the Eurasian plain had to precede that expansion. They were forced to consolidate partly because of the pressures exerted on them by other nations, especially Scandinavians from the north and Islamic Khazars from the south. These Slavs of the Russian plain formed themselves into three main linguistic groups—Great Russians in the central districts, Little Russians (Ukrainians) in the southeast, and White Russians (Belorussians) between the Poles and Lithuanians in the west and north and the Great Russians to the west. The Polovtsi drove the Russians into the lands populated by Finno-Ugrians and thus compelled them to lay the foundations of the large principality of Vladimir-Suzdad (the heartland of Mongol Russia) from which they expanded. This heartland had initially been part of a non-Slavic empire under Ghengis Khan, and his successors dominated a land extending from Samarkand in Central Asia and the Volga, Kazan, and the Don river basins, and occupied by different nationalities. Although they freed themselves from the Mongols in 1540 in the final phase of Russian national consolidation, this early unification under the Mongols left an indelible mark on the linguistic composition of the Russian Empire, and on Russian attitudes to Asian as opposed to Western or European languages.

It was not until 1552–54, when Ivan IV conquered the Khanates of Kazan and Astrakhan, that the seal was set on the transformation of the small Russian state into a multinational, polyglot empire. With the acquisition of the North Caucasus in the middle of the sixteenth century, the period of very extended colonization rapidly got under way. For two centuries, until the time of Peter the Great in the eighteenth century, Russia pushed northward to the province of Archangel, eastwards into Siberia, and southward beyond the Caucasus. They incorporated such linguistic groups as Nenets, Komi, Permeans, Vogul, and Ostiak, and later the more numerous Mordvin. Other linguistic and ethnic groups like the Karelians and Estonians in the northwest, the Tatar, Finnic, and Chuvash to the east, and the Lithuanians, Jews, Germans, and others on the Baltic seaboard were incorporated by the Russians. Not until after the death of Peter did the advance to the territories of Central Asia occur. There the Uzbeks, Kirghiz, and Kazakhs, speaking traditionally important languages, had long established themselves in the lands they have continued to occupy. The North Caucasus, including Daghestan with its thirty-two distinct linguistic groups, became a Russian possession only in

1813. South of the Caucasus, Georgia became a protectorate in 1783, and in 1831 eastern Armenia was annexed.

To facilitate linguistic shifts to Russian in all these new territories and among numerous and very different linguistic groups, religion and the educational system were employed as agents of assimilation. For instance, in 1802 the Ministry of Enlightenment established six educational administrative districts with "curators" to represent them in St. Petersburg. Two of them were concerned with the national minorities. In 1803, a special law was passed for the Vilna district (Lithuania and White Russia) in an attempt to eliminate Polish political and linguistic influence. Georgia, after its annexation, was included in the minority district of the Caucasus. In the Transcaucasus after 1831, the Russians established a network of elementary and secondary schools to attract Armenians. This system of education performed two functions: within the Russian heartland it was a conservative agency strengthening the center; on the frontiers it was an agent of change aiming to draw the younger generations away from their national languages.

As a result of these colonizing activities, the linguistic pattern of the Russian state changed enormously. In 1724, the number of unassimilated, non-Russians in the southern districts, alone, was over 2 million. By 1859, the figure was well over 4 million. At that time the total population of the Empire was 125 million, of which 30 million were nonRussians and 17.5 million of them were in the Asiatic part. Of this Asiatic population, 7.5 million inhabited the two main administrative divisions of Central Asia. (See Table 2.1)

At the end of the nineteenth and the beginning of the twentieth century, the "Asiatic destiny" of Russia, which motivated the early process of colonization and a great deal of later immigration, was stressed as much as was the "manifest destiny" of the United States. Dostoevski (1896) wrote "this conquest of Asia is necessary because Russia is not only in Europe but also in Asia; because Russia is not only a European but an Asiatic power. Not only that: in our coming destiny, perhaps it is precisely Asia that represents our main way out." Similarly, the linguist Trubetskoy (1927) maintained that the future of Russia did not lie in the elitist direction taken by the Western reform and acquisitions of Peter the Great, but "with the 'lower Layer' of the masses: this lower layer is a separate zone by itself which includes in addition to the Russians certain Ugrofinnic aliens together with the Turkic people of the Volga basin. In the East and South East this culture fuses in an imperceptible manner with the 'steppe' culture (Turkic-Mongolian) and through it with the other cultures of Asia." Jakobson (1969) followed Trubetskoy in stressing these Asiatic linguistic affiliations of Russia.

By the time of the Bolshevik Revolution and the subsequent massive industrial development with its associated immigration, Russia was an

TABLE 2.1. Central Asia 1897 Ethnic Composition (in thousands)

Division	Russian	Kazakh	Uzbek	Tatar	Turkey	Karakalpak	Uygur	Tadzhik	Dungan	European	Others	Total
Total	690	4,050	2,038	60	249	112	102	358	15	49	22	7,245
Steppe Kray	493	1,903	—	42	—	—	—	—	—	10	18	2,464
Akmolinsk	226	427	—	11	—	—	—	—	—	8	10	682
Semipalatinsk	68	605	—	10	—	—	—	—	—	1	2	685
Turgay	35	411	—	3	—	—	—	—	—	—	4	453
Ural	164	461	—	18	—	—	—	—	—	1	2	645
Turkestan Kray	197	2,147	2,038	18	249	112	102	358	15	39	6	5,281
Ferghana	10	260	1,139	1	—	19	41	97	—	5	—	1,572
Samarkand	14	71	518	—	—	—	61	245	14	11	1	860
Semirechye	95	790	15	8	—	—	—	7	1	1	4	988
Syr-Darya	45	952	365	5	—	93	—	9	—	10	—	1,478
Transcaspia	33	74	1	4	249	—	—	—	—	12	1	382

Source: *Russian Census*, 1897.

TABLE 2.2. Estimated Size and Distribution of Population of USSR Territory, 1897–1914

Area	1897	1914
Total	106,080	140,405
European Part	89,915	110,836
Siberia and Far East	5,750	10,001
Asiatic Steppes	2,466	4,956
Turkestan	5,281	7,158
Khiva and Bukhara	2,175	2,475
Transcaucasus	4,493	5,989

Sources: E. Z. Volkov, *Dinamika naseleniya SSSR za visem'desyat let* [*Dynamics of the Population of the USSR During 80 Years*] (Moscow, 1974); and F. Lorimer, *The Population of the Soviet Union* (Geneva, 1946).

extraordinary and complex multinational and multilingual state embracing 140 million people and over 150 languages. The details of the ethnic composition of the Empire are reflected in the first census taken after the Revolution in 1926. Table 2.2 gives a broad picture of the size and distribution of the population in the nineteenth century in territories which came to be included in the Soviet Union.

IMMIGRATION

Comparative Analysis

In the countries under review, immigration is distinguished from colonization because the colonists—Russian, Spanish, or English—aimed to establish their sovereignty in the areas to which they migrated. Accordingly, they acted not as individuals seeking only personal gain or satisfaction, but as groups possessing an identity and recognized as representing either their country of origin or their religion—the Quakers for instance. To that extent the colonists, whatever their personal interests, constituted corporate groups rather than collections of individuals. These links to their homeland are reflected in their attitude to assimilation generally, and to linguistic assimilation in particular. However, for immigrants in a postcolonial phase, though they may and very often do maintain a lively sense of their original affiliation, the institutions crystalizing that awareness are usually developed in and adapted to their new circumstances. Those institutions come to reflect attitudes to characteristics of the new country and especially the languages spoken there.

Immigrants do not intend to change the sovereignty of the host country: they come to stay and they accept—sometimes willingly, sometimes reluctantly—the existing situation, at least for as long as it suits them. Furthermore, however large the numbers of immigrants of any particular nationality and however much they prefer and are able to live and act in concert, their status as immigrants is ensured for them as individuals. Because of the quirks of history, peoples like the French and Germans may have a colonial as well as an immigrant presence in the United States. The dividing line is the Revolution, when sovereignty was transferred to an American government. In Britain, no distinction can be drawn between colonial and immigrant phases of linguistic assimilation— "internal colonization" is still the condition of all Celts except those in the Irish Republic.

The distinction between colonization and immigration holds for the Soviet Union as it does for the United States, and a revolution (that of 1918) is the dividing line there too. The Tsars imposed Russian sovereignty on the independent countries they incorporated in their empire, but since the Revolution and a new constitution sovereignty has devolved on all the peoples of the Union—Georgians, Armenians, Ukrainians, and Russians alike. Colonialism has ceased in theory and consequently all international migration within the Soviet Union takes on the character of internal migration. International immigration in the United States means movement across national boundaries from *external* origins, but in the Soviet Union it means movement across national boundaries *within* the nation-state. This has two consequences for language development. First, in theory if not in fact, all men and women wherever they are, whether they remain in a Union Republic (or similar administrative unit) that is their traditional home or have migrated to another Union Republic many hundreds or perhaps thousands of miles away, have the same constitutional rights to use and to be educated in their native language, as if they had never emigrated. Such linguistic rights are not found in most other countries. The Welsh language does not have the same status in other parts of Great Britain that it has within the national territory. So far as the United States is concerned, differential status of minority languages according to territory does not exist except for Spanish in New Mexico, which is recognized as an official language in the state constitution. Second, in the United States, international migration means the *reception* of new populations from abroad, but in the Soviet Union *as a whole* international migration takes on the same character as it does in the United States—it means the reception of new ethnic groups into a particular republic albeit from within the Soviet Union exclusively. In this respect, each Union Republic is a microcosm of the United States.

The policy of language rights in the Soviet Union has considerable significance for attitudes. Massive redistribution of so many different national groups has entailed the acknowledgment of a single lingua franca, Russian. Constitutionally, such a situation not only need not but should not have occurred. The titular language of a Union Republic such as Armenia, Georgia, Lithuania, the Ukraine, Tadzikstan, and so forth could well suffice as a lingua franca within its own territory. The needs of the federation could be met by a limited diffusion of Russian or by a network of international bilingualism as in the case of Switzerland. The status of Russian as a lingua franca derives almost entirely from the centralizing character of the Soviet Union. For this reason the function of bilingualism in the USSR and the United States, despite their opposed constitutional characters, are identical: the acquisition of a dominant language, either Russian or English, as a second language.

All but a few of the separate republics are inhabited by a stable indigenous majority that maintains the native language. Perhaps the main difference between the United States and the Soviet Union in respect of their linguistic diversity lies in the extent to which the languages are entrenched in large and traditionally associated territories, however many other indigenous or immigrant minorities may also inhabit those territories (Table 2.3). Apart from the Mexican-American and Amerindian population, this association between language and territory is not true of the United States. The position of the Celtic groups in Britain is that they, too, possess the advantage of territoriality which is the strength of the Welsh language. Similarly, the Irish language in the Republic rests on the

TABLE 2.3. Most Widely Dispersed Linguistic Groups, 1970

Language	Nos. in Thousands	% Dispersal[a]
Armenian		
Total in USSR	3,559	13.4
Total in Armenian SSR[b]	2,208	
Total in Azerbaydzhan SSR	484	
Total in Georgian SSR	452	
Total in Russian SSR	299	
Total in Turkmen SSR	23	
Azerbaydzhani		
Total in USSR	4,380	19.0
Total in Azerbaydzhan SR	3,777	
Total in Georgian SSR	218	
Total in Armenian SSR	148	
Total in Russian SSR	96	
Total in Kazakh SSR	55	
Total in Turkmen SSR	4	
Total in Kirghiz SSR	13	
Belorussians		
Total in USSR	9,052	20.0
Total in Belorussian SSR	7,290	
Total in RSFSR	964	
Total in Ukraine SSR	78	
Total in Kazakh SSR	198	
Total in Latvian SSR	95	

TABLE 2.3. *(continued)*

Language	Nos. in Thousands	% Dispersal[a]
Belorussians (continued)		
Total in Lithuanian SSR	45	
Total in Estonian SSR	19	
Estonians		
Total in USSR	1,007	8.2
Total in Estonian SSR	925	
Total in RSFSR	84	
Total in Latvian SSR	4.3	
Georgians		
Total in USSR	3,245	4.0
Total in Georgian SSR	3,131	
Total in RSFSR[c]	69	
Total in Azer SSR	13.6	
Total in Armenian SSR	1.4	
Germans		
Total in USSR	1,846	100.0
Total in RSFSR	762	
Total in Kazakh SSR (in 17 different Oblasts)	840	
Total in Kirghiz SSR	96	
Total in Tadzhik SSR	37.7	
Total in Latvian SSR	5.4	
Greeks		
Total in USSR	337	100.0
Total in Ukrainian SSR	107	
Total in Georgian SSR	89	
Total in RSFSR	58	
Total in Armenian SSR	5.7	
Jews		
Total in USSR	2,151	100.0
Total in RSFSR	808	
Total in Ukrainian SSR	777	
Total in Belorussian SSR	148	
Total in Uzbek SSR	103	
Total in Moldavian SSR	98	
Total in Georgian SSR	55	
Total in Azer SSR	41	
Total in Latvian SSR	37	
Total in Kazakh SSR	28	
Total in Lithuanian SSR	24	
Total in Tadzhik SSR	15	
Total in Kirghiz SSR	7.7	
Total in Estonian SSR	5.3	
Kazakhs		
Total in USSR	5,229	21.0
Total in Kazakh SSR	4,161	

TABLE 2.3. *(continued)*

Language	Nos. in Thousands	% Dispersal[a]
Kazakhs (continued)		
Total in Uzbek SSR	549	
Total in RSFSR	478	
Total in Turkmen SSR	69	
Total in Kirghiz SSR	22	
Total in Tadzhik SSR	8.3	
Kirghiz		
Total in USSR	1,452	15.0
Total in Kirghiz SSR	1,285	
Total in Uzbek SSR	111	
Total in Tadzhik SSR	36	
Total in Kazakh SSR	7.4	
Total in RSFSR	4.5	
Koreans		
Total in USSR	357	100.0
Total in Uzbek SSR	151	
Total in RSFSR	101	
Total in Kazakh SSR	78	
Total in Kirghiz SSR	9.4	
Total in Tadzhik SSR	8.5	
Kurds		
Total in USSR	89	100.0
Total in Armenian SSR	37	
Total in Georgian SSR	21	
Total in Kirghiz SSR	8.0	
Letts		
Total in USSR	1,430	6.0
Total in Latvian SSR	1,342	
Total in RSFSR	80	
Total in Lithuanian SSR	8	
Total in Estonian SSR	3.3	
Lithuanians		
Total in USSR	2,665	6.0
Total in Lithuanian SSR	2,507	
Total in RSFSR	190	
Total in Latvian SSR	41	
Total in Belorussian SSR	8	
Moldavians		
Total in USSR	2,698	15.0
Total in Moldavian SSR	2,304	
Total in Ukrainian SSR	266	
Total in RSFSR	88	
Total in Kazakh SSR	26	

TABLE 2.3. (*continued*)

Language	Nos. in Thousands	% Dispersal[a]
Mordvins		
Total in USSR	1,263	90.0
Total in RSFSR	1,177	
Total in Mordvin ASSR	365	
Total in Kazakh SSR	34	
Total in Tadzhik SSR	7.0	
Total in Kirghiz SSR	5.4	
Poles		
Total in USSR	1,167	100.0
Total in Belorussian SSR	383	
Total in Ukrainian SSR	295	
Total in Lithuanian SSR	240	
Total in RSFSR	207	
Total in Latvian SSR	63	
Total in Kazakh SSR	61	
Russians		
Total in USSR	129,015	18.0
Total in RSFSR	107,748	
Total in Ukrainian SSR	9,126	
Total in Kazakh SSR	5,500	
Total in Uzbek SSR	1,496	
Total in Belorussian SSR	938	
Total in Kirghiz SSR	856	
Total in Latvian SSR	705	
Total in Azer SSR	510	
Total in Moldavian SSR	414	
Total in Georgian SSR	397	
Total in Tadzhik SSR	344	
Total in Estonian SSR	335	
Total in Turkmen SSR	313	
Total in Lithuanian SSR	268	
Total in Armenian SSR	66	
Tadzhiks		
Total in USSR	2,136	14.0
Total in Tadzhik SSR	1,630	
Total in Uzbek SSR	457	
Total in Kirghiz SSR	22	
Total in Kazakh SSR	10	
Total in RSFSR	8	
Tatars		
Total in USSR	5,931	16.0
Total in RSFSR	4,578	
Total in Tatar ASSR[d]	1,546	
Total in Bashkir Oblast	945	
Total in 17 Other Oblasts	1,732	
Total in Krasnoyarsk Kray	63	
Total in Mordvin ASSR	45	

TABLE 2.3. *(continued)*

Language	Nos. in Thousands	% Dispersal[a]
Tatars (continued)		
Total in Mari ASSR	40	
Total in Uzbek SSR	578	
Total in Kazakh SSR	284	
Total in Ukrainian SSR	76	
Total in Tadzhik SSR	71	
Total in Kirghiz SSR	69	
Total in Turkmen SSR	36	
Total in Azer SSR	32	
Turkmen		
Total in USSR	1,525	8.0
Total in Turkmen SSR	1,417	
Total in Uzbek SSR	71	
Total in RSFSR	18	
Total in Tadzhik SSR	11	
Ukrainians		
Total in USSR	40,753	12.0
Total in Ukrainian SSR	35,284	
Total in RSFSR	3,346	
Total in Kazakh SSR	930	
Total in Moldavian SSR	507	
Total in Belorussian SSR	191	
Total in Kirghiz SSR	120	
Total in Uzbek SSR	115	
Total in Latvian SSR	53	
Total in Georgian SSR	50	
Total in Turkmen SSR	35	
Total in Tadzhik SSR	32	
Total in Azer SSR	29	
Total in Estonian SSR	28	
Total in Lithuanian SSR	25	
Total in Armenian SSR	8.4	
Uzbeks		
Total in USSR	9,195	15.0
Total in Uzbek SSR	7,734	
Total in Karakalpak ASSR	213	
Total in Tadzhik SSR	666	
Total in Kirghiz SSR	333	
Total in Kazakh SSR	208	
Total in Turkmen SSR	179	
Total in RSFSR	35	

Source: *Soviet Census, 1970.*

[a] Groups not indigenous to the USSR are 100% dispersed because they have no native territorial base in the country.
[b] SSR—Soviet Socialist Republic
[c] RSFSR—Russian Soviet Federated Socialist Republic
[d] ASSR—Autonomous Soviet Socialist Republic

assurance of maintaining such a base. This means that in the Soviet Union the native language as well as Russian has a status and maintains itself in the titular territories. In addition, though the status of the minority languages in a Union Republic is less prestigious than the titular language, they also may be taught and used in schools and at some levels of administration. The tension existing between the lingua franca and the other languages of the United States exists in the Soviet Union also. However, though there is a far higher level of acquisition of the lingua franca in the United States than in the Soviet Union, the United States has nothing like the complexity of minority bilingualisms recognized statutorily in administration, schools, and general social usage in the Soviet Union, arising from different colonizing processes and the differences in the processes of immigration that brought languages into contact.

RUSSIAN PENETRATION

Internal migration characterized Tsarist Russia after the Emancipation. This was partly a response to the economic conditions in the densely populated areas that had made Emancipation necessary in the first place. Although one direction of such migration was to the eastern frontiers, among non-Russian ethnic and linguistic groups little international migration occurred. Since the downfall of the Tsarist regime, Russian immigration had been heavy to the west and north and particularly into the vast Central Asian territories.

Explorers since the fifteenth century were interested in Asiatic Russia. Covering nearly 45 percent of the total territory of the USSR and inhabited by over fifty different ethnic groups, the imperial dynasties had not been greatly interested in the area. This has been attributed mainly to the reluctance of the great landowners of the central regions, who were tied economically to the interests of the Tsars, to lose through migration the abundant labor supply for their vast estates. But after the discovery of gold in the nineteenth century, an intense economic interest was aroused. At the end of the century, the imperial administration began to promote migration to Siberia as well as the Central Asian lands. Subsidization and the setting up of the All Union Migration Committee in 1925 accelerated movement beyond the Urals. The Trans-Siberian Railway also helped open up the area. Exiles, prisoners, and peasants swelled the number of migrants from 375,000 between 1801 and 1850 to 2.3 million by 1900. From 1900 to the end of the Revolution, over 3 million Russian and other Slavic migrants are estimated to have settled in the area.

There were no Russians in the East Siberian region at the beginning of the seventeenth century; a hundred years later they accounted for 40 percent of the population. This large nucleus of a Russian-speaking population subsequently assumed enormous significance because those who were attracted to the area tended to be members of the same language group. This is typical of immigration everywhere—like-calls-to-like in Chicago, New York, Toronto, London, or Birmingham as it does in Siberia. Thus, the ratio of Russians to the indigenous ethnic groups changed completely. Having been about proportionately equal at the start of the nineteenth century, the Russians became the majority (62 percent) fifty years later and have continued to increase.

The effects of such migration on language affiliation tend to be ambiguous or ambivalent, and this is true of Eastern Siberia. Though many of the small ethnic languages and dialects were submerged, the Russian presence was not entirely disadvantageous to the indigenous languages because the Russians gave a powerful stimulus to the economic development of the area and thus helped to stabilize the ethnic groups and their languages. For instance Buryats, Yakuts, and some of the Transbaykalian Tungus learned to make use of the new economic techniques introduced by the Russians—haymaking, storing, stabling of livestock, using firearms in hunting, and so forth. As a consequence, many ethnic groups became more stable demographically and economically, and they suffered less from inevitably unfavorable physical conditions and occasional natural catastrophes. Their rates of natural growth improved with higher birth and lower mortality rates, and they became stronger entities.

This was true of most groups. Of course, some like the Transbaykalian Tungus were russified, and others like Aga Buryats escaped that condition only by isolating themselves territorially and shunning contact. In other areas, however, Buryats did interact with Russians; where this occurred, Buryats not only assimilated to Russian, but in many instances they assimilated other minorities to themselves as was the fate of the Evenki. Similarly the Yakut, of Central Yakutia, increased their numbers and expanded to other territories. They assimilated other language groups and even some speakers of Russian. In some of these areas where the Yakut extended their territories, new linguistic and ethnic groups were produced. On the left bank of the Yenisey a new Turkic language, Khakass, came into being after consolidation of Turkic tribes and their assimilation of Southern Samoyed and Keti. In the Katanga region, a start was made in forming a new Yakut language, Dolgan, based on the assimilation of Yakuts, Evenki, Russians, and Northern Samoyeds. In the northeast of the region, the Yakuts continued to assimilate local groups like Yukagirs and Lamuts (Okladnikov, 1968). It is impossible to know if these linguistic developments would have occurred without the intrusion of the Russian-speaking element. But it is highly probable that the migration of the Russians was a strong catalyst that affected the interrelations of non-Russian languages.

Turkestan Kray had 200,000 Russians in 1897, 3 percent of the total population. In 1911, the number of Russians had increased to 410,000 (7 percent). In 1920, the Russians represented an even greater proportion of the turkestan population (See Table 2.4).

In the same period (1897–1911), the Russian penetration of the Steppe Kray had increased from 20 percent of the total population to 75 percent (Soviet Census, 1929). In 1934, the number of Russians in the territory now recognized as the Estonian SSR was 41,000; by 1959 they had increased sixfold and by 1970 over eightfold, to a total of 335,000 (Soviet Census, 1970). The history of nearly all the other Federated Republics is similar. Only in Georgia, Lithuania, and Armenia is the Russian element less than 10 percent of the total population. The flood of Russian immigration has been retarded in only one Republic, Georgia, where the total of Russians was reduced by 11,000 between 1959 and 1970. Elsewhere, the tendency has been very much in favor of Russian immigration. The average increase has been between 11 percent (Lithuania) and 14 percent (Belorussia, Uzbekistan, and Moldavia). The increase in Armenia was 17 percent and in Kirghizstan, Tadzhikstan, and Turkmenistan 13 percent. Apart from Georgia, the flow has been least in Azerbaydzhan (2 percent) and Estonia (4 percent). In only two Republics do the Russians number fewer than about one third of a million—Lithuania (268,000) and Armenia (66,000). Obviously, the size of the immigrant population has a great deal to do with the maintenance of its language.

The percentage of Russians has declined in nine Republics—the Russian Republic itself, Uzbekistan, Kazakhstan, Georgia, Azerbaydzhan, Kirghizia, Tadzhikstan, Armenia, and Turkemnistan. One of the principal reasons for the decline in Russia itself is the outflow of Russians to other areas. In the remaining eight Republics, the Russian proportion has fallen (in spite of a rise in total numbers) because of the higher natural increase among the indigenous populations and the fact that many other ethnic groups like the Russians have increased their representation as minorities in those Republics. Nevertheless, the decline of the Russian proportion does not diminish its influence. The larger the number of other linguistic minorites in any area, the greater the need for the lingua franca Russian.

TABLE 2.4. Numbers of Russians (in thousands) and Percent of Total Population in the Turkestan ASSR, 1929

Amu-Darya		Semirechye		Samarkand		Syr-Darya		Turkmen		Ferghana	
No.	%	No.	%	No.	%	No.	%	No.	%	No.	%
5.7	3.6	268.8	28.0	21	2.7	167	12.8	30	9	48	2.3

Source: *Soviet Census*, 1929.

TABLE 2.5. Growth in the Russian Representation in the Federated Republics, 1959–70

Republic	Total Population		Indigenous Population				Russian Population			
	1959	1970	1959		1970		1959		1970	
	No.	No.	No.	%	No.	%	No.	%	No.	%
RSFSR	117,534	130,079	—	—	—	—	97,844	83.8	107,748	82.8
Ukraine	41,869	47,126	32,158	77.0	35,284	74.9	7,091	16.9	9,126	19.4
Belorussia	8,056	9,002	6,532	81.1	7,280	81.0	660	8.2	938	10.4
Uzbekistan	8,261	11,960	5,044	61.1	7,734	64.7	1,114	13.5	1,496	12.5
Kazakhstan	9,153	12,849	2,723	29.8	4,161	32.4	3,950	43.2	5,500	42.8
Georgia	4,044	4,656	2,601	64.3	3,131	66.8	408	10.1	397	8.5
Azerbaydzhan	3,698	5,117	2,494	67.5	3,777	73.8	501	13.6	510	10.6
Lithuania	2,711	3,128	2,151	79.3	2,507	80.1	231	8.5	268	8.6
Moldavia	2,885	3,569	1,887	65.4	2,304	64.6	293	10.2	414	11.6
Latvia	2,093	2,364	1,298	62.0	1,342	56.8	556	26.6	705	29.8
Kirghizia	2,066	2,933	837	40.5	1,285	43.8	624	30.2	856	29.2
Tadzhikstan	1,981	2,900	1,051	53.1	1,630	56.2	283	13.3	344	11.9
Armenia	1,763	2,492	1,552	88.0	2,208	88.6	56	3.2	66	2.7
Turkmenia	1,516	2,159	924	60.9	1,417	65.6	263	17.3	313	14.5
Estonia	1,197	1,356	893	74.6	925	68.2	240	20.1	335	24.7

Source: *Soviet Census*, 1970; *Izvestija*, 1971.

NONDEMOGRAPHIC ASPECTS OF
RUSSIAN PENETRATION

The extent of Russian immigration is not, however, a precise indicator of the degree of Russian language dominance. In the case of the Kazakhs, demographic penetration is of the order of 42 percent; linguistic penetration is 1.1 percent. In Azerbaydzhan, the number of Russians is fairly high—10.0 percent; the switch to the Russian language, however, is low—1.2 percent. The respective figures for other nationalities are these: Latvia, 29.8 percent, and 1.4 percent; Kirghizstan, 29.2 percent and 0.3 percent. In other Republics, though, the reverse is the case. In Armenia, Russians account for only 2.7 percent of the population, but the loss of language is 8.6 percent.

Factors other than Russian immigration must be considered in assessing language maintenance and level of bilingualism. Equally important as the actual presence of Russians are (1) the size of the minority, (2) the length of the period of contact, (3) the geographical contiguity and cultural affinity (Belorussia) and (4) the relative acquiescence as in the case of Armenians, in the Russian political system, compared to their attitude to Georgians, Azerbaydzhanis, or non-Soviet groups like Turks. It will be seen (Table 2.6) that small nationalities such as those of the Far North and the Caucasus vary considerably in their attachment to the national language, and though the Russian influence is considerably less in the North Caucasus, the same variability is discernible there too. In Daghestan the use of Russian is increasing as a lingua franca in an area of great linguistic complexity. In 1897, 2.8 percent of the population spoke Russian; in 1926 it was 12.5 percent; in 1939, 19 percent; in 1959, 44.7 percent; and in 1970, 41.7 percent (1929, 1959 and 1970 Censuses). Even so, all but one of the Siberian nationalities have a lower degree of attachment to their national language than the lowest among the North Caucasians. The second most retentive among the Siberian nationalities is the Koryaki, with 9.5 percent loss of national language in 1959, and 18.1 percent in 1970; and the worst among the Caucasians are the Nogais with 9.4 percent in 1959 and 10.2 percent in 1970.

When it comes to the question of which language takes the place of the national tongue, as the latter gives way to another language, there is very little difference between the minorities—Russian is the almost inevitable choice, except for the Eveni and Evenki among the peoples of the North. The probable explanation for the exception of these two peoples is that they are closely related and relatively large for Siberian nationalities, they occupy extensive territories, and they are nationally self-conscious groups. They have given their name to a national Okrug and have withstood attempts to collectivize their reindeer herding. They are remarkably independent. However, it is probably their nomadic way of life, making only intermittent contact with Russian, that is the decisive factor.

TABLE 2.6. National Language Retentiveness and Russian Language Penetration among Siberian and Caucasian Nationalities

	Siberian and Far East		
	No. in Thousands	% Using Non-native Language	% Using Russian
Aleuts	.4	77.7	77.2
Itelmen	1.1	64.0	63.1
Selkup	3.8	49.4	48.4
Yukagir	.4	47.5	34.4
Evenki	24.5	44.1	8.7
Mansi	6.4	40.8	40.4
Orochi	.8	31.6	29.7
Saami	1.8	30.1	28.6
Udegei	1.4	26.3	22.4
Nivkh	3.7	23.7	23.2
Khanty	19.4	23.0	22.3
Keti	1.0	22.9	20.6
Eveni	9.4	18.6	5.7
Eskimos	1.1	16.0	13.0
Ulchi	2.1	15.1	14.8
Nentsi	23.0	15.3	5.5
Nanai	8.0	13.7	13.3
Koryaki	6.3	9.5	8.9
Chukchi	11.7	6.1	5.7

	North Caucasian Nationalities				
		Non-migrant		Migrant	
	No. in Thousands	% Using Non-native Language	% Using Russian	% Using Non-native Language	% Using Russian
Avars	270	1.0	.4	21.2	14.2
Dargins	158	.8	.6	11.1	9.9
Kumyks	135	1.1	.9	21.8	16.2
Lezgins	223	1.8	.9	31.4	26.3
Laks	64	1.5	1.3	20.9	14.2
Chechens	419	.2	.2	15.9	15.0
Kabardins	204	.8	.8	10.4	18.3
Adyges	80	1.9	.19	28.1	27.6
Ossetes	410	2.5	2.4	37.3	36.1
Karachays	181	1.0	.5	34.5	9.0
Ingush	106	.6	.5	21.1	20.4
Nogais	41	9.4	1.1	34.7	30.0

Source: A. A. Isupov, 1964: 40 *et seq.*

There is one other conclusion that suggests itself in comparing these two groups of minorities. Among the North Caucasians, who do not range over such vast territories, the opportunity for contact between the local languages is much greater than among members of the Siberian nationalities. For the peoples of the North, the probability of Russian contact compared with contact with other languages is greater than it is in the Caucasus. Consequently since such contacts as occur in the Caucasus are so various and of such long standing, and since the Caucasian languages in contact have about the same kind and degree of prestige, the bilingualism that eventuates does not lead to the replacement of the mother tongue. Contact with Russian among Siberian nationalities however it occurs, is apt to be decisive and to allow little chance of maintaining the mother tongue—Russian is an intrusive and not a neighbor language. The 1970 Census shows that 3 million of the non-Russian population have adopted Russian as their native language during the last 11 years, making a total of 13 million. Those who speak Russian as their native language amount to 129 million, 53 percent of the Soviet population. Those who have adopted Russian are the equivalent of one-tenth of those who speak it as their mother tongue. Furthermore the increase annually since 1959, if it continues at the same rate, would indicate the possibility that well over 40 percent of the present non-Russian population will have switched to, or adopted Russian by the end of this century. According to present projections, this means that over 69 percent of the population of the USSR will be Russian-speaking.

NON-RUSSIAN IMMIGRATION

The non-Russian immigration processes have two aspects: first, the in-migration of the nonindigenous nationalities into particular republics; second, the out-migration of an indigenous population to several other republics. Both are responsible for the redistribution and increased linguistic heterogeneity of areas of the Soviet Union. Both are interrelated and account for the decomposition of national linguistic populations.

In Table 2.7 the percentage out-migration (A) is the difference between 100 percent and the percentage of the nationality living in its native republic. The percentage in-migration (B) is the difference between 100 percent and the percentage of the total population of a republic represented by its indigenous population. The mean for A is 14.3 and for B 32. Each nationality is classified as Low (L) or High (H) according to whether it is below or above the mean.

Those ethnic groups who have high out-migration and low in-migration indices—that is, those who combine a high rate of emigration and highly stable indigenous population levels like the Russians, Azerbaydzhanis, and Armenians tend to be large language groups upon whom high emigra-

TABLE 2.7. Out-Migration and In-Migration Indices for Major Nationalities, 1970

	Russians	Ukrainians	Belorussians	Uzbeks	Kazakhs	Georgians	Azerbaydzhans	Lithuanians	Moldavians	Latvians	Kirghiz	Tadzhiks	Armenians	Turkmen	Estonians
A															
Percentage	18	12	10	15	21	4	19	6	15	6	15	24	38	8	8
Out-Migration	H	L	L	H	H	L	H	L	H	L	H	H	H	L	L
B															
Percentage	17	14	19	35	67	33	24	19	35	43	56	43	11	34	33
In-Migration	L	L	L	H	H	H	L	L	H	H	H	H	L	H	H

Source: *Soviet Census*, 1970.

tion rates have not yet made much impact and whose languages are therefore less threatened. Those with both out- and in-migration occurring at high levels are the most threatened.

Between 1959 and 1970 (See Table 2.8) the net gain by immigration to Central Asia was 1.2 million. Much of this represented a process of redistribution among the five Central Asian Republics, for instance Kazakhs migrating from the inhospitable steppe. The out-migration is best exemplified historically, with the exception of the Russians, by the Armenians. Although they do not have the highest percentage of dispersion, they have spread most widely. In the fifteenth century, many Armenians migrated to Byzantium, Cilicia, West Georgia, the North Caucasus, the Black Sea coast, the Ukraine, and Poland. In the eighteenth century, they had a considerable presence in Astrakhan, St. Petersburg, and Moscow, and in all these places they established schools. By 1885, the Armenian Church had to cater for significant numbers of Armenians in its five dioceses outside Armenia itself—Tbilisi, Karabakh, Shemakha, Astrakhan, and Bessarabia. They have preserved this long tradition of mobility. The Tatars are not far behind the Armenians. They are among those with the highest percentage of dispersion. Even before the accession of Catherine II in 1762, of the total of 5 million Tatars, 1.5 million constituted a diaspora with merchant colonies throughout Siberia, the Caucasus, Central Asia, and Western Russia. Diffusion is still characteristic of the Tatars. A more recent example of dispersion involves the Russians deporting Estonians: a total of 129,000 were removed in 1940–41 and 1945–46.

In the Central Asian Republics, the population changes have meant that some nationalities have become minorities in their own republics. Taking the Central Asian group as a whole, the proportion of the indigenous population dropped from 76 percent to 70 percent between 1926 and 1934; in 1959 the figure was 60 percent and by 1970 it had dropped

TABLE 2.8. Linguistic composition of the Populations of Each of the Union Republics (in Thousands)

	1959	1970
Russia RSFSR	117,534	130,079
Russians[a]	97,864	107,748
Tatars	4,075	4,758
Ukrainians	3,359	3,346
Chuvash	1,436	1,637
Bashkir	954	1,181
Mordvin	1,211	1,177
Daghestan Nationalities	797	1,152
Avars	250	362
Darghin	153	224
Kumyk	133	187
Lezghin	114	270
Lak	58	79
Tabasaran	34	54
Nogai	38	51
Rutyl	67	12
Agul	6.9	8.8
Tsakhur	4.4	4.7
Belorussians	844	964
Jews	875	808
Germans	820	762
Udmurt	616	678
Mari	498	581
Chechens	261	572
Kazakhs	382	478
Komi-Permyak	426	466
Ossetes	248	313
Buryats	252	313
Armenians	256	299
Yakuts	232	295
Kabardians	201	277
Peoples of the North	128	149
Nentsi	23	28
Evenki	24	25
Khanti	19	21
Chukchi	12	14
Eveni	9	12
Nanai	7.9	9.9
Mansi	6.3	7.6
Koryak	6.2	7.4
Dolgan	3.9	4.7
Nivkhi	3.7	4.4
Selkup	3.7	4.2
Ulchi	2.0	2.4
Saami	1.8	1.8
Udegey	1.4	1.4
Itelmen	1.1	1.3
Eskimos	1.1	1.3
Keti	1.0	1.2
Orochi	0.8	1.0

TABLE 2.8. *(continued)*

	1959	1970
Russia RSFSR (continued)		
Nganasan	0.7	0.8
Yakagir	0.4	0.6
Aleuts	9.4	0.4
Karelians	164	141
Tuvinians	100	139
Ingush	56	137
Kalmyk	101	131
Poles	118	107
Karachai	71	107
Koreans	91	101
Adyge	79	98
Gypsies	72	98
Azerbaydzhani	71	96
Moldavians	62	88
Georgians	58	69
Khakass	56	65
Finns	72	62
Greeks	47	65
Altay	45	55
Balkar	35	53
Cherkess	29	38
Ukraine SSR	41,869	47,126
Ukrainians[a]	32,158	35,284
Russians	7,091	9,126
Jews	840	777
Belorussians	291	385
Poles	363	295
Moldavians	242	266
Bulgars	219	234
Others (15)	665	758
Belorussian SSR	8,056	9,006
Belorussians[a]	6,532	7,290
Russians	660	938
Poles	539	383
Ukrainians	133	191
Jews	150	148
Others (12)	42	52
Uzbek SSR	8,261	11,960
Uzbeks[a]	5,040	7,734
Karakalpak	168	230
Russians	1,134	1,496
Tatar	448	578
Kazakh	407	549
Tadzhik	314	457
Koreans	142	151
Ukrainians	93	115
Kirghiz	93	111
Jews	95	103

TABLE 2.8. *(continued)*

	1959	1970
Uzbek SSR (continued)		
Turkmen	55	71
Others (18)	288	365
Kazakh SSR	9,153	12,849
Kazakhs[a]	2,723	4,161
Russians	3,950	5,500
Ukrainians	756	930
Tatars	189	284
Uzbeks	130	208
Belorussians	106	198
Uygur	60	121
Koreans	71	78
Dungans	10	17
Others (30)	1,158	1,352
Georgian SSR	4,044	4,686
Georgian[a]	2,601	3,131
Ossetes	141	156
Abkhaz	63	79
Armenian	443	452
Russians	408	397
Azeri	154	218
Greeks	73	89
Jews	52	55
Ukrainians	52	50
Kurds	16	21
Others (9)	41	44
Azerbaydzhan SSR	3,698	5,117
Azeri[a]	2,494	3,777
Russians	501	510
Armenians	442	484
Lezghin	98	137
Others (15)	163	209
Lithuanian SSR	2,711	3,128
Lithuanians[a]	2,151	2,507
Russians	231	268
Poles	230	240
Belorussians	30	45
Ukrainians	18	25
Jews	25	24
Others (8)	26	19
Moldavian SSR	2,885	3,569
Moldavians[a]	1,857	2,304
Ukrainians	421	507
Russians	293	414
Gagauz	96	125
Jews	95	98
Bulgarians	62	74
Others (9)	31	47

TABLE 2.8. *(continued)*

	1959	1970
Latvian SSR	2,093	2,364
Letts[a]	1,298	1,342
Russians	556	705
Belorussians	62	95
Poles	60	63
Ukrainians	29	53
Lithuanians	32	41
Jews	37	37
Others (8)	19	28
Kirghiz SSR	2,066	2,933
Kirghiz[a]	837	1,285
Russians	624	856
Uzbeks	219	333
Ukrainians	137	120
Tatars	56	69
Uygur	14	25
Kazakhs	20	22
Tadzhiks	15	22
Others (12)	144	201
Tadzhik SSR	1,981	2,900
Tadzhiks[a]	1,051	1,630
Uzbeks	435	660
Russians	263	344
Tatars	57	71
Kirghiz	26	35
Ukrainians	27	32
Kazakhs	13	83
Others (14)	89	114
Armenian SSR	1,763	2,497
Armenians[a]	1,552	2,208
Azeri	108	148
Russians	56	66
Kurds	26	37
Others (5)	21	33
Turkmen SSR	1,516	2,159
Turkmen[a]	924	1,417
Russians	263	313
Uzbeks	126	179
Kazakhs	70	69
Ukrainians	30	36
Armenians	21	35
Tatars	20	23
Others (11)	63	87
Estonian SSR	1,197	1,356
Estonians[a]	893	925
Russians	240	335
Ukrainians	16	28
Finns	17	19
Belorussians	11	19
Jews	5.4	5.3
Others (7)	15	25

[a] Titular ethnic group
Source: *Soviet Census*, 1959 and 1970.

even further, to 54 percent. Even in 1939 the Kazakhs were a minority (43 percent), and by 1959 they constituted less than a third of the population of the Republic. By 1970, they had increased their representation to 32.4 percent. By 1959, the Kirghiz had become a minority in their own Republic (40.5 percent), though their position had improved in 1970 to 43.8 percent. By 1970, the Tadzhiks had raised their proportion of the population of the Republic but only from 53.1 percent in 1959 to 56.2 percent in 1970. The same situation exists as well for Mari Oblast, Yakut ASSR, Khakass Autonomous Oblast, and the North Caucasus (See Table 2.8; Soviet Census, 1959 and 1960).

The Central Asian Republics, it is interesting to note, differ among themselves in the pattern of their outward migration, and this fact may affect the maintenance of their cultural integrity in ways that differ from the maintenance of their languages. For instance, only 10 percent of Kirghiz migrants, 6 percent of Tadzhiks, and 3 percent of Uzbeks, move out of Central Asia altogether. Relatively few move into different cultural areas, though they live in different language communities. Azerbaydzhanis have a similar reluctance to move into a novel cultural setting— only 2.4 percent emigrate to the RSFSR, 0.2 percent into the Ukraine. Naturally enough, Georgia with 5.2 percent and Armenia with 3.7 percent attract most of the Central Asian emigrants (Azerbaydzhan Tsifrakh 1964: 23). On the other hand, 30 percent of Turkmen emigrants (and 47 percent of Kazakhs) have left Central Asia altogether. It is probable that, for them, a movement outside the traditional culture will accentuate the risk to language. In this regard it is interesting that Tatars, who have a high dispersal index, tend to maintain their language in the areas which, though linguistically disparate, have close cultural affinities with them. The extent of language maintenance among Tatars who do not emigrate was 92 percent in 1959, but it was nearly as high among Tatars in Kirghizia (91 percent), Tadzikstan Tatars (91 percent), Kazakhstan Tatars (85 percent), and Turkmen Tatars (84 percent). For the Tatars, the adverse effect of emigration is modified by cultural affinities of a more general character.

This diversity and complex pattern of languages in contact is represented at every level of society—Union Republic, Autonomous Republic, Oblast, Okrug, town, and village. New industrial projects tend to attract very diverse peoples in large numbers. In Tashkent, for instance, 75 percent of the total population were native born in 1929, 9 percent were Russian, and 15.2 percent were members of other nationalities. After intensified industrialization and migration, by 1959 the indigenous population constituted less than 40 percent of the total, the Russian element had increased to over 44 percent, and other nationalities had risen to 20 percent. The composition of the population of the city of Dushanbe is as follows: Tadzhik 17 percent, Russians 43 percent, Uzbek 8 percent, Ukrainians 5 percent, Jews 3 percent, Mordvin 2 percent, Ossetian 1 percent, and other 5 percent. In many State farms of the Kazakh Republic, men and women representing fifteen to twenty-five nationalities now live together. Similarly a small, traditional village is not insulated from the effects of immigration. For instance, Goluboe village in Moldavia was settled initially by Czechs from a neighboring Guberniya. In 1880, 100 families helped to create the village. In 1911, ten families emigrated to Kazakhstan, though relations are still maintained between them. In 1930, Goluboe had a population of 822-236 Czechs, 296 Russians, 188 Moldavians, and 85 Bulgarians. By 1970, there were 5 major linguistic groups and 18 smaller linguistic groups in the village. The majority were Ukrainians, while the original Czechs make up no more than 22 percent. Eighty-eight of the 282 families were mixed (Larnin, O. V.).

It is to be expected that such heterogeneous situations will produce different types of language contacts, and Moldavia may be analyzed and described in such terms. The six largest linguistic groups in the Republic are Moldavian, Ukrainian, Russian, Gagauz, Jews, and Bulgarians. The following linguistic contact situations have been created: homogeneous Moldavian: heterogeneous but predominantly Moldavian; trilingual Russian/Moldavian/Ukrainian; bilingual Moldavian/Gagauz; bilingual Moldavian/Ukrainian; bilingual Gagauz/Bulgarian; with Jewish multilingualism existing involving any one or more of these languages and Yiddish. The Gagauz are thought to be of Turkic origin and they live for the most part in south Moldavia, with smaller numbers in the Ukraine, Kazakhstan, and Central Asia. In the Moldavian Republic, they often are bilingual in Gagauz and either Moldavian, Ukrainian, Bulgarian, Russian, or any combination of these languages. Their language has several lexical and grammatical layers resulting from their history of contacts through migration. Thus it is that the extreme heterogeneity of the Soviet Union is built up of innumerable microcosmic situations in multilingual villages and small townships.

BILINGUALISM WITH RUSSIAN AS A SECOND LANGUAGE

Although Russian bilingualism is a goal set by the government and is very emphatically a matter of educational planning and school instruction, one should not overlook the fact that Russian has been a significant component of unplanned and fortuitous bilingualism. In that sense it has entered into partnership with other languages, much as Georgian has done with Armenian. Large numbers who know a second language other than Russian will often know Russian, which they have learned normally in a mixed community or at school. It may very well occur without the intervention of the school. This is the case of Yakut, whose contact with the Russians predated any experience of the Russian language as a subject of school instruction. Since their arrival in their present habitat, the Yakut relationship with their neighbors has been in the direction of Yakut linguistic assimilation of others because of their superior culture. The second language learned by the Yakuts has been Russian, and they have done so because they have been in close contact with it for many decades. The same is true of Chuvash, of whom it is natural to expect that they should learn Russian because they have frequently constituted enclaves of various dimensions within a Russian context.

One of the most important factors affecting the acquisition or ignorance of Russian is, therefore, the contiguity of the group to a sizeable community of speakers of Russian. This will depend on the degree of geographic isolation they experience and consequently a second factor is the level of economic development and educational achievement which they manifest. These two considerations explain in part the comparatively low level of Russian bilingualism among, for instance, the Uygar, Mansi, Itelmen, Yukagirs, and Tuvin—all of whom have below 40 percent Russian bilingualism. Others like the Yakut, although isolated, are more advanced economically, and their need for Russian that much greater. A third factor is the nature and length of historical contact with Russian, which tends to raise the level of interest as well as achievement in Russian. This is true of groups like the Nogai, Cherkess, Udmurt, Mari and the Ossetes, who have mixed freely with Russians over the centuries. As a result, these groups have over 60 percent Russian bilingualism.

A fourth factor influencing levels of Russian bilingualism is the level of mature-language standardization, which is often related to the size of the given nationality. Such standardized languages as Ukrainian, Uzbek, Armenian, Azerbaydzhan, Georgian, Moldavian, Tadzhik, Kirghiz, and those of the Baltic nations are all associated with below the 40 percent level of Russian bilingualism. But for the self-sufficiency of their languages for all the purposes of contemporary life, as well as the possession by the nationalities speaking the languages of a highly advanced educational system, they would have produced a higher level of Russian bilingualism. Other language groups like the Ingush, Kabardinians, Kalmyk, and Balkar have a high level, partly because Russian is required to supplement their national language for many advanced purposes. At the same time it is true that some minorities like the Germans, who possess a highly advanced and modernized language, have a high Russian bilingualism rating; but this is because they are a highly urbanized group, they have had a long period of contact with the Russians, and they are a nonindigenous language group.

The position of the Jews is anomolous for, although like the Germans they possess an advanced language of international currency and are scattered among many Soviet nationalities, they still rate among the lowest of the groups in respect of Russian second language acquisition, no higher for instance than the Azerbaydzhanis. However, among the Jews the low level of Russian as a second language is combined with an equally low level of native language maintenance, whereas among the Azerbaydzhanis, the low level of Russian is combined with a high level of language maintenance. It may be that the Jews, for many reasons, prefer to claim Russian as their native language and their Yiddish or Hebrew as second languages. There is no such compulsion on the Azerbaydzhanis to adopt such a tactic. But however we look at the Jews in this matter, their case points to a general conclusion—a knowledge of Russian prepares the way for a shift of language affiliation. For instance, the Bashkir have a relatively low maintenance level and a low Russian-bilingualism level as well; so do the Evenki, Selkup, Itelmen, Orochi, and Yukagirs. The Russian that these nationalities have acquired rapidly becomes the first language. In which case the idea of Russian as a second language does not reflect the true status of Russian in the communities: the degree of Russian penetration is much greater than Russian second-language figures suggest, because having been a second language it has become the first language for many.

Non-Russian Bilingualism

This form of bilingualism involves knowing two or more non-Russian languages (sometimes in addition to Russian) and must be assumed to reflect the traditional relationship of contiguous language groups. It may be regarded as fortuitous, unplanned, and therefore a primary form of bilingualism since it gains virtually nothing from institutional support such as teaching. It should be noted that the figures in Table 2.9 (Column B) may not be a true reflection of the situation (though it is the best that can be provided) because many may have listed the language of their nationality as their second language. This is because they have virtually abandoned their native language or are in the process of doing so. This process of language shift is commonplace, and their second language is a kind of vestigial national language, their first language being in fact a "foreign" language. This happens among members of nationalities where the degree of language maintenance is low, and for that reason the figures may exaggerate the degree of bilingualism which involves retaining the national language and acquiring a non-native second language. Consequently, the additional language is already accounted for in reduced language maintenance figures.

What is least surprising is that speakers of the major national languages and nationalities with a million or more members are not required to learn a second language other than Russian and in fact do not. Apart from speakers of Belorussian, Armenian, and Ukrainian, none of the other major language groups have more than a 5 percent level of non-Russian bilingualism and most are in the 2 percent range. Interestingly, the Russians—who are normally regarded as the most exclusive nationality so far as

TABLE 2.9. Claimed Mother Tongues of the Soviet Union Together with
Two Estimates of Bilingualism, 1970

Nationality	A	B	C
USSR	93.9	3.0	
Russian	99.8	3.0	36.3
Ukrainian	85.7	6.0	36.3
Uzbek	98.6	3.3	14.5
Belorussian	80.6	7.3	49.0
Tatar	89.2	5.8	62.5
Kazakh	98.0	1.8	41.8
Azerbaydzhan	98.2	2.5	16.6
Armenian	91.4	6.0	30.1
Georgian	93.4	1.0	21.3
Moldavian	95.0	3.6	36.1
Lithuanian	97.9	1.9	31.9
Jew	17.7	28.8	16.3
Tadzhik	98.5	12.0	15.4
German	66.8	1.1	59.6
Chuvash	88.9	5.5	58.4
Turkmen	98.8	1.3	15.4
Kirghiz	98.8	2.3	19.1
Latvian	95.2	2.4	45.2
Daghestan Nationalities	96.5	8.9	41.7
Avar	97.2	5.7	37.8
Darghin	98.4	2.8	43.0
Kumyk	98.4	1.2	57.4
Lezghin	93.9	22.3	31.5
Lak	95.6	3.5	56.0
Tabasaran	98.9	10.2	31.9
Nogai	89.8	16.4	68.5
Rutyl	98.9	18.8	30.7
Agul	99.4	9.6	39.8
Tsakhur	96.5	43.5	12.2
Mordvin	77.8	8.1	65.7
Bashkir	66.2	2.6	53.3
Poles	32.5	12.7	37.0
Estonian	95.5	2.0	29.0
Udmurt	82.6	6.9	63.3
Chechen	58.7	1.0	66.7
Mari	91.2	6.2	62.4
Ossetes	88.6	10.7	58.6
Komi	82.7	5.4	63.1
Komi-Permyak	85.8	4.6	68.5
Korean	68.6	1.7	57.3
Bulgarian	73.1	7.9	58.8
Greek	39.3	14.5	35.4
Buryat	92.6	2.7	66.7
Yakut	96.3	1.1	41.7
Kabardinian	98.0	0.8	71.4
Karakalpak	96.6	3.6	10.4
Gypsies	70.8	16.4	53.0
Uygur	88.5	9.5	35.6

TABLE 2.9. (continued)

Nationality	A	B	C
Hungarian	96.6	9.8	25.8
Ingush	97.4	0.9	71.3
Gagauz	93.6	8.6	63.3
Peoples of the North	67.4	7.1	52.5
Nentsi	83.4	3.3	55.1
Evenki	51.3	7.5	54.9
Khanti	68.9	7.3	48.1
Chuchki	82.6	4.8	58.7
Eveni	56.0	17.6	48.4
Nanai	69.1	9.4	58.0
Mansi	52.5	5.6	38.6
Koryak	81.1	5.5	64.3
Dolgan	98.8	3.2	61.4
Nivkhi	49.5	5.6	48.3
Selkup	51.1	8.6	40.8
Ulchi	60.8	7.0	56.8
Saami	56.2	9.3	52.9
Udegei	55.1	10.1	46.0
Itelmen	35.7	4.3	32.5
Keti	74.9	2.0	59.1
Orochi	48.6	6.6	44.4
Nganasan	75.4	15.7	40.0
Yukagir	46.8	32.8	29.1
Kareli	63.0	15.1	59.1
Tuvin	98.7	0.4	38.9
Kalmyk	91.7	1.5	81.1
Romanian	63.9	16.3	28.5
Karachai	98.1	1.2	67.6
Adygei	96.5	1.4	67.9
Kurd	87.6	36.2	19.9
Finn	51.0	8.5	47.0
Abkhaz	95.9	2.8	59.2
Turki	92.3	31.2	22.4
Khakass	83.7	3.4	66.5
Balkar	97.2	2.5	71.5
Altai	87.2	3.2	54.9
Cherkess	92.0	2.5	70.0
Dungan	94.3	5.7	48.0
Iranian	36.9	12.7	33.9
Abazin	96.1	6.1	69.5
Aisor	64.5	14.7	46.2
Czech	42.9	21.4	35.6
Tat	72.6	15.3	57.7
Shortsi	73.5	5.9	59.8
Slovak	52.0	31.3	39.3
Other Nations	69.4	12.8	38.4

a Column A—percent of nationalities claiming national language as native tongue
b Column B—percent of nationality claiming to speak a second language other than Russian
c Column C—percent of those claiming a non-Russian language who have learned Russian as a second language
Source: Soviet Census, 1970.

concerns language acquisition—have a higher level of bilingualism than the Kazakhs, Azerbaydzhanis, Georgians, and the natives of the Baltic republics. However, this is due partly to the fact that large numbers of Russians, because of their contacts, cannot fail to learn the language of one or another of the many national minorities indigenous to and virtually forming enclaves within the RSFSR, like the Mari.

There are some exceptions to the generalization that the major nationalities are not concerned to learn a second language. Poles with 12.7 percent and Jews with 28 percent non-Russian bilingualism are instances. Their level of bilingualism is because their own languages are not recognized and because they tend to be largely dispersed communities. The nonindigenous, whatever the size of the population and the status of the language, are apt to have high levels of bilingualism. If they are widely scattered, the index of bilingualism tends to rise more appreciably. This is the case of Gypsies (16.4 percent) who occupy parts of Moldavia, the Ukraine, and the Central Asian Republics. The Tadzhiks (12 percent), too, are an exception to the generalization because their language has always experienced considerable Uzbek influence: Tadzhikstan has a large Uzbek minority, 23 percent of the total population. In addition, apart from Russians, Tadzhikstan is the home of over a quarter of a million people belonging to various minority groups including national minorities such as Tatars and Kazakhs. In such circumstances, it is not surprising that the Tadzhiks find it convenient, if not necessary, to learn one of the minority languages.

High levels of bilingualism characterize the small national groups, especially if they are minorities within larger linguistic communities, such as the Gagauz of Moldavia (8.6 percent) and the Tats in Azerbaydzhan (51.3 percent). It is also the case of nonindigenous but relatively stable minorities like the Kurds and Aisors of Azerbaydzhan and Armenia (36.2 percent and 14.7 percent respectively), the Slovaks (31.3 percent), Greeks in various Ukrainian villages and in Georgia (14.5 percent), and the Bulgarians of the Ukraine (7.9 percent).

Indigenous small and isolated nationalities, whose territories are extensive and therefore inhabited by scattered populations in contact with several other groups, have a higher level of bilingualism than large indigenous nationalities or nations. Thus, compared with Georgians, (1 percent) the isolated Evenki in northeast Siberia, with a scattered population of 25,000, have over 7 percent bilingualism and the Mordvin with a dispersal index of 63 percent have 8 percent bilingualism. To a somewhat less extent the same is true of the Tatars (5.3 percent) who are scattered throughout the RSFSR, Uzbekistan, Kazakhstan, Kirghizstan, Tadzhikstan, and Turkmenistan. The size of the scattered group and its relation to bilingualism is seen in the case of the Yukagirs, where a high level of bilingualism (32 percent) is combined with a very low level of native language maintenance (46.8 percent). Their language is being replaced by the languages of those with whom they are in contact, mainly Russians. They exemplify the situation where for many the original native tongue has become a second language. Sometimes a normally scattered and mobile nationality like the Nanai of North Siberia became settled either in collective farms or as part of the industrial labor force of cities such as Komsomolosk. This settlement process has tended to inflate their degree of bilingualism (9.4 percent), and the same is true of the Eveni (17.6 percent).

THE RESIDUAL CONGLOMERATE: THE LANGUAGES SPOKEN IN THE SOVIET UNION AND LEVELS OF BILINGUALISM

In view of the long history of Russian colonization and its continuance, the penetration of the Russian language into all the national territories of the Union, and the complex interplay of population movements among the non-Russians, what is the resultant picture of ethnic diversity and language contact in that country? We have already seen (Table 2.3) how the major languages are diffused through many parts of the USSR, just as Spanish and other languages are diffused in the United States. Table 2.8 offers a picture of the heterogeneous linguistic composition of the particular republics, and Table 2.9 offers a similar picture of the Soviet Union as a whole. It is an inventory of the Soviet languages together with estimates of two types of bilingualism—the one involves two non-Russian languages, and the second a national language and Russian.

Table 2.9 lists over 90 languages spoken by significant numbers in the Soviet Union. The 1970 census recognized 60 other languages, but they are spoken by very small numbers—between 50 and 200. There are approximately 130 million native speakers of Russian, 54 percent of the total Soviet population. In addition, as we shall note, it is claimed that over 13 million have learned Russian as a second language. Of the remaining languages, two are spoken by over 9 million, two by between 5 and 9 million, and another two by between 3 and 5 million. Four languages are spoken by between 2 and 3 million each and ten by between 1 and 2 million. Of the languages with fewer than a million speakers, three have between 500,000 and a million, eleven have between 250,000 and 500,000, fifteen between 100,000 and 250,000, ten have between 50,000 and 100,000, thirteen between 10,000 and 50,000, and fourteen between 1,000 and 10,000. Five major language families are represented in these "lesser" languages: (1) Indo-European including East and West Slavic, Iranian, Armenian, Moldavian, Greek, and so forth; (2) Altaic, including several Turkic languages, Mongolian languages like Buryat and Kalmyk, and Manchurian which includes Eveni and Evenki; (3) Uralian which includes Finnic languages like Karelian, Vespian, Mari, and so forth, and Ugrian which includes Hungarian, and Samoyed; (4) Caucasian, which has subfamilies like Abkhaz-Adygei, Chechen, and Iverian; and (5) the family of Paleoasiatic languages like Yakut, Eskimo, Aleut, and so forth. All these are indigenous to the present Soviet Union, and some are spoken as national languages outside the USSR. For example, there are exoteric languages like German, Polish, Hungarian, Greek, Persian, Yiddish, and Hebrew that are spoken by indigenous populations and by large numbers outside the Soviet Union.

The level of language maintenance among these diverse language groups has varied during the last fifty years. A few nationalities with fairly large populations, such as the Kalyks, Mordvins, and Jews, have tended to decline in level of maintenance. Other major nationalities raised the level of maintenance between 1926–59, and this was especially the case with the Armenians, Uzbeks, Turkmens, and Azerbaydzhanis. The Georgians and Armenians have higher levels of language maintenance than forty years ago, as do the Central Asian and Eastern nationalities. The Daghestanis have also raised the percentage claiming the national language.

The fate of the language among the smaller nationalities appears to be directly related to their size. The largest among them, such as the Avar and Lezgin, have a higher proportion speaking the native language. The same is true of the Bashkir. The smaller minorities preserve their native language much less. This is true of the Nogai and especially of the Peoples of the North, such as Evenki, Khanti, Selkup, Saami, and Itelmen. Among these smallest language groups the exceptions are the Mansi and Nanai who have raised the level of their language maintenance.

CONCLUSION

The extent of immigration and the strength of territoriality as they affect languages have to be measured in several ways—the size of the immigrant population, the rate or intensity of movement, and the degree to which the immigrants are diffused in their new country. Of the Soviet ethnic groups, territoriality and linguistic concentration are identified most strongly with Georgians, Lithuanians, and Letts. On the other hand, of the major Central Asian ethnic groups, the Tadzhiks have the highest percentage of dispersion. The ethnic groups who have no territorial heartland or base, either because they have been denied the opportunity of possessing one (like the Jews), or because they represent foreign populations (like the Poles, Czechs, Bulgarians, Germans, and Greeks), and are dispersed all over the Soviet Union are difficult to include in any account of heterogeneity due to migration because they have no national territory from which to emigrate. Minorities like Bashkirs and Chuvash within a large Union Republic (especially in the RSFSR) tend to have a high percentage of dispersion. Very low percentages of dispersion (1–2 percent) characterize isolated ethnic groups, whether they are relatively large like the Yakuts (296,000) or small like the Abazins of the North Caucasus, Itelmen of the Far Northeast (1,300), or Eskimos (1,300). These are peoples who are tied almost inextricably to the lands they occupy, and the occupations they have pursued for centuries. Their linguistic stability is associated with their high level of territorial integrity. Unlike the universality of English in the United States, Russian is not nearly as pervasive because of the strong territorial base for major non-Russian languages. In some areas Russian is indigenous, in others it is integral to the community and very extensive, but in others it is not at all well known.

Furthermore, the United States has been the recipient of far greater numbers of immigrants than there have been emigrants from the United States or reversed immigrants. Consequently, international migration for the United States is effectively in-migration. In the Soviet Union *as a whole*, the concept of in-migration has no meaning since all migration is redistributive; however, in the respective Union Republics (microcosms of the United States), international migration is open-ended and not entirely redistributive. Nonindigenous linguistic groups can move into new areas. Therefore, the position of a particular Soviet language in the Soviet Union—either the nation-state as a whole, or within its defined homeland titular area, or in particular areas outside the homeland—is the consequence of the combined operation of international in- and out-migration. In the Soviet Union the Russian language, like some of the minority languages, is an "intrusive" language in many large areas; however, some of the Soviet minority languages are indigenous and nonintrusive. The size, intensity, and extent of the diffusion of migrant groups affect Russian no less than the minority languages—these are questions of Russian as well as minority languages penetration, which is not the case in the United States except for the Mexican-American and Amerindian homelands.

Three

Internal Colonization and the Decline of Celtic Languages

INTRODUCTION

The Celtic-speaking periphery of Britain—Scotland, Ireland, and Wales—as well as Brittany, the Celtic area of France, were never uniform economically, culturally, or linguistically. Different variants of Celtic were spoken: Irish and Scots Gaelic together with Manx, which is virtually dead, being members of one group; Celtic, Welsh, and Breton members of the Celtic groups that includes Cornish, now completely dead. Their linguistic divergences were accompanied by religious differences. Irish and Bretons were and remain firmly Catholic, while the Scots and Welsh are equally firmly Protestant. As we shall see, the processes of their colonization differed also. But in spite of these very real differences, they share very much more. The Irish Sea was a cultural center from protohistoric down to medieval times. It has been amply demonstrated (Bowen, 1965) that constant movement in the so-called Age of Saints knit together the areas around the Irish Sea. As in the Mediterranean, it became a culture area reflecting earlier pre-Christian times as well as a Celtic Christian tradition.

They have been disadvantaged largely because they were the victims of a firmly pursued policy of colonization by the English. None of the four nations, not even the Scots who have preserved more of an indigenous political, administrative, and legal system than any of the others, possessed a strong center that could create a cohesive and comprehensive social entity. Such centers characterized the colonizing nations—France was centered on the Isle-de-France, Spain on Castile, and England on London and the neighboring counties. Because of the absence of a center, the nations of the periphery were as likely to suffer from internal dissension and unresolved conflict as they were to suffer the military intrusion and the political and social domination of the English. The absence of strong centers in the Celtic countries is not surprising. Once they had been drawn, however slightly, into the stream of colonial advance their social and economic development was outwardly oriented: to the extent that they grew at all they grew outward. Their economies were based on primary exports—the products of agriculture and stockbreeding and later the heavy extractive industries of coal and iron. Unlike the colonizing nations, the Celts did not possess strong dynasties. The strongest—the Tudors who were of Welsh descent—elected to identify with the center and so reinforced the attractiveness of that center for the aristocracy of the Welsh periphery. It is worth remembering that the English dynasty succeeding the Tudors were also rulers of Celtic Scotland and that James I was James VI of Scotland. Their cities were small, transportation networks were primitive, and communication with the external center easier in the case of Scotland and Wales than it was with regions within either country. Higher education, which could have supplied a native elite and a strong administrative cadre, was more attractive in Oxford or Cambridge.

The traditional aristocracy, the erstwhile princes of their nations, transferred their affiliation to England and adopted the English language. The Celtic peasantry, in Wales and Ireland nearly all of them speaking a Celtic language, like the peasantry in the areas north of the Lowlands of Scotland, were leaderless and without status. The three Celtic nations had a common ancestry and a strong affinity in social, economic, and legal traditions. They also shared other characteristics—a pastoral economy, a tribal organization, and a surviving Celtic monastic concept of Christianity. Other shared and less happy characteristics have also survived—inequality in economic development, cultural subordination, disenfranchisement of the native language until comparatively recently, and political dependence. The economic, cultural, and linguistic disadvantage that the Celtic-speaking peoples have suffered is not surprising since they have been largely confined to the Highlands for several centuries, and the speakers of Scots Gaelic have been there for over 1,500 years. Theirs are areas of low population density, contrasting with the high density of London and the southeast of England. They are all on the extremities of the British Isles, clinging as do speakers of Breton in France to peninsular localities where the landscape has been formed from the oldest and harshest of rocks. They have inhabited lands which have been described as "regions of hardship" (Fleure, 1918).

Before the Norman Conquest of England, considerable tension existed between English farmers and the marauding Irish, the Picts, and the Welsh on their borders. But in the eleventh century England was not itself sufficiently unified to make the dichotomy between the Celtic fringe and the gradually evolving center noticeably marked. It was the Conquest, by importing the Norman feudal regime, continental urban institutions, and reformist approaches to the Roman Church that accentuated the differences between Celts and the English and established a center-periphery dichotomy. "The tribal, mobile, disaggregative societies of the Irish, the Scots and the Welsh seemed irreconcilable with the richer, more highly centralized, feudal and manorial regime of Norman and Angevin England" (Pool, A. L., 1951).

As so often happens, the consciousness of objective differences was translated by the English into feelings of contempt for the Celtic nations, who were thereafter and to this day for that matter, doomed to be thought backward. This opprobrium, together with the self-seeking of the Celtic aristocracy that induced their migration to England, meant that aspects of Celtic culture, but more especially the languages, were condemned as inferior. In the fourteenth century a Scottish annalist referred to the Gaelic-speaking Scots of the North as a "savage and untamed nation . . . unsightly in dress, hostile to the English people and language and owing to the diversity of speech even to their own nation (namely those of the Lowlands)" (Dickinson, 1961). In Ireland, the English masters distinguished between the peace of the Pale which they inhabited and the lawlessness of the Celtic hinterland, and eulogized the civilized way of life of the English and their language in contrast to the manners, dress, and language of the wild Irish (Berry, J., 1966). Giraldus Cambrensis, whose loyalties were torn between his native Wales and his Norman-Welsh ancestry, denied to the Welsh the graces and accomplishments of civilized men whatever attributes of hospitality, wit, and devotion to individual liberty they might claim. Thus originated the stereotype of the Celt, and the dichotomy that has flawed the civilization of the Celtic lands ever since.

THE PROCESS OF COLONIZATION AND ITS RESULTS

Introduction

Our principal concern in this chapter is to follow the fate of the Welsh language in the wake of colonization and subsequent modernization—including economic growth, urban development, and immigration from England. The Welsh case is selected for several reasons besides an admittedly personal involvement. It is far better documented descriptively and statistically than the others, though this data may not always be easily available; it is the most closely bound to England geographically, the Highlands being separated by a Lowland buffer zone, and Ireland by the Irish Sea; colonization in Wales was the prelude to more intense industrialization and immigration than elsewhere among the Celtic groups; the system of bilingual education is more advanced in Wales than in Ireland or Scotland if we regard general acceptability by the total population as one criterion. For these reasons Wales offers the best ground for the investigation of current attitudes and rationales for bilingual education discussed in chapter 6: in focussing on Wales in the present chapter we are providing for a degree of thematic continuity. Finally, though Irish has been the strongest language in the past, proportionate to the total population it is no longer stronger than Welsh. So far as surviving in a modernized world goes, Welsh is far stronger in the urban areas, and it is in these urban areas that the fate of the Celtic languages will be decided. But we cannot treat the Welsh situation in isolation from the rest of the Celtic-speaking world, and for that reason some consideration is given to the remaining three Celtic-speaking countries—Scotland, Ireland, and Brittany.

Scotland and the Gaelic Language

The Anglicization of Scotland resulted fundamentally from the seepage of English influences within Scotland itself from before the eleventh-century, rather than any strong thrust on the part of the English themselves as was the case in Wales and Ireland. The Lowlands, between the Forth and Tweed had once been known as Lothian, part of the most northerly English principality of Northumbria. Late in the tenth and early in the eleventh-centuries, this land was incorporated by the kings of Scotland within their realm; thus, there was introduced by acquisition a completely English segment, and one which had little historical association with the Celtic elements to the North. The Lowlands, prosperous when it was acquired, became even more attractive to the poorer Northerners who were assimilated not to the English but to an English domain within the Kingdom of Scotland. Anglicization increased through the migration of increasing numbers of speakers of Gaelic and through the systems of education and administration. Yet, though it was anglicized rapidly, it maintained a national identity up to 1603.

When Anglicization was institutionalized by the Act of Union in 1707, the majority of Scots were unaffected either linguistically or culturally. But the Gaelic-speaking minority were still firm in their adherence to a traditional way of life and their language. In 1745, however, the Highlands were transformed forcibly—the clan system was destroyed and the language forced to retreat still farther. A hundred years later, in the middle of the nineteenth century, the Gaelic-speaking areas had been defined: the populous Lowlands were entirely English, but the Gaelic language remained strong in the sparsely populated Highlands and Islands. (See Figure 3.1.) Even today, whereas the whole of Scotland has a population density of over 170 per square mile, it is only 13.5 per square mile in the Gaelic-speaking areas. The area in which the language was spoken was vast, about half the total area of Scotland, yet the speakers represented only 8 percent of the population. About 20 percent of the whole population spoke Gaelic. Even within the Gaelic-speaking area there were weak spots, for example the proportion of Gaelic-speakers in the towns of Inverness and Stornoway was just above 50 percent.

The most numerous concentrations of Gaelic-speakers live in the Highlands and Islands—the counties of Argyll (7,825), Inverness (18,740), Ross, Cromarty (19,510), Sutherland (1,815) and the Highland District of Perth (2,060), the Outer Hebrides (Lewis and Harris, North and South Uist, Benbecula, and Barra), and the Inner Hebrides (Skye, Tiree, Coll, Mull and Islay). This Highland and Islands zone accounts for a total of approximately 50,000 Gaelic-speakers—62 percent of the total. In addition there are colonies in the Lowlands, including Glasgow (12,860) and 25,185 scattered in other areas.

The majority of the 18,000 Gaelic speakers in the cities and other dense urban areas are most probably first or second generation migrants from the Highland zone, and this is likely to be the case with many in the remainder of Scotland. (Stephens, 1976: 52-77) The level of Gaelic maintenance in the Highlands generally, and particularly in the remoter areas, is exceptionally high and stable. Between 1891 and 1971 the percentage of speakers of Gaelic in Kilmuir, for instance, has declined by only 3.1 percent from 94.2 percent to 91.1 percent. In other parts of the Highland zone, the language is less stable and there has been a marked deterioration. (See Table 3.1). The Mainland subzone of the Highlands has shown the most marked decline, and Gaelic has almost disappeared from the east coast of northern Scotland. In other areas the decline since 1891 has been from 54.6 percent to 2.6 percent (Alness), from 65 percent to 6.6 percent (Urray). North of the Firth of Lorne on the mainland Gaelic is still spoken widely, though here too there has been an obvious deterioration since 1891: for example, Gairloch from 91 percent to 46 percent, and Glenelg from 91 percent to 30 percent. In all these mainland areas the decline has been far greater among those between the ages of 3 and 14 years than among older groups. A report in 1961 (Scottish Council for Research in Education, XLVII: 70–1) showed that on the mainland only in some small parts of Argyll together with Ross and Cromarty are there primary schools in which more than 4 percent of the pupils speak Gaelic as their mother tongue.

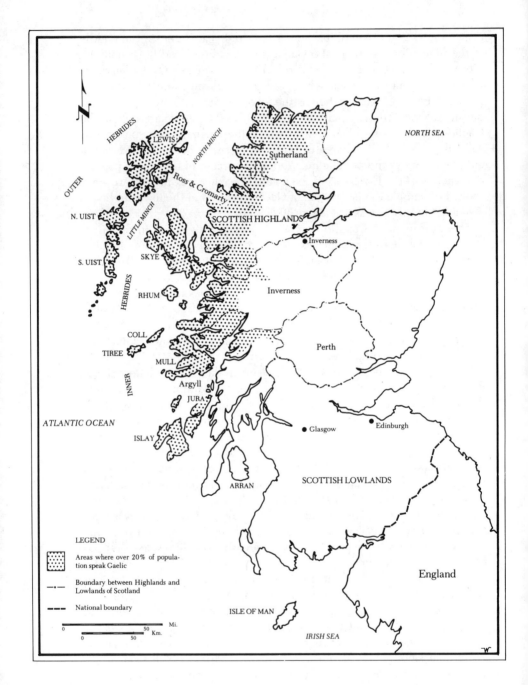

Fig. 3.1. *Gaelic in Scotland*

TABLE 3.1. Decline in the Number of Speakers of Gaelic in Scotland, 1891–1971 [a]

Census	Gaelic Only	Gaelic and English Total	% of Total Population	Total of Gaelic Speakers
1891	43,738	210,677	5.2	254,415
1901	28,106	202,700	4.5	230,806
1911	18,400	183,998	3.9	202,398
1921	9,829	148,950	3.1	158,779
1931	6,716	129,419	2.7	136,135
1951	2,178	93,264	1.8	95,447
1961	974	80,004	1.6	80,978
1971	477	88,415	1.8	88,892

[a] The Census of Canada 1931 recorded 30,000 speakers of Gaelic in Nova Scotia descendants of eighteenth-century immigrants. In 1971 a Scots linguist visiting Nova Scotia and Cape Breton estimated that there were 2,500 and 1,500 in the two areas, a total of 4,000. Source: Personal communication.

The second Gaelic-speaking subzone of the Highlands and Islands comprises the Inner Hebrides. None of the inshore islands of Argyll has above 46.9 percent Gaelic-speaking populations, and in most cases the decline has been of the order of 50 percent since 1891. In the remoter islands the majority are speakers of Gaelic, although here too the loss has been marked but less severe, of the order of 25 percent. In the islands offshore of Invernesshire, especially Skye, Gaelic is very well maintained: in none of the seven parishes of Skye is the proportion below 55 percent and in some instances (Kilmuir) it is over 91 percent. The Outer Hebrides, the third subzone of the Highlands zone, represents, with the exception of the borough of Stornoway, the most tenacious area linguistically as well as the most isolated. In the majority of the parishes the language is maintained by over 90 percent, though there have been losses that continue to be incurred and become greater the lower we go in the age groups. Eighty-three percent of the 3–4 year-old age group speak Gaelic, 89 percent of the 5–9 group, 93.4 percent of the 10–14 group while the 65 and over have a maintenance level of over 98 percent.

Taking Scotland as a whole, and particularly areas outside the Highlands and Islands, the future of Gaelic is unpromising. In the urban areas it ceased to be a significant part of the inheritance of the people many centuries ago. The remoter areas contribute much the greatest support to the language, and in those areas it is the older men and women who speak it most frequently and most fluently. There are important demographic considerations which tend to intensify the gloom. The population of the Highlands, irrespective of language, is moving away. It reached its peak of 201,000 in 1931 and since then it has declined steadily. The birthrate has been consistently lower than the Scottish average—in 1801 it was 2.7 percent compared with 3.5 percent for the whole of Scotland. In 1921–

30 the ratio was 1.7 percent to 2.2 percent. During important periods, the ratio of death to birth has generally been unfavorable to the Highlands. In 1851 the ratio was favorable, 1.7 percent to 2.2 percent, but since then it has been consistently the reverse. In the 1921–30 period, the ratio of death to birth was 1.5 percent to 1.4 percent.

Migration, too, has progressively damaged the structure of the population, leaving it disproportionately weighted with older men and women as the young adults left. For instance, whereas the percentage of the 65 and over in the whole of Scotland is approximately 1.2 percent, in the west and northwest it varies from 13 percent to 21 percent. In other words, the Gaelic-speaking population is thinly spread over a vast area; it is declining rapidly and aging. Improved transport and communications, together with the exploitation of oil resources in the seas around the northeast coast of Scotland, are already intensifying the influence of English. Political measures for devolving upon Scotland a greater degree of responsibility for its own affairs are unlikely to diminish that influence.

Irish

The history of England's colonization of Ireland is older than that of Scotland and almost contemporaneous with the colonization of Wales, for it was from there that the Norman lords usually embarked on their invasions of Ireland in the twelfth century. The pattern of lordships along the English-Welsh border was copied in Ireland where they were largely independent of the Crown. The main bridgehead was the Pale around Dublin which they strenuously attempted to enlarge against the resistance of the Irish tribal chieftains. In the sixteenth century, the unification of England under the Tudors enabled the English to attempt a more intensive campaign of colonization by means of the Virginia Plantation type of settlement, the most important example of which was Londonderry (1608). The failure of this plan led to large scale invasions by Cromwell and the allocation of Irish estates to new English colonists. By the end of the seventeenth century, the colonization of Ireland seemed on the face of it to be complete: English law was made to apply to all parts of the island and to all its inhabitants, and in the administration of this law the Irish language was proscribed. Use of the language was discouraged though in everyday affairs it was not prohibited. Acculturation to the dominant English life style was negligible, however, and while military and political domination of the whole land was the declared policy the most realistic practice was that which attempted to "compartmentalize" the two cultures. This policy was largely the reason for the English government's condemnation of the "degenerate English" who, adopting Irish customs and dress and possessing a smattering of the language were deemed to have "gone-native." The Statute of Kilkenny, 1366, prohibited the use of Irish by the colonists.

The Irish were as opposed to compartmentalization as they were to conquest or expropriation, and the main consequence of the attempt to colonize was outright war between the Irish and the English. The attempt to resolve that struggle later by actually separating the Protestant English of the North from the Irish speaking Catholics of the South has resulted in bitterness and slaughter. The effects of colonization have been catastrophic —a continuous population drain because of economic and social suppression in the past, as well as the decline of the Irish language. One of the principal causes of the decline of Irish has been the emigration of native speakers of the language (See Figure 3.2).

Ireland has always provided abundant and cheap labor for North American and English heavy industry as well as for building the roads, canals, and railways necessary to the expansion of that industry. The pull of better conditions elsewhere and the push of intolerable conditions at home (particularly the famines) meant that the population fell from its peak of over 8 million in 1841 to 3.9 million in 1881, 3.1 million in 1911 and just over 2.8 million at present. This drain on the population was especially marked in the period 1951–61 when the population fell by 146,000—over 5.0 percent. Since the number of urban inhabitants remained nearly stable during the decade, the loss must be attributed to rural emigration. If we add to the 146,000 the total arising from the natural growth rate which should have boosted the 1961 total, the net emigration from the republic during the period has been estimated at well over 412,000. During the nineteenth and twentieth centuries the drain for which emigration to North America and England must be held to account was in excess of 12 million. Not all of those who left were dominantly or perhaps even partly Irish-speaking, but since they were drawn in the main from the rural areas we are justified in concluding that most of them were at least bilingual and many of them monolingual Irish.

It has been estimated that approximately 50 percent of the population spoke Irish at the beginning of the nineteenth-century and, since the total population was then about 5 million, approximately 2.5 million spoke Irish. (See Table 3.2) In 1851, by which time the population had increased by 60 percent, the proportion who spoke Irish had dropped by 21 percent to a total of nearly 1.5 million. While the total population declined from 3,870,000 (all ages) in 1881 to 2,815,000 in 1961, a fall of 28 percent, the decline in the number of native speakers of Irish has been more precipitous: by 1881 it was just over 900,000, in 1891 the number was 664,000, and this fell to 540,000 in 1926. Since 1926 it has been estimated that not more than 10 percent of those who claimed Irish as a second language can be said to have mastered the language sufficiently to regard it as their language (Stephens, 1976). The vast majority have acquired it as a second language in the short time they were at school: a sharp increase overall in Ireland between 1926 and 1936 amounting to 120,000 (22 percent) stems from this reason. In 1971, the Irish-speaking

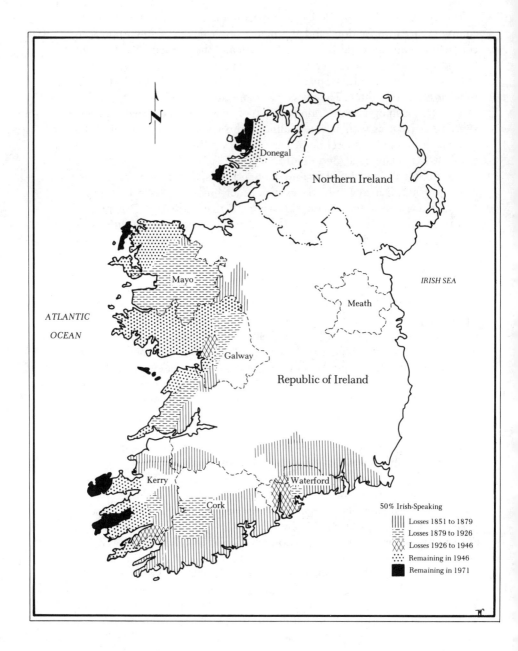

Fig. 3.2. Changes in the Distribution of Irish-Speaking, 1851–1971

TABLE 3.2. Numbers and Proportions of Irish Speakers, 1881–1971

	All Ages				Ages 3 Years and Over				
	1881	1891	1901	1911	1926	1936	1946	1961	1971
Speakers of Irish	924,781	664,387	619,710	553,717	540,801	666,601	588,725	714,000	789,310
Non-speakers of Irish	2,945,000	2,804,000	2,602,000	2,586,000	2,262,000	2,140,000	2,812,000	2,099,000	2,081,000
Total Population	3,870,000	3,469,000	3,221,000	3,139,000	2,802,000	2,807,000	2,771,000	2,815,000	2,870,310
% Irish Speakers	23.9	19.2	19.2	17.6	19.3	23.7	21.2	25	27

Source: Census of Population (Ireland), 1946, 1961, 1971.

population was 789,000; however, we should subtract the native Irish speaking population of the Ghaeltacht (55,000) from the overall total leaving us with a figure of 734,000 which is the total who have acquired Irish either as a first or second language elsewhere than the Ghaeltacht. Of these, no more than 10 percent can be regarded as having a satisfactory competency in the language—73,400. To this we add the native Irish-speaking population of the Ghaeltacht giving a total of competent speakers of Irish of 128,400 compared with the 1926 total of 540,000.

Though the majority of those who claim to speak Irish do not live in the Ghaeltacht, those areas are crucial for the maintenance of Irish. They were officially designated by a commission set up in 1925 as Irish-speaking areas, that is areas where in 1926 25 percent or more of the population spoke Irish. They further divided these areas into two categories: where Irish was spoken by over 80 percent of the population (Fíor Ghaeltacht); and where it was spoken by between 25 percent and 80 percent (Breac Ghaeltacht). These areas and the two categories were reconfirmed in 1956 and 1967. There are now seven Ghaeltacht areas in the southwest and northwest parts of the republic—parts of counties Donegal, Mayo, and Galway, and smaller areas of counties Cork, Kerry, Waterford, and Meath. A Language Enquiry set up in 1956 estimated that in the whole of the Ghaeltacht there were 193,00 speakers of the language in 1946; 104,000 in the Fíor Ghaeltacht and 88,000 in the Breac Ghaeltacht. By 1956 it estimated that the figures had fallen to 150,000 overall—two-thirds in the Fíor Ghaeltacht and one-third in the Breac Ghaeltacht. As percentages of the total populations of these areas there has been a decline overall from 48.3 percent in 1946 to 32 percent at present. The decline has always been greater in the less intensely Irish-speaking areas of the Breac Ghaeltacht; for instance, between 1946 and 1956 the decline in the Fíor Ghaeltacht was just over 4 percent from 76.5 percent to 72.4 percent. In the Breac Ghaeltacht, the percentage dropped from 33.7 to 25.3 percent, a loss of 8.4 percent. The total number of Irish in the Fíor Ghaeltacht in 1971 was 55,000, a decline of 14 percent from the 64,000 of 1961.

The 1956 Enquiry also looked into the language composition of the households in the Ghaeltacht. In Fíor Ghaeltacht, nearly 40 percent of the households used Irish as the only, or as the predominant, medium of communciation. In the Breac Ghaeltacht on the other hand, English as the exclusive language was used in nearly 90 percent of the households, and Irish was the dominant language of only 0.1 percent. Where both languages were used in the households of the Breac Ghaeltacht, Irish was said to predominate in only 0.9 percent, the remaining households claiming English as the predominant language. For all these reasons, the Breac Ghaeltacht is a transitional area, and the shift to English is at a higher level than in the Fíor Ghaeltacht. Very few use the language in the home and even fewer employ it in more public situations. Outside the Ghaeltacht, the large majority of those who claim to speak Irish have been taught it as a school subject for a few years, and the opportunity to use it in everyday life is limited. The Fíor Ghaeltacht is the home of the Irish language at present and its main if not its only hope for the future, and even there the number of speakers is declining.

Breton

Speakers of Breton do not belong to the English Celtic "periphery," but they are the second largest of the Brythonic Celtic stock and originated in Britain. They inhabit the northwest of France, an agricultural area with a strong and important fishing industry (See Figure 3.3). With a total area of 13,460 square miles, it has a population of nearly 2.6 million—7 percent of the population of France. Until the fifth century, the Breton peninsula and areas to the east of it were inhabited by Gaulish tribes, but with the invasions of Britain by the Angles, Saxons, and other Germanic peoples, a large proportion of the Celtic-speaking population of Cornwall and other western areas fled and settled in what was then known as Armorica. They began to expand eastwards from the peninsula and continued to do so until the tenth-century, when the Normans established themselves throughout western France. In 1532 Brittany was officially annexed to the Kingdom of France. In the last 1,000 years since their eastwards expansion was reversed, the Bretons have slowly but surely assimilated to French culture. Even among the peasants, who have always provided the great majority of speakers of Breton, the language has lost considerable ground to French—a process which began in the fifteenth-century.

The depressed condition of Brittany in the eighteenth-century was evident: it was "both administratively neglected and socially isolated" (Tilly, 25-27). Its geographical situation on the extreme northwest Atlantic peninsula coupled with its cultural (particularly linguistic) differences have been used to discriminate against it. It is and always has been staunchly Catholic, and since the Revolution it has been anti-Republican. Until the twentieth century, 80 percent of the population depended for their living on agriculture and even in the 1970s over 37 percent do so. Emigration has been an attractive prospect for the young: during the last century while the population of France as a whole increased by 135 percent, the population of Brittany has remained constant. In spite of a natural growth rate that was well above the national average, between 1831 and 1926, 1 million Bretons left the peninsula; in the years 1954 to 1962, those under thirty left at the rate of approximately 12,500 annually. Like the Ghaeltacht and the Highlands and Islands, age distribution has been severely distorted with this annual loss and an increase of well over 600 who are over sixty.

The French government issues no official figures for the Breton lan-

Fig. 3.3. Linguistic Regions of France

guage, and whatever estimates are produced are the results of individual investigation likely to be either unreliable or contradictory. According to an 1806 estimate, the number of speakers of Breton at the beginning of the nineteenth century was 967,000. By 1880, another observer estimated that the number had increased to 1 million, of whom 500,000 were monolingual speakers of Breton (Hardie, 1948). In 1926, the reknowned linguist Meillet put the Breton-speaking population at 1.4 million, while in 1928 a Breton survey published in the periodical Gwalarn estimated that about 1 million used Breton as their everyday language—75 percent of the population of Brittany. The linguist Dauzat maintained that the vast majority of these people were bilingual. In 1952, Francis Gourvil argued for a figure of 700,000 whose habitual language was Breton "and who used French only in case of necessity," while another 300,000 could speak Breton if they needed to. The reaction against the unfortunate identification of Breton nationalists with the German occupants of France and the Vichy collaborators during World War II tended to accelerate the shift from the Breton language. Thus, the most recent estimate *(Le Telegramme de Brest*, 1974) offers the figure of 44 percent as the level of language maintenance—685,000, a decline of approximately 31.5 percent since the 1952 estimate. Of the present number who are at all competent in the language, barely 18,000 are below 15 years of age, 5 percent of the total of those age groups. Of age groups 15 to 24, 23 percent of the total age group claim the language—56,750. The numbers of those between 25 and 64 amount to 423,000 (60 percent) and of those over 64 years to 168,000 (83 percent) (Stephens, M, 1976:363).

WALES

Introduction

The population of Wales (all ages), according to the Census of 1971, was slightly over 2.7 million. The total population 3 years of age and over was 2.6 million. Of this latter total, 20.9 percent (509,700) claimed to be able to speak Welsh to some extent, a decline of 5.1 percent since 1961 (26.0 percent). In 1971, 1.3 percent (32,725) claimed to be able to speak Welsh only, an increase of 0.3 percent since 1961. These are the very bare outlines of the demographic status of the Welsh language at present, and a more detailed analysis of the demographic condition of the language is presented in this chapter. Among the contributory causes of the decline of the Welsh language, the most crucial have been emigration to rapidly industrialized areas and the dense urbanization of key areas.

Even before the contemporary period, immigration was facilitated by the geography of the principality. While the moorlands and highlands have frustrated the consummation of the ultimate design of the invaders,

three points of easy access and communication have always invited penetration from across the border. Easy access is ensured along the northern
and southern low lying seaboard, as well as in the center along the upper
reaches of the river Severn. The central, rugged mountainous heartland,
however, has helped to delay total collapse of the Welsh language. In
these central, low population density areas agriculture and sheep farming
have been the traditional occupations. South Wales—apart from the rich
agricultural area of the Vale of Glamorgan, the eastern parts of Monmouthshire, and parts of Carmarthenshire and South Pembrokeshire—is characterized by narrow valleys and long defiles reaching into the foothills and
fringes of the central massif. The geographical and topographical variety
has contributed to a complex distribution of the two languages as well as
to great regional differences in social and economic development.

In justifying a more detailed examination of the background to the shift
in language affiliation in Wales than in Scotland, I suggested that the
Welsh language has been and still is more deeply involved in the transition to an industrialized modern society than either Gaelic or Irish. This is
reflected in the level of Welsh industrialization and has a lot to do with
both the higher status of the language in schools as well as with the
language. In fact, as we look at data concerning nonagricultural occupations in the British Isles, we find that up to 1851 the level of such employment at 50 percent was virtually identical for England, Wales, and Scotland
and much lower in Ireland at 25 percent. After 1851, the transfer to
industrial occupation accelerates except in Ireland which was static. In
England, the level of nonagricultural occupations reached 85 percent in
1961, the figure for Wales was only slightly lower at 79 percent, but for
Scotland it was much lower—57 percent. (Censuses of England and Wales,
Scotland and Ireland, 1851 to 1961). While Wales is well ahead of the
other peripheral areas in industrialization, it lags behind the center. However, as we shall note, the spread of industrialization in Wales was extremely uneven and was largely restricted to Monmouthshire and Glamorgan in the south and to a lesser extent the northeast corner bordering on
England. The least populated areas of Wales, therefore, retain the most
distinctive characteristics of Welsh culture. The strongholds of that culture were in the small rural communities of peasant life, among the less
skilled workers, and the nonconformist religious congregations. The Welsh
language was for a long time the most distinctive element in that culture.

In the new industrial areas the position was very different. In 1840, a
report on the state of education in mining districts of South Wales (Tremenheere, 156) described "the heads of the valleys where most of the largest
iron works in South Wales are collected (as) susceptible of but scanty
culture. . . . The people are for the most part collected together in masses
of from 4 to 10 thousands. The homes are ranged round the works in rows,
sometimes 2 to 5 deep, sometimes 3 storey high. . . . It is not unusual to

find that 10 individuals of various ages and sex occupy 3 beds in 2 small rooms— volumes of smoke from the furnaces, the rolling mills and the coke hearths are driven past according to the direction of the wind." It was estimated that over two thirds of the children "for whom daily instruction should be provided do not attend day school." (ibid, 158).

Such desperate conditions were not created but rather were accentuated by the coming of industry—internal colonization that had depressed the principality for centuries had simply taken a new form. The institutions that the English center had imposed upon Wales—the Church, the legal system, the schools—disseminated purposefully and effectively an influence against the Welshness of Wales. The gentry who had earlier identified with national aspirations were drawn into the English vortex, and their abandonment of the language and the Welsh way of life had traumatic effects.

The decline of the language begins to be recorded very soon after the Act of Union of 1536 stated Henry VIII's intention to "reduce them [the Welsh] to the perfect Order, Notice and Knowledge of His Laws of this His Realm and utterly to extirpate all the singular and sinister usages and customs differing from the same. . . ." The Welsh language was the most obvious of these "singular" influences, and for that reason it was enacted that "henceforth no person or persons that use the Welsh speech or language shall have or enjoy any manner of office or offices within the realm." Nevertheless, the English language had very little hold on the country. Even in the administration of the law, the local courts and some of the Quarter Sessions used as much Welsh as English since most of the pleaders knew no English. Elizabeth I accepted the view that "similarity and agreement in religion rather than speech best promotes unity" (Williams, G., 1967:40, 77). Therefore, most of the pressure on the Welsh came from the Church. At all levels, from bishops to the parish priest, the Welsh language was denied a place. Complaints were addressed to the Queen, as they had earlier been addressed to the Pope (ibid., 135), about the absence of Welsh prelates; but like the Pope who after 1370 showed little concern, the Crown was passive and the Church was much more negligent (ibid., 139–40, 177–78).

With the Act of Union, the geographic area we know as Wales today was defined. The boundary that was fixed accords reasonably well both with those which were reflected in the building of Offa's Dyke, but also with the language divide, although there was evidence of English infiltration to the west of the line, particularly along the valleys. Ecclesiastical records show that the border counties such as Radnor were largely Welsh speaking in the eighteenth century. In 1805, Welsh was the dominant language for the agricultural population "except upon the border—where the vile English jargon . . . has crept into use" (Richards, 95). The western border of the English county of Hereford was sufficiently Welsh as late as 1860 for Church notices to be written in Welsh and English. At the beginning of the last century, then, Wales was overwhelmingly Welsh, and that this was the case in spite of conquest and neglect was due partly to the fact that the economy of the principality remained predominantly agrarian and largely self-supporting. There were few towns of even moderate size and communication which had not developed much beyond what they had been at the end of the Middle Ages. There was another reason, namely the political status of the central government in respect to Wales: it was never hostile as it was to Ireland because the Welsh presented no threat as did the Irish or the Scots. The Welsh had been effectively neutralized when the gentry succumbed to the superior attractiveness of the English language and the English way of life. They might, and most of them did, speak Welsh because they could not help it in the running of their estates. They spoke English, however, because they wished to do so—it offered them opportunities of advancement and the cachet of what they regarded as English refinement.

English Immigration and Linguistic Diversity in the Celtic Areas

Nearly a thousand years after the unification of England and well over 500 years after the conquest and colonization of Wales, the population of the principality remained predominantly Welsh-speaking. For instance in 1750, "even in the three reckoned English counties, viz Monmouthshire, Hereford and Shropshire . . . most of the inferior people speak Welsh" (Davies, E. T., 59). Well into the nineteenth century the western valleys of Monmouthshire were entirely Welsh and the use of the language extended down to the seaport villages and towns. In 1840, an observer claimed that over two thirds of the total population of Wales still spoke Welsh and of these more than half were monolingual. The Commissioners of 1844 spoke of South Wales exhibiting the "phenomenon of a peculiar language isolating the mass from the upper portion of society." In 1848, an estimated 400,000 were monolingual Welsh, 200,000 had a slight acquaintance with English, another 200,000 spoke English well, while 100,000 spoke only English (Mills, 64). Two-thirds of the population were Welsh speaking. In 1858, in a representative area of North Wales with a population of 52,000 there were "probably from 44 to 47 thousands who may be said to speak and know Welsh only, while of the remaining 5,000 a large proportion amounting to at least two-thirds though conversant to a greater or lesser extent with English use Welsh as their vernacular language." Even in South Wales the same investigator estimated that 74 percent to 77 percent spoke Welsh habitually. The schools serving these areas maintained a high level of Welsh though they reflected the increasing influence of English on the older children, and a growing disparity between the incidence of the language in North and South Wales (Table 3.3).

TABLE 3.3. Competence in English and Welsh among Pupils of Some Schools in North and South Wales, 1858

	Children under Ten Years				Children over Ten Years			
	Total	Good English	Imperfect English	Welsh Only	Total	Good English	Imperfect English	Welsh Only
North Wales	903	110 (12%)	437 (46%)	356 (39%)	557	239 (43%)	244 (44%)	74 (13%)
South Wales	374	111 (29%)	160 (44%)	103 (28%)	212	133 (63%)	67 (32%)	12 (5%)

Source: Commission of Enquiry into the State of Popular Education in England and Wales, Vol. II. *Reports of the Assistant Commissioners* (London, 1861), Appendix D., p. 631.

For children under ten years of age, the level of Welsh language maintenance was high, though appreciably higher in North Wales than in the South. Among the older children the decline amounted to a loss of 28 percent in North Wales and 35 percent in the South, due no doubt to the influence of exclusively English instruction in the schools and increasing contact with English outside school. Ravenstein, in his pioneering investigation of the distribution of the Celtic languages, calculated in 1879 that Welsh was spoken by 934,500 persons—81 percent of the population 3 years and over. Wide variation in the estimates—with the exception of Ravenstein's—arises from the partial coverage of any investigation and partly because the estimates were intuitive. Nevertheless it is unlikely that the proportion of the Welsh-speaking population was less than 80 percent in the middle of the nineteenth century, and in some areas it was even higher than that.

INDUSTRIALIZATION AND MIGRATION

The abnormal growth of the population of Wales—like that of the United States—is a reflection of the development of industry, especially in South Wales (See Table 3.4). Before 1750 the economy of Wales was pastoral and depressed; only in a few lowland areas was it possible to cultivate sufficiently large arable acreages to make farming prosperous. Industrial activity was fitful and isolated. For most of the people of South Wales, the economic life of the area was centered on the local fairs and markets where the products of agriculture and domestic industry were displayed for sale. Migration was limited to traveling between such fairs and had barely progressed beyond what was characteristic of the late Middle Ages. Coal was extracted by individual farmers only where it outcropped on their land. Since the beginning of the eighteenth century, furnaces and forges using this coal had sprung up in small and scattered hamlets in areas like South Pembrokeshire which, once the real industrial revolution had got under way, lapsed into an almost exclusively agricultural economy. In the areas of South Wales where these early and spasmodic ventures were to grow into centers of world industry in coal mining and in ferrous and nonferrous metallurgy, very few people—not more than thirty to fifty workmen to one enterprise—were employed (John: 6–8). Even with the help of English capital, the local landowners who owned the coal and iron deposits expanded the required work force but recruited them locally with some support from neighboring Welsh-speaking villages and townships.

Where such protoindustrial units were close to the English border, as was the case in Monmouthshire and North East Wales (Flintshire), English-speaking workmen from across the border two or three miles away were attracted. Consequently, the mineral working villages tended to become bilingual though still dominantly Welsh. For example in Flintshire at least seven parishes arranged an English service monthly. In Wrexham which straddles the border, special provision was needed for immigrants. Here the services were "in English every other Sunday with a sermon in the evening for which there was a subscription made by the miners who are Englishmen that work at the mines" (quoted Pryce, W. T. R., 1972: 351). The villages remained Welsh to all intents and purposes. Analyses of the early censuses indicate that lifetime migration into the region tended to be short distance and primarily from within Wales. The migration followed a clearly defined path from the valley of the Clwyd eastwards to the Dee valley and toward the English border. The Ruthin area was an intermediate station or point of transit attracting monolingual Welsh migrants from the uplands and enabling them to acquire some English in the Norman settlement towns before sending them on to the coalfields. Not until toward the beginning of the nineteenth century, with the acceleration of the development of the iron industry, did any ambitious industrial development reach Wales. Between 1850–1914, the iron industry increased in importance and extended its geographical distribution into the coastal strip. The period 1914–39 is remarkable for the decline of the extracting industries characteristic of South Wales, leading to economic depression and out-migration. Finally, from 1939 to the present, there was a reorientation of the Welsh economy toward a more diversified and sophisticated industrial pattern.

These industrial changes were made possible by and in turn have led to large increases of population in a few areas. This selective increase is characterized first by considerable migration within Wales and later by large numbers coming from England (Table 3.5).

The rural counties have traditionally been regarded as the bulwarks of the Welsh language—namely Anglesey, Caernarvon, and Merioneth in North Wales, Radnor (largely English by the middle of the last century), Brecon, and Montgomery in Mid-Wales, Cardigan, Pembrokeshire, and Carmarthen in Southwest Wales—are usually heavy losers by out-migration almost from the beginning of the era of intense industrialization in 1850. They contributed very considerably to the satisfaction of the early manpower requirements of the industrial growth areas like Flintshire in North Wales and Glamorgan in the South. Because of such local migration, the population of the Southwest Wales coalfield increased nearly sixfold. The period of general industrial depression between 1920–36 helped to reverse the process of out-migration from the rural Welsh-speaking areas only slightly and accelerated out-migration from the industrial areas.

It is possible to distinguish four periods of migration. Up to 1850, the needs of Welsh industry were met largely by migration from the neighboring Welsh counties with some support from the southwest counties of

TABLE 3.4. County Distribution of Population of Wales and Percentage Decennial Differences (in thousands)

Year	Wales Total	Wales % Diff.	Anglesey Total	Anglesey % Diff.	Brecon Total	Brecon % Diff.	Caernarvon Total	Caernarvon % Diff.	Cardigan Total	Cardigan % Diff.	Carmarthen Total	Carmarthen % Diff.	Denbigh Total	Denbigh % Diff.
1801	587	—	34	—	32	—	42	—	43	—	67	—	60	—
1811	674	13.0	37	9.0	38	18.0	49	17.0	50	15.0	77	15.0	64	6.0
1821	771	17.0	45	22.0	44	16.0	58	18.0	58	16.0	90	16.0	77	19.0
1831	904	12.0	48	8.0	48	9.0	66	13.0	65	12.0	101	12.0	84	17.0
1853	1,163	14.0	57	9.0	61	2.0	68	3.0	71	4.0	111	5.0	93	5.0
1871	1,413	10.0	51	-3.0	60	0.5	106	28.0	73	1.0	116	2.0	109	8.0
1901	2,013	13.0	51	—	54	-1.0	123	6.0	61	-5.0	135	5.0	138	10.0
1911	2,421	20.0	51	—	59	9.0	125	-0.5	60	-2.0	160	19.0	145	10.0
1921	2,656	9.6	52	1.0	61	3.0	130	4.5	61	2.0	175	9.0	155	8.0
1931	2,593	-2.0	49	-3.0	58	-4.0	121	-7.0	55	-8.0	179	3.0	155	1.0
1951[a]	2,599	0.2	57	7.0	57	-0.5	124	3.0	53	-3.0	172	-2.0	171	4.0
1961	2,644	2.0	52	-8.0	55	-3.0	122	-2.0	54	1.0	168	-3.0	174	2.0
1971	2,731	3.0	60	15.0	53	-4.0	123	1.0	55	2.0	162	-4.0	185	5.0

TABLE 3.4. (continued)

Year	Flint Total	Flint % Diff.	Glamorgan Total	Glamorgan % Diff.	Merioneth Total	Merioneth % Diff.	Monmouth Total	Monmouth % Diff.	Montgomery Total	Montgomery % Diff.	Pembroke Total	Pembroke % Diff.	Radnor Total	Radnor % Diff.
1801	40	—	72	—	28	—	46	—	48	—	56	—	19	—
1811	47	17.0	85	19.0	31	10.0	62	4.0	52	8.0	61	5.0	21	15.0
1821	54	14.0	102	20.0	34	9.0	72	15.0	60	16.0	74	16.0	22	5.0
1831	60	5.0	126	24.0	36	6.0	98	35.0	66	9.0	81	9.0	25	14.0
1851	68	6.0	232	46.0	39	4.0	157	29.0	67	1.5	94	7.0	25	—
1871	76	12.0	398	36.0	47	10.0	195	13.0	68	1.5	92	-1.0	24	-2.0
1901	84	11.0	860	41.0	49	1.0	297	17.0	55	-5.0	88	-1.0	22	-3.0
1911	93	14.0	1,121	30.0	46	-6.0	396	33.0	53	-4.0	90	2.0	21	-3.0
1921	107	15.0	1,254	12.0	45	-1.0	450	14.0	51	-4.0	92	2.0	22	4.0
1931	113	6.0	1,203	-2.0	43	-2.0	435	-3.0	48	-6.0	87	-5.0	21	-4.0
1951	146	15.0		-1.0	41	-1.0	426	-1.0	46	-1.0	91	2.5	20	-2.5
1961	150	3.0	1,230	2.2	38	-6.0	445	2.0	44	-1.0	94	1.5	18	-5.0
1971	175	17.0	1,256	2.0	35	-8.0	461	4.0	43	-2.0	99	5.0	18	—

a No census during World War II.

Source: *Census of England and Wales: General Report and Appendices*, 1801–1971 and *Census of England and Wales: Language Spoken in Wales and Monmouthshire* (Language Supplements) 1871–1971 (London: Her Majesty's Stationery Office).

TABLE 3.5. Net Population Change per Thousand because of Migration in Each Welsh County, 1851–1971

County	1851–61	1861–71	1871–81	1881–91	1891–1901	1901–11	1911–31	1931–51	1951–71
Anglesey	− 25	+ 96	+ 58	− 32	−31	− 35	+ 13	+ 49	+ 4
Brecon	+ 35	− 46	− 98	− 47	−48	− 21	− 34	− 11	+ 4
Caernarvon	− 19	+ 33	+ 18	− 32	− 9	− 43	− 15	− 2	− 2
Cardigan	− 62	− 45	− 99	−133	−63	− 21	− 34	− 11	+ 4
Carmarthen	− 58	− 48	− 33	− 45	−43	+ 67	+ 10	− 65	0
Denbigh	− 6	− 44	− 27	− 22	−16	+ 1	− 9	− 4	+ 7
Flint	+158	− 24	− 51	− 82	−24	+ 21	+132	+120	+40
Glamorgan	+133	+ 45	+144	+166	+54	+ 92	−131	−109	0
Merioneth	− 61	+106	− 12	− 62	−54	−104	+ 14	− 14	+13
Monmouth	− 32	+ 35	− 65	+ 59	− 4	+119	−123	−111	+ 3
Montgomery	− 72	− 75	− 96	−118	−90	− 80	− 50	− 64	−11
Pembroke	− 54	− 74	− 81	− 99	−64	− 73	− 35	− 24	− 5
Radnor	−115	− 83	−146	−118	−90	− 80	− 50	− 64	−11

Source: Extracted from *Census of England and Wales: General Reports*, 1851–1971.

England. This compares with the early phase of industrialization in the Soviet Union and contrasts with the United States where early industry was more dependent on foreign than on local labor. The major turning point in population movement in Wales did not occur until about 1850, when the southwest counties of England became the main source of labor. The second phase lasted to 1906 and was greatly facilitated by the new communication network. The third phase from 1910 onwards saw the outward migration of Welshmen into both England and the United States. Within a decade, the long-term in-migration process was reversed. But this did nothing to ameliorate the demographic condition of the language. After the first internal migration phase, which completely disrupted the linguistic homogeneity of South Wales, out-migration could only aggravate the condition. The fourth period, from the end of the last war to the present day, has seen the retardation of the process of outward migration, the stabilization of the industrial population, and a change in the nature of inward migration. The population became extremely selective and professional in its composition and, to that extent, less permanent than inward migration tended to be in the second phase.

The history of immigration into Wales is largely, though not entirely, the history of changes in the economic life of the South Wales coalfield. Northeast Wales was also involved but to a lesser extent. Even by the mid–eighteenth century it was clear that the highest population densities in Northeast Wales were to be found in the exposed coalfield. By 1801, the distributional contrasts between the eastern coalfield of Flintshire and Denbighshire and the rural west had been further intensified. The rural parishes had lost to the coalfield a proportion of the Welsh-speaking population large enough to offset the natural growth of previous decades in the western uplands. Laborers were attracted by higher wages in the coalfield and pushed out by the economic difficulties the farming communities experienced at the end of the Revolutionary Wars. Farms were amalgamated and the reclamation of waste land was halted so that agriculture was able to support fewer and fewer people. In addition, the old lead mines of the northeast were closing (Pryce, 1972:320).

Glamorgan and Monmouth were, however, much higher in the order of urbanizing counties next after London, Durham, and Lancashire in the middle of the nineteenth century. In South Wales, urbanization was strongly associated with the accelerated development of the coal mines and iron works. Considering one indicator of urbanization—population growth—the urbanization of Glamorgan was faster and more intensive even than that of the Durham coalfield in the north of England. By 1871, the urbanization of the British Isles was concentrated in the north (Durham and Lancashire), the Midlands (Staffordshire and Warwickshire), London, and the two South Wales counties (Glamorgan and Monmouthshire). Furthermore, urbanization following industrialization and migration in

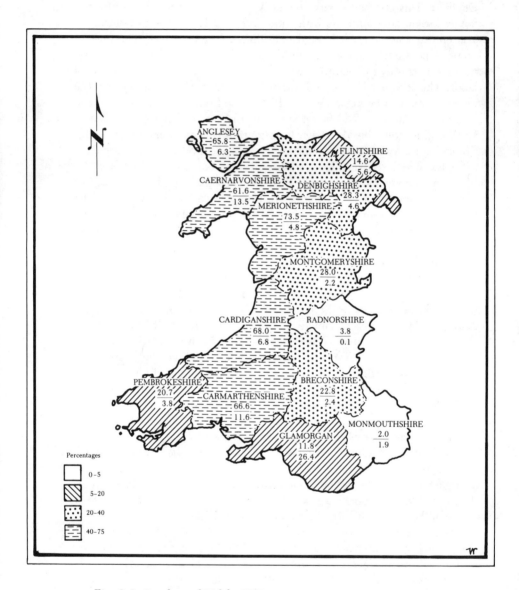

Fig. 3.4. Speakers of Welsh, 1971

Wales did not spread to other counties, although the urban population of the principality generally increased because of migration into the coal mining counties.

Unlike Glamorgan, Monmouthshire is one of a dozen counties in England and Wales that do not show simple migration patterns. While developing her own industries, for which she depended on English-speaking labor from across the border (as well as from the same Welsh resources as Glamorgan), Monmouth also contributed greatly to Glamorgan's population growth. In the 1840s, the coal deposits of Merthyr and its neighborhood, together with those of the Rhondda, began to be exploited in earnest. Colliers in the valleys of Monmouthshire moved into Glamorgan to promote the exploitation. In the decades (1851–61, 1871–81, and 1891–1901), a combination of in-migration mainly from England and out-migration to Glamorgan resulted in a net negative migration balance (Table 3.5). The number of inward migrants did not offset the number of Glamorgan-bound out-migrants, but actually intensified the rate of decline of the Welsh language in Monmouth—the in-migrants were almost all English, and a large proportion of the out-migrants were Welsh-speaking. Glamorgan, on the other hand, has a "special place in the history of internal migration in Britain," (Friedlander and Roshier, 1966) and belongs to a group of English and Welsh counties that experienced a net positive gain in the first period (beginning in 1851) and net losses thereafter. Between 1801 and 1851, the population of Glamorgan more than trebled from 71,000 to 232,000. The county was still largely agricultural, with a population density at the end of that period less than that of rural counties like Cornwall or Somerset; that is, 253 compared with 259 and 289 per square mile. During the next sixty years, while the population of England and Wales as a whole rose by only 80 percent (1.1 million), there was more than a five-fold rise in Glamorgan. Over half a million of these were immigrants.

Using their "migration index," Friedlander and Roshier (1966) estimate that in 1851–61 Glamorgan (of all the counties in England and Wales) witnessed a flow of migrants second in its strength only to that of another Welsh county in the midst of industrialization—Flintshire in the northeast. In the next decade, 1861–71, Glamorgan was second only to London and the home counties. During this phase, well over 70 percent of the immigrants were recruited from neighboring Welsh counties in addition to Monmouthshire (23,000), Cardiganshire (15,000), Pembrokeshire (37,000), Carmarthenshire (57,000), and Brecon (21,000). Thus, having been second in the list of gaining counties from 1851 to 1871, Glamorgan reached the top of the list in 1871–81: Over 57 percent of the migrants came from England (Table 3.6). The flow continued until 1911. This was due to the greatly increased production of coal involving the addition of more than 116,000 miners between 1871 and 1911. Of these, 67 percent

TABLE 3.6. Total Numbers Born Outside Glamorgan and the Proportion of the Total Population, 1861–1951

Date Census Return	1861	1871	1881	1891	1901	1911	1921	1931	1951
Total in Thousands	116.8	117.9	180.8	260.6	297.8	390.9	280.0	261.0	254.0
Proportion of Native Population	36%	34%	35%	38%	34%	35%	22%	21.5%	21%

Sources: Extracted from *Census of England and Wales: General Reports*, 1861–1951.

were recruited from neighboring English counties—Somerset, Gloucester, Devon, Wiltshire, and Hereford.

There was, therefore, both a massive rise in the number of migrants and, equally important, a decisive shift in the area of origin (Table 3.7). When the total number of in-migrants was held to no more than 21,000 (1861–71), three of every four migrants were Welsh. As the numbers increased to 74,000, 108,000, and finally in 1911 to 128,000, the Welsh contribution fell to one in every two. Between 1861 and 1911, the number of nonnative-born inhabitants of Glamorgan increased to 390,000—which represented the residuum of nearly 430,000 migrants, over 55 percent of them English monolinguals. The ratio of nonnative to native-born fluctuated slightly between 38 percent and 34 percent between 1861 and 1911, and this nearly constant ratio at a time of rapid rise in the total population is due to the equally constant reinforcement of Welsh migrants. After 1911, the nonnative to native proportion fell to 21 percent because of the cessation of in-migration (Table 3.7). But the Welsh language continued to decline because the second and third generation migrants —though native born—were predominantly if not exclusively English-speaking.

The fate of the Welsh language in Glamorgan is due partly to the fact that industrialization began in the strongest Welsh-speaking areas—the hills—and was fed by migrants from other Welsh-speaking areas. This is the first phase. It is a consideration of this phase that has led some researchers (Thomas, B., 1962) to maintain that industrialization and immigration did not affect the Welsh language adversely. Their contention is valid only for this first phase. During the second phase, however, the balance of cultural advantage finally swung decisively to the side of anglicization and with it went the last hope of preserving a Welsh culture on the coalfield (Jones, P.N., 1969: 92). The second phase was characterized by a predominantly English labor supply, which was massive but extended over a relatively short duration. The first phase gave the Welsh language an opportunity to adapt to change; the second phase, however, was too intense and too rapid to assimilate the English. This fact was stressed by the Commission of Enquiry into Industrial Unrest which noted that until 1894 "the inhabitants, in many respects, showed a marked capacity for stamping their own impress on all newcomers, and communicating to them a large measure of all their own characteristics. Of more recent years the process of assimilation had been unable to keep pace with the continuing influx of immigrants." The fate of the Welsh language is inextricably associated with the inflow of English immigrants and the outflow of Welsh-speaking rural people into the industrial and linguistically diverse areas of South and Northeast Wales and later to England and America.

The changes did not occur uniformly throughout Glamorgan. The rate of migration and population growth varied from district to district. The

TABLE 3.7. Glamorgan Immigrants and Percentages According to Areas of Origin, 1861–1911 (in thousands)

| Date of Census Return | Total of Migration to Glamorgan | Welsh Counties | | | | | | | | | | | | Total of Welsh Migrants | Welsh Migrants % of Total | Migration from England | |
		Anglesey	Brecon	Caernarvon	Cardigan	Carmarthen	Denbigh	Flint	Merioneth	Monmouth	Montgomery	Pembroke	Radnor			Total	%
1861–71	21.0	—	2.1	—	1.5	5.7	0.1	—	0.1	2.3	0.4	3.7	0.4	16.3	78	4.7	22
1871–81	74.7	—	3.6	0.3	4.1	4.9	0.2	0.1	0.2	10.1	1.4	5.8	0.7	31.4	43	43.3	57
1881–91	108.8	0.6	4.3	1.9	7.6	9.3	0.7	0.4	1.6	10.5	4.1	5.5	1.4	48.2	44	60.6	56
1891–1901	105.0	0.4	4.2	1.0	3.8	11.6	0.3	0.3	1.1	13.5	1.4	7.1	0.7	55.4	53	49.6	47
1901–11	128.5	1.0	3.8	3.9	2.9	6.8	1.1	0.3	2.5	11.6	2.2	5.5	1.3	42.9	33	85.6	67

Source: Extracted from Census of England and Wales: General Reports, 1861–1911.

most rapid changes were experienced in Merthyr and the Rhondda Valleys. The former, at one time the center of the country's iron industry, and the latter an area truly representative of the coalfield, are situated at the "tops of the valleys" almost within the mountainous Welsh heartland. In 1851, Merthyr had a population of over 50,000, over 40 percent of whom came from other Welsh counties and 38 percent from neighboring Welsh-speaking districts within Glamorgan. Only a small portion of the remaining 20 percent came from England. The significance for Welsh speakers of the historical isolation of the uplands of Glamorgan from the effects of the Norman and Tudor occupation of Wales and consequent anglicization soon emerged. Unlike the low lying areas of the county, the Rhondda Valleys and Merthyr had remained Welsh-speaking. Consequently, of the immigrants into Glamorgan, the Welsh-speaking element was almost invariably attracted to the coalfields in the hills. In 1808, it was claimed that "the workmen of all description at these immense works (at Merthyr) are Welshmen. Their language is entirely Welsh" (John, 1960: 62). It was natural, therefore, that Welsh-speaking agricultural workers seeking industrial employment would prefer Merthyr to the English-speaking lowland agricultural areas. The English migrants, however, were initially drawn to these more linguistically congenial agricultural lowlands rather than to the coalfields. For example, in 1891 the 252,000 lifetime immigrants in Glamorgan were divided almost equally between the Welsh and English. However, so far as the coalfields were concerned, Welsh migrants outnumbered the English by four to three. Outside the coalfield the ratio of English to Welsh migrants was reversed—it was nearly five to two. Of the total of Welsh migrants into Glamorgan, 80 percent went into the coalfield. They were motivated to migrate by the prospect of relatively high wages, but their choice of destination was influenced considerably by linguistic and cultural considerations.

The traditional linguistic and cultural character of Merthyr and the Rhondda drew Welsh immigrants to those areas, and their presence, in turn, reinforced that tradition. In a period of rapid transition they ensured that the inevitable process of anglicization was delayed because the Welsh were able to absorb without being overpowered by the English. In 1840, before long-distance migration began to affect Merthyr, but at a time nevertheless when, because of short-distance movement, the population of the town and surrounding villages had increased from 13,000 to 85,000 in less than 40 years. The religious situation—reflecting the linguistic division between the Church and nonconformist sects—was highly favorable to the latter, there being nine times as many chapels as churches. In one small but typical area of the town, consisting of two very long rows of tenement houses "standing behind each other, close to the works and a fair average of the whole, seventeen of the twenty families were Welsh; ten of the husbands could read Welsh and four of the wives could read the

Welsh Bible" (Tremenheere). In 1846, only 12.3 percent of the population were English, and this small proportion declined within 5 years to 9 percent. Twenty years later the position had not altered greatly, though the children were rapidly becoming bilingual. "In such towns as Merthyr, Aberdare and others where the different races converge large numbers speak English for the purpose of necessary intercourse with their neighbors, who beyond the very scanty nomenclature used for this end [they] are entirely ignorant of that language. Welsh is their vernacular for the fireside, for general conversation and for all the ordinary purposes of life. . . . They would be recent emigrants from the agricultural western districts of Wales. However, among the children knowledge of English is in advance of the population. In these instances the parents have been longer located in the district and the children are native to or brought there very young, and from intercourse with companions of their own age and other sources they not only are habituated to English in their earliest years but acquire and make more use of English abroad than they do of Welsh at home" (Jenkins, 1861: 453). Nevertheless, in assessing and acknowledging the value to Welsh language maintenance of the concentration of Welsh migration on Merthyr and the Rhondda, that concentration deprived other areas in Glamorgan on the border between the lowland English-speaking and the upland Welsh-speaking of similar much needed Welsh language support. Consequently, outside the coalfield the language collapsed very rapidly. But because of this early reinforcement of the Welsh population of Merthyr and the Rhondda Valleys at the beginning of its industrial expansion, these areas remain centers of Welsh language and culture.

Migration and Rural Areas

Without exception the predominantly rural counties—those in central Wales and the isolated north and southwest, Anglesey, Brecon, Cardigan, Montgomery, Pembroke, and Radnor—manifest a regular and continuous outward migration. Of all the counties in England and Wales that lost residents in the period after 1851, the Welsh rural counties rank among those with the highest proportion of out-migration. Apart from Merioneth and Caernarvon (which reached their population peaks in 1901 and 1921 respectively), the rural population peak is achieved before 1871 (Table 3.4).

Since 1801 the rate of population increase in the rural and traditionally Welsh-speaking counties has been comparatively slight. All the counties, other than those that became the centers of industry, had a total population of 359,000 in 1801. In 1971 the population of the same areas was 834,000—an increase of 130 percent while the total increase for the whole of Wales was 364 percent. The three industrial counties had an eleven-fold increase. The rural Welsh-speaking counties made their highest contribution to the total population of Wales at the beginning of the nineteenth century. In 1801, Carmarthenshire was only approximately 10 percent lower in population than Glamorgan (63,300 and 70,900 respectively). In 1831, Carmarthen was over 25 percent lower (100,700 and 126,600 respectively), and in 1851 the population of Glamorgan was twice that of Carmarthen (110,600 and 231,800 respectively). By 1871, when the industrial development of Wales was being pursued vigorously, Glamorgan had increased its population since 1801 by a multiple of twelve, Carmarthen and Brecon by a multiple of three, and Denbigh by a multiple of five.

The agricultural depression of the middle of the nineteenth century, together with the shortage of labor in the iron industry, combined to make the Welsh-speaking areas of West Wales an attractive recruiting ground to the ironmasters of Glamorgan. They sent agents into Pembrokeshire to hire workmen, paying them 5 pounds for every fifty they secured (John, 69). The depopulation of these areas has been portrayed as producing a pattern of concentric circles with Merthyr at the center, and the nearest areas being drawn upon first (John, 64). For example, in the 1820s the neighboring parishes made their greatest contribution to the industries of Merthyr, but not until 1845 did the almost completely Welsh-speaking areas of West Carmarthen and Pembrokeshire make theirs. In the southwest coalfield in 1851, nearly 90 percent of the labor force was local or drawn from neighboring Welsh-speaking counties. The majority of the remainder, approximately 10 percent came from southwest England.

During the present century and up to 1971, while the total for the whole of Wales has increased by 73,000, (41 percent) the population of rural Wales has declined by 53,000 (−8.2 percent). The most intensely Welsh of the rural areas had even more serious losses: Montgomery 12,000 (22 percent); Cardigan 6,000 (10 percent); and Merioneth 14,000 (28 percent) (Table 3.2). During the last 100 years, the population of rural Mid-Wales has fallen by over 25 percent. In the present century alone, the decline is over 17 percent as compared with a 50 percent increase in Wales as a whole (Table 3.4).

The recognized pool of Welsh speech has become increasingly shallow. In terms both of actual numbers and of proportions of the population, the balance has shifted progressively to South Wales; after 1911, however, the English Midland counties have increasingly attracted rural emigrants, thus accentuating even more the Welsh language losses. The decline of rural Wales, though, cannot be attributed exclusively to out-migration. The rate of natural increase has almost invariably been unfavorable to the rural areas, and this disadvantage has tended to increase over time. The rate of natural increase for England and Wales from 1951 to 1961 was 4.5 percent and for Wales alone 3.4 percent. During the same period in the Mid-Wales rural counties, it was only 0.4 percent. In the two most thoroughly Welsh-speaking counties, Merioneth and Cardiganshire, deaths exceeded births, and in three counties—Caernarvon, Cardigan, and

Merioneth—the decline in natural growth has been greater than out-migration by 8.5, 14.8, and 6.6 percent respectively.

The depopulation of the Welsh-speaking rural counties was not a total loss to the Welsh language, any more than it has been to the local languages of the Soviet Union. In fact, apart from reinforcing the already urbanized indigenous and native-speaking populations of heterogeneous cities, Pokshishevskiy (1969b) claims that such depopulation may serve the indigenous language by intensifying the ethnic consciousness of its speakers. The question does not arise in the United States because the urban areas *depended* on immigrants who could be reinforced only from abroad.

The period from 1851 to 1871 in Wales is characterized by short-distance migration, much of it to and from adjacent counties. The condition of the language in South Wales at present would be much worse than it is if the migration from England had not previously—and simultaneously—been offset by the deployment of the internal resources of Wales. During the period from 1850 to 1871, about 70 percent of the migrants into Glamorgan came from the neighboring Welsh-speaking counties. A large proportion of these immigrants were monolingual Welsh or nearly so. But between 1871 and 1881 long-distance migration really set in and only 38 percent of the migrants came from the five neighboring counties: migration from the southwest counties of England, though, rose rapidly to 37 percent. One feature of the early short-distance migration that census figures cannot reveal, but which was of great importance, was its occasional or seasonal character. Farm workers and owners of small holdings in Carmarthenshire and Breconshire were accustomed to move into the iron works and mines of Monmouthshire and Glamorgan during the slack farming seasons and return home when the pressure of farm work required their presence. This constant mobility had two contrary consequences: it helped regularly to reinforce the existing Welsh character of the industrial area; it helped to break down the settled traditional Welsh pattern of rural life, to promote the acceptance of novel ideas, and to prepare the way for the forces tending toward the anglicization of remote rural areas. Such seasonal migration is also characteristic of the USSR and other parts of Europe. This aspect of migration assumed greater importance in the short period between 1876 and 1879 in Wales, when temporary recession drove large numbers of short-distance migrants back to the farms.

The Decline of the Welsh Language
BROAD NATIONAL TRENDS

So far we have analyzed the process of population change, and especially migration flows, in the whole of Wales and in the critical localities. Changes in the demographic status of the Welsh language have paralleled these national and local changes (See Table 3.8).

TABLE 3.8. English- and Welsh-Speaking Populations of Wales, 1891–1971

Year of Census	a Total Population in Thousands	b Welsh Only			c English and Welsh			d[a] Total Welsh Speaking (b + c)			e[a] English Only		
		1 Total in Thousands	2 1 as % of (a)	3 Percentage Difference from Previous Return	1 Total in Thousands	2 1 as % of (a)	3 Percentage Difference from Previous Return	1 Total in Thousands	2 1 as % of (a)	3 Percentage Difference from Previous Return	1 Total in Thousands	2 1 as % of (a)	3 Percentage Difference from Previous Return
1891	1,813	508.0	29.0	—	402	24.0	—	910	51.0	—	759	41.0	—
1901	2,013	281.0	14.0	−45	649	32.0	+61	930	46.0	+ 2	928	54.0	+22.0
1911	2,421	190.0	8.0	−36	786	32.0	+21	976	39.0	+ 5	1,108	46.0	+30.0
1921	2,656	153.0	6.0	−19	746	29.0	− 5	900	36.0	− 8	1,467	63.0	+33.0
1931	2,593	98.0	4.0	−36	820	32.0	+10	909	36.0	+ 1	1,552	64.0	+ 5.0
1951	2,472	41.4	2.0	−57	673	27.0	−19	714	28.0	−22	1,758	72.0	+13.0
1961	2,518	26.1	1.0	−38	629	25.0	− 7	656	26.0	− 8	1,862	74.0	+ 6.0
1971	2,602	32.7	1.3	+30	510	19.6	−20	542	21.0	−20	2,060	89.0	+20.0

a The totals of the language categories (d) and (e) do not, as they should, equal the totals in (a) because of omissions in language data returns. No Census was taken in 1941.

Source: *Census of England and Wales. Reports on Welsh-Speaking Population—Language Supplements*

The proportion of the population who are bilingual rose consistently until 1951, with one exception in the period from 1911 to 1921. It has been falling since, so that in 1961 the percentage was only slightly greater than in 1891—25 percent and 24 percent respectively. The decline in the proportion of monolingual speakers of Welsh has been extraordinary— from 29 percent in 1891 to 1 percent in 1961. The rise in the proportion of monolingual English is continuous, from 41 percent in 1891 to 74 percent in 1961. It is clear that the bilinguals are becoming monolingual English very rapidly, and the monolingual Welsh are becoming temporarily and transitionally bilingual. The only decade when this process of complete transference of language loyalty was retarded is 1921–31, the period of post-World War I recession followed by the onset of the international depression, when Wales experienced the highest rate of out-migration. With the almost complete disappearance of Welsh monolingualism, ex- cept among children between the ages of 3 to 5 years, there remained after 1931 no pool from which bilinguals could be produced. From that time onward the curve of bilingualism has declined from 32 percent in 1931 to 25 percent in 1961. While the population of Wales increased from 1.8 million in 1891 to 2.6 million in 1961, the number of monolingual Welsh dropped from 540,000 to 26,000. The population increase represent- ed a rise of almost 44 percent, but the number of speakers of Welsh— bilingual and monolingual—dropped by 16 percent. Looked at nationally, the outlook for the Welsh language has no variation, no complexities, no light and shade; but rather, it is characterized by a uniform and deep- ening gloom.

REGIONAL DIFFERENCES IN THE DENSITY AND THE DISTRIBUTION OF THE WELSH LANGUAGE

The description of the national trends in the demographic situation of the Welsh language, however, cannot do justice to the variation from one locality to another. The analysis needs to be pursued according to geogra- phic distribution, type of locality (whether urban or rural), and age and sex composition of the population.

The rural areas have been consistent recipients of a certain number of inward migrants. Because the majority of these are English-speaking and are focused on well defined and limited areas, their adverse influence on the Welsh language is concentrated and therefore more effective. For instance, the increase of the population of Cardiganshire between 1951–71 is due in large part to the inclusion of the expanded and predominantly English-speaking staff and students at the University of Wales, Aberystwyth. The hydroelectric construction project within the same county, manned by migrant labor (English and Irish) was also responsible for an increase in the county population. Similar large industrial and construction projects in Merionethshire have inflated the local populations with non-Welsh elements, and so have military establishments in Breconshire, Cardiganshire, and other Welsh-speaking rural counties. In Anglesey, the rise between 1961–71 is due entirely to the expansion of a service base, the construction of a nuclear electric generating project, and the establishment of a large nonferrous industry—all of them entirely alien to the county and drawing upon non-Welsh migrants. Where the populations of other rural areas have shown signs of natural increase, as for instance in the case of Welshpool (5 percent), Newtown (4 percent), and the borough of Montgomery (7 percent), between 1951 and 1971, the locations of the increases have been close to the English border, or along the River Severn and therefore within easy access to the English Midlands. Such rises in the population are unlikely to favor the maintenance of the Welsh language (See Table 3.9).

Two dimensions of the local incidence of the Welsh language must be considered as well. The first dimension is the proportion of the Welsh-speaking to the total population in the several localities. This is the measure of the local or regional density of Welsh speech, and is referred to as the "intensity index." The second dimension is the proportion of the national total of speakers of Welsh represented in any area, and this is what is designated as the "distributional index." The two indices represent different aspects of the demographic status of the Welsh language; moreover, as we shall see, they are negatively correlated in almost every locality (See Table 3.10). Most maps of the distribution of the Welsh language fail to reveal how the intensity of Welsh in any area is related to the density of the population of that area. Thus, one gains the impression that because an area is shown to have a high proportion of Welsh speakers, the population is also large. In fact, though, the higher the percentage Welshness of an area, the fewer there are who speak it because few people live there.

In 1891 the thirteen counties, in terms of the intensity of Welsh, were divided into three groups; five had a percentage of 90 and over—Cardigan, Anglesey, Carmarthen, Merioneth, and Caernarvon; four counties ranged between 51 percent and 68 percent—Flint, Denbigh, Montgomery, and Glamorgan; four counties ranged between 10 percent and 51 percent—Brecon, Pembroke, Monmouth, and Radnor. It is significant that the first group, the high intensity areas, were heavily if not exclusively agricultural with low population densities in 1891; the second group were either dominantly industrial or leaning in that direction with increasing population densities. The third group, those with lowest intensity of Welshness, are either on the English border or, as in the case of Pembrokeshire,

TABLE 3.9. Welsh-Speaking Population by Categories and According to Counties, 1971

| | All Persons Aged 3 and Over | | | Speaking Welsh | | | | | |
| | | | | Total[a] | | | Monolingual Welsh | | |
Area	Persons	Males	Females	Persons	Males	Females	Persons	Males	Females
Wales	2,602,000	1,261,000	1,341,000	542,000	255,000	286,000	32,000	15,000	16,000
Anglesey	56,400	27,600	26,000	37,000	17,800	19,100	2,500	1,200	1,200
Brecon	51,100	25,400	25,700	11,700	5,600	6,100	500	200	300
Caernarvon	117,900	54,600	63,100	73,100	34,200	38,800	5,100	2,500	2,500
Cardigan	52,900	25,400	27,300	35,700	17,000	18,700	1,900	900	900
Carmarthen	156,600	75,200	80,800	103,800	49,700	54,000	4,500	2,200	2,200
Denbigh	176,400	83,900	92,400	49,500	23,700	25,800	3,100	1,500	1,600
Flint	166,600	80,000	86,000	24,400	11,500	12,800	1,400	600	700
Glamorgan	1,999,200	581,400	617,500	141,000	63,900	77,000	8,600	3,900	4,600
Merioneth	33,800	16,000	17,800	24,800	11,800	13,000	2,600	1,300	1,300
Monmouth	439,100	216,100	222,900	9,200	4,500	4,700	600	200	300
Montgomery	41,200	20,500	20,600	11,500	5,800	5,700	500	200	200
Pembroke	24,300	46,200	48,000	19,400	9,400	10,000	900	400	400
Radnor	17,500	8,600	8,800	600	300	300	30	10	10

[a] Figures are rounded and totals are not sums of these numbers.
Source: *Decennial Language Supplements for Wales,* 1971.

possess an historic English language plantation, "little England beyond Wales." Monmouth, which is in the third category, was both an industrial county and on the English border, and its intensity index was nearly the lowest of all. It is noticeable, too, that counties in the high intensity Welsh group all appeared to behave in identical fashion during the period 1891–1961—their rates of the attenuation of Welsh appear to be exactly synchronized. The four counties with medium Welsh intensity ratings also behaved consistently as a group from 1891 to 1961, though less uniformly than the first group. Glamorgan and Flint suffered 66 percent and 60 percent, respectively, loss of Welsh intensity between 1891 and 1961 while Denbigh and Montgomery, which retain a considerable agricultural character, suffered losses of only 40 percent each. Monmouth in the third group is a vital case because the combination of its highly industrial development and its vulnerability as a border county resulted in a loss of 85 percent intensity in 70 years.

The relatively high intensity of Welsh speech in the first group of counties has been maintained in spite of population change. As in the case with all other counties their affiliation to the Welsh language has weakened, but not to the same extent as with all the other areas. Furthermore the Welshness of the whole of Wales has declined at a much sharper rate (from 52 percent in 1891 to 26 percent in 1961) than in the high intensity counties. The sharp distinction between the high intensity areas and the two other groups in 1891 has been accentuated in the last 70 years; a polarization emerged in terms of intensity of the incidence of Welsh,

TABLE 3.9. (*continued*)

				Speaking Welsh					
	Speaking English			Reading Welsh			Writing Welsh		
Area	Persons	Males	Females	Persons	Males	Females	Persons	Males	Females
Wales	509,000	239,000	269,000	448,000	208,000	240,000	297,000	185,000	211,000
Anglesey	34,500	16,600	17,900	32,400	15,500	16,900	31,100	14,900	16,200
Brecon	11,100	5,300	5,800	9,100	4,200	4,800	7,600	3,500	4,000
Caernarvon	62,900	31,600	36,200	65,000	30,200	34,700	62,200	28,900	33,200
Cardigan	35,800	16,000	17,700	32,600	15,300	17,200	31,000	14,600	16,300
Carmarthen	99,300	47,500	51,800	87,600	41,100	45,900	76,800	36,400	40,400
Denbigh	46,300	22,100	24,200	40,800	19,200	21,500	36,500	17,300	19,200
Flint	23,600	10,900	12,000	18,700	8,700	10,000	16,100	7,400	8,600
Glamorgan	132,300	60,000	72,300	107,300	47,100	60,100	84,900	37,400	47,500
Merioneth	22,200	10,500	11,700	22,800	108,000	11,900	22,100	10,500	11,600
Monmouth	8,600	4,200	4,300	6,200	3,000	3,200	4,900	2,400	2,500
Montgomery	11,000	5,600	5,400	9,900	49,000	4,900	9,000	4,500	4,500
Pembroke	18,500	8,900	9,500	15,900	7,600	8,300	13,900	6,600	7,200
Radnor	600	200	300	400	200	200	400	100	200

between the agricultural counties like Cardiganshire, Merionethshire, and Radnorshire, and the heavily industrialized counties like Monmouthshire, Glamorgan, and Flintshire, and the semi-industrial areas like Carmarthenshire and Breconshire.

This polarization has been aggravated by another characteristic of the demographic status of Welsh. The five counties in the high intensity group had a mean of 92 percent in 1891 and 75 percent in 1961, but they are low in the distribution index, contributing only 40 percent to the national total in 1891 and 1961. The industrial counties in 1891 had a relatively low mean intensity index, 50 percent in 1891, and a very low mean in 1961 of 18 percent, but they contributed far more than 50 percent of the total number of Welsh-speakers in 1891 and 1971. However intense or weak the local incidence of Welsh may be, this is not reflected in the size of contribution to the national total.

Generally speaking, industrialization is correlated with a declining density of Welsh speech. At the same time, if we exclude Monmouth which is a special case because of its position on the English border, industrialization is also correlated with an increasing proportion of the national Welsh-speaking total. The great majority of speakers of Welsh live in highly industrialized communities; though they maintain the Welsh language, their attachment to it becomes very much less assured. The polarization already noted between the agricultural and the industrial counties is unlikely to be purely demographic. The minority who live in the intensely Welsh-speaking areas are still closely attached to the traditions associated

TABLE 3.10. Welsh-Speaking Population of Each County, Intensity Index,[a] and Distribution Index[b] for 1891 and 1971

	Wales	Anglesey	Brecon	Caernarvon	Cardigan	Carmarthen	Denbigh	Flint	Glamorgan	Merioneth	Monmouth	Montgomery	Pembroke	Radnor
1891														
Welsh-Speaking Total	910,000	40,000	29,000	107,000	73,000	100,000	52,000	27,000	320,000	58,000	39,000	32,000	24,000	1,000
Intensity Index[a]	52.0	94.0	40.0	90.0	95.0	90.0	66.0	68.0	51.0	95.0	20.0	52.0	37.0	10.00
Distribution Index[b]	100.0	4.4	3.2	12.0	8.0	11.0	5.7	3.0	3.5	6.3	4.4	3.5	2.6	1.00
1971														
Welsh-Speaking Total	542,000	37,000	11,700	73,000	35,700	103,800	49,500	24,400	141,000	24,900	9,200	11,600	19,500	650
Intensity Index[a]	19.6	65.8	22.8	61.6	68.9	66.6	28.3	14.6	11.8	73.5	2.0	28.0	20.7	3.80
Distribution Index[b]	100.0	6.3	2.4	13.5	6.8	11.6	9.4	5.6	26.4	4.8	1.9	2.2	3.8	0.10

[a] *Intensity Index* is the Welsh-speaking total expressed as percentage of total population of each county.
[b] *Distribution Index* is the Welsh-speaking total of the county expressed as percentage of national Welsh-speaking total.
Source: *Census of England and Wales: State of the Welsh Language Supplements, 1891 and 1971.*

with the Welsh language and its folk ethos, and they consistently seek to promote the preservation of that ethos.

The majority of Welsh speakers, those who live in the industrial areas, while very conscious of being Welsh, are in process of developing a nontraditional, urbanized consciousness of that Welshness. They tend to see the language as an expression of a different Welsh ethos from that favored by the minority. While they recognize themselves as Welsh, and demand to be acknowledged as such by others mainly on the grounds that they speak the language, the other characteristics which the two groups associate with their Welsh identity are different.

A preliminary pilot study, for which the research and interpretation of data are incomplete, is being directed by the author to discover the perception among Welshmen of what it means to be Welsh. Two groups of Welsh-speaking adults were selected—one in a Carmarthenshire rural area and the other in Cardiff. Each group consisted of ten men and ten women, aged between 25 and 35. They were selected so as to provide a uniform sample in terms of economic status but with different occupations. They were asked to rate along a five point scale "personality traits" and "culture traits" such as "Born in Wales," "Welsh the mother tongue," "Welsh the second language," "tolerance," "self-sufficiency," "sociability," "sports loving," "friendly," "appreciation of Welsh literature," "fondness of music," "solidarity with occupational group (trade unionism)," and "degree of commitment to a religious denomination." On the personality scale, it appeared to be less important to the urbanized Welsh to have learned Welsh as a first or second language than it did for the rural group. Tolerance and sociability with other Welshmen was less important to the urban group also. On the other hand, the same urban group valued more highly than did the rural group self-sufficiency, love of sport, and friendliness with "outsiders" (non-Welsh-speaking inhabitants of the areas). On the cultural scale, the urbanized Welsh attached considerably less importance to attendance at religious services, and considerably more to solidarity with fellow workers. They appeared to have less concern for the enjoyment of Welsh literature and more for the appreciation of and participation in musical events. Each group gave equal importance to political affiliation, though the direction of their political interests varied considerably—the rural group being far more conservative than the urban. The one characteristic that stands out as constituting their concept of themselves as Welsh is their determination to be so regarded—it is a matter of choice rather than of possessing the attributes that might traditionally be thought to constitute Welshness. This was in the view of the majority more important than the degree of command over the language. Apart from the "self-identification" factor, the two groups in their attitude to the language see it as expressing a different way of life, a different ethos.

Within-County Urban and Rural Language Differences

Within most counties the rural areas are more *intensely* Welsh-speaking than the urban areas of the same counties. For instance, in 1901 the urban and rural intensity indices for Anglesey were 85 and 93, for Brecon 20 and 87, Caernarvon 80 and 96. The only counties where the intensity of Welsh was greater in the urban areas were Merioneth and Monmouth, but in each case the difference was not great (95 and 93, and 13 and 13, respectively). The same kind of relationship has continued down to 1961, and Merioneth is now no exception—69 urban and 77 rural. Further-more, overall the disparity has become larger for the rural areas, so that the rural-industrial polarization we noted as existing *between* counties is equally evident *within* counties. For instance, the disparity in Carmarthen rose from 17.5 percent in 1901 (the percentage difference between 79 urban and 93 rural) to 33 percent in 1961 (the percentage difference between 61 and 81). In Glamorgan the disparity rose from 22 percent (51 and 62) to 25 percent (20 and 25). These increases in the difference between the intensity of Welsh in urban and rural areas are repeated in all other counties.

As a national pattern, the majority of speakers of Welsh live in the industrial counties. This is not the case within each county. For instance, 72 percent of the total of Welsh-speakers in Anglesey lived in the rural areas in 1901 and 64 percent in 1961. The percentages for some other representative counties are these: Brecon 88 and 87; Cardigan 78 and 72; Carmarthen 70 and 62; Merioneth 54 and 59. In 1901 Monmouth was an exception, only 14 percent of its speakers of Welsh lived in the rural areas, largely because the dominantly rural areas are on the English border; it remained an exception in 1961 with a very low 8 percent in rural areas. However, the disparity between the distribution of Welsh in rural and urban areas has decreased between 1901 and 1961, so that a far greater number of speakers of Welsh in each county now live in the urban areas than did before. In Anglesey the percentage in urban areas in 1901 was 28, and in 1961 it was 36. In other counties the significant increases have ranged from 6 percent in Cardigan to 14 percent in Denbigh, the mean increase being 7.5 percent.

Glamorgan, like Monmouth, was an exception to the general pattern between 1901 and 1961 in having a higher proportion of Welsh in urban areas—66 percent and 65 percent. In Glamorgan as a whole little change occurred between 1901 and 1961 in the disparity between urban and rural areas either in the intensity of Welsh speech or in the proportion of the total number of the two types of area. But this was because Glamorgan, like Monmouth, was already very heavily industrialized in 1901. This overall picture of the stability of Glamorgan is deceptive, however, and an analysis of the key urban areas and three representative rural areas re-veals that the intensity of Welsh in urban and rural areas alike has decreased considerably in 70 years. The increasingly intense industrialization of Glamorgan has virtually cancelled, so far as the incidence of Welsh is concerned, the Welsh differences between urban and rural areas that we have noticed elsewhere. Since Glamorgan is the key to the maintenance and survival of Welsh, it seems inevitable that the majority of Welsh speakers will remain city residents (see Table 3.11).

So far as the intensity of Welsh speech is concerned, Cardiff urban area had more in common with its surrounding rural area than with the other urban areas, such as Merthyr, Swansea, and Rhondda in 1901 and in 1971. The urban areas of Merthyr, Swansea, and Rhondda have more in common with the surrounding rural area of Mid-Glamorgan centering on Bridgend than they have with other urban areas. The rural area of Bridgend has closer affinities linguistically with local urban areas than with other rural areas. In fact, the determining factor in these important cases within Glamorgan is not the urban or rural distribution of the populations, so much as the geographical location and its historical tradition within the process of colonization. The urban and rural areas in Glamorgan that are Welsh-speaking are so because they are situated outside the *historically* anglicized vale—either in the western or the northern valleys. The English-colonized areas remained rural while industry developed in the Welshry. The rural district of Gower, for instance, comprises a thinly populated, almost exclusively English-speaking area to the south and within the same administrative district a densely populated industrial coal and steelmaking district to the north. But the language divide in Gower has hardly anything at all to do with industrialization or urbanization. It is still situated almost exactly along the line limiting the Norman occupation of the peninsula in the thirteenth century (Williams, T., 1934, 1935). The growth of industry in the Welsh-speaking part of Gower between 1891 and 1921 is reflected in the increased intensity in the Welsh-speaking population of Gower, but this is strictly within limits laid down by prior events. The decline of Welsh in Gower after 1931 is consequent on the closing of the mines and steel-making plant and outward migration. Neither industrialization nor out-migration has moved the historical-geographical division between the two languages.

Outside Glamorgan the urban-rural factor is undeniably significant in consideration of the maintenance of Welsh, but it is difficult to estimate the degree of that significance. This is partly because the method by which the urban-rural factor is calculated in the census returns is no longer a reflection of the true character of an area. It is also partly due to the fact that on the one hand industrialization has not progressed far enough in most of the rural counties to permit of a substantive as distinct from administrative demarcation between urban and rural areas. On the other hand, in South Wales and Glamorgan especially industrialization has proceeded so far as to eliminate that distinction for any real purposes.

TABLE 3.11. Welsh-Speaking Population of Selected Areas of Glamorgan, 1891–1971 (in thousands)

	Cardiff (Urban)		Merthyr (Urban)		Swansea (Urban)		Rhondda (Urban)		Gower (Rural)		Cardiff (Rural)		Bridgend (Rural)	
	Nos.	%	Nos.	%	Nos.	%	Nos.	%	Nos.	%	Nos.	%	Nos.	%
1891	22	15	68	63	50	46	85	72	2.0	26	6.0	27	9.0	52
1901	12	8	36	55	28	54	66	64	2.0	35	5.0	23	8.0	54
1911	11	6	34	50	28	27	76	54	3.0	38	5.0	26	9.0	45
1921	9	5	30	40	42	22	68	47	3.0	39	4.0	12	9.0	39
1931	11	5	27	39	43	27	62	46	3.0	33	10.0	9	10.0	39
1951	10	5	15	36	31	20	31	30	3.0	27	6.0	8	7.0	21
1961	11	5	11	18	28	17	23	24	1.7	14	3.2	7	6.0	15
1971	13	2	6	12	21	15	11	13	2.3	17	2.1	6	4.5	9

Source: Census of England and Wales: Language Supplements, 1891 and 1971.

CONCLUSION

At the present time proposals exist at Whitehall to relax the "internal colonialism" that has continued to embrace Scotland and Wales even after the decolonization of what is now the Republic of Ireland. During the many centuries of Celtic colonization, the major agencies of territorial consolidation and unification have played their part in Wales as they have done in the United States and still continue to do in the Soviet Union. Strong dynasties have helped to create and maintain the dominance of the center (London) over the periphery (Wales). In two of the most critical periods, the dynasties were of Celtic origin—the Tudors and Stuarts. Military agencies created the holding fortresses along the marches; administration was centralized and made little concession to local differences; cities rose which helped to create satellite centers reflecting the established authority; transportation network with roads, rails, and canals opened the periphery to the influences of the center and directed the economy away from the periphery to that center; ethnic stratification built up into a class system whereby the capital and managerial skills were handled by the immigrants while the Welsh provided the manual labor and craft skills; religious institutions were imposed which attempted to alienate the Welsh from their traditional way of life and their forms of belief; finally an embargo was placed upon any prestigious employment of the Welsh language. These are the factors that account for the background of the decline of the Welsh language, but the main cause for the present linguistic situation is industrialization promoted by the massive and intense flow of English immigrants.

In the light of their present depressed condition, an attempt to measure the relative importance of these various agencies of domination might appear the merest sophistry. But within the limited area associated with modernization—industrialization, urbanization, and immigration—it is important to do so because these are the processes which are also contributing to changes in the linguistic situations of the USSR, the United States, Canada, and the so-called developing countries. This relationship is often misunderstood. A recent study of considerable value (Hechter, 1975) assessed the independent effects of industrialization and immigration in Wales and concluded "that the industrial context from 1921 onwards begins to explain increasingly more of the decline in Welsh speaking with time. On the other hand the effect of English migration tends to be muted over time. By 1951 industrialization explains relatively more of the decline in Welsh speaking than does English migration." The conclusions are not altogether invalid, but the reasons proposed—namely "that after 1911 large scale English migration to Welsh industrial areas ceases" and in "1951 and 1961 to the extent that English migrants settle in Wales it is more likely to be in the hinterland counties"—(ibid., 204) do not really touch upon the complexities of the problem.

Immigration occurred in two main phases—the first drew upon a local, mainly Welsh-speaking labor force. This reinforced the Welshness of the area in which they settled. In spite of its massive scale, the English immigrant flow tended first of all to be compartmentalized, the Welsh language survived albeit in more limited domains of usage and its speakers spoke a less "authentic" variant of the language. The actual process of massive immigration was short-lived, but its impact was permanent and pervasive. New immigrants were not required to continue the process of anglicization: Welsh-born second and third generations remain in Wales and these are the products very often of intermarriage. While the effect of actual English immigration from 1921 onward is muted, so far as the fate of the Welsh language is concerned the effects of immigration have been decisive and irreversible.

Four

The Evolution of Ethnic and Linguistic Diversity in the United States

INTRODUCTION

Ethnicity and linguistic affiliation have not been traditionally associated in the United States. The size of a minority in the United States does not always coincide with the numbers who actually claim to speak its language. In the Soviet Union, though, ethnic affiliation is identical in principle with linguistic affiliation—those who claim to be members of a particular nationality are assumed to speak the language. This does not always turn out to be the case in fact, so additional data are elicited concerning the numbers who use a different language as their mother tongue or who are bilingual in Russian or another national language. The British regard language as the only criterion of difference, and there is no other way (apart from geographical location) in which the Welsh can be distinguished from any other group.

Three different relationships between ethnicity and language are evident: the British practice is to ignore ethnicity and differentiate on the basis of language; the Soviet principle is to assume that ethnicity determines language affiliation; the United States until very recently differentiated only on the basis of ethnic origin, without much regard for any persisting linguistic component of ethnicity. Since other factors in addition to size of poulations affect the level of language maintenance, and

therefore of bilingualism, the elucidation of the relationship between
ethnic origin and language in the United States is postponed until those
factors have been discussed.

NORTH AMERICAN COLONIZATION

The United States

Though penetration of one ethnic group by another is seldom achieved
without some discord, it is an inevitable process exemplified at various stages in the historical development of nations. It does not need to be
traumatic, as is the case with colonization. The importance of distinguishing
between relatively peaceful and colonial penetration becomes apparent
when the different attitudes to language among those affected are considered. Conquest of a native language group tends to create permanent
resentment and, however long delayed its expression, there remains a
reluctance to accept the imposed language. It has been reflected in the
attitude of Indians to the Spanish language as well as to English, in
strained attitudes to English among the Mexican-Americans, as well as
among the French-speaking population of New England, to say nothing of
Canada. Colonization and consequent culture and language contact have
affected similar and sometimes identical communities differently, according to the different processes of colonization. In the Spanish-speaking
Southwest, Amerindian pueblos have demonstrated a wide variety of
strategies of accommodation. For instance, although they had begun to
separate well before the coming of the Spanish in the sixteenth century, it
was not until postcontact times that the Tiwa speaking communities,
largely because of differences in the contexts in which contact with the
Spanish was established, began to diverge. Three Tiwa groups (Taos,
Isleta, and Ysleta del Sur) stood in markedly different positions in relation
to the Spanish, the Athapascans, and the English. Taos stood at the
gateway to the Plains but was remote from and relatively free from the
harsher colonizing pressures of the Spanish; Ysleta del Sur was a forgotten
village and hardly touched. But Isleta guarded the entrance to the middle
Rio Grande and was a focal point of Spanish pressure from the beginning
(Leap, 1973).

Different experiences of contact created differences of attitude to the
intruding languages. In this context it is worth recalling what Dozier
observed about the different textures of bilingualism produced by differences in the manner in which Spanish contact was established among the
Yaqui and the Tewa. In the case of the former, the early Spanish colonials
used little coercion and in consequence "these Indians represent a group
where Spanish and Indian cultural traits are so intricately interwoven that
it is virtually impossible to isolate the indigenous from introduced traits.

On the other hand the behavior of the Spanish to the Tewa of New Mexico was far more coercive and repressive; it was under compulsion that they took over a great deal of Spanish culture" (Dozier, 1956: 146). As a result, though they did not entirely reject Spanish elements, they distinguished the novel features from their own very clearly. They have compartmentalized their culture and their behavior into two coexisting systems. This compartmentalization was evident also in their employment of the two languages.

Conquest and linguistic imposition within North America was not an invention of the Spanish. There are many instances of one Indian tribe being subordinated to and eventually merging with another, and some instances where such conflict results in widespread bilingualism because of the forcible injection of new ethnic elements into hitherto homogeneous groups. The Hano, seeking relief from the oppression of the Spanish in the Rio Grande, took refuge with the Hopi, and though the Hopi claim not to be able to speak Hano, they do understand it. All Hanos speak Hopi and many Hopis and Hanos have learned Navajo (Dozier, 1954: 292). The two areas where enforced contact, conflict, and conquest produced the most varied types of tribal bilingualism are California and the Pacific Northwest coast. The Karok and the Yoroki are reported as having been forced to learn each other's language (Powers, 44), and the same observer claims that "among the tribes surrounding the Hupa many Indians speak three, four, or five languages, including English" (ibid, 73). However, though there are numerous examples of such tribal bilingualism born of conflict, they are of comparatively little quantitative significance especially in the context of contemporary education.

The first external colonizers of the North American continent—for the most part unlike the Russians in Europe and Asia—had to make contact, not with large nations like the Kazakhs or Georgians, but with small indigenous tribes, who though they spoke several languages and had great cultural differences had close ethnic affinities. The earliest of these, the Paleo-Amerinds, having crossed the Bering Strait into Alaska were forced southwards by the Neo-Amerinds, later arrivals who came to dominate the continent. The Eskimos who formed a third division of these peoples remained on the far north and northeast coasts. The first newcomers to make contact with them were the Spanish who entered Florida in 1513 and in little more than a century following the arrival of Coronado had explored, developed, organized, and set up administrations in more than a third of North America. In the meantime, Britain had initiated its colonizing venture in 1583 with the discovery of New Foundland. The French in 1605 (Canada), the Dutch in 1623 (New York), and especially the Germans in 1683 (Philadelphia) contributed significantly to the initial phase of colonization which laid the basis for linguistic heterogeneity. The history of the colonizing ventures has also set the topographic pattern or the geographical mozaic of such heterogeneity, in spite of subsequent population mobility. The first French settlement was in Canada (1605), but twenty years later (1625) French Huguenots settled in Manhattan. They also colonized in Virginia, the Carolinas (1679) and Georgia, where they were most numerous in colonial times. In 1679 French Huguenots helped to settle Massachusetts and by 1700 there were 4,000 in Maine. By 1740, the French influence extended from Louisberg to Winnipeg, and French Catholics (Acadians) who were deported from Nova Scotia found their way to Louisiana in 1755. With the fall of Quebec to the British in 1759, the French influence spread even more to the United States because of the southward migration of the Québecois. The location of the contemporary French presence reflects these phases.

At the time of the French settlement, the Dutch had been in New York for two years (1623) and by 1774 had established themselves firmly there. The Dutch Reformed Church in New York and New Jersey had sixty-five congregations, some of which continued to have services in the Dutch language until 1890. The linguistic influence exerted by the Dutch through the publication of books in that language and through establishment of native language schools was considerable, but their quantitative contribution to the colonial population was inferior to the Spanish, French, and English. The total population of New Netherlands at the time of the English annexation of that colony was only 8,000. This was also less than the contribution of the Germans who were the last of the major colonists of North America, whose arrival in the "Concorde" ("the Mayflower of German immigration") in Philadelphia (1683) added a new dimension of linguistic heterogeneity. Germantown was established and became the center for distributing new German arrivals into surrounding counties of Pennsylvania. By 1727, the German population of that state alone had probably reached 20,000; less than 20 years later (1745), 25,000 more had settled there. Benjamin Franklin was confident that one-third of the population of the state were Germans. Nor did they restrict themselves to the area but moved along the Shenandoah valley into Virginia and North Carolina. By 1750, Germans were present on the colonial frontier from the head of the Mohawk River in New York to Savannah, Georgia. This German population produced its own newspapers, published its own literature, and imported German books from Europe. "Pennsylvanian Dutch" has been claimed as the oldest non-English colonial dialect still in use in the United States.

The importance of these major colonial ventures should not tempt us to disregard less spectacular colonial contributions to the linguistic diversity of the United States. For instance the Swedes settled in Delaware, Pennsylvania, Michigan, and New Jersey. Sephardic Jews, though they did not number more than 3,000 in 1776, had a colonial presence in New York in 1664. The Irish settlements of the colonial period began to appear in the second decade of the eighteenth century. In 1718 Maine had a small colony though most of the Irish at that time were attracted to Pennsylvania. Earlier than the Irish, the Welsh formed an enclave in Pennsylvania in 1683, but the linguistic influence of the Irish and the Welsh in colonial times was negligible. Very few of them did not speak or at least understand English as well as their native language before they sailed, and so far as the Welsh are concerned (the Scots too) their Protestantism reinforced their linguistic assimilation.

Though the population was dominantly British and English-speaking at the end of the colonial era (1790), it was enriched by these other and very important ethnic and linguistic groups. The colonial contribution to the present diversity of the United States has been a competitive venture involving four very powerful and many less powerful nations. This has to be compared with the colonization of the Russian Empire which was the work of one nation alone. For that reason, while the present tendency in the Soviet Union is toward rigid uniformation, in the United States the underlying diversity of the colonial contribution is still a very significant influence. (See Table 4.1).

Canada

Except for the absence of any significant Spanish presence and the countervailing, relatively far larger representation of the French, the development of the linguistic pattern of Canada followed the same lines as the United States during colonial times. The Dutch (in 1609) were the first to establish themselves but in 1664 relinquished their claims to the British, who were there on trading ventures. The first real colonizers were the French. In 1605 they founded their first permanent settlement

TABLE 4.1. Composition of the Population of the United States, 1790

Country of Origin	Percent of White Population
Total	100.0
Great Britain and Northern Ireland	77.0
Germany	7.4
Irish Free State	4.4
Netherlands	3.3
France	1.9
Canada	1.6
Belgium	1.5
Switzerland	0.9
Mexico	0.7
Sweden	0.5
Spain	0.8

Source: W. S. Thompson and P. K. Whelpton *Population Trends in the United States,* p. 91, from 7h Congress, 2d Session, Senate Document 259.

in the Annapolis valley and in 1608 they established a fortified post at Quebec and thereafter the French consolidated their hold on the Canadian heartland by working west and north of the Great Lakes establishing permanent settlements as they went. The British followed, and after four or five years they established a base in New Foundland in 1610. Several more British colonizing ventures followed and these were consolidated in 1637. In 1715 the French, by the terms of the Treaty of Utrecht, recognized the exclusive sovereignty of Britain in Canada; in 1714 the Hudson Bay Company claimed virtually the whole of the territory to the north of the 49th parallel for Britain. Other linguistic groups arrived only after the British had established their sovereignty. The first Germans, for instance, did not arrive until toward the end of the seventeenth century. These and other contributions to the Canadian mosaic are more appropriately dealt with when we come to consider immigration.

North America was an extension of European culture and peoples in the colonial period. In terms of human geography, "western Europe and northern America are to a large extent mirror images of each other: there is no break but a progression. The geography of America is that of Europe in new terms" (Watson, 114–5).

LINGUISTIC CONFLICT IN NORTH AMERICA

Amerindian Bilingualism

The most pervasive of all conflict bilingualism arising from colonization in the United States has been from the interaction of Indian languages, Spanish, and English. The sequence of Spanish and English conquest of the Southwest, for example, produced complex bilingual and multilingual situations in several communities. One instance is the Sandia Pueblo on the outskirts of Albuquerque where the inhabitants speak Sandia (a Tiwa dialect), Spanish, and English. Men and women over 60 years are almost completely bilingual in Sandia and Spanish but tend to be ignorant of English. Those between ages 40 and 60 are reasonably fluent in all three languages, and those between 20 and 40 speak English as their primary language while some of them speak Sandia though somewhat hesitantly. For these younger Sandias, the influence of Spanish is seen only in the use of Spanish words that have been incorporated into the Sandia basic stock. The youngest group, those up to 20 years, do not speak Sandia, though they may well be able to understand it. What Spanish they know has been acquired as a foreign language in high school. English is their primary language and the only language of normal conversation in the Pueblo (Brandt, 46–50). This multilingual situation is common in other such communities with conflicting languages, and it has a historical basis. The addition of the Spanish language to such Pueblo dialects must be considered an important acquisition. Not all Pueblo adults spoke Spanish, but the records reveal that during the revolt of 1680 and after the reconquest of 1692–93 communication between Pueblo Indians and Spaniards presented no difficulties. It is very probable that even at this early date the Spanish language had become a lingua franca among the Pueblos. "By adopting Spanish as the language for communicating with the outside world the individual Pueblo linguistic communities retained their own indigenous languages as tools for retaining and perpetuating the cherished and closely guarded customs and beliefs" (Dozier, 1970: 69). They have continued the same attitude toward English.

Generally speaking, when Indian and European languages came together rarely did a significant number of Europeans learn the Indian language, and for this reason the level of Spanish or English bilingualism among the Pueblos was often high. They compartmentalized the native and the intrusive languages and so were better able to adapt to the immense social changes they experienced, as occurred in the nineteenth century when white settlers came into their basin in large numbers. "The Indian nomadic pattern was broken, with permanent settlements being formed on a number of small reservations. . . . Since there are permanent settlements there are now bounded speech communities" (Miller, 1975: 5). Similar developments occurred on the Plains where, as the result of pressure from white settlers, the classic Plains culture was developed (Sherzer, 774). Generally speaking, the stable tribal organization with well defined territorial limits evolved during this period (Driver, 340). Having learned to endure one conflict of languages, most Indians were slow to shift from Spanish to English dominance and English oriented bilingualism took a long time. It was not until the 1940s that the English in the Southwest exceeded the number of speakers of Spanish and established themselves as the dominant group. By 1950, the number of New Mexican residents with Spanish surnames (including the Rio Grande Pueblos) comprised only 37 percent of the total population and by 1960 the figure had dropped to 25 percent.

Although Alaskan natives learned Russian until the mid-nineteenth century, especially in Quebec Province where a large proportion lived, the influence of English colonizers has prevailed most strongly in the north. In 1740 the total population of Alaska (74,000) was completely native, but by 1970 83 percent of the total population of 302,000 were English-speaking. The relative distribution of native and nonnative populations in the area varies considerably and this affects the pattern of language dominance. For instance, in the southwest region the native population is almost double that of the nonnative—17,364 to 9,315. In the northwest part the dominance of the native population is even greater, 51,150 to 10,656. In the southeast the nonnative population is over four times the size of the native, but in the interior region the proportion is five to one in favor of the natives. However, of the total of 302,000 inhabiting Alaska, nearly 55 percent occupy the south central region and there the native population is outnumbered by 15 to 1—154,069 to 9,723 (Darnell, 1972b: 154, 157). It is not simply that the future of Alaskan languages such as Inuit is precarious: in the large communities of Nome, Kotzebue, and Barrow where the English-speaking populations have very considerable economic and cultural power, languages like Eyak, it has been alleged, are "victims of genocide and white greed" (Krauss, 1973a: 933). In any case, the prospects for a long-term bilingual community are precarious.

Conflict Bilingualism

As did the Indian languages, Spanish suffered considerably as a result of conflict with English. Until 1846, following the foundation of the first permanent settlement in New Mexico, Spanish had been a successful colonial language in the American Southwest. After 1846 and more especially after the Treaty of Guadalupe Hidalgo in 1848, Spanish ceased to be a sovereign, colonial language in the United States and the English language became pre-eminent. The original colonizers were themselves colonized, and Spanish became the subordinate language. The history of the Spanish-speaking population of Puerto Rico is also that of a sequence of colonizing activities, phases of conquest suffered by the indigenous Indians and then subsequently by their conquerors and colonizers.

Conquests, whether of the indigenous Indians or of the first colonizers, have consequences for bilingualism which differ from those resulting from more peaceful and later penetration of the United States by immigrant languages. A residue of natural resentment motivates (partly though not entirely) the pressure for the recogniiton of the subordinated languages in the present educational system. To recognize that "the politics of envy" are as powerful and as natural in language planning as they are elsewhere in society does not invalidate the legitimate claims that are made for bilingual education on other and more rational grounds.

The difference between other colonizers like the Germans and Dutch and the French is illuminating in this respect. In 1970, the fourth largest language minority in the United States were the French-speaking bilinguals. They were the fifth largest in 1960 (See Table 4.6). The greatest numerical concentration is in the old French colonial enclave of the northeast region in New England—962,000 constituting 2.1 percent of the population of that region. Within the region the largest number of French bilinguals is in Maine 123,000, 12.9 percent, Connecticut (116,000, 12 percent) and New Hampshire (96,000, 13.7 percent). The next largest number of French bilinguals is in the southern region (799,000), and the greatest proportion of French to the total population of the state is in Louisiana (569,000, 15.8 percent). During the post-colonial period up to 1961, these areas continued to draw new foreign-born French immigrants:

the northeast has attracted the highest number, 242,000, constituting 5.9 percent; and the southern region including Louisiana has 476,000, 3.6 percent. Presumably, the strength of the French language in those areas prior to English conquest is still influential in attracting a disproportionate number of new French arrivals, and in motivating the maintenance of the language.

German is the second largest non-English colonial language in the United States (see Table 4.6) but, while very strong ties to the language remain, this attachment does not express itself in antagonism toward English. The situation of the French is very different. In France as well as in North America, the consciousness of the former sovereign status of the French language in parts of North America compared with its current subordinate status, undoubtedly motivates the strong efforts that are made in North America and in France to maintain the language of North America. In those areas where the language possessed high status prior to conquest by the English, the language remains most prevalent. The French of New England were forced by economic circumstances resulting from English expansionism in Canada to move from Quebec, but they continued to regard themselves as sojourners waiting to return north. In 1758, the 3,000 French-speaking Americans refused to acknowledge the English language in Acadia and sought refuge in Louisiana, and by 1770 1,000 more had followed them. They strove by means of a network of educational, cultural, and religious institutions to maintain French as a sovereign language in that community. In Louisiana, which the French established in 1799, the status of French was institutionalized, and this lapsed only at the beginning of this century. Until 1866 both French and English were taught in the schools, French being the primary language. Even after 1866, when English was declared the sole language of instruction, French continued to be an official language until 1914. Both the Acadian French of New England and the French of Louisiana represent the consequences of English colonization and subsequent linguistic subordination. The tenacity of their hold on the French language and their attitude to English may be partial manifestations of the consciousness of colonial conflict.

IMMIGRATION
Voluntary

Until the early nineteenth century, immigration was not a critical problem for the United States. From the beginning of the European revolutionary wars (1776) to the Peace of Vienna (1815), movement from the Old World was not numerically significant. During a period given over to consolidating political as well as social institutions, when traditional attitudes needed to be clarified or re-oriented, the assimilation of ethnically and linguistically diverse populations presented very little difficulty. (See Table 4.2).

TABLE 4.2. Immigrants by Country of Origin, 1820–1974 (in thousands)

Country	1810–1974 Nos.	%	1820–1860 Nos.	%	1861–1900 Nos.	%	1901–1950 Nos.	%	1951–1960 Nos.	%	1961–1970 Nos.	%	1971–1974 Nos.	%
All Countries	46,710	100.0	5,916	100.0	14,054	100.0	20,560	100.0	2,515.0	100.0	3,321.0	100.0	1,981.0	100.0
Europe	35,888	76.0	4,679	79.0	12,707	89.0	15,980	78.0	1,375.0	53.0	1,123.0	34.0	452.0	23.0
Northwest Europe	12,925	27.0	3,164	54.0	6,071	42.0	3,676	18.0	381.0	15.0	343.0	10.0	87.0	4.4
Britain	9,500	10.0	764	13.0	2,251	15.0	1,359	6.5	252.0	10.0	247.0	7.0	63.0	3.1
Denmark	362	0.8							11.0	0.4	9.0	0.3	2.5	0.1
Norway	854	1.8	41	0.8	1,368	9.0	989	4.2	23.0	1.0	15.0	0.5	2.1	0.1
Sweden	1,269	2.7							21.0	0.9	17.0	0.5	3.2	0.2
Belgium	200	0.4							18.5	0.8	9.2	0.3	2.6	0.1
France	740	1.6							51.0	2.0	4.5	1.4	13.5	0.6
Central Europe	11,998	26.0	1,523	23.0	4,244	30.0	4,990	24.0	601.0	24.0	292.0	9.0	95.0	4.9
Germany	6,948	15.0	1,428	22.0	3,495	25.0	1,129	6.0	478.0	18.0	191.0	5.7	42.0	2.2
Poland	499	1.1	2		163	1.0	260[a]	1.2	10.0	0.4	53.0	1.6	15.0	0.8
Czecho-slovakia	137	0.3							1.0	—	3.0	0.1	3.9	0.1
Austria									67.0	2.7	20.0	0.6	11.0	0.2
Hungary	4,311	9.2							37.0	1.4	5.0	0.2	3.5	0.1
Yugoslavia	103	0.2							8.0	0.3	20.0	0.6	20.0	1.0

TABLE 4.2. (continued)

Country	1810–1974		1820–1860		1861–1900		1901–1950		1951–1960		1961–1970		1971–1974	
	Nos.	%	Nos.	%	Nos.	%	Nos.	%	Nos.	%	Nos.	%	Nos.	%
Eastern Europe	3,415	7.5	2	—	829	7.0	3,977	19.0	1.0	4.0	6	0.2	5.0	0.2
USSR and Baltic	3,349	7.2	1		670	6.0	2,711	12.5	0.5	—	2	0.1	3.0	0.1
Finland	32	0.1							5.0	0.2	4	0.1	1.5	—
Southern Europe	6,705	14.5	32	—	1,133	8.0	4,635	23.0	260.0	10.0	421	13.0	249.0	13.0
Italy	5,259	11.3	13	—	927	7.0	3,824	18.0	185.0	7.4	214	6.4	111.0	5.8
Greece	619	1.3							47.0	1.8	86	2.6	62.0	3.2
Spain	243	0.5							8.0	0.3	45	1.3	23.0	1.2
Portugal	399	0.9							20.0	0.8	76	2.3	53.0	2.8
Asia	2,143	4.5	43	0.8	328	2.0	609	3.0	153.0	6.0	428	12.9	552.0	27.0
China	480	0.1	50	4.0	250	0.3	93	0.4	10.0	0.4	35	1.0	41.0	2.0
Japan	396				10		250	1.2	46.0	1.6	40	12.0	26.0	1.3
Americas	8,172	17.5	176	3.0	1,039	8.0	3,498	17.0	1,000.0	40.0	1,762	52.0	696.0	34.0
Canada	4,037	8.6							377.0	13.0	413	12.0	86.0	4.0
Cuba	369	0.8							78.0	3.0	208	6.3	95.0	4.7
Mexico	1,849	4.0	17	—	10	—	803	4.0	299.0	11.0	453	13.7	301.0	15.0

a From 1899 to 1919, Poland is not recorded separately.

Sources: Taeuber and Taeuber, *Peoples of the United States in the Twentieth Century*, 1971. U.S. Department of Justice: Immigration and Naturalization Services. *Annual Reports*.

Regarded in purely quantitative terms, immigration has obviously been the most influential factor in promoting widespread bilingualism in the United States. The 1970 Census recorded well over 60 minority groups with populations of over 5,000 in each case. Even in 1850, over 15 percent of the total population of 23 million were of foreign stock (foreign born together with those of foreign or mixed parentage). Although the proportion has declined because of the increase in proportion of the native born together with fluctuations in the numbers of immigrants, the size of the foreign stock has increased to 31 million. After 1850 immigration to the United States accelerated and also became more diverse ethnically and linguistically. The decennial totals (all countries) rose from 143,000 to nearly 6 million reaching a peak of nearly 9 million between 1900 and 1910. The total (all countries) during the forty years from 1860 to 1900 was double that of the forty years from 1820 to 1860, and in the period 1900 to 1950 it increased by 50 percent. The tempo of immigration is an aspect of the intensity of language conflict in the United States, and this contrasts with the long history of stable contact in areas of the Soviet Union like the North Caucasus, or Wales, or which historically has characterized European bilingualism generally. It is this change in intensity of contact that leads to conflict.

Of the total of immigrants between 1820 and 1860, Europeans accounted for over 79 percent, ıd for 89 percent between 1861 and 1890. The proportion of the total number of immigrants from Europe during the 154 years from 1820 to 1974 is 76 percent, though the decennial proportions have declined from 89 percent (1861–1900) to 23 percent (1970–74). However, the contribution of the various regions of Europe differed considerably. From 1821 to 1860 the proportion of the grand total accounted for by northern and western European nations averaged 54 percent while central Europe during the same period accounted for 23 percent, eastern Europe less than 2 percent, and southern European nations even less. A second phase of immigration began around 1860 and continued until around 1920 and passage of the Immigration Act. This phase was characterized by a marked shift in the relative size of the contributions from northwest and central Europe, in favor of eastern and southern areas. Eastern and southern European nations took up an increasing share of the flood of immigrants. Changes in the dimensions of immigration from these regions went hand-in-hand with a shift in the character of the immigrant communities. The first phase was dominated by immigration from industrialized and highly literate countries. The second was dominated by immigrants from underdeveloped and poor agricultural communities with very low literacy ratios. Of the European countries most deeply involved, Great Britain and Ireland have been foremost, accounting for nearly 10 million. The total from these two countries rose from 764,000 (1820–60) to over 2 million in the next forty years (1860–1900), during which period the Irish immigrants outnumbered those from the rest of Britain. The British and Irish contribution has declined steadily from 1901 to 1950 (15 percent of the total) to 1970–74 (3.1 percent of the total). The non-Irish Celtic contribution (Scots and Welsh) was very much smaller than the Irish; the Scots tended to be identified with the Irish largely because of the Scots presence in Northern Ireland. The Welsh were attracted mainly to Pennsylvania and New York where place names such as Bryn Mawr and Merion still bear witness to their settlements. Their main New York focus was Oneida County, but, like all other Welsh immigrants, they were quickly and easily assimilated since they were bilingual in English and their native Welsh before their departure.

Mexican immigration was fairly light until 1900, but during the next twenty years nearly 600,000 Mexican immigrants entered. The proportion Mexican immigrants represent has been steadily increasing, from 4 percent in 1901–50 to 11 percent in the next decade, then 13.7 percent in 1960–70 and at present 15 percent.

The total Asian contribution to date has amounted to less than 5 percent of the total of all countries: it began to accelerate from 1870 onwards and especially during this century. The figure rose from 42,000 (1820–60) to 328,000 between 1861 and 1900 and 609,000 between 1901 and 1950. After a decline in the period 1951–60, it has begun to grow even faster than before. Even more impressive than the rise in total numbers is the increasing share they represent, rising from 0.8 percent in 1820–60 to 27 percent in 1970–74. It is no exaggeration to say that the period 1961–74 represents a shift from European to Asian immigration comparable in kind, if not as yet in dimensions, to the shift from northwestern European to southern and eastern European immigration during the last forty years of the nineteenth century. The trend continues to accelerate in the post-Viet Nam War era with Southeast Asian refugees—many of them "boat people"—fleeing their homelands.

"Induced Migration"—Refugees and Displaced Persons

Refugees and displaced persons are a very special category of immigrants, and their peculiar status undoubtedly influences their attitude to the dominant culture and language of the United States as well as to those of their native country. Unlike the voluntary immigrant, they are not motivated mainly by economic considerations nor impelled by any sense of adventure—though both considerations may be present. The cause of their migration is political, and very often they retain a tenacious hold on the possibility of return to their countries of origin. Among those who best exemplify this attachment to their homeland are perhaps the Cubans, the Poles, and the Ukrainians. Most immigrants are attached in one way or another to their country of origin—in the case of the refugees and displaced persons that attachment is qualified for a time by a social and political conviction and by a natural resentment at having had to emigrate at all.

World War II caused many millions to be transferred from one country to another, and, in the process, many thousands were left homeless and often stateless. The Displaced Persons Act of 1948 authorized the entry of such persons into the United States. Subsequent enactments were made in 1953 (Refugee Relief Act), in 1958 (affecting mainly Hungarians) and in 1960 and 1965. Cubans were admitted under an Act of November 1966. Between 1948 and 1955, over 400,000 refugees were admitted, and since that time 580,173 additional refugees have gained admittance (see Table 4.3).

As is the case with voluntary immigrants, the majority of refugees

TABLE 4.3. Refugees by Country of Birth, 1954–74

Country of Birth	1954-74	1974
All countries	580,173	25,650
Europe	304,667	5,990
Austria	5,664	27
Bulgaria	3,143	126
Czechoslovakia	10,907	165
Estonia	690	—
France	1,358	17
Germany	22,039	9
Greece	19,067	28
Hungary	50,884	528
Italy	60,329	67
Latvia	1,704	—
Lithuania	1,857	1
Netherlands	17,423	1
Poland	18,112	580
Portugal	5,003	2
Romania	14,274	602
Spain	7,978	662
USSR	8,033	409
Yugoslavia	48,984	2,771
Asia and Near East	59,913	3,186
China	20,493	1,548
Indonesia	15,901	1
Israel	779	6
Japan	4,358	2
Korea	4,438	2
Palestine	897	9
North America	206,747	16,131
Cuba	205,364	16,087
Africa	8,372	392

Source: U.S. Department of Justice, *Immigration and Naturalization, Annual Report, 1974.*

originate from Europe. In 1974 the Asian total was slightly more than half the European total, and this reflects the same shift of emphasis that we noted in respect to the voluntary European immigration flow after 1860. The countries most affected by the turmoil of World War II in Europe—central, eastern, and southern Europe—contributed more refugees than the northwest. Refugees from North America are almost entirely Cubans. In most instances, populations belonging to the same ethnic and linguistic groups represent both voluntary and induced immigrants. These differences among national contingents suggest a possible stratification of some immigrant populations—for example between those who arrived before and those who arrived after 1950. In the Cuban communities such a stratification is known to exist between the refugees who have arrived recently and the "old" Cuban immigrants, many of whom came at the end of the nineteenth century. A similar stratification exists among Mexican-Americans—those who came during the colonial period versus the later immigrant. Few of these minorities are homogeneous populations: they were not homogeneous before their departure and differences in the circumstances of that departure may help to reinforce cleavages. This has considerable relevance to immigrant attitudes to languages and culture.

THE RESIDUAL CONGLOMERATE

Options for Immigrants

Before we move from a consideration of the process of immigration to its demographic consequences in the United States, five aspects of that process need to be emphasized briefly since they, more than anything else, have determined those consequences.

First, differences within a particular immigrant minority may be due to circumstances characterizing their places of origin (villages, districts, and regions) and the form of their settlement in the United States, all of which as we shall see have implications for language maintenance and education. Immigrants may originate from all over a country as did the Norwegian Quakers of Minnesota. In some cases, however, the particular area of Europe concerned may be a small township or village: almost all the Rumanians of Woonsocket (Rhode Island) came from the village of Frashari (Galitzi, 88). In other cases they may originate from a more extended area, a number of adjacent villages centering perhaps on one market town as did the Norwegians of the Fox River settlement of Illinois who came from around Stavanger (Blegen, 76). In yet other cases a whole province may have contributed to the group of immigrants, as happened with the Rumanians of Chicago who came from the Banat region at the beginning of this century (Galitzi, 88).

Irrespective of the area from which they originated, immigrants have tended to differ according to the type of settlement they prefer. Immigrants may disperse immediately on arrival, but this has not been the history of any large numbers of them. Instead they initiate or gravitate toward group settlements, of which we may distinguish three types. The first are those founded by organized groups of laborers recruited to work in a specified area, like the Welsh miners and steelworkers who settled in Pittsburgh and Cleveland, or political and religious refugees like the Welsh Quakers of New England, and the Mennonites of Pennsylvania, or the Dukobars of British Columbia. The second category consists of chain settlements that evolve from being no more than two or three families to a considerable group by attracting friends and kindred from their places of origin. The Puerto Ricans of New York and New Jersey are perhaps the best examples. The third category consists of settlements which have evolved on account of their gravitational attraction of new, independent immigrants, as well as those who initially settled elsewhere. Many of the concentrations in the larger American cities from the mid-nineteenth century onwards, like the Norwegians of Wicker Park, Chicago, have been formed by such a process of gravitation. The "old" Cubans tend now to gravitate from distant places to Miami.

Such gravitation settlements have exerted an important influence on language maintenance. It is well known that immigrants who traveled independently or as organized groups lost much of their close group allegiances in the desperate struggle to establish economic self-sufficiency in the United States. Such struggles persuaded many to gravitate toward larger concentrations of their respective nationalities. Blegen has argued that in gravitating towards their own kind they sought the people "who had come out of the very valley, the *bygd* from which they themselves hailed" (p. 75). Though there is disagreement concerning this particular aspect of gravitation (Price, 175), no one has challenged the general proposition concerning the importance of chain and gravitational immigration to the maintenance of ethnic loyalties including the language.

This involved immigrants from different regions and provinces—with even different customs and dialects—assimilating to each other. For instance, Polish settlements by means of schools and associations of various kinds created an awareness of the Polish heritage that subordinated differences born of district, regional, and provincial allegiances. They generated forces that increased and strengthened their own cohesiveness and consolidated their "territorial" position. They obtained, in this way, greater control of the local educational system and could influence the curriculum of the local schools. So great was their influence that an intense adverse reaction, from the "host" society, was produced. In Pennsylvania, where "immigrant control" tended to be most effective, after years of dispute and conflict the state in 1854 cut off all financial aid to the "ethnic church schools" and then crippled the German local schools by refusing to train teachers in any language but English. In 1911 they enforced the exclusive use of English as the teaching language. The type of group settlement favored by immigrants exerted considerable positive and negative influence on bilingual education.

The second and third aspects of immigration are quantitative: the massiveness of the process of immigration is unprecedented and unique. Between 1790 and 1974 the size of the total population exploded from just under 4 million to just over 211 million. Its diversity is equally formidable: well over 60 ethnic groups with a minimum memberhsip of over 5,000 each and some as large as 8 million (Table 4.6). The fourth, and perhaps the crucial factor, is that this diversity was achieved not by *phasing* the reception of *successive* nationalities but, on the contrary, by their *simultaneous* reception. Unlike colonial processes or conquests where one group is able to stamp its identity before its successor appears (as in Britain and the Soviet Union), immigration of the kind witnessed in the United States was concurrent. In Britain the population has successive layers—Celts, Romans, English, Normans, and so forth and each succeeded the other about every four centuries. Similarly in the central Asian areas of the Soviet Union, the populations have been influenced by successive conquests—the Russians being only the most recent. In the United States, though, only the Native American populations have been rolled over by successive conquests.

In such a predicament only three alternatives appear to have been available to the postcolonial immigrants: as peripheral ethnic groups arriving together in large numbers, they could organize themselves so as to adjust to an existing focus or center, namely the dominant Anglo culture and its language; or they could remain completely independent peripheries unrelated to each other or to the center; or they could strive to become competing centers and hope in time to become dominant, at least in a particular region of the United States. All these alternatives have appealed to different minorities from time to time. Germans were attracted to the last alternative, as were the French to some extent. They hoped to establish their own commonwealths in America. Populations with pretensions to varying degrees of exclusiveness, or refugees with high expectations of being able to return to their native countries, have been attracted by the second alternative. That course, however, is open only to a relatively small, geographically concentrated group, and only religious sects have successfully pursued it. Most immigrants have instinctively adopted the first alternative. They have been impelled to do so partly because of their geographical dispersion which makes it difficult to maintain an organized and influential, independent center. Additionally, the length of time an immigrant group takes to establish itself necessitates adjustment to the existing center for reasons of survival. Even more importantly, they emigrated as individuals or very small groups and during the period of adjustment there were few if any ways in which they could act corporately. Finally, whatever their motives for emigrating, they were undoubtedly imbued with a strong belief in the reality of the ideals and values enshrined as the "American dream" which made adjustment to the existing center not only desirable but almost a moral imperative. That being the case, if we look at the situation as it might have appeared to the immigrants themselves, and not in the light of what contemporary ideologies and theories of political or social organization suggest is desirable, the criticism leveled at the way in which diversity came to be organized around an existing core or vortex which drew everything to itself appears to be misdirected.

It is particularly misdirected if the fifth aspect of immigration is recognized, namely the intensity of the process (the combined effect of very large numbers and a relatively short time span). Nevertheless, though the processes of assimilation may have been necessary or inevitable from about 1850 to 1950, it does not rule out the possibility that at the present time a different policy recognizing the need to regard minorities with their cultures and languages as more or less autonomous peripheral centers is required. A pluralistic society may not have been possible or even desirable during the formation of the United States, but now it may be both possible and desirable.

That it is possible is due to several factors. It is true that although there are important regional and ethnic differences, the United States possesses a characteristic culture that is not the exclusive possession of any group or region, though some groups and regions may represent it more than others. This characteristic culture is partly the result of the contact of so many ethnic cultures, each contributing something to the whole. It is partly a superordinate culture, standing above all national cultures though here again some national cultures may be closer to it than others. It is nevertheless discontinuous with the traditional cultures of all ethnic groups —Anglos as well as others. It is a scientific, technological, industrial, and urban culture; one in which political attributes tend to replace religious qualities. It is the characteristic culture of a modern or modernizing society, and in that sense it is not only characteristic of the United States, but most clearly represented in that country.

This culture of the modern society is fundamentally Western European in origin, generated almost simultaneously with the intensification of immigration to the United States. Consequently, the characteristic United States culture and its high level of homogeneity (though not of uniformity) may be explained by the preponderance of immigrants of European origin. This was itself a unifying principle. However unconscious they may have been of the fact, the immigrants originated from a fairly homogeneous culture area, one which was itself the creation of a long history of linguistic convergence dating from Greco-Roman times. Whatever else it may have achieved, the European dominance ensured a fundamental unity and continuity of culture; the English language, whatever may be said of the contribution of English culture, enabled that homogeneous culture to express itself as an autonomous phenomenon, offering stability and the hope of permanence to its values. The United States now possesses a national identity that subsumes real ethnic differences. Because of the strength of this national identity, such ethnic differences can be tolerated, a pluralist society may be conceived, and so perhaps strengthen the existing national identity. The diverse elements have made themselves known and have developed an American voice when a multiplicity of voices without a coordinating principle would have been distracting to say the least. No doubt minorities should have been allowed from the beginning, if they wished to project variants of the American voice, but it is doubtful whether they would have wished to do so and equally doubtful whether the balance of advantage to them as ethnic groups or to the whole nation would have favored their attempting it.

Demographic Consequences—Reinforcement

The importance of immigration for language lies largely in the creation and endurance of non-English-speaking populations. These groups represent the residuum or precipitate of the accumulated foreign stock. The nature of this residuum is not due to the extent of immigration alone—geographic dispersal or concentration, urbanization, intermarriage, and differentiations of age and sex also play their part in determining the character as distinct from the dimensions of the residuum (these we shall discuss in the next sections). The size of the residuum, though, is related to reinforcement—the numbers replenishing the foreign stock. The proportion of the total current population which this residuum represents reflects also the self-generating capacity of the native population, to which naturally the foreign stock contributes in the third and subsequent generations (see Table 4.4).

The foreign-born appear through migration and disappear partly through death and partly through remigration. Their American-born children, though of foreign stock, are "native of foreign or mixed parentage." In turn their children, though born to the first generation descendants of the foreign-born, are merged in the general population, that is "native of native parentage." The total population of the United States consists therefore of a series of nativity categories or cohorts, but the relations between such cohorts are flexible and in constant flux: migrants add to the number of foreign born; their children add to the native population of foreign or mixed parentage; and in turn their children add to the native children of native parentage. Each cohort has its own attitude toward, and use for, its ethnic language, as well as its own level of competence to handle it. The relative proportions of the foreign stock to the native population and the rapidity with which the foreign-born and their chil-

TABLE 4.4. White Population of the United States According to Nativity, 1890–1970 (in thousands)

Year	Total Population of U.S.	Total White Population		Total of Native Parentage		Foreign White								
						Both Parents Foreign		Mixed Parentage		Foreign Born		Total Foreign Stock		
		Total	%	Total	%[a]	Total	%[a]	Total	%[a]	Total	%[a]	Total	%[a]	
1850	23,192	19,750	85.0	Not available		Not available		Not available		2,241	9.7	Not available		
1860	31,443	27,000	98.0	Not available		Not available		Not available		4,097	13.0	Not available		
1870	38,558	33,700	88.0	22,771	59.0	2,324	6.0	3,100	6.7	5,494	14.2	10,800	28.0	
1880	50,156	44,480	89.0	28,568	57.0	3,960	7.0	4,500	9.0	6,860	13.7	15,900	31.0	
1890	62,847	55,101	88.0	34,476	62.0	8,085	12.0	3,419	5.0	9,122	13.0	20,625	36.7	
1900	75,994	66,809	88.0	40,949	61.0	10,632	15.0	5,014	7.0	10,214	15.0	25,800	36.6	
1910	91,972	81,732	88.0	49,489	61.0	12,916	14.0	5,982	7.2	13,346	16.1	32,300	36.2	
1920	106,022	94,303	96.0	58,422	62.0	15,695	14.8	6,992	6.8	13,713	14.1	35,881	37.1	
1930	129,203	110,287	90.0	70,401	63.0	17,408	13.5	8,495	6.7	13,983	11.0	39,886	31.2	
1940	131,669	118,215	90.0	84,125	72.0	15,184	11.7	7,974	5.8	11,419	9.0	34,390	26.5	
1950	150,697	134,938	89.0	100,805	71.0	14,816	10.1	8,763	5.9	10,161	6.7	34,133	22.7	
1960	179,326	158,838	89.0	125,759	71.0	14,320	8.3	8,964	4.1	9,294	4.9	33,079	17.3	
1970	203,210	178,119	88.0	146,231	74.0	14,632	7.1	8,522	4.2	8,734	4.2	33,974	15.5	

[a] Percentage of the Total White Population

Sources: U.S. Census of Population, 1950: Special Reports —Nativity and Parentage. Statistical Abstract of the United States, 1975. Table 39.

148

dren are absorbed into the native population depends upon such secondary factors as differential birth rates of native cohorts and marriage and
fertility rates of the foreign-born. These in turn reflect national characteristics, cultures, and religions as well as social and economic characteristics. It is these secondary factors which determine, in the long term, the
linguistic profile of the total ethnic group.

The number of foreign born increased from 2 million in 1850 to 8
million in 1970, but during the 1930s the number reached a peak of nearly
14 million. In spite of the fact that as a proportion of the total white
population the foreign-born after rising to 16.1 percent in 1910 has declined to 4.2 percent in 1970, they still represent a very strong reinforcement of the native ethnic composition of the United States. The foreign-
born account for 30 percent of the foreign stock.

The foreign-born are only one segment of the foreign stock. In 1970
second generation immigrants accounted for 4.2 percent of the total population and 70 percent of the foreign stock. Consequently, the age distribution
of this foreign stock is relevant in estimating the salience of their linguistic
standing. In 1890, almost 40 percent of the foreign-born was aged 25 to
44. In 1920 and 1930, the age structure began to change in favor of the
older groups so that by 1960 33 percent of all foreign-born were 65 or
over. Similar changes have occurred in the cohort of "natives of foreign or
mixed parentage." For example, in 1910 the proportion under 15 years
was 38.3 percent, and in 1940 it was barely 19 percent; by 1960 it had
declined still farther to 10.9 percent. Those between 25 and 44 in the
cohort gradually increased their representation from 27.6 percent to 33.7
percent, while the age group 65 and over in the same nativity cohort
became an even larger segment increasing from 1.4 percent to 6.5 percent and then to 12.7 percent. "The first and second generation heritage
of the great migrations involves generally an aged foreign-born population
and a generally aging population of the native born of foreign or mixed
parentage" (Taeuber, 177). The grandchildren of the original participants
in the great migrations are also maturing and at the same time being
absorbed at an accelerating rate. So far as education is concerned the
problem of bilingualism (as an effect more particularly of the great migrations) will tend to resolve itself in the normal evolution of time. Demographically it will cease to be an issue save in respect of the foreign-born
children and adults, some of their children and a diminishing proportion
of the grandchildren. In so far as it remains a substantial problem it will
be mainly in respect of Native American populations and the Spanish
Americans. They are groups who are not only the probable but almost
certainly the long-term clients of a developing bilingual program in education. They can replenish their aging stock of native speakers from indigenous sources independently of foreign sources because they have
disproportionately high growth rates. Furthermore, they have firm and
historical territorial bases.

Self-Perception of Ethnicity among the Native Population

The minorities not dependent on immigration for reinforcement (artificial self-reproduction) are the long-term targets for any successful policy of bilingual education, but in addition a potential of massive support for ethnic languages exists in the ethnic consciousness of the other minorities in and beyond the third generation. Given the example of the pressure for bilingual programs exerted by Spanish Americans and the Native Americans, other ethnic groups could very well become vocal in their demands.

Since 1969 the Current Population Survey of the United States has attempted to supplement objective immigration data with data from more subjective sources, in particular the self-perception of ethnic origin (see Table 4.5). This innovation had been anticipated to some extent by changes in the Soviet census. In 1926 the Soviet census required information concerning actual national origin as does the present U.S. census. In 1939 the USSR substituted a subjective criterion, namely ethnic preference or choice of affiliation. The principle of identifying ethnicity with linguistic affiliation was not modifed; instead, ethnicity became a matter of individual judgment. The United States innovation of 1969 is somewhat intermediate between a statement of origin and a statement of chosen affiliation. Ethnic origin in 1969 was determined on the basis of a question asking for *self-identification,* what a person *perceives* as his origin. Obviously the farther removed the interviewee is from the "first generation immigrant cohort," the greater the possibility of that perception being idiosyncratic. In any case, that so many who could not otherwise be identified (being native of native parentage) had indicated minority affiliation, is an indication of the strength of the support for particular ethnic groups in third and subsequent generations.

The 1970 census classification of first and second generation immigrants (Table 4.6) recognized 2,598,000 as French, but over 5 million recognized themselves as being of French origin (Table 4.5). Over four times as many Germans recognized their German origins as were enumerated in the census as Germans; for other ethnic groups there were twice as many Poles, six times as many Russians, and over twice as many Italians. The pool of ethnic support, though, is becoming shallower, especially in respect of the European participants in the "great migrations" and their descendants. Between 1971 and 1973 the self-identified French declined from 5,189,000 (2.4 percent of the population) to 3,939,000 (1.7 percent). The German self-identified declined from 25,662,000 (12.1 percent) to 20,517,000 (10 percent), Italians from 8,733,000 (4.1 percent) to 7,101,000 (3.2 percent) and the Poles and Russians commensurately. Nevertheless, apart from European groups, the general tendency has been for ethnic consciousness to increase. This is due partly to considerable recent immigration from non-European sources and especially the shift to Asian im-

TABLE 4.5. Self Perception of Origins, 1969–73 (in thousands)

Origin	1969		1971		1972		1973	
	Total	%	Total	%	Total	%	Total	%
Total population of U.S.	198,214	100.0	202,854	100.0	204,840	100.0	206,295	100.0
English	19,060	9.5	31,006[a]	15.0	29,548	14.0	25,993	12.1
French	In "other"		5,189	2.4	5,420	2.3	3,939	1.7
German	19,961	9.9	25,662	12.1	25,543	12.1	20,517	10.0
Irish	13,282	6.6	16,326	8.0	16,408	8.0	12,240	6.0
Italian	7,239	3.7	8,733	4.1	8,764	4.1	7,101	3.2
Polish	4,921	2.0	4,941	2.1	5,105	2.3	3,686	1.4
Russian	2,152	1.1	2,132	1.0	2,188	1.0	1,747	0.8
Spanish	9,230	4.6	8,957	4.2	9,178	4.3	10,577	5.0
Mexican	5,073	2.5	5,023	2.3	5,254	2.3	6,293	3.0
Puerto Rican	1,454	0.8	1,450	0.7	1,518	0.7	1,548	0.7
Other	106,653	54.0	84,692	42.0	85,130	41.0	97,593	46.1
Not reported	17,635	8.5	15,216	7.3	27,556	8.0	22,902	10.9

[a] Includes Scots and Welsh.

Source: *Statistical Abstract of the United States*, 1975. Table 40.

TABLE 4.6. The Population of the United States by Nativity and Parentage, 1970[a]

Country of Origin	Total (All Nativity Cohorts)	Native Parentage	Foreign Stock Foreign and Mixed Parentage	Foreign Born
Total	203,210,158	169,634,926	29,955,930	9,619,302
English	160,717,113	149,312,435	9,706,853	1,697,825
Celtic	88,162	9,734	32,969	45,459
Norwegian	612,862	204,822	313,675	94,365
Swedish	626,102	113,119	381,575	131,408
Danish	194,462	29,089	107,155	58,218
Dutch	350,748	90,713	132,204	127,834
Flemish	61,889	12,064	29,024	20,801
French	2,598,408	1,460,130	727,698	410,580
Breton	32,722	7,252	15,439	10,031
German	6,093,054	2,488,394	2,403,125	1,201,535
Polish	2,437,938	670,335	1,347,691	419,912
Czech	452,818	148,944	233,165	70,703
Slovak	510,366	86,950	340,855	82,561
Hungarian	447,497	52,156	234,088	161,253
Serbo-Croat	239,455	24,095	132,296	83,064
Slovenian	82,321	9,040	54,103	19,178
Dalmatian	9,802	3,038	4,748	2,016
Albanian	17,382	1,571	8,283	7,528
Finnish	214,168	58,124	117,754	38,290
Lithuanian	292,820	34,744	162,888	95,188
Other Baltic	19,748	1,231	8,309	10,208
Russian	334,615	30,665	154,673	149,277
Ukrainian	249,351	22,662	130,054	96,635
Georgian	747	179	157	421
Rumanian	56,590	5,166	25,369	26,055
Yiddish	1,593,993	170,174	985,703	438,116
Romany (Gypsy)	1,588	1,252	180	156
Greek	458,699	56,839	208,115	193,745
Italian	4,144,315	606,625	2,512,696	1,025,994
Spanish	7,823,583	4,171,050	1,956,293	1,696,240
Portuguese	385,300	62,252	162,749	140,299
Basque	8,108	1,852	4,087	2,169
Armenian	100,495	13,758	48,414	38,323
Persian	23,923	1,555	4,037	17,329
Hebrew	101,686	19,691	45,883	36,112
Arabic (all)	193,520	26,734	92,045	73,657
Southern Semitic	1,354	380	216	758
Hamitic	948	445	217	286
Swahili	3,991	2,040	812	1,139
Libyan	410	265	86	59
Niger-Congo	6,537	1,055	1,221	4,261
Sudanic	2,543	336	1,347	860
Turkish	24,123	1,811	5,666	16,646
Other Uralic	15,191	765	3,016	11,410
Altaic	974	306	251	417
Hindi	26,253	1,249	2,987	22,017

TABLE 4.6. *(continued)*

Country of Origin	Total (All Nativity Cohorts)	Native Parentage	Foreign Stock	
			Foreign and Mixed Parentage	Foreign Born
Other Indo-Aryan	22,939	731	2,342	19,866
Dravidian	8,983	635	813	7,535
Korean	53,528	2,756	16,024	34,748
Japanese	408,504	82,886	207,528	118,090
Chinese (all dialects)	345,531	30,764	124,407	119,260
Tibetan	352	183	50	119
Burmese	1,581	248	177	1,156
Thai	14,416	1,178	1,543	11,695
Malay (all)	10,295	2,019	1,267	6,915
Filipino	217,907	8,336	57,073	152,498
Polynesian	20,687	12,006	3,725	4,956
All Native American	268,205	254,859	7,537	5,809
All others	880,779	350,126	341,483	189,170
Not reported	9,317,873	873,081	348,645	96,147

^a According to national language of country of origin

Source: U.S. Bureau of Census, *United States Summary*, 1970. Table 192.

migration. No doubt it is also due in part to the higher regard in which the principle of ethnicity is held and to the greater social and political leverage exerted by minorities.

The ethnic diversity of the country and the considerable potential of many linguistic groups are indicated by these groups. They represent most of the language families of the civilized world, though many, like Tibetan (352), Libyan (410), Georgian (757), are represented by insignificant numbers of immigrants. Apart from the Native American, all groups are reinforced continuously by the arrival of new native-speaking immigrants. This is most clearly the case with Spanish, which because of the proximity of Puerto Rico, Cuba, and Spanish-American countries, and the common frontier shared with Mexico ensure a steady and indeed massive reinforcement annually. The level of reinforcement compared with existing American membership is even more pronounced among the smaller groups. This is because they tend to have shorter histories of immigration to the United States and therefore have a much smaller native presence. For example, the percentage of foreign-born speakers of Arabic is 37, Armenian 35, Rumanian 47, Japanese 39, Russian 48, and Chinese 53. In some cases, too, —especially the Spanish and the Native American groups—the differential birthrate is well above the national level. From the standpoint of the long-term planning of bilingual education, these facts have at least two implications. First, if the Germans and Poles or the Swedish and Norwegians decided to promote vigorously a demand for bilingual education—as have the Spanish, Italians, and Asians—their present overall numerical strength, to say nothing of the prospects of continuous reinforcement, would appear to justify them. That they are less inclined to do so than the Spanish, Italians, and Asians suggests there is more to the claim for bilingual education than overall ethnic and linguistic strength; for instance, considerations like the distribution of that population and the level of their economic and social development must be accounted for.

Second, because the more recently established and therefore smaller groups are represented by higher percentages of foreign-born (and therefore native-speakers of the immigrant languages), their ties with the language and with the associated cultures are closer. They compensate by intimacy for what, at the moment, they lack in numerical strength. Even in the short-term, however, their numbers are likely to increase rapidly, as the Asians have done in the last ten years. From whatever standpoint we regard the American educational situation, little justification exists for the belief (or the hope) that is sometimes expressed that the influence of bilingualism is likely to diminish, though the relative importance of different national and ethnic categories may shift. Demographically such a shift will be toward the salience of the Spanish-speaking, the Native American, and the Asian elements.

Distribution of Minority Language Groups

INTRODUCTION

The size of an ethnic group is a primary consideration in determining whether or not to set up a program of bilingual education, but other considerations also affect the viability of such a program. For instance, the number who are currently able and willing to speak the language is not an absolute determinant. No matter how attenuated the grasp of the language in the population, if a determined and influential group of native speakers exists then the recovery of a language can be engineered against powerful odds. This is exemplified by the remarkable recovery of Hebrew. Furthermore, if bilingual education is meant to satisfy only minimal criteria—for instance teaching the native language without using it to teach other subjects—then the size of the group need not constitute more than a single class of children of school age. Where a bilingual program is meant to satisfy the major part if not the whole of the education of a child, economics of scale are a fundamental administrative consideration and the size of a group to be recruited for a particular school becomes a vital factor in planning. The impact upon educational planning of overall size of the group nationally is reduced because of decentralized administration. Schools are locally controlled institutions and thrive best where they reflect local conditions. This is truer of the teaching and use of an ethnic language than it is of teaching a foreign language or mathematics and science, where the strength of the demand is unlikely to reflect local as against national considerations.

Whatever the overall national size, the geographical distribution of a language group is a crucial consideration. The pattern of distribution helps to determine where particular programs are needed now and likely to be required in the future. From the standpoint of those who plan national policy for the education of bilingual children, the overall size of the linguistic group determines the salience of that language in the general plan. It is equally important, however, to know how diffused the speakers of the language may be, in what kinds of areas (rural or urban) they are located, to what other language groups they are in proximity, and where they are concentrated regionally. Given satisfactory local concentration, the internal structure of a group is also significant—age and sex distributions and fertility rate are determinants of the self-reproduction of the group irrespective of reinforcement by immigration or gravitational migration from inside the country.

The national dimensions of the many language minorities are evident in Table 4.6 and it will be apparent that irrespective of their absence in many large areas of the United States, their overall size makes it virtually impossible for them to be ignored on a national level. This applies to the Spanish especially, and to the Italians to a lesser extent. In other instances the justification of bilingual education is determined by their regional concentration, and it is particularly so with the Amerindians. There are several languages, like Russian, in the United States claiming more than 10,000 speakers, but these people are spread so thinly over the country that they cease to offer adequate recruitment to bilingual programs —except in one or two densely populated cities like New York. Moreover, the decision in *Lau v. Nichols* (1974) implied these groups would find it difficult in law to claim special treatment.

On the other hand, much smaller national groups are so concentrated in certain localities, in many cases isolated, that a bilingual program becomes the most logical provision. For instance, in Alaska as well as on Indian reservations, or in deracinated groups on the outskirts of large cities, small isolated communities can justify bilingual education while much larger national but dispersed groups fail to do so. Title VII programs have been found to be successful among fewer than thirty Ute children in Cortez, Colorado, fewer than fifty Pomo children in California, and fewer than fifty Seminoles in Florida. Furthermore, it should be emphasized that however large or small the local minority may be, it is not its size relative to the total population (its relative dimension) that matters, but the actual numbers to be catered for: thirty children can be catered for in a city of 400,000, though less conveniently than in a township of 2,000. A great deal depends on the degree of geographical concentration of the small group, whatever the size of the city or town. A minimum or a workable number of students is important for other reasons. Teachers and materials have to be provided and their availability in any area is largely justified by the numbers of students satisfying the relevant or stipulated criteria.

The *proportion* of a minority to the total population becomes significant on grounds other than those we have mentioned. In the eighteen cities that have over 10,000 Spanish-speaking students, including Los Angeles (over 100,000), Montebello, California (14,000), Harlandale, Texas (13,000) and Newark, New Jersey (17,000), it is obvious that numbers irrespective of relative size indicate the need for bilingual programs as well as the possibility of ensuring their viability. In other words, the ratio of Spanish to total population in such cities is hardly relevant. It becomes a consideration when the ratio is such as to affect attitudes to the minority language. Where the ratio is high, as in Bell Gardens and Culver City, California (21.7 percent and 13.4 percent Spanish-speaking respectively), there is sufficient background support to the language to ensure that unfavorable attitudes can be neutralized. This is true also of larger cities like Denver, where 16.8 percent of the population speak Spanish. Therefore, looked at demographically, there are four aspects of language population distribution to be considered: first, the overall national dimension tends to establish the *salience* of the minority within the national plan or system; second, the distribution of the language population helps to determine the *viability* of the bilingual programs; third, the proportion of a particular minority to the total population helps to determine the *acceptability* or otherwise of a bilingual program; and, finally, the degree of linguistic heterogeneity in any locality—whether only one or several different language groups are represented—helps to determine both the *type of bilingual school organization* and its *relationship* to the total system.

DISTRIBUTION OF IMMIGRANTS

The distribution of immigrants within the United States has been a complex process governed largely by two dominant principles: the attraction of large industrial areas and cities; the close interrelationship of new-immigrant distribution with the internal movement of their older (and by definition) native nativity-cohort.

The proportion of the total population of the United States and each division attributable to the three main foreign-stock and first generation native cohorts as well as the changes in those proportions between 1890 and 1970 are given in Table 4.7. Apart from the Pacific states where the influx of Asians between 1960 and 1970 has boosted the number of those of foreign stock, the regions which in 1960 had high numbers as well as high proportions of the national total of those of foreign stock (Mid-Atlantic, East North Central and New England) now have reduced num-

TABLE 4.7. Composition of the White Population by Nativity[a]

| | Native | | | | | | | | Foreign-Born | | | |
| | Native Parentage | | | | Foreign or Mixed Parentage | | | | | | | |
Division[b]	1890	1930	1960	1970	1890	1930	1960	1970	1890	1930	1960	1970
United States	54.9	57.3	70.3	83.5	18.4	21.1	13.3	11.0	14.6	11.4	5.2	4.5
New England	51.8	38.8	61.0	69.5	23.0	37.5	26.5	24.0	24.2	22.5	10.0	7.0
Mid-Atlantic	50.8	43.6	59.7	73.4	25.8	32.2	21.9	19.4	21.6	20.1	9.9	8.8
East North Central	53.9	57.3	72.3	84.4	25.8	26.0	14.4	12.0	18.6	12.9	5.1	4.0
West North Central	56.0	64.3	80.2	88.0	23.9	24.7	13.1	10.0	17.4	8.1	2.5	1.5
South Atlantic	57.2	65.9	70.8	92.1	3.6	4.0	4.4	4.9	2.3	1.9	2.0	2.8
East South Central	62.3	70.5	75.8	98.2	3.1	2.0	1.3	1.3	1.6	0.6	0.4	0.5
West South Central	58.4	69.8	75.4	92.4	6.8	7.0	5.7	5.0	4.8	3.6	2.0	1.9
Mountain	51.9	64.3	80.1	86.7	23.4	21.5	11.4	10.0	21.2	10.1	2.0	3.0
Pacific	47.4	54.5	70.3	76.6	23.5	25.1	15.9	15.0	22.8	16.5	7.2	7.8

[a] Expressed as percentage of total area population.
[b] See Table 4.10 for listing of states in each division.

Sources: U.S. Census 1890. Vol. IV *Special Reports, Nativity.* Table 3. U.S. Census 1930. Vol. IV *Special Reports, Nativity.* Part 3, Chapter A, Table 3. U.S. Census 1960. *Special Reports, Nativity.* Table 3. U.S. Census 1970. Vol I, Part C.

157

bers and shares of the national foreign stock total. The areas previously having low proportions now tend to show an increase in percentage of foreign stock, though these downward and upward shifts in proportions have done comparatively little to equalize the national distribution of foreign stock. What a comparison of the 1960 to 1970 figures indicates is the stability of the distribution of first, second, and third generation immigrants, and this current stability has a strong historical foundation.

From 1930 onwards, as is to be expected in view of the increased immigration control, the proportion of the total population which is of native parentage has increased considerably—from just over 57 percent in 1930 to 83 percent in 1970. Although the proportion of foreign stock to the total population is higher in New England than elsewhere, the actual numbers of the foreign stock are much higher in the Mid-Atlantic States, next highest in East North Central and Pacific States. New England has the fourth largest group of foreign stock. The United States is tending increasingly toward distributive homogeneity in spite of continued immigration. The rise in the level of those of native parentage coincides with a gradual decline in the proportion of second generation immigrants (foreign and mixed parentage), and this decline is uniform in its national distribution, apart from New England where the high proportion in 1970 (24 percent) is a slight increase over the 1890 figure (23 percent) though reflecting a sharp decline since the turn of the century and more particularly since 1930. In spite of increasing homogeneity, that is the proportion of native to foreign stock, there are considerable differences in the distribution of second generation immigrants (measured in terms of percentage of the total population of any area), as evidenced by the difference between New England and East South Central states, or Mid-Atlantic and South Atlantic states. The same disparity is reflected in the distribution of the foreign born. Although the size of this nativity cohort has declined sharply everywhere except in the South Atlantic states, the differences between the divisions are wide, varying from 7.8 percent (Pacific states) to 0.5 percent (East South Central).

Table 4.8 lists for 1960 the proportion of the national total of thousands of foreign stock (first, second, and third generation) which is taken up by each division of the United States, and for 1970 the comparable foreign stock figures as well as the figures for first and second generation immigrants separately. A comparison of 1960 and 1970 serves to emphasize the fact that from 1890 onwards the distribution of the national total of immigrants has been relatively well established, excepting the Pacific states where the new Asian immigrants have tended to concentrate. The share of the national population of foreign stock has tended to shift from the Eastern divisions (New England, Mid-Atlantic, East North Central and West North Central) to the Western and Southern states. But (again with the exception of the Pacific states) there is no dramatic immigrant popula-

TABLE 4.8. Nativity and Percentage of the U.S. Total of Each Nativity Cohort, 1960 and 1970 (in thousands)

	1960				1970					
	Foreign Stock				Foreign Stock		Foreign-Born		Native of Foreign or Mixed Parentage	
Division	Total	% of Division			Total	% of Division	Total	% of Division	Total	% of Division
United States	34,050	100.0			33,575	100.0	9,619	100.0	23,956	100.0
New England	3,870	11.3			3,617	10.7	929	9.6	2,688	11.2
Mid-Atlantic	11,098	33.0			10,284	30.5	3,190	33.0	7,094	30.0
East North Central	7,129	19.8			6,297	18.7	1,584	16.4	4,713	20.0
West North Central	2,425	7.1			1,951	5.8	290	3.0	1,661	6.9
South Atlantic	1,714	5.0			2,409	7.1	879	8.9	1,530	6.7
East South Central	218	0.6			236	0.7	60	0.6	176	0.7
West South Central	1,329	3.9			1,469	4.3	378	3.9	1,091	4.9
Mountain	1,046	3.1			1,098	3.1	246	2.5	852	3.8
Pacific	5,222	15.3			6,214	18.6	2,064	21.5	4,150	15.0

Sources: U.S. Census, 1960. Vol. I. U.S. Census, 1970. Vol. I. Part C.

159

tion shift. From an examination of Table 4.7 and 4.8 it would appear that the overall incidence of bilingualism in the New England states (independently of the sizes of specific groups) will decline rapidly during the next twenty years provided the pattern of immigration remains stable. It is already declining in the Mid-Atlantic states, but the dimension of the problem in those states is so great that even a relatively rapid decline will not be felt in the schools for several decades. The incidence of bilingualism in the schools is likely to become more marked in the Pacific, Mountain, and East North and West North Central states.

A concentration of limited numbers of one ethnic group presents a greater problem than much larger numbers spread among several immigrant groups. We need to know how far the immigrant population in any division or state is limited to one or two linguistic minorities and what proportion of the total divisional population is represented by specified groups. This information is given in Tables 4.9 and 4.10.

So far we have analyzed the existing national as well as specific ethnic group distribution. Data useful in forming a view about whether the most recent nativity cohort (foreign-born) of each ethnic group are drawn to the areas historically associated with it are given in Table 4.11.

In the case of the French, it appears that there is a shift in the attractiveness of the historically associated areas. Whereas 37 percent of the total of the French ethnic group live in New England and 27 percent in West South Central, only 8.2 percent and 2 percent respectively of the foreign-born live in those areas. At present, in fact since 1940, the most attractive areas for the French (judged by the residence of the foreign-born) are the Mid-Atlantic and the Pacific states. On the other hand, the proportions of the foreign-born living in traditional German areas and of the total German ethnic group in those areas correlate fairly closely. The four most German states traditionally are in the East North Central, Mid-Atlantic, West North Central, and Pacific divisions (in that order). Apart from West North Central states, the other areas bear the same relationship to each other in attractiveness to the most recent German-speaking immigrants— Mid Atlantic 33 percent of total German foreign-born, East North Central 22.5 percent, Pacific 17 percent. In the case of the Italians, since they have a higher ratio of foreign-born to recent and subsequent immigrant generations, it is to be expected that the distribution of the foreign-born should conform closely to the distribution of the total and it proves to be so—44 percent of all Italians and 51 percent of the foreign-born live in the Mid-Atlantic states while New England and East North Central remain second and third in order of attractiveness to the recent Italian immigrants as they have been for their predecessors. South Atlantic and Pacific states though, are becoming more attractive to Italians as they have become also for Germans. A close conformity between area distribution of

TABLE 4.9. Ethnic Composition of the United States (Selected Groups), 1970 (in thousands)

Division	Total Population All Ethnic Groups	Total Ethnic Population					Ethnic Total as % of All Group Total in Area					Ethnic Total in Area as % of Total of Same Ethnic Group in U.S.				
		French	German	Italian	Polish	Russian	French	German	Italian	Polish	Russian	French	German	Italian	Polish	Russian
United States	203,212	2,603	6,092	4,144	2,438	334	1.2	3.0	2.0	1.2	0.1	100.0	100.0	100.0	100.0	100.0
New England	11,845	905	157	500	327	28	7.9	1.3	5.2	2.6	0.7	32.0	0.3	12.1	13.0	8.4
Mid-Atlantic	37,189	286	1,393	1,804	828	151	0.8	2.5	6.2	2.7	0.4	11.6	22.0	44.0	32.0	49.0
East North Central	40,248	204	1,785	545	422	5	0.5	2.4	1.4	1.8	0.1	7.8	29.0	13.4	17.0	1.4
West North Central	16,318	67	1,038	63	78	1	0.4	6.2	0.3	0.4	—	2.6	17.0	1.5	3.1	0.3
South Atlantic	30,671	148	373	194	113	14	0.4	1.1	0.6	0.4	0.9	5.8	6.2	4.7	4.5	4.2
East South Central	12,863	25	71	19	7	1	0.2	0.4	0.2	0.05	—	0.9	1.2	0.5	0.3	0.3
West South Central	19,318	700	308	62	55	3	3.5	1.5	0.3	0.3	—	27.0	5.1	1.5	2.2	1.0
Mountain	8,281	42	239	57	22	5	0.5	2.5	0.7	0.5	—	1.4	4.0	1.4	0.9	1.4
Pacific	26,527	241	776	379	98	29	0.8	2.5	1.2	0.4	—	9.0	12.5	9.0	4.0	8.9

Source: U.S. Census of Population, 1970. Vol. I. Part IC.

TABLE 4.10. Leading Foreign Stocks in Each Division, 1970

State	Leading Countries of Origin and % of Division or State
New England	French (7.9), Italy (5.2), U.K. (2.5)
Maine	French (13.8), U.K. (1.2), Ireland (0.7)
New Hampshire	French (13.1), U.K. (1.6), Ireland (1.1)
Vermont	French (10.4), U.K. (1.6), Italy (1.1)
Massachusetts	French (8.2), Italy (5.2), Ireland (3.8)
Rhode Island	Italy (7.7), French (7.0), U.K. (3.6)
Connecticut	Italy (7.5), French (4.2), Poland (3.4)
Mid Atlantic	Italy (6.2), Poland (2.7), Germany (2.5)
New York	Italy (7.3), USSR (3.1), Poland (3.1)
New Jersey	Italy (7.2), Germany (3.1), Poland (3.0)
Pennsylvania	Italy (3.8), Poland (2.1), Germany (1.7)
East North Central	Germany (2.4), Poland (1.8), Italy (1.4)
Ohio	Germany (1.8), Italy (1.6), Poland (1.1)
Indiana	Germany (1.2), Poland (0.7), U.K. (0.6)
Illinois	Germany (1.8), Poland (2.7), Italy (2.1)
Michigan	French (4.0), Poland (2.4), Germany (2.1)
Wisconsin	Germany (5.3), Poland (1.6), Norway (1.2)
West North Central	Germany (2.9), Norway (1.2), Sweden (1.1)
Minnesota	Germany (3.6), Sweden (3.0), Norway (3.0)
Iowa	Germany (3.6), Sweden (0.7), Norway (0.7)
Missouri	Germany (1.7), Italy (0.6), U.K. (0.5)
North Dakota	Norway (6.3), USSR (5.4), Germany (3.4)
South Dakota	Germany (4.0), Norway (2.8), USSR (2.1)
Nebraska	Germany (4.2), Czech (1.3), Sweden (1.2)
Kansas	Germany (1.9), USSR (0.8), U.K. (0.7)
South Atlantic	Germany (0.9), Cuba (0.9), U.K. (0.8)
Delaware	Italy (2.2), U.K. (1.5), Poland (1.3)
Maryland	Germany (1.5), Italy (1.3), USSR (1.2)
District of Columbia	Germany (0.7), U.K. (0.7), USSR (0.7)
Virginia	Germany (0.7), U.K. (0.7), French (0.5)
West Virginia	Italy (1.0), U.K. (0.5), Germany (0.4)
North Carolina	Germany (0.3), U.K. (0.3), French (0.2)
South Carolina	Germany (0.4), U.K. (0.3), French (0.2)
Georgia	Germany (0.5), U.K. (0.3), French (0.2)
Florida	Cuba (3.7), Germany (1.8), U.K. (1.7)
East South Central	Germany (0.4), U.K. (0.2), Italy (0.2)
Kentucky	Germany (0.7), U.K. (0.2), French (0.1)
Tennessee	Germany (0.3), U.K. (0.2), French (0.2)
Alabama	Germany (0.4), U.K. (0.3), Italy (0.2)
Mississippi	Germany (0.2), Italy (0.2), U.K. (0.2)
West South Central	Mexico (3.7), Germany (0.8), U.K. (0.4)
Arkansas	Germany (0.5), U.K. (0.2), French (0.2)
Louisiana	Italy (0.8), Germany (0.4), U.K. (0.3)
Oklahoma	Germany (0.8), U.K. (0.4), French (0.3)
Texas	Mexico (6.4), Germany (0.9), U.K. (0.4)
Mountain	Mexico (2.4), Germany (1.6), U.K. (1.4)
Montana	French (3.0), Germany (2.2), Norway (2.1)

TABLE 4.10 *(continued)*

State	Leading Countries of Origin and % of Division or State
Mountain (continued)	
Idaho	French (1.5), U.K. (1.5), Germany (1.4)
Wyoming	Germany (1.7), U.K. (1.6), French (0.9)
Colorado	Germany (2.0), USSR (1.2), U.K. (1.2)
New Mexico	Mexico (3.7), Germany (0.7), U.K. (0.6)
Arizona	Mexico (6.4), French (1.5), Germany (1.4)
Utah	U.K. (2.7), Germany (1.3), French (1.1)
Nevada	Italy (1.6), French (1.6), Germany (1.4)
Pacific	Mexico (4.3), French (2.4), Germany (1.8)
Washington	French (4.0), Germany (2.1), U.K. (1.8)
Oregon	French (2.5), Germany (1.9), U.K. (1.4)
California	Mexico (5.6), French (2.2), U.K. (1.9)
Alaska	French (2.2), Germany (1.2), U.K. (1.0)
Hawaii	Japan (13.7), China (2.7), French (0.8)

Source: U.S. Census of Population, 1970. Vol I Part C.

all Polish (as well as of all Russian) immigrants and the distribution of the most recent immigrants in these ethnic areas can be observed. So far as the smaller minority groups are concerned, foreign-born Scandinavians remain leading elements in their historical American localities—West North Central States, particularly Minnesota, Iowa, South and North Dakota, Nebraska as well as in East North Central States, particularly Wisconsin, and in Montana. The Czechs remain firmly rooted in Nebraska, which continues to attract most of these new immigrants.

The regional breakdown offered in Table 4.12 fails to reflect the actual degree of concentration of Asian Americans. San Francisco in the West and New York City in the Northeast are the two localities mainly involved, and within those two cities very limited localities are affected. In New York, for example, School District I serves a part of the Chinese population, but it is District II that caters for the majority—5,000 in six elementary and one junior high school. One elementary school has a 99 percent concentration of Chinese children, the average concentration being 50 percent. What is true of the Chinese is equally true as a general rule of the Japanese, who, with a population of nearly 600,000, are the largest Asian American subgroup—one third of these in the 1960–70 count being foreign-born.

It is important in considering the kinds of provision which should be made for ethnic and linguistic subgroups to note not only the diversity and the relative sizes of those groups but also their geographic distribution and differences between rural and urban elements in particular areas. These distributional differences may be closely correlated with difference of attitude to the ethnic group and its language, as well as attitude to the desirability of a bilingual education.

TABLE 4.11. Selected Foreign-Born Population and Their Distribution in the United States, 1940–70

Division		French			German			Italian			Polish			Russian		
		1940	1950	1970	1940	1950	1970	1940	1950	1970	1940	1950	1970	1940	1950	1970
United States	No.	79,940	107,924	416,000	919	984	1,201	1,429,890	1,427,000	1,025,000	993,459	861,184	386,000	1,040,000	864,000	209,000
	%	100.0	100.0	100.0	100.0	100.0	100.0	100.0	100.0	100.0	100.0	100.0	100.0	100.0	100.0	100.0
New England	No.	3,275	9,902	34,140	31,649	38,187	51,278	208,003	205,000	140,555	105,953	91,363	51,638	98,346	81,638	51,638
	%	9.0	9.5	8.2	3.0	4.0	4.0	14.0	14.0	14.0	11.0	11.0	14.5	9.2	9.1	23.0
Mid-Atlantic	No.	34,937	42,140	106,000	418,174	406,016	405,323	864,890	817,244	510,395	476,481	411,416	116,093	587,238	484,996	64,371
	%	45.0	42.0	25.0	43.0	41.0	33.0	60.0	57.0	51.0	47.0	47.0	33.0	57.0	58.0	32.0
East North Central	No.	12,653	16,157	41,550	281,224	262,695	275,685	189,194	194,257	141,666	322,229	271,120	142,217	153,591	129,203	20,071
	%	13.0	11.0	10.0	30.0	27.0	22.5	14.0	14.0	14.0	33.0	30.0	38.0	15.0	14.0	10.0
West North Central	No.	2,609	4,101	7,283	65,507	97,472	70,348	22,295	22,233	12,496	25,064	20,573	8,348	66,501	49,625	990
	%	3.0	4.0	1.3	6.0	10.0	5.3	1.5	1.5	1.2	2.5	2.3	2.6	6.6	6.7	7.5
South Atlantic	No.	2,856	6,683	36,234	24,361	38,699	104,407	28,203	37,545	42,552	23,330	25,599	18,974	36,529	40,442	11,771
	%	3.2	6.6	8.8	2.5	3.8	8.3	2.0	2.5	4.2	2.3	3.0	5.0	3.6	4.5	5.3
East South Central	No.	679	1,220	2,269	5,859	8,283	13,869	4,174	5,078	3,375	2,205	2,302	1,648	4,095	3,499	536
	%	0.6	1.0	0.5	0.5	0.8	1.1	0.3	0.3	0.3	0.3	0.25	0.4	0.4	0.3	0.2
West South Central	No.	2,607	3,765	8,747	12,864	22,911	34,555	11,162	12,212	7,944	5,427	6,250	3,354	9,274	7,948	1,407
	%	3.0	3.2	2.0	1.3	2.4	2.5	0.8	1.1	0.7	0.6	0.9	0.8	0.9	0.9	0.7
Mountain	No.	1,324	3,215	9,140	11,027	18,419	42,668	9,509	15,856	10,482	3,816	4,471	4,032	18,973	17,128	2,261
	%	1.5	3.2	2.3	1.2	1.9	3.5	0.7	1.1	1.0	0.3	0.5	1.0	1.8	1.8	1.2
Pacific	No.	15,000	20,743	63,308	69,915	91,699	203,530	81,940	115,362	91,529	19,235	28,010	22,571	66,337	80,367	32,934
	%	19.0	20.0	15.5	7.0	10.0	17.0	5.5	9.0	9.1	1.9	3.0	5.6	6.6	9.9	16.0

Sources: U.S. Census of Population, 1940. Vol. I. U.S. Census of Population, 1950. Vol. I. U.S. Census of Population, 1970. Vol. I. Part C.

TABLE 4.12. Geographic Distribution of Asian Americans

| | North East | | North Central | | South | | West | |
	1960	1970	1960	1970	1960	1970	1960	1970
Japanese	4	8	6	7	4	5	86	81
Chinese	23	27	8	9	7	8	63	57
Filipino	6	9	5	8	6	9	83	74

Sources: U.S. Census of Population, 1960. *Subject Reports: Nonwhite by Race*, PC(2)–IG, Tables 4 and 5. U.S. Census of Population, 1970. *Subject Reports: Japanese, Chinese, and Filipinos in the United States*, PC(2)–IG.

DISTRIBUTION OF INDIGENOUS GROUPS

So far we have described the processes of colonization and immigration in creating ethnic and linguistic diversity. By the languages of colonizing nations we mean those "that established sovereignty in the New World and consequently have been able to maintain themselves at the expense of others" (Haugen, 1956: 19). Many *colonial* languages competed for sovereignty with the English language in various regions—Dutch, Swedish, Portuguese, French, and Russian among them. The last named survived in Alaska until 1867 when it ceased to be the administrative language. None of the others were able to maintain their mainly localized sovereignty as administrative languages or to expand their sway, as the English language did. Consequently while still maintaining a "colonial" association in their original settlements, their strength in the United States now depends on past and continuing immigration. For all practical purposes they have to be regarded as immigrant languages. There are two groups that differ essentially from the immigrant-language population whose progress we have followed. First, the Spanish within territories that the United States either conquered or "acquired" were also a colonial power. They exercised sovereignty in virtue of the Mexican context, flourished at the expense of the Indians, and because of continuous reinforcement (partly on account of migration and partly on account of a disproportionately high birthrate) they flourish in relation to the English-speaking population. To that extent Spanish is different from the immigrant languages. In the Southwest the relations of English and Spanish may still be said to be those of two competing colonial languages. The other group is the indigenous Amerindian, and it is to the contribution of these groups to ethnic diversity that we turn our attention first.

American Indians

Although they represent only 4 percent of the total population of the United States, the total of Indians, Eskimos, and Aleuts is increasing rapidly. It has been assumed that prior to the European colonization of

America, 800,000 Indians and Eskimos lived in the area of the present-day United States. They declined to about 237,000 by 1900 (Krauss, 1973a: 796), but by 1950 the census reported 357,000 as a conservative estimate. Between 1950 and 1960 there was a 16 percent increase. On the face of it, the increases offer an encouraging prospect for the continued strength of at least twenty-five Indian languages (those with over 2,500 speakers), but the picture is deceptive. In many groups, the number of speakers under twenty years of age is few, and, though they may have increased their numbers, many have suffered a very severe diminution of their strength in relation to other languages spoken in their localities. For instance, in 1750 the Pueblos represented 12 percent of the total population of the areas in which they were located. The total population at that time was 870,000. In spite of an increase in numbers, the Pueblos are now less than 8 percent of the total population of the same area. Similarly between 1960 and 1970, Eskimos and Aleuts increased from 22,000 to 28,000 and from 5,700 to 6,300 respectively, representing increases of 26 percent and 10 percent. Nevertheless their proportion of the total regional population has declined.

Official estimates made by the Bureau of Indian Affairs (BIA), and in other counts of population on reservations, give figures higher than those of the U.S. census. Several tribes have made their own population counts, which record even higher figures than the BIA. In comparing official school records with the census count of those enrolled in schools, the census is as much as 50 percent below school figures.

American Indians are not vanishing. On the contrary they are increasing at a rate four times the national average (see Table 4.13). The total United States population increased by 13 percent in the decade from 1960 to 1970. The American Indian population increased by more than 51 percent. Navajos had a reported population of 9,000 in 1910; in 1970 the census recorded 96,743. Such an increase may be due in part to more

TABLE 4.13. American Indian Population of the United States, 1900–1970

Census Year	American Indian Population	Change from Preceding Census	
		Number	Percent
1970	792,730	269,139	51.4
1960	523,591	166,092	46.5
1950	357,499	12,247	3.5
1940	345,252	1,900	0.6
1930	343,352	98,915	40.5
1920	244,437	−32,490	−11.7
1910	276,927	39,731	16.8
1900	237,196	—	—

Source: Office of Special Concerns. *A Study of Selected Socio-Economic Characteristics of Ethnic Minorities Based on the 1970 Census, Vol. III: American Indians.* HEW Publication No(Os)75–122 Table A I.

efficient enumeration; certainly as more Indians take up permanent residence in urban areas, they are less likely to be overlooked. However, higher figures result mainly from the continuing favorable birthrate, reduction in infant mortality, and the effects of greater self-identification by many Indians, who for many years had become anonymous in the general population.

The figure most widely quoted in reference to the total 1970 population of American Indians and Alaskan natives—763,594—is 64,000 lower than the actual total arrived at by the Census Bureau. Adding those Eskimos and Aleuts living in Alaska to the total American Indian population would bring the reported Indian and Alaskan native population in the United States to 827,268. Even this figure is conservative because it does not include the Eskimos and Aleuts living outside of Alaska, for which no data are available.

The problem of determining who is and who is not an Indian is another issue that has undoubtedly affected the count of Indians. In 1970, race was defined on the basis of self-identification by respondents. For persons of mixed parentage who were in doubt as to their classification, however, the race of the person's father was used. Some 38 percent of all married Indian women have non-Indian spouses, and of all births registered as Indian in 1970 more than one-fourth had an Indian *mother* and a *non-Indian father*. By present census definition, however, if the race of the child is not clearly defined on the census enumeration forms, children would be enumerated by the race of their fathers. Yet this definition is contrary to most Indian family patterns, where children identify with the culture of their mothers. The children are raised by and learn the language, the culture, and the customs of their mothers. Where Indian tribes maintain clanship patterns, the clan affiliations are usually passed down from generation to generation through the women of the tribe.

The difficulties of ensuring a satisfactory bilingual education for the Amerindian population are several. The most obvious problem is that many tribes have only a relatively few members, irrespective of their ability to speak the languages. Another difficulty is the large number of different languages spoken by them, some at comparatively low levels of stabilization and development. A final difficulty is that the Amerindian languages as a whole are distributed very widely over North America, and any one of the moderately sized or large groups may be represented in several states.

Table 4.14 offers an estimate of numbers belonging to many Indian language groups in the United States. Many of the languages have very few possible speakers, and where this is the case the probability is that those speakers are adults and usually at an advanced age. Chitimachan (in Louisiana) is a case in point, as also are those languages with no more than 50 possible speakers—Chinookan (Oregon and Washington), Modoc (Or-

TABLE 4.14. Amerindian Languages in the United States

Language	Number of Speakers
Eskimo-Aleut[a]	
Eskimo	
Yupik	13,000
Inupik	15,000
Aleut	700
Algonquian	
Central	
Cree	30,000
Chippewa/Ojibwa	40,000
Menominee	3,000
Fox/Sauk	1,600
Shawnee	300
Potawatomi	1,000
Eastern	
Malecite	600
Passamaquoddy	300
Western	
Blackfoot	5,000
Cheyenne	3,000
Arapaho	1,000
Kutenai	400
Salishan	
Okanagon	1,000
Kalispel	700
Others	1,000
Wakashan	
Makah	500
Na-Dene	
Haida	100
Tlingit	1,000
Athapaskan	
Apachean	
Navajo	140,000
Tonto	500
Jicarilla	1,500
White Mountain	4,000
San Carlos	3,000
Masckakero	1,000
Pacific Coast and California Athapaskan	100
Northern	
Kutchin	1,000
Ingalik	100
Tanaina	400
Ahtena	500
Koyukon	1,500
Tutchone	500
Chipewyan	3,000

TABLE 4.14. *(continued)*

Language	Number of Speakers
Penutian	
Chinookan	50
Klamath	
Klamath	100
Modoc	50
Maidu	100
Zuñi	3,000
Mewok	50
Shahaptian	
Yakima	1,500
Nez Perce	750
Others	500
Hokan-Siouan	
Cadoan	
Pawnee	500
Arikara	250
Wichita	200
Chitimachan	10
Iroquoian	
Mohawk	1,000
Oneida	1,000
Seneca	2,000
Cherokee	10,000
Karok	750
Keresan	
Western	
Acoma	600
Laguna	3,000
Eastern	
Zía	300
Santo Domingo	1,000
San Felipe	1,000
Santa Ana	300
Cochiti	500
Muskogean	
Western	
Choctaw	10,000
Chickasaw	2,000
Eastern	
Muskogee	10,000
Seminole	300
Alabama	300
Palaihnihan	100
Siouan	
Dakota	4,000
Teton	10,000
Yankton	1,000
Assiniboin	1,000
Winnebago	1,000

170 / *Chapter 4*

TABLE 4.14. *(continued)*

Language	Number of Speakers
Hokan-Siouan (continued)	
Omaha	2,000
Crow	3,000
Others, such as Osage, Iowa	1,500
Washoan	100
Yuman	
Yuma	1,000
Mohave	1,000
Others	2,000
Aztec Tanoan	
Kiowa Tanoan	
Kiowa	2,000
Tiwa—Taos, Isleta, Sandia	1,200
Tewa—San Juan, Hano, etc.	1,500
Towa—Jemez	1,200
Piman	
Papago	5,000
Pomo	200
Uto-Aztecan	
Shoshoni	5,000
Comanche	1,500
Ute	3,000
Southern Pacute	2,000
Hopi	4,000

[a] Krauss (1973a) estimates 34,000 of which 22,000 are Yupik

Source: Compiled from data in the studies on Indian languages in Vol. 10 *Current Trends in Linguistics*, ed. T. A. Sebeok; see especially in ibid., the checklist by Herbert Landar, "The Tribes and Languages of North America: A Checklist," pp. 1253–1444.

egon), Mewok (California), and so on. If we assume that 500 possible speakers may constitute a satisfactory base for a viable language (provided other circumstances like geographical concentration and favorable age distribution are met), we are left with twelve languages with between 500 and 1,000 possible speakers, twenty-three with between 1,000 and 2,500, eleven between 2,500 and 5,000, six between 5,000 and 10,000, five between 10,000 and 20,000, two with up to 50,000, and one, Navajo, with nearly 150,000. Apart from the Navajo, given the small numbers who claim in surveys to speak the Indian languages "usually" and that even when they are not diffused over a wide area they are often part of heterogeneous Indian, English, Spanish, and immigrant language communities, the provision of an Indian language education for more than a very few tribes is a dubious possibility. When, therefore, their very considerable diffusion is taken into account the problem is even more immense (see Table 4.15).

TABLE 4.15. Distribution of American Indians in Selected States

A Location	B Indian Population	C Mother Tongue % of Population	D Language Groups Represented with Estimated Totals for Each[a]
California	91,018	20	Muskogean (100) Pacific Coast Athapaskan (100) Maidu (100), Mowok (50)
Los Angeles		24	Karok (750), Palaihnihan (100)
San Francisco		26	Washoan (100), Yuma (1,000) Pomo (200), Shoshoni (5,000)
Washington	33,386	13	Okanagon (1,000), Salisham (1,000)
Seattle		14	Wakashan (500), Shahaptian (1,500) Chinookan (50)
Oklahoma	97,731	30	Fox (1,600), Shawnee (300)
Oklahoma City		24	Polawatomi (1,000), Cheyenne (3,000)
Tulsa		19	Arapaho (1,000), Pawnee (500) Wichita (200), Kiowa (2,000)
Arizona	95,812	76	Navajo (140,000), Other Apachean (7,500)
Phoenix		34	Mohave (1,000), Other Yuman (2,000)
Tucson		78	Papago (5,000), Paiute (2,000) Hopi (4,000)
New Mexico	72,788	70	Jicarilla (1,500), Zuñi (3,000)
Albuquerque		39	Keresan (7,000), Tiwa (1,200) Tewa (1,500), Towa (1,200)
South Dakota	32,365	29	Chippewa (40,000), Caddoan (250) Dakota (4,000)
Alaska	51,519	72	Yupik (13,000), Inupik (15,000) Aleut (650), Haida (100) Tlingit (1,000), Northern Athapaskan (7,000)

[a] Estimates of mother tongue totals for each language (col. D) are based on Vol. 10 *Current Trends In Linguistics*, ed. T. A. Sebeok. The numbers quoted for each language may be spread over several states.

Source: Data in columns A, B, and C: U.S. Office of Special Concerns. 1970. Table E.6 of *Study of Selected Socio-Economic Characteristics of Ethnic Minorities*, Vol. III.

Indians, Eskimos, and Aleuts are distributed throughout the United States, though very unevenly. Almost half of them live in five states—Oklahoma (77,000), Arizona (95,800), California (91,000), New Mexico (72,700), and Alaska (51,500). Thirteen other states have Indian populations of over 10,000, so that 85 percent of the total live in about a third of the states. Their distribution is likely to become more widespread, since 22 percent of all Indians in 1970 lived in states other than those in which they were born; this mobility is expected to accelerate. (Office of Special Concerns, *A Study of Selected Socio-Economic Characteristics of Ethnic Minorities Based on the 1970 Census*. Vol. III: *American Indians.*) In turn greater mobility will tend to erode the language affiliation of many Indians;

this wider distribution, however, is unlikely to decrease the present density of their presence in the traditional localities because of very favorable birthrates, which ensure that they are increasing at four times the national average—especially in the rural areas (ibid., p. 7).

Spanish Americans

Data concerning the subgroup composition of the Spanish-speaking population are presented in Table 4.16. The difficulties encountered in seeking to encompass such diverse subgroups in the census are considerable and too absolute a reliance should not be placed on such data. The percentage error in the 1970 Spanish-American figures amounted to 16.6 percent overall, ranging from an overcount of 60 percent (Central and South Americans) to undercounts of 38.8 percent (Mexican Americans), 34.6 percent (Cubans), 33 percent (others), and 8.3 percent (Puerto Ricans). Even granting the increases that must have occurred between 1970 and 1973 such discrepancies are serious and should be noted whenever 1970 figures are quoted. The use of the term *Spanish American* tends to obscure the considerable heterogeneity that exists among them, arising from differences of origin, differences in the history of their incorporation into the United States, and differences of current life style, as well as in the variants of the Spanish they speak.

Following the war with Mexico in 1848 and their incorporation under the Treaty of Guadalupe Hidalgo in that year, the Mexican-American population in the Southwest—itself originally a colonial power—entered American society as a conquered people. Subsequent additions to the Mexican-American population have tended to erode the original composition of the group as well as to stratify the current composition along historical lines. Consequently attitudes to Spanish vary as much as does attainment in the language. Some speakers still try to conform to the model of Spanish spoken in metropolitan Spain. Others know little and care less for the original status of the language; some speakers are monolingual Spanish, some are bilingual, and some do not speak Spanish. Heterogeneity arising from differences among the Mexican-Americans is reinforced by differences between them and other Spanish-speaking groups.

Most of the Puerto Rican population in the continental United States arrived since 1950, and they do not have a history of life in American society comparable to Mexican-Americans. The Mexican-Americans, close though their ties may be with Mexican culture, consider themselves to be permanent members of continental American society. The majority of Puerto Ricans, although they have the same economic motives for immigration, tend not to regard their residence in America as permanent. Similarly the post-Castro Cuban arrivals in the United States tend for the

TABLE 4.16. Number of Persons of Spanish Origin, 1970 Census and 1973 Amendment

Sub-Group	1970	% of U.S. Population	% of Total South American Origin	1973 Total
Total Spanish	9,072,602	4.5	—	10,577,000
Mexican Origin	4,532,435	2.2	50.0	6,293,000
Puerto Rican Origin	1,429,395	0.7	15.8	1,548,000
Cuban Origin	544,600	0.3	34.6	733,000
Central and South American Origin	1,508,866	0.7	16.6	597,000
Other Spanish Origin	1,057,305	0.5	11.6	1,406,000

Source: U.S. Census of Population, Current Population Reports, *Persons of Spanish Origin in the United States, March 1973.* Series P-20, no. 264.

173

present at least to regard their move as temporary; most continue to hope for a change in political circumstances in Cuba that would enable them to return. Cubans, who immigrated earlier and settled in the area of Tampa, Florida, regard themselves like the Mexican-Americans as permanent members of American society.

Only about 5,000 Cubans belong to this earlier phase of immigration, and their presence has been submerged by the arrival of 265,000 legal Cuban immigrants between 1960 and 1970. Barely 18 percent of Cuban Americans were born in the United States. Like other immigrants they have tended to settle in areas where there was already a similar ethnic representation, and 45 percent of them made Florida their destination. This concentration served to draw dispersed Cuban Americans to Florida so that at present approximately 50 percent live in that state.

In addition to these three subgroups of speakers of Spanish, 1.5 million Spanish-speakers have come from South and Central America together with natives of Spain. Consequently different varieties of Spanish are spoken in the United States, and, though these differences should not be exaggerated, they are important because, among other things, they affect the appropriateness of whatever material is prepared to teach Spanish or to teach other subjects in Spanish. Differences of dialect and Spanish cultural orientation may hinder the deployment of native Spanish-speaking teachers if they have been brought up within one subgroup and wish to teach in another. The history of Puerto Rico—the interaction of Spanish, African, and Taino elements—ensured that a Puerto Rican creole evolved during the centuries of Spanish rule and the Spanish spoken was markedly distinct from standard American Spanish (Craddock, 1973: 469). Little attention has been given to Cuban Spanish, either the earlier (Tampa) or the later (Miami) varieties. Mexican-American has been the only variety studied with any degree of thoroughness, and the speech of New Mexico has been well described (Craddock, 1973; Bowen, J.D., 1972).

The general category of "speakers of Spanish" is not homogeneous, but additionally there is little uniformity within any one subgroup. Reference has been made to the early nineteenth century "Tampa" Cubans and the more recent arrivals. The same is true of the Puerto Ricans. Studies by J. Steward (1956) and Mintz (1966) established the diversity of cultures within Puerto Rico, and this diversity is reinforced and increased by the influences on immigrants exerted by varied aspects of mainland Spanish-American and Anglo cultures, which vary depending upon where they settle in the United States.

The greatest range of differences within any subgroup is exemplifed by Mexican-Americans. This diversity is to be expected in view of the long history and clearly differentiated phases of their involvement in the life of the Southwest. They possess at least two distinct modes of speech: one a survival of the genuinely colonial Spanish of the original Hispanic inhabitants; and the second the speech of the waves of Mexican immigrants.

There are also the undoubted differences in the speech habits of urban and rural (village) Mexican-Americans—differences that are not so characteristic of Puerto Ricans and Cubans, who have only a small rural proportion (Madsen and Shapira, 1970). Moreover the great distances between Mexican-American communities—the two largest concentrations in California and Texas are separated by more than a thousand miles—means communication between them is hindered. The mass media, radio, T.V., and the press (to the extent that they use Spanish)reflect regional varieties and so accentuate—rather than soften—the effects of distance. Nevertheless, it would be wrong to disregard the very genuine recognition among most speakers of Spanish that they share a common language and culture. Chester Christian, on the basis of his long experience of teaching Hispanic students in Texas, maintains that "no matter what form of Hispanic background they have, they live within the same frame of reference of Spanish culture, even going back as far as several centuries" (Christian, C. C., 1973:192).

Three important considerations are suggested by the data in Table 4.17. In the first place, the overall diffusion of Spanish is remarkably even, except for the states of Texas, Colorado, New Mexico, Arizona, and California. In fact, Spanish is more evenly and widely spread than any other minority language, and for that reason the Spanish language constitutes a national problem in a way that no other minority language does. Second, the wide and even distribution is supported by heavy concentrations in particular states and groups of states, providing the same kind of

TABLE 4.17. Age Distribution of Spanish Americans, 1970

1 State	2 % Spanish Origin	3 % of 2 Under 5 Yrs.	4[a] % of 2 Under 18 Yrs.
Total U.S.	4.6	8.4	34.4
Northeast States			
Maine	0.4	8.5	35.1
New Hampshire	0.4	8.9	38.5
Vermont	0.6	8.9	36.0
Massachusetts	1.1	8.3	34.2
Rhode Island	0.7	8.0	32.8
Connecticut	2.4	8.3	34.3
New York	4.8	8.1	33.7
New Jersey	1.9	8.2	34.4
Pennsylvania	0.4	7.4	33.6
East North Central States			
Ohio	0.9	8.6	36.1
Indiana	1.3	8.8	36.9
Illinois	3.3	8.4	35.2
Michigan	1.4	9.1	37.8
Wisconsin	0.9	8.6	36.3
Minnesota	0.6	8.7	37.7
Iowa	0.6	8.2	35.4
Missouri	0.9	7.9	34.6

TABLE 4.17. *(continued)*

1	2	3	4ᵃ
		% of 2	% of 2
State	% Spanish Origin	Under 5 Yrs.	Under 18 Yrs.
East North Central States (continued)			
North Dakota	0.3	8.3	37.5
South Dakota	0.4	8.2	37.3
Nebraska	1.4	8.1	35.1
Kansas	2.1	7.8	34.6
Southern States			
Delaware	1.1	8.9	34.9
Maryland	1.4	8.8	34.1
District of Columbia	2.1	7.9	30.5
Virginia	1.0	8.4	35.4
West Virginia	0.4	7.9	34.1
North Carolina	0.4	8.5	35.8
South Carolina	0.4	9.0	38.2
Georgia	0.6	9.1	34.7
Florida	6.6	7.4	32.2
Kentucky	0.3	8.4	35.9
Tennessee	0.4	8.2	34.6
Alabama	0.4	8.7	34.1
Mississippi	0.4	9.4	39.4
Arkansas	0.5	8.2	35.3
Louisiana	1.9	9.5	39.5
Oklahoma	1.4	7.7	33.2
Texas	18.4	8.9	36.5
Western States			
Montana	1.1	8.2	37.7
Idaho	2.6	9.0	38.5
Wyoming	5.6	8.5	37.8
Colorado	13.0	8.4	36.4
New Mexico	40.0	9.5	41.5
Arizona	18.8	9.0	37.3
Utah	4.1	10.6	41.7
Nevada	5.6	8.9	35.1
Washington	2.1	8.2	35.5
Oregon	1.7	7.8	34.4
California	15.5	8.2	34.8
Alaska	2.1	10.7	30.5
Hawaii	3.0	9.2	36.6

[a] In forty-two states together with the District of Columbia, Spanish-speaking or Spanish mother tongue is used for those families in which the head of the household or the wife report Spanish as the mother tongue. In five Southwest states, Spanish-speaking is equated with Spanish surname. In New York, New Jersey, and Pennsylvania it includes those of Puerto Rican birth or born in the U.S. with one or both parents born in Puerto Rico. Obviously the census data are open to large errors so far as ability to speak Spanish or the use of the language are concerned.

Source: Office of Special Concerns. *A Study of Selected Socio-economic Characteristics of Ethnic Minorities Based on the 1970 Census.* HEW Publication No. OS 75–120. Vol. I Table B.I, p. 22.

reinforcement of which the dispersed or immigrant Russians in Central Asia are assured by the reservoir of Russian in the R.S.F.S.R. or that dispersed Armenians are guaranteed by the existence of a very strong Armenian reservoir in the U.S.S.R. This is not available to any other group in the United States, with the exception perhaps of the Nàvajo. Third, the age distribution of the Spanish-speaking minority is comparable to the age distribution of the Anglos, and this normal distribution characterizes the minority wherever it is. This is not true of the Amerindian groups among whom the tendency is for those who speak the languages to be in the older age groups. Among immigrant minorities, the first and second generation speakers of those languages belong to older age groups.

The degree of Spanish American concentration together with the extent to which the principal Spanish-speaking subgroups are separated from each other are presented in Table 4.18.

Over 87 percent of the Mexican-American population live in the five Southwest states (See Table 4.19). Sizeable contingents are also found in the mid-West, notably Illinois, concentrated in and around Chicago (4 percent of the total Mexican-American population). Smaller communities are found in Kansas, Michigan, and Wisconsin. Bearing in mind that the criterion of identification was not identical on each occasion of the census, it is noteworthy that the Mexican-American population of the Southwest increased very considerably from 1930, and probably during an earlier period. Although the rate of increase decelerated between 1960 and 1970, that decennial increase is still very considerable.

The 1.4 million Puerto Ricans represent 0.7 percent of the total U.S.

TABLE 4.18. Main Centers of Spanish-Speaking Subgroups, 1970

Spanish Speaking Subgroup	Total in Thousands	%
Mexican-American		
Total in U.S.	4,532	100.0
Arizona	240	5.0
California	1,857	41.0
Colorado	104	2.0
Illinois	160	4.0
New Mexico	119	3.0
Texas	1,619	36.0
Puerto Ricans		
Total in U.S.	1,429	100.0
Connecticut	38	3.0
Illinois	87	6.0
New Jersey	139	10.0
New York	917	64.0
Cubans		
Florida	265	46.0

Source: Office of Special Concerns. *A Study of Selected Socio-Economic Characteristics of Ethnic Minorities Based on the 1970 Census*. HEW Publication No. OS 75–120. Vol. I Tables B-1 (p. 22) and H-1 p. 94.

TABLE 4.19. Population of Spanish Persons in the Southwest

Year	Total	% Increase	Criterion of Identification
1930	1,252,883	—	Mexican
1940	1,570,700	22.4	Spanish Mother Tongue
1950	2,281,700	45.3	Spanish Surname
1960	3,465,000	51.9	Spanish Surname
1970	5,008,000	44.6	Spanish Origin

Source: Office of Special Concerns. *A Study of Selected Socio-Economic Characteristics of Ethnic Minorities Based on the 1970 Census.* HEW Publication No. OS 75–I20. Vol. I Table I-2, p. 4.

population, but the important aspect of this figure from the standpoint of educational planning is that like the Mexican-Americans and Cubans they are heavily concentrated in a few areas—the tri-state area of New York (64 percent), New Jersey (10 percent), and Connecticut (3 percent). Illinois also attracts a large proportion of Puerto Ricans (6 percent).

The concentration of Cubans in Florida is not due exclusively to the choice made by new immigrants. Cubans with some years of residence in the United States have apparently been moving to Florida, drawn by the congeniality of the presence of members of their own subgroup there. Of all native U.S. born Cuban Americans in Florida, 19 percent were born in a different state, 75 percent of those in the northeast. This tendency to concentrate on one area, and to withdraw from other dispersed locations, while intensifying the urgency of a solution in Florida tends to rationalize the situation nationally. Unlike the Mexican-Americans and the Puerto

TABLE 4.20. Cuban Immigrants, 1960–73

Year	Total in Thousands	% Increase
1960	8.2	—
1961	14.2	75
1962	16.2	14
1963	10.5	−28
1964	15.8	50
1965	19.7	25
1966	17.3	−10
1967	33.3	31
1968	99.3	300
1969	13.7	−700
1970	16.3	25
1971	21.6	33
1972	20.0	−5
1973	24.1	20

Sources: U.S. Department of Justice, *Immigration and Naturalization Service, Annual Reports, 1960–73.*

Ricans, Cuban immigrants have not been as numerous since 1968 as they were between 1960 and 1968 (See Table 4.20). The rate of increase has not been steady, and from that point of view the Cuban subgroup poses very different long term problems from those posed by the others.

Current Linguistic Composition of the United States

SOURCES

So far as the non-Indian populations of the United States are concerned, we have attempted to analyze their origins and distribution and so produce a picture of the country's *ethnic* diversity. In dealing with the Amerindian populations, an attempt has been made to give rough estimates of their *linguistic* situation also. In the present section, estimates of the linguistic composition of the non-Amerindian populations will be offered. Although very valiant efforts have been made in the past to estimate and map the linguistic composition of the United States (see listing in Anderson and Boyer, Vol. 2, pp. 22–25) it was a frustrating exercise because of the absence of any firm data. Until 1975 various methods were employed to obtain such data—all of them unsatisfactory: counts by surname, ethnic origin, extrapolating the mother tongue claims recorded in the 1970 census, estimates of language dominance or proficiency in English, as well as the use of questionnaires designed to elicit information about the use of particular languages. Some states and school districts have attempted to refine these methods for purely local purposes. In 1974 the Educational Amendments to the Bilingual Education Act (1965) stipulated a "national assessment of the educational needs of children and other persons with limited English-speaking ability," and required the National Center for Educational Statistics to obtain information about the number of such persons. A preliminary survey was conducted by the Bureau of Census in July 1975, published as a supplement to the July 1976 Current Population Survey report (Special Studies Series P–23.60—*Language Usage in the United States*). The details available at present are limited to ten selected ethnic groups (Table 4.21), although information on all languages is published in the survey report.

The Current Population Survey took a sample of 45,000 households of which approximately 93 percent responded to the personal interviews of adult members of the household. The data in the regular Current Population Survey are for all persons fourteen years and over, but the language data are for children between the ages of four and thirteen years as well. The linguistic information now available covers claims to non-English languages as the mother tongue. This includes the language spoken in the home when those responding were children; those speaking the claimed mother tongue in households still speaking the language to some extent; those speaking the mother tongue as the *usual* household language; those

180 / *Chapter 4*

TABLE 4.21. Linguistic Composition of the Population of the United States—Excluding Indians, 1975

Item	Characteristics[a]	Source of Data	English	Other than English
	U.S. total for all languages 196.8 M			
1	Estimated nos. 14+ claiming language other than English as mother tongue	Waggoner pp. 10–13	—	27,670
2	(1) as % of ethnic *origin* or descent	Table 2	—	—
3	(1) as % of total U.S. all languages 14+	Table 4	—	17
4	Persons (4+) in households where languages other than English are spoken	Table 7	—	15,300
5	(4) expressed as % of total = 25.30 M	Table 5	—	100
6	% of non-English mother tongue claimants in households speaking that language	Table 5	—	55.0
7	Persons (4+) whose *usual* household language is claimed mother tongue	Table 8	185M	7,746
8	(7) as % of total mother tongue claimants	Table 5	—	35.0
9	Persons (4+) speaking language other than English—first or second	Table 15	—	18,719
10	Persons (4+) who do not speak English	Table 17	—	1,622
11	Persons (4+) in households claiming only English	Page 12	—	12,000 (45%)
12	Usual language spoken by individuals (4+)	Table 1*	188.800	6,587
13	(12) expressed as % of group mother tongue claimants	Table 1*	—	29.0
14	(12) expressed as % of total all languages	Table 1*	95.9	4.1
15	Second language spoken by persons 4 yrs and over	Table 3*	4,942	13,000

[a] in millions

Source: Waggoner, 1975, *Results of the Survey of Language Supplement;* Tables with asterisk from U.S. Department of Commerce, Bureau of the Census, *Special Studies Series P–23.60*

whose *individual* language (irrespective of the household) is not English; those who are bilingual together with an indication of the dominant or usual language; those who are monolingual in the ethnic or English language, and so on. Table 4.21 sets out this information as well as some which is legitimately inferred from it. In addition the survey gives details of the ethnic origin or descent of the population.

MOTHER TONGUE CLAIMANTS
(Items 1, 2, and 3 of Table 4.21)

In 1975 nearly 28 million Americans claimed to speak a language other than English in childhood (mother tongue), though this is no indication of

TABLE 4.21 *(continued)*

	French	German	Greek	Ital-ian	Port-ugese	Span-ish	Chin-ese	Filip-ino	Japan-ese	Korean	Other
Selected Languages[b]											
	2,200	3,900	0,600	3,900	0,300	6,500	0,600	0,300	0,600	0,200	0,870
	47	21	79	57	67	81	84	82	71	95	—
	8	15	2	14	1	22	2	1	2	0.6	—
	2,259	2,268	0,488	2,836	0,349	9,904	0,534	0,377	0,524	0,246	5,560
	9.0	9.0	0.5	11.0	0.4	39.0	0.6	0.4	0.6	0.2	23.0
	51.0	29.0	78.0	49.0	66.0	90.0	82.0	85.0	70.0	88.0	42.0
	0,285	0,157	0,161	0,252	0,143	4,819	0,353	0,122	0,109	0,123	0,952
	22.0	8.0	32.0	20.0	40.0	56.0	60.0	40.0	3.0	54.0	19.0
	1,452	1,389	0,384	1,879	0,279	7,243	0,475	0,317	0,372	0,182	3,748
	Below 50,000 each			0,148	Below 50,000	1,086	0,456	Below 50,000 each			0,172
	—	—	—	—	—	—	—	—	—	—	—
	0,270	0,132	0,124	0,447	0,110	4,027	0,280	0,112	0,111	0,090	0,812
	16.0	7.0	30.0	17.0	32.0	41.0	53.0	33.0	26.0	45.0	18.0
	0.1	0.1	0.1	0.2	0.2	2.0	0.1	0.1	0.1	—	0.4
	1,187	1,277	1,265	1,442	0,173	4,284	0,198	0,210	0,267	0,092	3,033

[b] in thousands

whether the mother tongue was still spoken to any extent whatever. This figure represents 17 percent of the total population of the United States. The largest group claiming a non-English mother tongue were those of Spanish heritage (6.8 million), accounting for 81 percent of that ethnic group and 22 percent of the total of non-English mother tongue claimants. The next largest group in this category were the Italians (3.9 million), 57 percent of the ethnic group claimed to have spoken the language in childhood, constituting 14 percent of the total of such claimants. The numbers and proportion of the other ethnic groups claiming the group language as the mother tongue are high for all the selected groups, especially German (3.9 million, 21 percent of those of German descent) and French (2.2 million, 47 percent of those of French descent). The smaller groups such as the Greeks and Asians tend to have the highest proportion of the ethnic minorities claiming the group language as their mother tongue. To some extent this is due to their generally being more recent immigrants than minorities like the French and Germans; this is particularly true of the Korean group.

MAINTENANCE OF ETHNIC LANGUAGE IN THE HOME (Items 4, 5, and 6)

Fifteen million non-English mother tongue claimants aged fourteen years and over belong to households where languages other than English were reported as being spoken, accounting for 55 percent of the 27.5 million aged fourteen and over with mother tongues other than English. Both totals are high even in relation to a total of nearly 197 million for all languages and bearing in mind also the assimilative tendencies which have prevailed. Of the individual languages, the nearly 10 million Spanish speakers are the largest group and account for 39 percent of the total non-English household language population. Ninety percent of Spanish mother tongue claimants live in Spanish-speaking households. The next largest group, German, with about 2.3 million accounts for 9 percent of the non-English total. Compared with speakers of Spanish, the proportion of those claiming German as their mother tongue belonging to households where it is still spoken is low—only 29 percent. In numbers the Italians are next to the Spanish in maintaining the language in the home, their total of 2.8 million accounting for 11 percent of the non-English total, and 49 percent of the total claiming Italian as their mother tongue. Although the French have almost the same number who belong to households where the language is spoken, and so account for the same proportion of the non-English total as the Germans, they differ in that more of those who claim French as their mother tongue belonging to French language households—51 percent compared with the German 29 percent. The French have fewer French mother tongue claimants than the Italians, but the proportion of those French claimants who belong to French households is higher than the proportion of the Italians—51 percent compared with 49 percent. The retention of the mother tongue as a household language at this level is higher among the smaller European languages, Greek and Portuguese, and the Asian languages than among the older and larger immigrant groups who have generally had a longer period in which to assimilate.

MAINTAINING THE ETHNIC AS THE USUAL LANGUAGE OF THE HOME (Items 7 and 8)

At the level of the *usual* use of an ethnic language in the home, it is only to be expected that the degree of maintenance should be lower; the actual numbers, however, still contribute significantly to the pattern of linguistic diversity. Thirty-five percent of ethnic mother tongue claimants belong to households where the use of the ethnic language is *usual*. Here again those of Spanish heritage are well ahead with 4.8 million, accounting for well over 60 percent of the U.S. total in this category. Over half, 56 percent, of those who claim Spanish as their mother tongue belonging to households where it is the usual language. Half a million Italians (7 percent of the U.S. total) claiming the language as their mother tongue belong to the same category of household, though the half million is only one-fifth of the total who claim Italian as their mother tongue. The highest proportion of mother tongue claimants in this category of household is represented by the Chinese—60 percent (353,000). The Germans, with 157,000 are at the bottom of the 10 selected ethnic groups in terms of the proportion of mother tongue claimants belonging to households using German routinely.

USUAL LANGUAGE, SPOKEN BY PERSONS 4 YEARS AND OVER (Items 12–14)

The categories of language maintenance we have analyzed thus far are related to *households* in which languages other than English are spoken to some extent or usually. There are individuals who speak the claimed mother tongue as their *native* language—"native" in this context meaning for adults the language they normally use. For children it means the language normally used by the parents. Some 6.5 million of those 4 years of age and over are in this category, constituting 4.1 percent of the total population. Speakers of Spanish are 2 percent of the U.S. total, the next largest groups being Italian (447,000), French (270,000), and Chinese (280,000). All groups except Korean (90,000) are represented by more than 100,000 who normally use the claimed mother tongue. The proportion of the total of mother tongue claimants which do use the language normally varies very considerably, the highest proportion being Chinese (53 percent); Koreans have a high proportion of mother tongue claimants who use it normally (45 percent), as do the Italians (41 percent). The proportion of German claimants actually using the language is the lowest (7 percent), the next lowest being French (16 percent) and Italians (17 percent). The *individual* use of the claimed mother tongue naturally is closely related to the household incidence of the language, and in fact little difference exists in the two sets of figures (see item 7 and item 12). Nevertheless, the proportion of mother tongue claimants in the "*individual* use" category (item 14) is lower in all cases than the proportion in the "household language" category (item 8). The household environment is conducive to greater use of the mother tongue, and clearly the household is the foundation for the individual's continued use of it.

PERSONS (4+) SPEAKING LANGUAGES OTHER THAN ENGLISH AS FIRST AND SECOND LANGUAGE (Item 9)

It is often difficult to conclude which of the two languages spoken by a bilingual is his first or his second. For this reason, the total use made of a particular language—either first or second—is important. There are 18.7 million in this category, with the largest group being speakers of Spanish (8.2 million). Speakers of Italian, French, and German are between 1.5 million and 1.8 million each, and none of the ten selected groups are represented by fewer than a quarter of a million, except the Korean.

MONOLINGUALS AND BILINGUALS (Items 10, 11, and 15)

Individuals who belong to households where languages other than English are spoken can be further classified by those who do not speak the ethnic tongue (item 11), those who do not speak English (item 10), and those who are bilingual (item 15). For the bilinguals, 13 million are English language dominant, but there are many for whom the ethnic language is dominant. More than 1.6 million were reported as speaking no English. The Italians (148,000) and the Spanish (1 million) had the largest non–English-speaking numbers; the numbers in all groups, however, represented very small proportions of ethnic mother tongue claimants.

At least 12 million (45 percent) of those claiming an ethnic language as their mother tongue do not speak it. The data on the proportion of mother tongue claimants who belong to various levels of ethnic language maintenance are summarized in Table 4.22.

Seventeen million aged 4 and over were reported to be bilingual in English and the claimed mother tongue, 8.8 percent of the total of all languages. Monolinguals in the U.S. accounted for 91.2 percent of the population (178 million) (item 13), the vast majority being speakers of English. Among those claiming the ethnic language as mother tongue, nearly 5 million claimed English as their second language (2.5 percent of the total "all languages"). Thus 12.5 million (approximately 6 percent of

TABLE 4.22. Summary of Data for Mother Tongue Claimants

Summary of Data	%
Mother tongue claimants	100
Numbers in households speaking mother tongue to some extent	55
Numbers in households speaking mother tongue usually	35
Individuals speaking mother tongue as native language	29
% shift from mother tongue to monolingual English	45

Source: Table 4.21 infra.

the total "all languages") are ethnic dominant bilinguals. The largest group in this dominance category are the speakers of Spanish, with 4.3 million speakers representing 2.2 percent of the total U.S. population. The next largest group of ethnic language dominant bilinguals are the Italians, followed by the Germans and the French, all represented by 1.75 million approximately.

Since the Spanish-speaking bilinguals are much the largest group a more detailed analysis of their situation is provided in Table 4.23.

There are 4.2 million speakers of Spanish for whom that language is second to English, and 72,000 for whom it is second to another non-English or ethnic language. There are 2.9 million Spanish-speakers for whom English is the second language.

On the basis of the data currently available, it is difficult to make a detailed analysis of the age distribution of those who belong to any of the categories of language maintenance (mother tongue claims, household usage, usual household language, usual individual language, and the various categories of bilingualism). Some conclusions can be drawn, however (See Table 4.24). Among the 27.7 million aged 14 years and over who claim an ethnic language as mother tongue (item 1), 1.6 million are between the ages of 14 and 18—giving an approximate average age group distribution of 300,000. Among the 28 million people aged 4 and over in households where a language other than English is spoken, 3.1 percent are between the ages of 4 and 5, 15 percent between 5 and 13, and 10 percent between 14 and 18—nearly 30 percent are of school age. The Spanish-speaking population, however, have 39 percent in the school age groups— 5 percent between 4 and 5, 21 percent between 6 and 13, and 16 percent between 14 and 18. The age distribution data of the other groups do not

TABLE 4.23. English or Spanish as Usual or Second Language

Usual and Second Language	No. in Thousands	%
Total	196,796	100.0
Usual language of person (age four or over)		
Usual language English, total	188,799	95.9
Usual language English, second Spanish	4,212	2.1
Usual language Spanish, total	4,027	2.0
Usual language Spanish, second English	2,934	1.5
Usual language other than English or Spanish	2,493	1.5
Usual language *not* reported	1,477	0.8
Second language of person (age four or over)		
Second language English, total	4,942	2.5
Second language Spanish, total	4,284	2.2
Other second language	8,143	4.1
No second language	177,964	90.4
Not reported	1,463	0.7

Source: U.S. Department of Commerce, Bureau of the Census 1975 *Special Studies Series P–23.60*, Table 5.

TABLE 4.24. Age Group Distribution of Those Who Speak an Ethnic Language (in millions)

| Categories | Total | | Age Groups | | | | | | | | | |
| | | 4-5 | | 6-13 | | 14-18 | | 19-25 | | 26-50 | | 50 and Over | |
	No.	No.	%	No.	%	No.	%	No.	%	No.	%	No.	%
1 Persons claiming ethnic mother tongue 14+	27,500												
Household language background (all groups)	28,650	0.978	3.1	4,376	15.0	2,795	10.0	3,304	11.0	9,089	30.0	8,113	27.0
2 Household language background Spanish	9,904	0.524	5.0	2,118	21.0	1,161	16.0	1,357	13.5	3,422	34.0	1,316	13.5
Usual household Language (all groups)	7,746	0.358	4.5	1,385	16.0	0.745	10.0	0.882	11.0	2,578	33.0	1,797	22.0
3 Usual household Language Spanish	4,819	0.262	5.5	1,056	22.0	0.557	11.0	0.601	12.0	1,606	33.0	0.737	15.0

TABLE 4.24. (continued)

Categories	Total	4-5		6-13		14-18		19-25		26-50		50 and Over	
	No.	No.	%	No.	%	No.	%	No.	%	No.	%	No.	%
Persons speaking mother tongue as first or second language (all groups)	18,119	0.508	2.7	2,226	12.0	1,474	8.0	2,031	11.0	6,639	35.0	5,842	31.0
4 Persons speaking mother tongue as first or second language (Spanish)	8,243	0.372	4.5	1,577	19.0	0.953	10.5	1,139	14.0	3,010	36.0	1,192	14.0
Persons who do not speak English (all groups)	1,622	0.970	6.0	73,000 [a]	4.6 [a]	0.460 [a]	2.5	0.183	11.5	0.608	38.0	0.615	38.0
5 Persons who do not speak English (Spanish)	1,086	0.890	8.0	50,000	4.0	0.340	3.0	0.156	14.0	0.424	39.0	0.344	30.0

Age Groups

[a] Estimates

Source: Waggoner, 1975, Results of the Survey of Language Supplement, Tables 7, 8, 15, and 17.

deviate to any great extent from the averages in this category (Source: Waggoner, Table 7).

The age distribution of those whose usual household language is the mother tongue does not differ much from that of mother tongue claimants—4.5 percent are between 4 and 5, 16 percent between 6 and 13, and 10 percent between 14 and 18. The school age groups account for 31 percent. Here again speakers of Spanish deviate from the norm: 5.5 percent are between 4 and 5, 22 percent between 6 and 13, and 11 percent between 14 and 18. The school age groups account for 39 percent (Waggoner, Table 8).

The possession of an ethnic language *only* is a characteristic of the very young or the elderly, and the general trends in age distributions of those who speak the claimed mother tongue (at whatever level) also favors the very young and the elderly.

Canada

The close cultural and economic ties between the United States and Canada, their geographical contiguity as well as the similar ethnic patterns permit us in this section on the United States to discuss Canada briefly.

Immigration proceeded at a much slower pace in Canada than it did in the United States (See Table 4.25). The linguistic diversity reprepresented by the immigrants was not as great, and the consequent heterogeneity in Canada was far less because of the smaller size of the immigrant minorities. In 1871, approximately 24 percent of the United States population was not of British, French, Spanish, or Indian origin; in Canada the proportion which was not Indian, English, or French amounted to less than 3 percent. This proportion increased to 9.8 percent in 1901 and to 23 percent in 1961. Of that nonindigenous and noncolonial population, the Germans were the largest part. Their number among the immigrants rose from 1,000 in 1901 (2.8 percent) to 33,000 in 1951 (17 percent), falling to 13,000 in 1961 (13 percent). These followed seventeenth-century German immigrants to New France and Nova Scotia. German religious sects, especially Mennonites and Moravians, settled in Upper Canada in the nineteenth century also.

Aside from the Germans, the Scandinavians and Dutch—at about 1 percent of the population—were the largest immigrant group in the nineteenth century. Norwegian and Danish farmers became homesteaders, and many Swedes came to work on the railways. The annual immigration rate of these minorities fluctuated, but in both cases the numbers ranged between 2,000 and 4,000, and their proportion of the total was approximately 3 percent. A significant proportion of Dutch and Scandinavian immigrants migrated from the United States and were already moderate-

TABLE 4.25. Ethnic Origins of Immigrants to Canada, 1901–61 (in thousands)

Year	Total All Countries	British[a] Total	%	French Total	%	Scandinavian Total	%	German[b] Total	%	Balkan Total	%	Russian[c] Total	%	Poland Total	%	Italy Total	%	Greece Total	%	Asia Total	%
1961	104	30	33	3.0	3.00	2.2	2.25	13.0	13.0	5.0	5.0	0.60	0.5	3.0	3.3	22.0	21.0	5.00	5.0	4.0	4.0
1951	194	37	19	7.0	3.50	6.5	3.50	33.0	17.0	10.0	4.5	9.00	4.5	13.0	6.5	25.00	12.5	3.00	1.5	3.0	1.5
1941	63	9	14	0.8	1.25	0.2	0.40	0.4	0.7	0.1	0.1	0.06	0.1	0.1	0.2	0.07	0.1	0.03	0.4	0.1	0.2
1931	27	17	62	3.0	11.00	0.7	3.90	2.0	9.0	0.8	3.0	0.60	2.0	0.6	2.0	0.60	2.0	0.06	0.3	0.4	1.0
1921	91	45	50	0.4	0.40	1.6	6.00	0.2	0.2	1.0	1.0	0.50	0.5	3.0	3.0	3.00	3.0	0.20	0.2	4.0	4.0
1911	331	144	43	2.0	0.75	5.0	1.30	9.0	2.3	4.0	11.0	19.00	6.0	6.0	2.0	7.00	2.0	0.60	0.2	8.0	2.0
1901	55	12	22	0.4	0.50	1.7	2.80	1.0	2.8	0.7	1.4	1.00	2.0	5.0	10.0	5.00	9.0	0.08	0.1	1.0	2.0

Source: Census of Canada, 1961. Series A 316–336.

[a] British includes English, Scots, Welsh, and Irish.
[b] German includes German, Austria, and Luxemburg.
[c] Russian includes population within the boundaries of the USSR.

189

ly assimilated on arrival in Canada. Icelanders in 1875–76 and Finns in the 1870s were represented by small groups.

Just as the importance of the north and western European countries declined in favor of southern and eastern European immigration to the United States, so Canada after the nineteenth century began to attract immigrants from those same nonindustrialized countries. The annual immigration rate of Italian immigrants rose from less than 5,000 in 1901 to 22,000 in 1961, and their proportion of the Canadian population rose correspondingly from less than 0.1 percent in 1901 to 2.5 percent in 1961. In 1901 fewer than 11,000 Italians lived in Canada; by 1961 the number had increased to 450,000. However, the increase in the number of Ukrainians was even more rapid: in 1901 they numbered fewer than 6,000, but by 1931 that number had risen to 81,000 and by 1961 to 473,000. Hungarians began to arrive in 1901 and by 1931 they constituted a sizeable minority of over 40,000, increasing to 126,000 by 1961—approximately 0.7 percent of the total population.

Asians, who had earlier preferred to drift south to California, migrated to Canada in the years after 1931. They were joined by others from Hong Kong and Canton to become laborers on construction work. Between 1901 and 1931 over 12,000 emigrated to Canada, and the number of Asians in the population increased to 84,000 (See Table 4.26). By 1961 this number had risen to 121,000.

In 1971, the ethnic composition of Canada was analogous to that of the United States and had developed along the same lines. The French, though, did not simply correspond to the Spanish of the United States in the population pattern; rather, they were a proportionately much larger and more cohesive minority. Further, the French minority have a longer history of more intense conflict with the English than do the Spanish-speakers. Immigrants from northwestern Europe constitute the larger element of the ethnic pattern. Among them those of British descent still amount to nearly a half, followed by the French. The indigenous Indians and Eskimos, as in the United States, are fewer than many immigrant groups. The European ethnic preponderance is greater, and the British element is somewhat less evident demographically in Canada than in the United States. Nevertheless, as in the United States, Canada too has a European and English-speaking base of unity and continuity of culture.

The linguistic and cultural dominance of western Europe is seen in the distribution of the population according to their claimed home language (See Table 4.27). Speakers of the two national languages—English and French—account for over 91 percent of the total population, the largest nonnational language groups being Italian, German, and Ukrainian, none of which accounts for 1 percent of the population. The change in language affiliation from first language (and still understood) to the most frequently employed language is a significant gain to the English language and a loss

TABLE 4.26. Ethnic Composition of Canada, 1871–1971 (in thousands)

Ethnic Origin	1871 Total	1871 %	1901 Total	1901 %	1931 Total	1931 %	1961 Total	1961 %	1971 Total	1971 %
Total Population	3,485.0	—	5,371	—	10,376	—	18,238	—	21,568	—
European	3,432.0	99.0	5,170	98.0	10,134	99.0	17,652	92.0	19,540	91.0
British	2,110.0	66.0	3,063	60.0	5,381	51.0	7,997	44.0	9,624	44.0
French	1,082.0	51.0	1,644	28.0	2,927	29.0	5,540	30.0	6,190	28.7
German	203.0	6.0	311	6.0	474	4.5	1,050	6.0	1,317	6.1
Hungarian	—	—	2	—	41	0.4	126	0.7	132	0.6
Italian	1.0	—	11	—	98	0.8	450	2.5	731	3.4
Jewish	0.1	—	16	—	156	1.5	173	0.9	297	1.4
Netherlands	30.0	1.0	34	—	149	1.5	429	2.3	426	2.0
Norwegian	6.0	0.2	12	—	93	0.8	148	0.8	179	0.8
Polish	—	—	6	—	145	1.5	323	1.8	316	1.5
Russian	0.6	0.2	20	—	88	0.8	119	0.7	64	0.3
Swedish	7.0	0.2	15	—	81	0.7	121	0.7	102	0.5
Ukrainian	—	—	6	—	225	2.2	473	2.6	580	2.7
Asiatic	—	—	12	—	84	0.8	121	0.7	286	1.3
Native Indian and Eskimo	23.0	0.8	127	2.5	129	1.0	220	1.2	315	1.5

Sources: *Canada Year Book*, 1948–49, p. 154; 1957–58, p. 137.

TABLE 4.27. Language Use in Canada, 1961–71.

| Language Group | Language First Spoken and Still Understood | | | | Language Most Often Spoken at Home[a] 1971 | |
| | 1961 | | 1971 | | | |
	No.	%	No.	%	No.	%
English	10,660,534	58.45	12,973,840	60.15	14,445,000	66.97
French	5,123,151	28.09	5,793,650	26,86	5,546,000	25.71
Italian	339,626	1.86	538,360	2.50	425,000	1.97
German	563,713	3.09	561,085	2.60	213,000	0.99
Ukrainian	361,496	1.98	309,855	1.44	145,000	0.67
Indian and Eskimo	166,531	0.91	179,820	0.83	138,000	0.64
Greek	40,455	0.22	104,455	0.48	87,000	0.40
Chinese	49,099	0.27	94,855	0.44	78,000	0.36
Portuguese	18,213	0.10	86,926	0.40	75,000	0.35
Polish	161,720	0.89	134,780	0.62	71,000	0.33
Magyar (Hungarian)	85,939	0.47	86,835	0.40	51,000	0.24
Netherlands	170,177	0.93	144,925	0.67	36,000	0.17
Croatian, Serbian, etc.	28,866	0.16	74,190	0.34	29,000	0.13
Yiddish	82,448	0.45	49,890	0.23	26,000	0.12
Czech and Slovak	51,423	0.28	45,150	0.21	25,000	0.12
Indo-Pakistani	4,505	0.02	32,555	0.15	23,000	0.11
Finnish	44,785	0.25	36,725	0.17	18,000	0.08
Spanish	6,720	0.04	23,815	0.11	18,000	0.08
Arabic[b]	12,999	0.07	28,550	0.13	15,000	0.07

TABLE 4.27. *(continued)*

| Language Group | Language First Spoken and Still Understood | | | | Language Most Often Spoken at Home[a] | |
| | 1961 | | 1971 | | 1971 | |
	No.	%	No.	%	No.	%
Russian	42,903	0.24	31,745	0.15	13,000	0.06
Japanese	17,856	0.10	16,890	0.08	11,000	0.05
Estonian	13,830	0.08	14,520	0.07	10,000	0.05
Lithuanian	14,997	0.08	14,725	0.07	10,000	0.05
Lettish	14,062	0.08	14,140	0.07	9,000	0.04
Danish	35,035	0.19	27,395	0.13	5,000	0.02
Romanian	10,165	0.06	11,300	0.05	4,000	0.02
Flemish	14,304	0.08	14,240	0.07	3,000	0.01
Swedish	32,632	0.18	21,680	0.10	2,000	0.01
Norwegian	40,054	0.22	27,405	0.13	2,000	0.01
Gaelic	7,533	0.04	21,200	0.10	1,000	—
Icelandic	8,993	0.05	7,860	0.04	1,000	—
Welsh	3,040	0.02	3,160	0.01	—	—
Other	10,443	0.06	41,830	0.19	33,000	0.15
Total	18,238,247	100.00	21,568,310	100.00	21,568,000	100.00

[a] Preliminary figures rounded to thousands. For final figures see 1971 Census Reports, Cat. No. 92-759 or 92-726.
[b] Includes Syrian
Source: *Canada Year Book*, 1972.

to French. The difference between English and French in terms of percent gain or loss of affiliation is reflected in and probably due in part to the distribution of the two languages across Canada. French is highly concentrated (in proportion to the total population of the provinces) in Quebec and New Brunswick, and therefore it does not stand to gain from the shift from minority languages that are distributed very widely across Canada. Irrespective of differences in prestige between French and English, the ubiquity of English is an overriding influence (See Table 4.28).

All the minority languages suffer from shift of language affiliation, presumably to one or another of the two national languages. Those which suffer most severely are Dutch, Ukrainian, Polish, Hungarian, Finnish, Danish, Swedish, and Norwegian, in that order. These include long-established languages in Canada, and an analysis of Table 4.27 reveals that the most recent languages in Canada are those that suffer least loss. This is similar to the situation in the United States where new immigrants, like those from Asia, suffer less in the short-term in assimilation than do immigrants from traditional European areas who are already strongly represented by assimilated former compatriots in the United States. The same differences in the distribution of the two languages accounts in part for the highly favorable status of English in the table of bilinguals (See Table 4.29).

TABLE 4.28. Numerical and Percentage Distribution of English, French, and Other Mother Tongues, 1961–71

Province or Territory		1961				1971			
		English	French	Other	Total	English	French	Other	Total
Newfoundland	No.	451,530	3,150	3,173	457,853	514,516	3,639	3,949	522,104
	%	98.6	0.7	0.7	100.0	98.5	0.7	0.8	100.0
Prince Edward Island	No.	95,564	7,958	1,107	104,629	103,102	7,363	1.176	111,641
	%	91.3	7.6	1.1	100.0	92.4	6.6	1.1	100.0
Nova Scotia	No.	680,233	39,568	17,206	737,007	733,556	39,333	16,071	788,960
	%	92.3	5.4	2.3	100.0	93.0	5.0	2.0	100.0
New Brunswick	No.	378,633	210,530	8,773	597,936	410,400	215,727	8,430	634,557
	%	63.3	35.2	1.5	100.0	64.7	34.0	1.3	100.0
Quebec	No.	697,402	4,269,689	292,120	5,259,211	789,185	4,867,250	371,329	6,027,764
	%	13.3	81.2	5.6	100.0	13.1	80.7	6.2	100.0
Ontario	No.	4,834,623	425,302	976,167	6,236,092	5,971,570	482,042	1,249,494	7,703,106
	%	77.5	6.8	15.7	100.0	77.5	6.3	16.2	100.0
Manitoba	No.	584,526	60,899	276,261	921,686	662,721	60,547	264,979	988,247
	%	63.4	6.6	30.0	100.0	67.1	6.1	26.8	100.0
Saskatchewan	No.	638,156	36,163	250,862	925,181	685,919	31,605	208,718	926,242
	%	69.0	3.9	27.1	100.0	74.1	3.4	22.5	100.0
Alberta	No.	962,319	42,276	327,349	1,331,944	1,263,935	46,498	317,441	1,627,874
	%	72.2	3.2	24.6	100.0	77.6	2.9	19.5	100.0
British Columbia	No.	1,318,498	26,179	284,405	1,629,082	1,087,253	38,034	339,334	2,184,621
	%	80.9	1.6	17.5	100.0	82.7	1.7	15.5	100.0
Yukon Territory	No.	10,869	443	3,316	14,628	15,346	450	2,592	18,388
	%	74.3	3.0	22.7	100.0	83.5	2.4	14.1	100.0
North West Territories	No.	8,181	994	13,823	22,998	16,306	1,162	17,339	34,807
	%	35.6	4.3	60.1	100.0	46.8	3.3	49.8	100.0
Canada	No.	10,660,534	5,123,562	2,454,562	18,238,247	12,973,809	5,793,650	2,800,852	21,568,311
	%	58.5	28.1	13.5	100.0	60.2	26.9	13.0	100.0

Source: Census of Canada, 1971. Series A 316-336.

TABLE 4.29. Numerical and Percentage Distribution of the Population Speaking One or Both of the Official Languages, 1961

Province or Territory	English Only		French Only		English and French		Neither English nor French	
	No.	%	No.	%	No.	%	No.	%
Newfoundland	450,945	98.5	522	0.1	5,299	1.2	232,447	0.2
Prince Edward Island	95,296	91.1	1,219	1.2	7,938	7.6	176	0.2
Nova Scotia	684,805	92.9	5,938	0.8	44,987	6.1	1,277	0.2
New Brunswick	370,922	62.0	112,054	18.7	113,495	19.0	1,465	0.2
Quebec	608,635	11.6	3,254,850	61.9	1,338,878	25.5	56,848	1.1
Ontario	5,548,766	89.0	95,236	1.5	493,270	7.9	98,820	1.6
Manitoba	825,955	89.6	7,954	0.9	68,368	7.4	19,409	2.1
Saskatchewan	865,821	93.6	3,853	0.4	42,074	4.5	13,433	1.5
Alberta	1,253,824	94.1	5,534	0.4	56,920	4.3	15,666	1.2
British Columbia	1,552,560	95.3	2,559	0.2	57,504	3.5	16,459	1.0
Yukon Territory	13,679	93.5	38	0.3	825	5.6	86	0.5
North West Territories	13,554	58.9	109	0.5	1,614	7.0	7,721	33.6
Canada	12,284,762	67.4	3,489,866	19.1	2,231,172	12.2	232,447	1.3

Source: Extracted from *Report of the Royal Commission on Bilingualism and Biculturalism* Book IV. Chapter V Language Transfer Patterns.

Part Three

Interpreting Theory

Five

Justifications of Bilingual Education: Rationales and Group Responses

RATIONALES: SOME DEFINITIONS AND FUNCTIONS

Much of the frustration teachers and students experience in their discussions of bilingual education may be attributed to their reluctance or failure to distinguish at least three levels on which any discussion of the subject occurs. To the primary level belongs the analysis of the characteristics and consequences of individual or societal bilingualism, for knowledge of which we have depended on contributions from linguistics, psychology, and social science. The second level will be discussed below, while to the third level belongs a consideration of the aims of bilingual education and the policies which should be pursued to realize them. Such policies range from an enthusiastic commitment and promotion of bilingualism to an equally firm resolve, as is the case in separatist ideologies, to eliminate the encroachment of bilingualism. Less extreme policies may set out to encourage bilingualism while ameliorating its disadvantages, or to compensate for its adverse consequences, or to accelerate its advantages.

Whatever policy is pursued tends to rely on objective knowledge of the characteristics and consequences of bilingualism rather than an interpretation of these factors. An important concern becomes an evaluation of the relative importance of the perceived advantages and disadvantages of bilingualism. Such decisions belong to the second level in which attitudes as well as rationales for languages and bilingual education are considered. A distinction is drawn between attitudes and rationales according to the degree to which an attempt is made to "state a case" for an attitude, or to formulate the attitude as a belief. Such beliefs are a form of hermeneutical understanding which is designed within a particular social and cultural tradition, and encourages the self-understanding of individuals and groups in their response to bilingualism and bilingual education. It helps to clarify the understanding of the various possible meanings of the concept *bilingual education.* The hermeneutical process is not concerned to state a belief in any objectively correct or idealized form of bilingual education (which is an illusion), but mainly to illuminate the range and relevance of its possibilities. In doing so the rationales help to promote a consensus, by establishing a group consisting of those who attribute a particular meaning to bilingual education, and for whom a particular form of bilingual education is the only one that is relevant, valid, or real.

We formulate and select rationales of bilingual education to conform to our personal or group interest in our present conditions. They are not abstract theories. Every rationale and every meaning attached to a rationale is a crystallization of the experience of a particular group. Evaluation and interpretation (what we refer to as rationales), or the modes in which we conceive the issues involved in the education of bilingual children, vary according to the history and current circumstances of those who formulate them. "Bilingualism is not a simple datum with either uniformly good or bad effects . . . as thinkers with a speculative method or approach have it" (Haugen, 1950). Furthermore, features favorably regarded in some communities may be considered unacceptable in others. Even in thoroughly bilingual communities, a knowledge of the two languages is not a necessary component of the good life. And when an individual does find it necessary to use a second language, no law of nature stipulates the degree of bilingualism required. Even in a thoroughly bilingual society, an individual to some extent chooses to be bilingual as well as the degree or quality of his bilingualism.

The most crucial discussions on bilingual education, then, are those occurring on the second level—the intermediate level of hermeneutic understanding, interpretation, and evaluation of our experience and our situation. This level provides the opportunity for a two-dimensional satisfaction, the first of which measures the comprehensiveness of the analysis of the primary data. The realism and range of the evidence made available for interpretation are vital in the final determination. The second dimension measures the intensity of the subjective response to bilingualism or the degree of commitment—affective and cognitive. Because of the element of subjectivity, rationales belonging to that category of propositions are not to be judged mainly for their truth or falsehood; rather, their primary function is to act as "lures for feeling" (Whitehead). That is, they appeal to or reflect the interest of an individual or group, and they do this within a framework of constraints imposed by the history and other characteristics of the community. Education does not mould men in the abstract but in and for a given society, and whatever the type of education provided in any country it has evolved in response—and remains in varying degrees responsive—to the interests of those who are in a position to make the provision as well as those for whom it is made. For example, methods and the criteria for selecting students for education differ, but the aim is always to serve the best interests of those responsible for the system. These interests are reflected in the rationales offered for the maintenance of the established system against innovative measures. Similarly, opposed interests are reflected in the rationales offered for the transformation, for instance, by the introduction of bilingual education.

Apart from their general character, rationales perform other functions. Bilingualism is an aspect of the culture of the group, but the responses of that group to bilingualism are seldom completely conscious or entirely explicit. Culture can never be wholly conscious nor can attempts to justify the promotion of any aspect of the culture be entirely explicit. For example, many of the important assumptions of the everyday life of a bilingual immigrant community are so deeply embedded as to make it difficult— and sometimes impossible—for them to explain their response to the kind of education offered their children. However, though they may not be able to formulate their own rationales concerning bilingualism and education, they are able to recognize a rationale that expresses their feelings. It is in this way that rationales "lure" into explicitness the latent feelings of a group. In doing so they act selectively, exaggerating some and disregarding other possible responses. Certain groups, especially those who are oppressed or form a permanent minority, are so committed to the overthrow or transformation of a given system of education that unwittingly they seize only on those elements in the interpretation and evaluation that tend to deny the legitimacy of the existing system.

To the extent that rationales are intended to lead to or guide programs of action, they partake of the nature of propaganda, and to some extent they are ideologies or proto-ideologies. In their capacity as forms of propaganda, they do not offer new knowledge about bilingualism or bilingual education. They are less concerned with cognition than with recognition; their aim is not to modify ideas (forms of orthodoxy) but to promote action (forms of orthopraxy). In this way rationales enable the group to see, sometimes even to create, an image of themselves: they use the latencies of the community. A rationale is a statement about the man himself, about his response to his own linguistic group and to other groups with which he is in contact. This is especially the case with immigrants or alienated minorities because rationales—like propaganda—are most effective where rootlessness is endemic. Like propaganda rationales may be based on scientific analyses (our primary level of discussion), but the use of the analysis is selective. Because of this selectivity, rationales limit rather than extend the channels of communication, a feature also common in propaganda. They tend to convince mainly those who are ready to be convinced, and they set up a system of rules whereby only selected forms of education for bilingual children are legitimized. From all this it must be conceded that rationales, like propaganda, are of the nature of a ritual act even though they assume the form of rational propositions. This is not surprising since the speech decisions made by bilinguals also have the same character; "for a man to speak in one language rather than another is a ritual act" (Haugen, 1958: 927). The elite among bilinguals tend to promote the "ritualizing of the symbols of traditional life . . . to withdraw traditional symbols from contact with impure influences, and on the other hand to attempt to impose traditional symbols on the impure world" of the out-groups (ibid: 933).

The ideological character of rationales arises because those who are deeply involved in formulating and proposing rationales for bilingual education see very selectively the situation of the linguistic, cultural, or ethnic groups. In certain situations ideological interpretations tend to obscure the real conditions of society. The world exists only with reference to the knowing mind, and the mental activity of the subject determines the form in which the world appears. This is characteristic of those who are most involved in bilingual education and bears a close relationship to the concepts advanced by Whorf (edited by J. B. Carroll) and the school of linguistic relativists, for whom the experience of phenomena is largely predetermined—either by language or the habit of mind which language reflects. In ideological thinking as well as in linguistic relativism, experience is inevitably distorted either by the perception of the individual subject or by the language of the individual. A further development of such ideological, relativist thinking is the claim that the determining factor is not so much the mind of the individual as that of the group—there is a transition from the unifying perception of the individual to that of the nationally differentiated *"folk* spirit."

Explaining why rationales for bilingual education have proliferated in recent years remains a problem. It cannot be due to the lack of previous interest in such a form of education because the history of this interest is almost coterminous with civilization itself. In looking for other explanations, we can identify three factors that may offer us some clues. First, problems of justification become general in an age when disagreement is more conspicuous than agreement. At present, there tends to be progressively less agreement about education within countries, and disagreements prevail or tend to prevail over consensus. However, not all those who are opposed to the consensus agree on the alternative, and consequently we have a proliferation of novel and alternative rationales. Second, a multiplicity of alternative proposals cannot be a problem in periods when social stability underlies and guarantees the consistency of a particular social philosophy. In nearly all the countries where bilingual education is a contentious issue, social life is fragmented. Bilingualism is often accused of being the cause of such segmentations, but in fact only in areas of long-standing social tension—as in Belgium or in Canada—do the problems posed by bilingualism become critical; and as a consequence of existing disputes there are attempts to offer alternative rationales for bilingual education. Third, multiplication of rationales characterizes a society where geographical mobility is accompanied by rapid movement between social strata, for it is in such societies that belief in the inviolability of accepted intellectual criteria is shattered. This is a characteristic of the United States. And finally, rationales are proliferated when intellectual activity is conducted less exclusively by a rigidly defined, self-perpetuating class and more by an unattached intellectual elite—Weber's *freischwebende Intelligenz*. All these considerations suggest that the proliferation of rationales for bilingual education, though not bilingual education itself, is the consequence of modernization.

Rationales for bilingual education make use of the evidence supplied by such disciplines as psychology, linguistics, and sociology, but in the last resort they reflect the attitudes of individuals or groups. They are essentially justifications for kinds of action directed toward predetermined ends, and they help to motivate those who accept them as the most valid reasons for undertaking or acquiescing to such action. Moreover rationales or their formulation are an expression of attitudes within a society and often involve a view of society that is ideological in its nature. Their formulation, therefore, is constrained by such factors as the vision of the end proposed by a system of education, the vision of the past of that community, and the popular view of the nature of bilingual education and its functions in relationship to a particular language and culture.

The proliferation of rationales for bilingual education is a characteristic of a fractured and unstable society. Their function, though, is to produce a period of hope for those who accept them, and they are heralded as forces contributing toward the creation of a better system of education. The constraints upon rationales for bilingual education are like the considerations referred to by A. N. Whitehead as "senseless agencies and formulated aspirations cooperating in the work of driving mankind from old anchorages" (Whitehead, 7).

Among the most important of these constraints, as John Rawls' (1973) book enables us to see, are the theories of social justice adhered to by a society or community interested in bilingual education. The foundation of any democratic society is the acceptance of such a theory of distributive justice, which sets the rules determining the fundamental rights of individuals and groups, the social and economic equalities and inequalities and the expectations founded on them. There are, of course, other fundamental social problems that affect justifications of bilingual education, including arranging the components of the social system in a comprehensible form, and ordering and maintaining a society's stability. But a large measure of agreement on conceptions of social justice is a prerequisite of a viable community whether it is linguistically homogeneous or not. We cannot understand bilingual education separate from the framework of a concept of social justice which such an education is meant to ensure. A system of education is meant to promote as far as possible the fair distribution of the "goods" which are produced within that society and these, in the United States, have been set out as "health, wealth, and the pursuit of happiness."

But concepts of social justice differ and that is one reason the form, structure, and justification of bilingual education will vary. Some multilingual societies argue that justice is done to the different groups when the benefit to society as a whole is maximized; accordingly, the advantages of the greatest number of the citizens outweighs whatever disadvantages may be experienced by minorities. This viewpoint has been termed the "utilitarian" concept (Rawls), and according to its language policy is justified by the extent to which the country as a whole becomes more efficient, stable, congenial, wealthier and stronger by recognizing or not recognizing minority groups and their languages. This is the concept which governs bilingual education policy, and language policy generally, in the Soviet Union.

The distribution of social roles among the different languages is determined not by whether the minority group and its associated language gains or suffers by such role distribution but by whether the Soviet Union as a whole (in effect the state) is a beneficiary. This view has almost always been held by colonizing and imperial powers. Sometimes the state gains by recognizing the different minorities, as was the case with the Persians who used a non-Iranian language throughout their vast empire while at the same time recognizing large numbers of ethnic languages locally. Sometimes the state believes it gains by ignoring the local languages, as was the case in the British Empire until almost the end of its supremacy and as has been the case in the United States until recently. The view cannot be dismissed out of hand, and its feasibility is at least arguable. There may be a time in the process of nation-building when it is more advantageous even to the minorities, immigrants and indigenous alike, that the claims of the state and the incipient nation should prevail. In such a case an unequal distribution of obligations and rights may be to everyone's advantage.

A variant of this "utilitarian" concept of justice regards all languages in a plurilingual society as candidates whose claims have to be weighed against each other. In this situation the goal is to achieve a balance that is the most just at a particular time and in respect of specified minorities. There is no single criterion for establishing a permanent balance of advantage. What this concept of justice as applied to languages envisages is a permanently shifting balance. Support for this or that language has to be continually adjusted according to educational, demographic, economic, or geographical criteria. This is basically the position in Switzerland, where language frontiers may be adjusted from time to time as in the case of Jura Canton. It is also the case in Belgium. According to the first principle of social justice and its variant, it is possible to justify providing full-scale bilingual education for all, or partial bilingual education for only one or two groups, or the refusal of any form of such education.

The second concept of social justice envisages a completely different set of possibilities. According to this concept, justice is what is inherently fair. All languages and all individual speakers have an innate claim to have their rights safeguarded in and for themselves alone. The loss or disregard of one language, diminishing its role or restricting its currency in society, is not made right by the fact that a larger number of people gain a greater advantage. The smallest and most insignificant language groups or individuals, like the largest and most powerful, have a right to exist and prosper irrespective of any calculation of profit and loss. This second principle of social justice between languages and between individuals speaking different languages has the advantage of being unequivocal. It has the disadvantage of being utopian, its realization fraught with difficulties. In spite of this difficulty, though, it exerts a powerful influence on linguists because it has a very close affinity to the relativist philosophy of Herder and Humboldt and to their notion that all languages are unique and therefore of equal value.

Other fundamental social considerations derive from these concepts. For instance, advocates of bilingual education agree that all language groups should be treated with equity, but they disagree on the question of whether such equality implies the right to press for the complete reorientation of the overall system of education as it exists or whether it simply implies the opportunity to profit equally from the existing system of education. The Soviet Union interprets the concept of equal opportunity in the latter and limited sense. In the United States, some ethnic groups or segments of some of them, especially those who are Spanish-speaking, adopt the former more radical proposition. However, other minorities, especially the descendants of older or more long-standing immigrant groups of European origin, like the Scandinavians and Germans or Dutch, adopt the more limited view.

Linguistic minorities in the free world, in seeking to realize the concept of equality in education, can follow one of three paths. First, they can seek to transform the total mainstream system so that all education is reciprocally bilingual. This is what has been achieved to a considerable extent in the Welsh system of British education. Second, the minorities can seek to advance within the existing system while modifying it at those points where it concerns them; this is being attempted in Scotland by speakers of Gaelic. This, it appears to some, is the course followed in the United States. The disadvantage of following this path is that it cannot hope to offer an integrated system of education within the country nor can it offer more than a series of bilingual programs as distinct from a system of bilingual education. Third, a minority or minorities can seek to set up a separate system or separate systems of bilingual education independently of each other and of the mainstream system and so create a segmented system of education. The Fleming-Walloon rift in Belgium and the French-English tension in Quebec and Canada are of this latter kind. It also appears to be the aim of some Amerindian groups in the United States. The justification of bilingual education so conceived would clearly relate to the political ideas of consociational democracy or segmented pluralism and would have reverberations far beyond the area of education. Obviously, none of these three alternatives is available in a totalitarian and authoritarian state like the Soviet Union where the system is uniform, albeit uniformly bilingual, in theory if not in actual fact.

Whatever view one takes of the justification of bilingual education, looked at from the point of view of social equality there are different ways of structuring that equality within the system of education, and different justifications of the different types of structures. For instance, equality may mean the complete integration of the system of bilingual education into the mainstream system thus ensuring that potentially the mainstream system becomes bilingual. This is the case in Wales where all types of school—elementary, secondary (Modern, Grammar or Comprehensive) and higher education—may be bilingual. In theory this is the case in the Soviet Union, also, although practice belies promise. On the other hand, bilingual programs may be structured in such a way that though the total system is pluralist, one element of the total complex is more prestigious than others; for instance, South Africa mandates different streams or tracks for different ethnic groups. In such a situation bilingual education is justified in the sense of ensuring separate development—linguistic apartheid. The fundamental importance—socially, politically, and linguistically—of such a policy for both majority and minority groups was revealed in the violence of the South African township of Soweto in 1976. A third method of resolving the problem of equality within the existing structure of education is to ensure "positive discrimination" in favor of groups who may have been disadvantaged historically. In America, this policy has been implemented spasmodically for Blacks, but it could very well be extended to include groups for whom a bilingual education as distinct from minority education is relevant. It is implemented in Wales where the schools in thoroughly Welsh-speaking areas—which have long-standing and acute problems of education because of the incidence of bilingualism and the disproportionate number of small rural schools—receive higher grants and have a favorable pupil-teacher ratio. For the same reasons, teachers are attracted to the heartlands of linguistic minorities in the Soviet Union by the offer of higher salaries. The structure of bilingual education that has been created accords with the concept of social justice approved by a particular society. One cannot understand the system of bilingual education, to say nothing of the curriculum structure and organization of a school, without first analyzing the conceptual justification.

The theories of social justice are to some extent abstract and general and do not go to the root of the justification of bilingual education. If we are to seek the ultimate justification we have to ask, "Who benefits?" By this we mean not so much which individual child so much as what level of the social structure—and specifically whether the system of education is governed by the needs of individuals or the wishes and aspirations of ethnic or national groups. Deseriev, writing from the Soviet Union, argues that "language policy should aim at the full development of human beings as well as the full development of each language community and region" (1974). The statement is meaningless. Nothing would be more satisfactory than the achievement of such a double aim, but that consummation is impossible. The *full* development of the one must involve some adjustment of the legitimate demands of the other.

The question to be asked is where the main thrust of the policy should be, whether toward the full development of the individual primarily or the full development of the group primarily. In practice it may so happen that a balance is struck that does not greatly harm individual or group aspirations. But unless there is a clear conceptual framework within which bilingual education is planned to achieve such an equalibrium, the result is apt to be unsatisfactory to both. In the Soviet Union the answer is simple and unequivocal—the education of the individual is subordinate to the demands and the needs of the group. The development of the individual is determined by the characteristics of his group. Deseriev implies that individual and group aspirations are not only compatible but synonymous; he imagines that the consequences of achieving the one are identical with the consequences of achieving the other. In fact, so far as concerns a democratic society, they may be irreconcilable.

This is not to say that the individual does not benefit from the advance of his group or that he does not contribute to that advance. But the fact that the two entities are in principle mutually supportive does not mean that they should not be considered separately in formulating policy. My group affiliation as a Welshman is not all that I am. I claim the right as an autonomous person to dissent from some of the goals the ethnic group may advocate; and even if I support the goals I claim the secondary right to dissent from the structural system which may be built to achieve those aims. The legitimate aims of the individual and the group to which he belongs may not necessarily coincide, and when it comes to the point of decision the autonomous person has the last word. Unquestionably, as John Stuart Mill argued in *On Liberty*, "the liberty of the individual must be thus far circumscribed that he must not make himself a nuisance to other people." Nevertheless the thrust of this approach to education and particularly bilingual education is best expressed in the words of Walt Whitman: "I swear nothing is good to me now save individuals."

Furthermore, whether or not individual and group aspirations are compatible or coincide in particular instances, the bases on which individuals and groups claim their right to decide the orientation of education differ. For the bilingual individual, certain rights (of which the right to determine the appropriate education he should receive is fundamental) are based on claims of natural justice. It is not circumscribed by any circumstance, and it is the foundation on which a democratic society is built. The justification on which a group claims the right to determine the orientation of a form of education is based on several considerations. It may be enshrined in a constitution or contract as it is in the Soviet Union, where the right to use and maintain the nationality languages is guaranteed by specific Articles of the Federal Constitution. The claim, on the other hand, may be based on political accommodations and adjustments worked out between nationalities and ethnic groups over a long period of time. Most agreements in a democratic society are arrived at in this manner, though sometimes only after a campaign of militant activism as was the case in Wales at the end of the last century, and even more so in Ireland. The claim to the use and maintenance of a minority language may be based on treaties made between conquered or incorporated minorities and the state, as was the case with some Amerindian tribes. But there is one thing in common to all these justifications for the use and maintenance of language—the claim is determined by and contingent upon some event having occurred in the past. The right in these cases is a convention rather than an inherent right or reflection of natural justice. Individuals may devolve to the group or the nation some of the innate rights they possess, usually to obtain greater security because a large group possesses greater political leverage than does the individual. But such a devolution of individual rights is an expedient, and the rights of the individual remain fundamentally inalienable.

Justifications claiming as the inherent right of any individual to have the opportunity to be educated to the limits of his capacity, or those that arise necessarily from theories of fundamental social justice applicable to all speech communities, may be regarded as universal justifications of bilingual education and are applicable to all minority groups at all times. There are secondary justifications, however, that change with the nature or the development of society, particularly economic development and modernization. The justifications change, becoming more comprehensive as the particular society advances. Just as bilingualism itself, as a linguistic phenomenon, is an aspect of social change, so too do the justifications of bilingual education as an institutional phenomenon reflect the nature of the change that is occurring or has already occurred. With changes in the level of modernization go shifts in the importance attached to particular scientific disciplines as well as development of new disciplines. To some extent, therefore, one may attribute changes in types of rationale to changes in the importance of the disciplines used to investigate bilingualism or to the emergence of new disciplines, forged in some instances for the purpose. The first discipline associated with the earliest attempt to explain bilingualism was metaphysics—theology or myth expressed in the belief in the Tower of Babel and the pathology with which bilingualism was associated. Vestiges of such theological preconceptions may be thought by some to be embedded in the theories of B. L. Whorf (1956), even though he attempted to validate the hypothetical concepts by empirical investigation using the discipline of linguistics. Many of the rationales based on the uniqueness and the inviolability of the native language, though, owe something to the survival of mystical and metaphysical approaches.

Such mythological and metaphysical explanations and justifications gave way to the more empirical efforts of the Sophists brought up in a multilingual world dominated by the interaction of Greek, Latin, and eastern Mediterranean languages. These efforts were directed to removing the study of languages from the realm of speculation. Inquiry into languages continued in Hellenistic times in the work of Quintillian who had pertinent things to say about the interaction of Greek and Latin during the early years of a Roman child. This same interest in language persisted in the Middle Ages in the remarks of St. Augustine on what might be regarded as an early instance of an "immersion" program whereby the child was educated in his second language. But it is not until the twentieth century and the change from philology to linguistics and the gradual introduction of strictly mathematical concepts in analyzing language contact that the explanation of bilingualism, and therefore the bases for its justification, become strictly scientific. This stage is characterized by studies of substratum, borrowing, phonological and other forms of "interference" and language change. Cassirer argues (Cassirer, *III*) that following the refinement of the quantitative approach a "new force begins to emerge. Biological thought takes precedence" and the psychological study of man claims attention. This development is characterized by an interest in the general laws governing learning. Particularly important for bilingualism was attention to language learning together with an appraisal of the consequences of the simultaneous acquisition of more than one language for cognitive development, the maturation of personality, and emotional stability. This phase builds on the earlier mathematical phase, and the instruments developed included intelligence tests, scales of linguistic background, word counts, and so on. These developments determine the direction of research and provide the framework within which bilingual education is justified. As these approaches fulfill their promise, new approaches are designed using other disciplines. During the last three decades we have witnessed a shift of disciplines in the study of bilingual education from psychology to social psychology, anthropology, and sociology. Each discipline contributes to a new formula for justifying bilingual education and explaining bilingualism.

It would be erroneous, however, to claim that changes in types of justifications occur because new disciplines become available. The disciplinary shift itself reflects and reinforces something more fundamental, namely a change in the structure and nature of society and therefore a redefinition of aspects of society that need explaining or justifying. The societal changes to which we refer can be regarded as aspects of the modernization of society, and we shall discuss changes in types of justification within the framework of modernization theory. The link between bilingualism and modernization is inevitable because the issues of bilingual education as we know it arise only when a society is in the process of modernization from its hitherto traditional status. Bilingualism itself as a linguistic phenomenon may be widespread and may have been so for millennia, but it is only when a society undergoes social, political, economic, and demographic shifts that bilingualism needs to be institutionalized within the system of government and therefore within educational institutions, whether these are for the elite or for the masses.

Such social changes describe the consensus that is necessary to scientific or pedagogic advance. During stable periods a paradigm or pattern of thinking is established "and the successive transitions from one paradigm to another via revolution is the usual developmental pattern of natural sciences" (Kuhn, 12). A crisis such as occurred during the Renaissance or the Industrial Revolution is a necessary precondition of the emergence of a new paradigm. The new conceptual model results from the accumulation of new data which loosens the former stereotypes, and it changes not only the meaning of established and familiar concepts but it offers a new interpretation of established facts and often necessitates a redefinition of the corresponding science (Kuhn, 102). This is what we refer to as a paradigm shift in bilingual education, for on at least four occasions the concept of that education has been redefined. So far as bilingualism and bilingual education are concerned, new paradigms and shifts from a "linguistic" through a succession of paradigms—cultural assimilation, psychological, and so forth—such as we describe in this chapter have led educationists to adopt new instruments with which to investigate the incidence of the phenomenon and to measure its extent in any individual case. These instruments have revealed new aspects of bilingualism and not least new aspects of the development of bilingual children and groups. The development of *institutionalized* bilingualism (within educational institutions) as distinct from *fortuitous* bilingualism (that which results entirely from force of circumstance, such as geographical contiguity) involves a paradigm shift, and the crisis of modernization is what makes such a shift necessary and inevitable. But it will be seen from the simplest reference to aspects of modernization that it affected the masses and the elites very differently. For the former it meant not merely participation in the political process, which necessitated literacy, but in those areas where modernization was most traumatically effective it involved a level of social degradation and very often of squalor which is difficult to conceive. For the elite modernization meant a consolidation of existing political power, additional economic advantage, and the opportunity to determine the direction to which the system of education inclined.

The process of modernization has been described and analyzed from several standpoints. Pye and Rostow emphasize modernization as the establishment of national identity; for Silvert it is the rationalization and secularization of authority; Deutsch regards modernization as a process of mobilization as well as of the differentiation of social roles with a high degree of specialization in the functions of institutions and individuals. For Almond and Verba modernization means the development of mass participation and the emergence of political awareness and capacity among those masses. This is also the view of Eisenstadt. For Rokkan and Bendix, modernization is synonoymous with the formation of a center and a governing elite. All these investigators identify different aspects of the same process, but modernization proceeds at various tempos and has distinct phases. Lerner has adopted a four stage model in considering modernization in the Middle East and Turkey. First urbanization, then in turn the development of literacy, the spread of mass media, and finally increased political participation. This has been admitted to be a highly simplified model, but it does serve to provide a frame within which we can analyze some of the problems occurring at particular points of the process.

The articulation of successive stages is important from the standpoint of bilingual education because each stage makes different demands on the development of language policy. As society moves from one stage to the next, a paradigmatic shift takes place in the rationales proposed. We have already described the first stage of modernization in three countries—the Soviet Union, Britain, and the United States. This is the stage of territorial consolidation or control over minorities and linguistic groups. In each case the result was the same: first the importation of a new language or languages—English in Wales, English and other colonial languages in the United States, and Russian in the USSR. Such territorial consolidation was a prerequisite of modernization, and the character of that consolidation, involving the interaction of several language groups, determines the character of the linguistic community. The resulting heterogeneity made inevitable the ultimate demand for a bilingual system of education.

The second stage of modernization in Britain was the revolution of sensibility that accompanied technological and scientific change. The revolution in sensibility was due in large part to the vast extension of knowledge as well as a change in attitude to the kind of knowledge that was considered relevant: it was knowledge that reflected and was produced by revolutionary technologies; it was abstract in nature and expression, scientific and to a very considerable degree discontinuous with everyday or normal experience, best exemplified by mathematics and physics. This second phase of modernization corresponds to the shift from the discipline of metaphysics to mathematics and other quantifying sciences. The United States replicated this stage of modernization.

The massive accumulation of knowledge, its discontinuity from everyday experience, and its insistence on the ability to handle new techniques made the traditional institutions of education—the home and the church—outmoded. Theology, the characteristic discipline of the church, was being replaced by new disciplines, and the family could no longer cope with the demands the new knowledge made upon it. Education had to be formalized anew in an old institution—the public school. In the heterogeneous areas of Britain, the territorial control exercised from an external center by an alien elite meant that education was carried out through the use of English, a foreign language to the minorities. A similar process occurred in the Russian Empire and continues to be the case in the Soviet Empire. Nevertheless, other factors existed and necessitated the use of the mother tongue, thus justifying the creation of at least an incipient system of bilingual education. Experience reinforced the early realization that the lingua franca could not guarantee literacy. The fundamental democratization of social consciousness gave a new prestige to the vernacular independent of its usefulness in initiating literacy. The Protestant Reformation, especially in Wales, emphasized the need for vernacular literacy because it was regarded as the only means of ensuring salvation. But it was equally well established that vernacular literacy (valuable though it might be) was in the last resort preparation for literacy in the major language—English. All these considerations justified bilingual education, but the vernacular entered into the scheme of things simply in order to facilitate the better understanding and later use of the lingua franca.

This transitional type of bilingual education was reinforced by the new sensibility modernization produced. Rationality replaced sentimental attachment to or continuity with tradition; efficiency and utility were the main criteria of relevance. The other aims of accumulating knowledge, contrary to the philosophy of the past, came to be the promotion of change. Francis Bacon maintained that "to generate change and superinduce a new nature or natures on a given body is the labour and aim of human powers"

(Novum Organum Aphorisms, Book 2:1). Along with the rationalistic and utilitarian approach to language usage, two other aspects of the modernizing spirit assumed significance—scientific skepticism and the demystification of sanctified institutions, of which the native language, like religion itself, was among the most prominent. Scientific skepticism and a more rational and pragmatic attitude toward the nature and function of the native language amounted to a reluctance to adopt Humboltian Romantic and metaphysical views of the nature of language. With the new spirit went a distrust of the intangible. Legitimacy was transferred from traditional and humanistic values to these new scientific guidelines. This philosophic realignment promoted the lingua franca as the basis of education of minorities because it was seen to represent the new spirit, which the peripheral languages and vernaculars did not.

The consolidation of control of territory and the concomitant evolution of a centralized bureacracy (alien to the minorities) constitute the first stage of modernization; the revolution in sensibility arising from technological revolutionary developments is the hallmark of the second stage. The most salient aspect of the next stage is industrialization and with it urban growth. These two aspects highlighted the need for literacy; this was most easily achieved initially in the vernacular, and industrialization gave a new status to the latter. Literacy is the justification of bilingual education in the third stage, and this literacy—albeit as a step towards a command of the lingua franca—involves both the lingua franca and the native language. Formal, popular education is the result of industrialization, representing an attempt to satisfy the need for a minimally literate and numerate work force so that industrial progress is facilitated and public order is maintained during rapid urbanization. In Wales, which became a major center of the industrial revolution, the need to use the non-English vernacular was recognized quite early. It was seized upon to promote a religious revival with a knowledge of the Bible as its foundation, but it also was a means of promoting the modernization of Britain. It was observed that "a country which did not permit the use of the vernacular is liable to suffer from evil conditions . . . whereby the majority of our countrymen are ignorant of the very language of the laws they are meant to obey. . . . Punishment and rewards are alike esoteric and consequently alike uninfluential upon those who must require their help" (Tremenheere, 1840). To be literate to the point where they could be a usable work force and be able to understand the laws which governed their social mobilization, the masses had to be taught their mother tongue as well as English. At this stage of modernization, therefore, bilingual education was synonymous with the acquisition of English as a second language in addition to the mother tongue, and the problem was to arrange the curriculum in such a way as to give precedence to English without losing the advantages which accrued from the mother tongue. This is the main thrust in the

Soviet Union at the present time, as it was thirty years ago and still is to some extent in the United States with Teaching English to Speakers of Other Languages (TESOL) programs. The governing paradigm of bilingual education as this stage of national development was linguistic.

Industrialization created more problems than could be dealt with simply by fostering the spread of literacy. It meant the dislocation of populations from their safe environments and the creation of a rootless proletariat. Disturbances occurred in the new steel and mining townships of South Wales, and these pointed to the importance of education in socializing and assimilating immigrant masses belonging to different social and language groups. Kay-Shuttleworth, one of the pioneers of public education, in a memorandum to the Privy Council in 1849 maintained that a "small band of teachers would be more effective in containing the disruptions than a regiment of soldiery" (Committee on Education of the Privy Council). In his novel *Sybil*, Disraeli, who as prime minister enacted a compulsory public school law in 1870, saw the issue as the creation of "one nation" where there were at that time "two . . . between whom there is no intercourse and no sympathy, who are ignorant of each others' feelings, thoughts and habits as if they were dwellers in different zones or inhabitants of different planets, formed by different breeding . . . ordered by different manners and governed by different laws." He was referring to divisions between the rich and poor in Britain generally, but to a considerable extent this division coincided in Wales at that time with differences between more or less identifiable ethnic groups. At this stage of modernization, bilingual education is intended for linguistic and cultural assimilation. In Britain, where the curriculum of the schools was determined by the School Codes formulated centrally by the Board of Education, cultural assimilation was promoted by the obligatory study of selected materials, uniform for the whole country and for all ethnic groups. The same purpose of ensuring a trained labor force motivated the Massachusetts Board of Education in the United States in the mid-nineteenth century.

Another aspect of modernization, reflected in the next phase and made necessary by the growth of technology and industrialization, is the differentiation of the roles of institutions and individuals in the complex society. In traditional societies, a single institution like the family or the church has to carry many social responsibilities. With modernization and increased social complexity, such undifferentiated role appropriation could not be maintained, social roles were separated and designated as the responsibility of specialist agencies, increasingly under the control of a central government. Differentiation and specialization of roles become the marks of this stage of modernization and of the third phase of bilingual education. In Britain, a paradigmatic shift occurred from emphasis on the three R's (Reading, Writing, and Arithmetic), which gave entirely objective criteria, to the three A's (Age, Ability, and Aptitude), which signify a shift toward a recognition of individual differences requiring differentiated education. It was a shift with which the name of John Dewey was associated. The paradigm governing bilingual education was no longer linguistic or cultural, but psychological. Bilingual education was judged by its success or failure in neutralizing alleged psychological handicaps of bilingualism, and it was expected that the possession of two languages promoted a richer and more rounded person.

The phases we have described have been preparatory to the phase at which modernized countries like Britain, the USSR, and the United States are at present—mass participation in the social and political domain. The achievement of this goal depends on the satisfaction of the earlier goals: literacy and some degree of consensus about social values (involving assimilation). In linguistically homogeneous countries, such participation involves the leveling of class differences; in heterogeneous countries, such a class leveling is almost inevitably synonymous with reducing ethnic differences and raising ethnic political consciousness. The political participation of different ethnic groups enables them to express their views on the education they should receive. Bilingual education, then, is a platform for promoting widespread political participation. The paradigm has shifted from the psychological to the political. The rationale is no longer simply linguistic, or simply cultural, or simply psychological, but all these as preconditions of the emergence of a new rationale associated with the concept of political pluralism. At this point in modernization, bilingual education is seen as quite explicitly concerned with the redistribution of political power.

CATEGORIES OF RATIONALES

Introduction

We have attempted to explain the importance and functions of rationales in promoting bilingual education, the circumstances influencing the formulation of such rationales, and particularly the relationship between modernization and bilingualism. In doing this we have also indicated how rationales reflect the conditions of social development and, therefore, are apt to change with changes in those conditions. Four main rationales have been identified—literacy, cultural assimilation, psychological differentiation, and political participation. The remainder of this chapter will deal with two types of rationales—the cultural and political. At the same time it needs to be emphasized that the cultural rationale with which we are concerned in this section is not necessarily that which motivated bilingual education in the phase intermediate between the phase of minimum literacy and the phase of psychological differentiation. That earlier phase was governed by considerations of cultural *assimilation*, and what we are now concerned with are the cultural rationales governed by cultural *pluralism*. These are, in the view of some, a preparation for political pluralism. With each shift of the paradigm which characterizes a phase of bilingualism, we discover a new component as well as a redefinition of earlier components. The minimum literacy of the early phase is not the kind of literacy we demand in later phases, nor are the cultural considerations of the earlier phase the cultural considerations which enter into the paradigm of cultural *pluralism*.

Analysis of the Literature

In the literature on bilingual education, the cultural and ethnic rationales formulated are varied and contradictory, but generally speaking they make the following propositions. First, bilingual education helps to establish or re-establish ethnic identity, sometimes referred to as developing an appropriate self-image among minority groups. Haugen points out the desire of the folk elite in Norway—during the controversies regarding the choice of language—for a bulwark against "indiscriminate acceptance of mass culture" (Haugen, 1966a: 286). The cultivation of New Norwegian grows from the need "to preserve among us anything that . . . has native distinctiveness" (Haugen, 1966a: 286). A similar opinion emerged from various reports published between 1956 and 1970 in Malaya that emphasized the importance of bilingual education as a "major component in the building of Malaysian national consciousness." Those who have observed the process in Malaya find it "abundantly clear that ethnicity is at the heart of the meaning of education" in that country (Nash, 6–7).

In other cases the defenses of bilingual education are centered on the individuals rather than the group itself, stressing the need to regard the system of education as a means of enabling the student to adjust to his complex social and cultural environment. Coser, following Georg Simmel, maintains that the conflict, which is inevitable in situations where languages and cultures interact, "is a form of socialization" (Coser, 28); the conflict of values often revealed in such situations helps in the establishment of group identity and to maintain the satisfactory functioning of groups. "Only where there is conflict is behavior conscious and only there are the conditions for rational conduct present" (Coser, 20). Consciousness of ethnic identity enables one to adjust rationally to complex and often potentially divisive situations. Such a view of "ethnic identification" is not shared by other commentators. For instance, in the 1969 Cannes conference on "Aspects of National and Ethnic Loyalty" (Taijfel, 1970), it was claimed that education stressing ethnic awareness, "as an organizing concept in structuring experience of the world makes it difficult to conceive of alternative systems of organization which may be equally valid and more valuable in determing the child's attitude towards a variety of human groups" (ibid., 135). This suggests that education channeled toward ethnic identity facilitates ethnocentrism.

Other ethnocultural rationales refer to the inherent values and traditions which are candidates for maintenance. These are often assumed to be synonymous with the concept of the "ethnic group," and religion and language are included more frequently than most other aspects. However, it is not so much the content of traditions that is of general interest, but their functions. Content can vary from group to group while the functions of traditions remain the same. In an era of radical discontinuities in almost all aspects of social life, and when such discontinuities are not simply experienced but sought with increasing persistence, there is a value in continuity. More and more, individuals are coming to appreciate this, especially members of ethnic groups moving out of a traditional way of life. Tradition and the maintenance of tradition can, in such circumstances, be inherently valuable. Furthermore, as Max Weber insisted, tradition is an important source of authority, and in a rapidly changing world it often appears eminently desirable to those involved in such change. Not only is tradition a form of authority, but the nature of the tradition—the content or the pattern of the culture that is communicated to succeeding generations—is the criterion of legitimacy. Tradition is the authority for behaving in certain ways, and the legitimate behaviors are those tradition offers. Finally, tradition is an available consensus. Agreement among people is necessary for the minimum of comfort and convenience; agreement freely arrived at is normally open to be modified, but to do so it is always useful to have a consensus from which to inaugurate whatever modifications may be necessary. Of course, all those functions are perfomed by tradition in monolingual, homegeneous societies. But traditions are far more important in complex societies where languages and cultures interact and conflict, and where, because of the changes brought about by such interactions, some means of guiding and possibly controlling the rate of change may be necessary. Bilingual education by emphasizing tradition offers this advantage.

The Relationship of Language and Culture as Well as Ethnicity

WEAK AND STRONG ARGUMENTS

Ethnic and cultural arguments for the development of bilingual education are typically based on one of the following propositions. First, however we define it, biculturalism offers some advantages in the system of education, and a knowledge of the two associated languages in certain circumstances may be a means of acquiring those advantages. This is the "weak" argument for bilingual and bicultural education. The second, "strong" argument stipulates a *necessary* relationship between language and its associated culture. The advantages of a bicultural education, it is argued, can be realized only if one becomes bilingual, and there is no way of becoming bilingual unless one is also bicultural. This argument is incontrovertible if, as some linguists believe, words always involve much more than language alone can convey. In their view, the mere fact of employing a word may establish or destroy important and formidable participations even on a mystical level. All our experience is so connected with words that it is impossible to distinguish between what is derived from words and what is not. This conception of how language and our social awareness, or culture, are inextricably intertwined was stated by C. W. von Humbolt, who insisted that "language is the very organ of a people's being" (1903–60: 56). The theme was taken up by Sapir for whom language "does not stand apart from and run parallel to direct experience but completely interpenetrates with it. For the normal person every experience real or potential is saturated with verbalism" (Mandelbaum, ed., 1957). He suspected that "there is little in the functional side of conscious behavior in which language does not play the most important part" (Sapir, 1921: 130). According to this view, there is no pure experience of phenomena, and our social or cultural experience is built on an unacknowledged foundation of presuppositions assimilated with our mother tongue and its associated culture. So much is this the case that it is impossible to understand a language without also understanding and indeed living the associated culture. Evans-Pritchard (1937), for instance, in stressing that the language mirrors "the situational imperatives of society," describes how an argument concerning the power of their oracle which, when expressed in Zande appears as a complete vindication of their earlier system of beliefs, becomes instead a demonstration of the futility of Zande claims when translated into an alien language. This is one of the bases for the argument that bilingualism and biculturalism entail each other.

SUPPORT OF THE "WEAK ARGUMENT"

According to the first, weak proposition, biculturalism may benefit from but need not entail bilingualism; the second argument posits a reciprocal entailment. The first argument is supported by three secondary propositions. First, culture is not a uniform phenomenon: several levels of culture exist, and language is not equally involved in a knowledge or appreciation of all of them. A culture consists first of a range of artifacts that are marked by the style of a particular ethnic group. These artifacts may lie anywhere within a range of objects from tools, weapons, and household utensils such as pots and pans to those things that are part of religious ceremonial, and even the buildings in which the ceremonies are performed. The cultural component of a bicultural education may be confined to this level; though a knowledge of the language may be an advantage, some would maintain that it is not a *necessary* basis for an appreciation of them. Second, different groups are identified by behavioral characteristics. Greeting customs and modes of expressing sorrow or mourning, for instance, differ profoundly across cultures. In any program of bicultural education, a knowledge of them would be instilled, although it does not appear to some ethnologists that a knowledge of the language, especially at school level, is required to ensure adequate acquaintance with them. There are, thirdly, higher levels of symbolic behavior which it is agreed cannot be handled without some use of the associated language. Clearly the oral traditions of the group belong to this level of culture. A fourth level is that on which the institutional forms or activities of the group may be placed. These would include kinship systems and especially the religious and organizational aspects of the life of the group. Those who admit only a limited or restricted concept of the relationship of language to culture base part of their argument on just such an analysis. The extent to which bilingual and bicultural education takes account of the culture of a group and the extent to which the learning of a language may be thought necessary to the program will depend on the culture level with which it is proposed to acquaint the student. No hard and fast rule can be laid down about the language-culture relationship, and therefore no fixed definition of a bicultural program can be proposed.

Furthermore, even if the content of the bilingual education includes those aspects of culture which are placed on the third and fourth levels which we have distinguished, the degree of awareness or knowledge of them may vary. It is even possible that it will not require a knowledge of the language. The corpus of oral traditions may be explained in and may be translated into another language, and it is not unusual even in higher education in the United States to adopt this practice. Part of the aim of the bicultural program may be simply to instill some acquaintance with the cultural differences of the interacting groups, and an acquaintance with the language may not be necessary for this purpose. One can maintain that a knowledge of the language is necessary in a bicultural program only if acculturation is a goal. But even the extent of possible acculturation may be so limited that the involvement of language (in the stages of primary and secondary education) may be limited also.

The process of acculturation for a young child or even an adolescent can involve acquiring not two cultures but a contact or marginal culture for which it may be claimed only one language may be necessary. Usually the concept of marginality refers to individuals in the process of changing their cultural affiliation or are uncertain of it. It refers to a situation in which "a person is not a full member of a well organized and supportive group, and more precisely that he is on the margin of the social spaces of the groups involved. It is usually associated with social isolation and cultural estrangement and under certain circumstances self-estrangement and loss of personal identity" (Hopper, 25). Many bilinguals and monolinguals, however, find themselves in a situation where from birth they are acculturated to the results of interacting cultures. They share this bicultural conditioning with members of both groups. For instance, Welsh or Irish together with English may sometimes produce a literature of acknowledged merit, even of greatness which reflects this bicultural conditioning—the Anglo-Welsh of Dylan Thomas and others, the Anglo-Irish of William Butler Yeats and others, or the Francophone or Anglophone literature of Africa. Nor is this bicultural inheritance something which appears overnight. The history of Anglo-Welsh literature extends as far back as the seventeenth century. The existence of this literature, produced by what would be regarded as "marginal men," suggests that the contact or marginal culture fulfills the same functions as either or both the separate cultures elsewhere. A knowledge of the Welsh language was not in the possession and therefore not necessary to Dylan Thomas, nor was W. B. Yeats conversant with the Irish language. These are some of the considerations which have weighed with those who, interested though they are in both a bilingual and bicultural education, do not see a necessary relationship between them. They regard bilingual education as something separate from a bicultural education—neither of necessity entails the other. This appears to have been the basis of the policy of the Canadian prime minister, Pierre Trudeau, who "envisaged multiculturalism within a bilingual framework"—the diversity of cultures need not entail the encouragement of a similar diversity of languages (Porter, 284).

CRITICISM OF THE "STRONG ARGUMENT"

Those who adopt the set of propositions concerning the necessary relationship between language and culture face conflicting empirical evidence. In the first place, diversities of cultures may coexist with a single language. Many and significant differences exist between Anglo-American, Canadian, Australian, and other English-speaking cultures which are nevertheless expressible within a range of mutually intelligible variants of the English language. Conversely, homogeneity of culture may be associated with linguistic diversity. For instance, F. Salisbury (1962, 1) writes of the Siane group of "New Guinea as a congeries of culturally similar tribes. . . . The same general culture with local variations continues both east and west with no sharp discontinuities. . . . But the cultural and interactional homogeneity contrasts with the linguistic diversity."

A second consideration is that consciousness of cultural distinctiveness may not be correlated with increased interest in or the use of the associated language. Language is but one of the components of a culture and but one of the ways in which it may be symbolized. The decline in the number of

Welsh speakers is concurrent with the growth in the comprehensiveness as well as the intensity of interest in things Welsh among Welshmen who would not be able or wish to claim the language. Their undoubted Welshness may be expressed in a belief in the uniqueness of their musical talent, or it may be tied to an almost obsessive interest in Rugby football. Other ethnic groups symbolize their distinctiveness in various ways, the French in types of food and drink, for instance.

Third, a historical culture expressed for many centuries in and associated apparently indissolubly with a particular language may become independent of it. The appreciation of the Classical Hellenistic culture no longer necessitates understanding Greek and Latin. The Judeo-Christian culture, even among members of the Catholic Church which for over a millennium associated itself with Latin, is independent of any particular language. Indeed, its proselytization is seen to be feasible only on the basis of such a disassociation. Furthermore, there are *nonhistorical* cultures which, though they may begin by being associated with particular languages, have grown to be independent of them. The scientific-technological culture is unlike ethnic or national cultures in any of their forms and has set out deliberately to ensure as much discontinuity as possible between it and them. This scientific and technological culture is generally identified with the Western world, "but is in fact a uniform, cosmopolitan culture that can be found in any part of the world" (Benedict, 164). It is the consequence of new or the reinterpretation of old knowledge and is highly elitist. It is international because its content is equally relevant to all societies, because its operation is governed by an international network of elites, and because it has created for its own purposes institutions which though highly centralized have an international mandate. The culture is equidistant from all national cultures and is equally independent of the languages associated with those cultures. The fact that English, French, Russian, or German are the languages associated with the dissemination of the culture does not derive from the relationship of language to culture, but in each case this is a consequence of imperial power.

Ethnic Cultures and Ethnic Languages

THE INDICATORS OF ETHNICITY

This general discussion of the relationship between language and culture may prompt some educators to argue—and quite correctly—that when we discuss bilingual and bicultural education what is currently relevant is the relationship of *ethnic* cultures. Of particular interest are the ethnic cultures of minorities within a culturally and linguistically diverse society, as is found in the United States, the Soviet Union, various areas of Asia and the Pacific, of Africa and Europe. One part of the "ethnic argument" appears to be as follows: the ethnic culture is a necessary, definitive characteristic of the ethnic group. This culture is an abstraction from the ethnic group's interactive processes and may be regarded therefore as synonymous with the existence of the group. Their maintenance is interdependent. Second, the ethnic language is the necessary and definitive expression of the ethnic culture. The language is not just a component of the culture or just one means of symbolizing it, it is an indispensable element of that culture. If we are to establish a working foundation for a bicultural education, these two propositions merit some attention.

At this point we are not interested in differentiating ethnicity from such concepts as tribe or nation, but simply to ascertain what is required to constitute an ethnic group whether or not some of the characteristics may also be required in constituting other types of groups. The Soviet approach is summed up by Kozlov's definition: "The basic characteristics of an ethnic community are ethnic self-consciousness and a common name for themselves (self-naming), a common language, territory, peculiarities of psychological traits, way of life, and a definite form of social and territorial organization (or an aspiration to create such an organization)" (Kozlov, 1967). Biological origin, akin to racial distinctiveness, has been claimed as a constituent of ethnicity but it finds favor no longer among those who are concerned with education. However, a shared historical experience reaching back very often to a mythical common origin is still regarded as a salient feature. Among the most important bases for a shared historical experience, and a characteristic which plays an important part in ethnic consciousness, is "territory." For many, territory is important for mainly pragmatic reasons. Freeman (Bell and Freeman, 179) attaches importance to it because it ensures some degree of "locality, allows of social functions (such as production, consumption, socialization, social control) and cohesiveness, being shared by the community." This appears to be the stance taken by Francis: "The attribution of territory to ethnic groups in actually only a corollary to local affinity and size" (396). It is to be expected that the Soviet ethnologists should take the same view. Considerable truth exists in such statements, but locality or territory—though originating as a pragmatic factor—may be ideologized. For the Hopis and Yaquis, the "sacred land" concept is fundamental in their identity systems. Spicer sees these land-based identity systems, supernaturally sanctioned, as basic to certain types of ethnic identity (Spicer, 1972: 35, 41). If this is the case, it would certainly be a vital distinction between types of ethnic groups in the United States: on the one hand are the indigenous and fairly permanently located; on the other hand are the immigrant and diffused. This distinction has important implications for the acceptance of their ethnic arguments in favor of bilingual and bicultural education.

The indicators most frequently stressed, however, are those which may be classified under the rubric of "folk ways"—mores, attitudes, and styles of living. Kinship, religion, tribal or ethnic self-consciousness, and language enter this list of ethnic indicators. But more important than the list itself is the dichotomy implicit within it. On the one hand are the *objective* attributes of territorial identification: common history, language, and common economic organization. On the other hand are the *subjective* attributes: psychological identity, willingness to assert that identity in relation to other identities, and consciousness or perception of "belonging" (Michelena, 1974:239). Some conceive of the subjective attributes as defining ethnicity: "an ethnic group consists of those who conceive of themselves as being alike" (Shibutani and Kwan, 47). Similarly, in considering the ethnic conflict in the Swiss Jura, one observer quotes an inhabitant to the effect that "it is not because we happen to speak French but because we are not Bernese and can never be Bernese that we want to be separate from Berne" (Keech, 400). The observer himself assesses the situation as revealing that the actual differences in conditions regarding ethnic values, including the relevance of language are "clearly less important than the perceptions of those conditions" (ibid., 398). Perhaps Kuper is the most forthright in his evaluation of the significance of the subjective substance of ethnic difference: "There is flexibility in the relationship between the ideological emphasis on cultural difference and the actual extent of cultural difference. Ideologies may understate cultural difference when it is considerable or emphasize cultural difference when it is negligible" (Kuper, 1974: 17), and he points to the symbolic significance of language in the scheme of such exaggerations or underestimations.

There is a further dichotomy that is important when considering the need for a bicultural component of bilingual education. Some of the ethnic indicators may be core characteristics while others are secondary. Steward (1963: 37) regards the core characteristics as being those which reflect the "subsistence activities and economic arrangements," and the core includes social, political, and religious patterns closely connected with those arrangements. Innumerable other features may have great potential variability because they are less strongly tied to the core. These latter, secondary features are determined to a greater extent by purely cultural-historical factors; he includes language among them. The secondary features are part of the superstructure of ethnicity and their significance may change. Furthermore the secondary feature that carries the task of symbolizing ethnicity may not be the same in all ethnic groups: "Recent disputes in Western Europe have been based on differences in both race (England or France) and language (Belgium or Norway), but also in religion (Netherlands and Northern Ireland), nationality (Switzerland), and region (Germany)" (Peterson, W., 1975: 179).

UNRELIABILITY OF THE INDICATORS

In view of the differences between types of ethnic indicators or characteristics, it is not surprising that they do not invariably and unambiguously serve to distinguish between ethnic groups. One cannot be sure that the possession of this or that characteristic identifies one as belonging to this rather than that ethnic group. Two or more distinct ethnic groups may share common characteristics, such as language, descent, and religion. On the other hand, many ethnic groups are obviously not at all homogeneous as to their descent or religion (Francis, 397). If we disregard the total concept of "ethnic group" and consider only one of the characteristics of such groups, culture, it is difficult to discover what an *ethnic culture* may imply. There are undoubtedly types of ethnic cultures that are primordial or pristine. As concerns the Transcaucasian ethnic groups, to say nothing of the more isolated and smaller Peoples of the North, the success of attempts to modernize them, to popularize Slav or Western Soviet cultures among them is seldom commensurate with the effort expended. The indigenous populations of Central Asia are reluctant to participate in atheistic propaganda: Islamic marriage rites and observances still continue to be observed. Among Tatars there is considerable interest in Tatar language broadcasts from Kazan—40 percent of the population listen to them. Tatar folk music is popular not only in the rural areas but among professional people in towns and cities. Nevertheless, even the most conservative ethnic cultures, irrespective of the external pressures upon them to eradicate what are claimed to be the "vestiges of bourgeois nationalism," are changing. This change is not limited to single traits but extends to their general character. For instance, among Soviet ethnic communities, the professional stratum of ethnic cultures may or may not be more encouraged in Soviet times, but it cannot be denied that the establishment of professional organizations of ethnic writers, an ethnic theater, ethnic song and dance ensembles, radio, television, and publishing houses for ethnic languages have changed the defining characteristics of many ethnic cultures (Vasil'eva et al., 53). The same is true of the indigenous ethnic cultures of the United States: they tend to be led by modernized elites and directed as much toward an external consuming public as they are toward the satisfactory functioning of the group itself. For these reasons, providing a bilingual education in conditions such as obtain in the United States, the Soviet Union, Europe and most parts of Africa cannot be based on an identification with an "authentic" primordial or pristine culture.

Furthermore, independent of changes induced from within the primordial or pristine culture, many of them have been in contact with other cultures for several decades and in some instances centuries. The kind of contact which they have experienced is well evidenced: even the various Pueblo groups, though for the most part they were self-sufficient and self-contained, had many features in common because from very early times they traded with each other (Parry, 301). Changes in their cultures became inevitable because the internal structures of such cultures are in part products of the social relationships which the different groups have maintained with each other (Spicer, 1972: 6). One of the results of such structural changes in culture is the emergence of the professional stratum noted to have occurred in the Soviet ethnic groups. A Chicano literature, supported by private foundations, has developed in the Southwest. The Quinto Sol publishing house issues a quarterly, *El Grito*, and an antholo-gy, *El Espejo*. The contents are sometimes in English, sometimes in both English and Spanish as well as in Spanish only, and they often follow patterns which are clearly English. The same tendencies are observable among Indian groups.

In the Soviet Union and the United States similar conclusions are reached concerning the reality of ethnic distinctiveness. In the former it is claimed "that the ethnic culture is made up partly of characteristics specific to a particular nationality but partly also of characteristics which they share with others because of mutual influence" (Kholmogorov, 26). In the American Southwest, the consequences are outlined as follows: "There is both a reality and an ideal of fluidity, of boundarylessness among ethnic groups of the region. There is a reality in the sense that boundaries are easily crossed, that change of identity on the part of indi-viduals happens constantly and frequently. There are certain mechanisms built into the social system which individuals use freely for learning and the necessary behavior characteristics of the other group and so of moving out of the group in which they began life" (Spicer, 1972: 58).

Ethnic identification is further complicated by the pervasive influence of industrial urbanization. American Indian groups like the Pueblos were accustomed to a large communal life, but the processes which now engulf the smaller ethnic groups of Europe (Welsh, Irish, Basques, Fries, and so on), Africa, the Soviet Union, and the United States are of a different dimension. The consequences of this are ambivalent: in the first place urbanization tends towards homogeneity and a leveling of cultural differ-ences; but simultaneously, and in spite of such a leveling, it results in an intensification of ethnic consciousness. Indeed it may be argued that contemporary ethnic consciousness is the consequence of urbanization or influences radiating from urban centers. However, the ethnic consciousness thus intensified is radically different from the traditional ethnic conscious-ness. For instance, a crucial difference is that it is a literate consciousness. An urban ethnic consciousness imbues the group with new cultural habits and needs, and these in turn require new forms of expression. Furthermore, the customary view that the traditional homeland, the village, or the isolated community can best preserve distinctive ethnic, linguistic, and cultural traits and values and, therefore, best facilitate the maintenance of the language and ethnic identity is not true. The leadership of ethnic groups tends to be provided by members who live in the towns and cities or have returned from them to their original homes. Sometimes the majority, if not the whole of the ethnic group, is urbanized. The towns and cities are the centers of publishing and broadcasting, and the media are increasingly becoming important to even the most isolated; the urban schools set the standards by which the others are judged. To this extent, though, the village may remain the idealized repository of the claimed ˙authentic culture, but in the contemporary world that culture is mediated by and through urban agencies and is colored by an urban consciousness (Pokshishevskiy, 53, 54). It is for this reason, it is said, that ethnic writers in Central Asian communities are "not saying anything—at least not anything couched in the old vocabulary, about the nationality question. . . . They de-emphasize the nationality principle (ethnic, multi-ethnic or other) while redefining the country" (Allworth, 1971: 18).

Another consideration also casts doubt on the usefulness of the criterion of "ethnic identity" as a rationale for a bilingual education. In the first place there may be difficulty in assessing objectively the group with which a person may be identified. Francis points to many factors which "not only forge together different ethnic elements into a new ethnic group but also divide an ethnic group or deliberately alter its structure, culture and character" (Francis, 397). Spicer cites instances in the United States of "cultures becoming differentiated in the course of their history, sending off variant forms that achieve a greater or less degree of independence from the parent stock" (Spicer, 12). Shibutani and Kwan speak of ethnic groups as "temporary alignments of people created by communication channels. . . . Ethnic groups disappear when consciousness of kind is altered, when people change their self-perception" (Shibutani and Kwan, 216–17).

Ethnicity as Protest

The original "ascriptive" character of ethnicity no longer claims much support except in the USSR. At one time it would be commonplace to regard an ethnic group as being composed of "primordial affinities and attachments—what a person is born with or acquires at birth" (Isaac, 30). Parsons, though agreeing that historically this was the case, declines to use the term partly because *ascriptive group* has become embedded in a sociological theory unrelated to this problem. Additionally, he recognizes that "there may be a certain optional rather than ascriptive character to ethnic identity" (Parsons, 57). Such primordial or ascriptive ties no longer hold—ethnicity is too fluid a reality to be amenable to such limitations. E. R. Leach (1954) and Barth (1969) in their study of Burma and the Pakistan border with Afghanistan (respectively) found that individuals and groups change their ethnic affiliations for purely pragmatic considerations; these culture and ethnic switches are recurrent and repetitious. Ethnic affiliation appears to be—or is in process of becoming—a voluntary act. Thus, Patterson describes the ethnic group as "the condition wherein certain members of society, in a given social context, *choose* to emphasize as their meaningful basis of primary, extrafamilial identity certain assumed cultural, national, or somatic traits" (Patterson, 308). He goes on to stress that "ethnicity is a *chosen* form of identification" (ibid., 309). There does not appear to be any categorical imperative to which putative members of an ethnic group should be required to respond.

In the absence of any substantive attribute to the ethnic identity rationale for bilingual and bicultural education, what is the basis of the strong response the proposition elicits? In the first place, enough *historical* substance to ethnic differentiations persists to ensure their being set up as symbolic instruments. Schneider points out that while it is true that "almost every family with historically different roots from Anglo-Americans identifies with some ethnic unit," the same is also true in a modified sense of the Anglos themselves—they identify with regional groups or types of community, like mid-Western farmers (Schneider, quoted in Parsons, 64). He maintains, though, that such ethnic identifications are devoid of content and may be referred to as "empty symbols." But almost by definition no symbol is empty—it either symbolizes something or it ceases to symbolize. In this case, ethnic identification may cease to symbolize ethnicity, but that only means that what is symbolized has changed—at present it symbolizes an attitude of protest.

It was argued in an earlier discussion of the stages in which rationales for bilingual education developed that the third phase was the individualistic or psychological stage. In this, the justification was the facilitation of the individual's rather than the group's well-being. The change toward an individualistic rationale has been accompanied by a decline in the authority of impersonal motives and norms. Furthermore, the multiplication of roles played by any one individual in contemporary society is a destructive process because the individual finds it more and more difficult to assume a "social" personality. Multiplicity of roles means a desocialization of personal identity. The society in which he plays such a conglomeration of roles becomes ever more distant, more contrived, and more abstract. In these circumstances individuals, especially those changing from a traditional to a post-traditional, urban, and modernized society, seek some anchorage. Their amorphous awareness of some kind of more meaningful past, one bound up with a cohesive, close, and supportive group, offers them that kind of anchorage. The nature of that group may no longer be relevant in a contemporary society, but it can be made to symbolize something different from what they have. David Bell has expressed the condition authoritatively and elegantly: "Ethnicity in this context is best understood not as a primordial phenomenon in which deeply held identities have to re-emerge but as a strategic choice by individuals who in other circumstances would choose other group memberships as a means of gaining power and privilege. In short it is the *salience* not the *persona* which has to be the axial line for explanation" (Bell, 171). Economic, political, cultural, and a host of other disabilities coincide, but it is ethnicity, as the most evocative of symbols, that carries the weight of these other demands. Doubtless the justification of any system of education, and especially the content of the curriculum, rests to a large extent on their ability to fulfill non-economic demands, such as an appreciation of the arts and a cultivation of physical well-being. But the intangibles of education are hardly likely to be satisfied if the education that a child receives fails to recognize the primary economic requirements of development. Because, through force of circumstances, such as the historical subordination of the "outsider," ethnicity has become synonymous with—or made to represent—nonethnic, economic, and other material characteristics, education needs to be evaluated according to the extent it recognizes the student's ethnic affiliation or origin.

PLURALISM

What Does It Mean?

"DEMOCRATIC PLURALISM"

Ethnicity as a rationale for bilingual education is related to the advantages and the necessity of a pluralist society. The difficulty in using this term is that it has had a long history in the United States, but with a very different meaning from that which it has now acquired. The Anglo-American pluralist society as it has usually been conceived consists of a homogeneous political culture within which various governmental and other agencies, parties, interest groups, the press, and so on have their own special functions and play different roles. The democratic system functions insofar as these different interests balance and check each other. The pluralism is that of competing and conflicting functions within a framework of "national interests." Society, according to this view, is not organized as one system but in several different ways and on several levels. These different levels may be occupied by different parts of the population, who may use different mechanisms and suborganizations to effect their different purposes. They have a network of relations to each other as well as with the total social organization working from an acknowledged center. Judge Learned Hand referred to this fact when he maintained that we have "come to think of the problem of democracy as that of its minorities," a point of view which was taken one step farther by Walter Lippman, for whom "every country is a mass of minorities."

The traditional democratic pluralism has also been given the name "liberal pluralism." Such pluralism is characterized "by the absence even prohibition of any legal or governmental recognition of racial, religious, language, or national origin groups as corporate entities . . . and a prohibition of the use of ethnic criteria of any type for discriminatory purposes or conversely for special or favored treatment" (Gordon, M. M., 1975: 105). It is difficult to imagine how a system of bilingual education can be introduced without some degree of "positive discrimination," if only to neutralize the effect of earlier "negative discrimination" resulting from a reluctance to take account of the needs of bilinguals. To that extent "liberal pluralism" offers no support to bilingual education.

ETHNIC PLURALISM

This form of pluralism, which is one of the bases of the argument for bilingual education, is of a different kind. It is partly a restriction of the liberal pluralism, in so far as it conceives of the minorities mainly as ethnic rather than interest groups. It also represents a considerable hardening of the flexibility of the original approach to pluralism in so far as it proposes that ethnicity should be a *determining* criterion for whatever other affiliations members of the ethnic group may wish to maintain. Being a Puerto Rican or Chicano, or a Navajo means, according to the new concept of ethnic pluralism, that not only do you behave as a member of the ethnic group should, and support its dynamism, but that your other interests—in recreation, reading, occupational associations, and so on—center upon and reflect the groups's own organizations. An individual may play any number of different roles in a nonsegmented pluralist society, some of which may coincide with his ethnic group affiliation and some of which may be irrelevant to or even conflict with that affiliation. Thus Parsons refers to this kind of pluralism "by virtue of which a typical individual may play multiple roles no one of which can adequately characterize his identification as a 'social' personality" (Parsons, 60). However in segmented or ethnic pluralism the roles identified with membership of the ethnic group do—and alone—provide that adequate social identity. Ethnic pluralism, of the kind that is becoming more attractive to many minorities, is segmented pluralism rather than traditional democratic pluralism. It consists of segmented sociological groups which can establish effective cultural and political cohesion and make cultural, economic, and political claims on the total society on the basis of ethnic group identity. Sometimes these cohesions are direct and primordial, and it is these which are referred to usually in discussions concerning the promotion of bilingual education. If, as some claim, it is doubtful whether pluralism (of whatever kind) is anything more than a form of social stratification (Braithwaite, 1938: 121), it is still a fact that ethnic groups have become the major functional stratum in contemporary society, because many other minority interests—especially economic and occupational interests—coincide with ethnicity.

DIFFERENCES IN ETHNIC PLURALISM

Apart from the confusion that may arise from failure to distinguish democratic pluralism from the ethnic segmented variant, difficulties arise from the use of different terms—as substitutes for "pluralism" in some contexts and in others to refer to very different concepts. First, we have to distinguish between the uses of "plural" and "pluralist" which are sometimes invoked as if they were synonymous. The former refers to a verifiable fact, whereas "pluralist" refers to a society that pursues a social *policy* of encouraging or recognizing a multi-ethnic society. Plurality may exist where the policy is explicitly opposed to its maintenance. In the Southwest of the United States and the whole of the Soviet Union, we may identify the contiguous presence of many languages and many cultures. But there is no doubt that a policy of "pluralism" is only partially implemented and some would say completely ignored. Other terms have been used to describe the fact of plurality as distinct from the theory of pluralism. For instance, a "plural society" may be referred to as a "composite society"—one in which "the groups are so closely interdependent that they could not be separated without vital damage" (Parry, 309). Other terms which are used for "plurality" include these: "feudal societies with cultural bifurcation" (Kuper, 1974: 238); multiple societies, segmented societies, and segmental societies (McRae, passim). However, the term which tends to be most frequently confused with "plural societies" is "heterogeneous societies." Confusion may be eliminated if the former is taken to describe a total society composed of clearly distinguished strata or groups of whatever kind; "heterogeneous" is taken to suggest the existence of a society that is so compounded of groups of distinctly different ethnic origins and that have become so comingled that however members of the groups feel about their past they can only with extreme difficulty, if at all, be distinguished as functionally different. The heterogeneous society is closer to the composite society than it is to the plural. One of the issues that needs to be clarified in relating ethnic pluralism to the promotion of bilingual education is the criteria or the major indicators of a plural as opposed to a composite or a heterogeneous society.

A third consideration in the analysis of the concept of pluralism is the existence of different levels or types of pluralism, even when we restrict the use of that term to primordial or ethnic groups. Gordon identified eight responses to the question, "What would you say is meant by cultural pluralism?" Among the eight statements it is possible to distinguish three different attitudes: the first implies no more than a recognition of the harmonious co-existence of different groups as a simple fact. No question of the value of such a situation is implied (Gordon, M. M., 1964: 16; statements 1, 6, and 7). Second, there is a recognition that such differences are valuable and should be encouraged, suggesting that we have moved from the identification of plurality to support for "pluralism" (Gordon, ibid; statements 2, 3, and 4). Third, there are statements that postulate not only that differences exist, but that these differences are subordinated to a "total American culture" or "within the framework of this nationality" (Gordon, ibid; statements 4 and 8). The important distinctions are those which should be made between the second and third categories of statements. The second category would not imply an overarching or superordinate cultural structure such as exists in the American and Soviet systems. In both countries, whatever distinctions are allowed to exist between the various minorities themselves, and between them and the majority Russian or English cultures, the latter are still regarded as superordinate or representing the Soviet or the American culture. The third category does assume such an overarching culture. Segmented pluralism can be regarded either as a network of equivalent cultures, or as a system of pillars "sustaining an overarching unity above the diversity of the nation's social structure" (Lorwin, 1970: 34). The difference is important from the standpoint of bilingual education: equivalent segmented pluralism would involve the provision of bilingual education for all students of whatever ethnic group. In the United States, Anglos as well as speakers of Spanish, Indian, or other languages—according to the linguistic complexion of the area in which the students lived—would have a distinct curriculum. In the Soviet Union, it would mean that Russians living among Georgians would be required to learn the local language just as Georgians would be required to learn Russian or some other locally significant language. If pluralism is conceived as pillarized segmentation, the culture which tends to represent the overarching unity of the society—English or Russian for example—would have a prestige position and the educational policy would be characterized by transitional bilingualism. According to the first concept of pluralism (equivalence), bilingual education would become a mainstream system. According to the second (pillarization), bilingual education would remain peripheral, the mainstream being Russian or English oriented.

The Relevance of Pluralism to Bilingual Education

BILINGUAL EDUCATION MUST BE BASED ON STRUCTURAL PLURALISM

The major theorists of pluralism as it has come to be conceived more recently are J. S. Furnival and M. G. Smith and the progression of their ideas is relevant to a discussion of bilingualism in education. Furnival maintained a clear division between the economic market activities of a plural society on the one hand and its cultural activities on the other. While the economic system is something to which all the different groups belong (an overarching superstructure), there are other aspects of their lives which they do not experience in common: these he regarded as cultural and communal. Smith recognized three levels of pluralism: the lowest is "cultural pluralism," the next or intermediate level is "social pluralism," and the highest is "structural." The intermediate level is characterized by an element of social segregation while the third level reflects the incorporation of all groups into the total society, but differentially or unequally. Smith's first formulation attached by far the greatest importance to the first level, cultural pluralism, which is defined as different and incompatible forms of social behavior characterizing the plural society. Most of the discussion concerning pluralism and its relevance to bilingual education has been concerned with this level. However, in later formulations of the theory of pluralism, Smith moved to a considerably different level of discussion. He came to insist that the cultural differences need to be structured.

Cultural differences which were not explicitly institutionalized were not a sufficient foundation for the establishment of a viable pluralist system. Cultural differences were unlikely to endure unless they were structured—in terms especially of functional kinship systems, religion, rules of property and economy, which not only marked them off distinctly from other group systems but remained functional to the group's contemporary activities. Segmentation implies lines of distinct cleavage, and the cleavage must be sufficiently deep and durable to enable the different groups to peruse a functionally distinctive way of life. Pluralism, although it can seek support in a historical tradition, cannot survive simply because of traditions alone. These segments have been termed *familles spirituelles*, and *Weltanschauungsgruppen* (Lorwin, 1970: 33). Horace Kallen, one of the earlier theorists of the American "melting pot" appears to have had a clear view of the direction a pluralist society would take and his views also reflect the later progression of Smith's views of pluralism in other countries. The United States, Kallen maintained, was "in [the] process of becoming a federal state not merely as a union of geographical and administrative unities but also as a cooperation of cultural divisions, as a federation or commonwealth or national cultures" (Kallen, 116). However, these cultures might be federated, equivalently or subordinately, and he clearly foresaw the inevitability of segmentation and the need for structural or institutional support for the different elements of the cultural and social segments.

INFLUENCE OF MODERNIZAITON ON STRUCTURAL PLURALISM

This is not surprising since the tendency toward institutional or structural segmentation is inextricably bound up with the processes of modernization and urbanization. Kuper and Smith (1969: 7–9) point out that low level or exclusively cultural plurality is associated with spatial distance and is an inverse function of the tightness of the communication network. Haug has also demonstrated (Haug, 300–03) that such plurality is correlated positively with a scattered population, a low level of urbanization, a high proportion of the population in agriculture (67 percent+), a low level of political integration, and a nonelitist political leadership. All these features are represented in the American Southwest, which is one of the most articulate areas so far as pluralist aims are concerned. "Remoteness, isolation, great area, small population, general aridity, widely scattered sources of water, absence of major economic attractions—help to explain the characteristic of the region we are met to discuss—its social plurality" (Parry, 306). Such characteristics explain the strength of exclusively cultural pluralism; they do not explain, however, the present demand for institutionalized or structured pluralism, and indeed persistence of such conditions would make the viability of such structured pluralism doubtful. It requires a degree of modernization for the different cultures to justify different structures and institutions in our society, without which the cultural differences themselves as functional entities could not prevail.

One would therefore expect that pluralism is, in Kuper's view, one of the three theories relevant to the consideration of social change. But it is also because of the effect of social change (induced by modernization and urbanization) that some have claimed that the dynamism has gone out of pluralism (Lorwin, 1970: 57). Clearly, only one form of pluralism has ceased to claim theoretical adherence, because the evidence is overwhelming that the development of other types of pluralism is acquiring increased acceptance. It is the *exclusively* cultural form which tends to have lost its appeal. Mass societies and the collapse of village life, the atomization of the "community," and depersonalization of many aspects of the daily life of ethnic groups have eroded the culturally distinctive foundations of those who do not have the support of structured and institutionalized cultural activities (Kuper and Smith, 18). Thus, in the Soviet Union, the more industrialized republics, though still culturally distinct, pay more attention to structured pluralism and have been granted the greater degree of what autonomy is available. Because of the importance of *structured* pluralism, the beneficiaries of the diffusion of power from the center (Hough, 1972: 34) have been the leading specialized institutions and establishments of power. It is not argued here that cultural differences are not the premise on which other forms of pluralism are based, but simply that those cultural differences have to be reflected in "concrete isolates of *organised* behavior," which is what is meant by structures and institutions in this context.

Pluralism, as a relevant consideration in the development of bilingual education, has to be regarded as a continuum stretching from a sentimental attachment to, but no longer functional reliance on, the cultural traditions of the group—or at least of those aspects of the culture which do not necessarily disadvantage one who is attempting to accommodate to a nonethnic way of life. At the other extreme is an incipient form of nationalism, where the institutions of the ethnic group form a cohesive, self-subsistent cluster. The range of pluralism is from the most amorphous or tenuous cultural differentiation to the most clearly segmented societies. In the middle range are various societal organizations: those societies that are segmented but federated on the basis of equivalence; and others which are federated but "pillarized" within the framework of a superordinate national organization. In the United States and the Soviet Union, as well as in some European countries, and in Africa, ethnic groups are found who conceive of themselves as representing each of these different stages of pluralist developments from heterogeneous to segmented pluralism. The descendants of European immigrants to the United States— Germans, Poles, and Italians for instance—however much they are attached emotionally to the traditions of their ancestors are tending more and more to be integrated at the structural and institutional levels with other elements of the population of the United States. Only where the distinctive institutions—like law, religion, kinship systems, tribal or group government —demarcate a particular group functionally from other groups are they able to claim a pluralist status rather than membership of a heterogeneous society.

A plural society must take account of two sets of facts: first, the extent to which specified groups are culturally differentiated; second, the level at which the institutions which support differentiation operate *functionally* in contemporary society. Both these considerations are matters of fact and open to objective analysis. They do not depend on subjective attitudes of ethnic identification and affiliation or attitudes to ethnic traditions, though it should be repeated the latter are important considerations in maintaining a pluralist society. They may be material causes of such pluralism, but they are far from being sufficient causes. People of Welsh ancestry in the United States still retain their close ties with Wales and return periodically. Some of them even speak the language. But they have no claim to enter as an ethnic group into an American pluralist society—the institutions which would serve to distinguish them from others no longer function. At the other extreme, the Amish have maintained their distinctiveness because they have institutionalized or maintained their traditional ways. Between these two cases are those groups who maintain important institutional aspects of culture which are not duplicated elsewhere in the United States, including language, a governmental system, kinship systems, and the control of a designated territory. To this group belong the Indian communites and at a slightly lower level of distinctiveness certain Spanish-speaking communities. In the United States, therefore, as in other multi-ethnic societies like the Soviet Union, the pluralist justification of bilingual education is not a uniform problem. Looked at from a point of view of advancing the pluralist argument, many types of ethnic groups exist who do not appear to be in a strong position to claim bilingual education. Other groups are in an extremely strong position.

The Institutional Basis of Cultural Pluralism

THE MEANING OF ETHNIC INSTITUTIONS

Social institutions, as we have suggested, are "the concrete isolates of organised behaviour. Each institution comprises a mutually supportive set of values, rules, activities and social relations" (Despres, 11). The institutions usually referred to in the discussions of ethnic group maintenance are language, law, economic organization, governmental systems, marriage, and kinship systems. The importance of these institutions depends partly upon their centrality to the way of life of the group. First, some of them (such as religion) may be less central now than they may have been; second (to some extent an aspect of centrality), an institution may be vital since it involves most other institutions, as may be the case with language; third, the distance between the institutions of the group and similar institutions outside the group is an operative factor—thus religion though important to Catholic Spanish-speaking groups in the Southwest does not of itself set them off as a distinctive group within the United States; and fourth, the very number of the institutions which are still functioning within the group is important—for instance, in many cases language appears to be the only distinctive feature of a group, all other institutions having become functionally obsolete. In such a case it is doubtful whether distinctive membership of a "pluralist" society can be justified simply on the foundations of the possession of a distinctive language. This may very well be the case in Wales at present, in Brittany, and in numerous of the smaller nationalities of the Soviet Union. Again, it should be stressed that the possession of a separate language may not be a sufficient justification for a bilingual education and that language alone is not an argument for a pluralist society. A pluralist justification may not be appropriately proposed for bilingual education, but there are other linguistic justifications for a bilingual education. One is the need to use the native language to initiate education and to prepare for literacy in the major language.

The importance of the institutionalization of differences lies in the fact that it is the institutions rather than the individuals or the group that carry the culture and the distinctive life of the group. The institutions are "organized and integrated to form the community. . . . Equipped with a material outfit and obeying norms which bind the members of the group and that group only, and with a social organization including a central authority the members of the *institutions* carry out a type of behaviour through which they achieve a definite purpose and contribute in a definite manner to the work of the culture as a whole" (Malinowski, B., 1945: 153), a work which cannot be performed by the individuals separately or the group acting as a whole. There is no reason why these institutions should remain the traditional institutions—they will indeed change in order to remain functional. What is required is that in changing they should not cease to set off the group as a distinctive unit. For instance, institutions have been borrowed historically by the Navajo from Puebloan, Spanish, and Anglo sources, modified to fit Navajo patterns and incorporated in the fabric of a distinctive Navajo culture (Young, R. W., 167). The Tribal Council is an example, since it has "provided the stimulus and framework within which the Navajo Tribe has emerged as a political entity" (ibid., 167). Their system of education is also influenced by Anglo conventions. The existence of a formal system of education as a distinct institution among them before this century meant that the introduction of the mainstream system of education was "an intrusive element, tolerated but not part of the Navajo culture" (ibid: 166). It has, however, at long last begun to be digested into that Navajo culture. The existence of an educational institution prior to Anglo influence made the incorporation of a modified system possible. The same has been noted in respect of the Hopis of Arizona. They reacted unfavorably to the suggestions that their children should receive an Anglo boarding-school type education, not that they disputed the advisability of learning English but "because they said they had an educational system of their own" and they did not think it necessary to adopt an alien system in order to acquire one element of the curriculum (Spicer, 1972: 43). Here, Spicer claims, was a Hopi educational policy well formulated in the light of the information they possessed of the English system and in line with their indigenous institution. It is one of Malinowski's theses that culture contact means that institutions come into existence which cannot be attributed to either parent culture, but which are wholly new. He calls this the "three column approach" (Malinowski, 5). If it is true, as Emile Van den Brande (1967: 450) maintains, that "the future belongs to the *class* which knows how to create its own institutions," it is equally true for the *ethnic group*, especially in a multi-ethnic society.

DISREGARD OF EDUCATION AS AN INSTITUTIONAL VARIABLE IN ETHNICITY

In the relationship between cultural and social pluralism on the one hand and bilingual education on the other, seldom is education, among the significant institutions of a group, discussed. This is due to several factors, one of which is that the concept of pluralism has grown out of that of class stratification. There is no case of the emerging classes claiming distinctive educational systems: they invariably claim access to the provision made for the dominant classes. However, ethnic groups often do possess distinctive educational institutions of their own; they may even demand access to other educational systems, but above all they demand the elaboration and improvement of their own, either independently of the mainstream or by incorporating elements of the mainstream system. But whatever the reasons for the comparative disregard of education hitherto as one of the ethnic institutions, it is now emerging as one of the most salient institutions of ethnicity. Religion has come to exert a less coercive influence as society is secularized. Law, which in the past was enforced as well as articulated as part of the religious system, depends increasingly for its understanding on the level of education.

At present, therefore, a dichotomy exists between the influence of formalized structures of government among such groups as the Hopi and the indigenous structures of tradition, custom, and religious influences on their concept of law (Sekaquapetawa, 239). Integration of members of ethnic groups into a mobilized society depends more and more on levels of literacy. The use of technology and the knowledge of science required for living in even isolated and unsophisticated communities point to the appropriation of the functions and significance of some of the more traditional institutions by a contemporary formal system of education, as well as to an increase in the influence of the traditional system of education. As important as is any of the cultural and social considerations already mentioned, only the system of education demands a period of compulsory attendance on the part of all the young and only the system of education in a modernized society competes with the home for the child's allegiance. In a literate society, the maintenance of the ethnic language depends upon the school. Because of the importance of education as an institution, it is not surprising that many countries are increasingly segmented according to the type of school attended by the children rather than along religious lines as they have traditionally been. This is so in Belgium, Switzerland, the Soviet Union, and Wales. The system of education is the main means of institutionalizing linguistic affiliations. And the linguistic, in turn, determines all other types of affiliation—political, voluntary associations such as those concerned with sport, occupations, and so on (McRae, 1974: 21). Yet, analyses of the pluralist society seldom give to educational institutions the same careful attention they give to other institutions, nor do they give the impression that they regard education as a central institutional concern of ethnic groups.

TERRITORIALITY AS AN INSTITUTION IN ETHNICITY

Another institution important for the development of bilingual education among different types of ethnic groups in the United States as elsewhere is territoriality. We have mentioned earlier the difference between ethnic groups in their territorial distribution as well as in their attitude to the relevance of territory. Indeed, Spicer postulates a "dichotomy among such groups on the basis of the meaning of the land in the identity system" (Spicer, 1972: 42). In his interpretation, the possession of an identifiable territory can be either a merely pragmatic consideration (the need to remain together in order to communicate) or a sacred trust irrevocably identified with ethnic identity; both views, though, recognize the importance of a distinctive territory. However it is regarded, possession of territory serves to reinforce ethnic distinctiveness, it adds a physical to a cultural dimension, and in a real sense it acts to legitimize cultural integrity. This is particularly important in considering the claims of the Indians. Only in connection with them is an ethnic definition of land ownership explicit in the laws of the United States. This may be due partly to the earlier policy of concentrating the Indians, and the related concession confirming their rights, to those lands. But their ethnic identity systems "have as an important element the symbol of roots in the land supernaturally sanctioned, ancient roots, regarded as unchangeable" (Spicer, 1972: 41). In this case territoriality is as much an institution as religion, law, kinship, and the system of education.

Not all such territorial considerations amount to an institutionalization of that factor. For instance, however much European immigrants may concentrate on particular cities or even states, they cannot and do not claim the same importance for their possession of those localities as the Indians do. It may be said that immigrant groups, in respect of their presence in the United States, are all equally without an abiding home. The Indians, wherever they may dwell in the United States, still believe in, and are institutionally entitled to conceive of, a particular land as their home. In a different sense this can be said of the Spanish elements of the Southwest: they may not have the same quasi-religious attachment to

New Mexico, Southern California, or Texas as do the Indians, but the land is their ethnic and traditional home and their attachment to it is part of their ethnic identity. To that extent it is as institutionalized as the land of the Indians is in their ethnic composition. Other speakers of Spanish in the United States—Puerto Ricans and Cubans—do not have a similar territorial heritage. The importance of this issue is that the concept of territoriality effectively distinguishes between types of ethnic groups in the United States. Furthermore, the difference is fundamental to a consideration of the types of provision that should be made for their education, and of the validity of their claim to a bilingual education on grounds of ethnicity and cultural pluralism. Nor is it a consideration affecting the United States alone. An examination of the provision of bilingual education for ethnic minorities in the Soviet Union highlights the distinction between ethnic groups who retain their ethnic territorial bases (however limited), and those who have dispersed as immigrants to other republics within the Soviet Union, no matter how large their original ethnic group or nationality may be. It is the tendency for quite small minorities who have remained in their homeland to be encouraged to develop a bilingual system of education, especially in primary schools. Apart from Russian immigrants who, for various reasons are able to continue to use their native language in the most complex linguistic situations, dispersed ethnic groups are seldom able to maintain a system of bilingual education (Lewis, 1972: 253).

Conclusion

DISADVANTAGES AND ADVANTAGES OF ETHNIC PLURALISM TO BILINGUAL EDUCATION

From the standpoint of education, what are the advantages and disadvantages of social pluralism of the ethnic variety which we have described? And by implication, what contribution can a bilingual education offer to the maintenance of pluralism? In the first place, it cannot be said that pluralism is unequivocally an advantage or disadvantage from the standpoint of the stability of society, on which a satisfactory education is based, and toward which education contributes. Some, like Daalder (1971: 20) claim that social pluralism has facilitated the development of a stable and legitimate social structure in such countries as Switzerland and the Netherlands. It may also be argued that pluralism is one way in which the reconstitution of national multi-ethnic society can best be achieved (Lorwin, 1965). If this were the case, the value of pluralism would be incalculable and the indirect contribution of bilingual education commensurate with it. However, not all observers agree; pluralism, it has been claimed, begets pluralism: the pluralist society is a necessarily fissiparous phenomenon.

Once the unified organization is disrupted there is no stopping the process of division. The history of the Old World since the rise of nationalism and the Reformation is the history of increased divisiveness. The breakup of empires has seen in turn the breakup of the former constituent elements of those empires. In that sense pluralism may be a disadvantage. This is certainly the case if the pluralist elements claim national or quasi-national status. Furnivall concluded that "nationalism within a plural society is itself a disruptive force, tending to shatter and not to consolidate its social order" (468). It is difficult to conceive of a satisfactory educational system in a fundamentally unstable society. Kuper maintains that in the pluralist society of the kind with which we are concerned, "there is no promise of progress to interracial solidarity or to racial equality" (Kuper, 1974: 237). If this were the case a bilingual system of education would be meaningless. Parsons, while seeing the advantages of social pluralism, appears to stipulate that ethnic pluralism should coincide with other forms of group identification if it is to neutralize the unfavorable attributes of polarization (Parsons, 82). However, it is difficult to see how this crosscutting by other interests is to be facilitated since the very roots of social pluralism based on ethnicity is to inhibit interests that do not focus on ethnic affiliation. The tendency, therefore, appears to be to regard social pluralism in Harold Isaac's words—as a "massive re-tribalization" (30) or—in Ralf Dahrendorf's —as "refeudalization—the return to ascribed as against achieved characteristics as determinants of social stratification" (161).

However, all is not lost, nor is the picture entirely gloomy. One justification for social pluralism is the inherent value of diversity, deriving from the undoubted fact that there is no single overarching standard of values in terms of which all behaviors, attributes of individuals and groups, beliefs, and acts can be evaluated. The highest ends for which men have striven are often quite incompatible with one another. Their incompatibility, however, does not diminish the value of any of them. We cannot emulate all cultures or all great men. Malinowski proclaimed that the "essential freedom of an individual depends on the multiple, diversified and differentiated constitution of society which we find in many cultures. . . . The business of life is carried on by a number of institutions (constituting different cultures). The greater the autonomy within each of them the more opportunities there are for an individual to choose his adherence" (166). Nevertheless, such a diversity is best cultivated within some wider framework. In Western Europe, for instance, the cultures of the separate nationalities (derived ultimately from the same sources) flourish best in interaction and interrelation; similarly, in the Soviet Union, it is argued, the cultures of the many separate nationalities have grown in the ambience of close interdependence within a unified system. It could be argued as well that the cultural pluralism of the United States will be productive if, together with differentiation of roles achieved by groups that are free to develop their autonomous existence and strengthen their solidarity, they accept at the same time obligations, loyalties and responsibilities that transcend their immediate affiliations and are directed toward a broader community—recognizing at a higher level the existence of a national culture.

Not only is diversity inherently valuable, it is also functionally or instrumentally valuable. Just as there is an inherent value in freedom (the importance of being able to determine one's own fate), so there is an instrumental value because it justifies protest—there is a freedom *to* and a freedom *from*. In much the same way diversity has a value in and of itself, as well as a value in opposing implacable tendencies of contemporary society which, though they too are valuable (and in any case almost inevitable), have to be limited. Diversity has to be encouraged as a counter to the unbridled development of uniformity and homogeneity. Pluralism, partly institutionalized by means of systems of bilingual education, helps to maintain diversity and simultaneously (because of the recognition of the lingua franca) helps to ensure that this diversity is encompassed by a more comprehensive unity.

This is the concept of bilingual education (looked at from the standpoint of pluralism) in the Soviet Union. It is the implementation of the policy of "two streams" (Dva potoka), and the two streams carry the individual student toward "inter-ethnic" or international friendship and understanding. A Latvian republic Honored Teacher, G. A. Spungins, writes: "The experience of the joint instruction of Latvian and Russian children has shown the fruitful effect of this method on fostering feelings of international friendship and love and respect for all peoples of our multinational homeland in the children" (*Current Digest of Soviet Press*, XVIII: 14). The same attitude is expressed by the Minister of Education for the Kirghiz Republic, Kanimetov (*Pravda*, January 4, 1974): "In our opinion schools in which lessons are conducted in several languages create the necessary pre-conditions for correct solutions of the problems of internationalist upbringing of students. Instruction takes place in Russian, Kirghiz, Uzbek, and Tadzhik in parallel classes." Empirical evidence of the value of such bilingual programs is forthcoming as a result of an investigation in the Tatar ASSR: "It is characteristic that Tatars who have graduated from mixed or Russian schools have a more favorable attitude and enter into personal interethnic contacts more often than those who have attended single medium schools. Of those who attended Tatar medium schools 90 percent have positive attitudes toward jobs in ethnically mixed work forces . . . while among those who attended bilingual schools the figure is 96 percent" (Drobizheva, 8–9). A bilingual education is one means of ensuring that a segmented pluralist society, as is the case in the Soviet Union, some Western European countries, and as may be the case in Canada, does not develop into a segregated society.

In any multi-ethnic society, the types of bilingual education appropriate to the different ethnic groups will not be identical in each case. The concept of pluralism relates in different ways to the different types of ethnic groups, and these types are to be found in most multi-ethnic societies. They are, first, the indigenous, whether primordially indigenous (autochthonous) or historically indigenous (by conquest or incorporation). The difference between these two types can affect the viability of pluralistic rationale for bilingual education, but it is doubtful whether it need affect the actual type of provision that is made. The second type of ethnic group consists of those who, though not indigenous to the United States, like Puerto Ricans, nevertheless have claims which differ from those of European or Asian immigrants. In addition, they may have close linguistic ties with existing ethnic groups in the United States. Thus, whatever is justified for the Spanish-speaking of the Southwest could hardly be denied to Puerto Ricans or Cubans, although they belong to basically different ethnic categories. The third type of ethnic group is the European or Asian immigrant who, whatever other rationale they may offer for a bilingual education, are not entitled to claim the justifications which the Indians, Chicanos, or "immigrant" speakers of Spanish claim. If these distinctions are valid, it follows from what we have discussed that the type of bilingual program appropriate to each kind of group has to be different. For instance, a transitional bilingual education which, on these arguments, does not offer a satisfactory program to the Chicanos may be the only appropriate program for Italians.

We conclude, then, that the justification any type of ethnic group has for using the concept of cultural pluralism as a rationale for the development of bilingual education does not depend upon the group's subjective awareness of a traditional culture. Instead, it must be based upon the existence of distinctive and objective institutions which give concrete and functional meaning to that subjective awareness. In other words, cultural pluralism—to justify bilingual education—has to be structured or institutionalized. And finally, two of the most important institutions that should be present to justify a bilingual education are a system of education that retains some of the distinctiveness of the group—this applies very much to the Indians—and territoriality—which applies mainly to the Indians, in a different way to the Spanish of the Southwest, less to immigrant speakers of Spanish, and hardly at all to European or Asian immigrants. Since this argument appears to be favorable only to perhaps two of the ethnic types we have distinguished, a caveat has to be entered: we have been concerned with only one argument or rationale for bilingual education, namely ethnicity and cultural pluralism. Other arguments are put forward which favor other groups far more than those in the present context, and it may be (and in fact I believe) that such rationales are more important than those based on cultural pluralism.

POLITICAL RATIONALES

Political and Cultural Rationales

Political and cultural rationales are so closely intertwined that separate analysis of their relevance may sometimes appear to be somewhat contrived. Nevertheless the general distinction is valid, and it has to be made especially in the area of bilingual education where political motivation may often be disguised in cultural terms. For the purposes of this discussion, political (socio-economic) rationales have to do with the structure of society, with the system of government, and with the distribution of power. Cultural considerations, on the other hand, pertain to values and meanings as they have built up through history and formed a tradition. A set of political considerations are necessarily bound up with action, whereas cultural considerations and values could still be real and vital even if they found little response in immediate action at any one time or place. Political rationales invoke the idea of obedience—or at least acquiescence—whereas cultural considerations call forth responses such as belief.

Political rationales do not enter into all forms of bilingual education. For instance, bilingual education provided by religious organizations is not motivated by political considerations unless, as in the case of the education of Jews in the Soviet Union, it infringes upon the claims of the political system, the party, or the state. With popular or mass systems of education provided almost exclusively by the state in some form or another, we have to take account of political rationales. This is certainly the case in Israel where the Hebrew language is considered to be a necessary characteristic of the state of Israel. Because Hebrew is a second language for a large proportion of the immigrants before their arrival in Israel, the system of education to which they are introduced must take account of a necessary bilingualism. Association of language with political considerations occurs in the Soviet Union where bilingual education, and more particularly the study of Russian among the nationalities, is regarded as important not only to political well-being but to the well-being of the Party: "the study of the Russian language is important not only for pedagogical reasons but also because it is inseparable from the political work of the Party" (*Okutucilar Gazetasi*, Tashkent, 1967). It is not surprising, therefore, that the highest percentage of bilinguals (Lettish/Russian) in Latvia is to be found among members of the Communist Party (95 percent) and the Communist League of Youth (90 percent) while among the politically unaffiliated the proportion is 63 percent (Kholmogorov, 1970: 315). Bilingual education in the Soviet Union is only one aspect of the political "problem of the nationalities," and the interest in bilingualism is derived from its relevance to the solution of that particular political issue.

The existence of a political rationale for any form of education, including bilingual education, does not entail the politicization of pedagogy.

Thus, while no one would deny the existence of political motives in promoting bilingual education among Chicanos and Puerto Ricans, the outcome has to be seen as better instruction in English and better opportunities to learn science, other languages, and mathematics, because of either greater competence in English or of the use of the mother tongue. Nevertheless bilingual education, like mainstream education, is conceived by its proponents as well as its adversaries as being about the redistribution of power. "A theory of instruction is a political theory in the proper sense that it derives from the consensus concerning the distribution of power within the society—who shall be educated and to fulfill what roles" (Bruner, 1969: 69). One of the former missionaries in the Cameroons, Hermann Skolaster, reported on the avidity of the indigenous population to become bilingual: "The German language was the magnet that attracted them. The indigenous inhabitant wanted to speak, to hear, and to understand the language of the Master of the country" (Fonlon, 34). Haugen reports that in Norway, by adopting a particular language policy—support for Landsmol—"the Venstre party struck a blow for national sovereignty by giving freer reign to Norwegian elements in that language" (Haugen, 1966a: 38). Later the Labor party in Norway argued that "the language movement is an important step in the rise of the common people" (Haugen, 1966a: 103).

Social Stratification and Bilingual Education

The acquisition of one language, whatever other language might be learned, must be related to the stratification of society, and in particular the wish to eliminate it altogether or to rearrange the strata. The desire of the Guarani-speakers in Paraguay to advance the usage of the language is partly a consequence of their demand that members of the upper classes, who normally speak Spanish, should shed some of their prestige and influence. Social stratification associated with bilingualism was equally evidenced in nineteenth century Poland: the upper class preferred Polish while the peasants preferred Russian dialects (Chadwick, H. M., 25). In the United States, the demand for bilingual education is associated with civil rights guaranteed by the state and monitored by the whole panoply of the legal system. (U.S. Commission on Civil Rights, 1975). But in turn the demand for the implementation of these guarantees (and the corollary of bilingual education) is but one aspect of the emergence of hitherto depressed groups (ethnic or otherwise) who see in education properly adjusted to their characteristic way of life a means of accelerating their emergence. Malherbe recounts the riposte of a Zulu chief to whom the advantages of the vernacular were being elaborated: "Yes, that may be so, but if I know only my own language I am no better than a chicken scratching around for its food in a narrow pen. If however I know the white man's language I can soar like an eagle" (Malherbe, 1961: 21). It may be the fear of their soaring like eagles, however, that accounts for the debilitation of the educational opportunities offered by the state to such people, an education which would be necessarily bilingual. It is equally true, both in the United States and in the Soviet Union where the reluctance of the dominant ethnic groups to learn nationality languages is equally pronounced, that their lack of involvement in bilingual education is often due to the fear of granting prestige to such languages and, by implication, to those who speak them. Meeting the demands of the nationalities for a truly bilingual education will not affect the prestige of the dominant group so long as the latter remain entirely and uncompromisingly committed to the Russian or the English language. The political rationale for bilingual education is unlikely to be realized until the system of education is reciprocally, not simply unilaterally, bilingual. The dominant language will remain a status symbol, as it was in Norman England, and remains the case in Wales, Ireland, and such large confederations as the USSR and the USA.

Ultimately, the power which bilingual education is conceived as helping to redistribute and which is the core of a political rationale, is economic power. Those who live in the Irish Gaeltacht and who learn English do so because it possesses an economic advantage. In the United States, advocates and opponents of bilingual education often focus their arguments on the consideration of job opportunities—the desire for or the fear of losing jobs. In Canada, Lieberson emphasizes there is "definite evidence of a structural pressure towards bilingualism generated by occupational demands" These linguistic pressures vary between occupational categories as well as across languages. "Relatively few men who are labourers, craftsmen or in transportation, communication and service occupations" are bilingual (147). Similarly in the USSR "the positive role of bilingualism is indicated by the close correlation between a more fluent knowledge of Russian and a high level of education and socio-occupational vertical mobility" (Gubolgo, 95). Mobility, both geographic and socio-occupational, are fundamental rationales of a bilingual education. Parents opt for Russian-medium schools in the Ukraine or in other non-Russian-speaking areas because fluency in that language is necessary to the pursuit of higher education in universities outside their republic. The custom of living on isolated farms in the Soviet Union inhibits the spread of bilingualism; but more important than that, a rural upbringing creates the desire to become bilingual as a means of escape (Kholmogorov, 316). In Wales, too, the same argument has been advanced as a major justification of bilingual education. Accepting the fundamental value of the Welsh language, leading educationists of the late eighteenth and early nineteenth centuries argued that English was a liberating force because the Welsh "have been too long committed to their language excessively" (Rowlands, 1886: 45).

The knowledge of English, a member of Parliament claimed in 1847, "would liberate the now poor and depressed monoglot Welshman from his mountain prison" (Williams, W., 1848). The argument was almost totally economic in its orientation. In securing English, another official observed in 1858 that the Welsh would have the opportunity to avoid "the dirty and arduous labours which they are forced to undertake when the prestigious and less exacting work is available only to Englishmen and Scotsmen" (Rees, 1858: 36). Almost the same year a leading religious leader warned his compatriots to "prepare themselves by a superior English education so that they may not be mere hewers of wood and drawers of water" (Kilsby Jones, 1859: 213). In the more restricted area of teaching, it is often forgotten how important bilingualism is to teachers, irrespective of whether they themselves are involved in teaching bilingual children. Although in the village schools of Tanzania, which are fairly homogeneous, children can be taught entirely in their mother tongue, it is necessary that the teachers should have Swahili to allow easy mobility between villages.

Unification of the State—A Negative Rationale

There are two aspects of the involvement of language in unification. The first is the promotion of maximum communication, irrespective of the political organization of the state. Wherever two or more languages are spoken, a common language is an obvious advantage; and this is true whether the state is a completely monolithic organization with a uniform political system, or a pluralistic and possibly segmented system. Whatever happens in Canada, or the United States, in the movement towards pluralism (whether cultural only or cultural and political), a large number of people will need to know two languages—one of which is English. If we consider within the Soviet Union only the Russian Republic, the same is true—the members of the small nationalities such as the Bashkirs and Mari, or the Peoples of the North, will need to know Russian if they wish to live outside their restricted enclaves and to be in a position to profit from industrial and technological advance. The argument based on *political* unification is somewhat different: basically it is identical with the "melting pot" analogy. Theodore Roosevelt was among the most trenchant of its advocates in the United States. "Any man who comes here . . . must adopt the institutions of the United States and therefore he must adopt the language which is now the native tongue of her people. . . . It would be not merely a misfortune but a crime to perpetuate differences of language in this country" (1917). This was also the Tsarist approach emulated by Stalin, in spite of Lenin's opprobrious comments on "Great Russian chauvinism." Even today that approach has not been eliminated in the Soviet Union; while the equality of all languages is proclaimed, in fact considerable differentiation of social usage exists among languages—the prestigious domains like science and technology are appropriated by Russian (Lewis, E. G., 1975). Nor is the discouragement of national languages in the Soviet Union restricted to the Union itself since the dream of a "single, universal lingua franca" is kept alive and is part of the justification of a federal lingua franca (Gubolgo).

The vision is more limited in Wales, but still beguiling. A Royal Commission in 1875 pronounced that "intelligent and educated Welshmen put forth the bilingual theory as a last resort to secure the perpetuity of the Welsh language. But such a theory that a whole population will and for all time keep up two languages when only one is necessary to society" is merely proof of intellectual perversity. Such a stance was supported in 1831 by some of the Welsh intelligentsia themselves, who argued Britain should be bound by a uniform language. "Under one sceptre, a common code of laws with common interests it was desirable if but one common language prevailed" (Blackwell, 76). If the Welsh themselves took this view it was not surprising that the English, even a great humanist like Matthew Arnold, should subscribe to it: "Whatever encouragement individuals may think it desirable to give to the preservation of the Welsh language on grounds of philological or antiquarian interest it must always be the desire of a Government to render its dominions . . . homogeneous and to break down the barriers to the freest possible intercourse between the different parts of them" (1853: 16).

Accepting the need to maintain the native language at least transitionally, the stress on the acquisition of a second, major language like English or Russian has nearly always been related to the need to ensure stability. This political rationale for bilingual education has two strands, one of which is the desirability of promoting the prestige of the acquired language. The second is the stability of the state of which the minority are members. This theme is constantly iterated in the Soviet Press, for example: "While not forgetting to promote the development of the Azeri language it is essential that constant attention should be paid to the propaganda and study of Russian as the most powerful weapon for strengthening mutual relations and solidarity of the Soviet peoples" (*Yazyki literatura zapinski*, 17 May 1972). Naturally, then, language would be associated with the maintenance of law and order, and this was the case during the rapid industrialization of South Wales and the pressure to ensure the beginnings of a bilingual education. Because a bilingual education was not available to all social classes "evil circumstances arise . . . wherein one side is disposed to depreciate whatever is Welsh while the other looks with suspicion on whatever is English" (Royal Commission, 1881).

While there is a considerable emphasis on the positive rationale of acquiring two languages, there is also a highly negative strand in the political rationale—the attack upon nationalistic pretensions as a means of emphasizing the value of the auxiliary major language. Arutiunian, the head of the Soviet Academy of Sciences' Institute of Ethnography, following his massive investigation of attitudes among Tatars, concludes that one of the most crucial functions of teaching and learning Russian among those whom he studied is to weaken "nationalist prejudices" and national cultural narrow-mindedness (Mordvinov, 1950). Other writers take pains to stress this opposition to the retention of national affiliations: "The attempt to restore obsolete cultural traditions and customs and life, to take the path of idealizing the past," is deplorable since it leads to disunity *(Kommunist,* 1966: May 1970–71). In Wales the attack on the preservation of Welsh was mounted because it was associated with national identity and, in the minds of critics, with potential disunity: "Our language is the foundation of our distinctiveness. . . . To lose our language would be to lose part of our claim to be independent" (Derfel, 1864). In the last resort, however, the views of the minority striving to slough off economic subordination, whether in Wales, the USSR, or the United States, tend to conform to those of the working classes in Norway reported by Haugen— problems of the means of communication are secondary when compared with economic well-being. "What does it matter if one says "groten i gryten" or "grauten i gryta" (porridge in the pot) so long as the worker has enough of it" (Haugen, 1966a: 113). The nadir of interest in bilingual education and of the promotion of Welsh in Britain coincided with the years of economic depression in the twenties and thirties.

Bilingualism and Political-Social Change

Bilingualism in a popular or mass system of education is always associated with political and social change. Such change is reflected and promoted by bilingual education. For our purposes, social and political change can be identified with the three aspects of modernization—homogenization of culture, differentiation of hitherto undifferentiated groups or occupations within society, and demographic heterogeneity. Such changes lead to greater political centralization and consequently to the promotion of a lingua franca. Changes of the kind we have referred to are associated with large-scale industrialization and urbanization, and this has been a characteristic of the development of bilingual education in the USSR and in Wales during the period of the pressure toward providing such an education (Lewis, E. G., 1974).

Modernization tends to produce changes which appear to move in contrary directions according to the social and economic development of the countries concerned. Where an ethnic group is moving from a traditional to a post-traditional phase—as was the case in Wales in the nineteenth century and is currently the case of many Soviet nationalities, some indigenous minorities in the United States, and the Republic of South

Africa—the tendency in education is to stress the traditional values and languages. This results from the fear of their disappearance and because it is only when that fear is aroused through contact with others that the traditional values—including the valued language—emerge into consciousness. Simultaneously, the ethnic language is promoted because in many cases it is the only feasible instrument of fundamental literacy. During this phase of social and political development, bilingual education is justified for traditional ethnic reasons. Modernization generates a movement from an affective relationship to a community toward a more rationalized relationship to a group of institutions that constitute a political structure. As a result, the idea of a "tradition" becomes more abstract, no longer a total way of life so much as a set of beliefs, and later not even a set so much as a congeries of isolated beliefs. In such a situation, the relationship of an ethnic language is less to a total traditional way of life than to separate elements or features. Attitudes to language in each context tend to be rationalized and so become parts of an ideology. Once attitude becomes an ideology it becomes a consciously directed force, making for social and political change, and tends to acquire its own accelerating momentum in promoting that change.

Where a country or ethnic group has already reached a post-traditional phase, as is the case currently in Wales, many of the Western or Slavic nationalities of the USSR, and the European immigrant minorities of the United States, the tendency is to promote changes which cut across ethnic divisions. Social-developmental justifications of bilingual education are substituted for the traditionalist justifications. One consequence of this has been a rapid shift towards unilateral as opposed to reciprocal bilingual education. This is the case in Wales, the Republic of South Africa, and the Soviet Union. In the United States bilingual education has always been unilateral (transitional), and the movement toward promoting reciprocal bilingual education is due to a political militancy, one which cannot find expression in the USSR or the Republic of South Africa and is inhibited in Wales by the demographic and economic weakness of the minority. In Wales the shift to unilateral bilingualism is reflected in the movement among school-age children away from Welsh monolingualism (9 percent in 1951 and 6 percent in 1961) while at the same time there was an increase of 25 percent in the proportion of Welsh children who claimed English as their native language. In the Soviet Union the shift is reflected first in the decline in the number of schools where the national language is the teaching medium—in Azerbaydzhan a 27 percent fall between 1955 and 1969. Second, an increase in the number of "bilingual schools," namely those which are created especially to provide for dual medium instruction (Russian and the national language). These schools, created ostensibly to further internationalism among school children, are powerful instruments for the promotion of Russian. Thirdly, there has been a very impressive development of schools in "nationality areas" where the medium of instruction is the second language, Russian. In Daghestan 400 such schools exist; in the Ukraine 14 percent of the schools are second-language medium schools. In very few nationality areas is the proportion of the children in such Russian-medium schools below 35 percent (Lewis, E. G., 1972; 192–6).

Bilingualism and Social-Political Tension

Bilingualism is ambivalent in its effect on social and political relations within a heterogeneous community: it helps both to create tension and to bridge the differences between groups. A recent commentator on bilingual education in the United States has correctly reported on the fear of possible divisiveness which arises from the promotion of bilingual education (Malitz, 24), and this is certainly one of the major premises on which the educational policy of the Soviet Union is based. It is well-nigh universal. For instance, Ruth Johnston reports a Polish immigrant family in Australia as saying: "I make my children speak Polish. I like them to keep two languages. I want them to speak Polish at home. We often have arguments about it. The younger one speaks Polish, the older ones don't want to. I feel completely Polish. I shall be a Pole to my death. . . . My children must be the same" (282). Such intrafamilial discord is inevitably reflected sooner or later within the larger society.

The probability is that no social unit exists in which convergent (homogenizing) and divergent (differentiating) trends are not inseparably interwoven, but the different direction of those processes may be more likely to lead to conflict in multinational and multilingual developing communities (found in the Soviet Union and the United States) than in homogeneous, advanced societies. The complex structure of linguistically heterogeneous, developing communities increases the instances where there are different uses of the languages associated with distinct spheres of action and at various levels of development. Such possibilities of conflict arise from the fact that segments of traditional areas co-exist with intrusive and unintegrated aspects of more modern areas of social experience and activity. For instance, in the Soviet Union (and this is equally true of the United States and African countries) "the drawing together of nations in the economic, social, and political ideological spheres has proceeded faster than in the cultural-linguistic sphere . . . aspects of spiritual culture retain a large degree of their original national colour" (Vestnik Akad. Nauk, November 1972: 3-11). In the new and expanding Soviet cities, the varying rate of development of ethnic groups moving in from the surrounding rural areas and co-existing with very different groups in respect of language development creates tension. Related to this is the fact that the unintegrated areas of social experience are associated differently with the lingua franca and the nationality or minority languages.

Of course conflict does not necessarily mean hostility between groups or between speakers of two languages—hostility means a predisposition to promote actual conflict, whereas conflict may be no more than tension and a recognition of different, possibly irreconcilable interests while at the same time behaving tolerantly. Hostility is not likely to be consonant with a pluralist attitude, while if there is any meaning at all to pluralism it must be able to ensure some mutual willingness to accept a consensus with dissentience.

Nevertheless, it will be of no assistance to those who are engaged in bilingual education to conceal the fact that tension and conflict are bound to be associated with bilingualism. A group defines itself in contact with other groups, and to the extent that value is attached to a language the contact with speakers of other languages will entail tension. In fact the closer the contact and the greater the degree of accommodation which the groups effect the more intense the tension is likely to be (Coser, 168). However, bilingual education may be an institutional means of channeling such conflicting interests in ways which do not threaten the cohesiveness of the social and political system. It is very often the case that groups who know they have to live together choose one aspect of social life which does not necessarily threaten co-existence as a focal point of conflict— tension about a symbolic activity (of which language is perhaps the most obvious) becomes a substitute or surrogate for conflict about matters which, if they were allowed to lead to hostility, would threaten the "commonweal." There are conflicts which are the very basis of a relationship and others which concern less politically and economically vital issues. Frustration which inevitably arises when any two people or groups of people live together have to find their symbolic means of expression. Boundaries of inviolable interests have to be set so that the business of living together may then proceed with minimum amounts of frustration. If bilingual education becomes a fundamental and crucial issue to more than the intelligentsia, it can be assumed that the real problem is not bilingualism but some associated features, usually economic deprivation, depression, or political disenfranchisement. Bilingual education as a cry is only a means of drawing attention to such discontents and if heeded early may help to drain off the more deep-seated malaise. Bilingual education is necessarily associated with conflict, and the conflict it is associated with is "unrealistic" rather than "realistic" (Coser, 48–53).

This is the case in the Soviet Union. The language policy adopted for a particular school helps to maintain the major thrust of social and political development without categorically denying or violating the special places of the ethnic group. Whatever its disadvantages, bilingual education in the USSR does facilitate the necessary modernization of society and ensures greater opportunities for more varied experience, at different levels of sophistication, for most of the children. Furthermore, the system of bilingual education in the Soviet Union is the principal means of rationalizing the relationship between several languages. In spite of possible disadvantages and inevitable distresses to those who are affiliated to small minority languages, such a rationalization is necessary in a vast multilingual society. To the extent that the various languages have institutional (in this case school) support, linguistic heterogeneity can be made tolerable and can be transformed into a *structured* plural society. This is basically the aim of the USSR at least over the immediate or short term. An unstructured linguistic heterogeneity is rich soil for conflict and open hostility, and this situation characterizes the United States and several other multilingual societies.

CONCRETE REACTIONS TO THE DIFFERENT TYPES OF RATIONALE AMONG ETHNIC GROUPS

As a result of an analysis of the international literature on bilingual education, a lengthy list of propositions purporting to justify bilingual education was discussed with small groups of teachers in Wales and later with similar groups in Scotland and the United States, belonging to different ethnic groups. From these discussions emerged a number of propositions concerning the rationales which had been discussed with the groups and which we have already described. A selection from among these propositions was made, based on the subjective judgement of the members of the groups who were concerned with children of all ages. The final set of propositions was administered to different samples of teachers in Britain, the United States, Belgium, and Sweden (in the latter case concerning European immigrants). The returns from the last two countries were incomplete and no use could be made of them. Those who participated in the United States and Wales (100 in each case) were asked to respond on a five-point scale, and the results are shown in Table 5.1. The propositions are listed according to the category of rationale with which it is associated and the results of this empirical enquiry are discussed in each case, except where extensive discussion has already occurred.

Types of Rationales and Associated Propositions

LINGUISTIC RATIONALE

Five propositions concerning this rationale were included:
1. Where two languages are in contact, one influences the other through borrowing, grammatical, and phonological change. A bilingual education helps to control such influences.
2. A bilingual education promotes greater consciousness of the nature and working of a language and leads to linguistic sophistication.
3. Being educated in two languages and two ways of expressing ideas gives the speaker greater flexibility of communication.

TABLE 5.1. Acceptability of the Rationales for Bilingual Education

| | | | | Samples | | | Wales | |
Category of Rationale	Means of Consolidated Sample	University of Texas, Austin	Texas School Agency	University of New Mexico, Albuquerque	Dade County Florida	Hunter College, New York	English Area	Welsh Area
Linguistic	3.10	2.75	3.82	3.60	2.57	2.97	2.91	3.35
Cultural	3.90	3.60	3.70	4.41	3.60	3.40	3.31	4.32
Psychological	4.70	4.37	4.14	4.85	4.30	3.60	4.30	3.32
Socio-Political	3.50	3.02	2.90	3.30	3.40	3.60	2.54	3.95
Pedagogical	4.75	4.35	4.04	4.53	3.70	4.36	5.20	4.07

Source: Survey by E. Glyn Lewis, 1968-1975.

254 / Chapter 5

4. Languages have different characteristics and attributes. For these reasons languages are worth having for their own sake.
5. A bilingual child is likely to be less advanced in each of his two languages (for example in vocabulary) than a monolingual child is in his. The only way of limiting or counteracting this disadvantage is a formal bilingual education.

In some instances bilingual education is conceived in terms simply of acquiring an additional language, just as classical languages were acquired in the age of enlightenment. In fact it was stated in the evidence to one of the Commissions of Enquiry in the nineteenth century in England that the acquisition of a second language in Wales could substitute for the teaching of Latin and have comparable advantages. A second element in this category of linguistic rationales is the argument that languages have emotional values, learning a new language would be like having an aesthetic experience. A variation on this argument is that a bilingual child acquires two systems of verbal music. These arguments refer to the alleged inherent qualities of a language. A different kind of linguistic argument is advanced when it is claimed that a bilingual child enjoys greater flexibility of linguistic usage, a greater range of choices is open to him. This is only an extension of the argument that the acquisition of more than one regional or social dialect offers more choices to the monoglot child.

Among the most important of the linguistic rationales is a belief in the value of maintaining or even recovering a language for its own sake. With this rationale goes also the justification of bilingual education as the basis of academic linguistic studies, that such studies are valuable in themselves irrespective of their contribution to a broader education, and that the bilingual child is better able than a monoglot to undertake such linguistic studies. There has been a tendency to deny this proposition, but it is important to remember, I believe, that the Jews, with nearly 3,000 years of bilingualism and bilingual education behind them, have come to be regarded as among the most linguistically sophisticated people.

Taking the total sample in the United States and Britain (Table 5.1), the linguistic rationales appeared to elicit the least support. They are less important in the Dade County sample and most important in the Texas Agency sample than elsewhere. There is an interesting difference in the response of the two Welsh samples. The responses of subjects in every one of the samples reveal a highly idiosyncratic approach but the difference between the two Welsh samples suggests that the linguistic environment (predominantly English or Welsh respectively) influences judgment: where the emerging language (Welsh) is not normally used, less attention is drawn to its exclusively linguistic attributes than is the case where it is much more normally used. This conclusion seems to be supported by the fact that among teachers in strong Spanish areas (Texas

Agency and New Mexico) compared with New York, for instance, the means for this variable are relatively high.

CULTURAL/ETHNIC RATIONALES

Five propositions concerning these rationales were included.

1. A bilingual education ensures that a minority ethnic group safeguards its original native culture while participating in modernizing and innovating tendencies.
2. In so far as the ethnic language is closely associated with traditional religious observances, a bilingual education safeguards religious institutions and religious sentiments.
3. A bilingual who does not receive a bilingual education is likely to be at a greater disadvantage in both cultures than a monolingual is in either. A bilingual education is necessary in order to take full advantage of the two cultures.
4. A bilingual education promotes ethnic identity by making explicit and maintaining the differences between the groups.
5. A bilingual education helps to limit ethnocentricism and to promote tolerance between language groups.

More urgent than the linguistic rationales in Wales, the United States, and the U.S.S.R. at the present time are the arguments which can be categorized as socio-cultural or ethnic. Several, sometimes contradictory, cultural-ethnic rationales are proposed, among them being the following: bilingual education is said to promote or preserve the identity of the ethnic groups involved, with pride and confidence being engendered in the members of the group. This is one of the main arguments in Canada for the development of bilingual education among the French of Quebec.

The level of support for the cultural and ethnic rationale is fairly uniform except in New Mexico and the Welsh-speaking area, where the means are relatively high. On the other hand, this set of propositions carries less weight in the English-speaking area of Wales than anywhere else. Taking all the sample, the weight attached to ethno-cultural rationales is only slightly higher than that attached to the set of linguistic propositions.

INDIVIDUALLY ORIENTED OR PSYCHOLOGICAL RATIONALES

The five propositions were the following:

1. A bilingual education assists the emotional and intellectual development of bilingual children by ensuring the use of the mother tongue.

2. A bilingual education, by helping to ensure a greater consciousness of the socio-linguistic environment, facilitates the ability to control that environment.

3. Without a bilingual education a bilingual's personality may be impaired because important aspects of the tradition or traditional values may be ignored or lost.

4. A bilingual education ensures for the bilingual a sense of security (derived from identification with his kin group, and at the same time fulfillment of outward reaching psychological demands (derived from contact with the contact group).

5. In so far as a particular language tends to impose itself upon the way a speaker of the language thinks, an education in more than one language offers greater independence of thought.

If we take the total sample, the psychological rationales appears to be nearly the most salient category. Furthermore, apart from New York and the Welsh area, this category is given greater importance than any other. So far as concerns the Welsh-speaking area, the lower ranking of this category may be due first to the supreme importance attached to ethno-cultural arguments and to the powerful part played by the pedagogical propositions. The arguments concerning the form and structure as well as the purely teaching aspects of bilingual education have been far more intensive in the Welsh-speaking than in the English-speaking area. New Mexico stands out as the sample which attaches very considerable importance to the psychological arguments.

SOCIO-POLITICAL RATIONALES

The five propositions were these:

1. A bilingual education helps to undermine the political prestige of dominant groups.

2. A bilingual education helps to ensure a more open society and a stronger democracy involving equal participation by all ethnic groups.

3. In a society already divided by different language affiliations, a bilingual education helps to reconcile conflict.

4. Concern for developing a bilingual education helps to drain off aggressive manifestations in areas of social and economic controversy.

5. In a bilingual community, a bilingual education is an economic necessity since it taps potential but unmanifested sources of talent.

The support for socio-political rationales, as suggested by the data of the empirical investigation, is moderate compared with that given to other rationales. Among the United States samples, the teachers in the Texas School Agency favor this set of propositions less than any other samples. The reason may be that the sample drew upon a very dispersed group of teachers compared with Austin, Albuquerque, Dade County, or New

York. For that reason political consciousness of the possibilities of bilingual education may be less developed. It is noteworthy that samples from the highly urban areas in the United States have the highest means for this category. However, this is not true of the Welsh samples where the English area is highly urbanized and the Welsh sample drawn from predominantly rural areas. The level of support for political rationales is lower in the English area of Wales than in the United States, while the Welsh-speaking area sample offers greater support than any United States sample. The reason for the differences between the United States urban and the Welsh urban, and the United States rural and the Welsh rural samples has to do with the historical background of bilingualism in the two countries. The Welsh have had a long history of militancy in this matter based on pockets of rural areas where the proportion of Welsh to English is very much higher than in the urban areas. It should also be realized that the situation of those who maintain a Welsh consciousness is that of a conquered people—similar to that of the Amerindians—not like that of the urban immigrants of the United States.

PEDAGOGICAL RATIONALES

Five propositions concerning the pedagogical rationales were included.
1. A bilingual education helps to ensure closer and more sympathetic relations between school and neighboring community.
2. Teaching the mother tongue is helpful in facilitating the acquisition of a second language.
3. A second language like Spanish offers the same kind of enrichment that a classical language like Latin or Greek used to be relied upon to provide.
4. Learning a second language is a good basis for learning a foreign language.
5. An educational program should reflect as a matter of principle the important positive characteristics of a community.

This category of rationales has to do with the school as a formal institution with its functions in respect of the subjects taught (especially the two languages), the relation of the school to the students' homes, and to the neighboring society. It does not constitute a very coherent set of propositions nor does it differ essentially from any similar set of propositions that might be made in respect of mainstream education in a monolingual country. For that reason the pedagogical rationales, whatever the propositions may be in which the rationales are stated, tend to reflect and intensify the support given to all the other categories. In the last resort, since the enquiry was concerned with bilingual education, all the categories are oriented towards the schools. But in each of the other categories it is a particular aspect of the relationship of bilingualism to the schools that was in question. Here the focus is on the school as a principal agent. Rationales concerning a particular aspect of bilingualism receive different levels of support (according to the samples considered) but the pedagogical rationales concentrate the support which is prevalent, whatever the special justification may be.

It is not surprising, therefore, that the pedagogical rationales receive, over all samples, the greatest degree of support. Taking the individual samples in the United States, the support is highest in New Mexico and lowest in Dade County. It is surprising that this should be so in the latter case since the schools have played an important part in and focused attention on the promotion of bilingualism. Between the two Welsh samples there is considerable disparity. The greater importance attached to this set of propositions by the English-speaking sample may be explained by the fact that the problem of bilingual education in Wales is almost exclusively a matter of teaching Welsh to the English speaking children. The prevalence of English is such that even in the most thoroughly Welsh-speaking areas the difficulty of acquiring English is not remotely comparable to the difficulty of acquiring Welsh in the English areas. Consequently, in the latter areas the pedagogical issues have a considerable relevance and figure prominently in discussions about the feasibility of bilingual education.

Conclusion

When the questionnaires containing the propositions were administered, it was hypothesized that political rationales would not be the most favorably received by the respondents because these propositions represent the latest phase in the development of an acceptable justification of bilingual education. It was also hypothesized that this would be the case in the United States even more than in the other countries because of the recency of the development of interest in bilingual education in that country. These two hypotheses have been supported to as satisfactory a degree as the smallness of the samples would allow. Political rationales tend to have a low rating except in the two areas of Wales and New York. In Wales, this may be because that country has probably the most mature system of bilingual education of any of the countries in which we were interested, so that all the other justifications of bilingual education have long been met, and arguments other than the political ones no longer capture the interest of proponents or opponents. Any new argument concerning bilingual education in Wales has probably to be derived from socio-political considerations. In New York, the Puerto Rican minority is probably more concentrated, closely knit, and effectively mobilized, and possibly more subordinate economically than other minorities in the United States. For these reasons, socio-political arguments are likely to have greater cogency among the Puerto Ricans of New York than they have among other minorities.

The most clearly acceptable aspects of the political rationales are those dealing with economic considerations or those taking a positive stance in respect of the possibility of neutralizing conflict. The least acceptable political rationales envisage bilingual education as an agent of conflict or as the medium for promoting it. New York is again an exception, and this is in line with the strong approval of political rationales in that sample and the existence of an undercurrent of social conflict in the city. This is not the case in Wales for several reasons: because the Welsh linguistic minority is not economically subordinate; because there is complete intermixture of the English and Welsh-speaking group socially and geographically; and because in spite of some political tension the political party working toward a greater measure of independence has always played down the issue of language much to the annoyance of more extremist Welsh groups.

An empirical enquiry of this kind proved impossible in the Soviet Union. Had it been undertaken there is hardly any doubt that two levels of response would have emerged. Among the political hierarchy and party members, bilingual education would have been justified very strongly for political reasons—as a means of social and political unification or assimilation to the Russian language. For them, bilingual education is synonymous with the learning of Russian as a second language. Among the less ideologically committed or convinced, the probability is that the linguistic rationale would have been strong since the Russian language is a necessary language whatever views may be held about the political system. But above all else, the pedagogical rationale would have been approved since it would grant status to the strong minority languages and satisfy pride in rich historical cultures.

It cannot be emphasized too strongly that the results of this empirical enquiry have a limited value, partly because of the small samples but mainly because a much larger number of propositions should have been included in each category. Consequently, the enquiry touched upon only a small number of teachers and included no other professional or nonprofessional people. It also touched upon only a very small sample of the propositions that are normally advanced for or against bilingual education. With these important reservations, though, the enquiry—the first of its kind— proved very illuminating.

Six

Attitude to Languages in Contact

INTRODUCTION
The Importance of Attitude

The study of attitude to languages in contact and to the institutionalization of such contact in political organizations, administrative agencies,
and especially the system of education, is important for a variety of reasons.
A comparison of such attitudes in different bilingual countries or among
different linguistic groups in the same country increases the value of such
studies. Before language-education policies can be formulated, we need
to know the extent of the use of particular languages in various social
contexts and how the functions are being extended or restricted. If we are
to understand such issues, we need to know what forces determine the
different categories of language (majority and minority, lingua franca, and
ethnic languages), the direction in which those influences are exerted
(whether favorably or unfavorably, as well as their relative importance). It
is equally important that we should have some understanding of the way
bilingualism and the attitudes it helps to form determine, or at least
influence, the total structure of a society. For instance, whether it tends
to lead in specific cases to a fundamental restructuring of institutions (in
the extreme case to the separation of group institutions), or whether it
results in a restructuring of individual views about society, in the direction of tolerance of different languages, or alternatively toward an attitude

that ignores differences. It is unlikely that anyone will deny the importance of attitudes in determining the extent of current usages of a language, the prospect of their extension, and the kinds of prestigious contexts in which it will be used or denied use.

For these reasons, attitude is as important a dimension in the structure of a society as are other more tangible forces—like the size of the language group, age distribution, and so on. Many would say that the importance of a particular language in society derives in very large part from the attitudes which are adopted toward it. The structure of a heterogeneous society, whether that heterogeneity is ethnic, linguistic, religious, or socio-economic, is largely the result of the conflict or the convergence of attitudes to the various components of social diversity. Any policy for language, especially in the system of education, has to take account of the attitude of those likely to be affected. In the long run, no policy will succeed which does not do one of three things: conform to the expressed attitudes of those involved; persuade those who express negative attitudes about the rightness of the policy; or seek to remove the causes of the disagreement. In any case knowledge about attitudes is fundamental to the formulation of a policy as well as to success in its implementation.

This consideration is reinforced by the fact that in some instances a language policy is in fact largely if not principally concerned with inculcating attitudes either to the languages or to the speakers of those languages. In the Soviet Union during a critical period in policy making, Premier Kruschev argued in favor of promoting the Russian language not simply because Russian "was a powerful means of international communication . . . and of bringing other peoples into contact with the wealth of Russian and world culture," but because the learning of Russian was a means of "strengthening friendship among the peoples of the USSR" (*Pravda*, 25 December 1958). One of the most important influences bringing the peoples of the USSR together in friendship was the study of the Russian language by a large section of the population (*Vysshaya Shkola*, 20 April 1973: 1). The poor teaching of Russian in Georgia, so frequently and vehemently lamented by the administration (*Zarya Vostoka*, 10 July 1973), is an indication of the known failure to create favorable attitudes toward Russian among the Georgians and to diminish their intense loyalty to their native tongue. The practical, immediate importance of attitudes derives partly from the fact that attitude is perhaps the one dimension of child behavior teachers can modify.

A Definition of Attitude

Attitudes either are, or help to create, mental sets. These mental sets often constitute a cluster of preconceptions that determine the evaluation of a task, a situation, an institution, or an object before one actually faces it. Asch has pointed out that "the most significant function of attitudes is to restrict and bias the psychological field" (1952: 47). Consequently, "the decisive effect of attitudes is to distort perception (ibid:47). If attitude is synonymous with or creates a set of preconceptions and these preconceptions lead to possible bias, we should, in such a sensitive field as language maintenance, try to discover and if need be change attitudes very early. It is known that once preconceptions are allowed to harden into an image or stereotype of the language, the culture related to the language, or the people who speak it, it is not easily changed by experience. Attitude is determined, therefore, by the objective situation, its complexity, or its novelty, but just as much by a desire for approval or the avoidance of disapproval, among other needs. This approval or disapproval is a function of the society or the group to which the student is in some way related, together with his attitudes to those groups. For instance, a potential determining factor is the importance a school attaches to maintaining the mother tongue, but the effect of that factor will vary according to whether the attitude of the student to the school itself is positive or negative. Such considerations were recognized by Arsenian: "National, religious and political sympathies or antipathies determine the affective tone or the attitude of a bilinguist toward the second language and they introduce, therefore, important differences among bilinguals (Arsenian, 1945: 69). (Equally, they affect attitude to the maintenance of the mother tongue.) Similarly, the important work undertaken or directed by Lambert underscores the significance of stereotypes of languages and speakers of those languages, as well as the nature of a student's *disposition* toward what a language is thought to stand for.

Perhaps the most comprehensive definition of attitude is that given by Cattell: "An attitude is not a frozen stance, or any mental analogue thereto, for example a temporary set, but a structure which like any other mental structure, is influenced from repeated appearances of behavioral responses of a certain trend—the attitude separates out as a species within the genus, habit, because it is an oretic (connative-affective) habit, not a skill or cognitive habit" (1957:442). An attitude, therefore, is distinguished from a passing interest, a short term or immediate task-motivation because its basic characteristic is its preservation. While an attitude, as Cattell's definition implies, is revealed and known only in terms of particular behavioral patterns or situations, it is not specific to any particular situation. In fact, the important thing about attitudes is that though they may be modified by the adoption of certain procedures or by changing the circumstances in which they are relevant: attitudes are in fact relatively stable and enduring; this characteristic was specified very early by Muller and Pilzecker (1900).

A second characteristic of attitude implied in Cattell's definition is that it is based upon concepts of value. Attitudes are affective states producing a motivating power directed toward a goal that has been identified as valuable or significant to the individual or appears to be a necessary part of the culture of a group. These goals, all of which are relevant to the learning of languages, may be of several kinds: some relate to the acquisition of knowledge or knowing more about the world; others refer to even more basic or primitive drives, such as the satisfaction of hunger and thirst or the escape from poverty; and still other motives are the desire to dominate or lead others, or to affiliate to certain groups—the promotion of interpersonal ties. Many attitudes to language are adopted as the price of admission to groups or communities on which a value is set, or as a means of enhancing the status of the group or community to which an individual belongs. Attitude to maintenance and acquisition of language in certain kinds of bilingual situations reflects and may be governed by such needs and social values.

A third characteristic of attitude is that it is fundamentally a disposition or preparedness to act, or a focusing process. Sarnoff's (1962) summary of the contemporary view is that attitude is a *disposition* to react favorably or unfavorably to a class of objects. Allport, (1965:4) in an earlier treatment came to the same conclusion: "An attitude is a mental and neural state of *readiness* organized through experience exerting a directive or dynamic influence upon the individual's response to all objects and situations with which is is related (ibid., 18). Operationally, therefore, a study of attitude to learning or to maintaining a language involves not simply a description of the attitude, but equally importantly an analysis of actual language behaviors as well as of the conditions in which the attitude finds expression. Clearly no matter how favorable a child's attitude to maintaining his mother tongue or to acquiring a second language may be, he is not likely to maintain a favorable attitude long if the learning conditions militate against him. These conditions include the status of the language in the home and in society, the place of the two languages in the school, general environmental influences, and the recognition by the teacher of the need to suit the instruction to the capacity and strength of the learner.

Since an attitude may be defined in the same terms as a predisposition, it is not unusual to find varying degrees of discrepancy between attitude and actual language behavior. This is particularly true in bilingual situations where, almost by definition, attitude is always quite complex. A potential conflict exists between attitudes toward each of the two languages and potential conflict within the attitude to one or other languages. To understand an attitude, therefore, it is not sufficient to describe it, but we have to elicit information about the way in which attitude is realized in action or behavior. Such behavior can, of course, be of several kinds, for instance the influence one language is allowed to have on another—interference—but we are mainly interested in the *use* of the two languages.

Finally, attitudes toward language and language learning have cognitive and affective aspects or components. An attitude is generally recognized as carrying considerable feeling—it represents to most people their emotional response to an object, a situation, or an institution. But it is important to stress that some attitudes have cognitive aspects, and this means a person has beliefs about both a language and the place it should occupy in relation to other languages in a heterogeneous society. He tends to rationalize or conceptualize his attitude. Abstract concepts (with degrees of abstractness and formality varying with age and maturity) have an important role to play in socially-acquired attitudes. Even young children form ideas about a language and about what speakers of the other language are like. As they grow older, they form very clear ideas and develop beliefs about what the two languages stand for and what kind of use they have for them. In other words, the two languages are placed in cognitive and even ideological contexts. They are sometimes taught ideas about their own language, their community, or ethnic group. This cognitive element in attitude, while it does not reflect exactly the affective state, can be assumed to cover many affective aspects of attitude. Nevertheless, considerable dissonance between cognitive and affective aspects of attitude are present.

Different Aspects of Attitude to Language

When we speak of attitude to language we may have one of several things in mind. It may be that we are referring to the student's attitude to the process of learning a language. If this is what we mean, we would have to include in our study more than a consideration of language; for example the student's attitude to learning in general—how lazy, indifferent, or opposed he is to formal instruction in any subject. We may be referring to the student's perception of the characteristics of a language, a perception which will involve a comparative judgment of the languages in contact where one may be regarded as more elegant or musical or rich than the other. A third approach is to consider attitude to the developmental possibilities of a language—how those who are concerned with language planning or with the teaching of a language conceive its future; how far and at what expenditure of time, money, and expertise one language in a multilingual society can be developed to meet contemporary needs in the light of the availability of other languages which can be promoted more economically. This dilemma faces multilingual societies, the component parts of which are at different levels of development. Thus the Soviet Union, having created alphabets together in some cases with written and teaching materials, abandoned the planning of some languages and ceased to promote them by means of such institutions as the press and schools. The United States, so far as concerns the languages of the Native

Americans, has in the past acted on the assumption that very few of them needed to be promoted or developed. The same attitude characterized administrators' and educators' assessment of the viability and the developmental prospects of the Celtic languages in Britain.

A fourth possibility is to consider attitude toward the current uses of a language, the current distribution of roles between the languages in contact, as well as to changes in the distribution of those roles. There are implicit in such attitudes some important moral considerations and judgments that tend to carry weight with those who are involved in decision making. In a heterogeneous society (and any other for that matter), some form of distributive justice must be present, some principle that guides the apportionment of whatever the society has to offer in the way of rights, privileges, and opportunities. (I am indebted to John Rawls, *A Theory of Justice,* for the basic argument developed here, which I adapt to language groups.) The extent to which a society is fair as between individuals or between groups speaking different languages is an aspect of our study of attitude. Some multilingual societies adopt toward languages a utilitarian attitude and argue that justice is done within the society when the benefit to society as a whole is maximized irrespective of how individual groups may fare. Justice is done to all languages when the good of the majority of the total population outweighs whatever disadvantages are caused to the speakers of some few languages. This is basically the approach of the Soviet Union. The distribution of linguistic roles argued for by Dešeriev (1974) is meant to satisfy this principle. Diminishing the role of Georgian, Yakut, or Mordvin may be planned legitimately if the good of the USSR as a whole (synonymous with Russian in this case) is maximized. A variant of his utilitarian attitude is to consider all languages in a heterogeneous society as candidates whose claims have to be weighed against one another to achieve a balance between languages that is the most just at a particular point. No single criterion of balanced advantage exists. Sometimes it is political, sometimes religious, sometimes demographic. This is largely the attitude adopted in Belgium; from time to time the balance between the two principal languages is adjusted so as to ensure a just equilibrium between them according to a variable criterion. To some extent this is the approach in Canada toward the two major national languages.

The second main philosophical basis for attitude formation relies on a totally different concept of what is right for the different language groups. Justice is what is inherently fair, and all languages—like all individuals or groups of individuals—have an essential inviolability. The loss or disregard of one language or the diminution of its social roles is not made right by the greater good to the society derived from promoting another language either permanently, as in the Soviet Union, or temporarily, as in Belgium. I take this to be the view of Fishman. It means that the roles of a language should not be planned in such a way as to diminish it, nor should a society such as the United States or Canada, while forgoing language planning, permit the market to favor a particular language and diminish another, either temporarily or permanently.

In considering attitudes we may not be referring to individuals, to groups, or to national orientations that influence policy in respect of a language. We may not be concerned with a language as such so much as with the types of programs offered by schools which may vary considerably even within a particular ethnic group or national system. There may be consensus about the value of a language and of a bilingual education and a fair uniformity of attitudes to them, but attitudes about how to realize the agreed aims may vary.

Attitudes are derived not only from philosophical or moral stances, but also according to such mundane considerations as socially derived needs and their nature and strength. We have already mentioned such needs, including the need for knowledge, for instance. Children are encouraged to become bilingual because of the prospect of acquiring new knowledge while maintaining contact with the traditional resources of knowledge. Second, the need to satisfy hunger and thirst and to avoid pain, the hedonic context. Both languages may be necessary to a child if he is to earn a living in a bilingual community, and the economic urge and the attractions of social mobility are very strong. Third, sometimes a student is attracted toward a new language because of its social, scientific, or cultural prestige. Fourth, a student may decide to learn a second language because, while he is determined perhaps to remain firmly within his native language group, he wishes to form close attachments to another group speaking another language. In extreme cases such a need to affiliate to another language group may lead to a complete shift of language. There is a fifth need which determines the attitude of some, though only a minority of students. The satisfaction of becoming bilingual may be unrelated to any ulterior motives. It is a quasi-aesthetic determinant and though it is probably very subordinate to the socially derived needs already outlined, it is not an insignificant consideration in the analysis of attitudes among bilinguals.

General Characteristics of Attitudes to Language

Apart from the characteristics of attitudes we have already referred to, seven attributes can be identified which play a key role in determining the influence an attitude may exert on the maintenance of a language in contact with another. The language may be *central* to the group's value system. It may be closely associated with religious observances and with the maintenance of a way of life. Clearly where a language plays a central role, attitudes to it tend to be conservative and to some extent ideologized. Such an attribute is related to a second, namely the *rigidity* of attitude to language or the degree of resistance it offers to change. This in turn is related with a third attribute, the *stability* of an attitude, how far a particular attitude has persisted through time and therefore what indications there are of any propensity to change in the future. These three attributes, centrality, rigidity and stability, are closely associated without being in any way identical with each other. They determine more than any other attributes the influence an attitude may have upon the maintenance of a native language and upon the degree of approval given to the intrusion of a second language.

A fourth attribute is the *explicitness* with which an attitude to language is expressed, the degree to which an attitude is articulated verbally so that linguistic behavior may be reinforced by the inculcation of a set of beliefs about the language, either in the form of myths or dogma. Related to this fourth attribute is what, for the want of a better word, we may call the *quality* or *texture* of an attitude. This refers to the relative weight borne by cognitive and affective elements. In some instances groups and individuals are so strongly attached emotionally to a language that it is difficult for them to recognize the bases of their adoption of it. In other cases the attitude is so completely rationalized, rightly or wrongly, that the basis of the adoption of the attitude may be disguised. The sixth attribute, the *pervasiveness* of an attitude among the group, depends very largely upon agreement over certain beliefs about the language. A consensus needs to exist regarding the cognitive components, whether expressed as myth or dogma. The affective components, though usually far more intensely experienced, are less stable. Because of this the seventh attribute, the *intensity* with which an attitude is experienced or approved, whether negatively or affirmatively, has a great deal to do with its texture, or the amalgam of cognitive and affective elements that it represents.

Frequently this attribute of intensity attracts the greatest attention from those who are interested in measuring attitudes. Nevertheless, it would be wrong to believe that any important language attitude can be plotted upon a simple scale or that it was likely at any time to be unequivocal. Fishman (1965), for instance, has pointed out that a child may be willing to learn an ethnic language in a group (at school) when he declines to use it at home. Similarly, Herman, in describing the situation in Israel, points to the conflict that can occur in one and the same person between his individual needs and capacities on the one hand, and on the other the demands of the group to which he decides to be affiliated. "One situation may correspond to the person's own need to speak a particular language (for example the language in which he is most proficient); the other may correspond to the norms of his group, which may demand of him the use of another language (for example the national language) which he may speak with difficulty. There may be a conflict between personal needs and group demands. . . . The individual behaves as if he were in an overlapping situation consisting of both the immediate and the background situation" (Herman, 150).

In considering the make-up of an attitude, therefore, it is best to envisage a cluster of related attitudes or motives, possessing varying kinds of patterns and degrees of interrelatedness to one another. The components of the cluster may possess similar referents or objectives. Since we are concerned with the study and the improvement of attitude to language in a bilingual situation, we are inevitably more interested in the conflict of attitude and attempts to resolve that conflict than we are in attitude to one particular language. The kind of bilingual situation which we study necessitates the acceptance of the two languages, with possibly competing loyalties. Consequently any attitudinal change must be within the context of conflict resolution rather than simply the improvement of attitude in one direction or of attitude replacement. Of course the presupposition of this argument is that conflict can be resolved—but since this is the necessary presupposition to the promotion of bilingual education anyway, it is required logically and pragmatically. It is the only one by which educators can work.

Dissonance exists between attitudes toward the two languages; and within the attitude to one language a somewhat similar dissonance or equivocation may occur. A third kind of conflict or dissonance is often observable between a student's attitude toward either of his two languages and his attitudes to other important aspects of his personal objectives or goals. None of us is all of one piece, and it would be an extraordinary person who exhibited no conflict of loyalties or revealed no inconsistencies of attitude. Even if all the attitudes informing a particular conflict are consciously acceptable to him, the individual obviously cannot respond in any way that will provide simultaneous and optimum expression. Nevertheless, inconsistency or ambivalence is painful or at least uncomfortable for most of us. In consequence we strain toward some kind of symmetry in various ways—sometimes by avoiding situations that provoke such inconsistencies, and so far as language is concerned, by selecting our linguistic affiliations in various contexts very carefully. Sometimes we do it by changing one or other of the terms of the conflict, abandoning one or another of the languages for a particular purpose or for all purposes. Or we learn to tolerate the inconsistency, which is probably the richest pattern of attitudinal symmetry and one of the main justifications of bilingualism.

Some people can tolerate greater degrees of language conflict than others. This variability in conflict tolerance may be a function of personality as much as it is a function of the strength of the members of the cluster of attitudes. However we attempt it, "a need will be felt by the person or group whose inconsistencies in valuation are publicly exposed to find a means of reconciling the inconsistencies. . . . The feeling of need for logical consistency within the hierarchy of moral valuations . . . is in its modern intensity a rather new phenomenon. With less mobility, less intellectual communication, and less public discussion, previous generations were less exposed to one another's valuation conflicts" (Festinger, 49). One aspect of modernization as it affects the sensitive area of language loyalty and maintenance is that the explication, the ideologization of attitudes, exacerbates inevitable but hitherto suppressed conflict. A true bilingual education, no matter how well the two languages have been taught, has done virtually nothing if it has not helped to reduce such conflicts, or to reconcile some of them.

Components of Attitude

STATUS

Attitude is such a general term that it tends to lose much of its value unless it is analyzed and exemplified. What is of interest are the components of an attitude, and this is what concerns those who are involved in considering language policy in education. To elicit information about such components of attitude several questionnaires were administered to very dispersed groups of Spanish-speaking students, and to teachers drawn from the University of New Mexico (Albuquerque), University of Texas (Austin), Hunter College (New York), the Texas Education Agency, and Dade County, Florida. The questionnaires had been designed and used previously among several hundred students and teachers in Wales. The

TABLE 6.1. Perceived Importance of the Specified Variable in Promoting the Status of Spanish

Variable	Means	S.D.	Rank Order
1 Officially recognized in courts of law	1.40	1.60	10
2 Officially recognized in public administration	2.70	1.75	7
3 Required for official appointments	1.24	1.40	12
4 Taught in primary and secondary schools	6.32	2.30	2
5 Taught in colleges and universities	3.10	1.71	6
6 Used to teach other subjects in schools	6.47	3.65	1
7 Used to teach other subjects in colleges and universities	3.43	1.83	5
8 Used frequently on radio and TV	4.30	2.30	4
9 Used frequently in nationally recognized press	5.41	2.75	3
10 Used in scientific publications	1.51	2.10	9
11 Used frequently in business and commerce	1.80	1.41	8
12 Used in public worship	1.37	2.53	11

Source: Survey by E. Glyn Lewis, 1968-1975. Unless otherwise noted, the source of the tables in this chapter is the research conducted by Lewis between 1968 and 1975 in Wales and the United States of America.

first questionnaire, summarized results of which are in Table 6.1, assumed that attitude to language may be indicated by views concerning the prestige or status of a language.

The majority identified the status of Spanish with its place in schools and colleges—items 4 to 7, which are rank ordered 2, 6, 1, and 5 respectively. Items 8, 9, and 10, which are concerned with the mass media, the press and scientific publications, are rank ordered 4, 3, and 9 respectively, and come second to the items concerning the use of Spanish in schools. Public administration and justice (items 1, 2, and 3) and business (item 11) are rank ordered 10, 7, 12, and 8. The low rating of these items probably reflects the current standing of Spanish in these domains of use, and may not actually reflect how the samples regard the importance of these domains for the prestige of Spanish. Nevertheless, however we interpret them, the responses do indicate that the use of Spanish in such circumstances is not regarded at present as adding to the prestige of Spanish. Finally, religion is referred to in item 12 and is rated 11, and we can conclude that attitude to Spanish among this sample is not favorably affected by its association with religious observances. The results of this questionnaire suggest that the institutionalization of bilingualism is identified significantly—perhaps dominantly—with the schools, because the differences in means as between items 4 through 7 and the next highest group—the media (items 8 and 9)—are considerable. Other institutions like courts of law and the churches do not compete with schools. Bilingual education is seen by those connected with schools as fundamental to the standing of Spanish in society.

It is worth noting that 46 percent of those who attach a great deal of importance to Spanish in the schools and colleges also attach great importance to item 1 in Table 6.9—studying Spanish helps in obtaining a job. Also 67 percent of those who attach great importance to item 9 in Table 6.1 ("use in the press") regarded item 4 in Table 6.9 (Spanish for the purposes of reading books and periodicals) as being important.

The same questionnaire had been administered previously to a sample of Welsh-speaking adults—stratified according to language dominance and socio-occupational status. Table 6.2 records the differences between the dominant-English (whether professional or manual workers) and the dominant-Welsh samples. For instance, on the whole, the dominant-English samples attach more importance to the use of Welsh in commerce, and less to the use of the language in schools and colleges. The dominant-English sample regard the use of Welsh in public administration as less important than does the dominant-Welsh sample. Taking the total dominant-English and the total dominant-Welsh samples, however, there is considerable similarity in the relative importance they attach to the variables, especially the importance of Welsh in public worship, the use of the language to teach other subjects in schools and colleges, the teaching of the language in schools, the use of Welsh in the administration of justice, and the appearance of the language in scientific publications.

TABLE 6.2. Perceived Importance of Specified Variables in Promoting the Status of Welsh

Variable	Language Dominance	Socio-occupational status			
		Professional		Manual	
		Mean	S.D.	Mean	S.D.
1 Officially recognized in courts of law	Welsh	4.46	2.1	3.41	1.7
	English	4.63	2.4	4.71	2.4
2 Officially recognized in public administration	Welsh	4.86	2.0	2.79	3.1
	English	4.15	3.1	3.14	1.7
3 Required for official appointments	Welsh	4.15	2.3	2.92	0.8
	English	2.69	1.7	2.31	2.3
4 Taught in primary and secondary schools	Welsh	4.59	1.8	4.67	2.4
	English	3.35	1.7	4.75	2.9
5 Taught in colleges and universities	Welsh	3.72	2.3	3.41	1.6
	English	3.21	1.1	3.41	2.4
6 Used to teach other subjects in schools	Welsh	4.32	2.2	2.34	1.6
	English	2.66	1.2	3.10	2.1
7 Used to teach other subjects in colleges and universities	Welsh	2.85	0.3	2.10	1.4
	English	1.51	0.4	1.92	0.6
8 Used frequently on radio and TV	Welsh	4.17	1.8	3.78	2.3
	English	3.10	2.9	4.43	2.1
9 Used frequently in nationally recognized press	Welsh	3.57	1.8	3.91	1.7
	English	4.13	2.0	4.61	1.8
10 Used in scientific publications	Welsh	4.68	3.5	4.67	2.0
	English	5.12	2.7	4.75	2.4
11 Used frequently in business and commerce	Welsh	3.40	1.6	4.10	2.1
	English	4.79	2.4	4.90	3.1
12 Used in public worship	Welsh	2.81	1.3	3.51	2.3
	English	1.67	0.8	1.50	1.7

Source: Lewis survey.

Apart from the use of Welsh in commerce, which the Welsh-dominant do not regard as important, the two professional subsamples are generally in agreement. The main disagreements relate to public administration and the use of Welsh in schools (more favorably regarded by the Welsh-dominant professionals) and the use of Welsh in the press (less strongly supported by them). Apart from the fact that the Welsh-dominant manual workers give a higher rating to the use of Welsh in worship than do the English manual workers, the differences between these two subgroups are not particularly noteworthy.

Very considerable differences exist between the United States samples and the Welsh samples taken as a whole. Disregarding the categorizations of the Welsh sample, the latter differ from the Spanish bilinguals in attributing much more importance to the use of the native language in the administration of justice, in scientific publications, and in trade and commerce—for the reason perhaps that the Welsh language is already being used in these areas—as well as for teaching law and science at the university. In such a case a favorable attitude has grown out of experience. On the other hand, the Welsh sample (largely because of the attitude of the dominant-English) consider the use of Welsh to teach other subjects in schools and colleges as much less important than do the Spanish bilinguals. Both samples, Welsh and American, agree on the importance of teaching the native language in schools and its use in the press.

APPROPRIATENESS

The perception of the appropriateness of using a particular language, in specified domains, like the expression of what domains of usage promote the status of language, is an indication of attitude. Table 6.3 sets out the results of a questionnaire administered to 100 bilingual adults in Wales categorized according to language dominance and age. Each category consisted of 25 subjects. The domains of usage are specified.

The age group does not make much difference in the domains which are thought most appropriate for the use of Welsh among the Welsh-dominant or English-dominant adults. The use of Welsh in public worship takes precedence in both language categories and both age groups. The family is regarded as the next most appropriate situation, except among the older dominant-English groups, by whom it is regarded as the least important. The use of Welsh as a medium at school or at work is regarded as the least appropriate except among the younger dominant-English group. There appears then to be a general consensus regarding the areas of usage where Welsh is appropriate. At the same time, apart from the use of Welsh in public worship, the means are relatively low, and we can conclude that Welsh is not regarded as highly appropriate in any domain.

TABLE 6.3. Perception of Appropriateness of Welsh compared with English in Specified Situations

| | | Domain or Usage | | | | | | | | Means for Consolidated Domains | |
| | | Worship | | Family | | At School or at Work | | Among Friends | | | |
Language Dominance	Age	Means	S.D.	Means	S.D.	Means	S.D.	Means	S.D.	Means	S.D.
Dominant Welsh	18–25	3.12	2.10	2.31	1.40	1.69	1.12	2. 9	0.7?	2.32	1.40
	35–50	3.59	3.14	2.48	0.95	1.56	0.75	1.61	1.1?	2.37	1.31
Dominant English	18–25	1.48	0.85	1.01	2.12	0.85	1.13	0.63	1.14	1.02	1.00
	35–50	2.03	1.14	0.45	1.31	0.90	1.31	1.04	0.9?	1.15	1.10

Source: Lewis survey.

274

GENERAL ASPECTS OF ATTITUDES—STUDENTS

Before we discuss particular aspects of attitudes to a language, like interest or perception of its usefulness for instance, let us examine more general aspects. This examination was undertaken in depth among school children and adults between 1970 and 1974 in Wales. In the school investigation a stratified sample of 57 junior schools yielded 1,750 children in three localities of varying bilingual intensity. Twenty-seven secondary schools yielding 3,650 students were also selected, 21 from the three linguistic areas referred to, and six, irrespective of area, from among the total of schools which have been created in recent years to give Welsh a more prominent place in the curriculum and to use it more frequently and intensively to teach other subjects. Recruitment to the last group of schools is voluntary and highly selective, reflecting high motivation among parents to maintain Welsh. The secondary school sample consisted of 2,200 17-year-old and 1,350 14-year-old students. Thurstone-type tests were administered to all junior and secondary school students.

The investigation revealed marked differences in attitude according to age and type of linguistic environment. Table 6.4 shows that the attitude to Welsh becomes increasingly less favorable in all areas and types of school as the students grow older, and increasingly favorable to English. In types of schools where English is generally favored (category C), the disparity between Welsh and English attitudes increases. In schools where Welsh is generally favored (categories A, B, and D), the disparity decreases to the extent that at 14+ there is an attitudinal switch from Welsh to English except in Category D (See also Figure 6.1.)

In nearly half the sample population, and particularly in category A, B, and D schools, the distribution of "attitudes to Welsh" responses is either highly favorable, or highly unfavorable to the language, with a correspondingly very limited number of neutral responses. The curve of the distribution in Figure 6.2 shows a peak covering the mean scores 3 to 4.5 and a secondary peak covering the mean of 7.3. The distribution of the scores for English are almost unimodal in all types of school, and the percentages of the scores falling within the neutral zone were usually much higher than they were for Welsh.

Between 1966 and 1968 a group of researchers, including myself, conducted a national survey of educational attainment in Wales (NFER/WJEC 1969) which took into account attitudes to the subjects of the curriculum, including Welsh and English. Children of 7+, 10+, and 14+ were included in the numbers in each group sample were 2,500, 3,263, and 3,651.

At 10+ girls were more favorable to English and Welsh than were the boys, and this is continued in the 14+ age group. It is also apparent that

TABLE 6.4. Mean Scores of Attitude to Welsh and English on Thurstone Tests

	Types of Linguistic Area							
	A = 68–81% Welsh		B = 48–55% Welsh		C = 3–26% Welsh		D = Welsh Medium Schools	
Ages	Welsh	English	Welsh	English	Welsh	English	Welsh	English
10+	4.86	4.81	5.16	4.92	5.92	4.58	3.70	5.63
12+	4.20	5.45	4.78	5.16	5.50	4.82	3.55	6.43
14+	3.97	5.87	4.22	5.66	5.39	5.06	3.21	6.75

Source: Schools Council for England and Wales—*Study of Attitudes to Welsh and English*, 1974.

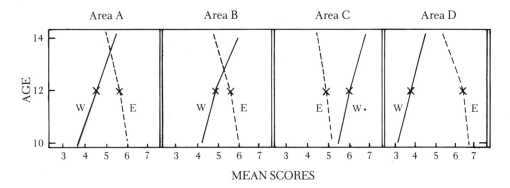

Fig. 6.1. Change of Attitude to Welsh and English According to Age and Type of Area

among both boys and girls the attitude to English is more favorable than the attitude to Welsh, and that the difference is greater among boys than girls. The linguistic environment correlates have not been included in Table 6.5. However, attitude to the Welsh and English language correlates positively to the intensity of Welsh and English respectively in the environment. It is interesting to note also that the percentage expressing positive attitudes to English in Wales was higher than it was in England. Attitude to English is distinctly more positive than attitude towards Welsh in both age groups. Thus 71.5 percent of the 10+ group and 76.8 percent of the 14+ group held positive attitude to English whereas in the case of Welsh the percentages were 39.3 percent and 44 percent respectively.

Fig. 6.2. Frequency Distribution of Attitude Scores

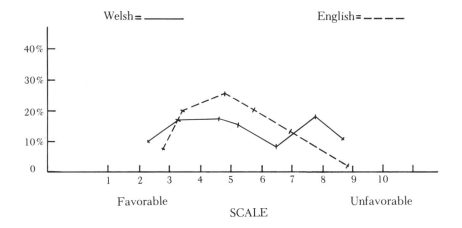

TABLE 6.5. Indices of Attitude toward English and Welsh[a]

	Boys		Girls		Boys and Girls	
Age	English	Welsh	English	Welsh	English	Welsh
10+	2.95	4.23	2.45	3.58	2.70	3.91
14+	2.96	4.31	2.48	3.33	2.74	3.86

[a] The lower the index, the more favorable the attitude.

Source: *Survey of Educational Attainments in Wales*, 1969. National Foundation for Educational Research and Welsh Joint Education Committee, Table XL.

GENERAL ASPECTS—ADULTS

A Thurstone-type test was administered to two different adult samples, each of 100 subjects between the ages of twenty and thirty (Table 6.6). The first was drawn exclusively from Area B (48–55 percent Welsh), and consisted of competent bilinguals. The second, consisting of monoglot speakers of English, was drawn equally from Area B and from Area C (3–26 percent Welsh). The distribution of the scores of the first (bilingual) sample showed, first of all, that the deterioration in attitude to Welsh among the school children continued among adults, the mean score of attitude to Welsh being 3.8 (S.D. 2) which is considerably less favorable than the least favorable among the group of school students in the same area (4.22). A consistent progression is found in attitude to English— mean 6.14 (S.D. 2.1) which is far more favorable than the most favorable student attitude in the same area.

The second sample, which was evenly divided according to linguistic area, was further divided according to length of residence in Wales. Attitude is more favorable to Welsh, and is less favorable to English among bilinguals (column 1) than among monolingual English-speakers in both areas, irrespective of length of residence. Among monolinguals, attitude to English and Welsh remained fairly constant irrespective of area of residence (compare columns 2 and 4, and 3 and 5); but increasing length of residence, independent of area, correlates with a more favorable attitude to Welsh (columns 2 and 3, 4 and 5) and a slightly less favorable attitude to English (columns 2 and 3, 4, and 5). Irrespective of differences in area or length of residence, the attitude of monolinguals (English) to English is much more favorable than their attitude to Welsh, and the disparity between the two attitudes among monolinguals is much greater than is the disparity among bilinguals.

The same Thurstone-type questionnaire was administered to a different sample of 100 bilinguals distributed throughout Wales. These were within the age group thirty to fifty years, and the sample was categorized first according to language dominance and then according to socio-occupational status (See Table 6.7).

TABLE 6.6. Attitude to Welsh and English among Bilingual and among Monolingual English Adults in Two Linguistically Different Areas

| | Bilinguals | Monolinguals | | | |
| | | Area B | | Area C | |
		Residence 2 Years	Residence 10 Years +	Residence 2 Years	Residence 10 Years +
Mean of Attitude to Welsh and S.D.	3.8 (2.2)	2.6 (1.6)	3.2 (2.5)	2.9 (2.4)	3.1 (2.5)
Mean of Attitude to English and S.D.	6.14 (2.1)	6.9 (1.8)	6.75 (1.7)	6.95 (2.0)	6.8 (1.9)
	1	2	3	4	5

Source: Lewis survey.

279

TABLE 6.7. Attitude to Welsh among Adults

| | Socio-Occupational Status | | | |
| | Professional | | Manual | |
Language Dominance	Mean	S.D.	Mean	S.D.
Welsh	3.42	2.03	3.64	2.41
English	4.03	2.76	5.75	3.05

Source: Lewis survey.

Irrespective of linguistic category, the attitude to Welsh is more favorable among the manual workers than among those in professions. But the difference is much greater concerning the English-dominant bilinguals (0.22) than among those whose dominant language is Welsh (1.72). If we take account of language dominance, socio-occupational status, type of linguistic environment, or length of residence in Wales, we can conclude that among adults, attitudes to English tends to be much more favorable than attitudes to Welsh. The greatest difference arises from the linguistic category of the subsamples—between dominant English and dominant Welsh bilinguals, and between monolingual English and bilinguals.

INTEREST

So far we have considered attitudes to any of the three languages (English, Welsh, and Spanish) in fairly general terms. We now need to investigate more specific aspects, and the first of these is interest, which we define largely in terms of the motivations determining attitude. These motivations may be immediate personal involvement—items 1, 2, and 8, for instance, in Tables 6.8 and 6.9; or long-term (items 3, 5, and 6); or they may be mainly affective in tone (items 2, 4, and 8); or more utilitarian (items 1, 3, 5, and 7). The same questionnaire was administered to the Welsh- and Spanish-speaking bilinguals. The Spanish-speaking sample was small (forty) and random. The Welsh sample was stratified according to lan-

TABLE 6.8. Interest in Spanish

Parameters	Mean	S.D.
1 My marks in Spanish are better than in other subjects	2.93	1.50
2 I like Spanish more than most subjects	4.21	2.11
3 I want to continue with Spanish in college	3.05	1.35
4 Spanish gets more interesting as I continue with it	3.31	1.53
5 I want to speak more languages than English	3.60	1.47
6 I hope to be able to use Spanish in my future career	2.71	1.61
7 I think everyone profits from learning Spanish	2.77	1.84
8 I owe it to my parents to speak Spanish well	3.66	2.30
Consolidated Means	3.23	2.31

Source: Lewis survey.

TABLE 6.9. Interest in Welsh

Parameters	Language Dominance	Age Groups 12+ Mean	12+ S.D.	14+ Mean	14+ S.D.
1 My marks in Welsh are better than in other subjects	Welsh	2.15	0.57	2.95	0.46
	English	1.76	1.00	0.79	2.00
2 I like Welsh more than most subjects	Welsh	3.05	1.14	2.76	2.31
	English	2.76	0.84	0.93	1.72
3 I want to continue with Welsh in college	Welsh	2.98	2.28	0.94	2.10
	English	2.10	1.21	0.85	1.23
4 Welsh gets more interesting as I continue with it	Welsh	2.86	0.49	3.41	2.41
	English	2.53	1.32	2.62	2.29
5 I want to be able to speak more languages than English	Welsh	3.20	2.40	4.31	4.65
	English	3.92	2.75	3.12	1.87
6 I hope to be able to use Welsh in my future career	Welsh	2.88	1.70	3.40	3.19
	English	1.21	2.00	1.42	2.01
7 I think everyone in Wales profits from learning Welsh	Welsh	3.50	2.62	3.21	2.58
	English	2.62	3.05	0.93	1.65
8 I owe it to my parents to speak Welsh well	Welsh	4.10	2.41	3.67	3.71
	English	0.75	2.10	0.59	0.81
Consolidated Means	Welsh	3.10	1.20	3.08	1.40
	English	2.20	2.40	1.50	2.50

Source: Lewis survey.

281

guage dominance and age. It numbered 200 shared evenly among the four subgroups. The Welsh sample was stratified according to language dominance and age. Each stratum was evenly divided between the two subgroups—12- and 14-year-olds. Consequently there are 50 members in each of the strata.

No consistent pattern of responses emerges from comparing the items reflecting immediate motivation (items 1, 2, and 8) and long-term motivation 3, 5, and 6), although on the whole the tendency is more in favor of the Spanish language being regarded as satisfying immediate rather than long-term requirements. The difference between responses to items 2, 4, and 8 (affective responses) and items 1, 3, 5, and 7 (utilitarian) is more consistent as well as more marked—favoring Spanish as the language regarded as satisfying emotional rather than utilitarian needs.

A more detailed examination of the Welsh sample was possible and is presented in Table 6.9. The Welsh-dominant students among the 12+ age group register stronger support for these items reflecting a long-term motivation for learning Welsh than those items reflecting an immediate interest. The 14+ age group, however, reveals an opposite tendency—a slightly greater support for items reflecting an immediate interest, except for item 5 where the value of Welsh is related specifically to the value of English. Interest in the immediate significance of Welsh among the 14+ age group suggests a certain lack of conviction about the future social significance of the Welsh language. To the English-dominant students of both age groups, it is the long-term value of Welsh that appeals; this is especially the case among the older group. The means for the immediate interest items are very low and among both Welsh- and English-dominant groups it declines with age. Among the Welsh-dominant group, the attitude to the long-term value of Welsh becomes slightly more favorable, while among the English-dominant group both aspects of attitude become less favorable.

If we look at the other categories of items—affective (2, 4, and 8) and utility (1, 3, 5, and 7)—Table 6.9 suggests that among the Welsh-dominant group support for the affective items declines with age, while support for the utility items increases with age. Among the English-dominant group, support for both categories declines with age. If, instead of comparing the two age groups, we compare the support for the two-item categories in a single age group, Table 6.9 suggests that among the Welsh-dominant group of 12 years and 14 years of age support for affective items is lower than support for utility items. The same is true for both age groups of English-dominant bilinguals.

We can summarize our conclusions thus: among Welsh-dominant and English-dominant students, greater interest is expressed in the long-term value of Welsh and in its utility. The interest in the immediate significance of Welsh declines with age among both types of bilinguals. The one exception is that the 12+ Welsh-dominant group are more interested in the short-term as opposed to the long-term significance of Welsh, and this we would expect with very young students. So far as the affective and utilitarian dichotomy goes, both age groups in both categories of bilinguals reveal stronger interest in the usefulness of Welsh, and relatively speaking the difference in level of support increases with age.

A comparison of responses of the Spanish bilinguals (U.S.A.) and the Welsh bilinguals reveals a divergence at each point. The United States sample favors the immediate and affective significance of the Spanish language; the contrary was present in the Welsh survey. It would have been interesting, but impossible in the time available, to have stratified the Spanish-speaking sample and so add to the possibilities of comparison. But it is possible to hypothesize that the differences we have noted are due to the generally greater acceptability and tradition of the use of Welsh in education, in public, and often formal, official domains.

USEFULNESS

Because of the evidence that the attitude of Welsh-speaking bilingual students tends to favor the long-term and utilitarian significance of the Welsh language, it was decided to probe further. For the contrary reason, namely the apparent lack of interest among Spanish bilingual students in the utility of that language, it was decided to use the same questionnaire in an attempt to discover whether there were any (and if so what) aspects of the usefulness of Spanish which the students might value in spite of the general lack of interest in utilitarian issues. Since the Spanish data is simpler to handle we will analyze that first in Table 6.10.

The eight statements belong to different categories of usefulness: eco-

TABLE 6.10. Perception of the Utility of Spanish among Students

Aspects of the Usefulness of Spanish	Mean	S.D.
1 Studying Spanish may help to get me a good job	3.00	1.78
2 I need to study Spanish because it is in the curriculum	1.89	2.11
3 I need to study Spanish because it is used to teach some other subjects	1.82	2.14
4 I need to study Spanish in order to read Spanish books	2.89	0.96
5 Studying Spanish will help me if I need to study another language	2.49	1.34
6 Studying Spanish will help me to make Spanish-speaking friends	4.52	3.13
7 Spanish will help me to communicate with a greater variety of people	3.93	1.76
8 Spanish will help me to know and appreciate the way of life of Spanish speaking people	3.76	1.92
Consolidated Means	2.92	1.45

Source: Lewis survey.

nomic (item 1); scholastic and academic (2, 3, and 5); social communication (6, 7, and 8); and usefulness for cultural activity such as reading (item 4). Table 6.10 suggests that the aspects of the usefulness of Spanish which are most highly regarded are those which belong to the broad context of general social communication—informal interpersonal relations. The least valued are those associated with academic achievement and economic life. The value of Spanish in the domain of culture (reading) relates more closely to the less highly valued economic and academic domains rather than to other domains. Spanish is considered useful in those aspects favored in Table 6.8—the immediate personal values of the language.

In the Welsh samples (Table 6.11), no tendency is seen comparable to that of the Spanish bilinguals to polarize the utilitarian values according to whether they are economic or social. The Welsh samples have a greater spread or range of uses for the language, tending to encompass all aspects of the utility of Welsh. Thus, among the Welsh-dominant 12+ age group, attitude is determined by the inclusion of the language in the curriculum, the importance of Welsh literature, and the prospects of a job for which Welsh would be an advantage. A similar spread of interest emerges among the 14+ age group. Both age groups of the Welsh-dominant bilingual attach relatively less value to Welsh as a means of enriching interpersonal communication.

The opposite is the case with the English-dominant age groups. They attribute a relatively high evaluation to Welsh as a means of enriching interpersonal communication, but they give a relatively low value to the economic usefulness of Welsh, its usefulness in providing an insight to Welsh literature, or as a basis for acquiring another language. Most of the differences between the Welsh-dominant and the English-dominant bilingual students of both age groups may be attributed to the fact that for the former Welsh is their native tongue, and they take the importance of Welsh for interpersonal communication for granted and are more aware of what the emergence of the language into economic and academic life offers.

It is noteworthy that the values among both linguistic groups tend to diminish between 12+ and 14+, and that they are lower among both age groups of the English-dominant bilinguals than among the Welsh-dominant group.

Because of the apparent agreement among Welsh bilinguals concerning the economic value of the Welsh language, it was decided to take the matter further and investigate how a sample of adults evaluated the consequences to them of the ability to speak the two languages (see Table 6.12).

The sample consisted of 200 adults between the ages of thirty and fifty drawn from the whole of Wales and distributed equally among the four strata. The first thing to note are the relatively high means for Welsh

TABLE 6.11. Perception of the Utility of Welsh among Students

Aspects of Usefulness	Language Dominance	Age Groups			
		12+		14+	
		Mean	S.D.	Mean	S.D.
1 Studying Welsh may help to get me a good job	Welsh	3.78	2.13	4.56	2.31
	English	2.63	1.05	1.35	2.21
2 I need to study Welsh because it is in the curriculum	Welsh	4.57	3.12	2.15	1.75
	English	4.35	2.14	3.01	1.94
3 I need to study Welsh because it is used to teach some other subjects	Welsh	3.51	1.21	3.12	2.31
	English	4.63	1.78	4.71	1.98
4 I need to study Welsh in order to read Welsh books	Welsh	4.21	1.97	3.97	2.34
	English	3.53	2.71	2.31	1.47
5 Studying Welsh will help me if I need to study another language	Welsh	2.34	2.11	1.73	2.00
	English	3.67	2.32	2.44	1.64
6 Studying Welsh will help me to make Welsh-speaking friends	Welsh	2.10	1.10	0.67	1.31
	English	4.52	2.11	3.21	2.10
7 Welsh will enable me to communicate with a greater variety of people	Welsh	2.32	2.56	0.47	2.13
	English	3.97	1.31	4.25	2.32
8 Studying Welsh will help me to appreciate the Welsh way of life	Welsh	3.14	1.07	3.92	2.05
	English	4.70	2.79	4.91	3.21
Consolidated Means	Welsh	3.64	1.84	3.57	1.67
	English	3.51	1.98	3.37	2.41

Source: Lewis survey.

TABLE 6.12. Perception of the Economic Consequences of the Ability to Speak Welsh and English

	Language Dominance	Socio-Occupational Status			
		Professional		Manual	
		Mean	S.D.	Mean	S.D.
Consequences of the ability to speak Welsh	Welsh	5.22	2.14	3.73	1.3
	English	4.79	1.46	2.97	1.6
Consequences of the ability to speak English	Welsh	6.90	2.15	4.85	2.0
	English	8.45	3.91	6.96	2.9

Source: Lewis survey.

among the dominant-Welsh and dominant-English professional groups and the much lower means for Welsh among the manual workers. This may be due to the number of teachers and clergy in the professional groups. In any case, this result confirms the results shown in Tables 6.9 and 6.11. Second, the dominant-English professional and manual groups appraise the economic consequences of Welsh lower than the dominant-Welsh groups. This probably reflects partly their confidence in using Welsh and partly (and consequently) the lower frequency of their resort to Welsh. Third, all groups give a much higher rating to the consequences of using English, and the position of the dominant-English in relation to the dominant-Welsh is now reversed.

The sample of forty-five Spanish-speaking adults in the United States was very diverse in location, age, occupational status, and, so far as I could ascertain, in the nature of their language dominance (see Table 6.13). They were asked the same type questions used in the Welsh sample, and the results bear out those we have touched upon. Spanish was rated lower than was Welsh, even lower than the responses given by manual workers in Wales. The rating given to English is higher than that given by any of the Welsh groups, except the dominant-English professionals. The higher rating of English is probably a reflection of the lower rating of Spanish in the United States compared with Welsh in Wales.

Only the most tentative conclusions can be drawn from comparing Spanish and Welsh bilinguals. First, a clear polarization of attitude is held by the Spanish bilinguals, a marked inclination to emphasize Spanish as a language of interpersonal and broad social communication and an equally marked disinclination to value Spanish in terms of its academic or economic usefulness. Among the Welsh bilinguals, there does not appear to be such a marked dichotomy: some interpersonal, cultural, academic, and economic aspects are valued highly and some are not. The range of the Welsh students' attitude to Welsh is comprehensive. The Welsh language in Wales is used nationally over a great range of affairs and circumstances— used in as many domains as English though not as extensively in some of them—and it seems probable that interest in and the perception of the usefulness of Welsh is influenced by the current situation of the language. A favorable or unfavorable attitude grows out of the soil of use or neglect as the case may be. This being the case, the results in both the Welsh and Spanish cases reflect the current situation of the respective languages as

TABLE 6.13. Perception of the Economic Consequences of the Ability to Speak Spanish and English

	Mean	S.D.
Consequences of ability to speak Spanish	3.22	1.14
Consequences of the ability to speak English	7.34	2.27

Source: Lewis survey.

much as and possibly more than they do attitudes as such. If we wish to improve attitudes we need to give the language an opportunity to show what it can do.

CONTENT OF ATTITUDES—STUDENTS

From a more detailed examination of the items which constituted the several questionnaires, it is possible to develop a content analysis of the attitudes to the two languages—especially in Wales— and to offer a tentative categorization of those elements. The first thing to be said is that it becomes more evident than ever that the nature of the response, from item to item in the questionnaires, varies consistently according to the area from which the subjects were drawn. For instance, the percentage responses of students in categories A, B, and C (Table 6.4) on the English scale ("English should be taught all over the world") was in the range 40 percent to 60 percent varying according to age and area, but the percentage response in category D was half that, in the range 23 to 33 percent varying according to age. In the same list, the item "English is a beautiful language" produced a range of 40 to 60 percent in favor among all students except category D where the percentage was 21 percent. It is likely that attitude to the two languages, and especially Welsh, is a function of the linguistic character of the locality, and individual variance within localities is limited. Though it was not possible to investigate the influence of linguistic environment in the United States, it is probable that the same influences prevail.

Attitude to Welsh among children appears to have four major components. The first of these is a factor that we may term general approval—"I would like to speak Welsh for the fun of it," "Welsh is a language worth learning," "I like speaking Welsh," and so on—and the average favorable response is 68 to 75 percent. The second factor is commitment to practice— represented by such statements as, "I want to maintain Welsh to enable Wales to develop" (50 percent); "Likely to use Welsh" (40 percent), "There are more useful languages than Welsh" (38 percent). Responses to items in the Spanish questionnaires appear to be in line with the Welsh responses. While general approval was very favorable to Welsh, response to items which might be taken to imply a practical decision to implement approval was relatively unfavorable. One indication of the apparent reluctance to take practical steps to promote Welsh is the fairly high percentage of responses in favor of individual choice in deciding to study Welsh, "Welsh should not be forced upon non–Welsh-speaking pupils" (75 percent); "The learning of Welsh should be left to individual choice" (78 percent). Spanish, which is associated far more unequivocally with group maintenance, might have a different tendency.

The third factor in attitude to Welsh is national tradition—represented by, "The need to keep up Welsh for the sake of tradition" (68 percent); "We owe it to our forefathers to preserve Welsh" (78 percent); "The Welsh language should be preserved because it is a sign of Welsh nationhood" (65 percent). This, together with the first factor of general approval, is the most important aspect of attitude to Welsh. The fourth factor, economic importance, also plays a significant role. For instance, Welsh was considered to offer advantages in seeking good job opportunities by 61 percent in Welsh-speaking areas, and in the English-speaking areas just over 50 percent thought that Welsh was important in Welsh economic life. As we have noted, this factor is far less impressive in the Spanish bilingual context. So far as Welsh is concerned, three factors—general approval, traditional nationalism, and economic importance—produce favorable responses, and the other factor, a commitment to practice, produced unfavorable responses on the whole.

Attitude to English also has four major components, three of which correspond closely to components of the attitude to Welsh—general approval, commitment to practice, and economic and educational importance —and all received very favorable responses. The fourth component of attitude to Welsh, traditional nationalism, finds no place in the attitude to English, and is replaced by a factor we may term *necessary bilingualism*. This factor is expressed in favorable responses to such statements as, "I should not like English to take over from the Welsh language" (65 percent); "The English language is killing the Welsh language" (80 percent); "The Welsh should speak both languages" (72 percent); "English should not be more important than Welsh in Wales" (68 percent). The existence of this fourth factor in attitude to English is in line with the nature of the curve of distribution of total responses to English (Table 6.4). It is unimodal and to that extent is devoid of extreme antipathy to Welsh or extreme commitment to English in Wales, but there is a degree of tolerance that is remarkable among relatively young children.

CONTENT OF ATTITUDES—ADULTS

The 100 bilinguals referred to in Table 6.6 submitted themselves to a second test designed to ascertain their beliefs about the Welsh language, the relative importance to them of those beliefs, and their conceptual significance. The initial preparation and pretesting of the instrument indicated the existence of five categories or groups of concepts about the Welsh language. The order of their apparent importance, with exemplifying statements, follow. First were familial and local considerations—the language is important to family life, whether at home or in formal worship, and it is vital to the integrity of small groups. The high means of items 5, 7, and 8 of table 6.10 indicate it applies to Spanish also. The second was ethnic considerations—the Welsh language is the symbol of

Welsh life, and the institutions of Wales are meant to preserve Welsh traditions. Welsh and Spanish bilinguals both stress the value of their language in close interpersonal relations. The third were personal considerations—Welsh does not promote the kind of progressive outlook I approve of, and it does not provide for an adequate range of aesthetic experience in literature, the theater, and the media. Social communication was the fourth consideration—Welsh promotes exclusiveness, and it is of little use in making contact with the world outside Wales. In view of the world language status of Spanish, it is improbable that this is the case among Spanish bilinguals. Finally, there were the linguistic considerations —the Welsh language has not developed sufficiently to meet the demands of modern society, industry, and science, and it is difficult to learn. For the reasons already stated, this opinion is unlikely to be present for Spanish bilinguals.

ASSOCIATION OF ATTITUDE TO LANGUAGES AND LANGUAGE USAGE

So far our attention has been focused on two of our main areas of comparison—Britain and the United States—and upon the attitude to language in those two countries. However, there are several other indices of attitude, the most important of which is actual language behavior—for instance, which language is chosen in particular situations, and the extent to which shift of language affiliation occurs. It is here that the Soviet contribution to the understanding of attitude to language is most fruitful. Soviet socio-linguists tend to work back from observed changes in the use made of the different languages to discover changes in attitude toward different aspects of ethnic identity, including language. Consequently, Soviet socio-linguists are greatly interested in the failure of native language affiliation to coincide with other aspects of ethnic behavior, and in the discrepancies that occur between the linguistic behavior of the same person, in the same family, or in the same group. But in their research, the basic postulate is that a connection exists between changes in attitude and changes in language behavior (Gubolgo, 1972: 33).

Language behavior in this sense can take several forms. For instance, in the Soviet Union the choice of school—either Russian or native-language medium—is indicative of an attitude. It is not without significance for an understanding of attitude that 90 percent of those attending Russian-medium schools in Armenia are Armenians (Bilinsky, 1962: 141). The preference for one language over another in social situations of different kinds is another index of attitude (Lewis, E. G., 1976). But the most categorical of all indices of attitude is language shift, which occurs in most cases without a corresponding change of ethnic affiliation. For instance, Mordvins who live in the Tatar ASSR and have adopted the Tatar language have preserved their ethnic identity. This situation is common among other peoples of the Volga and Urals (Terent'eva, 44). This phenomenon is well marked among all ethnic groups in the United States, but especially among Amerindians.

However, no definite association between attitude and behavioral changes can be established. Behavioral changes are not determined exclusively by changes of attitude, and we cannot measure attitude change by investigating behavioral changes alone. Geography helps to determine language behavior independently of attitude: remoteness confirms language loyalty while contact promotes change. Intermarriage and urbanization are forms of linguistic contact just as the internationalization of culture serves to change attitudes. Some institutions, like religious organizations, on the other hand tend to reinforce favorable attitudes to the mother tongue. These factors, which we analyze more fully later, are common to our three countries of major interest. However, there is one factor determining usage directly, and as a consequence determining attitude indirectly, which differentiates the Soviet Union from Britain and the United States.

All languages in either the United States or Britain are not on an equal footing and are not able to compete on the basis of "fair play" for the support in usage among the various minorities. Instead, the English language enjoys great advantages. In the Soviet Union not only does the Russian language enjoy the same relative advantages as English in Britain and the United States, but it is the *policy* irrespective of personal or group desires to increase that advantage. Efforts are made to increase the numbers speaking Russian, and to extend the range of its supremacy by ensuring that certain usages are reserved for Russian and denied to minority languages. Like English, Russian is to be allowed the advantages of the "free market." As Dešeriev remarks: "There is no need to regularize too strictly the development of social functions of . . . Russian. . . . Matters are different with the planning of the development of the social functions of the Abaz language" and he might have added Georgian and other major languages (Dešeriev, 1952: 9). If a language has the opportunity to be used it will attract a favorable attitude, but where it has a history of denial unfavorable attitudes will prevail. This was one point of comparison between Welsh and Spanish. To the extent that usage is planned, attitude is planned also. This is the difference between the Soviet Union on the one hand and Britain and the United States on the other.

ATTITUDE IN RELATION TO COMPARATIVE SOCIAL FUNCTIONS AND LEVEL OF KNOWLEDGE

No study of attitude would be remotely adequate if it did not at least touch upon the uses to which languages in contact are put and the comparative knowledge of them. For our purposes, we shall use data from questionnaires completed in Wales and the United States as well as data from studies in the Soviet Union by Soviet scholars.

Modal Usage

The first aspect of usage and knowledge to be investigated was in the area of modes of linguistic functions—listening, speaking, reading, and writing. The same questionnaire was used in Wales and the United States but the Welsh sample was stratified (see Table 6.14 and Table 6.15).

Generally speaking, the means for the use of Spanish compared with English are not high, the lowest being in respect of writing and the highest in respect of listening. The two more formal modes, reading and writing, are lowest in rank order and this confirms what other data have suggested about favorable attitudes to Spanish being mainly in respect of close interpersonal and informal social contacts.

The 100 adults in the Welsh bilingual sample were stratified according to language dominance and age. As was the case with Spanish, the means for Welsh as compared with English tend to be low, and lower, except for listening and speaking, among the Welsh-dominant groups than the English-dominant. As with Spanish, the two more formal modes have the highest means, and this is true of all four groups. The older Welsh bilinguals, whether Welsh- or English-dominant, have higher means than the younger groups—except in reading and writing. Invariably, the English-dominant age groups have lower means than the Welsh-dominant age groups, and in fact the interest of the former in reading and writing Welsh irrespective of age is comparatively negligible. Based on this data, the situation of the Spanish bilinguals within the United States is not dissimilar to that of the Welsh bilinguals taken as a whole, and it is more favorable than the situation of the English-dominant bilinguals in Wales.

Knowledge of Languages—Welsh and English Students

It goes without saying that attitude alone does not determine preference for either language in any of its modes. A great deal depends upon relative competence, just as there is a reciprocal association between competence and attitude.

Two comparatively recent surveys involving large samples of students have been undertaken in Wales measuring competence in Welsh and

TABLE 6.14. Distribution of Modal Spanish Usage

Language Mode	Mean	S.D.
1 Listening to Spanish compared with English	3.86	2.80
2 Speaking Spanish compared with English	3.76	2.30
3 Reading Spanish compared with English	2.39	1.20
4 Writing Spanish compared with English	1.97	1.30
Consolidated Mean	3.24	2.51

Source: Lewis survey.

TABLE 6.15. Distribution of Modal Welsh Usage According to Language Dominance and Age

Language Mode	Language Dominance	18–25		30–45	
		Mean	S.D.	Mean	S.D.
1 Listening to Welsh compared with English	Welsh	3.91	3.80	5.41	2.60
	English	2.22	1.80	2.79	2.00
2 Speaking Welsh compared with English	Welsh	3.49	2.20	4.42	3.80
	English	1.36	1.80	1.79	0.84
3 Reading Welsh compared with English	Welsh	3.08	2.15	2.61	2.30
	English	0.75	1.20	1.01	1.20
4 Writing Welsh compared with English	Welsh	2.01	1.80	1.76	2.30
	English	0.07	1.10	0.61	1.45
Consolidated Means for All Modes	Welsh	2.35	2.06	3.76	2.75
	English	1.43	1.95	2.07	1.82

Source: Lewis survey.

English. The first, "Attitudes to Welsh and English in Wales" (Schools Council, 1974), measured attainment in Welsh as a first and as a second language as well as English for three groups—10 years, 14 years, and 16 years of age (see Table 6.16). The number of students in each age group was over 1,000.

Just as attitude to English is more favorable than attitude to Welsh, so is attainment in English higher than attainment in Welsh as a first or second language in all groups. Similarly, the lower attainment in Welsh as a second language among English-dominant bilinguals compared with attainment in Welsh among Welsh-dominant bilinguals of all age groups corresponds to similar differences in attitude among the respective linguistic categories. It is also the case that attitude to Welsh becomes less favorable with age as also does level of attainment.

The second national survey we shall report was conducted between 1960–68 by a group of researchers advised by the present writer. Several aspects of the curriculum were studied, but we are at present concerned only with aspects of language. Table 6.17 is a summary of a sample of children drawn from the most thoroughly bilingual areas where the intensity of Welsh was high.

The results recorded in Table 6.17 bear out some of the results in Table 6.16 and have similar implications in respect of possible correlations between attitude and attainment. Attainment in the two aspects of English tested is higher in both age groups than attainment in Welsh, and there is an increment in respect of age in English and Welsh attainment.

Knowledge of Welsh and English—Adults

The sample of adults tested for attainment was much smaller than the school survey. The tests were limited to the Welsh language since at this age (30 to 40) the issue of competence in English is hardly relevant in Wales.

All those who were included in the sample on which Table 6.18 is based were English-dominant bilinguals between the ages of thirty and forty. They were equally shared according to socio-occupational status and then according to length of residence. Only forty were included. Their competence was judged by two investigators who asked the subjects to read a short passage of Welsh, on which they were questioned and replied orally. They were finally asked to write five sentences on the passage which formed the basis of the test. All were assessed on a five point scale. The first result to note is that there is considerable improvement in both socio-occupational groups according to length of residence and that the degree of improvement is roughly equivalent in the occupational groups. Invariably the professional group—irrespective of length of residence—have a higher competence in Welsh than the manual workers. The rank

TABLE 6.16. Attainment in Welsh as a First and Second Language as well as English among Bilinguals

	Age Groups								
	10+			14+			16+		
	Welsh[1]	Welsh[2]	English	Welsh[1]	Welsh[2]	English	Welsh[1]	Welsh[2]	English
Means	63.25	34.07	64.80	48.18	40.67	51.95	43.14	38.35	46.42
S.D.	23.67	17.50	22.99	15.90	17.80	16.71	14.05	17.30	8.76

Welsh[1] = Welsh as First Language. Welsh Dominant Bilingual.
Welsh[2] = Welsh as Second Language. English Dominant Bilingual.
Source: Schools Council for England and Wales, *Survey of Attitudes to Welsh and English*, 1974.

TABLE 6.17. Attainment Means in Aspects of English and Welsh among Bilinguals

	Age Groups							
	10+				14+			
	English Language	English Reading	Welsh Language	Welsh Reading	English Language	English Reading	Welsh Language	Welsh Reading
Means	94.0	91.7	88.2	88.3	97.4	95.1	90.8	89.1
S.D.	1.2	1.5	1.4	1.7	1.4	2.4	1.9	1.7

Source: National Foundation for Educational Research and Welsh Joint Education Committee, *Survey of Educational Attainments, 1969.*

TABLE 6.18. Knowledge of Welsh among English-Dominant Bilinguals (30 to 40 Years of Age)

Aspects of Welsh Competence	Socio-Occupational Status	Length of Residence			
		5–10 Years		11–20 Years	
		Means	S.D.	Means	S.D.
1 Understanding spoken Welsh	Professional	3.67	3.00	4.34	2.13
	Manual	2.17	0.58	3.78	2.74
2 Reading Welsh	Professional	3.09	1.47	4.16	1.31
	Manual	2.03	2.00	3.12	0.98
3 Speaking Welsh	Professional	2.51	1.41	2.93	1.47
	Manual	1.79	0.83	2.42	2.00
4 Writing Welsh	Professional	1.32	1.11	2.10	1.34
	Manual	0.97	1.31	1.35	0.79
Consolidated Means	Professional	2.52	1.48	3.40	1.78
	Manual	1.74	1.21	2.66	2.10

Source: Lewis survey.

order of modal usage (Table 6.15) is identical with actual competence as tested on this occasion, except that reading ability in Table 6.18 is placed higher than speech ability among all groups. This is not unexpected since reading Welsh (like reading Spanish) is less difficult than reading English, for instance, because of the regular phonetic character of the alphabet.

Knowledge of Language—Soviet Union

As we have suggested earlier, the most unequivocal index of the relation of attitude to and competence in a particular language is "language shift." The latter does not mean that knowledge of the forsaken language has disappeared, but that relative competence in the two languages has switched. For this reason, the census data concerning the lack of consistency between ethnic affiliation and choice of language—the choice, usually of Russian, as the first language of a member of a non-Russian nationality—reflect a shift both of attitude and competence. According to the 1970 census (Lewis, E. G., 1972: 133–9) in 32 of the 100 nationalities numbering over a thousand, 5 percent though retaining their ethnic affiliation claimed Russian as their first language. For seven nationalities, the language shift was between 20 percent and 30 percent, and for nine the percentage was over 50. The speed and extent of this process is determined by several factors—age (the younger are more prone), urbanization, intermarriage, and so on. And as is to be expected these factors, as we shall note, influence not only the ultimate shift but the level of competence in the intermediate stages.

More detailed investigations have been conducted in specified localities. Perhaps the major issue that interests the researchers is the level of attainment in Russian among non-Russian nationalities. It is significant that Georgia, which is usually the most reluctant of nations to conform to Russification and whose attitude to Russian is lukewarm, is constantly being criticized for the quality of its Russian. In 1973 (*Zarya Vostoka*, 10 July 1973: 1) a sharp rebuke was administered: the quality of Russian had declined, its teachers were inferior, and the University of Tbilisi (the capital) "had opted out altogether. Even people with higher education, scholars, scientists, engineers, University and school teachers, and party leaders even, have a very poor knowledge of Russian."

A survey conducted by Arutiunian (1973b) investigated the competence of four groups in Tbilisi (see Table 6.19) drawn from two academic institutions, a factory and a collective farm. Those in the sample all claimed a knowledge of Russian, but in no group was there a 50 percent fluency in Russian, and Georgian was by far the superior language among all but the scientists of the Mechanics Institute. The great majority of the total sample remained Georgian-dominant bilinguals. Similar results were obtained in

TABLE 6.19. Level of Competence in Russian and Georgian

	Competence of % of Samples		
Sample	Not Fluent in Russian	Russian Inferior to Georgian	Fluent in Both Languages
1 Mechanics Institute	15	37	48
2 Linguistics Institute	24	52	24
3 Factory	50	40	10
4 Collective Farm	60	30	10

Source: Arutiunian, 1973b: 8.

an investigation of bilingual Tatars. Gubolgo (1972: 27) found that among those corresponding largely to the third and fourth groups in the sample in Table 6.19 (manual workers), only approximately 16 percent spoke Russian competently; among those employed in mental work, less than 40 percent were fluent bilinguals. Similar results were obtained among Karelians (Klement'ev, 1971: 41). Among members of the highest socio-occupational groups, over 37.1 percent admitted to not being fluent in Russian. For those in the intermediate occupational groups, nearly 60 percent did not claim to be fluent in Russian, while among manual workers the figure was 79.8 percent. The percentage of the total sample who claimed to be fluent in Karelian was over 90 percent. Among the Letts (Kholmogorov, 1970), acquaintance with the Russian language (judged on the minimal base of "acquaintance") is relatively high—78 percent claimed to be familiar with the language. There is here, too, a great disparity between occupational groups. Only 48 percent of manual workers, compared with 98 percent of professionals, claimed to know Russian.

Language Activities—Welsh and Spanish

Three questionnaires were submitted to students and adults in Wales to elicit information concerning the use of Welsh as compared with English. The first survey dealt with the students' use of Welsh in school (see Table 6.20). The 200 who constituted the sample were drawn from several areas and were stratified according to language dominance and age.

Irrespective of age, the English-dominant bilingual students resort to Welsh far less frequently than do the Welsh-dominant students. It is also the case that both groups—Welsh- and English-dominant bilinguals—resort to Welsh far less frequently as they grow older. Of the four domains of usage specified, both linguistic groups in both age groups use Welsh more frequently in informal, interpersonal communication—like speaking to other students—than on more formal occasions—like speaking to teachers. These conclusions bear out the results of the attitude analyses.

A second questionnaire was submitted to 200 Welsh-dominant adults stratified according to socio-occupational status and age (see Table 6.21).

TABLE 6.20. Welsh Activities in School According to Language Dominance and Age

| Welsh Activities | Language Dominance | Age Groups | | | | |
| | | 12+ | | 14+ | | |
		Mean	S.D.	Mean	S.D.
1 Communicating with teachers	Welsh	3.90	1.78	3.20	1.57
	English	2.76	2.14	2.93	2.10
2 Communicating with students	Welsh	4.68	1.47	4.17	1.73
	English	3.10	2.26	2.56	2.03
3 Communicating in recreational activities	Welsh	5.30	1.47	4.45	2.12
	English	3.98	2.21	3.21	1.95
4 Communicating in formal extra class activities, e.g., discussion groups	Welsh	3.15	2.03	2.67	2.31
	English	2.45	1.04	2.17	1.85
Consolidated Means	Welsh	4.26	1.51	3.62	2.34
	English	3.07	2.73	2.94	2.08

Source: Lewis survey.

TABLE 6.21. Welsh Language Activities of Welsh-Dominant Bilingual Adults

		Age Groups			
		18–25		30–45	
Activities	Socio-Occupational Status	Mean	S. D.	Mean	S. D.
1 I read Welsh newspapers and magazines	Professional	2.23	2.40	5.70	2.40
	Manual	1.07	1.70	1.58	2.00
2 I listen to Welsh language radio and	Professional	3.10	2.50	4.10	2.30
TV programs	Manual	2.15	2.40	3.71	2.60
3 I discuss general topics with other Welsh-	Professional	1.56	2.00	3.56	2.80
speaking friends	Manual	1.03	1.90	2.68	1.90
4 I correspond in Welsh with friends and relatives	Professional	1.67	1.30	2.10	2.30
	Manual	0.73	1.70	1.97	2.10
5 I visit homes of Welsh-speaking friends	Professional	2.23	2.40	3.25	1.70
	Manual	2.80	2.20	3.72	2.90
6 I attend Welsh language societies and clubs	Professional	3.76	1.80	1.45	2.00
	Manual	1.62	2.20	1.05	1.80
Consolidated Means for all activities	Professional	2.42	2.70	3.47	4.10
	Manual	1.56	2.40	2.61	3.20

Source: Lewis survey.

This was also administered to an unstratified sample of Spanish bilinguals in the United States.

The first point to note is the comparatively low consolidated means for both occupational groups at both age levels. The manual workers participate in Welsh language activities less frequently than the professionals, in both age groups, and the difference increases with age. The professional sample included school and university teachers and clergy, as well as university students in the age group 18 to 25. It should also be noted that the movement to maintain the Welsh language is led and supported far more by the professional intelligentsia than by manual workers. The more frequent resort to the use of Welsh by the professionals is to be expected. Second, the participation in Welsh language compared with English is greater among the older group, irrespective of socio-occupational status. This is inconsistent with the data in respect of both linguistic groups among students; it is consistent, however, with the tendency in Wales to polarize support for Welsh (among the very young, up to 12 years of age, and the older groups, especially 50 years and over). The activities in which Welsh is most frequently used among the younger groups are attendance at Welsh societies, listening to radio, and visiting Welsh-speaking friends. The speaking on formal occasions and writing of Welsh are not frequently in Welsh. Among the older groups, the most frequent activities are reading, listening, and visiting Welsh-speaking friends. The order of frequency of the activities of the adult sample follows very closely the pattern of "distribution of modal usage" reported in Table 6.15.

The opportunity was taken in Wales to probe more deeply into the Welsh-language activities of a group of adults spanning the younger and older groups reported in Table 6.21. These were Welsh-dominant bilinguals between the ages of 25 and 35 and stratified according to socio-occupational status (see Table 6.22).

Generally speaking, the lead taken by the professionals in the use of Welsh is confirmed by an analysis of these results, with some few exceptions. The consolidated mean reveals the professionals as more frequent users of Welsh; but in public situations—more particualrly in public worship —the manual workers are ahead. The same is true of interpersonal relations —more particularly among friends—and occupational contacts other than work (for example, trade unions). This reflects the greater range of personal contacts crossing the language divide enjoyed by the professionals. At almost every transactional level the professionals use Welsh more frequently than the manual workers. This is true of their use of Welsh according to topics. These two categories of activities are those which reflect most clearly (and recognizably) the insistence of the Welsh-dominant professional groups, especially in this age group, on the recognition of the use of the Welsh language. This has been noted earlier. There is nothing in

TABLE 6.22. Use of Welsh Compared with English among Welsh-Dominant Bilinguals (Age Group 25-35)

		Socio-Occupational Status			
		Professional		Manual	
Activities		Mean	S.D.	Mean	S.D.
A	Public situations				
	1. Meetings of organizations	5.32	1.75	4.12	2.32
	2. Street conversations	5.78	1.68	5.21	2.10
	3. Sports meetings	3.75	2.31	5.43	1.75
	4. Church and chapel	5.79	1.94	5.85	3.42
	Consolidated Means	5.24	2.27	5.31	2.95
B	Interpersonal situations				
	5. Family	5.81	1.84	5.67	2.73
	6. Friends	3.42	2.13	4.21	1.32
	7. Occupational contacts other than work	2.11	1.00	3.10	3.85
	Consolidated Means	3.74	1.75	4.06	2.17
C	Transactions				
	8. Local shopping	4.40	1.64	4.56	2.35
	9. Banking and business	3.72	0.85	1.73	0.75
	10. At work	3.11	2.05	1.48	1.52
	11. Contacts with public administrators	2.64	0.88	1.35	1.67
	Consolidated Means	3.03	2.40	2.50	2.00
D	Topics				
	12. National politics	6.52	1.75	4.50	1.34
	13. Local affairs	5.04	1.32	4.72	2.15
	14. Religion	5.71	2.45	5.94	3.21
	15. Education	5.13	1.57	4.10	1.25
	16. Household affairs	4.71	3.21	4.89	2.17
	Consolidated Means	4.46	2.78	4.03	3.15

Source: Lewis survey.

the Welsh situation which reveals more clearly the importance of the intelligentsia among the Welsh-dominant bilinguals in shaping the attitude to Welsh and in determining that more frequent use of Welsh should reinforce favorable attitudes.

The questionnaire used to elicit the data for Table 6.21 was submitted to the Spanish bilinguals of the United States. A random sample of 100 was taken. Apart from the fact that "speech" activities are more frequent than any of the others (see Table 6.23), the pattern of response among the Spanish bilinguals is very similar to that of the Welsh groups. Besides "speech" activities, listening to radio and reading are the most frequent; the least frequent is written correspondence. The distinction between informal and formal language activities, and the greater frequency of participation in the former, is consistent with the findings about attitude that we have noted earlier.

TABLE 6.23. Spanish Language Activities of Adults

Activities	Mean	S.D.
1 I read Spanish newspapers or magazines	2.91	2.00
2 I listen to Spanish-language radio and TV	3.82	1.78
3 I discuss general topics with other Spanish-speaking students	4.96	2.20
4 I correspond in Spanish with friends or relatives	1.98	1.00
5 I visit homes of Spanish-speaking friends	2.73	2.40
6 I attend Spanish language societies and clubs	4.47	2.50
Consolidates means	3.40	1.92

Source: Lewis survey.

Language Activities—Soviet Languages

The Soviet studies to which reference has been made tend to use the framework of dichotomies like "home and work," or "manual and intellectual activities." But before we refer to some of the data, one important point must be stressed. In Britain and the United States, the main interest lies in attitudes to and the use made of ethnic or minority language— Welsh or Spanish, or other minority languages in the United States. The situation of the world language, English, is almost the measure of the use of the minority language and the interest in it. The reverse is the case in the Soviet Union: there what may be taken for granted in bilingual areas are the ethnic languages, and their situation is the measure of the intrusion both in attitude and use of the world language, Russian, which is the locally emerging or intrusive language. How far such a fundamental situational difference affects attitude—that is, to what extent intrusiveness, measured by increasing numbers of native speakers of a particular language, whether it is the lingua franca, like English and Russian, or a minority language, like Welsh or Spanish—affects attitude to the languages in contact has not been studied. It is undoubtedly a suitable, even valuable, area of comparative research.

Terent'eva (1972) studied the differential use of Tatar and Russian among the Tatars of Kazan either in the home or at work. Forty-six percent spoke Tatar exclusively in the home compared with 17 percent who spoke Russian exclusively and 37 percent who spoke both. At work, the proportion speaking Tatar and Russian were reversed—only 5 percent spoke Tatar exclusively as against 48 percent who spoke Russian and 47 percent who spoke both languages. When attention was confined to the home and the sample was drawn from both Tatars and Russians—irrespective of whether Russian or Tatar was their first language—both groups used Russian predominantly: 93 percent of Russians who were native Russian speakers and 83 percent of Russians who were native Tatar speakers, as against 0.36 percent and 16 percent respectively who used Tatar. When those of Tatar nationality are considered, of those who spoke Russian as their native language 54 percent used Russian, 19 percent used Tatar, and 20 percent used both languages; while of those who spoke Tatar as their native language, only 12 percent used Russian as against 46 percent who used Tatar and 35 percent who used both languages in the home. From this it is evident that the main determinants of use are the advantageous associations (political, literary, scientific, and so on) of the Russian language and not the ethnic affinity of the speakers nor the traditional association of language and ethnicity. The same is true in Wales and in the United States (frequency of usage and favorable attitude are the preserves of the "big battalions.")

The dichotomy between home and work interested Kholmogorov also in his studies of the Letts. He found that while 78 percent of the Letts claimed to know Russian, the use of that language in the home of native speakers of Lettish was negligible—an average of 7.4 percent claimed to do so. The difference between the Letts and the Tatars may be explained largely by the urban characteristics of the Tatar sample and the very long and intense Russian influence on Kazan and Tataria generally. History and urbanization, as they are in the United States and Britain, are influential factors in determining language usage in the Soviet Union.

The highest proportion of Letts using Russian in the home was among seamen (mobile workers, 9.8 percent), semi-skilled farm equipment operators (9.7 percent), and government employees (8.2 percent). Of the Letts who used Russian in their work or for their intellectual satisfaction whether at work or at home, the highest proportion who used it on the job were found among professionals in the arts, teachers, and physicians (70 percent). Government employees infrequently used Russian in their jobs, presumably because their work involved contact with the majority of Letts. The average use of Russian for intellectual satisfaction was lower than at work, and in this the greatest use of Russian was made by students (64 percent), government employees (60 percent), and engineers and technicians (58 percent). Here again the association between type of work and the use of the languages in contact is not dissimilar to that which we discovered in Wales.

Two other variables, both of which we have referred to in respect of Wales—age and level of education—have been studied for the Karelians. Klement'ev (1971) established the tendency for the younger group (16–19) and the older (40–49) to polarize concerning knowledge of Karelian and use of the language at home; this is as compared with the intermediate age group (25–29), who recorded lower percentages than either of the two polar groups (See Table 6.24). The youngest and oldest groups, compared with the intermediate group, are more fluent in Karelian, they speak Karelian more frequently than Russian at home, and they use Karelian more often at work—whether exclusively or with Russian.

Kholmogorov also established a close association between age and knowledge of Russian among Letts. The number of persons knowing Russian is

TABLE 6.24. Linguistic Characteristics of Age Groups

Characteristics	16–19	25–29	40–49
Fluent in Karelian	39.1	31.7	75.3
Speak at home			
Karelian only	45.3	31.2	44.2
Russian only	31.9	36.1	19.6
Both	22.8	33.5	34.4
Speak at work			
Karelian only	8.8	4.5	22.0
Russian only	58.3	67.6	34.5
Both	32.9	26.9	42.8

Source: Klement'ev, Table 1.

inversely proportionate to their ages—90 percent up to age 20, and then declining almost uniformly to 47 percent at ages 51 and over (Kholmogorov, Figure 3.6). Level of education is also an important factor, as it is in Wales. The percentage who spoke Karelian fluently declined and those who spoke Russian increased with the number of years of schooling they had received (See Table 6.25). The same is true in respect of the frequency with which they spoke Karelian or Russian at home or at work.

Home Background

The variables closely associated with attitude (expressed either verbally or behaviorally) in Wales and the Soviet Union are age (among students and adults), socio-occupational status, language dominance (expressed in the Soviet Union in terms of whether a subject regards the ethnic language or Russian as his native language), and level of education. In addition to these, length of residence is closely associated with attitude in Wales, while urban/rural differences and the home and work dichotomy have been found to have a bearing on the problem in the Soviet Union and Wales.

TABLE 6.25. Level of Education and Linguistic Process (in % of sample)

Linguistic Characteristics	Education		
	Up to 4 Years	4-6	7-9
Fluent in Karelian	85.2	77.7	57.6
Fluent in Russian	4.7	9.1	20.2
Fluent in Both	10.1	13.2	22.2
Karelian only at home	50.7	50.3	41.3
Russian only at home	10.5	15.3	26.1
Both languages at home	36.4	32.6	32.6
Karelian only at work	27.6	20.2	14.0
Russian only at work	27.0	32.0	43.3
Both languages at work	44.9	47.4	41.5

Source: Klement'ev, Table 3.

One important group of variables has to do with home background. Though some home background variables have been found recently to be closely associated with the attitudes of foreign language students (Lewis and Massad, 1975), little has been done in any country to study the specific association between home background and bilinguals. It was decided to prepare a more detailed study and to provide the basis for possible hypotheses by including in Wales a questionnaire on parental encouragement. Parents were stratified according to sex and language dominance.

Generally speaking the mother's attitude (irrespective of language dominance) is more influential in promoting the use of Welsh than is the father's, especially for children's use of Welsh with grandparents, in school, and for reading (See Table 6.26). The influence of both English-dominant parents is less than that of the Welsh-dominant parents and this is particularly the case in the use of Welsh in school or at play—these are areas of social function outside the immediate influence of the home. It is noteworthy that the encouragement to use Welsh with members of the family declines with the successive generation involved—from grandparents to parents to siblings. The means of parental influence are lowest in respect of the situation over which the parents have least control—radio and television, where the vast majority of transmissions are in English. In any further investigation it will be hypothesized that home background varia-

TABLE 6.26. Parental Encouragement of Children to Use Welsh

| | | Linguistic Character of Parents | |
| | | Dominant Welsh | Dominant English |
Context of the Use of Welsh	Parent	Mean	Mean
1 To grandparents	Mother	3.62	3.51
	Father	3.21	3.00
2 To either or both parents	Mother	2.75	2.65
	Father	2.93	2.16
3 To brothers and sisters	Mother	2.31	2.09
	Father	2.15	1.93
4 At play	Mother	3.10	2.31
	Father	2.95	1.76
5 In school	Mother	3.79	2.17
	Father	2.95	1.97
6 Listening to radio/TV	Mother	2.00	1.67
	Father	1.68	1.31
7 Reading	Mother	2.92	2.32
	Father	2.45	1.43
Aggregated Means	Mother	3.92	2.38
	Father	2.63	1.89

Source: Lewis survey.

bles are more influential than school variables, especially so far as concerns the minority language. And that, furthermore, the relative importance of home background variables and school variables among bilinguals are the reverse of their importance among foreign language students.

ATTITUDE TO BILINGUAL EDUCATION

So far we have discussed some data arising from studies of attitude to languages in contact. Attitude to the institutionalization of such contacts, though probably associated closely to attitude to the languages themselves, especially in education, need not necessarily be identical with the former. Attitudes to the institutionalization of the social phenomenon of bilingualism (whether in administration, education, business life, or religion) are important, perhaps as important as attitudes to the native language itself. Promoting bilingualism to a recognized place in society (not simply acquiescing in the fact of its existence) may be an extension of attitude to language, but there is no necessary and unambiguous relationship between attitude to language and attitude to the institutionalization of the interrelationship of languages in contact, more particularly institutionalization within the education system. We cannot infer from attitude to a *native* minority language what is likely to be the attitude to teaching and using it in school at various stages in the system and for varying degrees of comprehensiveness in the curriculum. Nor is it possible to correlate attitude to a *second* language and to its inclusion at various levels in the curriculum. This is partly because bilingual education is influenced by considerations other than language—for example, attitude to schooling generally, among both students and parents; student and parent aspirations in respect of education and employment; as well as beliefs held about the kinds of schools the students should attend. Other factors influencing bilingual education through the determination of attitudes to schooling are the social and economic circumstances of the family (whether urban or rural, for instance) and the degree of linguistic heterogeneity in the schools area. These factors have been found to be influential in Britain and in the ten countries recently studied (Lewis and Massad, 1975) where English was taught to non-native speakers of the language. They have also been found to be influential in the Soviet Union, and there is no reason to doubt that they would be similarly involved in the creation of attitudes in the United States, though the relative importance of the various factors would undoubtedly vary.

Since detailed studies of attitudes to bilingual education were conducted in the United States and Britain, and because the evidence from the Soviet Union is more circumstantial, we will consider the Soviet Union first.

Soviet Union

We have already analyzed the various rationales or justifications which are offered for bilingual education in the Soviet Union, where such education is referred to invariably as learning Russian as the second language. In their constitution, the choice of type of education which a child is given is the privilege of the parents, but the exercise of this right is not left to chance. Irrespective of the social pressures exerted by prestige and the planned roles of the Russian language, parents are always guided in their choice of type of school. "The parents' choice must in no circumstances be left to take care of itself. The press, radio, the public, must conduct insistent explanatory work among parents" *(Uch. Gaz.,* 14 November 1971). Nevertheless the attitude of parents to a minority language or to the Russian language determines the choice of the school, and when the teaching language of the school is changed this is invariably attributed to "parental pressure," for instance, it was reported that "persistent efforts were made to organize secondary education in the Abkhasian language. . . . Finally, however, . . . parents appealed to the government to change the language of instruction" (ibid.).

The choice of type of school affects not only the child's level of attainment in his two languages, but also his differential use of them for various social functions and, by implication, attitude toward them. Kholmogorov discovered that the different social functions for which Lettish and Russian were employed by 17- to 19-year-old bilinguals were closely associated with types of school (See Table 6.27).

The one important point to notice is that while the type of school does have an association with differential social functions of the languages, the influence of the Lettish-medium school is far less effective than the Russian-medium school. This is especially evident in the choice of language for reading, radio, and television enjoyment, and use in the school. Only the home use of either language coincides with type of school. Drobizheva (1971), in her study of Tatars, attempted to correlate type of school to attitude toward aspects of ethnicity, including language. She found it "characteristic that Tatars who have graduated from a mixed or Russian school have more favourable attitudes and enter into personal inter-ethnic contacts (involving language) more often" than those attending Tatar-medium schools (8).

Choice of school itself is an index (however partial, and however affected by official pressure) of attitude to the language which characterizes the school. In other words, the effect of the type of school is not to create attitudes, but to reinforce those which helped to determine the original choice. Of such schools, we can identify first those where the teaching language is the native tongue and those in which Russian is used. Where

TABLE 6.27. Use of Lettish and Russian According to Type of School (percentage)

Students	At School		In the Home		Social Functions In Reading		In Watching TV	
	Lettish	Russian	Lettish	Russian	Lettish	Russian	Lettish	Russian
Studies taught in Lettish to eleventh grade	100.0	89.0	100.0	6.2	100.0	67.0	100.0	100.0
Studies taught in Russian to tenth grade	53.0	100.0	14.5	100.0	20.0	100.0	20.0	100.0

Source: Kholmogorov, Table 3.1 (extracted).

Russian is the teaching language in the first grade, it follows that it continues to be so to the end. The minority language school may shift to Russian-medium instruction at any stage, and in the majority of cases this occurs when students enter secondary schools.

It does not always follow that verbal expression of a favorable attitude to Russian-medium schools coincides with the actual choice of such a school by parents. For instance, Arutiunian (1969) found that among village Tatars 60 percent of the parents favored such a school, but only 25 percent of them chose it for their children. Furthermore, the attitude to Russian or native-language school is associated with attitude to other ethnic indices; as Terent'eva claims, "There is a definite relationship between the relative number of schools with instruction in the language of the indigenous nationality and all other indices defining the direction of the ethnic processes" (46). The choice of school and other ethnic processes are influenced very considerably by attitudes of parents, the ethnic composition of the area, and especially the degree of ethnic heterogeneity. Schools may be situated in areas inhabited by several ethnic or linguistic groups, and here it would be possible to establish separate ethnic or language schools. However, neither exclusively Russian nor exclusively single-ethnic schools are favored either by the administration or parents in such areas, if they have a choice of "multinational schools." Where many groups attend the same school, the language of instruction often is in Russian, though there are many instances of multilingual instruction. The attitudes of the administration favors multiethnic as opposed to separate schools, being influenced by Lenin's insistence "that we must strive for a merging of children of all nationalities into one school in a given area . . . we must decisively oppose any movement to divide the school in terms of nationalities" (Lenin, 1962). It is for this reason that, though the 917 Azerbaijani children attending a school in Daghestan could very easily be organized in a separate single-ethnic school, they are nevertheless part of a school of 1,400 students comprising eight other nationalities.

Such bilingual schools, therefore, are not forced upon administrators or parents simply because of the degree of local heterogeneity: they are preferred even when an alternative organization is available, since they safeguard the native tongue (which is the teaching language for students who opt for it) as well as offering an opportunity to acquire Russian and to be taught in it if that is the choice. Attitudes to bilingual teaching are very favorable, but not uniformly so. Of the different occupational groups in Latvia (Kholmogorov, Table 5.2), the "best favorable" were physicians (66.2 percent) and government workers (76.2 percent) and the "most favorable" were engineers and technicians (100 percent) and teachers (91 percent). It is impossible to obtain any information about whether those who are least favorable would prefer separate Lettish-medium schools, or schools where the medium of instruction is the second language—Russian.

On the one hand, government workers and physicians have the lowest indices of Russian language attainment (75 percent and 77 percent), and their low approval of bilingual teaching might be governed by their wish for Russian-medium schools to increase their competence in Russian, or for Lettish-medium schools because of their favorable attitude to that language. I suspect that the low level of approval for bilingual schools among government workers and physicians, but their preference for Russian (in spite of low attainment), is because they are the highest among all occupational groups in favoring friendly relations with Russians in the localities (Kholmogorov).

Generally speaking, however, the degree of favor accorded bilingualism in Latvia is high and characterizes all nationalities in that republic: Letts 81.2 percent approval, other nationalities 84.5 percent. Opposition was limited to 3.8 percent among Letts and others.

Wales

Two questionnaires were administered in Wales and the second of these was used in the United States also. One of the main obstacles to the understanding of attitude to bilingual education has been our ignorance of how important such programs are to parents as *compared with other aspects of the school provision.* For this reason it was decided to attempt to measure attitude to the learning of Welsh which, rather than English, is the crucial factor in any such education in Wales relative to other subjects.

The sample of parents (100) was drawn from various areas of Wales and consisted of equal numbers of Welsh-and English-dominant, professional and manual worker parents (See Table 6.28). The students (100) were between the ages of 15 and 18 and were selected so as to represent the same stratification as the parents; that is, each parent was represented by one child, and where any parent had more than one child within the age group 15 to 18 the oldest was selected. The sample of parents consisted of 32 fathers and 68 mothers, and the students were divided 43 boys and 57 girls. The first point to note is the relatively low consolidated mean for the teaching of Welsh in respect of parents and students. Second, apart from the items on the relative importance of Welsh and social studies and extra-curricular activities, the students have a more favorable attitude to Welsh than the parents have. For the parents, the most important subjects, compared with Welsh, are a foreign language, science, English, and mathematics. Among the students, the teaching of Welsh compares unfavorably in importance with a foreign language, mathematics, and science. In spite of differences in the relative weight attached by parents and students to Welsh and the other subjects, both groups tend to give the same place to Welsh in the hierarchy of school subjects and its place is

TABLE 6.28. Attitudes of Welsh-Speaking Parents and Their Children to Learning Welsh in Comparison with Other Subjects of a Bilingual Program

| | Sample | | | |
| | Parents | | Students | |
Variable	Mean	S.D.	Mean	S.D.
1 Learning Welsh is more important than having more time for English	1.22	1.78	2.56	1.47
2 Learning Welsh is more important than having more time for a foreign language	0.97	1.31	1.24	0.76
3 Learning Welsh is more important than having more time for a science	1.14	1.03	1.47	0.93
4 Learning Welsh is more important than having more time for mathematics	1.30	2.11	1.32	1.21
5 Learning Welsh is more important than having more time for social studies	2.59	1.43	2.28	1.19
6 Learning Welsh is more important than having more time for extra-curricular activities, like drama	3.09	1.79	2.39	0.78
Consolidated Means	2.51	1.86	1.98	1.14

Source: Lewis survey.

relatively low. This would suggest that whatever may be the attitude to bilingual education taken on its own and unrelated to the curricular consequences of its introduction, a low level of importance is attached to it for the teaching of the subjects of the curriculum and, in this case, promoting the minority language. We need to bear this in mind in considering attitudes to *forms of bilingual education*, where it is already assumed that such an education is acceptable in principle.

One hundred parents, stratified according to linguistic environment and according to whether they were bilingual or monolingual English, were sampled (See Table 6.29). All had children of school age.

Items 1 to 5 in Table 6.29 refer to the possibility of increasing the comprehensiveness of bilingual education from the minimum (item 1) to the most realistically complete bilingual system. Items 6 to 8 are concerned with ways of organizing the bilingual school; item 9 is concerned with the cultural component. Irrespective of language environment, the attitude of bilingual parents improves with the comprehensiveness of the program offered: the more comprehensive the preferred alternative the greater the support. The same is true to some extent of the monolingual English parents in Welsh areas. However, they do not greatly favor the teaching of Welsh to their own English-speaking children up to 10 years of age (item 5). The monolingual English parents in the English areas give most support to the second item, which allows their own children to opt out of learning Welsh altogether. Generally speaking, the bilingual parents are

TABLE 6.29. Attitude of Welsh-Speaking and Non-Welsh-Speaking Parents to Specified Forms of Bilingual Education for Their Own Children

| | | Parent Group | | | |
| | | Welsh Speaking | | English Speaking | |
Types of Programs	Type of Area	Mean	S.D.	Mean	S.D.
1 Teaching and using English with only casual reference to Welsh	Welsh	0.78	2.25	2.75	1.85
	English	1.31	2.05	3.12	2.25
2 Teaching and using English and teaching Welsh only to those who speak it	Welsh	1.32	1.43	3.64	2.41
	English	2.76	2.04	6.25	3.21
3 Teaching English and Welsh to all but using English as the only medium of teaching	Welsh	2.43	1.87	3.67	2.41
	English	3.31	2.51	3.98	1.88
4 Teaching English and Welsh, using English for most of the time but also using Welsh during the first two years of the junior school to those who speak it	Welsh	2.76	1.95	5.41	3.25
	English	3.64	2.32	4.25	3.41
5 Teaching and using English and Welsh with all students to the age of 9–10 with English becoming the exclusive teaching language	Welsh	3.62	2.57	3.63	2.32
	English	4.13	1.87	2.63	1.57
6 Teaching and using both languages for all students but on alternate days	Welsh	4.32	2.56	1.79	0.85
	English	3.14	2.31	0.92	2.41
7 Separate streams in the same school, each following a program in its own language but also teaching the second language	Welsh	4.85	3.25	3.45	1.25
	English	3.72	2.42	2.64	0.95
8 Separate schools—Welsh and English exclusively but also teaching the second language	Welsh	4.79	3.21	3.92	2.56
	English	3.92	1.85	1.85	1.75
9 How do you regard the teaching of Welsh culture in the program?	Welsh	6.72	3.42	4.62	3.52
	English	7.45	4.76	3.67	2.56

Source: Lewis survey.

anxious to promote Welsh as both a second and a first language and to have it used as a teaching language even for those whose native language is English. They concede, though, the advantage to all students of transferring at some point to English. The English-speaking parents in Welsh areas are in favor of bilingual education in principle, and they do not prefer the first item to the others. But they do not on the whole favor a bilingual education for English-speaking children. Thus, after discussing the minimal alternative, they opt very definitely against item 5 (a comprehensive system) and they favor strongly item 2 which ignores Welsh as a second language.

Items 6 to 8 refer to the *organization* of bilingual schools. Here the bilingual parents differ according to their language environment. Those in the English areas favor entirely separate single-medium schools while those in the Welsh areas prefer "streamed" schools—one school with single-medium stream or tracks. Doubtless these differences arise from the fear in the English area that unless Welsh is isolated so far as possible from English it will succumb to its threat. In the Welsh areas it may be felt that such isolation is not necessary to maintain the language in view of the environmental support, and that the English-speaking children in the English-medium streams will be exposed to a strong native Welsh influence in school to reinforce that of the environment. The least favored alternative organization is that in which the two languages are used as teaching languages for all students on alternative days.

This is true of English-speaking parents also, irrespective of language environment. Of the two alternatives remaining to the English-speaking parents, those in the Welsh areas prefer separate language medium schools, feeling possibly that the mother tongue (English) will be better served in the English-medium school, especially since the language environment favors Welsh. English parents in the English areas prefer the streamed school, possibly because in an English environment the English language is not under threat; further, they may believe that advantage should be taken of a Welsh environment in school to facilitate the acquisition of Welsh as a second language.

The strongest support for a cultural component in a bilingual program comes from the Welsh-speaking parents, and especially those in English-speaking areas, where the heritage is threatened. Among the monolingual English parents, those in Welsh-speaking areas favor a bicultural component more than those in the Welsh areas, possibly because they have experienced the Welsh culture and have come to value it.

The United States

Attitudes in the United States range from clear and explicit opposition to bilingual education in any form, through hardly concealed indifference, to detached approval in principle, to various levels of support, including

thorough commitment to its promotion. Indifference to it may characterize any level of society. For instance, in 1975 at the annual meeting of the
state governors, of the twenty-four items proposed for discussion, state
involvement in bilingual education was not favored for discussion by any
of the governors. State legislators listed the subject twenty-first in order
of importance, 7.8 percent supporting its inclusion. What is even more
striking is that state commissioners of education placed it even lower,
twenty-third on their list, only 8.8 percent supporting its inclusion. While
it is true that the states are not immediately, directly, or exclusively
responsible for bilingual education, the fact that the problem impinges on
aspects of urban and minority affairs, as well as on aspects of civil rights,
and that a large number of states have significant bilingual populations
would lead one to anticipate a greater interest if not considerable involvement on the part of the states' leaders.

Generally speaking, minority groups (where they have given it thought)
and many Anglo parents support bilingual education as a general principle for both minorities and majority groups. This is expressed partly in
the greater actual involvement of some parents—"schools are finding that
parents do care" and are bringing their influence to bear on the type of
bilingual education which is offered (Fernández, 1973). A study conducted
in the public schools of Albuquerque (Gutiérrez, 1972) found a favorable
attitude to bilingual education among parents, especially the younger
ones, irrespective of socio-economic status. In a very different area altogether, Alaska, the Bureau of Indian Affairs (Juneau Area Office, 1973)
investigated the views held by people in the rural areas. One of the major
issues about which those who were interviewed expressed a concern was
bilingual education. With some exceptions, they were strongly in favor of
its provision. Parents who come to support bilingual education do so very
often after expressing earlier objections, which arose from their feeling
that religious matter was being taught (National Institute for Bilingual
Education, 1973: 40). Other parents support the program because teaching and using the native language (Crow in this instance) tends to "help
the children learn English better" (ibid., 29).

However, opposition of a very fundamental sort is expressed by some
parents even in those minority groups that have led in the promotion of
bilingual education. Resistance to the enforcement of bilingual education
among New York Puerto Ricans has come from some Hispanic parents. In
one school district, they successfully instituted a lawsuit after the promul-
gation of the Aspira Consent decree to ensure that any bilingual program
was voluntary. The attitude of such parents is that a bilingual education
serves only to prolong an undesirable umbilical relationship with the
country of origin (Shaw: 110). Among other minorities, for instance the
Crow Indians, it is believed that teaching and using the mother tongue
should be the responsibility of the home and to that extent, while they

approve a public system of general education, they are averse to supporting any bilingual program (Spolsky and Cooper, 1978: 340).

Because doubts exist about bilingual education—if not outright hostility to it among some minorities—it is not surprising that other people react unfavorably to it. Some do so on the grounds that schools should be more concerned with imbuing a sense of pride in their new home country and its language instead of encouraging a reluctance to learn it. Some of the opposition is due to a vested professional interest in maintaining the existing instructional situations: part of the disfavor with which it is regarded by teachers' organizations, especially in New York City, arises from the fear they have that nonbilingual teachers may lose employment and that a decline in the required standards for entry to the profession may result. In the House of Representatives hearings on the Bilingual Education Act (1974), before the general Subcommittee on Education of the Committee on Education and Labor of the 2d session of the 93d Congress, official representatives of the American Federation of Teachers opposed "the separate bilingual license and nonmerit appointments of bilingual teachers" since in their view there was a danger of dual standards in the profession (Hearings: 375–6). A school superintendent expressed the fear of many nonbilingual teachers that they might be displaced (ibid., 421). This fear is echoed by some parents who envisage the possibility of their children "being taught by a teacher who cannot speak English, [or] who speaks broken English" (ibid., 425). Not infrequently the question is asked by some in positions of authority, "why it is now imperative that we spend tax money to preserve the cultures of Spanish-speaking people" coming to the United States (ibid., 97). A variant of this complaint is the argument about discriminating in favor of some minorities—"we didn't help the Irish, we didn't help the Italians in the past, why should we now help the Spanish community?" (ibid., 425). These may be irrational objections, ignoring the commitment to equal opportunity for individual improvement, but they reflect the climate in which more profound attitudes are formed.

The questionnaire used in Wales (see Table 6.29) on alternative levels of bilingual education and of organizing it was administered to 100 bilingual (Spanish) teachers and educators of bilingual teachers in the following areas: New Mexico; Texas; Dade County, Florida; and New York. Because of the difficulty of stratifying the total sample in a manner similar to what was done in Wales, the United States teachers were asked to evaluate the alternatives from the point of view of what might be acceptable to the Spanish-dominant population and to the English-dominant population (irrespective of whether the latter were bilingual).

In the United States, support for bilingual education, on this evidence, increases with the comprehensiveness of the bilingual provision, when it is looked at from the standpoint of the Spanish-dominant (See Table 6.30).

TABLE 6.30. Attitude of Spanish-Speaking Teachers to Specified Forms of Bilingual Education

| | Language Group | | | |
| | Spanish Dominant | | English Dominant | |
Type of Bilingual Education Program	Mean	S.D.	Mean	S.D.
1 Teaching and using English with only casual reference to Spanish	1.65	0.78	3.12	1.45
2 Teaching and using English and teaching Spanish to those who speak it	2.74	1.84	3.47	2.25
3 Teaching English and Spanish to all but using only English as a medium	3.37	1.21	2.53	1.76
4 Teaching Spanish and English, using English most of the time but also using Spanish during the first two years with those who speak it	3.94	2.30	2.93	2.54
5 Teaching and using Spanish and English with all students in the first four grades but English becoming the exclusive medium	4.32	1.75	2.76	1.35
6 Teaching and using both languages with all students but on alternate days	3.14	1.25	3.41	1.21
7 Separate tracks in the same school, each following a program in its own language but also taking the appropriate second language	4.51	2.76	5.13	3.65
8 Separate schools, exclusively Spanish or English-medium, but teaching the second language. The school may be entirely separate or an annex or a mini school	5.76	2.47	7.10	3.22
9 How do you regard the teaching of Spanish culture in the program?	4.26	1.85	6.61	4.31

Source: Lewis survey.

318

The contrary is the case when it is regarded from the standpoint of the English-dominant, to whom the least bilingual alternative (item 1) receives the greatest support and the most comprehensive alternative (item 5) receives the least measure of support. Looking at the alternative organizations of bilingual education (items 6 to 8), separate schools are regarded as most advantageous to the Spanish-dominant group, with streamed or tracked bilingual schools second. The English-dominant group has a similar preference, except that in their case the support for separate schools is much greater. The cultural component of bilingual education is favored more for the English-dominants, possibly to compensate for the assumed lack of attractiveness (from their point of view) of the comprehensive bilingual education program.

Let us conclude by attempting very tentative comparisons of the three systems of bilingual education we have analyzed. First, bilingual education in its less comprehensive forms (items 1 and 2) receives more support in the United States from the point of view of the minority (Spanish-dominants) and less support from the point of view of the English-dominants than it does in Wales when looked at from the standpoint of ethnic language group irrespective of the language environment. Second, bilingual education in its most comprehensive form listed here (item 5) has greater support in the United States among the Spanish-dominants than it does from any of the sample strata in Wales. It gains less support when viewed from the standpoint of the English-dominants than it does from any of the Welsh groups, except the English-speaking parents in the English-speaking areas. Generally speaking, therefore, in both English-speaking countries it is the minority which favors the development of bilingual education, and its support is commensurate with the positive role played by the minority language.

It is difficult to compare the Soviet Union and the English-speaking countries directly because, whereas increased comprehensiveness in Wales or the United States means greater prominence for the minority language (Welsh or Spanish), in the Soviet Union it means increasing the role of the lingua franca—Russian. Though a direct comparison is difficult, it can be inferred that as support for that bilingual education increases there is decreasing support for the minority or the ethnic languages. Generally speaking, the Russian attitude to bilingual education coincides with the attitude of the English-dominants in Wales and the United States; at the same time though, evidence of greater support for bilingual education exists among the English dominants than there is among the Russians.

So far as the organization of bilingual education is concerned, a comparison of the mechanics of such an organization is fairly straightforward. The Welsh vary in their support for streamed or separate schools according to the linguistic environment and the language affiliation of the parents. In the United States, separate schools are more strongly approved for both

Spanish- and English-dominant students. In the Soviet Union, the separate school has little support (unless it is an exclusively Russian-medium school); instead, the bilingual school (streamed in our terms) is most strongly approved. The mechanics of the organization of such schools, however, disguises a radical difference between the English-speaking countries and the USSR in the justification of such schools. In Wales and the United States, separate schools are preferred to streamed schools because the former ensure some measure of isolation from the overwhelming influence of the lingua franca. In the Soviet Union, streamed schools are approved for exactly the reason they are disapproved in the English-speaking countries—they allow the prestigious language to be reinforced. One is justified in concluding that the English-speaking countries are beginning to adjust the instructional balance in favor of the minority languages, but the Russians are mainly concerned to extend the influence of the dominant Russian language.

Seven

Needs, Policies, and Programs in Bilingual Education

So far we have attempted to identify and illustrate the operation of some of the variables associated with heterogeneous societies and which, for that reason, serve to make bilingualism a necessary or at least a desirable element in their systems of education. Among the most important of these societal variables are the type of linguistic community, the historical development of bilingualism and bilingual education in such communities, population change arising from conquest, colonization, and other forms of migration as well as urbanization, levels of social and industrial development associated with the process of modernization, attitudes to the vernaculars and to their place in education, and finally beliefs about the cultures with which the languages are associated and about how close or necessary that association is or should be in the system of education. These are primary variables or factors, in the sense that they help to account for the existence of bilingualism in a society—they are *material causes* of bilingualism. Not all of these variables are simultaneously or successively present in a heterogeneous society, but in the total absence of the most important of these factors the question of bilingual education—except as an elitist provision or foreign as distinct from second language introduction—hardly arises. In this final chapter we shall be concerned with three possible outcomes of the interaction of these primary variables.

The most immediate educational consequences of language contact or linguistic heterogeneity are those that concern the behavior of individual children. There are influences upon their development—cognitive, affective, social, linguistic, and academic—and especially upon their response to whatever system of schooling is offered to them—in other words, their ability or willingness to attend schools. Bilingualism creates specific individual *needs* that have to be met. Another set of outcomes are the linguistic policies made necessary or actually pursued by those who are responsible for shaping an education appropriate to the bilingual situation of such children. Even widespread bilingualism does not result in widespread, partial, or for that matter any form whatever of bilingual education. The linking of bilingualism as a societal linguistic phenomenon with bilingual education is accomplished through linguistic policy. The third set of variables, therefore, includes the variety of programs designed to implement bilingual education policies.

IDENTIFYING LANGUAGE MINORITY NEEDS

The United States

In a bilingual society, the minority student needs as a minimum to be able to speak two languages, his mother tongue and the lingua franca. The optimum provision is an education that is as comprehensive and as satisfying to members of a minority as the mainstream system is to the English-speaking student. Between the minimum and maximum requirements lies the need for providing an education that ensures, through the use of the mother tongue, that the student has an equal chance to "achieve" academically. The minimum requirement involves simply the inclusion of an additional subject—English as a second language. The intermediate requirement involves simply substituting the mother tongue instead of, or in addition to, English as a teaching language. The maximum requirement takes us beyond individual programs and involves the establishment of an *alternative system* of education, like that provided in such bilingual countries as Belgium, Wales, Ireland, South Africa, and Malaysia.

In the United States, even the minimum requirement is not being met in the education of the vast majority of the 2.5 million children of limited English-speaking ability. It is estimated that over 75 percent of the 330,000 Asian-American children enrolled in schools speak little or no English and are not being catered for (National Advisory Council, 1976: 27). In 1974–75, over 50,000 Italian immigrant students with severely limited English language skills entered the schools of New York (ibid). A report on conditions in Texas prior to 1970 claimed only 20,000 of the 600,000 students of Mexican-American origin were able to profit in any way from a bilingual education (Lara-Braud, 5). In New York State, an estimated 300,000 students are categorized as non-English-speaking and, so far as their education is concerned, deprived (Regents of the University of the State of New York, 1972: 5). "The most distressing incidence of academic failure . . . occurs among a group of children who are handicapped by a language barrier in the classroom—those 160,000 children (in New York State) whose native language is not English and whose difficulty comprehending English significantly impedes school performance" (Committee on Education, 1974: 3).

In New York City between 1961 and 1971, in spite of increasing awareness of the students' language problems, the percentage of pupils with English-language difficulties rose steadily (See Table 7.1). Seen as a proportion of the ethnic group itself, rather than of the total registered school population, the figures are even more distressing. In 1972, of all the non-English school population, 14.1 percent were rated as having difficulty with English. Of the individual ethnic groups, the speakers of French, mainly Haitians and involving relatively few students (4,214), had the highest percentage of difficulty, 64.3. The next highest group was the non-Puerto Rican speakers of Spanish, 59.8 percent; followed by Greek students, 45.9 percent; Italian, 43.9 percent; Chinese, 41.7 percent; and Puerto Ricans, 38.7 percent (Regents of the University of the State of New York, 1972: 18).

New York is not atypical of other large concentrations of immigrant students. Being ignored for these pupils is the minimum requirement for the bilingual education of United States minorities—a knowledge of English. In this situation the intermediate requirement, namely, providing an equal opportunity to achieve academically, must be in default since the students are taught in a language they do not understand. The data on the academic attainment of linguistic minorities as compared to the achievement of Anglos are proof that the intermediate requirement has never been met. A half century ago the Merriam Report appeared (1928), and

TABLE 7.1. Pupils with English-Language Difficulties, New York City

Year	Total No. Students Registered	No. with Difficulty	% of Total Register
1961	1,004,000	88,904	8.9
1962	1,027,000	87,075	8.5
1963	1,045,000	87,782	8.4
1964	1,054,000	88,714	8.4
1965	1,065,000	92,786	8.7
1966	1,084,000	102,460	9.4
1967	1,109,000	110,447	10.0
1968	1,121,000	118,492	10.5
1969	1,123,000	121,733	10.8
1970	1,141,000	135,425	11.9
1971	1,146,000	122,515	10.7

Source: Board of Education of the City of New York, *Educational Progress, Research and Statistics*, 1972.

since then attention has been repeatedly focused on the low achievement of Indians. H. D. Anderson (1935: 361) was among the earliest to point to the failure of the schools to meet the requirements of the Indians. At about the same time, Austin (1934) assessed the achievement of Pimas; O. D. Smith (1932) worked with students in Santa Fe; Zimmerman (1934) studied the mathematics achievement of a particularly large sample; and a decade later S. A. Peterson (1948) reported for the University of Chicago enquiring into the low academic achievement of fourth, eighth, and twelfth grade Indian students. Peterson's work was replicated in 1953 by Anderson and others (Coombs et al., 1958). A 1964 report (Wax, 25) may be taken to summarize the general conclusions of nearly forty years of repeated assessment: "The results of a recent program of testing were dismaying." A former commissioner has referred to this adverse conclusion as a "familiar and by now dreary statistic" (Nash, 1966).

The academic needs of Spanish-speaking populations are equally well documented. A substudy of the Grebler, Moore, and Guzman investigation (1970) was undertaken by Carter (1970). He emphasized, from actual assessment and classroom observation in the Southwest, the lack of satisfactory educational programs for speakers of Spanish. A more comprehensive study for the federal government, the Commission on Civil Rights Reports (1971), concluded that the schools Mexican-Americans attended were by their very organization and management unable to satisfy the needs of the bilinguals. On every achievement criterion used, the needs of minorities were not met, largely because of the disregard of the mother tongue as a teaching language, adverse attitudes to minority culture, and low teacher expectation of Spanish achievement.

What is true of the Southwest probably applies to a greater degree among Puerto Ricans, especially in New York and New Jersey. In 88 schools having 50 percent or more Puerto Ricans, 81 percent of fifth graders in 1972 were below grade level in reading; of these, 20 percent were over one but below two years retarded, and 47 percent two years or more. Of the eighth graders, 86 percent were underachieving; 31 percent were four years or more below grade levels; 12 percent were one to two years behind. Only 19 percent of the fifth graders and 14 percent of those in eighth grade were at or over grade level (Regents of the University of the State of New York, 1972: 7). The New York Puerto Rican achievement record is very low, but it is not atypical of the pressing minority needs of the rest of the United States. In 1966 (Coleman), language minorities were found to lag well behind students in the minority group. By the twelfth grade, the Mexican-American was 4.1 years retarded in mathematics, 3.5 years in language attainment, and 3.3 years in reading. Puerto Ricans in the whole of the United States were 4.8 years behind the national norm in mathematics, 3.6 years in language, and 3.2 years in reading. Asians were less handicapped but nevertheless retarded to the extent of 0.9 years in mathematics, 1.6 years in language, and 1.6 years in reading. On tests of general information—including humanities, social, and natural sciences—the median twelfth grade score was 43.3 for Mexican-Americans, 41.7 for Puerto Ricans, 44.7 for Native Americans, and 49.0 for Asians. The score for majority-group students was 52.2 *(Commission on Civil Rights*, vol. 3, 1972). The longer such students remained in school the greater the gap in achievement levels became.

The greater the heterogeneity of the areas in which students live and the schools operate, the greater the likelihood of spasmodic or nonattendance at school. Erratic attendance in turn accounts for poor achievement as much as does the inappropriateness of lessons and instructional techniques. At the same time, it is important to stress that the failure of the schools to attract and to hold the minority language students as successfully as they hold the majority is due to a considerable extent to basic economic considerations, which are nevertheless inextricably associated with their language status. Young Mexican-Americans, Puerto Ricans, and Indians begin to work at a very early age. Those who do not enter the labor market look after the family. For instance, D. D. Atkinson (1955) reported that many Utes "became involved with parental responsibilities at a very early age" and are forced to discontinue their schooling (MSS, 3). Poor health, a result of the poor economic conditions which in turn account for young children of the minority groups having to work, is another cause of poor attendance. Bonner (1950), in her study of the Cherokees, found that a high dropout rate stemmed in part from "ill health and needed at home." These findings should alert all involved with bilingual education to the social and economic factors affecting students. Where bilinguals are members of economically depressed minorities, as in the United States, whatever may be done by the school in terms of better instruction, more suitable curricula, and a recognition of the mother tongue is likely to fail unless the root causes of their distress, which are economic and social, are removed. Bilingual education, though it will improve economic and social status, is unlikely to be the whole answer. It is virtually impossible, however, to measure the extent to which linguistic disabilities create or exacerbate economic needs, nor can the extent to which such unsatisfied economic needs create or perpetuate linguistic disabilities be determined.

Having entered such a caveat, it remains true that the schools themselves, geared as they are to the requirements of the majority, contribute a great deal to a failure of "holding power." What they do and how they do it engender in the minority student a lack of interest, indifference, or hostility, although the situation is improving. For instance, in 1960 only 13 percent of all rural Indians 14-years-of-age and over were high school graduates. By 1970, the percentage had risen to 23. Similarly with urban Indians: the graduates rose from 25 percent in 1960 to 42 percent in 1970. This improvement is not reflected in the figures for Indians completing college, where the improvement is little more than 1 percent in the same period (Office of Special Concerns, 1974: Vol. III, 38). Only 3.5 percent of all adult Indians 16 years and over, one third of the percentage for the nation as a whole, had completed college in 1970. The same disparity occurs in the figures for median years of schooling: for instance 12.1 years (U.S. total) compared with 10.4 years (Indian). School retention rate, the percentage of each age group enrolled, shows a similar disparity: for 14- to 17-year-olds, the U.S. total is 93 percent and for Indians 87 percent (ibid., 40).

Not all minority groups compare so unfavorably with the overall United States percentages. The median years of schooling for Japanese, Chinese, and Filipino students of 16 years and over is above the U.S. total—12.5 years in the first two groups and 12.2 years in the case of Filipinos, compared to 12.1 years for the U.S. total. It should be remembered, however, that the total U.S. percentage is depressed by the very low percentages for non-Asian minorities. The Japanese and Chinese also have the advantage over the rest of the United States in respect of school enrollment. Japanese and Chinese enrollment rates are much higher—59 percent and 62 percent compared with 54 percent nationally. On the other hand, the rate for Filipinos is lower, 46 percent (U.S. Census, 1970: 67–70, 77, 80). The attractiveness of schooling to Asian Americans reflects the motivation as well as the economic situation of the minorities. The Japanese and Chinese, though their economic status may be low, are attracted to the schools—however inappropriate the fare may be. The fact that they are also mainly from urban communities is a factor to be taken into account when comparing them with Indians and speakers of Spanish.

The educational level of the Mexican-American students (9.3 years) tends to be lower than those of the Native Americans (10.4 years) and the national average (12.1 years). If we take the males alone, since this is more favorable to the Mexican-Americans, while approximately 22 percent of all U.S. males 16 years and over have not gone beyond the eighth grade, the figure for Mexican-Americans is nearly twice that. Only 2.3 percent of all Mexican-Americans graduated from college, which is less than a quarter of the proportion of the total U.S. population. The Puerto Ricans, a predominantly urban population, have only a slightly better record than the Mexican-Americans: the median years of schooling is better by approximately 0.2 percent. However, the percentage of Puerto Ricans with eight or fewer years of schooling is below the Mexican-American proportion by 4 percent, and there are fewer Mexican-American than Puerto Rican college graduates (2.3 percent as against 2.5 percent). The Spanish-speaking population also has a poor enrollment rate. In the total U.S. population, approximately 93 percent of students between 14-and 17-years-of-age are in high school. Among Mexican-Americans, approximately 84 percent are in school, 9 percent below the national average. The enrollment rate of Puerto Ricans in the whole of the United States is lower still—approximately 70 percent, 21 percent below the national average. In the city of New York, the Puerto Ricans fare even worse with only 44.8 percent of them registered in high school (U.S. Census, 1970: 47–8).

The needs of the Cuban-American population are just as great. The percentage of poorly educated young people (45 percent) is as high as the Mexican-Americans and Puerto Ricans—47 percent and 44 percent respectively. The percentage of Cuban Americans who have graduated from high school (44 percent), though much higher than among other Spanish-speaking groups (27 percent), is still 11 percent below that of the total U.S. student population. Such figures place the total Cuban-American community in a favorable light, but the situations of subgroups of Cubans vary considerably. Thus, while 35 percent of all Cuban-Americans aged 18 to 24 in Florida are enrolled in school, compared with 32 percent of all United States students of the same age, only 28 percent of the Cuban-Americans in New York and New Jersey are enrolled.

The classroom differences between the socio-cultural needs of the language minority groups and those of the majority are easily distorted by relying on stereotypes both of culture and of the minority groups. For instance, the low self-concept of Indian students, referred to in the Coleman report, inferred from the Havinghurst study (1957), and generally built into the image of the Indian student, may simply reflect the linguistic status and social conditions of his upbringing. Linguistically and economically he has little if any control over his environment—he cannot affect the circumstances of his life and this is reflected in his feelings about himself. How he looks upon himself reflects how others look upon his language. In other respects and in favorable or even neutral surroundings, though, his self-image is positive. Naylor (1971) goes farther and concludes from his investigations that the stereotypical notion of ethnic cultures is a myth. Furthermore, the culture of any group is not unchanging; indeed, if it is worth taking into account within the system of education, it will change according as the social and physical environment of the group changes. Spicer (1972) argues that "the internal structures of the various cultures of the Southwest are in part products of the kind of social relationships which the different groups have maintained with one another and those have changed decade by decade in response to requirements of new population distributions, changing technology, development of new economic systems, differing political environments," and so on (MSS, 8). The "culture needs" of the students change, but however they change and whatever form the needs take, their satisfaction demands a recognition of those needs by systems and schools adopting appropriate policies.

It would be unwise to exaggerate the differences between the minority language and the majority culture, or to polarize the differences because they appear to be great. Nevertheless differences do exist; they are significant enough to merit their being taken into account, and generally speaking they are ignored or their relevance is underestimated. Apart from the difference between the general concept of Indian culture and Anglo culture, there are differences between categories of Indians. The Navajo regard themselves, and promote their ideas about education, as a nation. The Pueblos "will not surrender their independence for a unity beyond the single Pueblo village" (Dozier, 1970: xi). But whatever intragroup difference there may be, the differences between minority language groups and the majority are greater. "Indian society and culture have produced a series of values which contrast sharply from those of the dominant white group. In social interaction, Indians put the emphasis on good relations with neighbors—characteristically Indians are not talkative. . . . Important contrasts also exist between whites and Indians with respect to attitudes toward work and activity—a utilitarian philosophy among White Americans as against a contemplative one among Indians" (Dozier, 1967b: 400).

There are equally significant differences between the Mexican-American and the dominant culture. Zintz (1963) categorizes such differences as follows: subjugation to/mastery over nature; present/future time orientations; universalist/particularist perspective and level of aspiration; saving/ sharing, and so on. Other investigators, like Ramírez and Castañeda (1974), prefer a simpler categorization—identification with family, community, and ethnic group; personalization of interpersonal relations; status and role definition in family and community; and Mexican Catholic ideology.

The differences between a minority culture and the dominant culture suggest that the educational needs of both cultural groups are distinct. Given this bilingual situation, and if it is not recognized in the system of education, it is disadvantageous to the minorities, Thus, the concept of an alternative system of education is justified. But the intragroup differences, which may be considerable, are such that only programs that arise out of the immediate cultural environment of the children have any hope of being accepted. For instance, in the case of the Native Americans there are several levels of acculturation to the dominant society arising partly out of geographical mobility and urbanization. They differ greatly in relationship, or lack of relationship, to traditional tribal organization as well as religion. Consequently, it is to be expected that their life styles should vary. Some, whatever their distribution are completely assimilated, others still adhere faithfully to their historical traditions. Apart from changes that are due to the impact of a new civilization and the influence of new geographical and social environments to which they have moved, there are divergencies in attitude that arise from the way in which their community is organized. The Apache retain the open and receptive characteristics of a formerly nomadic people, while the Pueblos have always valued a settled way of life and have inherited a "closed" attitude. These differences have an important bearing upon their attitude to their own languages and those of others, as well as to the approval or encouragement of intertribal and other forms of bilingualism. Dozier (1970) has remarked on the conservative attitude of the Pueblos to their language. Such differences of attitude express themselves as different educational needs, differences of need that are increased by ethnic, cultural, and language contact.

While those who design the curricula for the education of bilingual children need to be precise in their analysis of cultural differences, all that is needed at this point is to indicate that the differences exist, that they are important, and that they need to be built into the alternative educational program. It is not necessary, at this point, to decide whether these differences are ethnic or of socio-economic origin—whether the Mexican American culture is a traditional national culture or a culture of poverty (Casavantes, 1970). What is important is that *their* culture has been ignored in a way in which the dominant culture has not, and that this disregard has created very urgent individual needs.

By whatever criterion we choose to use, language minorities in the United States are handicapped severely because of a failure to teach them English and to take account of the consequent advantages of bilingual education, and by the failure to meet adequately their needs within the present school system. Performance over the whole of the academic curriculum is very much below the national norm with levels of enrollment and length of participation in formal education also considerably substandard. Even when full consideration has been given to such nonschool related variables in academic performance as culturally determined variance in attitudes to schooling, the effect of rurality upon some (like the Indians and Mexican-Americans), and the low economic status and consequent poorer average health, the conclusion is inescapable that the types of linguistic communities, the schools as they are organized at present, the orientation of the curricula, and the virtual disregard of the mother tongue as a teaching language must take the greatest share of responsibility for the school failure of minorities.

On the evidence that has been adduced, the minorities are entitled to a choice of alternative systems of education, adapted to their inherent characteristics and needs, and capable of ensuring that their contribution to the whole of American society is commensurate with their capacities. Such alternative systems are unlikely to develop by evolutionary processes from the present established system or result from piecemeal modifications of it. National characteristics and national needs appear to change relatively slowly and, in any case so far as the United States is concerned, have not been marked for over two hundred years by radical departures from the traditions inherited from Western Europe. However, the needs of the minorities cannot be met by the traditional system whatever concessions it makes to them, partly because they are minorities, but mainly because they are immigrants from a great diversity of countries, possessing little if any English on arrival and brought up to conform to different ways of life. For these and other reasons, the immigrants lack the sense of security that would enable them to profit from the education they are offered, even if they could understand their teachers, and having understood, found the instruction relevant to their circumstances.

Past failure has resulted in the accumulation of stresses that now constitute a threat not simply to the schools but to society at large. No one would attempt to deny that society is changing, but the main characteristic of Western society is that it seeks change consciously and deliberately. This is true of relatively homogeneous societies, but truer still of ethnically and linguistically heterogeneous societies such as the United States. Yet the system of education in that country is dedicated to the preservation of existing institutions and the prevailing mores; and, if it does seek to meet the challenge of novel ideas and unprecedented social movements, it attempts to do so by slight and uncoordinated modifications. Nevertheless, the relationship between immigration, the maintenance of a foreign tongue, and the disenchantment with academic standards in the schools and colleges place the role, function, and style of bilingual education high among the problems to which attention should be directed. "A further factor influencing the interpretation of these relationships is the long-term movement of the United States into an information-based society. Right now some 55 percent of the work force is in the information business, presumably the widest road to upward social mobility is the ability to collect, handle, and interpret information, the bulk of which is in some printed form and in English" (Hearings, 1977: 435–6).

The problem facing teachers and educators is exacerbated by the fact that the causes of their difficulties (great though they be) are not stable nor their movement predictable, but increasing in their influence at an accelerating rate. For instance, the proportion of immigrants to the United States is increasing: 25 percent of the annual population increase is due to this factor. About 36 percent of such immigrants are under twenty years of age. The racial composition of the school-age population is changing and will continue to do so at an accelerating rate. In 1980 minorities will compose 17.4 percent of the elementary school population compared with 16.2 percent in 1975, while the increase in secondary schools will rise by 1.2 percent from 15.4 percent to 16.6 percent. This increasing proportion of immigrants would present a less acute problem to the schools if they were dispersed fairly evenly throughout the country, but in fact they are drawn into the vortex of city life. Thirty-seven percent of them settled in the fifteen largest cities, and of the remaining 63 percent most of them gravitate to less densely populated cities, while very few go to rural areas.

While the schools as they exist at present fail to meet the needs of their existing students, there is a tendency, forced by the number of young mothers at work, to recruit children at earlier ages. In theory at least, it is possible for children to be in schools (which are providing an admittedly inadequate service) for increasingly longer segments of their lives. "About 49 percent of both white and nonwhite 3- to 5-year-olds entered school in 1975. This is a 91 percent increase on the preprimary enrollment since 1964" (Hearings, 1974: 173). This is only one of the factors that has diminished the influence of the family as an important factor in child socialization at a time when the school is also failing. A child now entering the first grade may have been exposed to a variety of preprimary education, including day-care programs. He may have been involved in Headstart or related programs and most certainly he would have had increasing numbers of hours of exposure to television. The size of the family has declined so that grandparents and siblings exercise a less effective role in the education of the very young. The relationship between school and community at large has changed in important ways in urban areas: "as one looks at a sample of large cities—Atlanta, Chicago, Denver and so forth—one finds that the present minority school-enrollment in almost every case is substantially above the percentage minority-population of the city as a whole." Thus the disparity between school and community minority composition in Atlanta is 85 and 52 percent; Denver 47 and 11 percent; and St. Louis 70 and 41 percent.

These are some aspects of the background to school failure among both minorities and the majority. The system suffers extreme stress so that teaching is neglected, and the level of education of all students, of whatever racial category, declines. Cultural shock is not confined to immigrants; but among immigrants, as well as those who live with them at school, culture shock results in disenchantment with school and society. The influx of large numbers of youths from Hong Kong, for instance, results in all the classic dislocations of immigrants. "The consequence is that what had been a model community in terms of behavior is experiencing an unfamiliar upswing in delinquency. One can contemplate the parallel and associated difficulties within the school system" (Hearings, 1977: 453). Again there is an increase overall in the dropout rate of students. The failures of the school affect both minority and majority groups both as to delinquency and to dropouts. However, the rate among the non–English-speaking students is 30 percent higher than it is among the Anglos. This is a bleak picture, one made worse because of the rapidity with which changes occur. "The present and the past are decreasingly satisfactory models for the future, particularly the future of the educational system" (Hearings, 1977: 287).

Demography, a branch of the social sciences dealing with the determinants and consequences of population change, treats of such variable and measurable phenomena as birth, marriage, death, and the size of the family, the density, distribution, and mobility of populations. Demographic data can be tested for their accuracy and, because they are concerned with long-term secular trends in society, the interpretations can be adjusted from year to year. The data and the interpretation of the data as they relate to bilingual education point to the need not simply for a radical reappraisal of the existing educational system, but also for the creation of alternative systems. Only in this way can the injuries that are being perpetrated at present first be compensated for, and the more serious and more numerous injuries that demographic data predict during the next decade be avoided. The beneficiaries of such alternative systems would not be minorities solely: "if the bilingual education of students whose primary language is not English, particularly in big cities, overstresses the system so that the job is done badly, the level of education of English-speaking students may also be reduced, further accelerating the decline of the urban school system" (Hearings, 1977: 35).

The question is not whether alternative systems are required or who would be the beneficiaries. It is rather how can the emergence of such alternatives be encouraged, and what general philosophy should guide the acceptance of the concept of alternative systems? There is no single answer to what the alternative systems should be like. If there were, the alternative would soon become the new establishment. The alternatives must grow spontaneously from the needs and the visions of many groups with different attitudes to education and the ends to be served by any educational institution. The concept of alternative systems is polyphonic: no voice can be reduced or modified to coincide with another within the community. The idea of alternative systems is polyphonic, but within the context of the nation it is also harmonic since the alternative systems should be born out of tolerance and so be able to produce and reflect a communion of intellect and spirit that embraces the interests of the whole nation.

One thing one can say is that though minorities should be allowed greater freedom to create their own systems, freedom is not the determining factor. The release of an artist's instincts is only a precondition; and the removal of frustrations will not produce a work of art. It is what the artist brings to meet the released powers that will determine the quality of the work. The freedom of the minority groups to determine their own systems is simply the launching pad; where and how far they go is determined by their willingness to accept the constraints to which any worthwhile achievement is subject. Intellectual effort, tolerance of different styles of thinking and behaving, resilience in the face of failure, a care for what is relevant in the past and ruthlessness in sweeping away the irrelevancies of historical traditions—all these are required of those who demand alternative systems.

Wales

The needs of bilinguals in Wales are, in principle, similar to those of bilinguals in the United States or any other heterogeneous society. However, the linguistic situation is less complex than is the case in the United States, the numbers of minority students considerably fewer than in the United States, and the system of education, which takes account of bilingualism though conducted and administered locally, is organized and planned nationally. Furthermore, that bilingual system has existed (with changes and improvements) for nearly a century. For these reasons, the Welsh evidence of bilingual student needs and a comparison of those needs and how they are met with the needs of the monolinguals is more easily described than the evidence from the United States or the Soviet Union.

Schoolmasters in Wales were among the first educators anywhere to undertake what were admittedly modest investigations of the consequences of bilingualism and to identify the needs of bilingual children. The earliest studies (Saer, 1922, 1928, 1932) were concerned with the relationship of bilingualism and intellectual development, as well as bilingualism and verbal ability measured by formal objective tests. Serious reservations were expressed about the validity of this type of investigation, concerns prompted by the repeatedly conflicting conclusions and the limited relevance to the practical problems of conducting bilingual schools and implementing a bilingual policy. As a consequence sociological variables were taken into account by researchers. Of particular practical import have been the several surveys undertaken by the Advisory Councils of the Ministry of Education of England and Wales, the Ministry of Education itself, the Welsh Joint Education Committee, the National Foundation for Educational Research for England and Wales and the Schools Council for England and Wales. These surveys have provided necessary information about the incidence of bilingualism in a heterogeneous society. Further, they discuss the relationship of different levels in attainment in key areas of the curriculum, like reading in the two languages and mathematics, to the degrees of bilingualism in individuals and in different areas of Wales.

BILINGUALISM AND INTELLIGENCE

For three years D. J. Saer (1922) investigated 1,400 bilingual children between the ages of 7- and 14-years in seven Welsh-speaking rural and urban areas, together with one school in an anglicized area. In all the schools English was the teaching language. The children were classified according to the level of their bilingual competence and were administered tests of ability to reproduce pure rhythms, tests of manual dexterity, the Stanford Binet-Simon and the Burt Scales of Intelligence (translated into

Welsh), as well as vocabulary and English and Welsh composition tests.
Though this early work has been criticized for faulty statistical techniques, it
compares favorably with later investigations in Wales. Saer's results were
confirmed by Frank Smith (1923) using different techniques. A summary
of these studies concluded "that under present day conditions and the
organisation of schools in Wales the child who has learned two languages
at an early age . . . by learning the second language during play and in
association with other children suffers less disturbance than those who are
obliged to learn the second language at school and continue to use their
mother tongue in their association with other children." But, though not
stated explicitly, the disadvantages of bilingualism and the very special
needs of bilinguals are implied (Saer, Smith and Hughes, 1924). F. Smith,
from his investigations of the development of bilingual children over
three years, concluded that "monoglot children between the ages of 8 and
11 years make better progress than bilingual children in their power of
expression, their choice of vocabulary and their accuracy of thought. So
far from bilingualism being an intellectual advantage it seems to be exactly
the reverse at least under present day conditions in the schools of Wales"
(1923: 282). These conclusions governed attitudes to bilingualism in Wales
for many years and reinforced the reluctance of educators to promote the
teaching of Welsh among native speakers of English, lest the disadvantages
of the minority should be duplicated among the majority who would thus
acquire new needs.

A study of monoglot English and bilingual children from Welsh families
was conducted in 1938 (Jones, W. R.) using nonverbal, concrete verbal,
and abstract verbal tests as well as tests of linguistic attainment of a
general nature. It was found that "bilingualism did not seem to be a
hindrance to thinking carried out in verbal terms" (10–18). Another study
by the same investigator collaborating with Stewart (1951) modified the
conclusions. They used adapted English tests to compare the performance
of monoglot English and bilinguals and found in the "results a highly
significant difference in favor of the monoglot group on the verbal and
nonverbal tests." When the results were adjusted to a common nonverbal
basis, the difference was substantially reduced, but still remained statistically significant. It was therefore concluded that the bilingual children" were significantly inferior to the monoglot children even after full
allowance had been made for initial difference in nonverbal, intelligence"
(3–8). These second set of results only served to confirm the studies done
earlier by Barke (1933), and Barke and Williams (1938). These researchers
found very little difference in the performance of monoglots and bilinguals
on nonverbal tests, but they concluded that the bilinguals were distinctly
inferior on verbal tests, especially when the verbal tests were administered
in the child's mother tongue.

More recent investigations have tended to reveal a consistent inclination for scores on nonverbal tests of intelligence to increase as the linguistic composition of the group became more English and less bilingual (Jones, W. R., 1955, 1959, 1960a & b; and Lewis, D. G., 1959). This conclusion was supported by a later study using largely the same techniques. It has also been suggested that these tendencies continued beyond the early university stage. In 1952, W. R. Jones investigated the performance of Welsh-speaking bilinguals on verbal and nonverbal tests and how their performance on the two types of tests compared with their English reading performance. This was the first study which even tentatively included any sociological variables, namely parental occupation. He concluded that because of their inferior English reading attainment, Welsh-speaking children could not be assessed satisfactorily on verbal tests given in English. This appears to have been the most conclusive, though not unexpected, result of a long series of studies into the relationship between bilingualism and intelligence among Welsh-speaking children. In 1959 a further study elaborated the treatment of the social background variables in an attempt to correct earlier misconceptions (Jones, W. R., 1959). On this occasion it was found that the crucial variable in the test performances of bilingual children appeared to be the type of locality, urban or rural, and the occupational status of the parents, and that everything else being equal bilingualism need not be considered a disadvantage. So far as the development of their intelligence is concerned, bilingualism may pose difficulties but they arise not so much from bilingualism itself as from the extent to which the specific and unique needs of such bilingual children are not met by schools and other social institutions.

BILINGUALISM AND ATTAINMENT IN WELSH AND ENGLISH AND IN OTHER SUBJECTS

Some evidence of the reading attainment of bilingual children is available from some of the researches to which reference has been made already, but in 1955 an investigation was undertaken in order to compare the reading attainment of mainly Welsh-speaking and mainly English-speaking bilinguals (Jones, W. R., 1955). The Welsh groups were reported as significantly inferior on the silent reading tests, and this was attributed to insufficient opportunity to acquire satisfactory aural and oral skills in their second language, English. Furthermore, the mainly English-speaking bilinguals were reported as inferior to monoglot English groups, and this was attributed to the fact that the bilinguals were required to learn Welsh as a second language. It was also suggested that even children of superior intelligence were handicapped because of the need to learn a second language. Among the ten year old students, it was found that the average reading age of the mainly Welsh group was 9.47 months lower than that of the mainly English group of the same age. Among the eleven year old students the difference was 10.8 months. When mainly Welsh bilinguals were compared with a mixed English and Welsh group the figures were 8.85 months and 10.16 months respectively.

Other studies have been conducted by the local authorities, and it is significant that most of these are concerned with estimating the English reading attainment of students rather than their attainment in Welsh, a recognition of the fundamental need to acquire the lingua franca. Monmouthshire published a Survey of Reading Ability in 1953. The most thoroughly Welsh-speaking authority, Merionethshire, undertook surveys in 1958 and 1960. It was reported that attainment in Welsh as a first language was extremely good and that the mainly Welsh-speaking bilinguals achieved a much higher standard of reading in their second language, English, than did the English bilinguals in Welsh, their second language. There was considerable difference between the standard of reading among urban groups, where the parents appeared to be in professional and nonmanual occupations, and the rural groups where the parents were mainly engaged in agriculture. The 1960 followup survey was concerned with the same students, now in secondary school. It was reported that, judged on the average scores for the whole county, the standard reached by the students at the age of thirteen—especially in English reading comprehension—was not significantly below that usually associated with monolingual English children in England, though the majority of the Merionethshire students had a predominantly Welsh background and English was the second language. This is largely attributable to the very heavy pressure on students to learn English in the Welsh-speaking areas. The needs of the bilinguals were recognized and the school curriculum took them into account.

Following the three surveys described in *Standards of Reading 1948–56* (H.M.S.O., 1960) which were conducted in 1948, 1952, and 1956 by the Ministry of Education, it was decided to undertake a separate study in Wales. This study would not only take account of standards of English reading, as had been the custom hitherto, but standards of reading in Welsh also, among bilinguals in different linguistic areas. This study was carried out in 1968. Samples were drawn for the whole of Wales—boys and girls whose first language was Welsh and those whose first language was English. The same measures were used for testing English (the Watts Vernon test) as had been used in all previous England and Wales surveys. For the specifically Welsh survey, a reading test similar to the English test was constructed in Welsh. For all Wales, pupils aged 15 score 8.8 points more than pupils aged 11; for all England, 8.4 points more (See Table 7.2). This gives a rough equation of 8 points to 4 years of average progress or 1 point for every 6 months. The difference of 3 points between junior pupils whose first language was Welsh and the other junior pupils in Wales can be regarded as a difference of 18 months and the difference of

TABLE 7.2. Standards of Reading in English

	11 Years	15 Years
All Wales	12.0	20.8
Pupils whose first language is Welsh	9.4	18.0
Other pupils	12.4	21.4
All England	13.3	21.7

Source: Lewis, E.G., 1968, extracted.

1.3 points between the average junior score for all Wales and that for all England as a difference of 8 months. For senior pupils, the difference is somewhat less—0.9 points or 5 months. The difference between English-speaking bilinguals in Wales and English-speaking pupils in England has been reduced considerably by the age of 15 though there is still a slight inferiority. There is an appreciable difference in favor of the English-speaking students in Wales at the junior and senior levels, though as one would expect the rate of progress of those who are learning English as a second language is slightly greater than that of those of the native speakers of English whether these are bilinguals in Wales or monolinguals in England (See Table 7.3). The rate of progress of the English-speaking pupils learning Welsh as a second language is hardly impressive: the level of attainment at 15 years is well below that of Welsh speaking pupils at 11. Furthermore, if the progress of the two languages, the Welsh-speaking bilinguals and the English-speaking bilinguals is compared, the former advance more rapidly in their second language, English, than do the latter in their second language, Welsh.

There is some evidence also of the relationship of levels of bilingualism to attainment in other subjects. Jones and others (1957) administered a mechanical arithmetic test, a problem arithmetic test, a test of silent reading in English, and a Moray House English test, together with a Welsh silent reading test and a Welsh adaptation of the Moray House test, to 11 year old pupils of schools in the most thoroughly Welsh-speaking areas. The total sample was divided into four groups—predominantly Welsh-speaking, moderately English-speaking, predominantly English-speaking, and moderately Welsh-speaking. It was found that the four groups did not differ significantly in mechanical arithmetic, though this

TABLE 7.3. Standards of Reading in Welsh

	Pupils Whose First Language Was Welsh	Pupils Whose First Language Was English	All Welsh Speaking Pupils
Pupils aged 15	22.9	13.6	20.5
Pupils aged 11	16.7	10.5	15.4
Difference between A and B	6.2	3.1	5.1

Source: Lewis, E.G., 1968, extracted.

test was uniformly presented in English. There was a significant difference in problem arithmetic between the Welsh group and the English group in favor of the latter, the test having been administered in English. But the performance of the moderately English-speaking group was better than the performance of any of the others. So far as concerns the English reading and the English usage (Moray House) test, the predominantly English group had higher scores than any of the others. The Welsh group's performance on the Welsh language tests was superior to the performance of the moderately English-speaking group. Bilingualism tended not to have any significant association with mechanical arithmetic and only a lightly adverse association with problem arithmetic. The influence of bilingualism on attainment in English and Welsh varied according to the degree of the student's bilingualism.

The most thorough-going assessment to date of the consequences of bilingualism and of the consequent needs of bilingual children in Wales has been the National Foundation for Educational Research and the Welsh Joint Education Committee cooperative investigation (1969). Samples of pupils aged 7, 10, and 14 were drawn from the whole of Wales. The sample was stratified according to type of school and the linguistic character of the area in which a school was located. The 7-year-old pupils were given tests in number concepts (English and Welsh versions) mechanical arithmetic, problem arithmetic (English and Welsh versions), English reading, and Welsh reading (See Table 7.4). The 10-year-olds were given English or Welsh versions of concept arithmetic and problem arithmetic, and mechanical arithmetic where instructions for the administration of the test were in English and Welsh. The language tests consisted of an English usage test, and English reading test, and parallel tests in Welsh (See Table 7.5). The 14-year-olds were given the same language tests in English and Welsh as the 10-year-olds. The mechanical arithmetic test was also identical. In addition to these tests there were a mathematics problem test and a mathematical insight test available in both languages (See Table 7.6).

The differences in the Welsh and English reading tests generally coincided with the linguistic character of the area—the English regions performing better in English and less well in Welsh. So far as concerns problem arithmetic, no significant differences between linguistic areas were found. This was not the case with mechanical arithmetic or number concept tests; in these the Welsh linguistic region tending to have higher scores in both tests than the moderately Welsh-speaking area. We can conclude that generally the needs of bilingual children vary according to the linguistic character of the area and, specifically, according to the type of learning to which they are exposed or are expected to undertake.

Among the 7-year-olds, performance in the language tests varied according to the linguistic character of the area. The more English the area,

TABLE 7.4. 7-Year-Old Pupils in All Schools According to Linguistic Area

| | | Sampling Areas[a] | | | | | | Wales | |
| | | A | | B | | C | | All Schools | |
		Mean	SE	Mean	SE	Mean	SE	Mean	SE
Number Concept	Boys	99.75	0.84	95.94	1.23	99.21	2.03	98.83	1.97
	Girls	101.73	1.48	100.02	1.52	101.18	2.20	101.11	2.05
Mechanical Arithmetic	Boys	102.48	1.39	98.70	1.23	98.02	1.30	98.73	1.24
	Girls	106.06	1.46	102.70	1.69	100.77	1.34	101.64	1.21
Problem Arithmetic	Boys	100.22	1.10	98.47	1.10	101.51	1.58	100.91	1.53
	Girls	98.16	1.44	100.34	1.75	100.18	1.62	99.96	1.51
Reading Comprehension	Boys	94.90	1.08	95.57	1.12	98.17	2.08	97.36	2.01
	Girls	97.76	1.34	101.92	1.00	103.31	1.64	102.48	1.56
Welsh Reading	Boys	93.85	1.47	77.97	2.50	74.08	1.12	77.33	1.05
(Prawf Darllen)	Girls	95.13	1.40	83.05	2.14	73.32	1.19	77.07	1.21
Number of Children	Boys	369		374		428		591	
	Girls	314		303		439		575	

[a] Sampling Areas: A = Local Education Authorities with 62–100% Welsh-speaking children.
B = Local Education Authorities with 17–25% Welsh-speaking children.
C = Local Education Authorities with less than 8% Welsh-speaking children.

Source: National Foundation for Educational Research and Welsh Joint Education Committee [hereafter cited as NFER/WJEC], 1969:34.

339

TABLE 7.5. 10-Year-Old Pupils in All Schools According to Linguistic Areas

| | | Sampling Areas[a] | | | | | | Wales | |
| | | A | | B | | C | | All Schools | |
		Mean	SE	Mean	SE	Mean	SE	Mean	SE
Concept Arithmetic A	Boys	98.20	1.05	98.78	0.72	100.83	1.29	100.14	0.95
	Girls	96.93	0.79	97.00	0.75	101.51	1.29	100.22	0.92
Concept Arithmetic B	Boys	98.78	1.16	98.60	1.08	100.22	1.29	99.77	0.95
	Girls	100.35	1.18	98.72	1.17	101.74	1.20	101.14	0.89
Problem Arithmetic	Boys	99.47	1.10	101.38	0.93	101.08	1.19	100.86	0.87
	Girls	99.00	0.89	100.24	0.78	101.10	1.28	100.66	0.93
Mechanical Arithmetic	Boys	98.66	1.21	98.88	0.91	98.92	1.06	98.92	0.78
	Girls	100.41	1.06	100.54	0.95	101.86	1.19	101.63	0.88
English	Boys	92.78	1.05	95.49	1.03	98.88	1.32	97.45	1.02
	Girls	94.24	1.00	96.23	1.06	102.56	1.60	100.45	1.02
English Reading	Boys	91.90	1.06	95.67	0.83	100.68	1.45	98.60	1.13
	Girls	90.49	0.94	94.18	0.76	101.32	1.24	98.72	0.99
Welsh	Boys	89.19	1.76	56.93	2.82	53.63	3.21	59.77	2.22
	Girls	90.92	1.68	58.65	3.13	53.95	3.32	60.36	2.45
Welsh Reading	Boys	89.27	1.98	61.05	1.98	58.88	2.15	64.04	1.60
	Girls	89.21	1.97	61.08	2.10	58.63	2.47	63.76	1.77
Number of Children	Boys	537		441		478		677	
	Girls	509		398		468		653	

[a] Sampling area as defined in Table 7.4.
Source: NFER/WJEC, 1969:36.

340

TABLE 7.6. 14-Year-Old Pupils in All Schools According to Linguistic Area

| | | Sampling Area | | | | | | Wales | |
| | | A | | B | | C | | All Schools | |
		Mean	SE	Mean	SE	Mean	SE	Mean	SE
Mathematics	Boys	99.46	0.84	104.05	2.81	103.99	2.84	103.39	1.26
	Girls	98.37	0.93	98.71	0.63	97.37	1.35	97.71	1.28
Mathematics Insight	Boys	97.94	0.86	102.50	2.60	102.20	1.04	101.67	1.27
	Girls	99.52	1.23	99.89	0.60	97.81	1.30	98.35	1.19
Mechanical Arithmetic	Boys	98.40	1.05	100.06	2.10	99.78	1.18	99.64	1.23
	Girls	100.83	0.65	101.37	0.65	101.58	1.54	101.45	1.99
English	Boys	94.93	0.78	99.34	2.84	99.48	0.76	98.85	1.23
	Girls	99.98	1.51	100.29	1.12	99.96	1.40	100.01	1.06
English Reading	Boys	94.48	0.55	100.23	2.62	101.85	1.25	100.61	1.31
	Girls	95.36	1.49	97.02	1.14	98.22	1.20	97.66	0.98
Welsh	Boys	88.03	2.29	65.82	2.69	58.98	2.22	63.92	1.42
	Girls	94.03	2.50	71.41	3.93	62.59	3.96	68.15	1.94
Welsh Reading	Boys	86.82	2.86	62.57	3.44	56.10	2.41	61.21	1.56
	Girls	91.88	2.63	66.92	4.98	57.76	4.15	63.73	2.00

Source: NFER/WJEC, 1969:37.

341

the better the performance in English and the poorer in Welsh. On the other tests, the English area schools tended to have higher scores—though in some cases the differences were only slight. If we compare 7- and 10-year-olds, it can be concluded that where the area becomes more homogeneously English, the needs of the students in it become less acute.

Performance on the language tests again varied with the character of the area. On the other tests, the moderately Welsh-speaking area *B* obtained higher scores than the other two areas, though the variations are not very great. When we consider all three age groups, some interesting conclusions may be drawn. It is clear that standards in English tend to be higher than those in Welsh, especially where the two are second languages. School performance varies among different bilingual strata according to age. The influence of differences in linguistic background appears to be least at age 7 and then increases as the pupils reach 10 and 14 years. When the pupils in the thoroughly Welsh-speaking area *A* were further classified according to their specific home background, the differences in achievement between the children from thoroughly Welsh, moderately Welsh, and thoroughly English homes appeared to conform to the differences between the broader linguistic areas and in favor of English. Where bilingualism has an important effect on performance, it appears to be confined to those aspects of the curriculum where language is the key factor. Where language is less important, as in certain types of mathematical skills, the influence of bilingualism in Wales declines. Basic to the satisfaction of the needs of bilingual children appears to be sound and continuous instruction in language. Whatever else may be included in the curriculum—for instance, a specifically cultural component—takes a subordinate place.

THE SOCIAL PSYCHOLOGY OF BILINGUALISM

The evidence from the United States, Wales, and elsewhere confirms the widely held view that bilingual children may be handicapped. This handicap does not appear to be a necessary consequence of being bilingual, but rather of being a bilingual whose specific needs are not met by the existing system of education. These are handicaps contingent upon being a speaker of a minority language, and though they may be long lasting requiring a continuing bilingual education, there is no evidence that the results are permanent or that the system cannot cope with them. Contingent and temporary handicaps have to be dealt with, and for that reason a remedial and compensatory approach is justified. This is far from arguing that such remedial programs are the main or only justifications. They are required also for reasons which have to do with the bilingual's emotional needs. These issues have been examined in the United States and Wales, but unlike those countries the psychological issues of bilingualism have been paramount in the USSR. Because of the long history of deprivation suffered by minorities, bilinguals everywhere tend to acquire needs arising from their being alienated from their own group; they are also handicapped from accepting what is valuable in the majority social group, especially in adolescence (Bryde). Derbyshire concluded that forced acculturation, which is the root of alienation, has an adverse effect on "integration of dominant value orientations and behaviors also" (1971: 36). Identity conflict is alleged to characterize Eskimo bilinguals (Sindell and Weintrob, 1972). Brophy and Aberle describe value conflicts which inhibit the satisfactory development of bilinguals, and their early withdrawal from school (1966). Delinquency, the propensity to drop out of school, and fragmented personality development are all laid at the door of bilingualism. Even such very specific speech defects as stuttering and stammering are included in the indictment. Brown (1953) found these defects to be more frequent among Slovak bilinguals in the United States than among the nonbilinguals. In Ghana, the ratio of stutterers was higher among bilinguals than among monolingual children, and this phenomenon which appeared to be absent in preschool age children increased as they moved up the school grades (Lewis, E. G., 1953).

Many of these psychological needs of bilinguals derive from possible conflict among the "roles of speech in human behavior of no less importance than in communication. Language is the means of regularizing and organizing the actual world . . . and on the other hand it is the agent of organizing behavior and of planning further actions" (Luria, 1932:412; 1961: 25, 38). It is this internal functioning of language, rather than its communicative function, that is related to the most important possible dangers to which an adversely situated bilingual may be exposed. Luria suggests that the acquisition of speech and the transition to a new cultural form of living "changes the structure of the psychophysiological processes" creating new psychological needs. The active system of speech is the "definite leading system" (1932: 412; 1959: 341) psychologically, and "introducing the possibility of conflict here produces destruction in that process upon which depends the whole structure of the act" (1932: 208). The inhibitory regulating functions of language are exercised most successfully in states of emotional equilibrium; they are much more perfect in a state of composure than during affect (ibid., 215). This regulatory function may be artifically destroyed by introducing certain conflicts. There is no necessary or inevitable conflict between the languages of the bilingual person, nor is there any necessary disadvantage to offset the many advantages of learning two or more languages. "These disturbances are referred not to the difficulty of associating [ideas] in a second language but exclusively to the necessity of transferring from one established setting to another" (ibid., 216). Speaking in a certain language the person creates a definite psychological setting and "transfer to a new setting, with a removal of the former setting, is evidently sufficient to cause neurodynamic disturbances" (ibid., 216). It should be sufficient to bring into collision such language settings in order "to evoke a conflict of two very complicated structural systems . . . with results in the neurodynamics of the subject." Luria's experiments enable him to claim that when the transfer from one language to another was sudden and unregulated, considerable conflict resulted which introduced "a series of very interesting and serious disturbances. . . . Sudden transfer to another language is combined with a very great destructive process" (ibid., 215).

The destructive process caused by unregulated or mishandled bilingualism is characterized by Luria in some contexts as a "reversion to more primitive mechanisms of thinking," called syncretism following the custom of Piaget and Claparede (ibid., 284n). All his experiments, he claims, confirm the danger of this reversion from more advanced to more infantile systems of reacting, in which very "capricious forms of response occur" (ibid., 68). The reversion is consequent on the lowering of the "functional barrier," a psychological process of cultural origin, the nature of which is determined to a large extent by the acquisition of language and by the characteristics of that language. The functional barrier is the basis of voluntary as opposed to unreflective reaction. The result of an emotional disturbance consequent on language conflict is to "weaken the inhibitory and restraining functions of the higher strata of the nervous apparatus. The higher regulating mechanisms suffer from the affect . . . resulting in a distortion and disorganizing of behavior" (ibid., 395). In the structure of a child's response, there is a regulating factor in which speech is an important element and any slight disturbance in the regulating system inevitably brings about a considerable distortion.

One form of the distortion is spasmodic speech behavior and hesitancy. Words function as meaningful units only in context, and it is in context that they form an elaborate network of associations. This network is thought to work more or less automatically and unconsciously as a broad source of transfer for conceptual learning and retention. Any impairment or even a slight disturbance of this associative network is bound to have adverse consequences at all levels. This is what happens when there is conflict between a child's choice of language, since such a conflict rouses emotional reactions and "the associative process in the affective state is entirely another structure than that which is observed in the normal associative network (ibid., 55). Luria pointed out that during conflict of language associations, the time expended in speech responses fluctuated. He also observed that together with rapidly flowing associations were very slow ones. The subjects he observed were not able, as a rule, to produce reactions with any degree of stability. This phenomenon he related to sudden transfer of language— "the subject when exposed suddenly to an unfamiliar word or one with which he is slightly familiar in one language attempts to think it out assimilating it to words whose meaning are known to him in another language (ibid., 284). Thus, given the word *letter* in English, a speaker of Russian responds with an English association *summer* because of assimilation with the Russian word *leto*, meaning summer. These confusions occur at the level of understanding words as well as in actually speaking a language.

The psychological disturbances to which Luria refers result not from the possession of two or more languages, but of conflict arising from unregulated transfer from one language to another—from conflict within the context of their employment. It is conflict in the relationship of the two languages that accounts for disturbances, and this relationship is determined partly by the way in which the two languages are acquired. It depends upon whether, for instance, they are learned in "coordinate situations" where the languages are learned at different stages of life, or, having been acquired, are kept separate by being used with well-recognized different groups. For instance, in school one language may be used only with a particular teacher and the other language with another, or with either parent exclusively. On the other hand, they may be acquired in "compound situations where both languages are acquired simultaneously in mixed language communities or are used indiscriminately without relating one language exclusively to one group or another" (Imedadze, 1967: 132). The setting is influenced also by the attitude of others to the two languages; a child either accepts the two languages as functionally equivalent and appropriate or is forced to hesitate in his choice. It is not the possession of the two languages which is the cause of disturbances, but instead uncertainty concerning their relationship. This uncertain or unorganized relationship results in capricious, unsystematic, and fitful switching from one to the other. These considerations are well within the capacity of the teacher to cope with provided he is first of all able to operate within a sound general policy for the treatment of bilinguals, one which discourages negative attitudes towards their languages. Further, the teacher can deal with the problem provided he is knowledgeable about the linguistic, psychological, and sociological aspects of the contact of languages in children. The problem of ensuring a satisfactory setting for each language and for a right relationship between the two settings is a pedagogical issue that can be solved by judicious attention to the circumstances of the child's need to use either language.

POLICIES

It cannot be denied that bilingualism may result in some disadvantages to individuals and groups. These disadvantages are incidental to bilingualism and not of necessity consequent upon it. Nevertheless, educators have to recognize the possible disadvantages and adjust educational policy in such a way that they can be avoided, neutralized, or compensated for. In almost all advanced or modernizing societies, the central government or some central institution oversees education—including language—policy. This is certainly so in European countries, and if at first glance it appears not to be the case in the United States, that appearance is illusory. Although the separate states have responsibility for education, the United States federal government intervenes more and more frequently on vital issues of policy. This occurs not only where, for instance, the Department of the Interior is involved with the education of the Native Americans, but in such matters as federally mandated initiatives to redress segregation, particularly with bussing introduced to overcome racial imbalances in schools. Congress has defined what bilingual education should mean to American schools and has set out the criteria for selecting those who are to be educated bilingually as well as stating the period during which such students are to be retained in bilingual programs. Equally involved in United States bilingual education policy decisions is the judiciary, ultimately the United States Supreme Court. Court interpretations of the various statutory provisions and acts of Congress together with their monitoring of the implementation of judicial decisions have set the course of bilingual education in the United States. There are differences in the way in which the United States and the European countries, including the Soviet Union, formulate policy, and there are differences in the extent to which their central governments are involved; but in principle whether it is the United States, the Soviet Union, Britain, or Switzerland, linguistic policy is made at the center of government. This is almost inevitable because language policy is only one aspect of an overall policy aimed at the integration of disparate elements in a heterogeneous society. The concern of the central government is to cooperate in maintaining some form of unity in diversity.

Linguistic policy is determined within at least three sets of parameters. In the first place, a heterogeneous society may comprise more than one large *national group*, all, some, or only one of which may be regarded as official and/or taught in schools. In this context, a *national language minority* implies the existence of an indigenous (not incorporated or immigrant) group having a recognized territory in which the core of the nation live. France is a country where there are several such nationalities with distinctive languages of their own. Of these nationalities, the Occitanie are the most numerous: 10 million of whom speak Languedoc. The next largest national group in France are the Bretons with 1.5 million in lower Brittany alone, 44 percent of whom speak the minority national language—namely Breton. There are 260,000 Catalans who speak their national language; 220,000 Corsicans who speak Corsican; and 90,000 Basques who are part of the Basque nation—all within recognized territories of France. In spite of the size and diversity of the national groups, only French is regarded as an official language and the other languages are taught only by agreement or with permission. The operative law governing language policy is that of 11 January 1951 which "favors the study and use of local languages and dialects within their own regions (Falch: 66). But the favorable attitude extends only to allowing or permitting such teaching and use. The United States also has indigenous nationalities such as the Amerindian tribes whose languages are also not official and are taught only sporadically. Other countries, like Ireland and Finland which consist of more than one nationality, grant official status to both languages, Irish and English in the one case, Finnish and Swedish in the other. Ireland distinguishes between the two official languages, Irish being regarded as the official and national language. In Ireland, students are required to learn both languages. In Finland, according to the law of 1922 and reenacted in 1962, unilingual and bilingual communities were designated. In bilingual communities, eighteen students is the minimum necessary to establish a bilingual school. In 1964, the law was amended so as to make a foreign language *or* the second national language obligatory. Each of the two national languages of Belgium, Flemish (50 percent) and Walloon (35 percent) are official, but within the territory associated with each language only the one appropriate national language need be taught. The district of Brussels (15 percent of the total population), however, is regarded as bilingual and both national languages are obligatory.

There are some countries consisting of more than one nationality where the diverse nationalities form a federation in which the nationalities are regarded as equal and all their languages official. The Soviet Union, Switzerland, and Yugoslavia are among the best examples of this federation of nations. The Swiss population consists of speakers of German, 73.3 percent (3.9 million); speakers of French, 22 percent (1.2 million); speakers of Italian, 3.9 percent (210,000) and Romansch, 0.7 percent (40,000). In Switzerland, the principle of territorial language means that—except in the three bilingual and trilingual cantons—instruction is in the territorial language and the learning of a second national language is not obligatory. Yugoslavia makes the distinction quite explicitly. In the 1971 census, all inhabitants were classified into two categories: those who stated their nationality and those who did not. The former were further classified into nations of Yugoslavia: Croatians, Macedonians, Montenegrins, Muslims, Serbs, and Slovenes. The second were classified as nationalities of Yugoslavia (that is, incorporated national minorities): Albanians, Bulgarians, Czechs, Hungarians, Italians, Rumanians, Slovaks, and Turks. The third, immigrant groups, included Austrians, Germans, Greeks, Jews, Poles, Gypsies, Russians, Ukrainians, and Wallachians among others. Neither Switzerland nor Yugoslavia can be said to "contain" their nationalities in the same way as France, because of its language policy, can be said to contain Brittany or the northern Basque territory.

Heterogeneity may also be due, entirely or in part, to the incorporation of nations or nationalities which are not historically indigenous to the country. Such is the case of the Mexican-American population of the Southwest. In Europe, Yugoslavia has incorporated nationalities; Austria has several, too, Slovenes and Croats in Carinthia, as well as Slovaks and Czechs. Hungary has over a quarter of a million Germans as well as significant numbers of Serbo-Croats and Rumanians. In Rumania itself there are over 700,000 Hungarians, accounting for 9 percent of the country's population. The German-speaking populations of Denmark, France (Alsace), and Belgium constitute incorporated national minorities. These incorporations are not to be confused with immigrant minorities, although the latter constitute sizeable proportions in countries which consist mainly of indigenous or incorporated nationalities.

Immigration, therefore, is a third cause of heterogeneous composites, and in some instances it may be the predominant cause. For instance, England is distinct from Britain, which includes indigenous nationalities like the Welsh, the Scots, and the Northern Irish. France is a case of heterogeneity where migration, from Africa and elsewhere, adds to the complexity without actually affecting policy. The several and distinct national groups in the Soviet Union and Yugoslavia have also been penetrated by large numbers of immigrants from within the Soviet Union and from within Yugoslav federated republics. The concentration of the nations and nationalities within their respective territorial boundaries is relatively high, though it differs from group to group. In the case of Yugoslavia, the coefficients of concentration (obtained by dividing the number of members of a nation in its core territory by the numbers belonging to the same nation living elsewhere in Yugoslavia) for the respective ethnic groups are as follows: Serbs 1.7; Croats 3.4; Slovenes 22.3; Macedonians 22.4; Montenegrins 2.9; Muslims 6.4; Albanians 2.4; and Hungarians 7.1. In fact, none of the nations or ethnic groups is unrepresented in any of the republics or autonomous provinces of Yugoslavia. A heterogeneous national composition of the population is especially notable in industrial centers. Thus, in the Commune of Pancevo, 67 percent are Serbs, 6.7 percent Hungarians, 6.0 percent Rumanians, 8.0 Macedonians, 2.5 Croats, and 3.7 percent members of other nationalities. The same is true of the Commune of Zenica, though the "mix" is rather different. In such circumstances the language policy has to be based on individual rather than territorial claims to ensure that large numbers of the population are not treated unfairly. The best example of an amalgam of immigrant populations is perhaps the United States where, except in respect of the Amerindian and Mexican-American populations, it would be difficult to envisage a decentralized language policy based on territorial claims.

Linguistic minorities in a heterogeneous society may be almost entirely concentrated—as is the case with the Lapps of Norway, the Serbs of East Germany, and other instances we have referred to. Such concentrated groups may be "nations" or "nationalities," historically indigenous or incorporated; or, they may be diffused minorities who may also be one of two kinds—those who have migrated from their own national territories within the country (as is the case in the Soviet Union and Yugoslavia), or those who have migrated from other countries, usually on the borders of their new homes (as is the case with immigrants to England or to the United States or Canada). In most countries the distribution of linguistically diverse populations reflects a combination of all three types of minorities. Nevertheless, the distinction between the groups in terms of their national status, whether they are nations of the country, nationalities of the country (that is, national minorities), or immigrant populations has to be taken into account in the assessment of language policy. As we have seen, countries with structural diversity—concentrations of national populations—may have, as in France, such a centralized policy that very little account is taken of even considerable linguistic diversity. In other cases, similarly structured diversity may be associated with a language policy which recognizes the linguistic autonomy of such territorial concentrations: in such instances, personal wishes, or individual difficulties, are accommodated pragmatically. This is the case in Belgium where territorial unilingualism is the basic policy, as well as of Switzerland, unless the territory is officially regarded as bilingual. In other countries with structured diversity, the territorial principle may be ignored to a considerable extent. In Yugoslavia, in spite of strong concentrations, a "personal criterion" in choice of language is fundamental to policy. This is the policy pursued by Denmark in respect of Greenland and the Faeroe Islands. In both cases, the national language is permitted rather than obligatory in the respective island territories of Faeroe and Greenland. In Greenland, from the third grade onwards, two types of schools are available. In the one case Greenlandic is the language of instruction and Danish is optional. In the other type of school, instruction is in Danish but religion and the Greenlandic language are taught in Greenlandic. Parents are allowed to choose which of the two types of school their children should be sent to. Similarly in Canada, French and English bilingualism is predominantly a matter for the province of Quebec, but even there the teaching of the French language is not obligatory for all students.

Policies for Bilingual Education–The Soviet Union

So far we have discussed the types of language policy which may be pursued by linguistically heterogeneous societies according to the way in which that heterogeneity is structured nationally. Such policies range from virtual disregard, as in France, to equality of educational status, as in Switzerland or Belgium, where that equality is expressed in unilingual territorial policies, or as in Yugoslavia where it is expressed in terms of individual choice of language of instruction. In this section the policies and programs of the three countries in which this study is most interested will be examined in greater deail, beginning with the Soviet Union.

POLITICAL CONFLICT AND LINGUISTIC POLICY

In the Soviet Union, though there may be shifts of emphasis, language policy does not develop or evolve—it expands, or contracts. And though it is customary nowadays to identify several stages in the formulation of this policy (Ablin), these correspond only to different relations between or temporary readjustments of the same elements.

The first phase, and the previous preparation for it before the beginning of the Revolution, is a reflection of the pluralist concept of Soviet culture; but during this period, which was favorable to the nationalities, doubt never existed that this was only one of two related forces. Among the resolutions of the Tenth Congress in 1921 (Resolutions, vol. I: 559), three stressed the recognition of the claims of the non-Russian peoples. However, these follow a resolution in which both the "national" and "centralist" elements in language policy are equally stressed, thus setting the interpretation to be given to the remainder:

    a. to develop and consolidate their *Soviet* statehood in forms appropriate to the conditions of national way of life of the various peoples.

    b. to develop and consolidate in the native language, justice, administration, and economic and governmental bodies composed of local peoples who know the way of life and psychology of the local population.

    c. to develop the press, theater, clubs, and educational establishments generally, in the native tongue.

    d. to establish and develop a wide network of courses and schools, general as well as professional and technical, in the native language.

As far back as the 1923 Congress, the two opposing points of view had been given equal opportunities for expression. The first, represented by Stalin and Ordzhonikidze advocated centralism; the second view was supported by the leaders from Georgia, the Ukraine and other areas, who pressed for a more federal approach. Lenin took no part in the discussions in 1923, but he let it be known that each republic should be granted extensive rights of its own. He spoke in private in favor of giving all the languages of the Soviet Union equal rights with Russian (*Kommunist*, September 1965: 26). The Ukrainian Mykola Skrypnic attacked the russification of the Ukrainians living in the RSFSR who had been denied their own newspaper and were not allowed to have their children taught in Ukrainian. The conclusion of the congress saw a resolution attacking Russian nationalism. Even so, within two years, attacks were made on the leaders of non-Russian minorities. In other words, even in this first phase when the general tendency was to favor a more liberal approach to nationalities and their languages, the conflict between the two tendencies was joined in theory and practice. Thus, Stalin at the same 1923 Congress, as witnessed his attack on "Great Russian Chauvinism," spoke of the need to "struggle on two fronts" in seeking to promote the Communist nationalities theory.

Within ten or fifteen years of the creation of the Soviet Union, and of the development of national schools in the Soviet educational system, good materials in national languages that had only recently acquired a script were being demanded. Complaints were made that a satisfactory range of books was not available, for instance in the languages of the Peoples of the North, such as Nenets. Several other very small nationalities were handled in the same way. The Peoples of the North were not alone in experiencing this development. As early as February 1921, under special decrees on the use of Russian and Kazakh in state institutions, the Kazakhstan authorities instituted universal bilingualism in the republic. In 1923, a central commission for the "indigenizing" of the state apparatus of Kazakhstan, and for the introduction of the Kazakh language for the conduct of business and education, was set up. In the Ukraine, too, the same steps were taken. As a result, "in view of the elimination of a government language and the decision to make all languages equal, the local population have the right to determine the languages used in schools, so long as the minority interests are safeguarded" (Weinstein, 1942: 129). The extent to which this latter proviso was respected is indicated by the fact that in 1927, 2.8 percent of those attending general education schools in the Ukraine were in separate Jewish schools, 1.4 percent in German, and 9 percent in Polish schools. Schools using one or other of the following languages were also established—Bulgarian, Czech, Hungarian, Tatar, Swedish, Greek, Assyrian, and Moldavian. In all, those attending such schools constituted about half the minority population of school age. If Russian was the medium of instruction for a school, the local population had the right to have a second language included in the curriculum.

The chairman of the supreme soviet of the republic of Azerbaydzhan, reflecting on the shifts in language policy implementation, commented that during the "first ten years of the Soviet regime there was respect for national languages at all times" (*Revolutsia i Natsionalnosti*, 1933). The *korenizatsiya* ("local-rooting"), whereby greater demands were made on and greater responsibilities given to local cadres in administration, affected the employment of teachers, in Armenia for instance. There, during 1925, the elementary school staff consisted of 80 percent Armenians and nearly all the secondary staffs were recruited locally (Matossian, 1962: 83). Even in 1938, 77 percent of all pupils were receiving instruction in Armenian language schools; 12 percent were in bilingual schools with Azerbaydzhan as the second language, and 2.8 percent were in Russian language classes (ibid., 190).

If the first phase of Soviet language policy favored pluralism, the next two decades—constituting the most important part of the second phase— saw a sharp change toward a centripetal movement and a diminution of the approval given to national and minority languages. It was a period of contraction. Late in 1927, the Central Committee of the Communist Party in the various republics drew attention to what they conceived as the danger of "petty bourgeois nationalism." In line with this shift of emphasis toward "centralism," large numbers of the creative intelligentsia who had encouraged the study of national languages were expelled from the party and many were "eliminated" *(Pravda,* 20 November 1961). The policy of *korenizatsiya* was abandoned. This affected the favorable attitude toward the local languages severely, especially in Turkestan, the Caucasus, Tartaria, the Ukraine, and Belorussia. However, this negative attitude was not absolute. In the case of Armenia, for instance, until as late as 1944 many concessions were allowed to Armenian national linguistic suscepti- bilities. In 1940, the new uniform orthography was modified in favor of Armenian traditional practice (Matossian, 1962: 164). The creeping shad- ow of the European war, and the growing fear of separatism, created suspicion of the loyalty of elements within some nationalities. Warnings were administered to Bashkirs and Tatars. Publications that had previously been promoted, advancing the claims of the national languages of Buryats and Kazakhs alike, were attacked; and rather than the praise that had previously been proffered to Georgian literature and language, it was now the custom to favor those who had in the past encouraged close relations with the Russian language.

During this period of centralist propaganda, it was customary first to stress the need to develop a Soviet patriotism, and then by an almost imperceptible switch to identify Soviet with Russian patriotism. Even prerevolutionary Russian influences on education were stressed. The work of the Orthodox missionaries which would normally have been the occasion for denigration, was praised. In view of these tendencies in propaganda, it is not surprising that the Russian language became more and more promi- nent in the national schools. For instance, before 1938 Russian was little favored in the non-Russian schools of Armenia. In 1937, there were only 470 teachers of Russian compared with 1,295 three years later in these same schools. In 1940, the Russian Pedagogical Institute was founded in Leninakan *(Kommunist* [Erevan], 3 July 1943). The promotion of Russian, of course, was statewide and not confined to isolated republics. In 1938, the Central Committee of the Party decreed the compulsory teaching of Russian, and also promoted the language by beginning the processes of successive changes of the national languages' scripts, first to Latin and then to the Cyrillic alphabet.

The second phase, especially after 1945, was a "lean" period for the national languages. One administrator who had reflected nostalgically on the first comparatively ten "fat" years, regretted that "for fifteen to twenty years the position of the languages had been endangered. They have not been used in schools or elsewhere and documents have been ignored because they have been written in the national language" (*Revolutsia i Natsionalnosti*, 1933). His concern was with Azerbaydzhan, but what had happened there was the case in other areas also. For instance, in Daghestan in 1928 a special commission had recommended the use of the indigenous languages of Daghestan for use in schools, and 12 such languages were recognized for this purpose—Russian, Kumyk, Azeri, Avar, Lak, Darghin, Lezghin, Tabasaran, Chechen, Tat, Adkvakh, and Nogai. Toward the end of the 1940s, the number had been almost halved (Bennigsen and Quelquejay, 1961: 23). In June 1950 the plenary session of the Union of Writers of Armenia condemned "nationalist isolation" in language and literature.

The third phase reveals a new readjustment of the language policy, a compensatory shift following the repressive, centralizing bias of Stalin. In 1962, conferences on nationalities policy affecting Central Asia were held in Tashkent and a month later in June at Dushanbe. In both conferences vigorous expression of opposing views concerning bilingualism occurred. These discussions were continued from 1963 to the end of 1969, beginning with a major conference in Frunze sponsored by the USSR Ministry of Higher Education and sections of the Academy of Sciences. This was followed by regional conferences in the Ukraine and Uzbekistan in 1964 and 1965. A followup conference was convened in Tiraspol, Moldavia and many of the participants of the conferences contributed to a great debate, which was extremely open, in journals like *Kommunist*, *Voprosy filosofii*, and *Voprosy istorii KPSS*.

Divergent views about language policy received their most thorough discussion in the arguments concerning Premier Nikita Khrushchev's proposal for the reform of education and for the rationalization of the place of the several languages in the curriculum. These discussions, whatever the actual consequences, were aimed to create or to establish a new equilibrium between centralist and pluralist dogmas. The discussions centered on Khrushchev's Thesis 19, concerning the position of languages in schools. This became the basis for part of the subsequent "Law on the Strengthening of the Relationship of the School and Life and on Further Development of the System in Education in the USSR" (*Pravda* 25 December 1958). Many educators had regularly complained that the school curriculum was not simply overloaded but also seriously unbalanced on account of the linguistic bias. This imbalance had a serious detrimental effects, particularly on the teaching of the sciences. Consequently, it was argued, the parents must be allowed to retain the right to select the language of instruction, as well as the language the child should learn as a class subject, wherever a choice was possible or necessary. Thesis 19 begins by restating that "instruction in the Soviet school is carried on in the native language." It then draws attention to the importance of Russian in the curriculum—"the powerful means of international communication, of strengthening friendship among the peoples of the USSR and bringing them into contact with the wealth of Russian and world culture" (ibid.). Having made these predictable points, Khrushchev took up the problem that some children in the "nationality schools study three languages—their national language, Russian, and one foreign language." These, so it is implied, are in addition to the language of instruction if it differs from Russian or the national language—as it might be, for instance, for Armenian children in Tbilisi, who would, if they chose to be educated in Armenian, be required to learn Georgian (the national language), Russian (the compulsory lingua franca), and a foreign language.

The thesis then proposed that the number of languages should be limited according to the parent's wishes. Khrushchev proposed that a parent should have the right to ask that a child should not be taught Russian if he attended a nationality school. If he attended a Russian-medium school, the child should have the option of omitting the native language. It is these proposals that were discussed at some length and with considerable acrimony at conferences and in the press in nearly all the republics and autonomous republics and in professional journals. During the Moscow conference to finalize the discussion, some proposed that "in schools of the Union and Autonomous Republics, the study of Russian and the native language should be obligatory on all pupils" (*Izvestiya* 24 December 1958). This certainly reflected the mood of Armenian educators. Similarly, voices were raised in the Azerbaydzhan press in support of the national language, often in preference to Russian. However, the dominant mood was expressed by Simonyan, Director of the School Administration of the Armenian Soviet Republic, who argued that Russian should remain a compulsory language for all, while the study of Armenian was made compulsory for all Armenians, irrespective of whether they attended Russian or other language medium schools (*Pravda* 12 December 1958). Almost identical views were expressed in Azerbaydzhan SR, where a proposal was made to delay the introduction of Russian until the fifth grade, so as to safeguard the national language. In the Baltic Republics, too, the debate revealed considerable support for the national languages. The Prime Minister of the Latvian Republic insisted that whatever the importance of Russian, the native language was necessary to everyone in the republic. He asserted that any change unfavorable to Latvian in the schools would be detrimental to the friendship of the Latvian and the Russian people.

Khrushchev's strategy was an attempt to balance opposing groups and moderate the persistent hardcore centralist dogmatists. Consequently, tendencies towards pluralism were supported by legal enactments. With Khruschev's removal in 1964 there was a reversal of policy, and in the current fourth phase the centralist point of view is reinforced. Some ritual acknowledgement is made of the existence of the pluralist point of view, and "the diversity of today's Soviet reality" is mentioned. But the problems created by such diversities, it is claimed, have been solved and have been "irrevocably consigned to the past" (Brezhnev; *Pravda* 11 April 1971). Henceforth the aim is to ensure a general uniformity. The centralist bias of the present period is well exemplified by the publication of an article, written by a Daghestan teacher in 1970 (Garunov). The writer seeks to make two points: first, that the linguistic situation of the villages and schools of Daghestan is complex and therefore difficult to administer satisfactorily. For instance, in one class alone in a small school more than six nationalities and languages are represented. Consequently "schools with a multinational intake of students and using Russian as the language of instruction, have become widespread in our multinational and socialist country, and this is a progressive phenomenon," compared with the provision of separate "national schools" (ibid., 14). The second contention is that the only acceptable policy, since it conforms with Lenin's views, is the denial of separate schools for language minorities. This intention the writer fulfills by selecting for quotation only those pronouncements of Lenin which favor such a policy, though in point of fact a review of Lenin's "nationalities theory" would show considerable ambivalence, and at best a support for the *dva potoka* "two paths." Garunov quotes Lenin to the effect that "we must strive for a merging of children of all nationalities into one school in a given area. We must decisively oppose any movement whatsoever to divide the school in terms of nationalities" (ibid., 7). Such separation along national divisions in education will only exacerbate latent community conflicts. The article refers to the supporting resolution of the Central Committee in 1913, to the effect that "separation of schools by nationality within any one country is unquestionably harmful from the point of view of democracy in general and the interests of the class struggle of the proletariat in particular" (ibid., 11).

SOVIET PROGRAMS OF BILINGUAL EDUCATION

The overall language policy of the Soviet Union has produced five types of schools; and the changes of policy have been reflected not in the abandonment of any one kind of school or the creation of an additional kind, but simply lesser or greater relative support for particular types. The most strongly supported by officials are the Russian-medium schools. These are of three kinds—the first cater to speakers of Russian within the Russian Republic where the Russian language, irrespective of its Soviet-wide status, would be the native language of the republic, just as Georgian

is of the Georgian Republic. The second kind of Russian-medium schools
are those in the Russian Republic which are attended by members of
non-Russian ethnic groups. Most of these non-Russians are minorities
native to the Russian Republic, for example, Chuvash, Bashkir, Yakut,
Evenki and many others. The third kind of Russian-medium schools in the
Russian Republic are those attended by non-national or immigrant minorities, for instance Armenians. They are rare, since groups of immigrants are very seldom large enough in a particular locality to establish a
school in which the minority language may be used. Also, immigrants
tend to approve of the choice of Russian. The fourth type of Russian-
medium school is that which is provided for Russian immigrants in other
Soviet Republics, which non-Russians also tend to select for their children.

Russian is the only Soviet language taught, after the second grade, to all
children in the Soviet Union as a first or second language; it is the only
language used in all Soviet republics as a medium of instruction in some
schools. In both the Russian Republic and in other Soviet republics,
Russian is being used increasingly as the teaching language. Within the
Russian Republic, between 75 percent and 90 percent of the pupils belonging to non-Russian nationality groups, like the Bashkir, attend Russian-medium schools (Lewis, E. G., 1972: 196). Outside the Russian Republic,
while the Russian-medium school attracts the Russian-speaking migrant
minorities in a republic, in some instances a higher proporiton of non-
Russians attend such schools. As many as three times as many children
attend such schools as might be justified by the number of native speakers
of Russian in the school locality, as is the case in Belorussia; in Georgia
and Azerbaydzhan the ratio is 2 to 1. The ratio is lowest in the Baltic
countries (ibid., 1972: 198).

To some extent the pattern of schools in the other republics is like that
of the Russian Republic. There are schools where the medium of instruction
is the language of the republic, for instance Georgian, and these schools
attract not only native speakers of Georgian but speakers of other minority
languages, for instance Armenian students in the Georgian capital Tbilisi.
In addition to the Russian-medium schools to which the Russian minority
in a non-Russian republic may be attracted, there are schools where other
minority languages are used as the media of instruction. All union as well
as autonomous republics employ the native language in some schools,
but not necessarily in all grades since schools which use the native language
in elementary grades frequently transfer to Russian at some stage, especially in secondary grades. All union republics also employ, in some
schools, a language other than its own. The Russian Republic has schools
where in addition to, or instead of, Russian any one of thirty-eight other
languages may be the teaching language. The Uzbek SSR employs seven
languages, the Kazakh, Georgian, and Tadzhik republics six each. In

Belorussia, Latvia, and Estonia, only two languages are used, the native language of the republic or Russian (Lewis, E. G., 1972: 184). There is no question but that such minority language schools are in decline. One Soviet educator has claimed: "During the period of developing Socialist construction, in the 1938–39 school session, Uzbekistan provided schools where instruction was conducted in twenty-two languages. The provision even made it possible for a Polish family to have its child taught in the mother tongue. The policy has recently led to parents choosing to send their children not to the minority school but to Russian medium-schools. There are in Uzbekistan now schools for minorities in only seven languages, and these are the neighboring Central Asian languages, in addition to Russian. At the same time, 50 percent of the Russian-medium schools consist of Ukrainian, Belorussian, Jewish, Armenian, Mordvin, Kazakh, and other minorities" (*Voprosy razvitiya*, 340).

Finally there are the so-called bilingual schools, those where two or more languages are employed in teaching two or more different ethnic groups. Some schools in Daghestan have representatives of as many as twenty-five nationalities. The city of Kzylorda in Kazakhstan in one school has representatives of thirty ethnic groups. While it would be unrealistic to expect that all, or even a few, of these in any one school could be used as teaching languages (and in fact the tendency is to use only Russian), the existence of a multiethnic enrollment has led to the establishment of some schools where more than one language is used. They were most popular during the first, liberal phase of language policy since they conformed to Lenin's desire to have all ethnic groups educated together. In 1927, 7 percent of the Ukrainian elementary schools used more than one language. In Kharkov, nearly 49 percent of the children were in such schools. (*Statistiki Ukranyi*, 1928: 20–1). Their popularity remained in some areas even during the second phase: in Azerbaydzhan the number of bilingual schools increased from 158 in 1940 to 340 at present (Lewis, 1972: 194). In Uzbekistan the percentage of schools rose from 10 percent in 1960 to 20 percent at present—well over a thousand schools. Comparable increases have occurred in Kirghizia. The rationale for the establishment of such schools is complex. In the first place, it is sometimes stated quite openly that though the child attending such schools may not actually be taught in Russian, yet since Russian tends to be the language of play, he acquires a ready facility in it. It is in any case recognized that in such schools the "common language of the pupils in all extra-class activities is Russian, which is the language of school administration" (*Norodnoye obrazovaniye*, 1965: 3, 9). On the other hand, more liberal motives are sometimes acknowledged. Secondary School No. 55 in Riga was reported in 1966 as having provided parallel Latvian and Russian classes for over six years, with the result that more than 1,000 Latvian and Russian children learned to live as one family. Both languages were used in all out of school activities. There are now over 240 such schools in Latvia, enrolling more than a third of the total school population. The intention is that any new schools that are established should follow this pattern. The director of School 55 claims that the experience of the joint instruction of Latvian and Russian children in such schools fosters mutual respect among the two linguistic groups (*Pravda* 5 April 1966).

Whatever the language of instruction, the native language of the union or autonomous republic, or the immigrant group language, and whatever kind of school organization is adopted—separate ethnic or bilingual (multilingual)—and whether the teaching language is changed or not at any grade, the choice of school and of language is in principle *personal*. "Pupils are given the opportunity to receive instruction in their native language. Their parents or guardians have the right to select for their children a school of their choice with the appropriate language of instruction. In addition to the language in which instruction is conducted, the pupils may choose to study the language of another people of the USSR" (*Uchitelskaya Gazeta*, 15 September 1970). This statement omits to refer to the fact that Russian is an obligatory *subject*, in addition to any other language, from grade two onwards.

Wales–Development of Policy

As in the Soviet Union and the United States, bilingual education in Wales was first inaugurated in schools conducted by churches. The most important of the religious leaders to promote such an education was Griffith Jones, an incumbent of the Church of England in Wales. His interest was the salvation of souls and the question which motivated his interest was, "Shall we be more concerned for the propagation of the English language than the salvation of souls?" And he supplies his own answer, "How much better is it that the Welsh people should be forever ignorant of the English language . . . than that they should live and die ignorant of what is necessary to their salvation, and which they cannot be instructed in (as they understand no other language) but in Welsh only" (Welch Piety, 1741 and 1744). Accordingly, he and his associates set up "circulating schools" where children and their parents were taught to read Welsh; the moral motivation of bilingual education, however, was not unequivocal. In 1847 the Commission of Enquiry into the State of Education in Wales (1847; Vol. II, 66) stated that "the Welsh language is a vast drawback to Wales, and a manifold barrier to moral progress." The vehemency of the criticism of Welsh aroused a correspondingly vehement repudiation which, contrary to the wishes of the government, created a very powerful support for the teaching and use of Welsh.

Such support was channeled by organizations such as Cambrian Ar-

cheological Association (1846), the Cambrian Institute (1844), the Cymmrodorion Society, and especially the Society for the Utilisation of the
Welsh Language. But, however great the support of these organizations,
the chief responsibility for the development of a bilingual education policy
lay with the Ministry of Education (earlier known as the Committee of the
Privy Council, which became the Board of Education for England and
Wales). Responsibility for ensuring that this policy was implemented lay
with Her Majesty's Inspectors of Schools appointed by the "Queen in
Council." In 1849 the Secretary of Education, Sir James Kay-Shuttleworth,
stated that the Privy Council "had directed their attention to the arrangements which would be required to carry into execution in Wales their
recent Minutes (covering the possible use of Welsh) and I am to assure
you that they are ready to appoint natives of the Principality having a
knowledge of Welsh language as Inspectors of Schools" (Kay-Shuttleworth,
Sir J., 1873).

Such inspectors fulfilled two functions: they examined the pupils annually
and they advised the Privy Council (later the Board or Ministry of Education). Their examination of the schools was conducted according to the
Codes and Regulations which directed what should be taught, and who
should be paid to teach. The first we hear of the introduction of any form
of bilingual education in Britain's state schools occurs in the Privy Council
Minutes of 1846–7: "A paper in Welsh and a paper in Gaelic are presented
to such teachers as desire to work them with a view of service in Welsh or
Highland Schools. Every teacher who passes a thoroughly good examination in one of these languages will be specially registered, and as often as
Her Majesty's Inspector certifies of any particular school that it is one in
which a knowledge of Welsh or Gaelic is needful in the teacher" extra
financial assistance would be available to the school. Although this provision
was omitted from the Codes and Regulations of 1860 (Board of Education
for Public Elementary Schools, Codes and Regulations), the hiatus in the
development of bilingual education was only temporary, and the Minutes
of 1846–7 (Committee on Education of the Privy Council) may be regarded
as the charter of bilingual education in Britain.

Since then the policy has developed and has provided for an increasingly
comprehensive program. In 1875 the code was revised and Article 19C(3)
stated: "In districts where Welsh is spoken, the intelligence of the children
may be tested by requiring them to explain in Welsh the meaning of
passages read." And this provision acquires a more or less permanent
status. Paragraph II of Circular 212 (Board of Education, 1882) issued to
Her Majesty's Inspectors, forming part of the Instructions for 1882, reads:
"In all cases where a dictation exercise is given the teacher may be
permitted, if he desires, to read the passage over to the children before it
is dictated by the Inspector. In Welsh-speaking districts the teacher may
be allowed to give out the whole of the dictation." In 1890, a definite

advance may be noted for in the footnote to Schedules I and II, in addition to what was included from 1875 onwards, we read: "and bilingual books may be used for the purpose of instructing the scholars." With this the Welsh language is introduced as a subject to be taught in the schools.

It took some time for further recommendations of inspectors to be accepted, and it is not until 1891 that the codes reflect the changing attitude. In that year Welsh was introduced into the curriculum as an "optional subject taken by individual children in the upper classes." This is what was meant by "specific subjects" as the footnote to Schedule IV—"Table of Specific Subjects of Secular Instruction"—makes clear: "Welsh may be taken as a specific subject provided that a graduated scheme for teaching it is submitted to and approved by the Inspector" (Committee on Education of Privy Council, 1891). In 1892 such a graduated scheme is included. It provides for three stages at each of which there are three types of work—formal grammar according to the most rigid classical tradition; translation from English to Welsh and from Welsh to English; and a piece of dictation from a prepared book in Welsh. In addition, the learning of verse was introduced at the second stage, and at the third stage "a short theme or letter in Welsh on a familiar subject."

In 1893 the cause of the vernacular was advanced still further: Welsh, in addition to remaining a possible specific subject, is placed in the group of "class subjects," optional subjects taken not by individuals at the top, but by whole classes throughout the school. As a result, in Schedule II of Class Subjects we have, as an alternative to English, "English taught bilingually." In Standards V, VI and VII, analysis and parsing of Welsh are expected. At this time, too, a grant was allowed for older scholars for the memorizing of poetry which might "if the Managers so desire, be taken from Modern Welsh poetry." Moreover, in order to qualify for the grant for singing, "in Welsh districts among the school songs taught during the year popular Welsh airs sung to Welsh words" might be included. There were three additional concessions. In the first place, in a footnote to Schedule I (Elementary or Compulsory Subjects) it was stated that "the instruction generally may be bilingual," and the implications of this are made clear. For composition in English might be substituted translation into English, the problems in arithmetic should be in both English and Welsh. In reading and repetition, the pupils were required to read fluently Welsh and English and were allowed to choose English or Welsh verse for repetition. In grammar and composition, it required "in Welsh districts parsing and analysis of simple sentences, with knowledge of the ordinary terminations of Welsh words. Writing in Welsh the substance of a story read once." Finally, in the revised instruction to Her Majesty's Inspectors (H.M.I.s) for the same year, 1893, emphasis was laid on the need to encourage a bilingual education. "It is desirable that the attention of teachers should be called to this question, and that H.M.I.s should encourage the practice of bilingual teaching by themselves making use of Welsh in testing children's intelligence."

That is as far as the English Codes take us until the separate formulation of the Welsh Codes; and it is clear that in the circumstances of those times, and with the theories of language teaching then prevailing, they had gone a remarkable way. This was reflected to some extent in the reaction of those directly responsible for the schools locally. In 1898 Monmouthsire passed a resolution in favor of introducing Welsh into every school, and actually began to do so. A year before that the Rhondda School Board appointed a specialist teacher of Welsh for its pupil teachers. In 1897 the Cardiff School Board asked the parents of their school children whether they wished to have their children taught Welsh. Of the thirty schools concerned, only two returned a majority against its introduction. Of the parents of the 13,492 children on registers, 8,124 asked for Welsh, and 1,866 opposed it.

In 1907, with the setting up of a separate Welsh Department of the Board of Education, with its own Permanent Secretary and Chief Inspector, the Board of Education attempted by every means to promote bilingual education. The first separate Code for Wales (1907) states: "The Board of Education wish that every Welsh teacher should realize the educational value of the Welsh language, and of its literature, which from its wealth of romance and lyric is peculiarly adapted to the education of the young" (Public Elementary Schools, Codes and Regulations). At the same time, in its Regulations for Secondary Schools in Wales, made almost simultaneously, we read: "In districts where Welsh is spoken, the language or one of the languages other than English should be Welsh. Any of the subjects in the curriculum may, where the local needs make it desirable, be taught in Welsh" (Board of Education, Regulations for Secondary Schools). So far as policy is concerned, all the necessary foundations of a comprehensive bilingual education were laid by 1907. What has happened since is the refinement of policy, its acceptance by increasing numbers, and its implementation by a flexible school system.

WELSH PROGRAMS OF BILINGUAL EDUCATION

The extent to which the local provision of education is bilingual, and the nature of the bilingual education, depend upon the linguistic character of the area. In every part of Wales, both English and Welsh are spoken by different proportions of the population. Furthermore, it would not be an exaggeration to say that even in the more thoroughly Welsh-speaking areas the command of English, after the age of 7, is high. For historical and demographic reasons, therefore, English is the customary language in Welsh schools, though in schools which are thoroughly Welsh in their background, the unmarked language is Welsh. Because of the diffuseness of Welsh throughout Wales (even the most thoroughly anglicized areas), and because the parents have the right to determine the language of instruction—a determination that is expressed not idiosyncratically but through their local representatives (local education committees, school managers, and boards of governors)—the programs range from almost zero recognition of Welsh to the teaching and the use of Welsh in all classes and to all students. The gradation of the provision of bilingual education in Wales conforms to one of ten options presented in Appendix 2.

All programs provide a strong bicultural component including Welsh and English history, nationally characteristic arts—music and dance—and so on. There is a wide variation between authorities in the allocation of time to the teaching of Welsh as a first or second language, ranging from 100 to 300 minutes a week. There are also considerable differences in the ages at which Welsh is introduced formally. Among primary age children sampled in the National Foundation for Educational Research and Welsh Joint Education Committee (NFER/WJEC) Survey (1969: 120) of the fifty-five schools in the Welsh-speaking areas that responded to a questionnnaire, all taught Welsh from the age of entry. In the English-speaking areas, Welsh was introduced under the age of five in 10 percent of the 100 schools sampled, in 18 percent under the age of six years, and in 22 percent under the age of seven. In approximately 71 percent of the English-speaking schools, Welsh was introduced at or slightly over seven years of age. Some of these schools introduced Welsh as second language as late as nine and ten years of age. Where English is concerned, considerable differences existed. In the English-speaking areas, English is taught from the beginning, but this is also the case in a less formal fashion in the Welsh-speaking areas, too. When it comes to the formal introduction of the language, however, the tendency is to introduce English as a second language later than Welsh as a second language: only 10 percent (as against 18 percent for Welsh) introduce English as a second language below the age of six years. The difference is accounted for by the belief that Welsh requires an earlier introduction in order to compensate for a weak societal support for the language in the English-speaking areas.

Secondary School Programs

Generally speaking, the same range of variety of bilingual programs for primary schools is offered at the secondary level. But there are some constraints on the organization of such programs that do not affect primary schools. In the first place, secondary schools after a certain stage, usually at ages thirteen to fourteen, offer students a choice of alternative subjects. In such cases, Welsh as a subject may be rejected in favor of an additional science, or art, or sometimes another language such as Latin. However, some schools do not regard Welsh as an option and continue to teach it to the end of the compulsory school age. The second constraint is the highly specialized orientation of the curriculum toward the end of the secondary stage as well as the highly selective intake of universities which depend on the Secondary School Advanced Level Certificate (seldom more than 4 subjects) as qualifying for entry. The advanced level stage (age 17–19) is of roughly first year university level and the specialist textbooks are usually in English. For these reasons, while the teaching of Welsh (both as first and second language) does not decline markedly, it tends to be replaced as a teaching language by English. The NFER/WJEC Survey (1969) reported that 30 percent of the Welsh-speaking schools taught Welsh for the whole period of schooling, 60 percent taught Welsh for five years and 10 percent for three years. Where Welsh was taught as a second language, 42 percent of the schools gave instruction for five years, 42 percent for four years, and 16 percent for three years. The amount of time available for Welsh in the secondary schools of the Welsh-speaking areas is comparable to that devoted to English. In the English-speaking areas, Welsh is taught on an average of three days a week during forty minute classes.

Table 7.7 indicates the amount of time during which different schools use Welsh or English as teaching languages.

Table 7.7 shows the results of an enquiry among a small sample of schools throughout Wales. Even in the least anglicized areas, 55 percent of the schools use the Welsh language for only 50 percent of the time. In the most anglicized areas, the use of Welsh in the schools included in this sample is negligible, 4 percent using Welsh for between one to twenty-five percent of the instructional time.

Higher Education

The seven constituent colleges of the federated University of Wales have a total of something over 15,000 students drawn from many countries, but mainly from England and Wales. Ability to understand Welsh is not necessary for entry, and the proportion of students who are able to speak Welsh is approximately 25 percent and declining as the university grows. However, the influence of the native speakers of Welsh among the university population is far greater than their numerical status would allow us to expect. Some of the colleges have residential hostels which are reserved for Welsh-speaking undergraduates. Some departments of the university—for instance Philosophy, History, Theology, Politics and Sociology, but in particular Education—teach some of the courses in Welsh and they have appointed members of the respective faculties with this purpose in mind.

The same considerations affect the colleges of education (the former normal colleges) established exclusively to prepare teachers for primary and lower grades of secondary schools. From 1956 onward, the use of

TABLE 7.7. Proportion of Time in Which Welsh is Used as Teaching Language

Type of Area	% and No. of Schools in Sample		Percentage of Schools with Indicated Proportion of Time for Welsh-Medium			
	No.	%	1%-25%	26%-50%	51%-75%	76%-100%
Least anglicized	57	46	25	30	28	8
Moderately anglicized	41	33	20	15	15	21
Most anglicized	26	21	4	—	—	—

Source: Schools Council, 1974: 219.

Welsh as a teaching language was firmly established in all colleges, but especially in two of the nine. In one of these, a student must follow the whole course exclusively in English or Welsh; in the other, he may follow only part of the course in Welsh or the whole course in English. In both colleges, a student who elects to follow a Welsh language course is required to follow a modified English course. Where students do not choose to pursue their general course either partly or wholly in Welsh, they are offered the opportunity to prepare for an endorsement of their Teacher's Certificate—a bilingual endorsement. This entails a concurrent three year course in the theory and practice of bilingualism in education, and it certifies that the holder of the endorsement is able to teach Welsh as a first and second language and English as a second language. It is assumed that he is able to teach English as a first language. Approximately 80 percent of the Welsh-speaking women students and 60 percent of the men pursue the course each year. Finally, whether they elect to study in Welsh or not, and whether they wish to obtain the bilingual endorsement or not, all students are required to follow a general course in the education of bilingual children with special reference to Wales.

The system of bilingual education in Wales is well established, with over a century of development: it is comprehensive in that it extends over the whole country and includes monoglot or dominantly English as well as Welsh-speaking pupils; it is supported by parents and it is based on parental choice. Unlike the system of bilingual education in the Soviet Union, its progress has been uninterrupted. In all probability this is because its development is governed by educational, developmental, or pedagogic considerations rather than by political goals as in the Soviet Union.

The United States

HISTORICAL DEVELOPMENT

A foreign student of bilingual education is bound to be struck by some paradoxical or contradictory positions as it is conceived, discussed, and administered in the United States. On the one hand, it has been argued that American bilingual education is no more than "sophisticated linguistic counter insurgency, a devious means of ensuring assimilation" (Kjolseth, 1972: 109). At the other extreme, it has been championed as the "noblest innovation" in American education (Gaarder, 1970: 1973). The first contention does not do justice to the flexibility and range of program provision or the options available, while the enthusiasm of the second is not justified because of a lapse in historical understanding. The history of bilingual education in the United States is as long as that of any system of bilingual education elsewhere in the world. It may not have lived up to its early promise and may only now be recovering its momentum, but it ceased to be an innovation with the arrival of the colonists, or the missionaries. During the nineteenth century, an estimated one million children attended bilingual public schools and many more profited at a much earlier date from a variety of "private" provisions. If, as we are entitled to do, we interpret bilingual education with only a moderate degree of liberalism, its past history in the United States is nothing to cavil at.

As early as 1568 the Jesuits organized in Havana a school for Indian children from Florida, and although many would not regard it as a "true" or "real" bilingual school it certainly catered to children who needed to speak two languages in and outside school. The point has been made time and time again that the "learning of at least some English by those for whom it was not the first language must have occurred in North America when early in the seventeenth century the colonists in Virginia and Maryland needed to communicate with American Indians. . . . The formal teaching of English . . . occurred very early, probably as an activity of missionaries" (Allen, 1973: 294). Subsequently, treaties between the government and the Indians provided for the establishment of schools in which the speakers of Native American languages were also taught English. Prior to the nineteenth century, the schools which took account, formally, of the minority languages by teaching and using them in the curriculum tended to be private, usually parochial schools. For example, German was being taught near Philadelphia in 1694. By 1775 there were 40 Lutheran and 78 Reformed schools, and in 1800 a combined total of 254 schools. Other German religious denominations, like the Mennonites, made a contribution also (Kloss, 1974: 216). Throughout the eighteenth century, school instruction in Pennsylvania, Maryland, Virginia, and the Carolinas was in German (Leibowitz, 1971: 6). Wisconsin in the nineteenth century spent a considerable part of its education budget on German textbooks and some districts of the state hired only German-speaking teachers. In 1839 Ohio decreed that German students attending schools that had no provision for German "and who desired to learn in the German language may attend a district German school" (Kloss, 1966a: 233). Other immigrant nationalities like the French, the Scandinavians, and the Dutch had similar schools where the mother tongue was used as a teaching language and English as a second language. The last quarter of the nineteenth century saw a considerable increase in French and Scandinavian schools as well as new schools for Lithuanians, Poles, and Slovaks. By the beginning of the twentieth century, over 120 parochial schools were conducted in French (LeMaire, 1966: 258).

The progress of bilingual schools—of which those we have referred to are only a small sample—was not uninterrupted: as a result of the intense and accelerated immigration at the end of the last century, involving poor, illiterate Catholics from Southern Europe, a spate of legislation was passed to ensure an "English only" educational policy. The thirty years from 1890 onward have been referred to as "the heyday of xenophobic legislation," and the U.S. Supreme Court in 1967 referred to the era as the "period of extreme nativism." Over thirty states made English the exclusive teaching language in public and private schools, and in seven of those states certification of teachers who used a language other than English in class could be revoked. (Zirkel, 409). The prejudice engendered by World War I made the continuance of bilingual education in both private and public schools virtually impossible, and up to 1957 public schools showed little interest in reviving the early interest. Even when it did revive there was no question of formulating a national policy, and so far as a national consensus existed it was in favor of an English-only system of education. Where specific provision was made for some form of bilingual schooling, it was again the private schools that took the initiative. Nevertheless, some public schools in areas of very heavy minority concentration at first displayed a strong commitment, which gradually became less pronounced. As in the Soviet Union, the development of bilingual education in the United States was initiated and supported by religious organizations. This was partly because all education was almost entirely within their range of interest and partly because they were closer in sympathy to minorities than were the public generally. As in the Soviet Union, too, interest in the United States oscillated: early enthusiasm among those who were in any way concerned gave way to reluctance and antipathy in the late nineteenth and first part of the twentieth century but more recently there is a new expression of the early encouraging phase. There are no signs as yet that the fourth and present reactionary phase of the Soviet Union will be replicated in the United States, though the possibility cannot be ignored in view of some Americans' reactions to developments in Quebec.

THE MEANING OF BILINGUAL EDUCATION

Within the United States, two contrasting approaches to an understanding of the meaning of bilingual education may be observed. The first is concerned with institutional aspects—what kind of school may rightly be regarded as bilingual. The second approach is concerned with individual or developmental aspects—what kind of program for a particular child, looked at over a period of four or five years or more constitutes a satisfactory bilingual education. Typical of the institutional or school based approach is the definition offered in the Draft Guidelines to the Bilingual Education Programs (ESEA: P.L. 90–247, 1968 in *Current Legislation on Bilingual Education*, 1975): "Bilingual education is instruction in two languages and the use of those two languages as mediums of instruction for any or all of the school curriculum. Such of the history and culture associated with the mother tongue is considered an integral part of the program." The 1974 Amendments included the following stipulation: "There is instruction given in both the native language . . . and in English in all courses or subjects of study." According to this definition a child who, at whatever age, is not taught all the statutorily required subjects in both languages would not be receiving a bilingual education, even though he might be taught both languages and though in the very early stages he might not have sufficient command of one of the languages to be able to profit from instruction by means of it. The school itself as a complete system may quite rightly be expected to use both languages, but to insist that bilingual education requires that every child at every stage should be taught in both languages is unsound.

The developmental approach to an understanding of the meaning of bilingual education, while setting as its goal the emergence of as satisfactory a bilingual program as possible, concedes the necessity for flexibility and disavows restrictive guidelines or limiting constraints on how the program is to be organized over the time available (four or more or fewer years as the case may be). Typical of such an approach is the statement of the Education Amendments of 1974 (ESEA: P.L. 93–380, 1974 in *Current Legislation on Bilingual Education*, 1975): "The term program of bilingual education means a program of instruction designed for children of limited English-speaking ability in elementary or secondary schools with respect to the years of study to which such a program is applicable, there is instruction given in and a study of English and to the extent necessary to allow a child to progress effectively through the education system the native language of the children of limited English-speaking ability . . . with appreciation for the cultural heritage." The criticism that may be justifiably leveled at this approach is that it conceives of the use of the native language as limited to the early stages of education, but at least it avoids the other error of inflexibility. The institutional approach to the interpretation of bilingual education is normative and prescriptive. It confuses the definition or interpretation of a bilingual school with what is required to make individuals bilingual to some degree or other. It confuses system and process.

Such normative statements are confused with statements of fact—what a bilingual education actually is. A large range of possibilities characterizes programs throughout the country, but a consideration of programs is distinct from a discussion of statements of policy about what bilingual education should be, a *selection* of this or that kind of program. The confusion of statements of policy with statements of fact leads to some disadvantages. Unless bilingual education policies in other countries coincide with that of the United States, it is difficult to compare the United States with them—like is not being compared with like and a possible extension of relevant experience is foreclosed. Furthermore, the development of innovative bilingual education programs in the United States is inhibited if what is a statement of policy (which is only one of very many possible policies) is assumed to be a definition of *true* or *real* bilingual education. There are as many bilingual education programs as there are situations which demand their introduction. The nature of the program will change according to changes in the situation, and toward these changes the bilingual program itself contributes. Bilingual education is determined by specific need, and the need changes as the program succeeds in meeting it. Looked at from the standpoint of the individual, there cannot be anything but the most minimal of definitions of bilingual education. Beyond the bare minimum, which is formal exposure to two languages, any number of programs may rightly be included within a definition, though whether in particular circumstances they are appropriate and whether they reflect policy are two other matters.

Being normative, the so-called definitions of bilingual education in the United States are the expressions of aspirations (limited or radical and comprehensive) and set out the goals proposed.

UNITED STATES POLICIES

Policy is decided and determined by those who, reluctantly or willingly, are prepared to pay for it. Central government policy is exerted through the Department of the Interior for Native Americans, the Department of Health, Education, and Welfare (HEW) for programs depending upon appropriations under various titles of the Elementary and Secondary Education Act (ESEA), or the influence of other organizations such as the Commission on Civil Rights. These agencies, though they directly affect only a relatively small area of the bilingual programs, ensure that the central government rather than individual states is the principal voice in policy.

This policy of the central government has four formal and three substantive characteristics. In the first place, it is limited almost entirely to minorities—though some very hesitant concessions are made to the possibility of enabling English-speaking children to become bilingual. Rhode Island empowers school districts "in the fullest extent possible to enroll a substantial number of English-speaking children in the bilingual programs provided that priority be given to children of limited English-speaking ability" (Rhode Island P.L., Chapter 54 Section 16. –54–5b; quoted in Lawyers' Committee on Civil Rights). Saravia Shore found that in 7 percent of the bilingual schools she investigated, it was obligatory for non-English mother-tongue students to take the bilingual program; in 20 percent both English and non-English students were required to take the program; and in the remaining 73 percent participation for non-English and English students was voluntary (Shore, Table 5.6). The restrictiveness of the general policy is only one disadvantage, besides which the full advantages of bilingualism are not exploited nationally. Additionally a considerable weight of unnecessary evaluation and testing, with its highly sophisticated machinery, is imposed upon a system that is hardly able to bear it. The language dominance and the level of language attainment of bilinguals have to be measured continually. No other system of bilingual education requires such measures to be taken because they are usually available to speakers who are dominant in either language. Only in the United States is the use of a particular language as the principal medium of instruction according to objectively ascertained level of ability in either language mandated by statute.

Second, the provision even in respect of minorities is for those of "limited English-speaking ability." Consequently, the ablest among minority children may often be deprived of a program from which, because of their ability, they may be best able to gain. Third, the provision is generally regarded as experimental, usually limited in time to no more than three or four years unless the school district decides to continue it. Whether a school renews the program or not, its experimental origins continue to be reflected in the tentativeness of the approach as well as in the number of different models even within a limited area, for instance New York City. Experiment takes precedence over commitment. For instance, the state of New Hampshire declares that bilingual education may be permitted as "experimental education programs" (Lawyers' Committee, 87). Indeed, some programs are set up not to offer a substantive teaching program but to diagnose or identify need. This is the case in Azusa Unified School District where the California Board of Education is sponsoring a project for children in kindergarten through fourth grade with the object of identifying the child's dominant language and assessing his educational needs.

Fourth, participation in bilingual programs is voluntary, even for those who are in greatest need of such an education. Students, as in the case of the Aspira of New York Consent Decree, may be withdrawn from programs by the parents. The influential Community Services Society of New York emphasize in their policy recommendations both the limited duration as well as the voluntary nature of the provision: "Where the child has mastered English . . . he should be transferred to classes instructed in English. . . . Participation in bilingual programs should be voluntary and require written permission of the parent" (City of New York, 1974: viii). In the light of the restricted entry into the program, the limited period for which it is available, and its experimental and voluntary nature, it will be seen that bilingual education is not envisaged as an integral part of the system. Indeed, it is peripheral and irrelevant from the standpoint of the great majority of the population, including large segments of minority groups.

The characteristics we have described are formal; they determine who receives bilingual education, for how long, and under what circumstances.

There are four other characteristics that have to do with its substance, which in turn is determined by the goals that are set as part of policy. In the first place, it is a *preventive* program. This is the more positive aspect of what is usually regarded as remedial education. If minority children are at a disadvantage because of a disregard of their bilingual or minority status, then one aim of the program should be to prevent such disadvantages from appearing. This is no different in principle from a program of literacy; for instance, if being illiterate is regarded as a disadvantage, one of the aims of education should be to promote literacy. It would be an advantage if those who are concerned with the theory and practice of bilingual education stressed this converse of the remedial rationale.

The remedial function, in present circumstances, is not an unworthy characteristic. The first purpose of a bilingual program must be to counter or neutralize the effects of inequality or deprivation in education where those inequalities and deprivations have not been forestalled by an adequate preventive program. If disregard of his native language places a minority student at a disadvantage, the use of the native language should be obligatory. If the obligation is not met from the beginning of their schooling, then some form of compensation and some remedies to counteract the initial deprivation are necessary. A system of education has to secure or repair the foundations before it can hope to ensure a satisfactory superstructure. This policy is inadequate only when it is envisaged as the total requirement, and unfortunately this appears to be the case in several states. For instance, it is state policy in Texas (Lawyers' Committee, 112–117) "that a compensatory program of bilingual education can meet the needs of these children and facilitate their integration into the regular schools curriculum." In the state of Utah the compensatory provision was interpreted not in educational terms but as having to do with economic difficulty or moral deviance, so that bilingual education was associated with "low income families . . . as well as foster children, neglected, and delinquent children" (Lawyers' Committee, 118). Remedies are required because of initial errors. The purpose of educational policy is to eliminate the possibility of error as far as possible, otherwise to remedy the defects which have not been prevented.

Another consequence of the pursuit of an exclusively compensatory program has been the tendency to regard the teaching of English as a Second Language (ESL) not simply as one of the components of a bilingual education but rather as its principal if not its only aim. In a heterogeneous society, especially one so complex as the United States, it is inevitable— particularly in the earliest phase of social consolidation—that an overriding concern should be the need to be able to use the lingua franca. This has occurred in all linguistically complex societies moving towards modernization. It was brought out most clearly within the context of education by the study of Puerto Ricans in New York in 1958 (City of New York,

Board of Education, 1958). The weakness of the ESL program, from the standpoint of policy, arises when it is made to appear as the be-all and end-all of bilingualism. Thus Arizona (Article 10, Sect. 15–202 in *Current Legislation on Bilingual Education*, 1975: pp 37–9) approves the inclusion of "special programs of bilingual education to the extent deemed necessary to improve or accelerate the comprehension of English." Texas and Pennsylvania take very much the same line, and they are representative of the states permitting bilingual education. However, emphasis on English cannot in itself be regarded as a weakness. The inadequacy appears when the entire program is for the purpose of accelerated English instruction enabling students to return to the class to be given an entirely English-medium program.

In the long-term, a preventive or remedial, compensatory program may be associated with either a policy that envisages the gradual shift of dominance to the second language or a policy that envisages the achievement and maintenance of an equitable balance between the two languages. Remedial and compensatory elements, as the structure of actual programs, are equally compatible with transition or maintenance aims: "In an education program of transitional bilingual education, the medium of instruction of all required subjects shall be the native tongue initially and then to an increasing degree in English" (Committee on Education and Labor, 1974: 146). The transitional program can be regarded in one of two ways. Regarding the structure of the program, its organization may be transitional without envisaging that the student is to be assimilated. It is not difficult to ensure that students maintain their mother tongue as well as their affiliation to its associated culture while the curriculum, especially in the secondary schools, becomes increasingly oriented to the second language. After a stage of education in which the mother tongue has been the medium of instruction, the curriculum can be taught increasingly in the second language without vitiating the status of the mother tongue.

This has happened in the schools of Wales over the last fifty years, where the structure of the curriculum has almost invariably been transitional but where there are nevertheless more students than ever who are able to speak Welsh, and where attitudes to it are generally favorable. Evidence from Wales also supports the contention that parents accept as the long-term eventuality the increasing assimilation of their children to English, while insisting on placing them in schools where the structure of the curriculum is such as to ensure the use of Welsh as the medium of instruction for most subjects throughout the secondary school. They see maintenance programs as a strategy for delay, the longer to establish Welsh, without unrealistically expecting that the students themselves will remain dominantly Welsh-speaking. Curriculum organization or structure is only one element in the implementation of a policy; other factors, such as attitude and family or neighborhood linguistic background, are often more important. At one time an extreme maintenance structure—the separation of the dominant English and dominant Welsh into two permanent tracks in the same school, each being taught their curriculum in the native language—was popular in Wales where it was thought to be the most effective means of maintaining Welsh. The system was abandoned because it was found that, despite the maintenance structure, attitudes and the influence of the school environment and the neighborhood were more effective in determining the fate of the language in the lives of the students. The maintenance structure was powerless against such influences. Similarly tracked or linguistically streamed schools, ostensibly native language maintenance structures, in the Soviet Union are in fact geared to a policy of Russification by the operation of the same factors which we noted in Wales. The structure of the program is irrelevant in terms of long-term aims in both countries. In the United States, too, neither the structure of the curriculum nor the intention behind its design ensure that a program is necessarily transition or necessarily maintenance. Structure and intention are two factors independent of each other and often differently oriented. Such a conclusion points to the need to produce separate typologies of policies and of structures rather than typologies of programs.

CENTRAL DETERMINATION OF POLICY

Because of the autonomy of the individual states to determine educational policy, it can be said in only the most general terms that an overall national policy exists which effectively determines how bilingual education is handled. Nevertheless, there is a general consensus concerning the importance of a federal role in view of the "embryonic stage at which bilingual education stands and because the national welfare is directly affected by the success of the educational system" (Committee on Education and Labor, 1974: 99). The federal government is also able to exert direct influence promoting bilingual education because of federal legislation, some of which concerns bilingual education only marginally. The passage of the Civil Rights Act (1964) gave the federal agencies considerable power of intervention in education, partly through the Office of Equal Educational Opportunity to which was delegated the authority to investigate compliance in matters affecting the education of minorities. In 1967 the Office of Civil Rights became responsible for monitoring the implementation of other agency requirements, and in 1970 the Department of Health, Education, and Welfare was authorized to enforce federal authority over bilingual education.

However, the Elementary and Secondary Education Act has done the most to extend the federal government's powers and responsibilities. By amendments in 1966, 1968, 1970, 1973, and 1974 the national interest became increasingly specific through the determination of means, the allocation and distribution of funds, and the establishment of the Advisory Committee and Council, but above all by a declaration of policy. It is stated (P.L. 93–380, Title VII Sect. 702. See Andersson and Boyer, 2nd ed., Appendix C) that

> "recognizing (i) that there are large numbers of children of limited English-speaking ability; (ii) that many of such children have a cultural heritage which differs from that of English-speaking children; (iii) that a primary means by which a child learns is through the use of such child's language and cultural heritage; (iv) that therefore large numbers of children of limited English-speaking ability have educational needs which can be met by the use of bilingual education methods and techniques; (v) that such children benefit through the fullest utilization of multiple language and cultural resources, the Congress declares it to be the policy of the United States in order to establish equal educational opportunity for all children to encourage the establishment and operation where appropriate of educational programs using bilingual educational practices, techniques and methods . . . and provide for children of limited English-speaking ability instruction designed to enable them while using their native language, to achieve competence in the English language."

The same act set up the "Office of Bilingual Education through which the Commissioner shall carry out his functions relating to bilingual education" with a Director of Bilingual Education.

The central government has two avenues along which it can travel in seeking to implement its declared policy. The first is by financial inducements and support for local agencies working according to the stipulations of the various titles of the Education Act, most of which have some relevance to bilingual education. Title I is concerned with economically deprived children, often identical with linguistic minorities; Title II involves the Equal Educational Opportunity Act; Title IV is the Indian Education Act; Title VI refers to the Office for Civil Rights and Title IX involves the Ethnic Heritage Program. But Title VII focuses central government intervention most clearly. There are disagreements about the merits of the policy, but whatever its adequacy it cannot be denied that a national policy exists and that there is machinery for its implementation. The United States Office of Bilingual Education is able to claim (*New York Times, 30 January 1977*) that a variety of federally funded programs are present in more than forty states, catering to nearly 170,000 students. Sixty-eight languages are represented in these programs, including forty Native American languages. By far the greatest number of students attend the schools of large cities such as Chicago or New York. In the latter city alone 60,000 Spanish-speaking pupils have been recruited to bilingual programs, while 5,000 study in Italian, Chinese, French, Greek, Arabic, Hebrew, and Russian.

The second avenue along which the central government can travel is by "law enforcement," the monitoring of the fundamental requirements of the Constitution as well as the specific enactments of Congress. Bilingual education then becomes a field for litigation and legal adjudication. After an ambitious but unsuccessful effort to mandate bilingual education in the *Tijerna v. Henry* case in 1969, the advocates of bilingual education did not have much success in the courts of law until the early 1970s with cases involving desegregation, starting with *U.S. v. Texas* (1971). The result of the desegregation decisions was to force a comprehensive plan of educational relief to Mexican-Americans, first of all in Texas and then for Puerto Rican pupils in Boston and elsewhere. The decision implied that the native language naturally entered into the program of instruction. Other litigation followed involving bilingualism but without the question of segregation, as in the *Serna v. Portales Municipal Schools* in 1972, the result of which was to create a federal constitutional right to bilingual education. The victory was short-lived because the decision in the *Lau v. Nichols* case (1974) limited the range of the constitutional right. The court found in favor of pupils of Chinese origin but did not stipulate as the means of meeting the needs of the Chinese students adherence to a bilingual policy as set out in the Educational Act. "Teaching English to the students of Chinese ancestry who do not speak the language is one choice. Giving instruction to the group in Chinese is another. There may be others." Encouraged by the *Lau* decision, the Office of Civil Rights (OCR) after a compliance review of 333 school districts issued a document entitled "Task Force Findings Specifying Remedies Available for Eliminating Past Educational Practices Ruled Unlawful under *Lau v. Nichols*." The office was forced to retreat from its original favorable stance in respect of bilingual education (Documented in Teitelbaum and Hiller, 16).

At about the same time as the Lau decision, Aspira of New York and the City of New York agreed on a consent decree mandating the establishment of bilingual educational programs for Puerto Ricans in New York City schools. Significant though the result was, the subsequent history of the case involving the rights of parents to withdraw their children and the realization that it has very limited precedent effect has tended to modify the optimism of bilingual educators in much the same way as did the retreat from the position taken in the OCR task force report. Similar retreats have occurred in the *Keyes v. School District No. 1, Denver* (1976) and in *Ortero v. Mesa Valley School District No. 51, Colorado* (1975). In the former case, the court reversed a decision in favor of a comprehensive bilingual and bicultural education program; in the latter the court found that "under . . . the law there is no constitutional right to bilingual/bicultural education."

In view of the traditional, and in some instances almost invincible prejudice against bilingual education among local educational agencies, recourse to the courts of law was to be expected. Since litigation could be taken to the United States Supreme Court, it was one way in which minorities could evade the entrenched obduracy of school districts and states. However, though recourse to law may be necessary, it is always a misfortune in education because the issues involved are bedeviled by adversary claims and counterclaims. Other disadvantages have also been suggested. One such disadvantage is inflexibility; to meet the requirement of "instruction in two languages," states that impose such a requirement in their bilingual programs insist that both languages should be employed at all stages. Massachusetts insists that all required courses should be duplicated in the two languages—dominant and second. It is impractical if standards of achievement, for example in mathematics and the sciences, are to be maintained. Furthermore, if this were adhered to, the very young students of limited English ability would not be taught in the native language for a long enough period to establish it satisfactorily (P. and E. C. Roos, 1975). Other criticisms directed against dependence on litigation are that it has proved ineffective, that there is inconsistency between the goals set out in the results of litigation and the known requirements of bilingual students, and finally the impact of a judgment is in any case limited because of its very specific and local provenance (Lawyers' Committee for Civil Rights). Litigation has made important contributions to the development of bilingual education, but the long strides forward are succeeded by significant retreats so that dependence on litigation as a means of formulating and ensuring the implementation of policy is unpredictable. The movement is one of fits and starts, and this can be avoided only by a firm national commitment—a national consensus concerning the meaning and implications of bilingual education.

The individual states do not conform to a single pattern of legislation or of policy toward bilingual education. This is because of their autonomy, their linguistic heterogeneity, and differences in attitudes to their ancestral languages among the ethnic groups. Only a few states specifically prohibit bilingual education, but among the majority there are different levels of acquiescence or approval: fourteen states make no provision; twenty-five permit such programs, and nine make them mandatory. Tables 7.8 and 7.9 cover legislation affecting bilingual education in the fifty states and American jurisdictions.

NATIVE AMERICAN POLICY

What we have described so far has been the more general area of national policy for bilingual education—those aspects which concern all minorities. But the Native Americans, though they come within the broad ambit of national legislation and litigation, have and always have had

TABLE 7.8. Legislation Affecting Bilingual Education in the Fifty States (1976)

State	Prohibitory[a]	No Provision[b]	Permissive[c]	Mandatory[d]
Alabama	X P/NP			
Alaska				X
Arizona			X	
Arkansas	X P/NP[e]			
California			X	
Colorado			X	
Connecticut			X	
Delaware	X P[f]			
Florida			X	
Georgia		X		
Hawaii		X		
Idaho	X P			
Illinois			X	X
Indiana		X		
Iowa	X P/NP			
Kansas			X	
Kentucky		X		
Louisiana	X P			
Maine			X	
Maryland			X	
Massachusetts			X	X
Michigan			X	X
Minnesota			X	
Mississippi		X		
Missouri		X		
Montana	X P/NP			
Nebraska	X P/NP			
Nevada		X		
New Hampshire			X	
New Jersey			X	X
New Mexico			X	
New York			X	
North Carolina	X P/NP			
North Dakota		X		
Ohio		X		
Oklahoma	X P			
Oregon			X	
Pennsylvania				X
Rhode Island			X	X
South Carolina		X		
South Dakota			X	
Tennessee		X		
Texas			X	
Utah			X	
Vermont		X		
Virginia		X		
Washington			X	
West Virginia	X P/NP			
Wisconsin	X P			
Wyoming		X		

Source: National Advisory Council on Bilingual Education, *Annual Report: Bilingual Education–Quality Education for all Children,* 1976.

TABLE 7.9. Legislation Affecting Bilingual Education in Non-State
American-Flag Jurisdictions (1976)

Jurisdiction	Prohibitory[a]	No Provision[b]	Permissive[c]	Mandatory[d]
Guam			X	
Panama Canal Zone		X		
Puerto Rico				X
Samoa			X	
Trust Territories		X		
Virgin Islands			X	
Washington, D.C.		X		

[a] Prohibitory   The jurisdiction has a provision requiring that instruction be exclusively in English.

[b] No Provision   The jurisdiction has no provisions specifying any language of instruction.

[c] Permissive   The jurisdiction has a provision that expressly or implicitly permits the use of a language of instruction other than English.

[d] Mandatory   The jurisdiction has a provision that identifies circumstances under which a local school district must provide instructional programs employing a language other than English.

[e] P/NP   Refers to both public and non-public schools.

[f] P   Refers to public schools only.

Source: National Advisory Council on Bilingual Education *Annual Report: Bilingual Education—Quality Education for all Children*, 1976.

special problems arising from their unique status. From the beginning, the federal government has been directly involved in formulating and implementing education policy for Indians and Eskimos. State involvement has been created by specific withdrawal of the central government from time to time, for instance in 1962 when Indian tribes were brought under the jurisdiction of states. But, although the direct involvement of the federal government has been pervasive since the late-nineteenth century, the missionary organizations of various denominations were first in the field. Their influence was most pronounced between 1568 and 1800, though their impact continued to be felt well into the present century. The shift away from employing missionaries to educate Americans accelerated from 1895 and was virtually completed by 1917 (Hopkins, 1972: 56). Although the missionaries were committed to the policy of assimilation, they worked more closely with local communities than did the agencies of the federal government and they had more sympathy for the use of the native language.

The development of the education of native American bilinguals in public schools of various kinds occurred in distinguishable but overlapping phases. During the first, the provision was in the hands of the federal government—mainly through the Bureau of Indian Affairs. Its orientation was assimilationist with little sympathy for the native language. Federal policy for the education of the bilingual native Americans was a precise reflection of political, internal-colonialist considerations, the main elements of which were always assimilation. The second phase coincided with the removal of Native Americans from original tribal lands, a process which, though it dates back to 1763, gained momentum after the first quarter of the nineteenth century. It meant the dispersal of groups speaking the same language. The third phase is identified with the consequences of the allotment of lands to individuals rather than tribes, and became effective from 1867. This resulted in further disintegration of tribal and language groups. The concentration of tribes within reservations largely coincided with the policy of allotment and ensured to some extent that the local language was safeguarded by physical boundaries. By the same token it ensured also that the language could hardly play a significant part in a rapidly modernizing society to which English alone became the means of entry. The full effect of this policy began to be felt after 1880. Then there was the extension of local state laws over tribes which facilitated rapid assimilation and which was proposed as early as 1829 by the states of Georgia, Alabama, and Mississippi, but was not effective until fifty years later. The 1960s saw a major Congressional hearing on Indian education which recommended increased Indian control and a National Indian Board of Education. This was a prelude to a more satisfactory place for the native languages and gave a new impetus to reforms which had been introduced in the time of John Collier. In 1934 the Indian Reorganization Act had been passed, and later in 1936 the Alaska and Oklahoma Supplements were introduced and enacted. This act was accompanied by a shift in educational goals as well as far greater encouragement for the native languages (Tyler, 1973: 135).

By 1971 the following languages were being used in the Indian schools: Micossukee in Florida; Navajo in Arizona, New Mexico, and Utah; Ute in Utah; Passamaquoddy in Maine; Crow, Northern Cheyenne, and Cree in Montana; Keresan and Zuñi in New Mexico; Cherokee, Choctaw, and Seminole in Oklahoma; Sioux in South Dakota as well as three Alaskan languages including Yupik. Most recently there has occurred the gradual shift of responsibility for their schools from the federal government to the Indians and Eskimos (Hopkins, 1972: 57). Such schools as Rough Rock and Blackwater in Arizona and Ramah Navajo Community School in New Mexico have been operated contractually by Indian communities since 1971. In all these developments, from a very unpromising initial phase, the progress toward the greater use of native languages has been slow but by and large relatively uninterrupted. It has been claimed that the Soviet Union is fifty years in advance of the United States in the treatment of minorities such as Eskimos; but it is necessary to stress that whereas the Soviet Union did at one time advance rapidly toward bilingual education among Eskimos, they have since retreated considerably so that there are few Eskimo schools where the medium of instruction is the native language after the first two years. The story of Eskimo bilingual education in Alaska and of Indian education farther south promised less but is on the way to achieving more.

The degree of autonomy possessed by school districts in relation to the state as well as of the states in relation to the federal authority means that the districts are not constrained to follow any one pattern of bilingual education. Furthermore, while there is an increasing consensus about the value of bilingual education in principle, there is no agreement about the form or direction it should take. Consequently, the variety of such programs is very great. In examining the various programs, the number of variables which may be taken into account is considerable: one theorist lists 400 variables with different combinations resulting, theoretically, in ninety so-called types of bilingual education (Mackey, 1978). Such a theoretical exercise is interesting but unrealistic and, from the standpoint of the teacher and administrator, unfruitful. More realistic approaches have been suggested by such investigators as Fishman (1965), and these tend to typify programs according to a limited and homogeneous set of variables. Fishman deals with the set concerned with the orientation or direction of the program—transitional, maintenance, or revival. There are other limited sets of variables which are equally relevant and are not to be confused with the set of direction variables. The first of these sets we have already discussed and have referred to as "characteristics of student entry"—who is eligible and for how long.

A third set of variables concerns the composition of the bilingual school. Schools differ in overall size, in the number of minority students enrolled, and in the number and proportion of those who are eligible compared with the overall and minority totals. Such considerations have an effect on the feasibility and the actual organization of the bilingual program, to say nothing of their effect on background, or non-instructional, factors in the success of a program. According to information extracted with the author's permission from *The Content Analysis of 125 Title VII Bilingual Programs* (Shore, 1974), the composition of bilingual schools is an important factor. At some schools, for instance New York P. S. 64, total enrollment is 935, of which 90 percent are minority language students. Of the latter, 35 percent are in the bilingual program. Other schools have as low as 33 percent minority students. In some schools, as high a proportion as 84 percent or as low as 12 percent are eligible for bilingual education. Given such differences in total school enrollment, size of minority group and of the eligible group, and the proportion of the latter to the overall and minority totals, the number of classes in which a bilingual education is provided at each grade level and throughout the school will vary a great deal. In some instances these enrollment figures will determine the kind of organization which is operated. Most elementary bilingual schools begin with kindergarten (67 percent) and a few with pre-kindergarten (15 percent). Some do not extend beyond third grade while others go from pre-kindergarten to sixth. In view of the fact that many of these bilingual programs have not been in existence for more than three or four years, and because they are transitional, it is not surprising that the number of grades in which bilingual education is offered declined from 89 percent at grade one to 12 percent at grade six to 6 percent at grade twelve.

The composition of the school is related to the area which it serves, and this is especially true of its linguistic and socio-economic character. Most bilingual schools cater for one minority group, but there are many which cater for several. Thus P. S. 2 in Lower Manhattan caters for unequal numbers of Chinese and Puerto Rican students. The South Shore High School in Brooklyn, with some 250 students who are eligible for bilingual education, recruits speakers of French, Spanish, Russian, Yiddish, and Hebrew. One school in New York enrolls students from thirty different countries—though many of these countries have the same language.

Sometimes students attend a school during the first two or three years where only one minority group is taught and then transfer to a school which is very much more linguistically heterogeneous. This is the case of Warm Springs in Central Oregon. Many other Native American bilingual programs are organized in schools having very mixed linguistic enrollments—for instance, Cheyenne, Eagle Butte, and Ponca City (Bureau of Indian Affairs, *Indian Educational Research Center Bulletin*, vol. I., 1975). The greatest degree of heterogeneity is exemplified in the Native American Boarding Schools which draw upon numerous and often distant communities; for instance, the school in Fort Apache, Arizona, has Navajo, Pima, Havasupai, White Mountain Apache, and San Carlos Indians.

Irrespective of their linguistic composition, the largest number of schools conducting bilingual programs and surveyed in 1974 (Shore) were in small cities, towns, or suburbs of cities (25 percent). In addition to these areas, 12 percent served inner city ghettos and 14 percent served major cities. A combination of major city and ghetto programs accounted for 38 percent with only 21 percent catering for entirely rural areas—although a number of programs recruited from both major city and rural areas. From this it will be seen that the issues of bilingual education are complicated by background, economic, and residential factors.

A fourth set of variables relate to the organization or structure of the bilingual program, either within the regular school or separately from it. Thus, bilingual programs may be organized in such a way as to separate the linguistic groups (to track or stream them) on the one hand, or on the other to allow of their being mixed or integrated. The legality of separation has been questioned. It is suggested that a bilingual program which separates children for the better part of any day violates Title VI of the 1964 Civil Rights Act, or regulations set out under the Emergency School Assistance Act (ESAA). The prohibition extends to segregation for more than 25 percent of the school day by recipients of ESAA funds, unless it is to promote "bona fide ability grouping as a standard pedagogical practice." The Office of Civil Rights, however, takes the view that a program which is part of a larger school containing non-minority students is acceptable as long as students are not separated for instruction in those subjects which do not involve verbal skills. Shore identified eight possibilities of the separate/integrated organization. Most of the schools which were investigated operated a combination of mixed and separated classes. Twenty-seven percent were organized as mixed classes exclusively; 8 percent never mixed language groups for any instruction. Between these two extremes were various combinations of separation and integration. Fifty percent separated the two groups for second or native language instruction while only 8 percent mixed the two groups for such instruction. Twenty-four percent separated the two groups for most academic instruction, 37 percent mixed the classes for some instruction in academic subjects, and 38 percent mixed the groups only for instruction in nonacademic subjects like art or music. Three percent had recourse to extensive individualized instruction. The percentages aggregate more than 100 because many schools employ more than one of the listed strategies.

Other aspects of school or curriculum organization cut across the separate /mixed dichotomy. For instance, some elementary bilingual programs employ a graded class system throughout from kindergarten to sixth grade. (New York School 64). Of those who use the grade system, some do so for only one of the language groups while combining two or more grades for the teaching of the other language group. This is the case of New York School 98 and New York School 52 which have a grade organization for English students and a multigrade system for the speakers of Spanish. The most thorough nongraded organization of both groups is exemplified by New York School 75, which operates an open plan system. Some schools, for instance Johnstown, Colorado,—whether they have an integrated or separate system—make use of small group instruction within each class. Such within-class grouping lends itself in many instances to effective team-teaching practices, as is the case in San Angelo, Texas, and Fox Point, Providence, Rhode Island (Salganik, 49).

Where separation has been adopted as the most convenient strategy, it may lead to separate schools and these may be of several kinds. In the first place, the separation of minority members may lead to the organization of a school within a school—a mini-school. The best example is the John S. Roberts Junior High School 45 in East Harlem, New York. This is a nongraded bilingual program catering for 150 students, 19 percent of the minority group, which in turn constitutes 60 percent of the total enrollment of the regular school. Three other mini-schools, with somewhat similar numbers, are located within intermediate schools of New York City. Sometimes the separate bilingual program is situated outside the regular school, constituting an annex. This is the case with New York School 83, catering for seventy students in a detached building administered independently of the regular school. Another instance is an elementary school with a kindergarten through second grade program located across the street from the regular school and administered independently. Though they are virtually independent schools, the annex type recruits its students from those who would normally attend the regular school. This is not the case with a third type of separate program—the magnet school drawing from several regular schools. The state of Michigan (Lawyers' Committee, 80), recognizing the need for such schools, has declared that "where fewer than 20 children of limited English-speaking ability are enrolled in school districts, an intermediate bilingual institutional support program may be set up drawing its students from several districts." (ibid.). New Jersey adopts the same policy. The use of this type of organization—recruiting students from several schools either within one district or from several which have very few students eligible for a bilingual program—is being advocated by increasing numbers of teachers and administrators.

A fourth set of variables has to do not with the nature of the entry into bilingual programs, the linguistic composition of the schools, where they are located, or their organization, but with the substance of the program—what is taught, in what languages and to whom, whether to both language groups or only the minority. The most pervasive, indeed almost a universal feature of bilingual programs in the United States is the teaching of English as a second language, but as in almost every feature of the bilingual program there are several options within the ESL provision. Only in a very small number of schools (2 percent) does the second language constitute a separate subject and no more—everything else in the program being the province of the native language. In 89 percent of the schools, the second language is taught as a subject but is also used as a medium of instruction. Nine percent do not teach the second language specifically, but ensure its acquisition by using it to teach the normal curriculum, especially such subjects as social studies. In 29 percent of the schools, however, the curriculum is divided between the native and the second language, some subjects being taught in one and some in the other language. Finally, a considerable number of schools (71 percent) use the material taught in the native tongue as the content of the second language lesson (Shore, Table 21.1). Although the ESL component is essential to almost all the bilingual programs, the tendency is to integrate the teaching of the second language with course content rather than to restrict such instruction to the ESL lesson.

The most extreme form of language-curriculum content integration is represented by the so-called immersion of students for almost all their instruction in the second language, whether this is English or the minority language. In the St. Lambert (Montreal) experiment, the language of immersion is French; in Culver City (California) the English-speaking students were immersed in Spanish. Considerable claims have been made for the success of these programs in terms of language acquisition and achievement in the basic subjects, but these claims are no different from those which were made for the achievement of selected Welsh-speaking students who were taught entirely in English up to 1900 and before the introduction of bilingual programs. Such claims are also being made for non-Russian-speaking students who are taught in Russian in the Soviet Union and are open to criticism as the instruments of Russification. In fact, the greater the success of the immersion program the weaker the argument for a program of education which emphasizes the value of the native language as the medium of instruction, which is a fundamental rationale of bilingual education. Furthermore, it has been suggested that such programs do not conform to the minimum requirements of the *Lau* decision. If a program of immersing non-English-speaking students in a regular English-only instructional program cannot be considered adequate, no sound educational arguments exists for maintaining that the immersion programs are acceptable in the case of English-speaking students.

Where both languages are used to teach the curriculum, at least four approaches have been adopted and three of them appear to be equally popular. The least acceptable is the alternate day approach whereby the curriculum is handled in the native language one day and the following day in the second language. This has been adopted in Montreal and the Philippines, as well as in Wales about twenty years ago. In the United States, it was introduced to schools in San Francisco which had approximately equal numbers of English and Spanish-speaking students. The classes alternated on successive days between the English and the Spanish-speaking teacher. A slight variation of the approach was adopted in the Culver City (California) program where teachers would handle a particular subject in English on one day and the following day would teach the same content in Spanish.

So far as medium of instruction is concerned, the most evident characteristic of the bilingual programs is flexibility. Only 10 percent of the schools investigated (Shore, Table 14.0) reported that the two languages were never mixed in any single lesson by teachers or pupils, whereas 17 percent reported constant switching by the teacher from one language to another in the same lesson. Sometimes the teacher used English and the para-professional translated (11 percent), and students used either language in responding to the teacher or the para-professional (10 percent). Where the teacher is reported as using only one language, in 12 percent of the schools the pupils were allowed to use either or both languages in the same lesson.

The subjects which are taught in both languages are determined by the terms under which the program is funded. Federally aided programs demand that all "the required subjects"—namely, those that are obligatory in the regular program, the core subjects, and those which are necessary for promotion and graduation—are taught in both languages. But bilingual education does not always mean that all children at any one stage in their program receive instruction in every subject in both langauges. What usually happens is that some courses are taught in one and other courses are taught in a different language. Nevertheless, there are programs which use the concurrent approach whereby both languages are used for all subjects in a particular class. Where textbooks and other materials are available, the subjects most frequently taught in the native language are social studies, mathematics, and aspects of the sciences. One consideration affecting many if not most bilingual programs is that, as is required in New Jersey (Title 18A, Ch. 35:20 in *Current Legislation on Bilingual Education*, 88–90), pupils of limited English-speaking ability shall be integrated fully with English-speaking pupils in those courses or subjects in which verbalization is not a predominant feature.

The bilingual programs which have been investigated appear to share a common characteristic: "an overwhelming majority of projects (94 percent) were two-way programs . . . with English mother tongue students learning Spanish or another language as a second language" (Shore, Table 9.2). The pioneer two-way program is that initiated in Dade County, Miami (Florida) and most clearly exemplified in Coral Way. After 1960, because of events in Cuba, over 200 Spanish-speaking students took up residence in Miami every week. By 1976, the number of children who were identified as requiring instruction in English as a second language had reached nearly 75,000, of whom 72,000 were native speakers of Spanish, with over 40,000 in elementary schools, 18,000 in junior high, and over 13,000 in senior high schools. All elementary and secondary schools now provide special English courses for non-native speakers of the language, and in addition eight elementary schools include in their curriculum some or other of the following—Spanish for native speakers of the language, Spanish as a second language, and the use of Spanish in teaching curriculum content to both English and Spanish language origin students. These courses begin in kindergarten; in 1975 one school had partial or complete programs through second grade, three schools through third grade, and four schools through sixth grade. It was expected that all eight schools will be offering complete programs in all grades by 1979.

All junior and senior high schools offer courses in English to non-native speakers of the language, as well as Spanish as a first and as a second language. In addition, seven junior high schools and four senior high schools teach at least some part of the curriculum in Spanish, usually though not exclusively to native speakers of Spanish. The proportions involved are 88 percent Spanish language origin and 9.5 percent English language origin students.

For the student of English language origin, the bilingual program comprises regular courses of instruction in English, Spanish as a second or foreign language, and curriculum content in Spanish. For the student of Spanish language origin, the program comprises English as a second language, Spanish as a first language, and curriculum content in Spanish as well as in English. A school which offers all these components is considered to belong to the Bilingual School Organization (BSO). All students in such schools need not participate in the total program, the only obligatory component being English for speakers of other languages (ESOL) for native speakers of Spanish. In the high school, provision is made for Spanish-speaking students who have graduated from elementary school courses in ESOL as well as for beginners in English. For the latter, the course is at three levels and includes ESOL, foreign-born maths, Spanish as a first language, and an exploratory, elective enrichment program in Spanish. For Spanish students who are of longer standing in the area, the bilingual program includes ESOL, bilingual science, bilingual social science, and Spanish as a first language. Courses in math are also included and these may be taken in both languages or in either. All students in the bilingual program must take Spanish.

The most ambitious aspect of the bilingual program is the use of Spanish as well as English in teaching native Spanish and native English-speaking students. This is a voluntary program designed to reinforce Spanish language skills, and it also imparts the concepts, skills, and knowledge that students would have acquired in the main stream monolingual English system. The overall aim is to develop cross-cultural understanding and to enrich the experience and social attitudes of students. For the Spanish language student, the course also provides the means of ensuring he is not disadvantaged in his academic studies because of the limited acquaintance with the normal language of instruction, namely English. Furthermore, to an even greater extent, the learning of the language and its use as a medium of instruction enhances the student's concept of self. To establish Spanish on a parity with English, the program includes as many as possible of the innovations in technique and content introduced into the main stream instructional program, such as reading and math "system approaches" and "discovery and enquiry strategies." At present the course is optional; but because of a marked national interest in ensuring equal educational opportunity for minority ethnic groups, the trend is to interpret the *Lau* Supreme Court decisions as necessitating curriculum content in the minority language as well as ESOL so as to comply with the Civil Rights Act. It is to be expected, therefore, that more schools in the area will offer greater opportunities to native speakers of Spanish to pursue their studies in that language. For the native speaker of English, it is likely that the program will be of interest since it offers a good opportunity to facilitate his knowledge of Spanish, which will make him a fluent bilingual without sacrificing achievement in the content subjects. The amount of time devoted to the use of Spanish varies from approximately 150 minutes per week in kindergarten to an average of about 600 minutes in later grades of the elementary school. The time devoted to the use of English varies from approximately 800 minutes per week to 1,500 minutes.

At the secondary level, curriculum content in Spanish is offered in at least one subject to bilingual English language students from elementary schools where they have been accustomed to instruction in Spanish, as well as to Spanish-speaking students from all the elementary schools in Dade County. Eight junior and three senior high schools are involved. The number of hours of instruction in Spanish is the same for both English-speaking and Spanish-speaking students, and it varies from two and one-half hours per week in kindergarten to fourteen hours in grade six. However, the schools vary in the amount of time they devote to this aspect of the program. The number of hours of instruction in English also tends to be the same for both language groups and varies according to school and grade from eighteen hours to twenty-five hours per week. Two schools have a more equitable distribution of time between Spanish and English: Coral Way and South Side devote fourteen hours to Spanish and sixteen to English language use, except in kindergarten where the figures are six and one-half hours Spanish and eighteen and one-half hours English.

The curriculum-content in the Spanish program enrolls 3,683; the degree of their involvement, though, varies. Some students take only one subject in Spanish, usually Science and Health, while others add math and fine arts. Some schools offer a full program taught in both languages to both English-speaking and Spanish-speaking students, while others restrict the use of Spanish to Spanish-speaking students. As we have noted, the degree of the use of English is far greater than the degree of Spanish usage. The subjects represented in the program at secondary level are social studies, science, mathematics, music, typing, and so on. At this level a total of 2,000 students are involved. It is to be expected that the students of Spanish language origin favor the program more than students of English origin, the proportions being approximately ten to one. At the secondary level, 90 percent of those involved are of Spanish language origin. The involvement of Spanish-speaking secondary students is less than at the elementary level, 23.3 percent of the eligible students in junior high and 3.87 percent in senior high schools participating.

Since Coral Way is the school which inauguarated the bilingual program, it is worth indicating some of the features of the program in that school. Of the total enrollment of 1,149, 86 percent are of Spanish language origin and are therefore eligible for the ESOL course. It is not surprising, therefore, that 30 percent of the students are below average or average in reading competence. All the 997 students who are eligible to enroll in the Spanish as a first language course have done so, and 66.7 percent of the

English language origin students are studying Spanish as a second language. All students in kindergarten through sixth grade participate in the regular program taught in English, and nearly all also participate in the curriculum content course taught in Spanish. In Coral Way, this course is science and health, mathematics, and fine arts in both languages in all grades.

CONCLUSION: THE MORALITY OF PLURALISM

Although some of the justifications of bilingual education and a pluralistic theory of society have been discussed earlier in this study, that earlier treatment was deliberately descriptive, avoiding any assessment of the value of one or another of the proposed justifications. However, the reader may very well prefer that the writer take a stand and declare what he has learned over and above a large amount of information—"What has the study of bilingual education taught you about society?" Such a question is perfectly legitimate to ask, and responding to it involves considerations of the worthwhileness, the value, and ultimately the morality of bilingual education, as well as its expediency and social convenience or inconvenience. Yet is it not a question that is often asked, and this may be due to the belief among teachers and parents that raising the problem onto a moral plane was to divorce it from reality, suggesting that bilingual education is an esoteric subject, unworthy of the attention of practical men and women. The contrary is true, for values, which are the substance of morality, whether we are prepared to acknowledge them or not, and at whatever level of sophistication we propose to formulate our arguments, inform all that we do. "Morality thinks with the philosopher" it is true, as Benedetto Croce remarked, "but it also shapes things like the artist, as it also labours with the farmer and the workman" (Croce, 55). Indeed the very essence of morality is that "it is capable of engendering passion and transforms itself into will and utility" (ibid.).

Any truly lively and comprehensive mental revolution is bound up necessarily with a moral reorientation and a new attitude to the problems of personal and social behavior. The mental and moral revolutions are associated in such a way that there exists between them a reciprocal reinforcement and amplification. The removal of "pluralism" from the area of social theory to the practical areas of social organization and education constitutes such a mental revolution, which carries with it profound implications for the present as well as the future. The treatment of pluralism belongs to the plane of morality as much as it does to the areas of intellectual analysis and practical reason. Consequently, any study of the coexistence of diverse nationalities and their associated languages within the same nation-state, could be accused of evading the weightiest question of all if it ignored the moral implications.

Not that value judgments are relevant to all aspects of linguistic and ethnic heterogeneity. As a social phenomenon, a plural society is neither good nor bad. It is a fact, like a birth or death, and as such we can be neither critical nor approve but simply accept or acquiesce. Though the conditions in which languages came into contact—including the result of such ineluctable forces as conquest, immigration, or transportation of slaves—may be morally reprehensible, the simple fact of the juxtaposition of races and languages, however caused, is only a fact of our human predicament. We may like or dislike it, but we cannot pass judgment on it. It is the way in which we deal with facts, how we behave in the presence of death, for instance, that invites such a judgment. It is our attitudes toward pluralism, our handling of its consequences, that raises moral questions. The present writer's own approach to the linguistic aspects of pluralism is best expressed by the French philosopher and poet Pierre Emmanuel: "whoever does injury to language also wounds man" (*The Universal Singular*, 229). He was writing of intellectual monsters, which the systematic deformation of language by totalitarian regimes had produced. But such regimes are not alone in inflicting "injury to language." We witness it wherever and whenever any nationality, native or immigrant, is frustrated in its devotion to its language.

It is the poet's task not only to seek out rare satisfactions in a fastidious use of words but also, perhaps more importantly, to restore to the simplest words which many have forgotten, their integral, everyday, and therefore sacred meaning. Similarly it is the task of the linguist, the student of society, and particularly the student of language in society, to maintain the integral character of the most insignificant language, and enable it to continue to reflect its authentic cultural ambience. At the same time, in a plural society languages do not exist in isolation, and it is no part of the linguist's or the poet's function to prevent the cross-fertilization of languages. A pedigree is safeguarded not by a refusal to propagate but by the choice of partners. It is not true that "spiritual and intellectual life of a higher order always grew out of the soil of intense mixing only" (Hertz, 308). But it is true that such higher order intellectual and spiritual life is encouraged by the contact of languages and cultures. The moral dilemma of a plural society is to promote advantageous and productive contact while simultaneously maintaining the separate languages and the speakers' pride in them.

Another question to be asked is, How far should we identify the system of education with our attitude, favorable or unfavorable, to a plural society, and to the maintenance or proscription of languages? We may agree that maintaining a language is a morally admissible activity, but if, in order to accomplish our aim, we endanger the social realization of another morally admissible end we are in a cleft stick. Values do not form a coherent and mutually supportive set: to do justice we may have to sacrifice some freedoms, and to achieve equality we may have to prejudice aspects of social justice. The use of a child's language is something to which he is morally entitled. He is also entitled to the best education possible, and the two entitlements may conflict. Language is not only a means of expression and communication. It is also a symbol of one's cultural and ethnic affiliation. Education, too, is not a simple process of enlightenment and the means of intellectual development. It is also a political agency, the means of maintaining the existing distribution of power or of redistributing that power. The attempt to maintain a particular language by means of the educational system is a political act, so that the assessment of the morality of language maintenance is conditioned by our understanding of the social and political consequence of its maintenance.

Then again, one of the elements in the morality of maintaining a child's native language is that he should have the most favorable conditions for free and unstultified development. But education is not at every stage dedicated to the encouragement of absolute freedom. On the contrary, as Ruth Benedict rightly argues "the life history of the individual is first and foremost an accommodation to the patterns and standards traditionally handed down in his community. From the moment of his birth, the customs into which he is born shape his experience and behavior" (1968: 2) and the educational system, formal and informal, is one of the principal means of ensuring such a process. Malinowski, while agreeing with Ruth Benedict, takes the argument farther: "phylogenetically man begins with culture and culture begins with trammels. Man is not born free as Rousseau wanted us to believe. He is born to a new freedom which can only be achieved by taking up the chains of tradition and using them; for paradoxically these very chains are the instruments of freedom" (1945: 33). Kant had anticipated him when he wrote of the eagle's ability to soar depending on the winds against which it had to strive. There is no absolute freedom, and the child depends on the education with which his group supplies him if he is to gain the freedom which, in turn, the achievement of personal identity may bring him to criticize.

These considerations are not surprising, but they mean that a cultural tradition must be open to development if it is to remain a living force. Fortunately, for those who believe in the value of a cultural tradition for its own sake and as a means of ensuring personal freedom, this is the case. "A tradition has no changeless centre to which understanding can anchor itself; there is no sovereign purpose to be preserved or invariable direction to be detected; there is no model to be copied, idea to be realized or rule to be followed" (Oakshott, 23). If the value of a traditional culture and its associated language are emphasized and their maintenance proclaimed as one of the principal functions of education, it is just as well we should realize how elusive a tradition is, especially since, in a plural society, no tradition is immune from the influence of contact with other traditions. A tradition is only partly normative, and so it lays no categorical obligations on those to whom it is offered as an inheritance. As George Boas wrote, "if a tradition is allowed to die out that is not because of sin" (79).

No matter how difficult it is to capture the essence of a cultural tradition, to understand the place of language within a particular culture or even to understand what is meant by a tradition, of one thing we can be certain, no individual can possibly achieve a personal identity or mature satisfactorily unless he has assimilated at least some of the core elements of the culture of his ethnic group or nationality. Having assimilated those elements he may be critical of them and disown others. But he is inextricably attached to the group and its culture: the one thing he cannot afford to do is to isolate himself from that tradition, for if he does he is not merely rootless, he is defenseless against anarchy. Isolated, an individual has no safeguard against the arbitrary restraint imposed by other people, or the arbitrary selection of types of restraint imposed by the state, or the arbitrary selection of classes of action to be restrained (like the use of a language in particular circumstances). The liberty of an individual is synonymous with the absence of arbitrariness.

It is true, as we have stated already, that restraints on individual liberty are imposed by membership of an ethnic group and by adherence to the values which inform its cultural tradition. But that restraint is moderated by the fact that no tradition is homogeneous, constant, or stable. A tradition characterized by such features would be as futile as that of the Japanese who destroy the Temple of Ise every twenty years only to rebuild it precisely as it was before. A cultural tradition which can be justified on moral grounds is always undergoing change in some peripheral respects while it maintains continuity at the center. It is able to maintain a satisfactory balance between change and stability because the work of a cultural tradition is not done by the community or nation as a whole, nor yet by individuals working independently, but by small, organized groups or institutions that are integrated into the community. The cultural tradition of a single group is characterized by such pluralism, and consequently the national tradition, if it is to reflect the contributions of the whole of society, is similarly segmented.

Education is one of the institutions whose function it is to maintain a traditional culture while at the same time encouraging it to develop attitudes which may be critical of some aspects of the tradition. It can be dedicated equally to inhibiting such possible changes: whether education moves in a critical or submissive direction depends on the political philosophy of the state. In a democracy, no matter how far it falls short of fulfilling its ideals, the system of education acts according to rules in which reference is made to the individual's personal experience as well as rules which have grown up in a long tradition. All these are controlled principally by experience of cooperating voluntarily in most aspects of the communities' activities, and by ethical action and reaction between individuals. These are the moral rules of freedom. On the other hand, rules that are based on doctrines and beliefs outside the experience of the individuals, and which dictate considerable claims of impersonality, power, privilege, and domination by identifiable groups, whether they are castes, classes, or ethnic (linguistic) groups, are immoral rules of oppression. The former system implies a willingness to accommodate an independent and critical spirit that is permitted a wide scope in choice and in range of options. Such independence encourages variety, and variety of cultural and social institutions implies "pluralism" as a philosophy of political organization.

However, the moral implications of pluralism do not cease to reverberate at this point, for we have to consider a further point—whether pluralism in language policy, in education, or social and political organizations is compatible with the claims of a superordinate unity, for instance national unity. If one of the preconditions of achieving personal freedom is the willing acceptance of the traditional values of one's ethnic group, it is arguable that the freedom of that group, in turn, is conditional on its voluntary acceptance of a higher authority. We cannot ignore the intensification of national rivalries or the increasing power of national states which feed their desire for power by dominating others. It would be a sad conclusion to the story of pluralism in the United States or Britain if it collapsed in a fissiparous process and disjunction. The greater the attractiveness of pluralism, the greater the need to ensure that it does not end in segmentation, but instead provides for differentiation as well as national integration, the separation and independence of the ethnic traditions as well as their contribution to an overarching national culture. The Soviet Union has set out deliberately to create such an overarching structure, the "Soviet culture" which takes precedence over national cultures and exists in a formalized ideology as the direction in which national cultures are set to move.

However, independent national traditions and cultures on the one hand and on the other an overarching sense of national unity in social, educational, and cultural matters can be reconciled differently than in the USSR. The moral justifications of both sides of the equation are not in doubt: what would undermine the morality of either is a perverse desire for segmentation, or an equally perverse will to dominate or seek a mechanistic unity. We can choose pluralism knowing that it does not necessarily require a doctrinaire unity to survive and contribute to the survival and enrichment of the nation. In academic life, Sidney Hook claimed that only one kind of unity was compatible with freedom of scientific, scholarly, and technological development. "It is not a unity of doctrine, but a unity which expresses itself in an uncoerced convergence of interests from various disciplines working on common problems" (Hook, 314). The same is true of the relation of ethnic cultural traditions and the culture of the nation within which they exist. The task of bilingual education is to maintain the traditional cultures, to further the development of the broad national culture as well as our understanding of it, and finally to provide the conditions whereby each type of culture reinforces and supports the other.

Appendix One
Census Returns: Some Reservations

INTRODUCTION

In Part Two we have relied for the largest part of our data on the official censuses of the United States, the Soviet Union, England, and Wales together with Canada, Scotland, and Ireland to a smaller degree. We are fortunate because these censuses, with all their shortcomings, are among the most carefully designed and organized as well as being interpreted by highly skilled scholars able to call upon technically sophisticated methods and instruments. The United States introduced the first census in 1790 and added questions concerning literacy (in English) for the first time in 1840. The United Kingdom inaugurated its national census in 1801 but delayed the introduction of questions concerning language (Welsh) until 1871. Similar questions are included for the inhabitants of Scotland in its separate census. These language questions apply only to those living in Wales and Scotland, irrespective of whether the inhabitants of other parts of the country are able to speak either language. The first census of any value to students of the USSR was the Russian Census of 1897, which contained no language questions. Although the census has been repeated almost without exception every ten years, their value does not extend back very far. Nevertheless they are of great value to the states concerned in respect of the demographic aspects of language, literacy, and education, but particularly because they lend themselves to the establishment of correlations between these and other variables.

A census of population may be defined as the simultaneous recording of demographic data by the government at a particular time, pertaining to all persons who live in the relevant territory. Although it may enquire about some aspects of the past history of individuals, for example the language spoken at home when the respondent was a child, it is meant to provide information about the occasion when the census is taken: it offers a still-life photograph. But the picture can only be as comprehensive as the number of questions and the correlations between the answers permit. Furthermore, though censuses are of relatively recent origin, it is long enough for us to be able to suggest some observations about trends in the past and to extrapolate cautiously into the future.

Though censuses are probably the most important, because the most comprehensive instruments at hand, they are not the only measures designed to provide data of the same kind. The Immigration and Naturalization files of the Department of Justice of the United States as well as the local police files concerning migrants within the USSR belong to the same kind of category. Then again, total national surveys of the school population of England and Wales published annually give valuable data that can be correlated with the census returns, while a specific survey of language comprising all students between certain ages has been found of great value to educationists and to sociolinguists in Wales and of interest to other countries (Lewis, E. G., 1953: WJEC, 1963). However, even more important are national sample surveys, such as that conducted on the status of the languages of the United States in 1975. As will be evident, the value of this sample survey is that because it was restricted in the numbers concerned, it could afford to be extremely detailed in the questions it posed. Second, because of the number of questions concerned with the same broad question, it was capable of sophisticated validation.

THE VALUE OF THE CENSUS

Data on languages spoken in any of our three main areas help us to identify nationalities or ethnic groups, and a census repeated a satisfactory number of times helps us to understand the direction of group assimilation or maintenance. Additionally, knowledge of the existence of ethnic groups speaking known languages gives us evidence concerning the distribution of those languages and the stability of their distribution. The three categories of language questions usually included concern the mother tongue of the respondents, the language most frequently or habitually spoken by them at the time of the census, and the ability to speak other, usually indigenous, languages. Sometimes the languages in which the organizers of the census are interested are specified, as in the case of England and Wales, Scotland and Ireland. In the case of the Soviet Union, the languages are not specified in the schedule but in the tabulation of results; languages spoken by fewer than an agreed number (usually about 300) are not included. Such data are correlated in the tabulations with such data as age, sex, urban/rural residence, country or locality of origin, and so forth.

A general census such as we have in mind is not specifically an instrument of linguistic research, rather its aim is predominantly demographic. But this contention must be qualified somewhat. Lieberson (1967, 286) has argued that though it is an excellent device for determining the frequency, distribution, trends, and correlations of linguistic change (especially of bilingualism), it is not appropriate for linguistic analysis per se. In the strictest sense this is perfectly correct, but Lieberson's claim cannot be accepted as it stands. For instance, in the Soviet Union the minority languages are at different stages of standardization and many of the dialects of those languages, spoken by many thousands in some cases, are regarded by their speakers as independent languages, an attitude shared by some Soviet linguists. The extent of the stabilization of any such language or cluster of dialects can be estimated by the proportion of the population of an ethnic group claiming a particular dialect in preference to another dialect of the same language. This is a "linguistic" fact revealing the convergence of dialects. a good deal of linguistic evidence concerning the relationship of the dialects of the Karakalpak group of dialects can be elicited from a close examination of the census returns for the mountainous areas they inhabit.

Apart from its fairly limited "linguistic" value, censuses have other disadvantages. It is too much to expect that a census is a complete enumeration of the population. In Wales children below the age of 2 are excluded from some tables, especially language. Some areas of the Soviet Union and India, though not entirely inaccessible, are sufficiently difficult to survey that there is no guarantee that a significant proportion of the population have not been excluded, and such isolated peoples are usually among the most conservative of their native language as well as being in long-term historical contact with speakers of dialects of other languages, as is the case in the upper areas of Daghestan. Even when there is no inherent difficulty in conducting a satisfactory census, it may be defective because of design errors. The 1921 and 1931 censuses of England and Wales failed to provide birthplace data and for that reason there are no data concerning the number and origin of immigrants into Wales for those periods. When we take into account also the fact that the 1941 census was abandoned because of World War II, it is clear that for the period 1911–51 —a time of fluctuating fortunes for the population of Wales—we have to rely on global figures of population change. Attempts to overcome this difficulty have been made and the present study has relied heavily on the conclusions and methodologies of students of population change in England and Wales during this period (Thomas, B., 1930; and Friedlander and Roshier, 1966).

Another disadvantage arises from the need to adhere to the two conditions of "simultaneity" (that all populations of a particular territory are enumerated at the same time) and "immediate location" (only those resid-ing at a particular place at the specified time are to be enumerated). Residence at a particular place at a specified time may be entirely fortui-tous, and the results may distort the results of the census. So far as Wales is concerned, it reduces the value of the picture of language distribu-tion. In Wales large residential schools, colleges, and universities may be situated in towns whose normal populations are small. Recruitment to these establishments is open to England and Wales and to students from abroad, and in fact, the proportion of students from England is much greater than the proportion from Wales. Consequently the census figures give a distorted picture of the situation—demographic and linguistic. For instance, in 1961, Cardiganshire, in which are located two constituent colleges of the University of Wales (Aberystwyth and Lampeter), had a disproportionately high number of young people between 15 and 24 years. Without these there would have been a dearth of young people in the county. This conclusion is supported by the fact that the 25–44 age group contained only 23.8 percent of the 1961 population compared with 26.2 percent in England and Wales. Since recruitment to these colleges is favorable to students from England, the linguistic distribution reflects the existence of a cyclic phenomenon, temporary but recurring migrant mono-lingual English populations.

Not only does the limitation of the Welsh Language Census to the inhabitants of the principality inflate the number of speakers of English in that area, but it means that we have no means of knowing the number of speakers of the language living in the rest of the British Isles, although we know that in 1961 13 percent of the male and 11.7 percent of the female population of England were born in Wales. Some, though not necessarily a large number of these, will be able to speak Welsh since we know of the existence of several places of worship in some of the largest cities that conduct parts of their services in Welsh. There are also flourishing Welsh societies in such cities. Consequently, migrants to Wales may already be Welsh-speaking, though born in England. A similar difficulty exists about the interpretation of data concerning migration within Wales because of the complexity of the linguistic distribution within the area. We can only infer the original language of the migrant, whether English or Welsh on the assumption that his language corresponds to the predominant language of his original place of residence. This assumption is fairly sound when we are concerned with migrants from England. It is also fairly acceptable when we are concerned with migration from the predominantly Welsh-speaking areas. But the assumption is less well founded as we consider migration from linguistically mixed areas in South Wales, for instance. This is an important consideration since the early migration was over short distances, and in a linguistically mixed area, and the migrants might be either exclusively English, or exclusively Welsh-speaking, or bilingual.

Even if it were possible to guarantee completeness and avoid fortuitousness, the validity or objectivity of the returns might still be questionable. Lack of consistency in the definition of the criteria to be observed is a serious disadvantage. Among these are changes in the "base age" for the enumeration of speakers of a particular language. In Britain, the first Welsh Language Supplement to the National Census adopted the base age of 2 years, but thereafter the age has been raised to 3. Then again, the criteria employed in determining the type of economic area in which the speakers of a language live are apt to be seriously in error. Within ten years, the introduction of new industries may change the earlier character of an area from being predominantly rural to being industrial and urban. This occurred in Soviet Central Asia and there are examples in such predominantly rural and Welsh-speaking areas as Anglesey and Merionethshire. This is true of the United States also. Bogue maintained that every criterion which was used in the United States to determine the socio-economic character of an area proved "satisfactory only in a very crude and approximate way" (1959: 75). The distinction between urban and rural has become virtually meaningless in Wales, partly because of the fact that while the designation of the administrative boundaries of rural and urban areas has not been changed for over half a century, the substantive nature of the areas themselves has changed considerably. This disadvantage has been accentuated because of the removal of county boundaries and the redistribution of some smaller areas among the eight new, larger administrative areas of Gwent, South Glamorgan, Mid-Glamorgan, West Glamorgan, Dyfed, Powys, Clwyd, and Gwynedd. Not unrelated to the difficulties arising from even small boundary adjustments are those which are due to the erosion of substantive difference between urban/rural areas, as distinct from merely administrative adjustments. The official urban/rural demarcations have in the main acquired a historical interest, and there are considerable urbanized populations in areas which are officially designated rural. In a small country, the comparative effects of urbanization are far greater than in a much larger one. In 1961, while the percentage of the urbanized population of England and Wales living in rural administrative areas was 1.6, it was more than four times greater in Wales alone—7.3 percent. Broadly speaking, the distinction between urban and rural is still relevant in respect of population density, but it is far less useful in comparing the distributions of language, sex, and age groups. In an area like South Wales, this is especially true. Correlations between economic background and language maintenance or shift have become meaningless in such cases.

Changes in the administration boundaries of regions or counties, to say nothing of small townships and larger towns, especially when we take into account the fact that policy for language and for schools is determined by the localities in the United States as well as in England and Wales, make it difficult to compile trend analyses of the incidence of languages, and especially to describe in any consistent fashion the direction of language policy. While it is still possible to institute micro-analyses of small habitations, it is not possible to build up any number of such micro-analyses into larger profiles because the boundary of smaller units are not alone in being the object of change. In the Soviet Union, changes have occurred between the boundaries of the constituent union and autonomous republics; and though these are not major changes and have usually been redrafted in terms of the ethnic composition of the areas concerned, a further element of uncertainty is added to the interpretation of the linguistic data.

We cannot rely on the regularity of the censuses in several countries. As we have already noted, no census was taken in the United Kingdom (as well as most other European countries including the USSR) in 1914. In the case of the latter the turmoil during the period 1917–38 made the returns unsatisfactory and little reliance can be placed upon them even when the results are available. Furthermore, even when a census is taken after such a period of turmoil, the devastation of the countryside and the annihilation of large portions of the population mean that what linguistic changes may now be recorded cannot be attributed to anyone or for that matter to any recognizable or agreed number of causes. It is estimated for the USSR that World War I, the Revolution of 1917, the subsequent civil war and its consequences reduced the population by over 4 percent. Collectivization in the 1930s accounted for only a slightly lower percentage loss, while actual and presumed—as well as projected losses—attributable in the 1930s to political uncertainties cannot be estimated precisely but must be calculated in many millions. World War II meant the loss of 15 million Soviet men and women. The spread of these losses over the large number of ethnic groups, linguistic, and dialectal divisions cannot be determined.

A major defect of the censuses we have had to deal with is the inconsistency in linguistic criteria. For instance, in Wales the terms "English only," "Welsh only," and "Welsh and English," are subjective and arbitrary, and may vary from person to person. It might be thought that in spite of this, the large numbers involved would neutralize possible discrepancies, but this ignores the fact that differences of personal interpretation may be a reflection of a fundamentally important socio-linguistic variable attitude.

Furthermore, the way in which individuals interpreted the categories has been inconsistent over the years. For instance, there is no doubt that in the earliest language returns many persons took "Welsh-speaking" to be synonymous with "Welsh only." This meant not only a bias in the returns of the first census, but an inflation of the proportion of bilinguals in later returns, when the so-called monolinguals labelled themselves correctly as bilinguals. In 1971 the census asked the question, Do you speak English? From the writer's own knowledge some interpreted this as meaning, Can you speak English? Others, as meaning, Do you actually speak English habitually or often or sometimes? The number of monolingual Welsh has been greatly inflated by the interpretation, Do you speak English habitually or often? being taken as correct.

In the Soviet Union, also, changes have been introduced in the criteria for judging what constitutes an ethnic group. In the 1926 Census an individual was required to state this in objective terms—his actual national origin (*narodnost*). In 1939 a subjective criterion was substituted—ethnic preference or chosen affiliation (*nationalnost*). The 1970 census attempted to elicit information not only concerning the nationality and national language of each person, but also the more general multilingual competence of each person, since it required him to name any other language in which he might be fluent. The number of nationalities does not bear any really exact relationship to the number of languages spoken in the Union, since many languages are used by groups that are not granted the status of nation. In 1926, 150 languages were officially recognized; since then, the number has been considerably reduced. At present newspapers are printed in well over 122 indigenous and foreign languages.

But perhaps one of the most serious difficulties to be encountered in dealing with census returns is that of translating "lifetime migration" figures into statements concerning language. However, so far as the United States and Wales are concerned, this difficulty is not crucial. Although seasonal and temporary migration are important, it is the *permanence* of the immigrant force that is the main factor affecting language loyalty: the regularity with which that permanent force is reinforced is also vital. Nevertheless, from the standpoint of language maintenance, the massiveness of the English migration into Wales, together with the relatively short period when that migration was in operation, have ensured that more sophisticated analyses of reinforcement provided by intercensal flow could add very little to the knowledge that is relevant to our particular need.

Another difficulty arises from the convenient assumption that is made in estimating the influence of migration on population change—that inward and outward migration in any one instance or locality negate each other (Friedlander and Roshier, 242). This assumption is useful only when we are concerned with very broad problems of overall densities of population. Once we begin to analyze the composition or the characteristics of total population—for example, age, sex, occupation, and language—it has to be abandoned. In fact, as we shall see, far from neutralizing each other, inward migration and outward migration accelerate and accentuate the processes of demographic linguistic change.

In the Soviet Union, while it is possible to obtain fairly accurate data concerning changes of population that have resulted from migration between census dates, such intercensal data are open to misinterpretations. In the first place, annual figures are based, in the main, on police registration of persons arriving and leaving. Such movements may have to do with any number of occasional and casual visits of more than a month's duration. Then again, it is difficult, if not impossible, to measure the permanence of the movements which are registered. An additional complexity in interpreting the statistics is the existence of migrational cross currents. The figures obtained from censuses and registrations are, in the last resort, the net results of a large number of movements in varying and conflicting directions. In order to establish with any degree of confidence the relationship between migration and language affiliation, one would have to know not only the net figure but also the group identity of those who left compared with those who arrived. Between 1956 and 1960, for every 100 departures from the Ukraine for Siberia, 143 moved from Siberia to the Ukraine. Out of every 100 persons who moved into Siberian cities, 16 represented additions to the urban population; the rest, 84 percent, filled the gaps created by immigrants who had left (Perevedentsev, 1966b, Part IV: 115). What is true of Siberia is equally the case elsehere for "most factors in population movement operate more or less identically everywhere" (ibid., 116).

CONCLUSIONS

The above observations are meant to accomplish two objectives. First to remind us that the interpretation of socio-linguistic data from census returns is a highly hazardous exercise, partly because the census is not geared to obtain such data or at least only to the same extent as it is geared to obtain a host of other data. Furthermore demographers have not developed the same sophistication, or even the same interest in interpreting the data we do possess respecting the correlations of language with other variables. Nor do we have the confidence about the correlations that might prove of most value. The second aim of these observations is to suggest that so far as concerns socio-linguistic studies, valuable though censuses will continue to be, we should regard with greater favor than we have heretofore supplementary and alternative procedures. The kind of sampling of language affiliation reported by Waggoner (1975) has considerable advantages over a total population census, especially so far as language is concerned. Information about the languages of a heterogeneous population does not rank very high among the priorities of those designing the census, so that the low cost of instituting a sample survey should commend itself to them. "Usually an efficient sample will cost about a tenth as much as a complete count" (United Nations, Department of Economic Affairs, 1954:28). Even more important, a sample properly carried out because the margin of error can be calculated precisely in advance gives a more accurate picture than the complete count. "The greater accuracy of a sample. . .will often much more than offset the sampling error, and the net effect may be better census information than if a complete count had been attempted" (ibid., 29).

Appendix Two
Structure of Bilingual Education in Welsh Elementary Schools

OPTION 1—TEACHING AND USING THE CUSTOMARY
LANGUAGE THROUGHOUT WITHOUT ANY FORMAL
RECOGNITION OF THE EMERGENT LANGUAGE

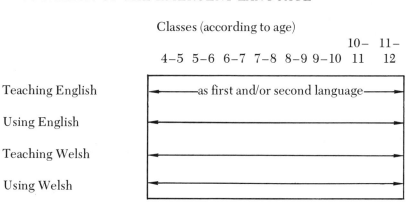

Classes (according to age)

	4–5	5–6	6–7	7–8	8–9	9–10	10–11	11–12
Teaching English	◄——as first and/or second language——►
Using English	◄————————————————————————————►
Teaching Welsh	◄————————————————————————————►
Using Welsh	◄————————————————————————————►

Note: Such programs are found only in almost completely English-speaking areas. Some programs of this type distinguish between participants for whom English is the native language and those for whom it is a second language. They may split classes, or place different groups in different classes.

403

OPTION 2—TEACHING AND USING ENGLISH THROUGHOUT
BUT ALSO TEACHING WELSH

    a) either to speakers of Welsh only
    b) or to speakers of both languages. The note to 1 is relevant to
       Option 2 also.

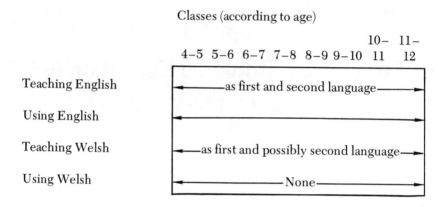

OPTION 3—TEACHING ENGLISH AND USING IT FOR MOST
OF THE TIME IN ALL CLASSES BUT ALSO TEACHING
WELSH FOR VARYING NUMBERS OF CLASSES AND
USING IT IN THE EARLY CLASSES TO TEACH
SPEAKERS OF WELSH ONLY

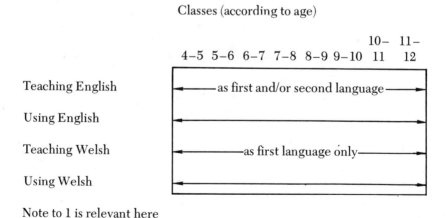

Note to 1 is relevant here

OPTION 4

a) Beginning with teaching and use of Welsh to speakers of that
   language and introducing English to the same group around ages
   7 or 8. Using English in later grades, but not using Welsh with
   speakers of English.
b) Same as for (a) above except that Welsh is taught as a second
   language to speakers of the customary language, English.

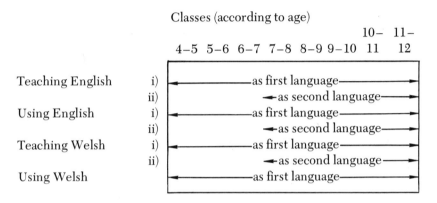

OPTION 5

a) In respect of those for whom it is the native language, teaching
   and use of Welsh from the beginning, introducing English
   as a second language also at the beginning and using it
   progressively.
b) In respect of those for whom English is the native tongue, teaching Welsh as a second language only, and not necessarily from
   the beginning.

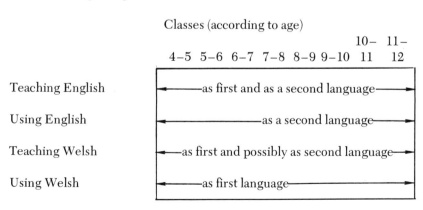

OPTION 6—TEACHING AND USE OF BOTH LANGUAGES WITH
BOTH LANGUAGE GROUPS FROM THE BEGINNING FOR
DIFFERENT SUBJECTS, BUT WITH ENGLISH BECOMING
THE ONLY MEDIUM OF INSTRUCTION IN LATER
STAGES FOR BOTH GROUPS

Classes (according to age)

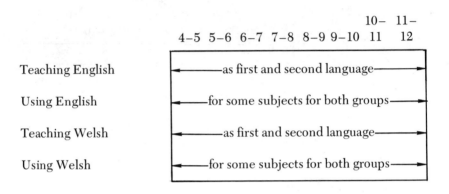

OPTION 7—TEACHING AND USE OF BOTH LANGUAGES
FROM THE BEGINNING TO ALL STUDENTS FOR ALL
SUBJECTS, BUT ON ALTERNATE DAYS

Classes (according to age)

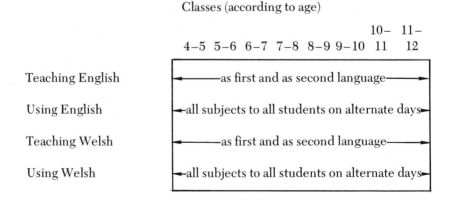

OPTION 8—WELSH TAUGHT AND USED FROM THE
BEGINNING. ENGLISH TAUGHT AS A SECOND LANGUAGE,
BUT NOT USED, OR ELSE USED ONLY IN EARLY
GRADES AS A TRANSITION TO WELSH. THESE PROGRAMS
ARE OFFERED IN SCHOOLS WHICH HAVE BEEN
ORGANIZED SPECIFICALLY TO MEET THE WISHES OF
PARENTS WHO CHOOSE TO HAVE THEIR CHILDREN
BROUGHT UP ALMOST EXCLUSIVELY WELSH. IN MOST
CASES HOWEVER THE PARENTS AND THE CHILDREN
SPEAK ENGLISH WITH EASE

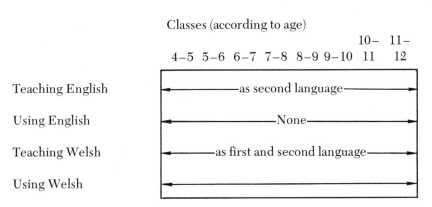

Classes (according to age)

	4–5	5–6	6–7	7–8	8–9	9–10	10–11	11–12
Teaching English	←————————as second language————————→							
Using English	←——————————————None——————————————→							
Teaching Welsh	←————as first and second language————→							
Using Welsh	←————————————————————————————————————→							

OPTIONS 9 AND 10—THESE INVOLVE THE CREATION OF
NON-NEIGHBORHOOD SCHOOLS, PARTICIPANTS BEING
WITHDRAWN FROM THE SCHOOLS THEY WOULD
NORMALLY ATTEND

a) In any one area speakers of Welsh (and speakers of English in
some instances) are withdrawn from neighborhood schools where
the numbers of speakers of Welsh are thought to be too few to
allow of the creation of a satisfactory program, in order to build up
a relatively homogeneous "Welsh school." The program provided
is usually of option 8.

b) In any one area Welsh and English speakers are withdrawn from
schools which cater to each group separately, and enrolled in one
school. But such a school provides separate programs for each
group. These would be option 8 (and its converse respectively) in
the same school either streamed or tracked.

References

ABLIN, F.
1970   "Decision Making in Soviet Higher Education: A Documentary History," *Soviet Education* 13:9–11.

ABRAHAM, R. D., AND R. C. TROIKE
1972   *Language and Cultural Diversity in American Education* (Englewood Cliffs, N.J.: Prentice-Hall).

ALATIS, JAMES E.
1970   *Bilingualism and Language Contact: Georgetown University Round Table on Languages and Linguistics* (Washington, D.C.: Georgetown University Press).
1978   *International Dimensions of Bilingual Education: Georgetown University Round Table on Languages and Linguistics* (Washington, D.C.: Georgetown University Press).

ALATIS, J. E., AND K. TWADELL
1976   *English as a Second Language in Bilingual Education* (Washington, D.C.: TESOL).

ALLEN, H. B.
1973   "English as a Second Language," in *Linguistics in North America*, Vol. 10 *Current Trends in Linguistics*, ed. T. A. Sebeok (The Hague: Mouton).

ALLPORT, C. W.
1965   In *A Handbook of Social Psychology*, ed. C. Mackinson (Worcester, Mass.: Clark University Press).

ALLWORTH, E. (ED.)
1971   *Soviet Nationality Problems* (New York: Columbia University Press).

ALMOND, G. A., AND S. VERBA
1965   *The Civic Culture* (Boston: Little, Brown & Co.).

ANDERSON, H. D., H. DEWEY, AND W. C. ELLIS
1935   *Alaska Natives: A Study of their Sociological and Educational Status* (Palo Alto: Stanford University Press).

ANDERSON, K. E.
1953   *The Educational Achievement of Indian Children* (Washington, D.C.: U.S. Department of the Interior, Bureau of Indian Affairs).

ANDERSSON, T.
1969   *Foreign Languages in the Elementary School* (Austin. University of Texas Press).
1971   "Bilingual Education: The American Experience," *The Modern Languages Journal* 55:427–440.
1974   "Bilingual Education and Early Childhood," *Hispania* 57:77–78.
1977   "Philosophical Perspectives on Bilingual Education," in *Frontiers of Bilingual Education*, ed. B. Spolsky and R. Cooper (Rowley, Mass.: Newbury Press).

ANDERSSON, T., AND M. BOYER
1978   *Bilingual Schooling in the United States* (2nd Ed.) (Austin. National Educational Development Publishers, Inc.).

APTER, D. E.
1977   "Political Life and Cultural Pluralism," in *Pluralism in a Democratic Society*, ed. M. Tumin and W. Plotch (New York: Praeger Publishers).

ARNOLD, M.
1853   *Report on English in Welsh Schools: Reports to the Committee on Education of the Privy Council* (London).
1923   *Thoughts on Education from Matthew Arnold*, ed. H. Huxley (London: Smith Elder).

ARSENIAN, S.
1937   *Bilingualism and Mental Development* (New York: Teachers College Press).
1945   "Bilingualism in the Post War World," *Psychological Bulletin* 42:2.

ARUTIUNIAN, I. V.
1969   "Preliminary Socio-Ethnographic Investigation of Tatar Materials," *Sovetskaia etnografiia* 4 (In Russian).
1972   "Socio-cultural Aspects of the Development and Convergence of Nations of the USSR," *Sovetskaia etnografiia* 3 (In Russian).
1973a   "Interaction of Cultures of the USSR Peoples," Paper for the Ninth International Congress of Anthropological and Ethnological Sciences, Chicago.
1973b   "On Certain Tendencies towards Change in the Cultural Aspects of a Nation," *Sovetskaia etnografiia* 4 (In Russian).

ASCH, S.
1952   *Social Psychology* (New York: Prentice-Hall)

ATKINSON, D. D.
1955   "Educational Adjustment of Ute Indians as Compared with Mixed Bloods and Native Whites at Union High School, Utah" (M.A. thesis, Utah State Agricultural College).

ATKINSON, D. F. C.
1952   *The Greek Language* (London: Faber)

AUCAMP, P.
1932   *Bilingual Education and Nationalism with Special Reference to South Africa* (Pretoria: State Press).

AUDEN, W. H.
1963   *The Dyer's Hand and Other Essays* (London: Faber).

AUERBACH, E.
1965   *Literary Language and its Public in Late Antiquity and in the Middle Ages* (London: Methuen).

AUSTIN, WILFRED G.
1934   "An Educational Study of Pima Indians of Arizona" (M.A. thesis, Stanford University).

AZERBAYDZHAN TSIFRAKH
1966   (Annual publication) (Baku: State Press) (In Russian).

BACON, FRANCIS
1879   *Novum Organum Aphorisms*
BAKER, J.
1795   *A Picturesque Guide Through Wales and the Marches*
BARBER, C. G.
1973   "Trilingualism in an Arizona Yaqui Village," in *Bilingualism in the South West*, ed. P. Turner (Tucson: University of Arizona Press).
BARKE, E. M.
1933   "A Study of the Comparative Intelligence of Children in Bilingual and Monoglot Schools," *British Journal of Educational Psychology* 3.
BARKE, E. M., AND D. P. WILLIAMS
1938   "A Further Study of the Comparative Intelligence of Children in Bilingual and Monoglot Schools" *British Journal of Educational Psychology* 6.
BARTH, F. (ED.)
1969   *Ethnic Group Boundaries* (Boston: Little, Brown & Co.).
BAUER, EVELYN
1973   Comments in *Proceedings of National Indian Bilingual Education Conference* (Washington, D.C.: U.S. Department of the Interior, Bureau of Indian Affairs).
BASKAKOV, N. A.
1960   *The Turkic Languages of Central Asia: Problems of Planned Culture Contact*, trans. (Oxford: Central Asia Centre).
1973   "The Scope of Abstract Influences on a Language Functioning in Complicated Inter-ethnic Relations (The Gagauz Language)." Paper prepared for Ninth International Congress of Anthropological and Ethnological Sciences, Chicago.
BELL, D.
1975   "Ethnicity and Social Change," in *Ethnicity: Theory and Practice*, ed. N. Glazer and D. Moynihan (Cambridge, Mass.: Harvard University Press).
BELL, W., AND E. FREEMAN (EDS.).
1972   *Ethnicity and Nation Building* (Beverly Hills: Sage Publication).
BENDIX, R.
1964   *Nation Building and Citizenship* (New York: John Wiley).
BENEDICT, R.
1968   *Patterns of Culture* (New York. Beacon Press).
BENNIGSEN, A.
1967   "The Problems of Bilingualism and Assimilation in the North Caucasus," *Central Asian Review* 15.
BENNIGSEN, A., AND C. M. QUELQUEJAY
1961   *The Evolution of Muslim Nationalities of the USSR and Their Linguistic Problems* (Oxford: Central Asian Centre).
BERRY, B.
1965   *Race and Ethnic Relations* (Boston: Houghton Mifflin).
1969   *The Education of American Indians: A Survey of the Literature* (U.S. Department of the Interior, Bureau of Indian Affairs).
BERRY, JAMES
1966   *Tales of the West of Ireland* (Dublin: Dolmen Press).
BILINSKY, Y.
1962   "The Soviet Education Laws of 1958–9 and National Policy," *Soviet Studies* 14:138–157.
1968   "Education of the Non-Russian Peoples of the USSR, 1917-67," *Slavic Review* 22:411–439.
BILLS, G. D. (ED.)
1974   *South West Areal Linguistics* (Institute for Cultural Pluralism, San Diego: San Diego University Press).

BLACKWELL, J.
1851   *Ceinion Alun* [In Welsh, *Selection of Works*]

BLEGEN, T. C.
1931   *Norwegian Migration to America* (Duluth: Northfield).

BLOCH, M.
1961   *Feudal Society*, trans. L. A. Manyon (London: Kegan Paul).

BLOOMFIELD, L.
1933   *Language* (New York: Holt).

BOARD OF EDUCATION, CITY OF NEW YORK
1972   *Educational Progress, Research and Statistics* (New York:n.p.).

BOARD OF EDUCATION (England and Wales)
1932   *Memorandum No. 1: Suggestions for the Consideration of Teachers*

BOAS, F.
1940   *Race, Language, and Culture* (New York: Macmillan)

BOAS, GEORGE
1960   "Tradition," in *Diogenes* 31.

BOGUE, D. J.
1959   *The Population of the United States* (Glencoe, Ill.: The Free Press).

BONNER, M. S.
1950   "Education and Other Influences in the Cultural Assimilation of the Cherokee Indians on the Quala Reservation in North Carolina" (M.A. thesis, Alabama Polytechnic Institute).

BOWEN, E. G.
1965   *The Age of the Saints* (Cardiff: University of Wales Press).

BOWEN, E. G. (ED.)
1966   *Wales: A Physical, Historical and Regional Geography* (London: Macmillan).

BOWEN, J. D.
1972   "Local Standards and Spanish in the South West," in *Studies in Language and Linguistics*, ed. E. Ewton and J. Ornstein (El Paso: University of Texas).
1977   "Linguistic Perspectives on Bilingual Education," in ed. B. Spolsky and R. Cooper, *Frontiers in Bilingual Education* (Rowley, Mass.: Newbury House Press).

BRAITHWAITE, C.
1938   *The Voluntary Citizen* (London: n.p.).

BRANDT, E. A.
1970   "On the Origins of Linguistic Stratifications: The Sandia Case," *Anthropological Linguistics* 12:46-50.

BRAUDEL, F.
1973   *Capitalism and Material Life, 1400-1800*, trans. Miriam Kochen (New York: Harper and Row).

BREZHNEV, L.
1971   "Comments," in *23rd CPSU Congress Report* (Moscow) (In Russian).

BRIGHT, W. (ED.)
1966   *Sociolinguistics: Proceedings of the UCLA Sociolinguistics Conference, 1964* (The Hague: Mouton).
1973   "North American Indian Language Contacts," in T. A. Sebeok ed., *Linguistics in North America* Vol. 10 of *Current Trends in Linguistics* (The Hague: Mouton).

BROPHY, W., AND S. ABERLE
1966   *The Indian: America's Unfinished Business (Report of the Commission on the Rights, Liberties and Responsibilities of the American Indian)* (Norman: University of Oklahoma Press).

BROWN, F.
1953   "A Comparative Study of Race and Locale on Emotional Stability of Children," *Journal of Genetic Psychology* 49.

BRUK, S. I.
1971   "Ethnodemographic Processes in the USSR Based on Materials from the Census of 1970," *Sovetskaia etnografia* 2 (In Russian).
BRUNER, J.
1968   *Toward a Theory of Instruction* (Cambridge, Mass.: M.I.T. Press).
1969   "Culture, Politics and Pedagogy," in *Saturday Review of Literature* May 18.
1976   "Psychology and the Image of Man," *Times Literary Supplement* December 17.
BRYDE, J. F., S.J.
1965   "The Sioux Indian Student: A Study of Scholastic Failure and Personality Conflict" (Ph.D. dissertation, University of Denver).
BUREAU OF INDIAN AFFAIRS (BIA)
1971-73   *A Research and Evaluation Report* (Albuquerque: BIA).
1973   *Proceedings of the National Indian Education Conference* (Albuquerque: BIA).
1974a   *Alaskan Native Needs Assessment in Education* 2 vols. (Juneau, Alaska: BIA).
1974b   "Educational Research Bulletin" (Periodical Publication; Albuquerque: BIA).
1974c   *Rough Rock School Evaluation* (Albuquerque: BIA).
1975   "Educational Research Bulletin" (Periodical Publication; Albuquerque: BIA)
1974–77   "Indian Educational Research Center (IERC) Bulletin" (Albuquerque: BIA).
CAMPBELL, R.
1972   "Bilingual Education in Culver City," in *UCLA (ESL Workpapers)* no. 6.
CANADA YEAR BOOK
            Annual Publication (Ottawa: Government Printer).
CARDENAS, J.
1975   "Bilingual Education, Segregation and a Third Alternative," in *Inequality in Education* (Center for Law and Education, Cambridge, Mass.: Harvard University).
CARROLL, J. B.
1975   *Teaching French as a Foreign Language in Eight Countries* (Stockholm: Almqvist and Wiskel).
CARTER, T. P.
1970   *Mexican Americans in School: A History of Educational Neglect* (New York: College Entrance Examination Board).
CASAVANTES, E.
1970   "Pride and Prejudice: A Mexican American Dilemma," *Civil Rights Digest* 3:22–27.
CASSANO, P. V.
1973   "The Substrata Theory in Relation to the Bilingualism of Paraguay," *Anthropological Linguistics* 15:406–426.
CASSIRER, E.
1959   *The Problem of Knowledge* (London: Kegan Paul).
CATTELL, R. B.
1957   *Motivation and Dynamic Structures* (London: Holt, Rinehart).
CENSUS FOR SCOTLAND
1930–71   *Decennial Reports* (London and Edinburgh: Her Majesty's Stationery Office).
CENSUS OF CANADA
1971   (Ottawa: Queen's Printers)
CENSUS OF ENGLAND AND WALES
1865-1971 *General Reports* (London: Her Majesty's Stationery Office).
1870-1971 *Decennial Language Supplements for Wales* (London: Her Majesty's Stationery Office).
CENSUS OF POPULATION (IRELAND)
1941–71   *Reports* (Dublin: Central Statistics Office).
CENTER FOR APPLIED LINGUISTICS
1968   *Styles of Learning among American Indians: An Outline of Research* (Washington, D.C.: Center for Applied Linguistics).
CENTER FOR LAW AND EDUCATION (HARVARD UNIVERSITY)
1975   *Inequality in Education* February 1977.

CENTRAL ADVISORY COUNCIL FOR EDUCATION (Wales)

1953   *The Place of Welsh and English in the Schools of Wales*, ed. E. G. Lewis (London: Her Majesty's Stationery Office).

1967   *Primary Education in Wales*, ed. G. V. Morgan (London: Her Majesty's Stationery Office).

CHADWICK, H. M.

1945   *The Nationalities of Europe* (Cambridge: Cambridge University Press).

CHADWICK, N. K.

1963   "The Celtic Parts of the Population of England," in *Angles and Britons*, ed. H. Lewis (Cardiff: University of Wales Press).

CHAFE, W. L.

1962   "Estimates Regarding the Present Speakers of North American Indian Languages," *International Journal of American Linguistics* 28:162–171.

1963   "Corrected Estimates of Present Speakers of North American Languages," *International Journal of American Linguistics* 31:345–346.

1973   in *Linguistics in North America*, ed. T. A. Sebeok op. cit.

CHAYTOR, H. J.

1966   *From Script to Print* (London: Sidgwick and Jackson).

CHOMSKY, N.

1976   Quoted in J. Bruner, "Psychology and the Image of Man," *Times Literary Supplement* December 17.

CHRISTIAN, C. C.

1973   "Criteria for Cultural-Linguistic Subdivisions in the Southwest," in *Bilingualism in the Southwest*, ed. D. R. Turner (Tucson: University of Arizona Press).

CHRISTIAN, J., AND C. C. CHRISTIAN

1966   "Spanish Language and Culture in the Southwest," in *Language Loyalty in the United States*, ed. J. A. Fishman (The Hague: Mouton).

CITY OF NEW YORK

1958   *The Puerto Rican Study* (New York: Board of Education).

1974   *Report on Bilingual Education* (New York: Department of Public Affairs).

COHEN, A. D.

1975   *A Sociolinguistic Approach to Bilingual Education* (Rowley, Mass.: Newbury House).

1976   *The Redwood City Bilingual Education Project*, Working Papers on Bilingual Education, no. 8 (Toronto: Ontario Institute for Study of Education).

COLEMAN, JAMES

1966   *Equality of Educational Opportunity* (Washington, D.C.: Government Printing Office).

COLLINGWOOD, R. G., AND J. MYRES

1931   *Roman Britain and the English Settlements* (London: Oxford University Press).

COLLYER, R. J.

1976   *The Welsh Cattle Drovers* (Cardiff: University of Wales Press).

COMBER, L. C., AND J. P. KEEVES

1973   *Science Education in Nineteen Countries* (Stockholm: Almqvist and Wiskell).

COMMISSION OF ENQUIRY ON THE STATE OF THE MINING POPULATION OF SOUTH WALES

1846–47 (London: Her Majesty's Stationery Office).

COMMISSION OF ENQUIRY INTO THE STATE OF EDUCATION IN WALES

1847   (London: Her Majesty's Stationery Office).

COMMISSION OF ENQUIRY INTO THE STATE OF POPULAR EDUCATION IN ENGLAND AND WALES

1861   (London: Her Majesty's Stationery Office).

1881   (London: Her Majesty's Stationery Office).

COMMISSION OF ENQUIRY ON EDUCATION IN ENGLAND AND WALES
1886–87   (London: Her Majesty's Stationery Office).
COMMISSION OF ENQUIRY INTO INDUSTRIAL UNREST (SOUTH WALES)
1917   (London: Her Majesty's Stationery Office).
COMMISSION ON CIVIL RIGHTS (U.S.)
1971   Vol. 1, Ethnic Isolation of Ethnic Americans in the Public Schools of the South-
          west (Washington, D.C.: Government Printing Office).
1972   Vol. 2, The Unfinished Education (Washington, D.C.: Government Printing
          Office).
1972   Vol. 3, The Excluded Students: Educational Practices Affecting Mexican Ameri-
          cans in the Southwest (Washington, D.C.: Government Printing Office).
1972   Vol. 4, Mexican American Education in Texas: A Function of Wealth (Washing-
          ton, D.C.: Government Printing Office).
1972   Vol. 5, Teachers and Students: Differences in Teacher Interaction with Mexican
          American and Anglo Students (Washington, D.C.: Government Printing Office).
COMMITTEE ON EDUCATION (N.Y.)
1974   Report on Bilingual Education, ed. L. S. Steinberg (New York Department of
          Public Affairs: Community Services Society).
1975   Report on Bilingual Education, ed. L. S. Steinberg (New York Department of
          Public Affairs: Community Services Society).
COMMITTEE ON EDUCATION AND LABOR, SUB-COMMITTEE ON EDUCATION,
HOUSE OF REPRESENTATIVES
1974   Hearings on Bilingual Education (Washington, D.C.: Government Printing Office).
1977   Hearings on General Issues in Elementary and Secondary Education (Washing-
          ton, D.C.: Government Printing Office).
COMMITTEE ON EDUCATION OF THE PRIVY COUNCIL (U.K.)
1840–60   Minutes
1858–   Codes and Regulations
COMMITTEE ON IRISH LANGUAGE ATTITUDES
1975   Report (Dublin: CILAR).
COOMBS, L. M.
1961   "Implications of Achievement Levels of Indian Students," in Conference of Co-
          ordinating Council for Research on Indian Education 1:8.
COOMBS, L. M., ET AL.
1958   The Indian Child Goes to School (U.S. Department of Interior, Washington,
          D.C.: Bureau of Indian Affairs).
COOPER, R. L.
1969   in M. L. Bender, Language in Ethiopia (London: Oxford University Press).
1977   "Bilingualism With and Without Schooling: An Ethiopian Example," Interna-
          tional Journal of Sociology of Language 14:73–88.
COOPER, R. L., AND J. A. FISHMAN
1974   "The Study of Language Attitudes," International Journal of Sociology of Lan-
          guage 3:5–20.
1976   "A Study of Attitudes," International Journal of Sociology of Language, 3.
COSER, L.
1964   The Function of Social Conflict (New York: Free Press).
COUNCIL FOR WALES AND MONMOUTH
1962   Report: The Welsh Language To-Day (London: Her Majesty's Stationery Office).
CRADDOCK, J. R.
1973   "Spanish in North America," in T. A. Sebeok, ed., Language in North America,
          Vol. 10 of Current Trends in Linguistics (The Hague: Mouton).
CROCE, BENEDETTO
1954   History as the Story of Liberty (London: Macmillan).

CURRENT DIGEST OF SOVIET PRESS
1965   Vol. 18
CURRENT LEGISLATION ON BILINGUAL EDUCATION
1975   Appendix D of Lawyers Committee for Civil Rights under the Law.
DAALDER, H.
1962   *The Role of the Military in the Emerging Countries* (The Hague: Mouton).
1971   "On Building Consociational Nations: The Case of Netherlands and Switzerland,"
          International Sociological Sciences Journal 23:888.
1973   "Building Consociational Nations," in *Building States and Nations*, ed. S. N.
          Eisenstadt and S. Rokkan (Beverly Hills: Sage Publications).
DADE COUNTY (MIAMI, FLORIDA)
1962   *The Cuban Refugee in the Public Schools of Dade County: Reports of January and
          October 1962* (Dade County: Board of Education).
1975   *Report to the Board of Education* (Dade County: Board of Education).
DAHRENDORF, R.
1959   *Class and Conflict in Industrial Society* (Stanford: Stanford University Press).
DARNELL, F.
1972a   *Education in the North: Conference on Cross Cultural Education in the Circum-
          Polar Nations* (Arctic Institute of North America: University of Alaska).
1972b   "Systems of Education for the Alaskan Native Population," in *Education in the
          North*, ed. F. Darnell.
DAVIES, E. T.
1957   *Monmouthshire Schools and Education* (Newport: Private).
DAVIES, REES
1973   "Race Relations in Pre-Conquest Wales," *Transactions of the Honorable Society
          of Cymmrodorion.*
DAVIES, THOMAS
1914   "Our National Language," in *Selections from Prose and Poetry* (London: Fisher
          Unwin).
DEPARTMENT OF EDUCATION AND SCIENCE FOR ENGLAND AND WALES
1960   *Standards of Reading* (London: Her Majesty's Stationery Office).
DEPARTMENT OF HEALTH, EDUCATION AND WELFARE (U.S.)
1976   *Task Force Findings and Report* (Washington, D.C.: Office of Civil Rights).
DERBYSHIRE, S.
1971   Quoted in *Bilingual Education for American Indians* (Washington, D.C.: U.S.
          Department of Interior, Bureau of Indian Affairs).
DERFEL, R. J.
1864   *Essays and Addresses* [In Welsh]
DEŠERIEV, Y. D.
1958   *Development of the National Languages of the New Nationalities* (Moscow: Moscow
          University Press) (In Russian).
1966a   "Development of the National Languages in the Soviet Period," *Yazyki narodov
          SSSR* (Part 1) (Moscow: Moscow University Press) (In Russian).
1966b   "Development and Mutual Enrichment of the Languages of the USSR," *Kommunist*
          113 (In Russian).
1974   "Social Linguistics," *Language in Society* 9.
DESPRES, L. A.
1968   "Anthropological Theory, Cultural Pluralism and the Study of Complex Socie-
          ties," *Current Anthropology* 9.
de TOQUEVILLE, A.
1965   *Democracy in America* (London: Oxford World Classics).
DEUTSCH, K.
1966   *Nationality and Social Communication* (Cambridge, Mass.: M.I.T. Press).

DICKINSON, W. S.
1961   *A New History of Scotland* Vol. 1(London: Nelson).
DIEBOLD, A. K.
1968   "The Consequences of Early Bilingualism in Cognitive Development and Per-
         sonality Formation," in *The Study of Personality*, ed. D. Price-Williams and M.
         McCord (New York: Holt, Rinehart and Winston).
DISRAELI, BENJAMIN
1846   *Sybil: or Two Nations* (London: Oxford University Press 1970 ed.).
DODD, A. H.
1940   "Welsh and English in East Denbighshire," *Transactions of the Honourable
         Society of Cymmrodorion.*
DODSON, C. J.
1968   *The Bilingual Method* (Aberystwyth: University College).
DOOB, L. W.
1947   "The Behavior of Attitudes," *Psychology Review* 54:135–54.
1957   "The Effect of Language on Verbal Expression," *American Anthropologist* 59.
1961   *Communication in Africa* (New Haven: Yale University Press).
DOSTOEVSKI, F.
1896   *Polnoe sobranie sochinenii* (Leningrad: Ak. Nauk SSSR) (In Russian).
DOWNS, J. F.
1973   Quoted in J. Sherzer, "Areal Linguistics in North America," in T. A. Sebeok, ed.,
         Linguistics in North America, Vol. 10 of *Current Trends in Linguistics* (The
         Hague: Mouton).
DOZIER, E. P.
1951   "Resistance to Acculturation and Assimilation in an Indian Pueblo," *American
         Anthropologist* 53.
1954   "The Hopi-Tewa of Arizona," *University of California Publications of American
         Archeology and Ethnology* 44.
1955   "Kinship and Linguistic Change Among the Arizona Tewa," *International Jour-
         nal of American Linguistics* 21, no. 3.
1956   "Two Examples of Linguistic Acculturation," *Language* 32:146–157.
1960   "The Pueblos of the Southwestern United States," *Journal of the Royal Anthropo-
         logical Institute* 90:146–160.
1961   "Rio Grande Pueblos," in *Perspectives in American Cultural Change*, ed. E. H.
         Spicer (Chicago: University of Chicago Press).
1966   "Factionalism at Santa Clara Pueblo," *Ethnology* 15:ii.
1967a   *Hano* (New York: Holt, Rinehart and Winston).
1967b   "Linguistic Acculturation," in *Studies in Southwestern Ethnolinguistics*, ed. Dell
         Hymes and W. E. Bittle (The Hague: Mouton).
1970   *The Pueblo Indians of North America* (New York: Holt, Rinehart and Winston).
DRIVER, H. E.
1961   *Indians of North America* (Chicago: University of Chicago Press).
DROBIZHEVA, L. M.
1971   "Socio-ethnic Features of the Personality and Ethnic Attitudes," *Sovetskaia etno-
         grafiia* 3 (In Russian).
DUNCAN, O. D.
1959   *Statistical Geography* (Oxford: Oxford University Press).
EDWARDS, J.
1651   Introduction to *The Marrow of Divinity*, by Edward Fisher.
EDWARDS, LEWIS
1860   *Literary Essays* [In Welsh]
EDWARDS, R.
1973   *Relevant Methods in Comparative Education* (Paris: UNESCO).

EHRLICH, H. J.
1973   *The Social Psychology of Prejudice* (New York: John Wiley).
EISENSTADT, S. N.
1954   *The Absorption of Immigrants: A Comparative Study* (London: Kegan Paul).
1961   *Essays on the Sociological Aspects of Political and Economic Development* (The Hague: Mouton).
1963   *The Political Systems of Empires* (New York: The Free Press).
1964   "Political Modernization: Some Comparative Notes," *International Journal of Comparative Sociology* 5 no. 1.
1965   *Essays in Comparative Institutions* (New York: John Wiley).
1966   *Modernization, Protest and Change* (Englewood Cliffs, N.J.: Prentice-Hall).
1973   *Tradition, Change and Modernization* (Englewood Cliffs, N.J.: Prentice-Hall).
EISENSTADT, S. N., AND S. ROKKAN (EDS.)
1973   *Building Nation States* (London: Sage Publications).
ELCOCK, W. D.
1960   *The Romance Languages* (London: Faber).
EMMANUEL, PIERRE
1957   *The Universal Singular* (London: Ples)
EMMENEAU, M. B.
1956   "India as a Linguistic Area," *Language* 32.
ENTWISTLE, W. J.
1936   *The Spanish Language* (London: Faber).
EVANS-PRITCHARD, E. E.
1937   *Witchcraft, Oracles, and Magic Among the Azande* (London: Oxford University Press).
EWERT, A.
1959   *The French Language* (London: Faber)
FALCH, J.
1973   *Contribution of a l'étude du Statut des langages en Europe* (Quebec: Laval University Press).
FERNÁNDEZ, E.
1973   Quoted in Kal Gazi, "Bilingualism and Bicultural Education: A Review of Research," *California Journal of Educational Research* 25.
FESTINGER,
1965   *A Theory of Cognitive Dissonance* (Evanston, Ill.: Wiley).
FILIP, J.
1956   *Keltvoe v Stredni Europa* [*The Celts in Central Europe*] (Prague: Czechoslovak Academy of Sciences and Arts).
1960   *Keltska Civilisace a jeji dedictivi* [*Celtic Civilization and its Heritage*[(Prague: Academy of Sciences and Arts).
FINLEY, M. I.
1959   "Was Greek Civilization Based on Slave Labor?", *Historia* 8:145–164.
FINLEY, M. I. (ED.)
1965   *Slavery* (London: Oxford University Press).
FIRTH, J.
1935   "The Techniques of Semantics," *Transactions of the Philological Society* 38.
FISCHER, J.
1970   *The Social Sciences and the Comparative Study of Educational Systems* (Scranton, Pa.: International Text Book Co.).
FISHBEIN, A.
1967   *Readings in Attitude Theory and Measurement* (New York: John Wiley).
FISHMAN, J. A.
1965   "The Status and Prospects of Bilingualism in the United States," *Modern Languages Journal* 15.

1966   *Varieties of Ethnicity and Varieties of Language Consciousness*, Monograph
          Series on Languages and Linguistics, no. 18 (Washington, D.C.: Georgetown
          University Press).
1968   "Sociolinguistic Perspective on the Study of Bilingualism," *Linguistics* 39:21–50.
1971   "Bilingual and Bidialectal Education" in *Conference on Child Language* (Quebec:
          Laval University Press)
1972a   *The Sociology of Language* (Rowley, Mass.: Newbury House Press).
1972b   *Language and Nationalism* (Rowley, Mass.: Newbury House Press).
1976   *Bilingual Education: An International Sociological Perspective* (Rowley, Mass.:
          Newbury House Press).
1977   "The Sociology of Bilingualism," in *Frontiers of Bilingual Education*, ed. B.
          Spolsky and R. L. Cooper (Rowley, Mass.: Newbury House Press).
FISHMAN, J. A. (ED.)
1966   *Language Loyalty in the United States* (The Hague: Mouton).
1968a   *Readings in the Sociology of Language* (The Hague: Mouton).
1968b   *Language Problems of Developing Nations* (New York: John Wiley).
1971a   *Bilingualism in the Barrio* (Bloomington: Indiana University Press).
1971b   *Advances in the Sociology of Language*, Vol. 1 (The Hague: Mouton).
1972   *Advances in the Sociology of Language*, Vol. 2 (The Hague: Mouton).
1974   *Advances in Language Planning* (The Hague: Mouton).
FLEURE, H. J.
1918   *Human Geography in Western Europe: A Study in Appreciation* (London: Williams
          and Norgate).
FONLON, B.
1969   "The Language Problem in the Cameroons," *Comparative Education* 5, no. 1.
FRANCIS, E. K.
1947   "The Nature of Ethnic Groups," *American Journal of Sociology* 52.
FRANCISCI, P. De
1969   *Primordia Civitatis* (Rome: Studi Classici).
FREEMAN, A.
1965   Quoted in Almond and Verba, *The Civic Culture* (Boston: Little, Brown).
FRIEDLANDER, DOV.
1970   "The Spread of Urbanization in England and Wales," *Population Studies* 24.
FRIEDLANDER, DOV., AND E. ROSHIER
1966   "A Study of Internal Migration in England and Wales," Parts 1 and 2, *Population
          Studies* 19 and 20.
FRIJDA, N., AND G. JAHODA
1966   "On the Scope and Methods of Cross Cultural Research," *International Journal
          of Psychology* 1.
FUCH, E., AND R. J. HAVIGHURST
1972   *To Live on this Earth* (New York: Doubleday).
FURNIVALL, J. S.
1948   *Colonial Policy and Practice* (London: Cambridge University Press).
GAARDER, B.
1970   "The First 76 Bilingual Education Project," in *Bilingualism and Language Con-
          tact*, Monograph Series, no. 23, ed. J. Alatis (Washington, D.C.: Georgetown
          University Press).
GALITZI, C. A.
1929   *The Study of Rumanian in the United States* (New York: Columbia University
          Press).
GARUNOV, E.
1970   "Schools with a Multinational Composition," *Narod. obrazhovanie* 3 (In Russian).
GEERTZ, C.
1973   *The Interpretation of Cultures* (New York: Basic Books).

GEZI, KAL
1973   "Bilingual-Bicultural Education: A Review of Research," *California Journal of Educational Research* 5.
GLAZER, N.
1977   "Cultural Pluralism: The Social Aspect," in *Pluralism in a Democratic Society*, ed. M. Tumin and W. Plotch (New York: Praeger).
GLAZER, N., AND D. MOYNIHAN
1970   *Beyond the Melting Pot*, 2nd ed. (Cambridge, Mass.: M.I.T. Press).
1975   *Ethnicity: Theory and Experience* (Cambridge, Mass.: Harvard University Press).
GONZALEZ, N. L.
1967   *The Spanish Americans of New Mexico: Mexican American Study Project* (Los Angeles: University of California).
GORDON, M. L.
1924   "The Nationality of Slaves in the Early Roman Empire," *Journal of Roman Studies* 14:93–111.
GORDON, M. M.
1964   *Assimilation in American Life: The Role of Race, Religion, National Origins* (New York: Oxford University Press).
1975   "Toward a Theory of Racial and Ethnic Group Relations," in N. Glazer and D. Moynihan, *Ethnicity: Theory and Experience* (Cambridge, Mass.: Harvard University Press).
GRAHAM, R. S.
1956   "Widespread Bilingualism and the Creative Writer," *Word* 12, no. 3.
GREBLER, L., J. W. MOORE, R. C. GUZMAN, ET AL.
1970   *The Mexican American People* (New York: Free Press)
GRIFFITHS, H. R.
1845   *Address on the Importance of Training Teachers in Wales.*
GUBOLGO, M. M.
1972   "Socioethnic Consequences of Bilingualism," *Sovetskaia etnografiia* 2 (In Russian).
GUGGENHEIM, F., AND A. HOEM
1967   "Cross Cultural and International Attitudes of Lapps and Norwegian Children," *Journal of Social Psychology* 73.
GUTIÉRREZ, L. P.
1972   "Attitudes Towards Bilingual Education: A Study of Parents and Children in Selected Bilingual Programs" (Ph.D. dissertation, University of New Mexico).
GWALARN (Breton Periodical)
        February 1927 and June 1950 (Rennes).
HAAS, M. R.
1945   "Dialects of the Muskogee Language," *International Journal of American Linguistics* 21, no. 3.
1973a   "American Indian Linguistic Prehistory," in T. A. Sebeok, ed., *North American Linguistics*, Vol. 10 of *Current Trends in Linguistics* (The Hague: Mouton).
1973b   "The Southwest," in T. A. Sebeok, ed., *North American Linguistics*, Vol. 10 of *Current Trends in Linguistics* (The Hague: Mouton).
HADDON, A. L.
1912   *The Wandering of Peoples* (Cambridge: Cambridge University Press).
HALL, R.
1974   *The External History of Romance Languages* (New York: Elseveier Press).
HANDLIN, O.
1959   *Immigration as a Factor in American History* (New York: Macmillan).
HARDIE, D. W. F.
1948   *A Handbook of Modern Breton* (Cardiff: University of Wales Press).
HAUG, M.
1967   "Social and Cultural Pluralism," *American Journal of Sociology* 73:294–304.

HAUGEN, E.
1950   "Problems of Bilingualism," *Lingua* 2:271–290.
1953   *The Norwegian Language in America*, 2 vols. (Philadelphia: University of Pennsylvania Press).
1955   "Problems of Bilingual Description," *General Linguistics* 1:1–9.
1956   *Bilingualism in the Americas*, Publication of American Dialect Society no. 26 (University, Ala.: University of Alabama Press).
1958   "Language Contact," in *8th Congress of Linguistics* (Oslo: Oslo University Press).
1966a   *Language Conflict and Language Planning: The Case of Modern Norwegian* (Cambridge, Mass.: Harvard University Press).
1966b   "Linguistics and Language Planning," in W. Bright *Sociolinguistics* (The Hague: Mouton).
1966c   "Dialect, Language and Nation," *American Anthropology* 68:922–935.
1971   "Bilingualism, Language Contact and Immigrant Languages," in T. A. Sebeok, ed., *Linguistics in North America*, Vol. 10 of *Current Trends in Linguistics*, (The Hague:Mouton).
HAVINGHURST, R. J.
1957   "Education Among American Indians: Individual and Cultural Aspects," in *Annals of the American Academy of Political and Social Sciences* 311:105–115.
HAVINGHURST, R. J., AND B. L. NEUGARTEN
1954   *American Indian and White Children* (Chicago: Chicago University Press).
HEARINGS. See Committee on Education and Labor.
HECHTER, M.
1975   *Internal Colonialism: The Celtic Fringe 1536–1966* (Los Angeles: University of California Press).
HEER, F.
1953   *The Intellectual History of Europe* (London: Weidenfeld).
HERMAN, S. R.
1961   "Explorations in the Social Psychology of Language Choice," *Human Relations* 16; and 1968 in *Readings in the Sociology of Language*, ed. J. A. Fishman (The Hague: Mouton).
HERTZ, F.
1944   *Nationality in History and Politics* (London).
HILLS, H. S.
1936   "The Effects of Bilingualism on the Measured Intelligence of Elementary Children of Italian Parentage," *Journal of Experimental Education* 5.
HOCKET, C. F.
1958   *A Course in Modern Linguistics* (New York: Macmillan).
HOLT, R. T., AND J. TURNER
1970   *The Methodology of Comparative Research* (New York: Free Press).
HOOK, SIDNEY
1952   In *The Social Implications of Scientific Progress—Mid Century*, ed. E. Burchard (New York: The Free Press).
HOPKINS, T. R.
1972   "The Federal Government as Agent of Cross Cultural Education in Alaska," in *Education in the North: Conference on Cross Cultural Education in the Circum Polar Nations*, ed. F. Darnell (Juneau: Alaska University Press).
1975   Comments in *Educational Research Bulletin* 3 (Albuquerque: Bureau of Indian Affairs).
HOPPER, E.
1971   *Readings in the Theory of Educational Systems* (London: Hutchinson).
HOUGH, J. F.
1972   "The Soviet System: Petrification or Pluralism?", in *Problems of Communism* 2.

HUMBOLDT, von C. W.
1903-60   *Collected Works*, ed. Leitzman (Berlin: Behr). Reprinted, Bonn: Dimmlers Verlag, 1960.
HUSEN, T. (ED.)
1967   *International Study of Achievement in Mathematics*, 2 vols. (Stockholm: Almqvist and Wiskell).
HYMES, D.
1967   "Models of Interaction of Languages and Social Settings," *Journal of Social Forces* 23:8–28.
1970   "Linguistic Aspects of Comparative Political Research," in *The Methodology of Comparative Research*, ed R. T. Holt and J. Turner (New York: Free Press).
IMEDADZE, N. V.
1960   "The Psychological Characteristics of Early Bilingualism," *Voprosy psikhologii* [*Problems in Psychology*], no. 2 (In Russian).
1967   "On the Psychological Nature of Child Speech Formation under the Conditions of Exposure to Two Languages," *International Journal of Psychology* 2:129–132.
ISAAC, H. R.
1975   "Basic Group Identity: The Idols of the Tribe," in *Ethnicity: Theory and Experience*, ed N. Glazer and D. Moynihan (Cambridge, Mass.: Harvard University Press).
ISAYEV, M. I.
1977   *National Languages in the USSR: Problems and Solutions* (Moscow: Progress Publishers).
ISUPOV, A. A.
1964   *Ethnic Composition of the Peoples of the USSR* (Moscow: Progress Publishers).
IZVESTIYA [ITOGI VESSOYUZNAYA PEREPISI NASELLNIYA—SOVIET CENSUS]
1958   December
1971   April
JACKSON, J. A. (ED.)
1969   *Migration: Sociological Studies* 2 (Cambridge: Cambridge University Press).
JACKSON, K.
1953   *Language and History in Early Britain* (Edinburgh: Edinburgh University Press).
JAKOBSON, R.
1945   "The Beginnings of National Self Determination in Europe," *The Review of Politics* 7:29–42.
1969   *Selected Writings*. Vol. 1 (The Hague: Mouton).
JANSEN, C.
1969   "Some Sociological Aspects of Migration," in *Migration: Sociological Studies* 2, ed. J. A. Jackson (Cambridge: Cambridge University Press).
JARAMILLO, MARI-LUCI
1977   "Cultural Pluralism? Implications for the Curriculum," in *Pluralism in a Democratic Society*, ed. M. Tumin and W. Plotch (New York: Praeger).
JENKINS, J.
1861   "Report on the State of Popular Education in the Welsh Districts of North Wales, Neath and Merthyr in South Wales," in *Commission of Enquiry into the State of Popular Education in England and Wales*.
JENSEN, H.
1970   *Sign, Symbol and Script* (London: Allen and Unwin).
JESPERSEN, O.
1925   *Mankind, Nation and Individual from a Linguistic Point of View* (Bloomington: Indiana University Press).
JOHN, A. H.
1960   *The Industrial Development of South Wales* (Cardiff: University of Wales Press).

JOHN-STEINER, V.
1970   "Cognitive Development in the Bilingual Child," in *Bilingualism and Language Contact*, ed. J. E. Alatis (Washington, D.C.: Georgetown University Press).
JOHN-STEINER, V., AND V. M. HORNER
1971   *Early Childhood Bilingual Education* (New York: Modern Language Association of America).
JOHN-STEINER, V., AND E. SOUBERMAN
1977   "Educational Perspectives of Bilingual Education," in *Frontiers of Bilingual Education*, ed. B. Spolsky and R. L. Cooper (Rowley, Mass.: Newbury House Press).
JOHNSTON, R.
1967   "Language Use in the Homes of Polish Immigrants to Western Australia," *Lingua* 18.
JONES, A. H. M.
1956   "Slavery in the Ancient World," *Economic History Review* 6.
JONES, EMRYS
1967   "The Changing Distribution of the Celtic Languages in the British Isles," *Transactions of the Honourable Society of Cymmrodorion*.
JONES, GRIFFITH
1740–46 *The Welch Piety, Letters to Society for Propagation of Christian Knowledge (SPCK)*.
JONES, H. R.
1965   "A Study of Rural Migration in Central Wales," *Transactions of the Institute of British Geographers* 37:31–45.
JONES, KILSBY
1859   *The Educational State of Wales*.
JONES, P. N.
1969   "Some Aspects of Immigration to the Glamorgan Coalfield," *Transactions of the Honourable Society of Cymmrodorion*.
JONES, W. R.
1938   "Bilingualism and Intellectual Development," *Higher Education* 6:10–19.
1955   *Bilingualism and Reading Ability in English* (Cardiff: University of Wales Press).
1959   *Bilingualism and Intelligence* (Cardiff: University of Wales Press).
1960a   *Bilingualism and Reading Ability in English* (Cardiff: University of Wales Press).
1960b   "A Critical Study of Bilingualism and Non-Verbal Intelligence," *British Journal of Educational Psychology* 14.
1966   *Bilingualism in Welsh Education* (Cardiff: University of Wales Press).
JONES, W. R., AND J. R. MORRISON, J. ROGER, H. SAER
1957   *The Educational Attainment of Bilingual Children* (Cardiff: University of Wales Press).
JONES, W. R., AND W. A. C. STEWART
1951   "Bilingualism and Verbal Intelligence," *British Journal of Psychology (Statistical)* 14.
JOSEPHY, A. M.
1968   *The Indian Heritage of America* (New York: Knopf).
JUGEMAN, F. H.
1959   "Structuralism in History," *Word* 15.
KALLEN, H.
1956   *Cultural Pluralism and the American Idea* (Philadelphia: University of Pennsylvania Press).
KARI, J., AND B. SPOLSKY
1973   *Trends in the Study of Athapascan Language Maintenance*, Navajo Reading Study, Report 21 (Albuquerque: University of New Mexico).
KASDAN, L.
1970   Introduction to *Migration and Anthropology: Proceedings of the 1970 Annual*

Meeting of the American Ethnological Society, ed., R. F. Spencer (London: University of Seattle Press).

KAY-SHUTTLEWORTH, J.
1873   *Thoughts and Suggestions on Certain Social Problems* (London: Longman).
KEECH, W. R.
1972   "Language Diversity and Political Conflict," *Comparative Politics*, April 1972.
KELLY, L. C.
1968   *The Navajo Indians and Federal Indian Policy* (Tucson: University of Arizona Press).
KHODACHEK, V. M.
1973   "On the Formation of Population in the Region of the Far North of the USSR," in *Problems of the Geography of Population and Labour Resources* (Leningrad: University Press) (In Russian).
KHOLMOGOROV, A. I.
1970   *International Character of the Soviet Nations* (Moscow: Mysl) (In Russian).
KJOLSETH, R.
1972   "Bilingual Education Programmes in the United States: for Assimilation or Pluralism?" in *The Language Education of Minority Children*, ed. B. Spolsky (Rowley, Mass.: Newbury House Press).
KLEMENT'EV, E. I.
1971   "Linguistic Processes in Karelia," *Sovetskaia etnografiia* 6 (In Russian).
KLOSS, H.
1966a   "Types of Bilingual Communities," *Sociological Enquiry* 31.
1966b   "Bilingualism and Nationalism," *Journal of Social Issues* no. 23.
1974   *The Bilingual Tradition in the United States* (Rowley, Mass.: Newbury House Press).
KLUCKHOHN, C.
1954   "Culture and Behavior," in *Handbook of Social Psychology*, ed. G. Lindzey (Cambridge: Addison-Wesley).
1962   *Culture and Behavior* (New York: Free Press).
KOMMUNIST (Moscow)
1965, 1966
KOMMUNIST (Erevan)
1943, 1956
KOZLOV, V.
1967   "On the Concept of Ethnic Community," *Sovetskaia etnografiia* 2 (In Russian).
KRAUSS, M. E.
1973a   "Eskimo-Aleut," in *Linguistics in North America*, in T. A. Sebeok, ed., *North American Linguistics*, Vol. 10 of *Current Trends in Linguistics* (The Hague: Mouton).
1973b   "Na-Dene," in T. A. Sebeok, ed., *Linguistics in North America*, Vol. 10 of *Current Trends in Linguistics* (The Hague: Mouton).
1973c   *The Alaska Native Language Center Report* (Juneau: University of Alaska).
KROEBER, A. L.
1939   "An Outline of the History of American Indian Linguistics," *American Council of Learned Societies Bulletin* 29.
KUHN, T. S.
1970   *The Structure of Scientific Revolutions* (London: The University of Chicago Press).
KUPER, L.
1969   "Plural Societies: Perspectives and Problems," in *Pluralism in Africa*, ed. L. Kuper and M. G. Smith (University of California Press).
1974   *Race, Class and Power* (London: Duckworth).
LADEFOGED, P., R. GLICK, AND C. CRIPER
1972   *Language in Uganda* (London: Oxford University Press).

LAMBERT, W. E., AND G. R. TUCKER
1972   *Bilingual Education of Children: The St. Lambert Experiment* (Rowley, Mass.: Newbury House Press).
LANDAR, M. J.
1973   "The Tribes and Languages of North America: A Checklist," in T. A. Sebeok, ed., *Linguistics of North America*, Vol. 10 of *Current Trends in Linguistics* (The Hague: Mouton).
LARA-BRAUD, J.
1971   *Bilingualism for Texas: Education for Fraternity* (Austin: Texas Conference of Churches).
LARNIN, O. V.
1971   "Social Demographic Aspects of Urbanization in the USSR," *Problemy urbanizatzii*, 32–45 (In Russian).
LAWYERS' COMMITTEE FOR CIVIL RIGHTS UNDER THE LAW
1975   *Model Legislation and Regulations for Bilingual-Bicultural Education* (Washington, D.C.: Center for Applied Linguistics, Arlington, Virginia.)
LAYMAN, M.
1942   "A History of Indian Education in the United States" (Ph.D. dissertation: University of Minnesota).
LEACH, E. R.
1954   *Political Systems of Highland Burma: A Study of Kuchin Social Structure* (London: Oxford University Press).
LEACH, J. N.
1971   "Cultural Factors Affecting the Adjustment of Puerto-Rican Children," Mimeograph. (Storrs, Conn.: University of Connecticut).
LEAP, W. L.
1973   "Language Pluralism in a Southwestern Pueblo: Some Comments on Isletan English," in *Bilingualism in the Southwest*, ed. P. R. Turner (Tucson: University of Arizona Press).
LEIBOWITZ, A. H.
1971   "A History of Language Instruction in American Indian Schools," in U.S. Department of Interior *Curricular Bulletin* 3 (Albuquerque: Bureau of Indian Affairs).
LeMAIRE, H. B.
1966   "Franco-American Efforts on Behalf of the French Language in New England," in *Language Loyalty in the United States*, ed. J. A. Fishman (The Hague: Mouton).
LENIN, V. I.
1918   *The State and the Revolution* (Berlin: Wilemsdorf Verlag Die Aktion).
1962   *The Economic Content of Narodism* (Moscow: Vol. 1 collected works)
LERNER, D.
1958   *The Passing of Traditional Society* (New York: Free Press).
LE TELEGRAMME DE BREST (Periodical)
1974   February 21.
LEVINE, R. A., AND D. T. CAMPBELL
1972   *Ethnocentricism: Theories of Conflict, Ethnic Group Behavior and Attitude* (New York: John Wiley).
LEWIS, B.
1961   *The Emergence of Modern Turkey* (London: Oxford University Press).
LEWIS, D. G.
1959   "Differences in Attainment between Primary Schools in Mixed Language Areas," *British Journal of Educational Psychology* 60.
LEWIS, E. G.
1968   "Reading Standards in English and Welsh," Mimeograph. (Cardiff: Welsh Office, Department of Education).

1972	*Multilingualism in the Soviet Union: Language Policy and its Implementation* (The Hague: Mouton).
1974	"The Sociological Bases of the Interaction of Soviet Languages," in *Forum Linguisticum* 1 and 2, ed. C. Gutknecht.
1976	"Attitude to Language among Children and Adults in Wales," *International Journal of Sociology of Language* 4.
1977a	"Cross National Study of Bilingual Education," *International Journal of Sociology of Language* 14.
1977b	"The Development of Literacy in the Soviet Union," in *Language and Literacy: Current Issues*, ed. T. P. Gorman (Teheran: International Institute for Adult Literacy Methods).
1977c	"The Present Language Situation in the Soviet Union," in *The Languages and Literatures of the Non-Russian Peoples of the Soviet Union: Papers and Proceedings of the Tenth Annual Conference*, ed. G. Thomas (MacMaster University, Canada).
1977d	"Bilingualism and Bilingual Education: The Ancient World to the Renaissance," in *Bilingual Education: An International Perspective*, ed. J. A. Fishman (Rowley, Mass.: Newbury House Press).
1978a	"Bilingualism and Bilingual Education: The Ancient World to the Renaissance," [expanded version] in *Frontiers in Bilingual Education*, ed. B. Spolsky and R. L. Cooper (Rowley, Mass.: Newbury House Press).
1978b	"Migration and the Decline of the Welsh Language," in *Advances in the Study of Societal Multilingualism*, ed. J. A. Fishman (The Hague: Mouton).
1978c	"Bilingualism and Social Change in the Soviet Union," in *Case Studies in Bilingual Education*, ed. B. Spolsky and R. L. Cooper (Rowley, Mass.: Newbury House).
1978d	"Bilingual Education in Wales," in *Case Studies in Bilingual Education*, ed. B. Spolsky and R. L. Cooper (Rowley, Mass.: Newbury House Press).
1978e	"A Comparative Study of Language Contact: The Influence of Demographic Factors in Wales and the Soviet Union," in *Language and Society* (ed. W. McCormack & S. Wurm) Proceedings of IXth International Congress of Anthropoligical & Ethnological Sciences (The Hague: Mouton).
1978f	"What Are the International Dimensions of Bilingual Education?" In J. Alatis, ed. *International Dimensions of Bilingual Education* (Georgetown University Round Table on Languages & Linguistics).
1978g	"Types of Bilingual Communication," in ibid.

LEWIS, E. G. (ED.)

1953	*The Place of Welsh and English in the Schools of Wales: Report of Central Advisory Council on Education* (London: Her Majesty's Stationery Office).
1965	*Bilingualism in Education: Report of UNESCO, U.K. Commission* (London: Her Majesty's Stationery Office).

LEWIS, E. G., AND CAROLYN MASSAD

1975	*The Teaching of English as a Foreign Language in Ten Countries* (Stockholm: Almqvist and Wiksell).

LEWIS, H.

1963	*Angles and Britons* (Cardiff: University of Wales Press).

LIEBERSON, S.

1964	"An Extension of Greenberg's Linguistic Diversity Measures," *Language* 40: 526–531.
1966	"Language Questions in the Censuses," *Sociological Enquiry* 36:262–279.
1967	"Theme," in *Description and Measurement of Bilingualism* (Toronto: University of Toronto Press).
1970	*Language and Ethnic Relations in Canada* (New York: John Wiley).
1975	"The Course of Mother Tongue Diversity in Nations," *American Journal of Sociology* 81, no. 1.

LIJPHART, A.
1960   "Consociational Democracy," in *Consociational Democracy*, ed. K. D. McRae (Toronto: McLelland and Stewart).
1971   "Cultural Development and Theories of Cultural Integration," *Canadian Journal of History* 5.
LINZ, J. J., AND A. MIGUEL
1975   "Differences and Comparisons: The Eight Spains," in *Comparing Nations: The Use of Quantitative Data in Cross National Research*, ed. R. L. Merrit and S. Rokkan (New Haven: Yale University Press).
LIVERSIDGE, J.
1961   *Britain in the Roman Empire* (London: Cape)
LORGE, T., AND F. MAGANS
1954   "Vestibule Versus Regular Classes for Puerto Rican Migrant Pupils," *Teachers College Report* no. 55 (New York: Columbia University Press).
LORIMER, F.
1946   *The Population of the Soviet Union* (Geneva: League of Nations).
LORWIN, V. R.
1965   "Belgium: Conflict and Compromise," in *Consociational Democracy*, ed., K. D. McRae (Toronto: McLelland and Stewart).
1970   "Linguistic Pluralism and Political Tension in Modern Belgium," *Canadian Journal of History* 5.
LOVEJOY, E.
1964   *The Great Chain of Being* (Cambridge, Mass.: Harvard University Press).
LURIA, A. R.
1932   *The Nature of Human Conflicts* [trans. 1967]. (New York: Washington Square Press).
1955   "The Role of Language in the Formation of Temporary Connections," *Voprosy psikologii* 1:73–87 (In Russian).
1956   "The Disturbance of Reading and Writing in Polyglots," *Fiziologicheskiy zhrnal SSSR sechenova* 2 (In Russian).
1958   "Brain Disorders and Language Analysis," *Language and Speech* 1, no. 1.
1959   "The Directive Function of Speech—Parts I and II," *Word* 15.
1960   "Verbal Regulation of Behavior" in *The Central Nervous System and Behavior*, ed. M. A. B. Brazier (New York: Macey Foundation).
1961   *The Role of Speech in the Regulation of Normal and Abnormal Behaviour* (Oxford: Pergamon Press).
1963   *Human Brain and Psychological Processes* (Moscow: Ak. Nauk) (In Russian).
1967   "Problems and Facts in Neurolinguistics," *International Social Sciences Journal* 19.
LURIA, A. R., AND C. S. VINOGRADOVA
1959   "An Objective Analysis of the Dynamics of the Semantic System," *British Journal of Psychology* 50.
LURIA, A. R., AND F. YUDOVICH
1959   *Speech and Development of the Mental Processes of the Child* (London: Pergamon Press). [Quoted from 2nd ed., 1966]
MACKEY, W. F.
1978   "A Typology of Bilingual Education," in *Bilingual Schooling in the United States*, ed. T. Andersson and M. Boyer (2nd ed., Austin: National Educational Development Publishers, Inc.).
MacNAMARA, J. (ED.)
1967   "Problems of Bilingualism," in *The Journal of Social Issues* 23.
MADSEN, M. C., AND A. SHAPIRA
1970   "Comparative and Competitive Behavior of Urban Afro-American, Anglo, Mexican-American, and Mexican Children," *Developmental Psychology* 3.

MAGNER, T. F.
1967   "Language and Nationalism in Yugoslavia," *Canadian Slavic Studies* 1.
MALHERBE, E. G.
1934   *The Bilingual School: A Study of Bilingualism in South Africa* (London: Longman).
1961   "Learning English in a Bilingual Country," *Proceedings of the English Academy of South Africa* (Natal).
MALINOWSKI, B.
1945   *The Dynamics of Cultural Change* (New Haven: Yale University Press).
MALITZ, F. W. VON
1975   *Living and Learning in Two Languages: Bilingual-Bicultural Education in the United States* (New York: McGraw Hill).
MANDELBAUM, D. C.
1957   *Selected Writings of Edward Sapir* (Berkeley: University of California Press).
MANN, H.
1844   *Seventh Annual Report to Massachusetts Board of Education.*
MANNHEIM, K.
1936   *Ideology and Utopia* (London: Kegan Paul).
MATHER, E.
1973   Cited by Krauss in T. A. Sebeok, ed. *North American Linguistics*, Vol. 10 of *Current Trends in Linguistics* (The Hague: Mouton).
MATOSSIAN, M. A. K.
1962   *The Impact of Soviet Politics in Armenia* (Leiden: n.p.).
MAYER, K.
1956   "Cultural Pluralism and Linguistic Equilibrium in Switzerland," in *Demographic Analysis: Readings*, ed. J. Spengler and D. Duncan (Glencoe, Ill.: The Free Press).
McRAE, K. D. (ED.)
1974   *Consociational Democracies* (Toronto: McLelland and Stewart).
MEAD, G.
1934   *Mind, Self and Society* (Chicago: University of Chicago Press).
MEILLET, A.
1951   *Linguistique Historique et Linguistique Générale*, Vol. 12 (Paris: Société de Linguistique de Paris).
MERIONETHSHIRE EDUCATION COMMITTEE REPORT
1958   *Report on the Language Survey* (Dolgellau).
1960   *Report on the Language Survey* (Dolgellau: n.p.).
MERRIAM, L.
1928   *Problems of Indian Administration* (Baltimore: Johns Hopkins University Press).
MERRIT, R. L., AND S. ROKKAN (EDS.)
1966   *Comparing Nations: The Use of Quantitative Data in Cross National Research* (New Haven: Yale University Press).
MICHELENA, J. A. SILVA
1973   "Dependent Nations" in *Building States and Nations*, ed. S. Eisenstadt and S. Rokkan, Vol. 2 (Beverly Hills: Sage Publishers).
1974   *The Illusion of Democracy in Dependent Nations* (Cambridge, Mass.: M.I.T. Press).
MILL, J. S.
1947   "On Liberty," in *Selected Essays*, ed. F. Alford (London: Beacon Press).
MILLER, W. R.
1972   "Obsolescing Languages: The Case of the Shoshoni Language," *American Indian Education*, Winter 1.
1975   "Ethnography of Speaking." Mimeograph. Salt Lake City: University of Utah.
MILLS, R.
1836   *The Duty of the Welsh to Retain their Language.*

MINISTRY OF EDUCATION, WELSH OFFICE OF EDUCATION
1927   *Welsh in Education and Life* (London: Her Majesty's Stationery Office).
1932   *Memorandum I–Suggestions to Teachers* (London: Her Majesty's Stationery Office).
1936   *Bilingualism in Primary Schools* (London: Her Majesty's Stationery Office).
1938   *Language in Secondary Schools* (London: Her Majesty's Stationery Office).
1953   *Curriculum and the Community* (London: Her Majesty's Stationery Office).
1960   *Standards of Reading* (London: Her Majesty's Stationery Office).
MINTZ, S. W.
1961   "Review Article on Slavery" by S. Elkins, *American Anthropology* 63.
1966   "Review of M. I. Finley, *Slavery* (1965)," *Higher Education* 10.
1970   "Some Aspects of Involuntary Migration and Slavery," in *Migration and Anthro-
        pology: Proceedings of 1970 Annual Meeting of Ethnological Society*, ed. R. F.
        Spencer (London: University of Washington Press).
MONMOUTHSHIRE EDUCATION COMMITTEE
1953   *Survey of Reading Ability* (Newport).
1960   *Report on the Language Survey* (Newport: n.p.).
MOORE, J. W., AND A. CUELLAR
1970   *Mexican Americans* (Englewood Cliffs, N.J.: Prentice-Hall).
MORDVINOV, A. E.
1950   "The Development of the Languages of Socialist Nations in the USSR," *Problems
        of Philosophy*, no. 3 (In Russian).
MULLER, G. E., AND A. PILZECKER
1900   *Experimenelle Psychologie*, Vol. 1 (Freiburg: Mohr).
NARODNI OBRAZOVANNIYE SSR. TSIFRAKH (Periodical)
1966   Moscow (In Russian).
NASH, PHILLEO
1966   "Education: The Chance to Choose," *Indian Education* (February).
NATIONAL ADVISORY COUNCIL ON BILINGUAL EDUCATION (U.S.)
1976   *Annual Report: Quality Education for all Children* (Washington, D.C.: U.S. Of-
        fice of Education: Office of Bilingual Education and National Institute of Education).
NATIONAL FOUNDATION FOR EDUCATIONAL RESEARCH AND WELSH JOINT
EDUCATION COMMITTEE [NFER/WJEC]
1969   *Survey of Educational Attainments in Wales* (Cardiff: WJEC).
NATIONAL INSTITUTE FOR BILINGUAL EDUCATION (U.S.)
1973   *Report* (Washington, D.C.: Department of Interior, Bureau of Indian Affairs).
NAYLOR, G. H.
1971   "Learning Styles at Six Years in Two Ethnic Groups in a Disadvantaged Area"
        (Ph.D. dissertation, University of Southern California).
NEW YORK TIMES
        June 21, 1976; January 3 and January 30, 1977; and May 2, 1977; articles on
        Bilingual Education.
NOAH, H. J.
1973   "Defining Comparative Education," in *Relevant Methods in Comparative Educa-
        tion*, ed. R. Edwards (Paris: UNESCO).
NORODNOYE OBRAZOVANIYE (In Russian).
NOVAK, M.
1977   "Cultural Pluralism for Individuals: A Social Vision," in *Pluralism in Democratic
        Society*, ed. M. Tumin and W. Plotch (New York: Praeger).
NOZICK, R.
1974   *Anarchy, State and Utopia* (New York: Basic Books).
NUMELIN, B.
1937   *The Wandering Spirit: A Study of Human Migration* (London: Macmillan).
OAKSHOTT, M.
1962   *Political Education* (London: Oxford University Press).
OFFICE OF SPECIAL CONCERNS
1974   *A Study of Selected Socio-Economic Characteristics of Ethnic Minorities Based*

on the 1970 Census. Vol. 1, *Americans of Spanish Origin;* Vol. 2, *Asian Americans;* Vol. 3, *American Indians* (Washington, D.C.: U.S. Department of the Interior).

OHANNESIAN, S.
1967   *The Study of the Problems of Teaching English to American Indians* (Washington, D.C.: Center for Applied Linguistics).

OHANNESIAN, S., AND W. W. GAGE
1967   *Teaching English to Speakers of Choctaw, Navajo and Papago* (Washington, D.C.: U.S. Department of the Interior, Bureau of Indian Affairs).

OKLADNIKOV, A. P.
1968   *Yakutia Before its Incorporation.* Arctic Institute of North America, Publication no. 8.

OKUTUCILAR GAZETASI (Teacher's Gazette) (In Russian).
1967

ORNSTEIN, J.
1951   "The Archaic and the Modern in the Spanish of New Mexico," *Hispania* 34:137–142.

ORR, J.
1953   *Words and Sounds in English and French* (Oxford: Blackwell).

ORVIK, J. M.
1975   *Definition of Bilingual Education in Alaska.* Mimeograph. (Juneau: University of Alaska).

PARK, R. E.
1950   *Race and Culture* (Glencoe, Ill.: The Free Press).

PARMING, T.
1972   "Population Changes in Estonia, 1935-70," *Population Studies* 25:55–78.

PARRY, J. H.
1972   "Plural Society in the Southwest: A Historical Comment," in *Plural Society in the Southwest,* ed. E. H. Spicer (New York: Interbook, Inc.).

PARSONS, TALCOTT
1975   "Some Theoretical Considerations on the Nature and Trends of Ethnicity," in *Ethnicity: Theory and Experience,* ed. N. Glazer and D. Moynihan (Cambridge, Mass.: Harvard University Press).

PATTERSON, T.
1975   "Context and Choice in Ethnic Allegiance," in *Ethnicity: Theory and Experience,* ed. N. Glazer and D. Moynihan (Cambridge, Mass.: Harvard University Press).

PAULSTON, C. BRATT
1974a   "Questions Concerning Bilingual Education." Paper for American Anthropological Association Conference, University of Pittsburgh, Pittsburg, Pa.
1974b   *Implications of Language Learning Theory for Language Planning Concerns* (Washington, D.C.: Center for Applied Linguistics).
1974c   *Ethnic Relations and Bilingual Education: Accounting for Contrasting Data.* Mimeograph. (Pittsburgh: University of Pittsburgh).
1976   *Language and Ethnic Boundaries.* Mimeograph. (Pittsburgh: University of Pittsburgh).
1977   "Theoretical Perspectives on Bilingual Education Programs." Paper for National Institute of Education Conference on Bilingual Education, Washington, D.C.

PEAL, E., AND W. E. LAMBERT
1962   "The Relation of Bilingualism to Intelligence, *Psychology Monographs (General and Applied)* no. 27.

PENNAR, J. I. (ED.)
1970   "Population Migration and the Utilization of Labour Resources," *Voprosy ekonomiya* (September).
1971   *Modernization and Diversity in Soviet Education with Special Reference to Nationality Groups* (New York: Praeger Publishers).

PEREVEDENTSEV, V. I.
1965   "Relation of Population Migration and Ethnic Convergence," in *World Population Conference Transactions*, 513–518.
1966   "Ethnic Factors in Population Movement," *Z. Ak. Nauk. Seores. Geog. IV*
1970   "Population Migration and Urbanization of Labor Resources, *Ekonomiya* 9
PETERSON, S. A.
1948   *How Well Are Indian Children Educated?* (Washington, D.C.: U.S. Department of Interior Indian Services).
PETERSON, W.
1958a   "Migration: Social Aspects," *International Encyclopedia of the Social Sciences*, Vol. 10.
1958b   "A General Typology of Migration," *American Social Sciences Review* 23:256–266.
1975   "On the Subnations of Europe," in *Ethnicity: Theory and Experience*, ed. N. Glazer and D. Moynihan (Cambridge, Mass.: Harvard University Press).
PHILIPS, S. V.
1970   "Acquisition of Rules for Appropriate Speech Usage," in *Bilingualism and Language Contact: Anthropological, Linguistic, Psychological and Sociological Aspects*, ed. J. E. Alatis. Monograph series no. 23 (Washington, D.C.: Georgetown University Press).
PHILPOTT, S. B.
1970   "The Implication of Migration for Sending Societies: Some Theoretical Considerations," in *Migration and Anthropology: Proceedings of the 1970 Anthropological Society*, ed. R. E. Spencer (London: University of Washington Press).
PIRENNE, H.
1925   *Medieval Cities* (Princeton: Princeton University Press).
POKSHISHEVSKIY, V. V.
1969a   "Urbanization and Ethnogeographical Processes," in *Problemy urbanizatsii* (Moscow: Ak. Nauk).
1969b   "Ethnic Processes in Soviet Nationalities," Sov. Etn. 5
1969c   "Population Migration in the USSR," *Priroda* 9:67–75.
POOL, A. L.
1951   *Medieval England* (rev. ed.; Oxford: Oxford University Press).
POOL, J.
1969   "Language Development and Language Diversity," *American Political Science Association* (September).
POOLE, DE SOLA
1972   "Plural Society in the Southwest: A Comparative Perspective," in *Plural Society in the Southwest*, ed. R. F. Spicer (New York: Interbook, Inc.).
PORTAL, R.
1969   *The Slavs* (London: Weidenfeld).
PORTER, J.
1975   "Ethnic Pluralism in Canadian Perspectives," in *Ethnicity: Theory and Experience*, ed. N. Glazer and D. Moynihan (Cambridge, Mass.: Harvard University Press).
POULTNEY, J. W.
1968   "Review of *Georgev 1966*," *Language* 44.
POWERS, J. F.
1965   *Brotherhood through Education: A Guide for Teachers of American Indians* (Fayette: Upper Iowa University Press).
PRAVDA December 12, 1958; December 25, 1958; February 20, 1961; November 20, 1961; April 5, 1966; April 11, 1971; January 4, 1974 (In Russian).
PRICE, C.
1969   "The Study of Assimilation," in *Migration Sociological Studies* 2, ed. J. A. Jackson (Cambridge: Cambridge University Press).

PRICE-WILLIAMS, D.
1969   *Cross National Studies: Selected Readings* (London: Penguin Books).
PRICE-WILLIAMS, D., AND M. McCORD
1968   *The Study of Personality* (New York: Holt).
PRYCE, W. T. R.
1971   "Parish Registers and Visitations as Sources," *Transactions of the Honourable Society of Cymmrodorion.*
1972   "Approach to the Linguistic Geography of North East Wales," *Journal of the National Library of Wales* 12.
PYE, L. W., AND W. ROSTOW
1965   *Political Culture and Political Development* (Princeton: Princeton University Press).
RAMIREZ, M. A., AND M. CASTAÑEDA
1974   *Cultural Democracy, Bicognitive Development and Education* (New York: Academic Press).
RAVENSTEIN, E. G.
1885   "The Laws of Migration," *Journal of the Royal Statistical Society* 48:167–305 and 52:241–305.
RAWLS, J.
1973   *A Theory of Justice* (Oxford: Oxford University Press).
REES, O.
1858   "The Welsh and the English Language," [in Welsh] *Traethodydd* 41.
REGENTS OF THE UNIVERSITY OF THE STATE OF NEW YORK
1972   *A Statement of Policy* (Albany: State of New York).
REICHARD, G.
1945   "Language Diversity among the Navajo Indians," *International Journal of American Linguistics* 3.
REISTRA, M. A., AND C. E. JOHNSON
1964   "Changes of Attitude of Elementary School Children," *Journal of Experimental Education* 32.
REVOLUTSIA I NATSIONALNOSTI (In Russian).
1933
REX, J.
1959   "The Plural Society in Sociological Theory," *British Journal of Sociology* 10.
RICHARDS, HENRY
1884   *Letters and Essays on Wales* (London: James Clarke).
ROBERTS, G.
1567   *Welsh Grammar*
ROBINSON, W. S.
1952   "Indian Education and Missions in Colonial Virginia," *Journal of Southern History* 18:152–168.
ROKKAN, S. (ED.)
1968   *Comparative Research Across Cultures* (The Hague: Mouton).
ROOF, M. K.
1961   "Soviet Population Trends," *Soviet Survey* (July-September).
ROOS, P., AND E. C. ROOS
1975   "The Massachusetts Transitional Education Act," in *Inequality in Education* (Harvard University: Center for Law and Education).
ROOSEVELT, T.
1968   Quoted in L. Snyder, *The New Nationalism* (Ithaca: Cornell University Press).
ROWLANDS, D.
1886   "Education," *Traethodydd* 21.
ROWSE, A. L.
1957   "Tudor Expansion: The Transition from Medieval to Modern History," *William and Mary Quarterly* 14.

ROYAL COMMISSION ON BILINGUALISM AND BICULTURALISM IN CANADA
1965   4 vols. (Ottawa: Queen's Publishers).
RUBIN, V. (ED.)
1960   *Social and Cultural Pluralism in the Carribean* (New York Academy of Sciences, Vol. 83).
RUSSIAN CENSUS
1897   *Tsentral'niy Statisticheskiy Komitet-Pervaia*
SAER, D. J.
1922   "An Enquiry into the Effects of Bilingualism upon the Intelligence of Young Children," *Journal of Experimental Psychology* 6
1928   "Psychological Problems of Bilingualism," *Welsh Outlook* 15.
1932   "The Effects of Bilingualism on Intelligence," *British Journal of Educational Psychology* 14.
SAER, D. J., AND F. SMITH, J. HUGHES
1934   *The Bilingual Problem* (Wrexham: Hughes).
SAFA, H. I., AND B. M. du TOIT (EDS.)
1975   *Migration and Development* (The Hague: Mouton).
SALGANIK, L. H.
1975   "Fox Point," in *Inequality in Education* (Harvard University: Center for Law and Education).
SALISBURY, F.
1962   "Notes on Bilingualism and Linguistic Change in New Guinea," *Anthropological Linguistics* 4.
SALISBURY, J.
1547   *A Dictionary of English and Welsh* (Reprinted 1877)
SAMARIN, W. J.
1966   "Self Annulling Prestige Factors among Speakers of Creole," in *Sociolinguistics*, ed. W. Bright (The Hague: Mouton).
SAPIR, E.
1921   *Language* (New York: Harcourt Brace).
1949   *Selected Writings*, ed. David G. Mandelbaum (Berkeley: University of California Press).
SARNOFF, I.
1962   *Personality and Dynamic Development* (New York: John Wiley).
SAVILLE-TROIKE, M.
1973   *Bilingual Children: Resource Development* (Washington, D.C.: Center for Applied Linguistics).
1974   "Problems in Apachean Historical Linguistics," in *Southwest Areal Linguistics*, ed. G. D. Bills (San Deigo: San Diego State University Press).
SAVILLE-TROIKE, M., AND R. C. TROIKE
1970   *A Handbook of Bilingual Education* (Washington, D.C.: Center for Applied Linguistics).
SCHEUCH, E. K.
1961   "Cross National Comparison Using Aggregate Data," in *Comparing Nations: The Use of Quantitative Data in Cross National Research*, ed., R. L. Merritt and S. Rokkan (New Haven: Yale University Press).
SCHERMERHORN, R. A.
1974   "Ethnicity in the Perspective of the Sociology of Knowledge," *Ethnicity* 1.
SCHOOLS COUNCIL FOR ENGLAND AND WALES
1974   *Study of Attitudes to Welsh and English: Report*, ed. D. Sharp (Swansea, Wales: University College).
SCOTTISH COUNCIL FOR RESEARCH IN EDUCATION
1961   *Gaelic Speaking in Highland Schools* (London: University of London Press).

SEBEOK, T. A. (ED.)
1973   *Linguistics in North America*, Vol. 10 of *Current Trends in Linguistics* (The Hague: Mouton).
SEKAQUAPETAWA, H.
1972   "Preserving the Good Things of Hopi Life," in *Plural Society in the Southwest*, ed. E. H. Spicer and R. H. Thompson (New York: Interbook, Inc.).
SHAW, F.
1975   "Bilingual Education: An Idea Whose Time Has Come," *New York Affairs* 3.
SHERZER, J.
1973   "Area Linguistics in North America," in T. A. Sebeok *Linguistics in North America*, Vol. 10 of *Current Trends in Linguistics* (The Hague: Mouton).
SHIBUTANI, E., AND E. KWAN
1965   *Ethnic Stratification: A Comparative Approach* (New York: Macmillan).
SHILS, E.
1972   *The Intellectuals and Powers* (London: University of Chicago Press).
1975   *Center and Periphery: Essays in Macro-Sociology* (London: University of Chicago Press).
SHORE, M. SARAVIA
1974   *The Content Analysis of 125 Title VII Bilingual Programs, 1969-70*. Mimeograph. (New York City: Hunter College).
SILVERT, E.
1966   *The Conflict Society* (American Field Science)
SINDELL, P. S., AND R. WEINTROB
1972   "Cross Cultural Education in the North," in *Education in the North: Conference on Cross Cultural Education in the CircumPolar Nations*, ed. F. Darnell (Juneau: University of Alaska).
SLAGER, W. R. (ED.)
1970   *English for American Indians* (Washington, D.C.: Bureau of Indian Affairs).
SMITH, F.
1923   "Bilingualism and Mental Development," *British Journal of Psychology* 13.
SMITH, M. G.
1957   "Social and Cultural Pluralism," in *Social and Cultural Pluralism in the Carribean*, ed. V. Rubin, New York Academy of Sciences, Vol. 83.
1965   *The Plural Society in the British West Indies* (Berkeley: University of California Press).
1969   *Some Developments in the Analytical Framework of Pluralism* (Berkeley: University of California Press).
SMITH, O. D.
1932   "Comparison of Full Blooded Indians, Sedentary and Nomadic on Achievement Tests." (M.A. thesis, University of Denver).
SMITH, S.
1973   See H. Landar in *Linguistics in North America*, ed. T. A. Sebeok (The Hague: Mouton)
SOMMERFELT, ALF
1938   *La Langue et la Société* (Oslo: Instituit pour l'étude comparative des civilisations).
SOVETSKIY KIRGIZ
1956   February 11 (In Russian).
SOVIET CENSUS
1929   Vseoiuznaia Perepis Naseleniia 1926 goda (Moscow) Izdanie Tsentral'ngo Statiiteschkogo
1959   Itogi Vseiuznoia Perepis Naseleniia 1959 goda (Moscow)
1970   Itogi Vseiuznoia Perepis Naseleniia 1959 goda (Moscow)
SPEAR, F.
1972   *Culture in the Southwest*. Mimeograph. (Albuquerque: University of New Mexico).

SPENCER, R. F. (ED.)

1970   *Migration and Anthropology: Proceedings of the 1970 Annual Meeting, American Ethnological Society* (London: University of Washington Press).

SPENGLER, J., AND D. DUNCAN

1956   *Demographic Analysis:Selected Readings* (Glencoe, Ill.: The Free Press).

SPICER, E. H.

1962   *Cycles of Conquest: The Impact of Spain, Mexico and the United States on the Indians of the Southwest* (Tucson: University of Arizona Press).

1972   "Plural Society of the South West," in *Plural Society of the Southwest*, ed. E. H. Spicer and R. H. Thompson (New York: Interbook, Inc.).

SPICER, E. H., AND R. H. THOMPSON (EDS.)

1972   *Plural Society in the Southwest* (New York: Interbook, Inc.).

SPITZER, L.

1948   *Essays in Historical Semantics* (Oxford: Blackwell).

SPOLSKY, B.

1969   "Attitudinal Aspects of Second Language Learning," *Language Learning* 19.

1970   "Navajo Language Maintenance: Six-Year-Olds in 1969," in *Conference on Child Language* (Quebec: Laval University Press).

1971   "Literacy in the Vernaculars: The Case of the Navajo," in *Studies in Language and Linguistics*, ed. J. Ornstein (El Paso: University of Texas).

1972   "Advances in Navajo Bilingual Education 1962-72," *Curriculum Bulletin* 13 (Washington, D.C.: Bureau of Indian Affairs).

1973   "Trends in the Study of Athabaskan Language Maintenance and Bilingualism," *Navajo Reading Study Report* 21 (University of New Mexico).

1977a   "American Indian Education," *International Journal of Sociology of Language* 14; and in *Case Studies in Bilingual Education* (1978), ed. B. Spolsky and R. L. Cooper (Rowley, Mass.: Newbury House Press).

1977b   "The Establishment of Language Education Policy in Multilingual Societies," in *Frontiers of Bilingual Education*, ed. B. Spolsky and R. L. Cooper (Rowley, Mass.: Newbury House Press).

SPOLSKY, B. (ED.)

1972   *The Language Education of Minority Children: Readings* (Rowley, Mass.: Newbury House Press).

SPOLSKY, B., AND R. L. COOPER (EDS.)

1977   *Frontiers of Bilingual Education* (Rowley, Mass.: Newbury House Press).

1978   *Case Studies in Bilingual Education* (Rowley, Mass.: Newbury House Press).

SPOLSKY, B., AND J. KARI

1974   "Apachean Language Maintenance," *International Journal of Sociology of Language* 2.

STATISTICAL ABSTRACT OF THE UNITED STATES

1975   (Washington, D.C.: Bureau of Census).

STATISTIKI UKRANYI

1928   (Annual Publication) (In Russian).

STEPHENS, M.

1976   *Linguistic Minorities in Western Europe* (Llandysul: Gomer Press).

STEVENS, R. P.

1965   "Bilingual Experience and Psycholinguistic Ability," *Canadian Journal of Psychology* 5.

STEWARD, J. (ED.)

1956   *The People of Puerto Rico* (Urbana: University of Illinois Press)

STEWARD, J. H.

1963   *Theory of Culture Change* (Urbana: University of Illinois Press).

SWADESH, M.
1948   "Sociologic Notes on Obsolescent Languages," *International Journal of Applied Linguistics* 14:728–732.
1954   "Perspectives and Problems in Amerindian Comparative Linguistics," *Word* 10.
SWAIN, M., AND M. BRUCK
1975   "Immersion Education for the Majority Child," *Canadian Modern Languages Review* 32.
SWAIN, M., AND H. C. BARRICK
1978   "Bilingual Education in Canada: French and English, in *Case Studies in Bilingual Education*, ed. B. Spolsky and R. L. Cooper (Rowley, Mass.: Newbury House Press).
SWAIN, M. (ED.)
1972   *Bilingual Schooling; Some Experience in Canada and the United States* (Toronto: Ontario Institute for Study of Education).
SWANTON, J. R.
1952   *The Indian Tribes of North America* (Reprint 1968; Grosse Point Michigan: Scholarly Press).
SWEET (edited by Karl E. Taeuber et al.)
1978   *Social Demography* (San Francisco: Academic Press)
TABOURET-KELLER, A.
1972   "A Contribution to the Sociological Study of Language Maintenance and Shift," in *Advances in the Sociology of Language*, Vol. 2, ed. J. A. Fishman (The Hague: Mouton).
TAEUBER, I., AND C. TAEUBER
1971   *Peoples of the United States in the Twentieth Century* (Washington, D.C.: U.S. Bureau of Census).
TAIJFEL, H.
1970   "Some Aspects of National and Ethnic Loyalty," *Social Sciences Information* 9: 119–144.
TATEVOSAYAN, R. V.
1971   "Methods of Analysis of Inter-Region Migration in the USSR," *Problemy urbanizatsii* (In Russian).
TEITELBAUM, H., AND R. J. HILLER
1976   *Bilingual Education: The Legal Perspective* (MSS: Center for Applied Linguistics, Washington, D.C.).
TERENT'EVA, L. N.
1972   "Some Aspects of Ethnic Processes in the Volga and Ural Region," *Sovetskaia etnografiia* 6 (In Russian).
THOMAS, B.
1930   "The Migration of Labour into the Glamorgan Coalfield," *Economica* 1:0275–292.
THOMAS, B. (ED.)
1962   *The Welsh Economy: Studies in Expansion* (Cardiff: University of Wales Press).
THOMPSON, W. S., AND P. K. WHELPTON
1933   *Population Trends in the United States* (Washington, D.C.: U.S. Bureau of Census).
TIMES (OF LONDON)
1965   July 7; article on Bilingualism.
TILLY, C.
1965   *Migration to an American City* (Newark: University of Delaware Press).
TORNEY, J., AND C. TESCONI
1977   "Political Socialization Research and Respect for Ethnic Diversity" in *Pluralism in Democratic Society* ed. M. Tumin and W. Plotch (New York: Praeger).

TOUSSAINT, N.
1935   *Bilingisme et éducation* (Brussels: Lamertine).
TOVAR, A.
1954   "Linguistics and Psychology," in *Linguistics Today,* ed. A. Martinet and U. Weinreich (New York: Linguistic Circle of New York).
TREMENHEERE, I.
1840   "The State of Elementary Education in the Mining Districts of South Wales 1839-40," Appendix to *Report to Privy Council Committee on Education.*
TRUBETSKOY, N.
1927   *K. problemy russkogo samozponaniia* (Paris: Sobranei statei) (In Russian).
TUCKER, D. R., AND A. ANGELAN
1973   "Some Thoughts Concerning Bilingualism in Education," in *Anthropology and Language Science in Educational Development* (Paris: UNESCO).
TURNER, P. R. (ED.)
1973   *Bilingualism in the Southwest* (Tucson: University of Arizona Press).
TYLER, S.
1973   *A History of Indian Policy* (Washington, D.C.: Bureau of Indian Affairs).
UCHITELSKAYA GAZETA (In Russian).
1965, 1970, 1971, 1973
UNITED NATIONS
1963–78 *Year Book* (Paris: United Nations).
UNITED NATIONS, DEPARTMENT OF ECONOMIC AFFAIRS
1954   *Handbook of Population Census Methods* (New York: Statistical Office of the United Nations).
URQUAHART, M.
1967   *Historical Statistics of Canada* (Cambridge: Cambridge University Press).
U.S. BUREAU OF THE CENSUS
1960   *Historical Statistics of the U.S.: Colonial Times to 1957* (Washington, D.C.: U.S. Bureau of the Census).
1975   *Statistical Abstract of the United States* (Washington, D.C.: U.S. Bureau of the Census).
1976   *Current Population Studies Series P-23.60* (Washington, D.C.: U.S. Bureau of the Census).
U.S. COMMISSION ON CIVIL RIGHTS
1975   *A Better Chance to Learn: Bilingual/Bicultural Education* (Washington, D.C.: Government Printing Office).
U.S. DEPARTMENT OF JUSTICE
1960–74 *Immigration and Naturalization Service, Annual Reports* (Washington, D.C.: U.S. Department of Justice).
USSR
        Successive Congresses of the Communist Party (Moscow) (In Russian).
VAN DEN BERGHE, R. L.
1967   *Race and Racism* (New York: John Wiley).
VAN DEN BRANDE, A.
1967   "Elements of Sociological Analysis of the Impact of the Main Conflicts in Belgian Life," *Res Publica:* 457–469.
VASIL'EVA, E. K., ET AL
1970   "Current Ethnocultural Processes in Udmurtia," *Sovetskaia etnografiia* 2.
VOEGELIN, C. F., AND F. M. VOEGELIN
1973   "The Southwest and the Great Basin," in T. A. Sebeok, ed., *Linguistics in North America,* Vol. 10 of *Current Trends in Linguistics,* ed. T. A. Sebeok (The Hague: Mouton).

VOLKOV, E. Z.
1974   *Dynamics of the Population of the Soviet Union During 80 Years* (Moscow: University Press) (In Russian).
VOLKOVA, N. C.
1967   "Problems of Bilingualism in the North Caucasus," *Sovetskaia etnografiia* 1:27–40 (In Russian).
VOPROSI FILOSOFII
1950   No. 3 (In Russian).
1976   No. 5 (In Russian).
VOPROSI ISTORII
1966   Nos. 1, 4, 6, 7, 9 (In Russian).
VOPROSI RAZVITIYA LITERATURNYZ JAZYKOV NARODOV USSR
1964   (In Russian)
VYSSHAYA SHKOLA
1972   June 20; December 15
1973   April 20
WAGGONER, DOROTHY
1975   *Results of the Survey of Language Supplement to the July 1975 C.P.S.* Mimeograph. (Washington, D.C.: National Council for Educationl Statistics).
WATSON, W. W.
1963   *North America: Its Countries and Regions* (London: Longman).
WAX, M.
1964   *Formal Education in an American Indian Community* (Michigan: Society for the Study of Social Problems).
1971   "Review of Havinghurst Summary Report," *Human Organization* 30, no. 2.
WEBB, E. B.
1952   *Indian Life in the Old Missions* (Los Angeles: Lewis).
WEBER, MAX
1947   *The Theory of Social and Economic Organizations* (Glencoe, Ill.: The Free Press).
WEINREICH, U.
1953a   *Languages in Contact: Findings and Problems* (New York: Publications of the Linguistic Circle of New York).
1953b   "The Russification of Soviet Minority Langauges," in *Problems of Communism*, 46–57.
WEINSTEIN, H. R.
1942   "Language and Education in the Soviet Union," *American Slavonic and East European Review* 23.
WELSH JOINT EDUCATION COMMITTEE
1963   *Language Survey* (Cardiff: Welsh Joint Education Committee).
WHATMOUGH, J.
1956   *Language: A Modern Synthesis* (London: Secker).
WHITEHEAD, A. N.
1965   *Process and Reality* (Cambridge: Cambridge University Press).
WHITELY, W. H.
1971   *Language Use and Social Change: Problems of Multilingualism with Special Reference to Eastern Africa* (London: Oxford University Press).
WHORF, B. L.
1956   *Language, Thought and Reality*, ed. J. B. Carroll (New York: John Wiley).
WILLIAMS, GLANMOR
1967   *The Welsh Church from Conquest to Reformation* (Cardiff: University of Wales Press).
1971   "Language, Literacy and Nationality in Wales," *Welsh Historical Review* 56.
WILLIAMS, TREVOR
1934   "Gower: A Study of Language Movement," *Archeologica Cambrensis* 16.

1935   "Language Divides in South Wales," *Archeologica Cambrensis* 17.
WILLIAMS, W.
1848   Letter to Right Honourable Sir John Russell (MSS).
WILLIAMS, W. O.
1964   "The Survival of the Welsh Language after the Union of England and Wales," *Welsh Historical Review* 2.
YAZYKI LITERATURA ZAPINSKI
1972   May 17
YOUNG, CRAWFORD
1976   *The Politics of Cultural Pluralism* (Madison: University of Wisconsin Press).
YOUNG, K.
1931   *Social Attitudes* (New York: Holt).
YOUNG, R. W.
1972   "The Rise of the Navajo Tribe," in *Plural Society in the Southwest*, ed. E. H. Spicer (New York: Interbook, Inc.).
ZACHRISSON, R. E.
1927   *Romans, Kelts, and Saxons in Ancient Britain* (Uppsala: Uppsala University Press).
ZARYA VOSTOKA (In Russian).
1956   No. 4.
1967   No. 2.
1973   No. 2.
ZAVATSKAYA, M.
1963   "The New System of Primary Education in Action," *Narodnye obrazovaniye* 12 (In Russian).
ZIMMERMAN, H. E.
1934   "The Indian's Ability To Learn Mathematics According to Degree of Indian Blood" (M.A. thesis, Kansas Teachers College).
ZINTZ, M. V.
1963   *Education Across Cultures* (Dubuque, Iowa: Kendall Hunt Press).
ZIRKEL, P. A.
1977   "The Legal Vicissitudes of Bilingual Education," *Phi Delta Kappan* 5.

Index

Commission of Enquiry into Industrial Unrest, 111

Commission of Enquiry into the State of Education in Wales, 358

Commission on Civil Rights, 364; Reports, 324

communication, 5, 7, 46, 107, 202, 211, 233, 246, 248, 284, 343; mass media, 175, 226

Communist League of Youth, 243

Communist Party, 243; Central Committee, 352, 355

community, 31, 37, 38, 135, 140, 233, 321, 391; Amerindian variables, 328–29; bounded, 21–22; enclave, 16–19, 21, 74; home background study, 307–8; importance, 335; isolated, 14–16, 155; latencies, 201, 203; mobility, 25–41; segregated, 24–25; settings, 13–41; settlement, 79, 90, 143–44; sources of heterogeneity, 4–5

commuting. *See* migration.

compartmentalization, in Ireland, 90–91; in the Southwest United States, 131, 135; in Wales, 128

Congress, of the United States, 317, 346, 374, 375; House of Representatives, 317; Subcommittee on Education, 317

"Concorde," 132

Connecticut, 136, 178

Constitution, of the United States, 375

conquest, compared to immigration, 136

Coombs, L. M., 324

Cooper, R. L., 33–34

Coral Way School, 387–88

Cork county, 94

Cornish language, 83

Cornwall, 49, 95, 109

Corsicans, 346

Cortez, Colorado, 155

Coser, L., 216, 251

Craddock, J. R., 174

Cree language, 379

Creek, Confederacy, 22, 23, 35; language, 22, 35

Croat nationality, 16, 18, 347, 348

Croce, Benedetto, 388

Cromarty county, 87

Cromwell, 90

cross-national studies, 5, 9

Crow, language, 316, 379; tribe, 316–17

Crown, the; 90, 99

Cuba, 153, 174, 385; immigrants to the United States, 6, 13, 24, 28, 37, 141, 142, 143, 144, 172, 174, 175, 178, 239, 242; language needs, 327

culture, 4, 33, 134, 224, 327, 328, 331, 390–91; and language, 217–21, 221–22; artifacts, 218; as unconscious, 201; behavioral aspects, 219; contact variables, 45–49, 130, 236; diversity, 240–41, 328; Hellenistic,

221; Judeo-Christian, 221; nonhistoric, 221; pluralism as a rationale, 216–42 passim, 243; Western European, 146

Culver City, California, 156; immersion program, 384

Current Population Survey of the United States, 150, 179

Cymmrodorian Society, 359

Cypriot nationality, 18, 24, 37, 73, 80, 163

Cyrillic alphabet, 352

Czechoslovakia, 34; language, 351; nationality, 18, 30, 37, 73, 80, 163, 347, 348

Daalder, H., 239

Dade county, Florida, 25, 254, 256, 258, 270, 317; program, 385–87

Daghastan, nationality, 4, 21, 80; region, 15, 50–51, 64, 250, 311, 353, 355, 357

Dahrendorf, R., 240

Danube, 37

Darghin language, 353

Darnell, F., 136

Dauzat, linguist, 97

Davies, E. R., 100

Dee, 103

Delaware, 132

delinquency, 343

demography, 26, 332; consequences of immigration, 147, 149; coefficient of concentration, 348; diffusion variables, 5–6; dispersal index, 78; distributional index, 119; group status, 349

Denbighshire, 107, 115, 119, 120, 124

Denmark, 18, 348, 349; language, 194, 349; nationality, 18, 188

Denver, Colorado, 156, 331

Department of the Interior, 346, 369

Department of Health, Education and Welfare, 369, 373

depopulation intensifying ethnicity, 116

deportation, 36, 40, 67

Derbyshire, 343

Dešeriev, Y. D., 207, 266, 291

Despres, L. A., 235

Detroit, Michigan, 28

Deutsch, K., 5, 211

Devon county, 111

Dewey, John, 215

diaspora, of Tatars, 67

Dickinson, W. S., 85

displaced persons. *See* refugees

Disraeli, Benjamin, 214

Dniester, 47

Dolgan, 61

Don river, 47, 50

Donegal county, 94

Donetsk Oblast, 24

Doob, L. W., 17

Dostoevsky, F., 51

448 / *Index*

Lamuts nationality, 61
Lancashire, 107
Landsmol, 244
langue d'oc, 17, 33
Languedoc, district, 17; language, 346
language, 202, 205, 213, 220, 223, 236, 370, 390; and psychology, 343–45; and unification, 246–48; appropriateness, 273; behavior, 290–91; catagories, 261; competency, 94, 147; conflict, 131, 134–37, 140, 250, 251, 259, 268–69, 269–70, 343–45; convergence in Europe, 146; diffusion, 48–49, 79; distribution, 118, 124, 127, 156; diversity, 14, 48, 55, 100; functions, 343; in contact, 32, 46, 47, 73, 74, 79, 130, 209, 308; "intensity index," 119; interference, 209, 264; learning, 264, 265; learning relative to other subjects, 312–13, 315; maintenance, 14–15, 25, 31, 32, 34, 37, 62, 64, 75, 79, 129, 137, 143, 144, 165, 183, 208, 226, 237, 247, 254, 330; maintenance and morality, 389–90; recovery, 154, 254; relative to culture and ethnicity, 217–21, 221–22; shift, 290, 298; stability, 14; status, 54, 55, 60, 264; study of status, 270–71, 273; study of usage, 290–91, 292, 298, 304, 305, 311–12; usefulness of studies, 283–84, 287–88; viability basis, 170. *See also* assimilation, attitudes, bilingual education, economics, *and by country*
Language Enquiry of 1956, 94
Lapps, 15, 31–32, 348
Lara-Braud, J., 322
Larnin, O. V., 73
Lau v. Nichols, 155, 375, 386
Lauricum, 37
Latin, 209, 221, 254, 257, 352, 362
Latvia, nationality, 80, 243, 299, 305, 309, 312; republic, 41, 64, 241, 243, 311–12, 357–58; policy, 354
Lausitz, East Germany, 17
Leach, E. R., 227
lead, 107
Leap, W. L., 22, 130
learning theory, 209
Lebanese, 28
Leibowitz, A. H., 366
LeMaire, H. B., 366
Lena river, 34
Lenin, 246, 311, 350, 355, 357
Leningrad, as St. Petersburg, 51, 67
Lerner, D., 211
Lewis, D. G., 335
Lewis, E. G., 7, 10, 23, 27, 37, 38, 239, 247, 248, 250, 290, 298, 343, 356, 357
Lewis, E. G., and C. Massad, 307, 308
Lezghin, language, 353; nationality, 80

Lieberson, S., 245
Liège, Belgium, 19
Libyan language group, 153
lingua franca, 60, 212, 213, 241, 248, 250, 304, 320, 322, 371; Azeri, 15; English, 39,, 336; English and Russian compared, 23; Russenorsk, 31; Russian, 54–55, 62, 64, 247, 319, 354; Spanish, 135
linguistic relativists, 202, 205
linguistics, 199, 203, 205, 209; paradigm, 214; task, 389
Linz, J. J., and A. Miguel, 4
Lippman, Walter, 229
listening, 292
literacy, 211, 212, 213, 215, 236, 237, 249, 371
literature, of Africa, 220; of Chicanos, 225; of colonial United States, 132; of Georgians, 298, 352, 354, 355
Lithuania, nationality, 30, 50, 80, 366; republic, 51, 54, 62
Little Russia, nationality, 50. *See* Ukraine
Lloyds, 49
London, 24, 61, 84, 107, 109, 127
Londonderry, 90
Lorwin, V. R., 231, 232, 233, 239
Los Angeles, 156
Lothian, 86
Louisberg, 132
Louisiana, 132, 136, 137, 167
Luria, A. R., 343–45 passim
Lutheran schools, in the United States, 366

Macedonians, 18, 37, 347, 348
Mackey, W. F., 380
Madsen, M. C., and A. Shapira, 175
Maine, 132, 133, 136, 179
mainstream education system. *See* education, mainstream
Malaya, 216, 322
Malherbe, E. G., 244–45
Malinowski, B., 236, 237, 240, 390
Malitz, F. W. von, 250
Manchurian language, 79–80
Mandelbaum, D. C., 218
Manhattan, 132, 381
"manifest destiny," 51
Mansi nationality, 74, 80
Manx language, 83
marginaltiy, 10–11, 219, 220
Mari, language, 80; nationality, 74, 78, 246; Oblast, 72
Maryland, 366
mass media. *See* communication
Massachusetts, 132, 214, 376
mathematics, 212, 324, 333
Mather, E., 21

University of Texas, 270
University of Wales, 118, 363, 365
Ural Mountains, 16, 41, 60, 291
Uralian language group, 80, 233, 248
urbanization, 107, 125, 147, 211, 213, 225, 233, 248, 291, 298, 305, 321, 328
Urray, 87
Utah, 23, 371, 379
Ute, language, 379; tribe, 155, 325
Uygur, language, 16; nationality, 23, 74
Uzbek, language, 74, 241; nationality, 16, 23, 25, 31, 50, 72, 78, 80; republic, 62, 353, 356, 357

Vale of Glamorgan, 98
Valencians, 49
variables. *See* institutional variables
Vasil'eva, E. K., 224
Vaughans, 49
Vespian language, 80
Vichy collaborators, 97
Viet Nam, war, 141
Vikings, 49
Vilna district, 51
Virginia, 132, 366
Virginia Plantation type of settlement, 90
Vladimir-Suzdad, 50
Voegelin, C. F., 32
Vogul language, 16, 50
Volkov, E., 26
Volga river, 40, 47, 50, 51, 291
Voprosy filosofii, participant in debate, 353
Voprosy istorii KPSS, participant in debate, 353

Waggoner, Dorothy, 188
Wales, 47, 49, 83–128 passim, 140, 208, 212, 221, 235, 238, 245, 247, 248, 249, 270, 322; colonization, 86, 97–100; economics, 98–99, 100, 102–127 passim; ethnic perception, 123; industrialization, 102–9, 213, 214; language, 11, 15, 30, 32, 33, 83, 86, 97–125 passim, 220, 273, 302, 333–35, 358–65 passim; language activities, 299–303; language affiliation, 98; language decline, 97, 115, 116, 118, 127; language maintenance, 102–114, 119; language regional differences, 118–21, 123, 124–25; language status, 54, 271; language studies, 273–320; migration, 26, 27, 33, 102–118; nationality, 32, 33, 47, 49, 83, 84, 85, 97–125 passim, 129, 133, 141, 144, 225, 234–35, 246, 247, 348; politics, 100. *See* attitudes, bilingual education, immigration
Wallachians, 347
Walloon, language, 347; nationality, 19
War of Liberation, 13
Warwickshire, 107

Washington, state, 35, 167
Washo tribe, 23
Waterford county, 94
Watson, W. W., 134
Watts Vernon test, 336
Wax, M., 324
Weber, Max, 203, 217
Weinstein, H. R., 351
Welshpool, 119
Wends, 17
Whatmough, J., 31
"white greed," 136
White Mountain Apache tribe, 381
White Russia, nationality, 50; region, 51. *See* Belorussia
Whitehall, 127
Whitehead, A. N., 200, 203
Whitman, Walt, 208
Whorf, B. L., 202, 209
Wicker Park, 144
Williams, Glanmor, 99
Williams, Trevor, 125
Williams, W., 246
Wiltshire county, 111
Winnipeg, 132
Wisconsin, 19, 163, 177, 366
Woonsocket, 143
word function, 344
Wrexham, 103
writing, 292
Wyoming, 23

Xenophon, 37

Yagnobi language, 16
Yakut, language, 34, 266; nationality, 4, 34, 73, 61, 74, 81, 356; republic, 32, 72
Yaqui tribe, 130, 222
Yeats, William Butler, 220
Yenisey river, 61
Yiddish, 73, 75, 80, 381
Yoroki tribe, 131
Young, R. W., 236
Ysleta del Sur, 130
Yugoslavia, 39, 40, 347, 348, 349; enclave, 18
Yukagir nationality, 15, 31, 61, 74, 75, 78
Yupik language, 379

Zande, 218
Zavatskaya, M., 26
"zero grades," 31
Zimmerman, H. E., 324
Zintz, M. V., 328
Zirkel, P. A., 367
Zulu chief, quoted, 244–45
Zuñi Pueblo, 39, 379

A Note on the Author

E. Glyn Lewis, educated at the universities of Wales and Oxford, has taught in both grammar schools and the University of Wales. For over twenty years he served in the Ministry of Education in London in charge of educational research affecting language teaching. Long recognized as an international authority, Dr. Lewis is the author of numerous studies on comparative bilingual education.